COVER:

Model by Ming Cho Lee
Bomarzo by Alberto Ginastera
Libretto by Mujica Lainez
Directed by Tito Capobianco
Opera Society of Washington (1967)
New York City Opera (1968)
(Photograph – Nathan Rabin)

FRONTISPIECE:

Setting by Santo Loquasto
King Lear by William Shakespeare
Produced by Joseph Papp's Shakespeare
Festival
Directed by Edwin Sherin
Costumes by Theoni V. Aldredge
Lighting by Martin Aronstein
Delacorte Theatre, Central Park (1973)
(Photograph – Fredda Slavin)

TITLE PAGE:

Setting and lighting by Neil Peter Jampolis
L'Incoronazione di Poppea
by Claudio Monteverdi
Libretto by Francesco Busenello
Directed by Frank Corsaro
Costumes by Kristine Haugan
Kennedy Center Opera House
Washington, D.C. (1973)
(Photographs – Neil Peter Jampolis)

LYNN PECKTAL

Designing and Painting for the Theatre

Harcourt Brace College Publishers

Fort Worth   Philadelphia   San Diego
New York   Orlando   Austin   San Antonio
Toronto   Montreal   London   Sydney   Tokyo

Contents

Library of Congress Cataloging in Publication Data Pecktal, Lynn
Designing and painting for the theatre. Includes index.
1. Theaters–Stage-setting and scenery. I. Title.
PN2091.S8P37 792'.025 74-31271
ISBN 0-03-011901-4
Printed in the United States of America
3 4 5 6 071 16 15 14 13 12

To my wife and sons—
Georgia, Steven, and Scott

Ruth Chapman
Fred Jacoby
John William Keck
Lucy Kroll
Ethel Johnson Meyers
Rita Pew
and Arnold Abramson

with appreciation

Preface

Designing and Painting for the Theatre is about the creation of scenery for theatre, opera, and ballet. It presents a realistic professional picture of the designing process from the point of view of both the stage designer and the scenic artist—esthetics, steps of a design's realization, and the progression of execution. More than 700 illustrations fuse with the text to give a sense, as well, of the beauty and excitement that can result from that process.

Chapter One discusses the principles and the initial steps involved in the designer's fulfillment of the playwright's intention along with career aspects and practical considerations about entering the profession of scenic design. The chapter also includes a wide representation of the work of established designers in many genres.

Each chapter is followed by the transcript of a conversation with one of ten outstanding American stage designers. In these wide-ranging talks, accomplished and successful theatre artists touch on personal philosophy and experience, their unique approach to their craft, and offer advice of interest to the working designer as well as the aspiring student. Although these discussions do not necessarily relate directly to the preceding text discussion, in sum they give a sampling of the opinions and experiences of designers whose work has spanned a good portion of the twentieth century and give stimulation, some exploration of advanced theories, and a sense of personal contact. Examples of the designer's work accompany each conversation.

Chapter Two explores the spectrum of the world of stage design, from New York—Broadway, the Metropolitan Opera, Radio City Music Hall, Off Broadway, Off-Off Broadway—to summer stock, professional resident companies, university theatre, and beyond. It also provides information about the designers' trade union and agents.

Chapter Three traces the evolution of a stage design from thumbnail sketches through research, models, renderings, floor plans, drafting, and lighting. As in the succeeding chapters, each aspect is extensively illustrated.

Chapter Four takes the reader into the professional scenic studio and pictures the final execution of the designer's ideas, from his finished sketches to completed scenery. The unique facilities and procedures of the Metropolitan Opera Scenic Studio are also discussed.

Chapters Five and Six offer detailed technical information about methods of drawing scenery, and basic as well as specific theatrical painting techniques.

Chapter Seven includes a large number of previously unpublished formulas for mixing paints, dyes, glues, binders, and special finishes; discussion of decorative effects, textures, and application of metallic leaf; and the use of special products.

Chapter Eight details the painting and handling of backdrops, discusses the use of scenic fabrics and gauzes, and includes formulas for starching and other treatments.

Chapters Nine and Ten show methods of painting framed scenery, decks, ground cloths, furniture, and creating sculptured three-dimensional scenery, molds, and metal scenery.

The techniques for executing scenery have been developed, refined, and used by master scenic artists through many years. Allowing for differences in budget and facilities, they are as applicable to the needs of the designer in a small school or community theatre as to the craftsman in a major commercial scenic studio. It is these techniques that make the scenery, no matter what the theatre in which it plays.

Designing and Painting for the Theatre has been so organized that it does not necessarily need to be read or taught in consecutive sequence after Chapter Three, although the present order has proved the most useful. Later chapters have also been constructed to afford ready reference in both text and illustration on specific areas and techniques.

Many people have been generously helpful during the evolution of this book. Acknowledgment is gratefully made to these stage designers for permission to include examples of their work and for supplying information and ideas: Boris Aronson, Howard Bay, John Lee Beatty, Eugene Berman, Rolf Beyer, Lloyd Burlingame, Charles Caine, John Conk-

lin, Virginia Dancy, Raoul Pène du Bois, Marsha Louis Eck, Ben Edwards, Karl Eigsti, Lloyd Evans, Peter Harvey, Desmond Heeley, Neil Peter Jampolis, David Jenkins, Don Jensen, John William Keck, Allen Charles Klein, Sandro La Ferla, Peter Larkin, Eugene Lee, Franne Lee, Ming Cho Lee, Frank Lopez, Santo Loquasto, Kert Lundell, Gordon Micunis, Jo Mielziner, David Mitchell, Robert D. Mitchell, James Stewart Morcom, Roger Morgan, Tharon Musser, Donald Oenslager, Robert O'Hearn, Lester Polakov, Helen Pond, Robert Randolph, David Reppa, John Scheffler, Douglas W. Schmidt, Herbert Senn, Oliver Smith, Frank Spencer, Robert U. Taylor, Rouben Ter-Arutunian, James F. Tilton, José Varona, Robin Wagner, Elmon Webb, Peter Wexler, and Ed Wittstein. Acknowledgment is also made to those designers and craftsmen whose work is shown in the production photographs and in the illustrations of the execution of scenery in scenic studios, and to the many photographers credited in the book.

Arnold Abramson and Charles Bender of Nolan Scenery Studios supplied helpful information and photographs of productions in progress. Fred Jacoby and John William Keck, now art director at Radio City Music Hall, both provided technical information and read portions of the manuscript. Thanks are also due other craftsmen, including Robert Motley, Ken Calender, Ben Kasazkow, Joe Ruggiero, Munro Gabler, Danny Blanch, Herman Thiele, Mike Gallo, Howard Rau, Vladimir Odinokov, and scenic artists at the Metropolitan Opera Scenic Studio.

Others whose special assistance is gratefully noted are: Danny Banks; Abe Kanter and Betty Coe Armstrong of United Scenic Artists Local 829; John H. Jackson and Patricia H. Robert of Radio City Music Hall; Rod Bladell, Lincoln Center Library for the Performing Arts; John Schwartz, Superior Photo Service; Mac Weiss, I. Weiss and Sons; Steve Wolf, S. Wolf's Sons; and Felipe Fiocca, Dazian's.

I am indebted to Kenney Withers and Paul Schmitt of Holt, Rinehart and Winston, as well as to Sandra Baker, Arthur Ritter, and John Reale. My editor, Ruth Chapman, has been involved with this book from its beginning and in its development. I am most grateful for her knowledge of theatre and for her patience, understanding, and wisdom.

Lynn Pecktal

New York

August 1975

ONE

Starting out as a young designer in the theatre

The scenic designer, like every creative artist, is highly individual, with strongly personal insights and sensitivities. Once the basic rules of the designing process are absorbed, the designer's artistic personality affects how they are put to work, but he is very much on his own in a field in which both common sense and talent are crucial. (Some seasoned designers say that no one can be taught to design in theatre, only inspired, encouraged, and stimulated.) It is also an area in which a designer's taste is the key to good or bad results; the overworked word *taste* is used here simply to indicate his selectivity in the work he puts on stage. Taste is to a great extent intuitive, but it controls the way a designer interprets and uses creative ideas.

The scenic designer must work both alone and as a vital collaborator in the definite, full realization of a theatre work. Jo Mielziner, whose credits have so far reached more than three hundred, including a staggering number of legendary productions in the American theatre since 1924, believes that the designer is a craftsman and only incidentally an "artist." Mielziner agrees that the scenic designer must be a "jack-of-many-trades," needing a sound working knowledge of more functional aspects of the theatre than any one of his professional collaborators. The fully practicing stage designer, in addition to everything else he must be, is a combination painter, sculptor, draftsman, architect, upholsterer, electrician, plumber, and all-round stage technician.

The designer's challenge and ultimate goal is to create the best possible scenery for a production, whether for Broadway, regional or university theatre, or summer stock. Ideally, the end result will serve well both the author and the director's interpretation of the work. Producing organizations vary, as do lavishness of production and economic limitations, but the general rules for designing in the theatre remain the same.

In this chapter, exploring the world in which the young designer today starts out, we examine the general facets of scenic design, then analyze two plays from a scenic designer's point of view. We also look at various types of stage and setting and at the basics of design and their application in sketches. The chapter ends with some thoughts about the choice of theatre as a career, means of gaining experience and background, and some practical hints on portfolios, résumés, and employment.

THE DEMANDS OF SCENIC DESIGN

Certain basic requirements of every stage work must be respected by the director and designer in preserving the integrity of the piece. According to the type of work (drama, musical comedy, opera, ballet, for example) and the director's aims, the scenic designer and the director are concerned with these esthetic and mechanical elements: place and locale, time and period, theme, mood, scenic style, social status of the characters, movement and position of the actors, and changing of the scenery.

Place and Locale

One of the earliest and clearest facts the designer learns about a production is where the action takes place. While the words "place" and "locale" can be used interchangeably, we frequently speak of the *place* as the type of area in which the action is set (an executive's office, a swamp, an artist's studio), and the *locale* as the geographic placement (New York City, the Everglades, Paris). The action of William Inge's *Bus Stop* unfolds in a street-corner restaurant (place) in a small town some thirty miles west of Kansas City (locale). We can imagine what *a* bus-stop restaurant would be like, but the locale tells us the distinguishing characteristics are Kansan.

Some playwrights, like Shaw and Ibsen, go into great detail to describe where the action of the play takes place; others, such as Shakespeare and Pinter, state their instructions very simply. For instance, in Act I of Harold Pinter's *The Birthday Party*, the playwright says: "The living-room of a house in a seaside town. A door leading to the hall down left. Back door and small window up left. Kitchen hatch, centre back, kitchen door up right. Table and chairs centre." This brief description may easily spark many ideas for a setting that would be proper for the play, but it sometimes takes a lot of exploratory concentration to decide (with the director's approval) which would be best for the overall concept.

Time and Period

Is the play timeless or is the action confined to a specific span? Discovering the time in a script involves several questions:

1. What is the designated *time of day*—dawn, morning, noon, afternoon, evening, or midnight? We begin at once to think of the type of lighting the set might need, as well as what the physical setting should be like during this time of day.

2. What is the *season* or month of the year—spring, summer, autumn, or winter? Is the climate warm or cool? Would windows and doors be open or closed? What kind of flowers, foliage, and shrubbery would be natural during this time? What is the weather—is it raining or snowing? Is the sun shining?

3. Is a *holiday* involved? Such special occasions as Christmas, New Year's, Easter, July Fourth, and Yom Kippur point up the use of set dressing associated with the holiday and contribute to the mood of the scene.

4. What is the *year* or years? Is the play set at the turn of this century, in the 1920s, 1930s, 1940s, or 1970s (contemporary)? Does it go farther back in time—to the eighteenth century, the Renaissance, the Byzantine period, or the Egyptian dynasties? Productions vary enormously in the year they are set: In the

OPPOSITE PAGE ONE
Setting by Douglas W. Schmidt
ANTIGONE by Sophocles
Directed by John Hirsch
Lighting by John Gleason
Repertory Theatre of Lincoln Center
Vivian Beaumont Theatre, New York (1971)
(Photograph—Martha Swope)

"John Hirsch, the director of ANTIGONE, wanted to convey the sense of the inevitability of war—life goes on, but war is with us forever. In talking with him, the idea came to me to use bas-relief as a symbolic gesture of this theme.

"In designing for a thrust stage, the most important visual element besides the back wall is the floor. The floor has to be complimentary and interesting. For ANTIGONE we did a nailed brass circular pattern design. We also built a pipe grid and lowered it about twelve feet from the real stage ceiling of the auditorium to try to keep the actor's energy contained and directed rather than dispersed into the flies."
—Douglas W. Schmidt

Stage design by Karl Eigsti
HORATIO by Ron Whyte
Music by Mel Marvin
Arena Stage, Washington, D.C. (1974)

STAGE DESIGN FOR AN ARENA PRODUCTION. The musical HORATIO concerns the life of Horatio Alger, Jr., from 1830 to around the turn of the century. This sketch is a scene late in the production when all the characters gather on stage with Alger seated at the desk. Eigsti not only incorporates figures as part of the overall design but also shows the many possible positions that actors may use in the setting. The window and door units (left and right) are above the southeast and southwest vomitories.

current popular hit musical *Pippin* the time is "780 A.D. and thereabouts, in the Holy Roman Empire and thereabouts"; the action in *A Little Night Music* takes place at the turn of the century in Sweden.

The year can also be classified as the *period* of the play insofar as it concerns a certain interval of time in history. The particular characteristics of such plays usually mean that even the most experienced designer must do research into styles current during that period, including architecture, furniture, fabrics, ornamental details, and

clothes (if the scenic designer is also doing the costumes).

5. What is the *span of time?* Do several years pass from one scene or set to the next, or is the action contained in the time it takes to see the play? Is there also a shift in locale?

Theme

The theme of a production, the subject that keeps recurring throughout the work, is stronger in some plays than others. A theme is sometimes a guide that can point up certain visual ideas to the scenic designer. It certainly does not mean that each play with a theme of love must have red hearts painted on the scenery or that a theme of death warrants black crosses in the setting, but the designer may find what he considers romantic architecture or get an idea for a morbidly or mysteriously painted sky. The theme can also be a guide to what would not be proper for the production. However, a designer may sometimes wish subtly to incorporate in a setting a shape, a color, or a texture that symbolically emphasizes some particular aspect of the theme. The audience is not always aware that a scenic designer has even considered a theme. As with mood, the observer in the audience can only sense emotionally if it is right or wrong.

Mood

The prevailing emotional tone of a scene can be one of many: frivolous, somber, decadent, tragic, foreboding, among others. A mood in the play can build in crescendo to a climax at the end of a scene, the end of an act, or can be spread throughout the entire play. Various moods can also exist within the individual scenes of a production. The mood of a scene, the distinctive quality that produces an emotional response from the audience, is established by many factors. The scenery itself does not carry the weight of the mood, although it and the lighting contribute greatly. Mood is created by the melding of all the work of the collaborators: scenery, lighting, costumes, directing, acting, choreography, dancing, music, and singing. Since the expression of a mood is subjective, the designers and director must come to an early agreement so that the various parts of the production will not be in conflict.

Mood is often what the audience responds to initially, when the curtain rises. After the first few minutes, the set itself should be such a natural part of the scene that it is not noticed.

Scenic Style

The new designer should not be worried or confused about finding a certain scenic style for each production. What is much more important is for the director and the designer to be flexible and resolve their ideas according to

Model by José Varona
THE SLEEPING BEAUTY
Act I: Aurora's birthday

Choreographed by Alicia Alonso
Théâtre National de L'Opéra, Paris (1974)

Paint elevation by Oliver Smith
Scrim backdrop "Paris park"
GIGI—musical based on the novel by Colette
Book and lyrics by Alan Jay Lerner
Music by Frederick Loewe
Directed by Joseph Hardy
Uris Theatre, New York (1973)
(Photograph—Arnold Abramson)

ESTABLISHING LOCALE AND MOOD IN A SKETCH.
The romantic feeling of Paris is captured in this sketch by the particular elements and the way they are rendered. Note the graceful shapes of the Eiffel Tower in contrast to a sky of horizontal washes, and the depth created by foliage and street lights in perspective. Mirrored discs were attached in the center of the street lights on the actual scrim.

the basic demands of the work; if a particular style evolves then, fine! Asked what scenic style they did a certain production in, some of the leading contemporary designers respond with a puzzled look and do not really classify each design according to style, but answer by saying "The scenery is realistic" or "the scenery is sculptural," or "abstract," "skeletonized," "architectural," "painterly," "romantic," or "nonliteral." As Edward A. Wright pointed out in *Understanding Today's Theatre*,[1] a director and a designer do what they feel is right for the work, and it is the audience that labels it. The chart, page 6 (adapted from his design), indicates what Wright considers the six most common scenic styles.

Social Status of the Characters

Are the characters in the play wealthy, comfortably off, or poor? Are they doctor, lawyer,

[1] © 1959. Chart on p. 6 reprinted by permission of Prentice-Hall, Inc., Englewood Cliffs, N.J.

or Indian chief? We find the answers to these questions of socioeconomic status in part by reading the playwright's cast of characters, but we learn more as the roles unfold and expand during the progress of the play. The social position of the characters is very much a part of developing costume designs. When reading a script, it is always a good idea to ask these questions if they apply to the production:

1. Who inhabits the setting? Man or woman (single or married), or a family?
2. What are their personal tastes?
3. Is the man or woman responsible for the condition of the setting? Are the walls, furniture, and props well kept or in disrepair?
4. Do the inhabitants collect material possessions? If so, what?

The answers can provide leads for the designer in developing what a set should be and what it should look like. Naturally, not all settings need to express social significance, and some —such as an abstract void, a forest, or a barren heath—cannot.

PURPOSE OR GOAL	_MODERN SCENIC STYLES_	_CONTRIBUTING FACTORS_
	Realism (naturalism) consistent convincing complete	
	Simplified realism no effort at completeness; unconvincing details eliminated	_Stylization_ Exaggeration to suggest period or mood _Symbolism_ One object represents another—or a great deal more
Helps actor to portray mood spirit emotion	_Impressionism_ less detail—only essentials to suggest locale and emotion	_Space Staging_ A light picks a scene out of a void and illuminates a portion of a
	Expressionism still suggests, but by distortion; tries to portray feeling in physical set	multiple or simultaneous setting which may suggest or represent a specific or a generalized locale— anywhere or everywhere
Helps actor by staying out of his way	_Theatricalism_ background decorated and used as background only _Formalism_ building or surroundings as they are	

The Movement and Position of the Actors

When discussing the movements and positions of the actors, we are also considering their characterizations and dialogue an integral part of the action on stage. With this in mind, the designer works with the director to plan the setting in terms of _practical movement_ (actors should be able to move comfortably, naturally, and safely) and _esthetic movement_ (while moving in a practical manner, the actors should be able to appear visually pleasing from the audience, always executing the action as the director has blocked it). In other words, the scenic designer is involved with the movements and positions of the actors in all areas on the stage—including where the actor stands, walks, dances, sits, climbs, lies, runs, or performs any other function on the physical stage. With the director's approval, the designer must plan the position and size of:

PLAYING AREAS

Consider first the kind of playing space demanded by the production. Are you designing:

1. A _ballet_, where the dancers need a large expanse of smooth floor on which to perform?
2. A _comedy_, where the actors need only a flat carpeted floor in an interior set?
3. A _musical,_ in which wagons come on stage with scenery and furniture, with some playing areas designated on the wagons and others on the stage floor?
4. A _drama_ with a unit set on a raked stage that has platforms, stairs, steps, and other levels?
5. A production that needs a large open space or a small enclosed space?

All the main playing areas—including the stage floor (or a portable deck covering the stage floor), platforms, ramps, raked stages, and levels—must be calculated by the designer according to the director's need for moving groups of actors or a single actor in the existing stage space. The size of the cast plus the required action in the play influences the design of the playing areas.

Platforms and various other levels not only break up a flat stage, they also make the stage picture visually interesting, especially for blocking large groups of actors. They also work well when a production does not require much furniture and the platforms can be used for both standing and sitting. The wise scenic designer is aware of certain important limitations (such as that a raked deck on too steep an angle makes an actor uneasy), just as he knows that the width of treads on a stairway should not be less than the height of the risers.

Setting by Ming Cho Lee
ST. MATTHEW PASSION
Directed by Gerald Freedman
Lighting by John Wright-Stevens
Costumes by Patricia Woodbridge
San Francisco Opera (1973)
(Photograph – Carolyn Mason Jones)

PROJECTIONS. Images projected on a front scrim can produce tremendous dramatic impact.

ENTRANCES AND EXITS

Major and minor entrances and exits should always be in good sight lines from the audience. For an important entrance, no position is better than upstage center. What more could an actor ask for than the long stairway Don Quixote descended in Howard Bay's setting for *Man of La Mancha* or the stairs Dolly drifted down in Oliver Smith's setting for *Hello, Dolly!* (or the boom on which Mack rides out over the audience in Robin Wagner's set for *Mack and Mabel*)? A minor entrance, like one in the downstage side wall of a setting, cannot always be so spectacular, but must be planned carefully.

Entrances do not always follow a traditional pattern. Today an actor may fly in from the wings (*Peter Pan*) or come down from the grid on a bridge (*Jesus Christ Superstar*), or climb up from a trap opening in the floor (Caliban in a production of Shakespeare's *The Tempest*). An actor can also enter from one side of the stage moving on a treadmill, or from behind a unit of scenery on a revolve.

As practical features of entrances and exits, the designer must plan to have doors open and close properly and be braced sufficiently. Doorknobs must turn, keys must open locks, latches must lift. Besides doors, the designer

7

is concerned with such other practical items as functional windows and shutters that must be used by the actors as part of their business in the play.

FURNITURE

While the furniture selected for a production may be arranged attractively, either a single piece or a group must be placed in the stage space to allow the actors movement between and around it with ease. To a great extent, placement of the furniture controls the flow of traffic in a production. An actor should always be as free as possible to move across stage, upstage, downstage, and diagonally. Each piece of furniture should relate nicely to the other pieces, the walls or surroundings, and the actor. Arrangements of chairs and tables should be grouped like a pleasant island of

forms whenever possible. Large bulky desks, breakfronts, armoires, and similar pieces are usually placed against the wall, as they would be in real life, so the actor does not have to compete with them for space. Objects like table lamps with tall shades can be planned so they never block an actor in his scene.

Even though furniture in various periods and styles may be lower or higher than the contemporary actor is accustomed to using, most often the height is adjusted accordingly. If this is not possible, a good playing height for the seat (and back) of the furniture can become a determining factor in its use. If the actors seem to be uncomfortable on the furniture, the audience can sense this and also become uneasy. Good chair-seat height is from 18 to 20 inches, and an average height for a table top is 29 to 31 inches. While it may be a contemporary trend,

Model by Boris Aronson
FOLLIES
Book by James Goldman
Music and lyrics by Stephen Sondheim
Directed by Harold Prince and Michael Bennett
Winter Garden Theatre, New York (1971)
(Photograph – Robert Galbraith)

"The bonus in FOLLIES was the arrival of the follies themselves . . . amidst the ruins and rubble. . . . Valentines and lace . . . symmetrical, colorful, painted, unexpected . . . a visual relief.

"I wanted to pay tribute to the institution of the theatre."   —Boris Aronson

Setting by Robert O'Hearn
DER ROSENKAVALIER by Richard Strauss (Act II)
Libretto by Hugo von Hofmannsthal
Staged by Nathaniel Merrill
Lighting by Rudolph Kuntner
The Metropolitan Opera, New York (1969)
(Photograph – Louis Melançon)

ELABORATE INTERIOR SETTING. Framed by a portal 52 feet wide by 30 feet high, O'Hearn's opulent interior of a Viennese palace during the reign of Maria Theresa includes stairs and balconies large enough to accommodate a cast of more than seventy singers. A floating painted ceiling is tilted for better visability by the audience. The center-entrance stairway ascends ten feet from an elevator below stage.

there are times when extra-high risers or uncomfortable period furniture is used by a director to force actors into behaving or moving in certain ways.

Upholstered chair and sofa seats that sink down, as well as mattresses, may have to be supported with something like $\frac{1}{4}$-inch plywood so they do not go down with the weight of an actor. Furniture is also sometimes fastened to the floor so it does not move from its original position during the action of a play. If furniture has to be moved by stagehands during the performance of the play and later repositioned, "spike marks" are indicated on the floor by small dots, squares, angles, or dotted lines made with paint or tape. For a play with several scenes, different colors are used. Paint or tape that glows in the dark is sometimes selected for changes during blackouts. Luminous tape is

also used on the edges of steps, platforms, and ramps, especially on carry-off steps, so the actors know where they are moving on the darkened stage. This is both a safety measure and a great timesaver.

PROPS

Props are items that are part of the visual picture in a stage setting, and the scenic designer is therefore responsible for designing, supervising, and approving them.

Set props: Pictures, paintings, draperies, mirrors, barometers, clocks, lamps, sconces, and other items pertaining to the set dressing.

Hand props: Objects such as cocktail glasses, cigarette boxes, books, flowers, briefcases, and telephones used by actors as part of their business in the action of the play. Hand props can also be set props.

9

Special props: Unusual props, like fountains that gush real water or statues that break away. The elevator used to lift the actor in the comedy with music *Good Evening,* designed by Robert Randolph, could be cited as a special prop. A special prop may or may not be touched by the actor but be one that pertains to the action.

Changing Scenery

While the average one-set show usually has only a change of set dressing, props, or furniture at the most, a multiple-set show involves far more work for the designer. He must decide how the different sets will change according to the sequence of the scenes and where the scenery not playing onstage will be stored. Scenery can shift *between scenes or acts* behind the house curtain or *during a scene* in one of two ways:

1. Without the audience seeing it. The scenery change can be concealed behind an "in one" curtain, behind other scenery, or in a blackout.
2. With the audience seeing it (*a vista*), which lets them participate and be involved in the change. This technique of changing scenery can be done in all types and styles of productions, and has come to be welcomed and accepted by the audience. When it is planned to take place rapidly and smoothly like choreography, a change of scenery with music, dialogue, and continued action by the actors creates a pace and excitement that the production would otherwise not have. Sometimes the scenery itself does not shift, but the lights will go to blackout, with a new scene introduced visually by a change of lighting.

Scenery may be shifted by one or more of the following methods, manually or electrically:

Wagons or wagon stages	Elevators or elevator
Flying units in and out	stages
Travelers	Sliding flats in grooves
Turntables	Hinged flats opening
Revolving stages	and closing
Jackknife stage units	Scenery moved *a vista*
Treadmills	by actors
Periaktoi	

ANALYZING A PLAY

Designers analyze a work they are starting out to design in ways they have found work best

for them, and certain types of production (opera, ballet, a musical comedy, for example) require different approaches. Dealing with a play, however, it is a common practice among established designers to progress through three readings: a first reading for enjoyment and generally to become acquainted with content; a second reading to establish mood, time, locale, flow of action; and a third reading to concentrate on position and movement of the actors and how the scenery will change.

As a study in designing a realistic play, let us plan a proscenium production of Henrik Ibsen's *A Doll's House,* which might well be considered a typical classical play by a repertory company or university theatre. This is a simple one-set play with no scenery changes. What follows is one way of going about designing this production, although a hundred designers assigned the play would undoubtedly come up with a hundred different designs.

THE CAST

Torvald Helmer, *a lawyer*	*Helmer's three small children*
Nora, *his wife*	Anne-Marie, *nurse at the Helmers'*
Doctor Rank	
Mrs. Kristine Linde	Helene, *maid at the Helmers'*
Nils Krogstad, *an attorney*	A porter

Detailed instructions from the playwright appear at the beginning of Act I in the script:

Scene: A comfortable room furnished with taste, but not expensively. In the back wall a door on the right leads to the hall; another door on the left leads to Helmer's study. Between the two doors a piano. In the left wall, center, a door; farther downstage a window. Near the window a round table with an armchair and a small sofa. In the right wall upstage a door, and further downstage a porcelain stove round which are grouped a couple of armchairs and a rocking chair. Between the stove and the door stands a small table. Engravings on the walls. A whatnot with china objects and various bric-a-brac. A small bookcase with books in fancy bindings. The floor is carpeted; a fire burns in the stove. A winter day.

We now know from Ibsen's description several facts about what is required for the play, but we must analyze each aspect of the characters and action in all three acts before coming to a definite conclusion as to what the overall scenic design should be.

Place and locale. The action takes place in the Helmer residence, Norway.

Time and period. Act I – The day before Christmas
Act II – Christmas day ⎤
Act III – The night after Christmas ⎦ —1879

Theme. The play deals with woman's emancipation in a masculine society, one of the first on the subject and a most important social drama at the time it was written. The theme in this production does not necessarily bear directly on what the scenic design should look like, except possibly that the room could lean toward being more masculine than feminine in appearance. However, we may infer this from the dialogue in Act III where Nora says to Torvald, "You arranged everything according to your tastes and I acquired the same tastes, or I pretended to—I'm not sure which." Nora also speaks earlier of wishing to have everything as Torvald wants it.

Mood. Ibsen called *A Doll's House* a modern tragedy. While we may imagine a mood of gloom and darkness, subdued colors and stark lines, is this what is called for in the script? The tragedy of *A Doll's House* is the hollow relationship between a man and wife. While the overall tone of the mood is serious, it fluctuates throughout the play. We may think of doing a setting like the one Ibsen called for and use changes of stage lighting to vary the set for the different moods.

At the rise of the first curtain, the audience should see a room in the home of a young couple with a moderate income who can afford comfortable surroundings and from all appearances have made a happy home together. It is a late winter afternoon and quite cold outside. We may see a fire burning in the stove and light shining through the windows.

Scenic style. Realistic.

Social status of the characters. Although Torvald is a lawyer and has been able to afford a maid and a nurse for the children, times have been difficult as a result of poor health, the launching of a career, and family problems in the last eight years; money has not been plentiful. Torvald is now on the brink of success with a titled bank position to begin soon. (A character analysis of each role will be helpful to the costume designer in discovering the individual tastes and preferences of the characters.)

The movement and positions of the actors. We know there are only two exceptions to the usual walking, standing, and sitting movement by actors: Nora plays hide-and-seek with the children in Act I and dances a wild tarantella in Act II, which requires sufficient space for her to whirl rapidly.

Besides the required furniture, entrances, and props already listed, we know that the business of the actors in the play makes it necessary to open and close real doors with keys in the locks, to have a porcelain stove with a door that can be opened so it appears that Nora is tending a burning fire in Act I and Torvald is burning the letter in Act III, to have a table with a cover so Nora can hide under it (Act I), to have a footstool by the sofa so Nora can be positioned there when she talks with Mrs. Linde (Act I), and so on. We must also not forget that very often a director and scenic designer will use certain theatrical license, taking arbitrary liberty to change something called for in the script to something else as long as it seems plausible to the action. In this case, it could be changing the stated position of a piece of furniture or substituting a regular chair for a rocking chair.

Changing of scenery. *A Doll's House* is a one-set play; the scenery does not move. Some furniture is shifted in Act III, and there are several props that come on and off during the three acts, including the Christmas tree with candles and red-paper flowers, assorted packages containing specific Christmas presents, a lamp, letters, bundles of documents, and embroidery.

Beginning work on the design. While a designer gets the essentials about the kinds and positions of the entrances and exits, the furniture, and other pertinent information from the script, it is up to him to use his imagination and skills to put these together and add any appropriate set dressing that will finish the idea of what the set should look like. Often it helps to remember that the visual appearance of a set should be completely natural for the character appearing in it, and that upon entering the set the character should become an integrated part of the scene, not just an actor standing in front of the scenery.

For basic dimensions, let us assume that the play is being produced on a stage that has a proscenium opening 34 to 36 feet wide. On such a stage, we might make the depth 17 to

Show curtain design by Eugene Berman
PULCINELLA
Music by Igor Stravinsky
Choreographed by George Balanchine and
  Jerome Robbins
New York City Ballet
Stravinsky Festival
New York State Theatre, Lincoln Center (1972)
(Photograph — Lynn Pecktal)

Eugene Berman made numerous sketches before arriving at
the design of the figure on the show curtain. Painted on
linen, the curtain was 60 feet wide by 40 feet high.
Drapery and a wide black border finished off the design on
the top and the sides.

OPPOSITE PAGE. Berman's sketch for three rolling
units in PULCINELLA. Designed to be moved by dancers
during the ballet, the units were painted on all sides.
(Photograph — Kenneth Pew)

20 feet (curtain line to back wall) and the height of the flats 14 to 16 feet, although these measurements could vary with each designer.

Once the entrances and exits and the furniture have been thought out (either working from ground plan to the elevations or the reverse, depending on the designer's method), other ideas emerge about what would perhaps be proper to put into that room. They are not mentioned in the script, but you might want to add a couple of side chairs, a small table, a couple of plant stands, paintings and other wall dressing, lamps and a chandelier for light sources.

More thoughts come forth. Since this play takes place in the Victorian era (1879) in Norway, we know from research something of what the architecture would most likely be — high ceilings, tall doors, lots of molding. The walls could be patterned with a wallpaper typical of the period and the carpet could also be patterned. The windows might have the heavy draperies of the era tied back over lace curtains. Architecturally, you might think of starting with designing the main door, an entrance that should be prominent in size and position in the room, then go on to establish the other doors, the windows, the placement of the piano, the stove, and the remaining furniture. Going back to the playwright's description at the beginning of Act I, we must remember that this is all put together with taste, but it should not look expensive.

All the while you are planning the setting, you should also be thinking of how the stage lighting will affect it.

TYPES OF STAGE

The scenic designer today may find himself or herself called upon to design settings for many kinds of acting area, although the proscenium or "picture-frame" stage opening is still more usual. These are the most frequent forms:

Proscenium stage. Audience views actors on a setting framed by a decorative arch separating the stage from the auditorium. Sometimes a proscenium stage has small side stages.

Proscenium stage with extended apron or thrust. The same type with an extended playing area in front of the proscenium arch, which brings the action nearer to the audience.

Open stages. Half- or three-quarter-round seating. Stage may be circular, semicircular, square, rectangular, or otherwise angular. Intimate relationship with audience and actors. Most scenery usually located at upstage wall.

Arena stage (theatre-in-the-round). Audience surrounds complete stage. More emphasis on costumes and props than scenery. Blocking and staging for viewing by audience on all sides.

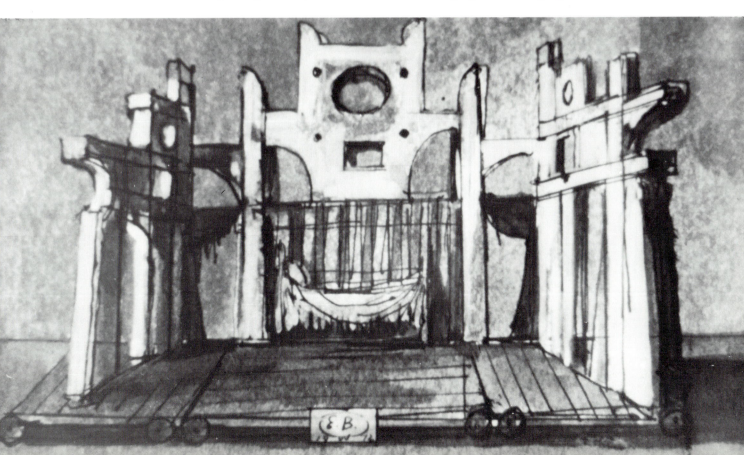

Stage may be circular, square, rectangular, or otherwise angular. Common stage in music tents.

Open-air theatres. Vary from proscenium stages (usually without the horizontal arch) to open stages. Semicircular seating is common.

Mobile street theatres. Audience can be positioned anywhere and view action from front, sides, or around complete stage.

TYPES OF STAGE SETTING

The architectural qualities of the stage (and sometimes the auditorium) affect the general choice of physical set that is workable for an individual production in a specific house. The general categories of stage setting are single sets, multiple (individual) sets, unit sets, and simultaneous scene settings. The range is nevertheless quite wide, since most of the categories can embrace elements from more than one of these characteristic setting forms:

Box setting
Wing, border, and backdrop setting
Portal, wing, border, and backdrop setting with profiled or three-dimensional set pieces
Set pieces in front of a cyclorama or backdrop
Drapery settings with props
Projected scenery on backdrops or cycloramas
An arrangement of platforms and levels.

A basic rule for productions with completely separate (multiple) sets is that all the settings should be in one scenic style, for overall unity. Even within this limitation the designer has good opportunity to be versatile, allowing much variety in mood within the nuances of the single style. This rule should not be violated without careful thought, but it has been sometimes successfully disregarded in designs for works in which the action takes place in numerous locales or covers a great time span, when some scenes are flashback, and when certain sets are conceived intentionally in a contrasting style.

Unit Settings

Instead of having a number of individual settings for a multiset show, a *unit set* can be designed to serve as a playing area for several scenes. The set should be interesting, yet neutral enough in overall feeling to sustain itself through the entire play. A unit set can be done in any style and period and range from the very simple to the very complex. All sorts of set pieces (drapery, banners, platforms, steps, furniture, and props) plus changes of stage lighting can be blended artistically to create many different effects. The most successful unit set is designed to relate honestly to the audience, not cleverly disguised to hide the fact that it has already been viewed in an earlier scene. A unit set may remain stationary, or parts may move. Or a whole set may move at one time, such as one on a revolving stage, and be designed like a lovely piece of sculpture so that when it turns we see all of the various finished surfaces.

Many classical works, such as multiset productions of Shakespeare, Euripides, and Sophocles, play beautifully on a very simple unit set. Notable examples of unit sets include Robert Edmond Jones' sets for *Hamlet, Othello, Desire under the Elms,* and *Richard III,* Lee Simonson's sets for *Marco Millions* and *Hamlet,* and Norman Bel Geddes' set for *Hamlet.*

A unit set may be chosen because it is:

1. Esthetically appropriate as a statement for the entire production, giving it unity and strength.
2. Practical in terms of budget and time to execute.
3. Practical for rapid and smooth scenic changes.
4. Both esthetic and practical as the simplest solution for the specific production.

Simultaneous Scene Settings

A *simultaneous setting* is one in which two or more individual sets can be viewed by the audience in the same scene and is one of the most difficult settings to design from the standpoint of both practicality and esthetics. Not only must this kind of set be well organized in terms of playing areas but it must be pleasing to the eye. In a simultaneous scene setting, the action can take place in various rooms in the same house, in various rooms in different houses, and in various sets in different locales. It may or may not include a portion of an exterior scene (street, sky, or other), or all of the individual sets may be outdoors. A variety of simultaneous scene setting can be created also by spotlighting actors in pools of light on a series of abstract platforms.

Stage design by John Lee Beatty
BATTLE OF ANGELS by Tennessee Williams
Directed by Marshall W. Mason
Circle Repertory Company
Sheridan Square, New York (1974)

INTERIOR SETTING IN AN OPEN STAGE PRODUCTION. An interior of a mercantile store in the Deep South becomes an intimate setting for the spectators (rendered far left and right) in this open stage production. The height of the room is emphasized by architectural elements such as poles, shelf units, wainscoting, ceiling details, and hanging fixtures.

Such well-known plays as *A Moon for the Misbegotten*, *A Streetcar Named Desire*, *Romanoff and Juliet*, *Five Finger Exercise*, *The Desperate Hours*, *Desire under the Elms*, *Tea and Sympathy*, and *Death of a Salesman* are works in which the playwrights intended several rooms in a single house to be shown onstage at one time. In this group of plays, Jo Mielziner's skeletonized set for Arthur Miller's *Death of a Salesman* is a legendary example of a simultaneous scene setting.

In deciding whether a simultaneous scene setting is practicable, the designer needs to be aware of these decisive questions:

1. Is there enough stage space on which to put all the different sets and required furniture, especially if second-story floors are involved?
2. Will the sight lines from the audience be good in all the individual sets?
3. Can each set be well lighted independently?
4. Can doors, windows, and other practical units be braced sufficiently so they do not shake during the action?
5. Will the overall setting have unity and be visually pleasing?

DESIGNING WITH A UNIT SET OR A MULTIPLE SET

One of the early decisions the designer and director of a multiset production must make is whether to use individual sets for each scene or to work with a unit set. Bernard Shaw's *Saint Joan*, which has been mounted interestingly both ways, is a good play to illustrate the factors that must be considered for that decision. Let us examine the list of sets in *Saint Joan*.

Scene 1. Castle of Vaucouleurs, spring 1429
Scene 2. Throne room, Chinon, late afternoon March 8, 1429

Scene 3. Orleans, bank of the Loire, April 29, 1429
Scene 4. Tent in an English camp, spring 1429
Scene 5. Ambulatory in the cathedral of Rheims, July 6, 1429
Scene 6. A great hall in the castle of Rouen, May 30, 1431
Epilogue. A royal chateau, June 1456

This is a very large production to design; it is equally challenging to direct and act. In design terms, we must first consider how much stage space is necessary for the action. There are 24 characters listed in the cast, plus more, depending on the number of ladies and gentlemen in the court, soldiers, and other extras the director may wish to add. From the characterization and dialogue of the actors, we realize they must walk, sit, run, kneel, bow, and march. Several groups must appear onstage simultaneously, particularly in the throne room, the ambulatory, and in the great hall, which means that we need a lot of open playing space.

The bulk and silhouette of the costumes of the period (1429 to 1456) require more visual and physical space than an ordinary production in modern dress. The long, flowing robes and trains need plenty of space to move, whether through groups of furniture and actors or through fixed arches and doorways. Further, the corners and edges on the surfaces of platforms, ramps, and steps must be smooth so that the fabrics of the costumes will not snag or tear.

Considering Multiple Settings

We know already from the scenes listed in *Saint Joan* that there are seven large sets that must change and that none is repeated. In a production of this scale a deciding factor in how to attack the scenic design is consideration of how

Setting by Lynn Pecktal
SAINT JOAN by Bernard Shaw
Directed by Adrian Hall
Lighting by Roger Morgan
Costumes by John Lehmeyer
Trinity Square Repertory Company
Providence, Rhode Island (1966)

ST. JOAN IN A MULTIPLE SETTING.   Like the six other settings in SAINT JOAN, this setting for the castle of Vaucouleurs (Act I) was designed primarily for soft scenery—cut leg drops, cut backdrops, and backdrops—to facilitate rapid scenery changes by flying units in and out. The three framed portal units remained stationary throughout the production. All pieces of furniture were carried off and on by stagehands, except the bed of King Charles the Seventh of France (Epilogue) which was mounted on a wagon unit.

the sets are going to shift. No matter how magnificent a scenic design is, the fact that it takes too much time to get one set off and another on always distracts from the designer's brilliance and reflects badly on his ability to solve the technical aspects of the production. A change that involves as much as 30 seconds seems long to an audience waiting in a darkened theatre, even if the scene changes are bridged with music.

The next consideration is the type of theatre where this production of *Saint Joan* is to be produced. Is it proscenium (with or without a thrust), an open stage (with scenery at one end), or arena stage (theatre-in-the-round)? Should the play be done with realistic or with stylized scenery?

We can at once logically eliminate the possibilities of designing *Saint Joan* completely realistically using full three-dimensional sets. Even if budget and time permitted, with the space on a proscenium stage (where this type of production would normally be presented realistically), the shifting of scenery would be an almost impossible feat. With one set on stage, six others would have to be stored, and rapid changes would be extremely complex, even with a revolve.

If the director and scenic designer are thinking of realistic scenery on a proscenium stage for this production, one of the best solutions will be realistic painting on two-dimensional surfaces (profiled wings and borders — framed or unframed — backdrops, draperies, and so on) combined with minor three-dimensional pieces, furniture, and props. The large units (wings, borders, backdrops) can easily shift by flying, the smaller scenery (any three-dimensional set pieces, furniture, props) can move on wagons with casters and so on. (This solution also works well with scenic styles other than realistic.)

When there is a difficult change of scenery to be made between scenes in a play like this, it is very helpful to a designer's planning if the director decides (and if it is possible) to have the intermission at that time.

Considering a Unit Setting

Another and easier approach, usable on all types of stage, is to design a unit set consisting of a series of levels, platforms, and steps that are neutral enough in size, shape, and color to remain onstage throughout the entire play. Certain fast changes can take place by adding or subtracting various units (steps, platforms, plugs, and the like). No matter what scenic style (skeletonized, fragmentary, or suggestive) the director and designer decide on, set pieces and props can be added according to what works for the visual and physical action, and the practicality of these units for the scene changes. Fortunately, the period of this play offers the designer a multitude of objects, patterns, and designs which can be easily found through research — such things as Gothic arches and throne chairs, cartouches, emblems, banners, and draperies.

Scenically, *Saint Joan* can also be produced on a much smaller scale, especially on an open stage or arena stage with minimal scenery. Changes of lighting, props, and furniture would then dominate the scenic picture. The contrast of shapes, patterns, and colors in the historic period provides enormous possibilities to create variety and interest in the production. The stage lighting, ever changing with movement, could also include the use of lighting projections. (For example, moving patterns might suggest fire when Joan is burned at the stake offstage or represent rippling water reflections during the scene on the bank of the Loire.) While Shaw's play does not necessarily demand a great deal of furniture (considering there are seven sets), it should be selected according to the period and each piece should make a pleasing visual statement.

So far in this chapter we have discussed the demands of scenic design, the different types of setting, and analyzed two plays. It is now appropriate to take a look at guidelines of design.

THE ELEMENTS AND PRINCIPLES OF DESIGN

As in all the visual arts, the scenic designer uses the elements and principles of design as a basis for his work in the theatre. They work hand in hand in a composition, and it would be difficult to separate one from the other; the experienced designer puts them to work without consciously analyzing each one. His intuition, discrimination, and observation tell him what to do. This section offers guidelines to the aspiring or beginning designer, to spark his imagination and to remind him of what may need to be explored further. (Nature, incidentally is one of the best sources in which to study the elements and principles of design.)

17

Stage design by José Varona
ATTILA by Giuseppe Verdi
Libretto by Temistacle Solera

Act I, scene 1
Directed by Tito Capobianco
Deutsche Oper, Berlin (1971)

When you look at the designs, models, and sketches throughout this book, notice consciously how the elements and principles of design are used in the various productions. This is good practice for any designer; it will also stimulate ideas of your own and should raise questions in your mind about how you might have designed the same productions.

As a cook uses ingredients according to a recipe to prepare a delicious meal, the scenic designer uses *the elements of design* (line, color, shape, texture, space) as his ingredients in a composition, organizing them according to *the principles of design* (balance, proportion, emphasis, rhythm, unity) to make a design that is appropriate, interesting, and exciting. Imagination and ingenuity blended with a bit of daring make the stage design unique.

Line

From our earliest associations of using it to write and draw, we know that line can be used in an incredible number of ways. Defined in mathematical terms, *line* means an extension of a point. A line can be straight or curved and move in any direction. It can be wavy, coiled, twisted, scalloped, circular, or zigzag. A line can also be long, short, narrow, wide, thick, thin, broken, crisp, or delicate.

SOME WAYS IN WHICH THE DESIGNER EMPLOYS LINE IN A COMPOSITION:

Line makes shapes and contours, defines boundaries.

Lines can be varied by being angular, broken, bent, or shaded with different thicknesses.

Curved and straight lines can be used to create rhythm.

Lines can be used to simulate texture.

A passive line can divide color from color, mass from space.

Lines in perspective can be used to create the illusion of depth.

Lines can be organized to express movement or motion.

Let us look briefly at the use of *line as a direction of movement*. Whenever you start the composition of a design, you may want to use certain directional movement in it and begin by roughly sketching some light lines on the paper or board to express your ideas. According to the mood of the scene you are designing, how do you visualize the direction of the movement? Do you sense strong horizontals, verticals, diagonals, or a combination? The list below contains a few simple examples of how we associate strong directional lines emotionally in a composition:

Horizontal lines (waves on the shore, a flowing river, hills, the horizon, beams overhead) suggest quietness, calmness, restfulness.

Vertical lines (columns, trees, striped patterns) suggest force, activity.

Horizontal lines combined with vertical lines (the framework of a building under construction, telephone poles on a plain, trees with spreading branches) suggest stillness, staticness, equilibrium.

Diagonal lines (patterns of clouds in a sky, lightning, crumbling and broken architecture) suggest action, excitement.

Many straight lines coming from a center (rays coming from the sun, a star, a firecracker or rocket exploding) suggest energy, vitality.

A line moving in a circle (a wheel, a moon, a sphere) suggests unity, completeness.

Curved lines (arches, drapery swags) suggest gracefulness, frivolity.

Lines that form sharp angles (scaffolding bracing, jagged rocks) suggest tension and conflict.

Apart from using line as a compositional element, some designers employ line drawing as a technique or style in their work. They may use their own personal drawing style or may pattern their method of drawing after such gifted artists as Jacques Callot, Albrecht Dürer, or other engravers and etchers. A definite line-drawing technique works especially well when the shapes are drawn with a pen on the sketch in black or sepia ink (usually having been sketched roughly with a pencil beforehand). The outlines of the shapes may be varied with straight, curved, long, short, or broken lines in different widths. The value of a shape can go from light to dark by using a series of parallel lines to shade it—a technique that depends on

Stage design by Douglas W. Schmidt
A STREETCAR NAMED DESIRE by Tennessee Williams
Directed by Ellis Rabb
St. James Theatre, New York (1973)

Schmidt's simultaneous scene setting was designed for the St. James Theatre with a proscenium opening 40 feet wide by 25 feet 8 inches high. The set depth was 25 feet.

first sketch

The Survival of Saint Joan — 1970

Peter Harvey

Sketch (ink and watercolor) by Peter Harvey
THE SURVIVAL OF ST. JOAN
Book and lyrics by James Lineberger
Music by Hank and Gary Ruffin
Conceived and directed by Chuck Gnys
Anderson Theatre, New York (1971)

INITIAL SKETCH FOR A ROCK OPERA SETTING. The rock concert form fused with a theatrical event led Peter Harvey to design a set with action flowing over the downstage center floor level, up each side of the stage on various levels, and under the central rock-band platform. The tree roots serve as support for the platform, the trunk the highest performing level where the burning and transfiguration of St. Joan take place.

how wide you make the ink lines and how far apart they are spaced. The direction of the lines may be horizontal, vertical, or diagonal. Even more variety and contrast can be obtained by crosshatching with the pen and ink. Some designers brush transparent colors over the design after the inking is finished; others apply opaque or transparent colors before inking.

In designing the ballet *Dim Lustre* for the New York City Ballet, Beni Montresor gave texture to the colors by using short scratchy lines and crosshatching on his setting of unframed cut leg drops and backdrops. Eugene Berman, in his inimitable drawing style, outlined many of his scenic and costume designs for ballet with black India ink, then painted the shapes with opaque and transparent colors, and came back later to add linear details with the ink.

Shape

Shape is concerned with both two-dimensional and three-dimensional form. In speaking of shape, we frequently think of it as the contour of a two-dimensional or flat object. Line, of course, is used to enclose space (area) to make shape. In discussing the term, we should have a clear understanding of *area* and *mass*. Area refers to the number of square inches within a two-dimensional shape and is always used to describe two-dimensional shapes. *Mass* describes either a two-dimensional or three-dimensional shape. We think of mass as describing a *two-dimensional shape* (a shape on a flat surface such as a backdrop or wings and borders) and how one *mass* of color relates to another, one *mass* of texture to another—how much is green, how much is yellow?—or a *three-dimensional shape* (the amount or extent of bulk within the shape) and how it relates to the total space on stage—how big is a sofa onstage? When we talk of mass in three-dimensional terms we identify the *shape* of the object (a cube, a ball, a cone, a cylinder, a pyramid) and the *size* (width, height, and depth or thickness). We are concerned not only with how one shape relates to another, but

Stage design by Donald Oenslager
LIFE WITH MOTHER by Howard Lindsay and Russel Crouse
Staged by Guthrie McClintic
Empire Theatre, New York (1948)
(Photograph—Peter A. Juley and Son)

RENDERING FURNITURE, PROPS, AND WALL TREATMENT IN AN INTERIOR SETTING. The setting for the living room of the Day country home at Harrison, New York, in the 1880s. Oenslager's sketch demonstrates the technique of rendering details in a period interior (summertime), especially in the furniture, draperies, props, and floral arrangements.

Setting by David Mitchell
MEFISTOFELE
Music and libretto by Arrigo Boito
Production devised and directed by Tito Capobianco
Staged by Elena Denda
Costumes by Hal George
Choreography by Thomas Andrew
Lighting by Hans Sondheimer
New York City Opera (1969)
(Photograph – © Beth Bergman 1974)

TEXTURES IN A SETTING. The Witches' Sabbath (Act II, scene 2). Textures were created by painting on both flat and three-dimensional surfaces—the translucent muslin backdrop, the plywood cutout trees, and the Styrofoam carved figures. Many vacuum-formed figures, slightly less than life size, hang above in front of the two open-work borders made of canvas cut-outs applied on opera net.

how it relates to the whole. The space or interval between shapes is as important as the shapes themselves. In *Visual Design*, Lillian Garrett explains: "Shape is concerned with the boundaries of masses. Three-dimensional forms are bounded by two-dimensional surfaces; two-dimensional forms are bounded by one-dimensional borders, or lines."

Scenically, we deal with all kinds of shapes: *geometric shapes*, two- and three-dimensional (circles, squares, rectangles, triangles, spheres, cones, cylinders); *shapes in nature* (leaves, snowflakes, flowers, eggs, cells, honeycombs); *nonobjective shapes* (blobs, fragments, puddles); and *invented shapes* (shapes we make up).

Color

Harmony of colors, as well as unity of all the other elements and principles of design, is always desired in a stage design. A good color sense is largely a product of intuition, association, and constant study. Every craftsman who is considering stage design seriously has presumably had some painting experience and is familiar with using color. Since the use of color is highly personal, it is important for the aspiring designer to have enthusiasm and experiment with color freely. While it is often more valuable to get experience by trial and error than to follow rigid principles, the young designer is expected to have a knowledge of the qualities of color (hue, value, intensity), the divisions of colors (primary, secondary, and tertiary), and other facets of color theory. If a review is necessary, the student can consult numerous publications in libraries or even obtain helpful booklets in any reliable art store.

There are no established rules for the use of colors on the stage, because each rule made on one production is broken on another. One learns to sense with a trained eye what colors would be appropriate for each production. For instance, for a realistic play like Chekhov's *The Three Sisters,* the overall colors would probably be muted and subdued. A Shakespearean tragedy like *Coriolanus* or *King Lear* might have a unit set of plastic forms in front of a cyclorama, all painted in very neutral tones, with additional colors supplied and varied by the stage lighting. In designing a stylish drawing room such as the one in Oscar Wilde's comedy *The Importance of Being Earnest,* you might make the colors very cheerful and pleas-

ant while still keeping them within the taste and the mood of the play. This is not to say that you always have to use bright set colors in the scenery for playing comedy; a great deal of the feeling can also be realized through the stage lighting. Neil Simon's comedy *The Sunshine Boys* is an example of a production where the hotel-room set, although designated to be drab and shabby and, like the characters in the play, having seen better days, was brightly lighted for playing comedy. It is a common belief among some producers and directors that there must always be bright lighting for playing comedy. Much of the feeling of color and mood in a setting is indeed dependent on the quality of stage lighting.

Bright and lively colors are usually in order for the typical Broadway musical comedy. However, the splashiest and boldest colors are those reserved for scenery like that for Radio City Music Hall productions, revues, ice

Stage design by John Lee Beatty
MOUND BUILDERS by Lanford Wilson
Directed by Marshall W. Mason
Circle Repertory Company
Sheridan Square, New York (1975)

RENDERING STAGE LIGHTING IN AN OPEN STAGE PRODUCTION
Beatty's rendering of stage lighting in this open stage setting displays illumination of the playing areas as well as captures the realistic positions of instruments in the theatre proper.

shows, circuses, rock concerts, jazz spectacles, and certain ballets, where the colors are at their fullest intensities. These productions often have dazzling effects created with Day-Glo colors, metallic flitter, mica, mirrors, sequins, Mylar, tracer lights, and moving lighting projections.

The handling of colors in a design is very important in terms of taste and mood. The choice of colors can express elegance in one set and garishness in another. For instance, if you are designing a lovely set like the living room of General Zandek's home in Howard Lindsay's and Russel Crouse's play *The Great Sebastians,* you might wish to limit the large expanses of scenery to colors like off-whites, raw-umber grays, and pale yellows with gold-leaf trim, and use such brighter accent colors as reds, greens, and golds in the smaller areas like the furniture, the draperies, and other set dressing. But for the Atlantic City boardwalk set in Thornton Wilder's play *The Skin of Our Teeth,* you might perhaps design the set with all sorts of wild, bold, gaudy colors in many shapes and sizes to convey the bizarre feeling of a typical amusement park.

Colors for a stage design can be selected not only because they are appropriate for the production and pleasant to look at, but also to produce a psychological and emotional reaction from the audience. We know that colors affect us through association. For example, red suggests gaiety, passion, fire; white purity, cleanliness; yellow cheerfulness, light, sunshine; green restfulness, spring; blue coldness, aristocracy, purity; purple royalty, luxury; black sorrow, darkness; gold power, royalty. Light colors are said to convey openness or a large space while dark colors seem oppressive and make objects appear heavier. Warm colors are

Stage design by Ben Edwards
MORE STATELY MANSIONS by Eugene O'Neill
Directed by José Quintero
Morosco Theatre, New York (1967)

THE DOMINANCE OF FOLIAGE IN A STAGE DESIGN. The effect of sun shining through foliage is created by contrasting patches of light leaves with dark ones, thereby also giving more depth to the overall design of this realistic setting.

Setting by Kert Lundell
THE CEREMONY OF INNOCENCE by Ronald
  Ribman
Directed by Arthur A. Seidelman
Lighting by Roger Morgan
American Place Theatre, New York (1967)
(Photograph — Frederick Rolf)

DESIGNING AN OPEN PLAYING AREA WITH LEVELS AND
STEPS. The drama takes place in a monastery on the Isle of Wight
and the castle of King Ethelred in 1013. While platforms and steps
on various angles were used in this setting, the main playing area
was kept open. The wooden platforms were covered with
Homosote and canvas, then painted. Other materials included
crating lumber for the walls and sheet metal for ornamentation.
The focal point, the unit at center, was created basically by tying
metal rings together.

exciting, cool colors soothing. We learn that warm colors (reds, oranges, yellows) tend to come forward and cool colors (blues, greens, violets) tend to recede. An illusion of greater depth in a stage design can be achieved by putting warm colors downstage and cooler colors upstage.

In thinking of the colors for a stage design, should you use a specific color scheme or one that you make up? Should your color scheme for a stage design be one that is monochromatic (variations of one color), complementary (using two complementaries like blue and orange), analogous (three neighboring colors like yellow, yellow-green, and green), or a combination of

several colors? An experienced designer may use his stored-up knowledge and create his own color scheme for a design, or he may pattern it from a painting, an illustration, a poster, a photograph, or some other work he finds appropriate and interesting.

If you are just starting out, remember that it is easier and simpler to begin by making a black-and-white thumbnail sketch (about the size of a postcard) with a pencil or pen and then establish your general colors by painting it. In the beginning it is also better to use only a few colors. Fine details and polish can then be developed after you see the results of the thumbnail and go on to making the larger sketch (usually $\frac{1}{2}$-inch scale) of the setting. Too, you usually get new ideas when going from colored thumbnail sketches to the $\frac{1}{2}$-inch-scale renderings.

Painting thumbnail sketches is extremely advantageous in designing a production that has several different settings, because you can see the contrasts of colors and moods that are created in the whole group of thumbnails before making larger sketches. If you are disturbed by one design, redo it before going on to larger sketches. When you are painting the thumbnails, it is always well to think about having good contrasts of colors in each individual sketch. Do you plan to make dark patterns against light ones, light patterns against dark ones, or dark-and-light patterns against middle values? As in a fine-art painting, the illusion of depth and perspective may be obtained in an overall design by making objects in the foreground dark, objects in the middle ground in medium values, and objects in the middle distance in light values. Besides colors, you should show contrast and variety in the line movement, textures, sizes, and shapes in each sketch.

Colors should always be thought out well so they are in good contrast with the skin tone of the actors and the colors of the costumes. Except for some unusual reason, a large expanse of color on a costume should not be an exact duplicate of a prominent color of the scenery. Such a color calls attention to itself and distracts from both the actor and the scenery.

Increased depth and plasticity can be achieved by the use of color on both two-dimensional and three-dimensional objects. This is mentioned here rather than in the scenic painting section because the designer should

Set sketch by Raoul Pène du Bois
KITTY
Paramount Pictures (1945)
(Photograph — Kenneth Pew)

always be aware of how a setting is going to be executed while he is designing it. While we may use the technique of painting with light, shade, and shadow (over the local color) on flat or two-dimensional units such as architecture on a backdrop, or when lining molding on a flat, we also frequently do the same on three-dimensional objects. For example, real molding with the local color applied is enhanced by painting it with light, shade, and shadow so it will "read" better from a distance, will "hold up" better visually under stage lighting, and in general match the same kind of painting done on any flat surfaces. (Three-dimensional molding must sometimes blend in with flat painted molding.)

To show even more contrast among three-dimensional planes, we may vary the colors. For instance, after the local color has been applied, this can be done by painting the risers of platforms, steps, and stairways a darker or lighter value of the local color, and sometimes a completely different color, when an object is meant to be purely decorative as well. This holds true for other three-dimensional objects: the sides of pilasters, the reveals of portals, the thicknesses of doors and windows.

Two-dimensional flats, even though designed to be positioned together in several planes, may be given contrast by varying the values. If you have three adjacent flats positioned in ground plan in a zigzag shape, you might make the first flat a bit lighter in value than the local color on the second flat, then make the third flat slightly darker. Inner corners made by two flats are often darkened to give more depth, atmosphere, and aging to the overall set. Flats and other scenery may be kept darker at the top so the whole visual picture of the setting makes the audience's eye concentrate on what is happening in the lower portion of the set.

Texture

Besides using colors (hue, value, and intensity) and patterns to produce contrasts on surfaces, texture is also used for enrichment. *Texture,* the surface quality of a material or object, makes us aware of how something feels even if we are seeing it instead of touching it. When thinking of using texture in a design, ask yourself what kind of effect you want it to express to the audience. Do you want to use a rough texture like erosion cloth in a cave setting to convey an

Costume sketch by Raoul Pène du Bois
KITTY
Designed for Paulette Goddard
Paramount Pictures (1945)
(Photograph — Kenneth Pew)

itchy and uncomfortable feeling? Or smooth materials such as vinyl coverings and mirrored Plexiglas in a superfuturistic laboratory to suggest slick, smooth, glossy surfaces? Or clear latex, flitter, and sequins to give a sparkling magical quality to foliage in a forest at night? Do you want the effect of bumpy and irregular cobblestones in a street painted on a flat surface or a three-dimensional material like Ozite rug padding applied on the surface, covered with canvas, and then painted to simulate them? It is always important to think of the impact you want to create on the viewer with texture.

Designers often use texture as direction to create a line movement, such as long bold strokes, or static texture to enrich an area with random dotting and spotting. Texture on a set can be created with line-drawing techniques (broken lines or crosshatched lines), painting, appliqués, or a combination of these. Texture in a design also includes such common items as carpets and drapery and upholstery fabric.

27

Thumbnail sketch by Peter Harvey
THE BOYS IN THE BAND by Mart Crowley
Directed by Robert Moore
Theatre Four, New York (1968)

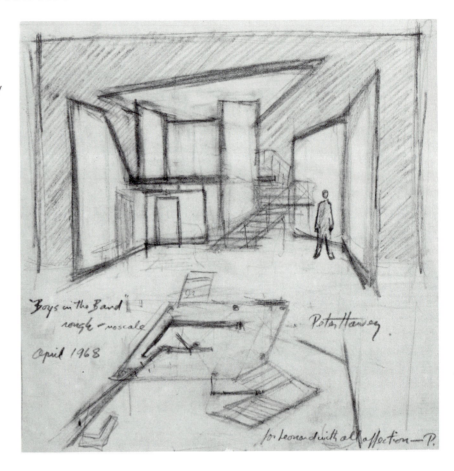

MAKING A THUMBNAIL SKETCH Peter Harvey's rough pencil sketch on drafting paper showing the set and plan for THE BOYS IN THE BAND.

Space

Because the theatre is three-dimensional, a designer should always concentrate on how a design will look in a three-dimensional space, even while making a sketch on a flat piece of paper. The fact that the stage designer creates both on the vertical plane of the proscenium and on the horizontal plane of the stage floor is why it is so helpful to work with models. The designer also has to bear in mind that a stage setting seen by the audience varies with every spectator's seat. The composition of your design takes on a different appearance when it is viewed from the orchestra, the mezzanine, and the balcony. If the production is being presented on an open stage or as theatre-in-the-round, even more angles are involved.

In thinking of the limitations of the stage space in which the setting will actually exist for a proscenium production, we may envision some imaginary boundary in space such as a cube or a rectangular box to define the three-dimensional volume. When creating a design, it is useful to make a sketch in perspective showing simple outlines of shapes to indicate how everything looks together in a composition, which may require several rough sketches before you are pleased with the design. In planning the organization of two-dimensional and three-dimensional shapes in space, the designer is concerned with not only the shapes themselves but also the space created between the shapes. We sometimes speak of positive and negative space; *positive space* is that which the mass occupies, *negative space* or *interval* is the space left around it. As with sculpture, the remaining space is important to the overall design. In essence, the designer must think of the relationship of one shape (or mass) to another, of mass to space, of one group of masses and spaces to another group of masses and spaces. Such principles as balance, proportion, emphasis, and rhythm must be considered as well.

The depth of the sketch of course is realized by drawing it in perspective. The perspective sketch is usually drawn as though one were looking at the setting from a center seat in the orchestra. (It works better to indicate some floor

28

Setting and lighting by James Tilton
SEASCAPE by Edward Albee
Costumes by Fred Voelpel
Directed by the author
Shubert Theatre, New York (1975)
Pictured: Deborah Kerr and Barry Nelson
(downstage), Frank Langella and Maureen
Anderman (lizards standing)
(Photograph — James Tilton)

Stage design by Ed Wittstein
ULYSSES IN NIGHTTOWN by James Joyce
Dramatized from Joyce's ULYSSES by
    Marjorie Barkentin
Directed by Burgess Meredith
Winter Garden Theatre, New York (1974)
(Photograph — Ed Wittstein)

Setting and costumes by Marc Chagall
DIE ZAUBERFLÖTE by Wolfgang Amadeus Mozart
Libretto by Emanuel Schikaneder
Production by Günther Rennert
Stage director: Bodo Igesz
Lighting by Rudolph Kuntner
The Metropolitan Opera, New York (1967)
(Photograph – Frank Dunand/The Metropolitan Opera Guild)

Costume sketches by Eugene Berman
PULCINELLA
Music by Igor Stravinsky
Choreographed by George Balanchine and
    Jerome Robbins
New York City Ballet – Stravinsky Festival
New York State Theatre, Lincoln Center (1972)
(Collection of the author)

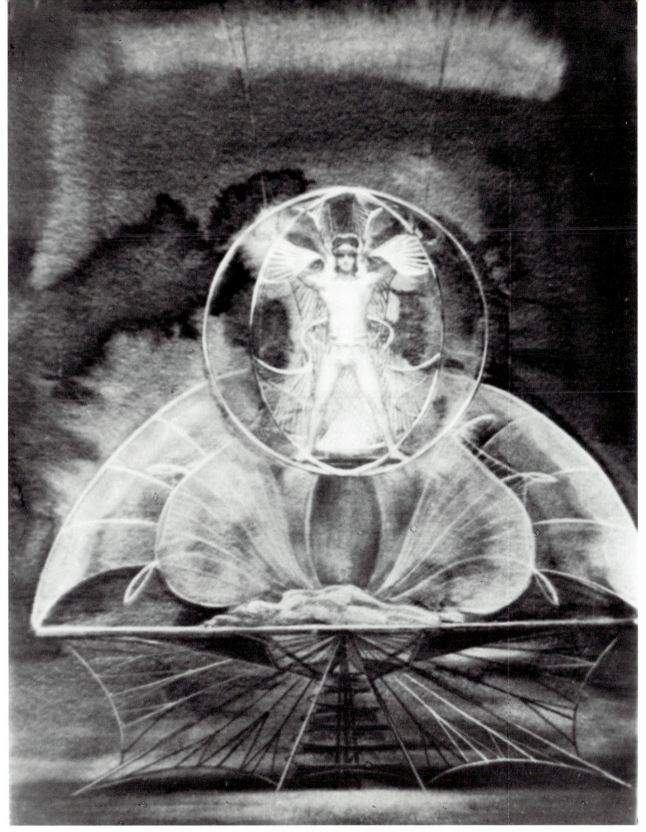

Stage design by Robert D. Mitchell
LA PERI
Choreographed by George Skibine
Paris Opéra Ballet (1966)
National Ballet of Washington, D.C. (1967)
(Photograph – Robert D. Mitchell)

USING LINE AS A DOMINANT FEATURE IN A DESIGN
Straight and curved lines are blended together to
form a graceful design in metal for this ballet setting.
The contoured frame of the unit on the floor, with
the top portion designed in the shape of a lotus
flower, was constructed of metal covered with gauze.
The 9-foot-diameter hoop sculpture above, on which
the dancer flies in, was made of metal only.

Stage design by Peter Larkin
GOLDILOCKS
Book by Walter and Jean Kerr
Music by LeRoy Anderson
Lyrics by Joan Ford, Walter and Jean Kerr
Directed by Walter Kerr
Lunt-Fontanne Theatre, New York (1958)

in the sketch, because this helps to establish the space between shapes.) Some designers who are not adept at perspective drawings may choose to make a model (rough or finished in color) and, as a permanent record of their work, have it photographed under dramatic lighting. But a knowledge of perspective is important in designing. You must be able to use it when laying out a drawing of architecture or a landscape on a backdrop, or when doing a drawing of a three-dimensional object to be built in perspective. Sometimes the perspective in a three-dimensional object is foreshortened (decreasing the depth of the actual object but still giving the illusion of depth). It is necessary to know the principles of perspective even if you only want to draw thickness pieces and reveals in perspective on scenery that is to be a series of flat profiles.

In the commercial theatre, the scenic designer is not always interested in showing a set sketch that conveys an extremely precise perspective drawing in which he has used a perspective grid in plotting out the lines, since accurate line drawings will have to be indicated on the drafting for building and painting. Instead, he may wish to give some character to the lines and to concentrate on the overall colors and mood of the scene.

An illusion of greater depth can be achieved

onstage by placing large two- or three-dimensional objects in front of small ones. For instance, a group of four flat arcade portals (positioned parallel with the apron and spaced equally) would take on their own perspective as they go farther upstage. However, as they continue upstage, the designer may wish to make each opening slightly smaller and vary the outline of each one slightly. To increase the depth further, colors could also become lighter in value as they continue upstage. In addition, depth in a setting can be enhanced by good stage lighting.

After the perspective sketch or drawing has been completed, colors, surface textures, and decorative details can be applied according to the technique of the designer. Rendering so that the shapes are modeled three-dimensionally with light, shade, and shadow increases the depths of the forms and the spaces between them. While the overall idea of the setting may be realized by making a painted sketch in perspective, we must now work out precise measurements (size and position dimensions) when doing the drafting, because we cannot scale dimensions from a perspective drawing. At this point, a model becomes invaluable, even though some designers figure out dimensions of a setting in the process of drafting plans, elevations, and sections. We must identify the shape of an object by figuring *size dimensions* (width, height, and depth) for each and *position dimensions* (where the object plays in the stage space). Is it a standing unit that rests on the floor, a hanging unit suspended from above, or a combination of the two? It is necessary that all of these dimensions and any other pertinent notes be placed on the drafting so that the scenery can be built, painted, and set up on stages as you wish in a successful spatial relationship.

Balance

In simple terms, *balance* is the equal distribution of visual weight on each side of the center line of a stage design. This visual weight is brought about by the combination of line, shape, size, color, texture, and placement. There are two basic kinds of balance, symmetrical and asymmetrical.

Stage design by Peter Harvey
LA GUIRLANDE DE CAMPRA
Music by Les Six
Choreography by John Taras
New York City Ballet
New York State Theatre (1966)

CREATING DEPTH WITH PERSPECTIVE. Harvey created a feeling of great distance in this near-symmetrical ballet design by placing the vanishing point on a high horizon line.

La Guirlande de Campra   Peter Harvey '66

Symmetrical (or *formal*) *balance* occurs in a composition when one side is a reverse and repeat of the other side. This type of balance can express a feeling of dignity, stateliness, or formality in a design. Although symmetrical balance tends to be the easiest to achieve in a composition, it nevertheless requires the touch of the imaginative designer. Instead of a design being completely symmetrical, most are usually considered nearly symmetrical, since there are variations in the colors (hue, value, or intensity), the placement of the furniture, the rendering of stage lighting, and so on.

Symmetrical balance works beautifully for certain productions, but on multiset shows it can become monotonous. Sometimes a designer will design symmetrical portals (wings and borders, cut leg drops) to frame multiple settings, then vary the individual settings within by making some symmetrical and others asymmetrical.

Asymmetrical (or *informal*) *balance* is not a duplication of the design on both sides of the center line, but the random yet careful organization of line, shape, size, color, texture, and placement in the composition. For a new designer, asymmetrical balance is very much like proportion in that it may be difficult to achieve in the beginning. On the other hand, asymmetrical balance can offer more freedom of creativity than symmetrical balance because of the numerous ways in which an asymmetrical design can be organized. It also allows for the creation of more movement and action in a design.

Model by Ming Cho Lee
BORIS GODUNOV by Modest Moussorgsky
Libretto by the composer
Outside the Cathedral of St. Basil, Moscow (Act III, scene 1)
Staged by August Everding
The Metropolitan Opera, New York (1974)
(Photograph — Nathan Rabin)

Stage design by Karl Eigsti
THE KARL MARX PLAY by Rochelle Owens
Directed by Mel Shapiro
American Place Theatre, New York (1973)

Choice between a symmetrical and an asymmetrical setting is governed most of all by the designer's taste and judgment. Both kinds of balance may express a dramatic quality for the production; when in doubt, experiment with both types while creating a design. You will know instinctively when you have discovered which works best for you and the production.

A remarkable source for further study of symmetrical and asymmetrical balance is the classic eighteenth-century *Architectural and Perspective Designs* by Giuseppe Galli Bibiena.

Proportion

Proportion is the relationship of one part of a design to another, the scale of one element in relation to another. Good proportion is present in a design when all parts relate nicely to each other and to the whole.

Poor proportions in a design (especially architecture and furniture) are as obvious to the trained eye as when the top of a building is out

of line with its proper vanishing point in a perspective drawing. Proportion is built into the talent of some designers, while others have to struggle with it. Being able to judge proportions well is largely the result of sensitive study, the constant observation of objects in everyday life, and the relation of that knowledge to the work put on stage.

We may say simply, "That picture is out of proportion to the fireplace," or "That chair is out of proportion to the table." Or we may talk about the proportion of the cornice to the wall, or the actor to the door. Because every piece of scenery on stage is considered large or small by comparison to the actor, the scale of all scenery should always be related to his scaled figure (average height 6 feet). This in itself lets us know we are on the right track when figuring out the initial proportions in a setting. In speaking of proportions, we are concerned not only with the relationship of one shape to another but also of one area of color to another, one texture to another, one interval (space between forms) to another, one mass to another, and so on.

Sometimes what we call ordinary proportions of shapes are varied to express a certain dramatic quality in a setting. We might design the great hall in the palace set of Verdi's *Aïda* with exaggerated towering proportions to convey a feeling of grandeur, whereas we might do the cellar set in Gorky's *The Lower Depths* in compressed proportions to suggest an intimate cellar resembling a cave.

If you are having trouble arriving at good proportions when beginning a design, try the following. First draw the outlines of the basic shapes on paper, cut them out, and then move them around on the outline of your composition. A decision by this method comes more easily.

Emphasis

That part of a design which catches our eye and holds our attention is the *focal point,* the center or area of interest. Some examples: the doors in *Medea,* the horizon in a perspective design, an elaborate table set for dinner, or the orchestra rising on the upstage elevator in *Over Here.* A design can have both a dominant point of interest and less significant or secondary areas of emphasis. Some of the ways we create emphasis in a design are by showing contrasts of colors (hue, value, and intensity), by using lead lines, by grouping or placement of objects, and by creating unexpected and interesting details. The rendering of stage light in a sketch is also important in stressing emphasis.

If we consider a show curtain or an "in one" curtain as individual scenic designs, we can

Stage design by Robert O'Hearn
L'ELISIR D'AMORE by Gaetano Donizetti
Libretto by Felice Romani
Act I, scene 2 – Village square

Directed by Nathaniel Merrill
The Metropolitan Opera, New York (1961)
(Photograph – Louis Melançon)

Setting by Eugene Lee
A MAN FOR ALL SEASONS by Robert Bolt
Directed by Adrian Hall
Lighting by Roger Morgan

Costumes by James Berton Harris
Trinity Square Repertory Company
Providence, Rhode Island (1974)
(Photograph — William L. Smith)

say that if they have *allover* or *repeat patterns* they do not necessarily have a focal point. Examples of repeat patterns are wallpaper patterns, lace patterns on a scrim, printed patterns, stripes, and checks. Examples of allover patterns include snowflakes, flowers, leaves, stars, and nonobjective shapes.

We must remember that the actor or dancer must always be the focal point within the overall stage setting.

Rhythm

Rhythm in a composition is the sense of regularity or recurrence of movement, the feeling of gracefulness and easy movement that the designer works for. Rhythm is what leads our eye from one part of a design to another in an easy manner at a definite pace. The eye likes to roam

and see a great many new things, but it must be given a sense of order to what it sees, to have direction and balance. Rhythm is an intrinsic part of life itself, and if we only look, we find it all around us.

Repetition and emphasis are the two most important factors in creating rhythm in a composition. We can express rhythm through the repetition of lines, of shapes, of colors, and through the way they are emphasized. For instance, suppose you were told that you should have seven arches in the walls of a stage setting. How would you design it? You know immediately that if you make all the arches the same size and shape, with the same spacing in between and the same colors for all, you will have a design that is monotonous and static. Instead, you apply your imagination in using repetition and emphasis; you think of varying the sizes and shapes

35

of the arches, of varying the spaces between them, of varying the colors and the values. You may put the arches in perspective, or add certain textures or patterns, or render the design as it would appear under stage lighting. In the end you organize the composition rhythmically, so that the eye viewing it can flow from one part of the design to another in a pleasurable, easy movement.

Another case where a feeling for rhythm is valuable in a stage design is the realization of an interior box set that has several doors, windows, bookcases, and a fireplace. We tend to think of these objects as basic rectangular shapes consisting of a lot of vertical and horizontal lines. While these objects could be positioned and proportioned nicely within the walls (flats), they would be unappealing and monotonous to the eye as an overall design. To create a pleasing

rhythm, you break up the feeling of so many straight lines by introducing some curved and diagonal ones. You might wish to add a curved arch, pediments over the doors, tied-back draperies with swags, or an oval mirror. The design could be further varied with other architectural units, items of set dressing, or groups of furniture to create a composition that leads the eye smoothly from one part of the setting to another. The possibilities are endless and, as in all design, the intellectual and the emotional work hand in hand.

Unity

Unity or harmony must exist within the stage design; it occurs when all the elements and principles of design are blended in the composition in such a way that they all seem to belong together. It is as important to know what to put into a design as to know what to leave out, or

Stage design by Marsha Louis Eck
MANON by Jules Massenet
Libretto by Henri Meilhac and Philippe Gille
Act 1 — The courtyard of an inn at Amiens
Directed by Tito Capobianco
New York City Opera (1968)
(Photograph — Kenneth Pew)

Stage design by Peter Larkin
WISE CHILD by Simon Gray
Directed by James Hammerstein
Helen Hayes Theatre, New York (1972)
(Photograph — Kenneth Pew)

The play takes place in the Southern Hotel in Reading, England, at the present time. The proscenium opening was 36 feet wide by 20 feet high. Notice that the double-room interior setting is designed on an angle.

where and when to introduce variety and contrast. One of the best ways to achieve unity in a stage design is to plan every aspect with a definite objective in mind. Unity in a composition depends not only on your creative ideas, but on your choice of materials and the techniques you use to render them on paper as well.

When a stage design is completed, you should ask yourself if you have organized line, shape, color, texture, and space according to balance, proportion, emphasis, and rhythm to achieve a sense of unity or harmony in the work.

STAGE LIGHTING

The composition and interest of a stage setting can be heightened enormously by the lighting design, whether it is general lighting or special effects (sunrise, sunset, moonlight, lightning, fire, rippling water, or projections of abstract light patterns focused on the scenery). Unlike

the other visual arts, a scenic design on stage can take on countless different aspects, depending on the lighting. The range can go from a set that has the lighting up full to a scene where all the lights are dimmed except those focused on a single actor.

Controlled stage lighting should be thought of as a vital element in the completion of a scenic design. The main functions of stage lighting are to provide visibility, reveal form, create scenic and dramatic composition, and create mood. Even though the scenic designer of a production may not design the lighting, he must be aware of all the visual and technical possibilities — how the set can be lighted, what effects he prefers, what instruments are needed, how much space should be allowed for them, and so on.

Sometimes in the early period of doing a show, a scenic designer (whether or not he is designing the lighting) will test a painted design

Design by Rouben Ter-Arutunian
NOAH AND THE FLOOD, a Ballet Oratorio for Television
Music from THE FLOOD by Igor Stravinsky
Choreographed by George Balanchine
CBS Television (1962)
Seraph from an iconostasis done as a model

or certain painted materials to see how they will look under stage lighting. This test is usually simulated in the designer's studio by using small spots with various color filters.

Rendering Stage Lighting in a Sketch

What really makes a stage design come to life dramatically is the rendering of stage lighting within the sketch. We are concerned not only with expressing the mood of the scene, but also with emphasizing visually the dramatic action that takes place within the setting as it will ap-

pear on stage. One knows at once that the concentration of light in the rendering should be focused on the main playing areas. For this reason it is often ideal to put an actor (two or three in various positions, or a group or groups) within the set sketch. The human figures should be drawn in the appropriate costume for the scene. Their position, posture, and gestures, indicative of the roles, further enhance the overall mood and dramatic feeling of the sketch.

The planning of the stage lighting in the rendering should be thought out well before work is actually begun, even though you may expect to get fresh ideas and make some changes along the way. You may prefer to have one or more sources rendered to show where the direction of light might come from. Is the light shining through the windows from outside, from the chandelier overhead, or from a purely arbitrary source? Is the direction of the light being rendered from front lighting, side-lighting, backlighting, or downlighting, or several of these?

To give good contrast and variety to the strong light shining on the actors, the rest of the scenery may be somewhat subdued. Perhaps you want the top and sides of the composition to be fairly dark while the remaining parts of the set have a nice general glow of light. Remember that a strong light shining on an actor in the set not only reveals the form of the actor, but the spill of the light around him helps to define the furniture, props, and scenery. When the strong light hits the actor from above, it highlights his form and casts a definite shadow on the floor (horizontal plane or otherwise). While doing the rendering and painting highlights on the sketch, also keep in mind that the reflected light bouncing from the floor may pick up bits of highlights in various parts of the scenery—the woodwork, molding, ornament, drapery texture, foliage.

After you have finished the sketch, put it away for a few days if time permits, then come back to it with a fresh eye. You may be surprised with the results; you will know immediately if changes must be made.

MAKING SKETCHES

The beginning designer should not be discouraged if he must do a great many sketches before being satisfied with one in particular. Some well-known designers make only two or three

Setting by Santo Loquasto
WIPE-OUT GAMES by Eugène Ionesco
Directed by Mel Shapiro
Costumes by Linda Fisher
Lighting by Lee Watson
Kreeger Theatre, Arena Stage, Washington, D.C. (1971)
(Photograph – George De Vincent)

Loquasto's abstract setting strongly emphasized textured surfaces – on the background, the wood-patterned painted floor, the leaning poles, and the scaffolding railing of sticks tied with rope. Pictured: Ned Beatty and company.

Costume sketches by Peter Wexler
LES TROYENS by Hector Berlioz
Libretto by the composer
Directed by Nathaniel Merrill
The Metropolitan Opera, New York (1973)

TOP: Priam, Dido
BOTTOM: Hecuba, Soldier

Stage design by Howard Bay
SOMETHING FOR THE BOYS
Music by Cole Porter
Book by Dorothy and Herbert Fields
Choreography by Jack Cole
Staged by Hazzard Short
Alvin Theatre, New York (1943)

sketches, but others make dozens before they feel they have achieved their best design for a production. Being an established designer does not mean that final ideas come in a flash.

In scenic design, good drawing is as important as good painting and vice versa. The new designer should also receive some consolation from the fact that even among established designers in the theatre this can vary. Some designers both draw and paint well, some draw well but do not paint well, some paint very well but draw poorly. Ideally, a designer should be adept at both.

Even though the scenic design you have created is intended to be the ideal one at the time the drawings and sketches are completed, many ideas and changes (practical and esthetic) can occur during the evolution of the final setting. Changes can come about:

1. When all elements of the setting are being constructed and painted in the scenic shop.
2. When it is assembled onstage in the theatre.
3. When it is being dressed and propped in the theatre.
4. When it is lighted.
5. When it is being tried out by the director and actors during rehearsal (usually up to opening night).
6. When the dress parade is held on the set with actors in costumes and makeup under stage lighting.

These changes in a scenic design can be anticipated in university and regional theatres as well as in Broadway productions.

CHOOSING THE THEATRE AS A CAREER

Starting out as a designer in the theatre, you may not have the advantage of a drama department

41

Model by Neil Peter Jampolis
LA BOHÈME by Giacomo Puccini
Libretto by Giuseppe Giacosa and Luigi Illica
An Attic Studio in Paris (Acts I and IV)
Directed by Bodo Igesz
Netherlands Opera, Amsterdam (1970)
(Photograph — Neil Peter Jampolis)

in which to study and develop your craft. You may be enrolled in a high school or a small college where plays are presented only as an extracurricular activity. Even so, you do not have to be handicapped by the lack of a program and facilities; if your interest in and enthusiasm for the theatre are strong enough, you can be stimulated to have more drive and ambition in wanting to learn about it. This may also be the time you will definitely decide to choose the theatre as a career rather than an avocation. Sticking to that decision can always be challenged even today by family and friends who think you should be involved in a more stable occupation. If the theatre is something you love and you want to be a part of, however, by all means give it a try. Do this as soon as possible by serving as an apprentice, a carpenter, or whatever in summer stock. *Any* experience working in the

theatre helps reinforce or reverse your decision. If you stay, there is a wonderful world of creative excitement and challenge awaiting you. And how high you set your goals for success in the theatre is up to you.

Gaining Experience and Background

The new designer gains widened knowledge about his work through:

1. *Practical experience.* By being an apprentice to a well-known designer, by designing anywhere — high school, college, university, stock, community or little theatre.
2. *Formal study.* By studying in a theatre program in a college, university, or drama

Stage design by John Lee Beatty
THE WAY OF THE WORLD by William Congreve
A Chocolate House (Act I)
A project (1973)

Stage design by John Lee Beatty
THE WAY OF THE WORLD by William Congreve
A Room in Lady Wishfort's House (Act III)
A project (1973)

school; by studying individual theatre design courses or courses in such related fields as painting, drawing (freehand sketching, drafting, perspective), and sculpture in which knowledge may be lacking.

3. *Attending and observing current productions.* By going to see as many new productions and revivals as possible, including all types of plays, ballets, operas, and other theatre pieces.

4. *Conversing with theatrical craftsmen.* By discussing design problems with contemporary designers and other theatre people.

5. *Designing projects.* By doing designs for shows. Even if these are unproduced, they expand skills.

6. *Reading critiques and reviews.* By keeping abreast of the good and bad aspects of current productions.

While a designer often works in both the commercial theatre and the educational theatre, he usually leans toward one or the other. Anyone selecting a career in scenic design should decide whether he wants educational theatre or commercial theatre. Both require talent and experience for advancement, but teaching and designing in the educational theatre place emphasis on academic degrees, while the commercial theatre does not. The commercial theatre makes its own demands: drive, the ability to survive in a highly competitive field, mental and physical stamina during periods of intense strain, skill in coping with a wide spectrum of complex temperaments.

Deciding on What to Study

If you are a design student trying to decide what to study, you may find it interesting and provocative to learn what working designers have to say about what they consider necessary as a background for stage design. Several designers expressed their candid opinions.

In response to this question, *Kert Lundell,* who designs at the American Place Theatre and for Broadway, replied: "I think a designer should assist when he first comes to New York, but for a very short time. That's one of the best ways. What he really should do is take a lot of classes that have nothing to do with theatre, like sculpture and painting. If I went back as far as graduate school and I wanted to be a designer, I would take three years in an art school, maybe one semester in theatre, and the rest in painting and sculpture and drawing—not so much learn-

ing how to make sketches, but just basic art."

Lloyd Evans, set and costume designer for the New York City Opera and art director for a daytime television dramatic series, had this to say about graduate school: "You go to an educational institution to get as much knowledge and as much practical experience as you possibly can. When you feel that you have accomplished this, it won't do you any good at all to get a master's degree in anything. If you are an artist, you will be able to perform. I feel that many people go to educational institutions for the wrong purpose. Yale collects a great number of students who wish to pass the United Scenic Artists exam and become a professional scenic designer or scenic artist. And they say to themselves, 'I have to go to Yale Drama School for three years in order to pass that exam.' They are really wasting their time. I feel that those crafts can be learned by designing. If you are a designer, a painter, a lighting designer, or a costume designer of a professional caliber, you will pass that exam. You will not learn to pass that exam by going to Carnegie Tech, Yale Drama School, or UCLA, or any other educational institution. If you are a mediocre designer, you will come out a mediocre designer."

"I think that master's degrees in theatrical arts are to give a person status in an educational institution if you are going to teach. Know why you are getting a master's degree or a Ph.D. in theatre. That Ph.D. or any other degree is not going to help you a tinker's dam as far as performing in the theatre is concerned. If you are going to perform, and feel you have the talent to perform in any theatre art, you will get the necessary tools and pass the test to work in professional theatre."

Asked what he thought was a necessary background for a young designer, *Douglas W. Schmidt,* who has designed for the Lincoln Center Repertory Company and for Broadway, responded: "I've had a radical turnaround from when I thought that a strictly professional theatre school is the best thing. I'm not so sure any more. I wish that I had had nothing to do with theatre until my graduate year in college. I'd like to have had a very strict and thorough grounding in the graphic arts. I don't think a month goes by that I don't say, 'Next year I'm going to go to the Art Students League and take some courses in figure drawing or something like that.' But, of course, I never get around to it because there is just no time. I did some teaching at Columbia in stage design, and now I'm teaching at Lester Polakov's. I see kids who have good ideas but can't express them graphically. They can't get them together or can't draw and paint. This has nothing to do with any one place, but in general there is not enough emphasis put on the language of visual representation—the graphic arts. I know every day I wish I had concentrated on it. Drafting is technical stuff that you can pick up or can assimilate in the course of being an assistant. But just sitting down with a pencil and drawing for two hours a day is a discipline that I never experienced, and I sure wish I had.''

Robert O'Hearn, whose sets and costumes have been seen in numerous productions at the Metropolitan Opera, also teaches at Lester Polakov's Studio and Forum of Stage Design and is very much aware of what young people need in preparing to be a stage designer. ''I think at least half of what a designer needs is really a drawing and painting style and graphics,'' O'Hearn says. ''Of course, you need imagination and a conception in designing, but you also need to really draw. Let's face it, in drawing costume sketches, it looks better if you draw a figure that looks like a human being. And I still think one should draw a tree that looks like a tree. Many times people tend to end up with only a skeleton made out of metal or something because they can't really draw a tree. The quality of painting is so important. Sometimes you have to do a drop that is nothing but painting, and I think so many young designers are really lacking in art training. Life drawing and painting technique are very important. You really need to be an artist and probably go to art school. And of course, you need drafting and the technical things to do your own working drawings.

''You could design without a high school degree, but I think anybody should have a college degree these days. It's just a general background, and you need that. . . . You should have a knowledge of both period painting and architecture, because so often you are doing things that take place in other periods; and you'd be amazed at how few students really know how to draw a classical column or a Corinthian capital, or a cornice, or how many divisions are in a cornice, or the proportion in them. No matter how abstract you're going to make a column, whether you do it in metal rods, or screen, or whatever, it has to have a certain basic function. People should buckle down and look at their architectural books and learn a few of these things.

''I think working as an assistant to a designer is an ideal way to get going. I've always thought the union should have at least a couple of classifications so that young, inexperienced people could work with a designer at a much reduced fee. They need that period in their training where they can develop.''

THE PORTFOLIO

A portfolio of your work is essentially what sells you as a talented designer to the producer or director who is not familiar with your work and is hiring. This collection of your best work —a folder of designs and sketches—is usually taken around to be shown to the theatrical entrepreneur after an appointment has been arranged. The most important features in a portfolio are good organization and an arrangement that shows as much versatility as possible. A well-rounded portfolio includes these items:

1. *Color sketches of the set design.* It is impressive to show a wide selection of work that can span the classics to the modern: realistic interiors and exteriors of dramas, from the very elegant to the very tawdry; sculptural and abstract sets of avant-garde productions and other serious works; light, stylish settings of musical comedy and plays. Dramatic scenes from operas and ballets always add variety. These may be shows that have been produced, as well as unproduced projects. Ten to twelve of these are sufficient, and mats should be kept to a minimum so they do not add weight and make the portfolio heavy to carry. Names of the shows are labeled, but dates are optional.

2. *Production photographs of the settings* (with or without the cast). These indicate how your designs were finally realized and how they appeared under stage lighting. It is always interesting to see the end results of a setting in contrast to the original set sketch.

3. *Photographs of models* (black-and-white or color). Imaginative models photographed under good lighting can be as effective as sketches for showing your design concept of a production. Four or five different shots of shows will suffice, if these are put in as supplements with sketches of the set.

Stage design by José Varona
ATTILA (Prologue) by Giuseppe Verdi
Libretto by Temistacle Solera

Directed by Tito Capobianco
Deutsche Oper, Berlin (1971)

4. *Examples of drafting* (originals or copies). Drafting can be floor plan, front elevations, details, and a section of the setting as it appears on stage. Not only do examples of drafting display your technical ability and practicality as a designer, but it is also most necessary to convey these points if you are applying for the position of assistant designer.

5. *Copies of reviews.* A couple of good notices from a reputable critic can reinforce your credits and experience and indicate just how you fared in designing for a particular production.

6. *Playbills or programs.* Like notices, these can emphasize your reliability and the caliber of the organizations or theatres in which you have worked.

7. *A copy of your résumé.* An up-to-date copy of your résumé is usually expected when the interview with your portfolio takes place, unless one has been sent previously. It is a reminder of your visit to the producer or director; many like to take notes and keep the résumé in their files for future reference, especially if there is not an opening at the time of the interview.

8. *Other designs.* If you also do costumes or lighting (or both), it is wise to put in some samples for these categories: four or five costume sketches or close-up production shots of the clothes (black-and-white and color); for lighting design, some effective production photographs showing special lighting features, such as projected scenic patterns.

THE RÉSUMÉ

A résumé lists exactly what you have done in the theatre and is a necessary item when you are seeking a job. Résumés should be neat, thorough, and to the point—keep to one page if possible, two at the most. The simplest way to summarize your experience is in typed outline form, using standard white 8½-by-11-inches typing paper. This information should be included:

1. *The title or position you are applying for.* Scenic designer, lighting designer, costume designer, scenic artist, property master, technical director, or technician. This may be one category or a combination, but it should stand out clearly so the reader can easily see it.

2. *Your name.*

3. *Full address and telephone number.*
4. *Education or training.* Colleges, universities, or drama schools, with degrees listed. Specialized courses and recognized instructors or professors with whom you have studied.
5. *Union* (if any).
6. *Productions you have designed.* It is customary to list your latest work first. This includes name of the show, the year, what organization or theatre, and what you designed (sets, costumes, or lights). If several productions were done for one particular theatre, make that the heading and let each show, year, and what you did follow.
7. *Shows for which you have been the assistant designer.* Again, the production, the year, designer, and the theatre are stated. If applicable, other positions in which you have worked (director, stage manager, producer, writer) can also be listed here, along with the show and year.
8. *Other work.* Mentioning other work in a related field demonstrates what you have done besides designing for the theatre and may be helpful in getting work when a designer's job is not in the offing. Among these may be architectural design, industrial design, display, graphic design, photography, sculpture, fashion design, and drafting. Any awards and honors should also be noted.
9. *Enclosures.* Including letters of introduction and reference from well-known people in the theatre (or other fields) reinforce your ability and qualifications in seeking a position with a new organization. It never hurts to add a personal touch with a covering note, saying when you are available and asking what the possibilities are for your working with the company to which you are sending the résumé.

If you are a new designer without contacts, you may have to search to find organizations to which you can send résumés. Some reliable places are:

Professional resident and repertory theatres throughout the country. A partial list can be found in the appendix.

Summer theatres, package houses, and musical tent theatres. Leo Shull's annual *Summer Theatre* ($3 by mail) has a comprehensive directory with a description of each theatre and who to contact.

Address: *Show Business*, 13 West 44th St., New York, N.Y. 10036. Tel.: (212) JU 6-6900.

Theatrical trade papers: *Show Business* and *Backstage*. From time to time they have articles seeking designers, artists, and technicians, both in New York City and elsewhere.

University theatres, particularly those with professional companies in residence.

Theatre Communications Group (TCG) accepts résumés and keeps regular files on designers, especially for regional and university theatres. Address: 15 East 41st St., New York, N.Y. 10017. Tel.: (212) 697-5230.

Other sources to check are:

Variety, the weekly trade paper covering all phases of the entertainment industry. Address: 154 West 46th St., New York, N.Y. 10036. Tel.: JU 2-2700.

Theatre Crafts Magazine (published six times a year). Features current articles and photographs of theatrical productions of every description. Subscription address: 33 East Minor St., Emmaus, Pa. 18049.

Theatre World, John Willis' annual publication. The complete pictorial and statistical record of the Broadway and off-Broadway theatrical season. Also includes professional regional companies, Shakespeare Festivals, and national touring companies. Crown Publishers, Inc., 419 Park Avenue South, New York, N.Y. 10016.

ACCEPTING A JOB

Ambitious young designers who want to get experience do not always negotiate about salary, simply because they are anxious to get experience and credit. The competitive nature of the theatre is such that there is always someone willing to take the job at the price offered. A designer's experience and the reputation he has made for himself has a lot to do with the salary or fee he can command. That is why young talented designers (and actors) without experience are willing to accept apprenticeships with theatres. This can work in several ways. The apprentice can pay, he can get only room and board, room and board with some pay, or he can get a small salary only.

If you are seriously interested in the theatre as a career, now is an excellent time to talk with (and listen carefully to) theatre people every chance you get—people in your school's drama department, members of community or other theatres nearby, especially the craftsmen who are actively involved in designing scenery, lighting, and costumes.

A CONVERSATION WITH JO MIELZINER

An ideal and stimulating thing would be an opportunity to sit down with several of the American commercial theatre's ranking designers, to be able to hear what they have to say about their work and their ideas about it, and how they approach and solve problems. Since that is not possible, this book includes at the end of each chapter a transcript of the author's conversation with one of ten notable, highly successful stage designers. These ten chats range widely, and each indicates something of the distinct individuality of an accomplished creator. In total they reveal a constant excitement about the work, although one finds little emphasis on the glamour of the world of the theatre; there is much more of dedicated drive, long hours of work, and the application of perceptive imagination in meeting the challenges of designing for the stage, in the informal and candid words of people who have earned real distinction and recognition in their intensely competitive field.

(Below) Stage design by Jo Mielziner
AFTER THE FALL by Arthur Miller
Directed by Elia Kazan
ANTA Washington Square Theatre
New York (1964)
National tour set
(Photograph — Peter A. Juley and Son)

(Opposite page) Stage design by Jo Mielziner
DANTON'S DEATH by Georg Buechner
Directed by Herbert Blau
Repertory Theatre of Lincoln Center
Vivian Beaumont Theatre, New York (1965)
(Photograph — Peter A. Juley and Son)

A Conversation with JO MIELZINER

Jo Mielziner took time to talk in his design studio in New York's landmark The Dakota, where he also maintains an apartment and where his neighbors include a great number of people in the arts. Born in Paris on March 19, 1901, Mielziner has virtually dominated the field of stage design in the United States for over half a century. Beginning with *The Guardsman* in 1924, starring Alfred Lunt and Lynn Fontanne, he has designed the settings and lighting for more than three hundred productions, of which an exceedingly large number have been major highlights in the theatre. He has been designer, co-designer, and consultant for more than nineteen new theatres. Most notably, he was the collaborating designer with the late Eero Saarinen of the Vivian Beaumont and Forum theatres at Lincoln Center. He has received numerous theatre awards, including five Tony Awards, five Donaldson Awards, and nine citations from the *Variety* Poll of Critics. Among his academic awards are four honorary degrees. Jo Mielziner is the author of two books, *Designing for the Theatre* (1965) and *The Shapes of Our Theatre* (1970). For the Metropolitan Opera he designed Gruenberg's *The Emperor Jones* in 1932–1933. Included in his long list of Broadway productions are:

Child's Play (1970)	*Fanny* (1954)	*Mister Roberts* (1948)
1776 (1969)	*Can-Can* (1953)	*A Streetcar Named Desire* (1947)
After the Fall (1964)	*The King and I* (1951)	*Street Scene* (1947)
Gypsy (1959)	*A Tree Grows in Brooklyn* (1951)	*Finian's Rainbow* (1947)
Sweet Bird of Youth (1959)	*Guys and Dolls* (1950)	*The Glass Menagerie* (1945)
Look Homeward, Angel (1957)	*The Innocents* (1950)	*Pal Joey* (1940)
Cat on a Hot Tin Roof (1955)	*South Pacific* (1950)	*On Your Toes* (1936)
Silk Stockings (1955)	*Death of a Salesman* (1949)	*Winterset* (1935)
The Lark (1955)	*Summer and Smoke* (1948)	*Strange Interlude* (1928)

Do you remember when you first became interested in the theatre?

I was exposed to the theatre as a small child because my mother was a journalist [the first woman correspondent for *Vogue* in Paris], and once a month she had to write an article covering theatre, fashion, painting, and architecture, and any artistic thing that was going on in Paris. So we used to be taken to things like the Russian Ballet and the theatre from the time I was six or seven. And I was brought up in an artist's studio. My father was teaching me the visual things—drawing and painting—from the time I was six years old. I did a French dray horse pulling a heavy wagon and one of the famous sculptors of that period, Andrew O'Conner, saw it and said could he have it cast? So my strong visual inheritance and what the good Lord gave me was very positive quite early.

When did you come to America?

I came to New York in 1909, when I was eight years old (I had gone to early school in France and England). And I had difficulties in the conventional school until the first year of high school in the Ethical Culture School, which started a new experiment in education. It was called the Arts High School, where a child, for instance, with a strong musical bent would be encouraged to spend a great deal of time on music and the history of music. Now with me, chemistry was the chemistry of color, history was the history of art. So I jumped from being low grade to being top of my class—in one year. I enjoyed it there.

But then at the end of my first year, I was offered a scholarship studying at the Academy of Fine Arts in Philadelphia . . . such a good scholarship that my family felt that they couldn't afford to give it up because it paid for my tuition and my living. So I left my last formal high school with one year of high school. That was the last of my education, academically. Earlier than that, here in New York, mother took us to the theatre and I went to Bobby [Robert Edmond] Jones' first production in 1915, when I was fourteen years old. I remember saying to my mother, "How beautiful the painting is. This would be a good way to earn a living." It was *The Man Who Married a Dumb Wife.* Jones also did the costumes as well as the setting.

Who were some of the other well-known earlier designers who influenced your thinking?

Well, later on, [Lee] Simonson and Joseph Urban. Urban, technically, was very brilliant. He had just come from Vienna, and the banker Otto Kahn felt the Metropolitan Opera scenery was old-fashioned and dark and colorless, so he paid for Urban to come to America to do productions—first at the Boston Opera and then at the Met. Later on, I was an apprentice and spent a year painting scenery in his studio. Besides being an apprentice there, I was an apprentice with Simonson and later on I was an apprentice with Jones for a year. So I had very good training.

Training which you cannot get today. . . .

Which our union prevents from happening and which is a most shocking kind of fact. In the first place, I've considered designing a craft and only unusually a fine art. You're a journeyman in the traditional sense of the word, not in the union sense of the word. Today the word *journeyman* refers to the money he gets and the hours he works. I'm thinking of journeyman in the classical sense, of a person who loves to work with his hands as a master of what he does, whose obvious interest is going to be paramount in his productivity, not his earnings or the number of hours he is going to take off. That's the tragedy of the modern labor movement when it comes to the crafts. We, who should be a union of supercraftsmen, are nothing but a skilled labor organization in the worst sense of the word. . . . Many unions are superior to ours, because they at least recognize the fact that they have to train the younger generation. We do nothing about it. We prevent students from being trained the only proper way, which is a true apprentice system. . . . I think every designer should have one or two students working as apprentices. I don't think they should do the final drafting, but they should assist the artist in all phases of his work. When I go to colleges and lecture, which I do quite often, I'm appalled at the lack of relationship between the reality of the profession and the theory that they teach. I've always urged that their top students should spend a year with a designer in New York, Chicago, Houston, San Francisco, or wherever. It doesn't have to be New York. Naturally, New York is still the production center of the United States, but it's fast growing to be less of a hub, which is a very good thing.

You have designed the lighting for all the shows you have done. How did this come about?

In the twenties in the average commercial Broadway production, lighting was simply turning on illumination, which was done by the production electrician. Directors would say, "Well, let's have nice bright comedy light," or "This is a mystery scene, just give me a follow spot here." It was very crude and insensitive, and much of it was purely functional rather than creative. And then there were exceptional people like Lee Simonson, Bobby Jones, and Norman Bel Geddes, who had been in Europe in their early training days and had been fascinated with what the German and Russian theatres were doing. Lighting in the English theatre was pretty much illumination in the pre-1930 period, and it wasn't until the thirties that designers in England were interested in theatre lighting. As late as ten years ago, they had been dominated by directors who always would say, "Oh, don't put on any color. Let's have nice white light. We saw our dresses in white light. Don't spoil them." And directors dominated the field. Now, the British theatre has been strongly influenced in lighting by American designers. When I first went over to London to do productions, Larry Olivier was horrified when I suggested having color filters in lights for the première of *Streetcar*, but he was good enough to at least let me try. And that's changed a lot. Now, of course, you find well-trained lighting designers in England.

But you have done lights on every production?

Yes, always. In fact, I've even lit another designer's production. I don't like to do it, but there was a case when Oliver Messel, a brilliant English designer, had trouble and he said he didn't know how to plan lights and would I do it? And with the management and with Oliver's acquiescence, naturally, I did it. I don't think it's an ideal thing, because I believe that the designer

Stage design by Jo Mielziner
OUT CRY by Tennessee Williams
Directed by Peter Glenville

Lyceum Theatre, New York (1973)
(Photograph—Peter A. Juley and Son)

should light what he designs. . . . A lighting designer doesn't light dust, he lights material and bulk, human beings, fabric. Therefore, who should know best how to plan it than the man who designed the production?

In the more than 300 productions you have designed, can you name a favorite?

No, not a favorite or even two or three favorites. There are so many out of that number; I suppose there are three or four dozen that I loved as plays and I loved as opportunities to work with a creative playwright and a creative director. And designing does become that when you meet head-on with a great play as I did, for instance, in *Streetcar* or *Death of a Salesman*. Fortunately, I had directors who knew how to use the designer's abilities. When you get a combination like that, designing can become part of the creative effort.

Can you comment on the fact that in so many of your shows you have created such a poetic feeling with lighting, gauze, and skeletonized scenery?

I've always been interested in creative brevity. Now, to say that brevity is the

soul of wit, of course, is just a clever phrase. Because if it is brief and what you say is not very interesting, then it certainly isn't wit. And it's the same with designing. If you eliminate nonessentials, you've got to be damn sure that the things you do put in are awfully good. They've got to be twice as good, because they stand alone to make a comment. I got interested in that first— selective realism as opposed to being an interior decorator. I was never very good at it. A lot of designers are doing a much better job of that sort. And I didn't believe in it. And I got to feel that even realistic plays didn't need realistic settings necessarily.

True theatre is a charade, in a sense, in which there are three participants: the actor–author combination versus the audience, and the audience back to the actor. Three-way—and it's a charade because you take part. Now, if you simply open up the fourth wall and look into the actual room, you are turning the audience into a collection of peeping Toms, but you're not necessarily exciting their interest. The average insensitive person applauds a pot that

is boiling over on a stove and a fire that's smoking, and they think it's clever. But photographs and films have always done that far better than we can. I think that's the technique that belongs there, and theatre will never die. But it will if we forget the fact that we have to be creative in our ideas visually, very much so.

Do you think of your work as having a particular style? After designing every conceivable type of production, is any one kind most exciting to you?

No. For instance, you look at Robert Edmond Jones' art work, and there's a "Jones look" in everything he did. Very positively, and most great designers have that. I think there's less of that in my work, maybe because—I don't know whether I'm more versatile or less— maybe I have less "great style." But certainly I've done everything from the most realistic to the most abstract. And I enjoy the challenge. I don't think even at my age that I am repeating myself, because I am constantly doing things even now that I've never tried before and my interest is broad.

What about directors?

51

Stage design by Jo Mielziner
LOOK HOMEWARD, ANGEL by Ketti Frings
Based on the novel by Thomas Wolfe

Directed by George Roy Hill
Ethel Barrymore Theatre, New York (1957)
(Photograph—Peter A. Juley and Son)

It's very hard when you work with a director who has no visual sense. That's terribly hard, because he or she is uncomfortable and you're uncomfortable. I've worked with directors like George Kaufman, a brilliant example and a brilliant man who had a tremendous ear. He was a writer, he was a director, but it was interesting. At rehearsals he'd pace up and down in back of the theatre never facing the stage, but listening. His comments to the actors were wonderful, and actors never complained because he was superb with them. But I've heard him at dress rehearsal tell a woman friend, "Now what does that look like? Is that dress good? Tell me what the set looks like." He was so insecure about himself, so when you did a drawing and showed it to him, that normally worried look on his face just doubled and his eyebrows went up and he squirmed. He was very uncomfortable and he'd say, "Well, am I going to like it?" or "What will this look like?" When a man says "What will this look like?" and he is looking at a model or a painting, you know that he is terribly insecure visually.

You have also worked with Kazan, Richard Rodgers, and Joshua Logan.

These are all people with great visual sense. I think that helps enormously, because not only do you do better work, but you do more for the director, because if you help in the decision of style, or make suggestions which the director accepts, or it stimulates his ideas of maybe a different style which deserves a more enriched approach, then you've got teamwork and you can help a great deal. If you're not a collaborator, the theatre is no place for an egocentric, egomaniac artist, and it's no place for an artist who wants to do "his own thing." The designer is the only person on the team who hasn't the privilege of changing his mind. The actor is constantly changing his mind, the director is changing up to the last dress rehearsal, and he's changing after the opening. But *you* can't change because the cost of scenery is too great. If you've been a hair off in the tone of a ceiling, you can't go up there and spray that ceiling "up" or "down." You're stuck with it. The costume designer has a bit of a break. When a star is

uncomfortable or you feel the thing is not entirely right, maybe they'll say, "Well, let's get her a new gown" or "Let's dye that shawl." But you don't dye that wall, the wall dyes you!

Do you prefer working on a play rather than a big musical, where you have to collaborate with so many people?

No, they're both fun. The musical has more of a challenge in certain departments—the presence of music, the timing. I remember some of the first. I don't know if I was the first, but I certainly was one of the first designers in the American theatre to work on the idea that changes were really open—not only in front of the audience, not by pulling out all the lights, but frankly in lighting it and having it move with the show. I had one musical once where I had a treadmill, and the furniture from one scene was rolling off stage, the backdrop was on a traveler and moving in the opposite direction, and George Balanchine had girls coming on dancing on their toes, moving on the treadmill against the motion. And that kind of change was so thrilling to Richard

Rodgers that in the next show I did for him, he said, "Let's do some more of that. That's fine, because then we don't pad and have a scene 'in one' while they're struggling to get the palace stairs together."

Do you prefer thrust stages or proscenium stages?

It depends upon the play. I did a production of *Caravaggio* a few years ago on an open stage in Cincinnati. That was a multiscene episodic drama about the painter Caravaggio, and the open stage was wonderful. It was in a theatre with highly banked seats around the thrust. I decided that all the effects to aid the play would be done with props and costumes and projections on the floor—nothing in the background, except one wall on which I threw some images. It was tremendously exciting, the sort of thing you couldn't do in a proscenium theatre. Now, if I was told the rest of my life that I could only work on one kind of stage, I probably would pick a proscenium stage as long as it had a decent apron.

When designing a show, do you sometimes get several designs in your mind and find it difficult to throw out some to reduce good scenery to a minimum?

No, unless I have complete lack of agreement with the director. And I like to sit down with the director very early before there are any sketches and talk to him about concepts, because even if it is the best design in the world, it's no good if the director isn't going to work with it. So the designer is always wrong, not the director. I once did, I thought, a very fine solution to a multiscene play where I oversold the idea of simplicity to the director. He was a brilliant director but, again, a man without a strong visual sense. And being that it was an enormous production, and being so busy getting it out, it was several weeks before I got to stop in at a rehearsal. I discovered to my horror that he was having actors pick up nonexistent phones and banging nonexistent doors, running up nonexistent stairs. He had completely forgotten that we had agreed "a flash of the simple" that told you where you were was better for a short scene that could move away very easily in the lighting. The result was, I was a complete failure in that job. The director, naturally, wouldn't change his mind, he went ahead. I had to either change scenery which the management couldn't afford, or I could accept the fact that I was a flop as a designer. You better be sure that he, the director, is aware of either your phraseology or the implication of your preliminary sketches.

Do you make rough preliminary sketches and then discuss them with the director?

As a rule, because I think visual things are more telling than oral things. But I always do them to scale. I'm so used to them, I can sketch up a quarter-inch or an eighth-inch to a foot without a scale rule, and I know that I'm within possibility. And I never do a visual thing that hasn't got a ground plan ahead of it. I'm thinking also, "How am I going to light the scene—where is the equipment going to be?" So my ground plans, the very first ones, usually have a symbol where the lighting equipment is going to be. That's terribly important.

Would you advise an aspiring designer today to learn as many aspects

Stage design by Jo Mielziner
GUYS AND DOLLS
Times Square
Based on a story and characters by Damon Runyon
Book by Jo Swerling and Abe Burrows

Music and lyrics by Frank Loesser
Staged by George S. Kaufman
Forty-sixth Street Theatre, New York (1950)
(Photograph—Peter A. Juley and Son)

Stage design by Jo Mielziner
PIPE DREAM—"Flop House"
Music by Richard Rodgers
Book and lyrics by Oscar
    Hammerstein, 2nd
Based on the novel SWEET
    THURSDAY by John Steinbeck
Directed by Harold Clurman
Sam Shubert Theatre, New
    York (1955)
(Photograph—Peter A. Juley
    and Son)

of theatre as possible—like getting some experience as an actor so he can see what is demanded of him?

Oh, I think it's a good thing. . . . I acted in stock one season in the summer and I spent a year as an apprentice in the Theatre Guild, although I was Lee Simonson's assistant and an assistant stage manager, I was also playing parts. And it helped me to overcome my strong feelings that actors were people who stood in front of my paintings.

When you go around the country what questions do students ask most?

Well, of course; "How do you get a job in New York?" The second question is: "Is it important that I learn how to build scenery?" And I would say, "No, it isn't." I think students in universities spend far too much time being free labor for the drama department—building and painting. It's true, it's good to learn how to paint scenery, but learning how to put a flat together is not going to help you in the professional theatre. You know perfectly well you can do your working drawings, but the shop that bids on it knows how to break it up. And principles you should know— general principles. But to spend a lot of time tearing down sets is only being free labor for the department. I don't think you learn anything as a designer doing it. You should do more painting and drawing, more working with actors, more reading of scripts and analyzing scripts. And sit down with a theoretical director—anybody who's studying play-

writing—and let him confront you as a director, and you confront him as a designer. See how you work something out. That's much more important than putting on hardware.

Nothing that you learn is useless. But you have just so many times and so many years in which to prepare for your career, and there is much to learn. Certainly a designer of the theatre has to be a jack-of-many-trades. But you can't be a jack-of-*all*-trades, and I think you've got to pick the ones that are important. Drawing and painting are essential. It's a means of communication. I pity the young designer who can't render, because you do have to render unto Caesar. And if you can't do it visually, it's rough. Now there are wonderful exceptions to every rule. John Bury, one of our finest designers living, doesn't draw at all, to speak of. But he has learned to overcome it. He does superb models, and he ends up by doing superb settings well lit, well designed, and very creative. I think he overcame it because he was brought up in the English theatre. Here in America, it would have been much tougher to get a job. Now he's so well established that there would be no problem.

Have you preferred designing for the theatre to designing for television or movies?

I've never done television. I've been a consultant. I spent six months under contract with CBS as a consultant in the problems of lighting many years ago when they first started. But I soon dis-

covered that lighting in television was done by engineers who had instruments in their hands and nothing in their heads. And they just depended on that needle. They had little sense of an artist's approach—how to see a thing. And they overlit and overlit. To make my report, I asked for an hour each day (in the early morning) with a small crew and a camera. I made tests, including tests with candles and oil lamps, and got beautiful pictures, even in those early cameras. But my report was quickly hushed up because the power of the engineers in the company was so great; they refused to accept it. However, to this day, I think I'm still right—that they overdo.

The reason I only did one film is that I discovered when you go into a Hollywood organization or any big film organization, they put patches over your eye. If your contract calls for being an architect, you're only allowed to look at moldings and the proportions of doors— ornament. You're not allowed to look at color. And if you're a color man, no form whatsoever, you just pick out colors. If you're a specialist at dados, they have dado specialists. They have prop specialists. And *no one eye* to give the quality. Now there are some beautiful pictures. I was very lucky in the one picture that I did—I got an Oscar. But I had a cameraman who knew me, admired my work, and was willing to be my "knight in armor." Every night he went down to the lab and saw to it that my color wasn't distorted by the engineers in the lab. And

54

on camera, he protected my design. So he really deserved at least two legs on that Oscar, if you can find two legs. I wouldn't go out there on a bet, except as a cameraman.

A director, naturally, can have a great deal to do with it—a director with a strong visual sense. A director alone can order. He can pick and choose people to do various things. But I think that tradition started when films left New York and the buttonhole finishers who became the financiers and the organizers of studios were so convinced that a machine that cut a thousand pairs of pants at one stroke was the obvious answer. You could do a better design if you had fifteen people doing it rather than one person doing it. Of course, that's completely wrong.

You have also been an architectural consultant for many theatres, including working on Lincoln Center with Eero Saarinen. How have productions worked out there?

I don't think for the most part that the thrust stage has been well used, because in many instances there were directors who had never had a thrust stage to work with. I think it has been very poorly used on the whole, with exceptions. Of course, both Eero Saarinen and I pleaded with the directors during the planning stages to have the two theatres, both of them for a single purpose. We said, "If we're going to have the big theatre an open stage, let's have the best open stage we can make,

and let's have the little theatre a proscenium, or reverse it. But let's not have dual-purpose theatres." But the directors of Lincoln Center were adamant and they were opposed to the board of management-directors, which was a pity. I think they were wrong. I think we would have been better off with a great big proscenium theatre upstairs. The Forum, I think, is very successful because no one has interfered with it—it was never finished. I had designed screens in the back which rolled in on a track to make it more intimate. But that has never been completed. They ran out of money because they had to pay for the Italian marble on the outside of the building. That's one of the things I'm screaming all over the country, and I've written books on the subject, trying to prevent foundation money from being spent on externals when internals were incomplete. This is happening all over the country, so I've been strong. I may have made myself unpopular, but if it's a voice in the wilderness, I think it's going to be heard. The Ford Foundation thought enough of it to finance a book that I wrote a few years ago called *The Shapes of Our Theatre.*

The real motive back of that is the plea that theatres be designed by theatre people—that architecture has nothing to do with theatre. You must have an envelope around your theatre, and there you need an architect. But the architect must certainly not be the person who vetos the shape of the theatre. And some of our

greatest architects have done astoundingly insensitive jobs costing millions of dollars, because they wouldn't listen to the technical people they had available.

Do you ever get time to take a vacation?

As a rule, in the spring I'm apt to go to Europe—either to do a production there or to do some research. One summer I had the privilege of being a member of the faculty at Salzburg in the American conference there, Studies in the Theatre. And that was very stimulating. I learned a great deal from that, as well as being a member of the faculty. And I usually go to London because I find the English theatre very stimulating. I like their training methods. They act out the classics in a way that none of us can touch—they're superior in that. They are not superior to us in musicals. And scenically and lighting-wise, I think they run from top-notch to a rather low average. I think the average production here is a little bit more interesting. There's still too much "safe" illumination and lighting in the English theatre. And they don't have the Off-off Broadway kind of daring, sometimes silly, and sometimes empty expressions. Although I don't agree with what Off-off Broadway does, it is an important place to learn in New York. Some of it is pretentious and brash, exhibition for an exhibitionist reason, or pornographic with pornographic appeal, which won't last too long. Pants are coming back and so are skirts.

Stage design by Jo Mielziner
1776 — Full Congress
Book by Peter Stone
Based on conception by
   Sherman Edwards
Music and lyrics by
   Sherman Edwards
Directed by Peter Hunt
Forty-sixth Street Theatre,
   New York (1969)
(Photograph — Peter A. Juley
   and Son)

TWO

Designing in
New York and
elsewhere

BROADWAY

Designing for Broadway is considered the zenith of success by the theatregoing public as well as by the industry itself. Here stars are born, photographs of the designer's work become part of theatre-history books; here shows become legendary. From this point of view, it *is* the top. The theatre designer who sets Broadway as his ultimate goal must view the overall situation realistically and be fully aware that to achieve this kind of success requires more than just being talented and having enthusiasm. It takes drive, discipline, dedication, and very hard work.

Just how does the stage designer get that Broadway show? Talent, years of study, and experience do not necessarily assure a designer steady employment in the New York theatre, although all of these are crucial. There really is no set pattern that can be followed to fulfill this goal. Many creative artists believe that the "break" will come sooner or later from hard work, getting to know the right people at the right time, and having patience and luck. But, even after the "break," it is often just as difficult to sustain Broadway success as to gain it.

To be able to earn a living in the theatre has never been easy, but to cope with the keen competition that exists on Broadway (and elsewhere), the designer must also be prepared to face frustration and disappointment. Like the actor and the director, he must know that this is a part of the work he loves and be ready to accept it. It is possible that the very successful designers have always been aware of this, and have approached their daily life with the attitude that their work and their success are the most important things in the world to them.

It is rare for an unknown designer to walk "cold" into a producer's office with his portfolio and come out with a contract in hand. Most jobs come about through some personal association or recommendation. It can be an association from anywhere—from stock, a regional group, or repertory theatre, where a multitude of brilliant shows are being staged. For the new designer, it is, of course, absolutely vital that he come to New York with some expertise in the field, and it is equally important that he build up a rapport with directors and producers along the way. The fact that he has previously worked

Settings and costumes by
Eugene Lee and Franne Lee
CANDIDE
Music composed by Leonard Bernstein
Book adapted from Voltaire by Hugh
Wheeler
Lyrics by Richard Wilbur
Additional lyrics by Stephen Sondheim
and John Latouche
Lighting by Tharon Musser
Choreographed by Patricia Birch
Directed by Harold Prince
Broadway Theatre, New York (1974)
(Photograph — Friedman-Abeles)

For Leonard Bernstein's CANDIDE, which was first revived at the
Chelsea Theatre Center of Brooklyn, Eugene Lee revamped the
Broadway theatre (a proscenium house) into one large playing arena
with spectators seated on benches and stools. Planked platforms and
levels form various patterns throughout the house. The orchestra is
shown in the foreground.

with a director who respects his talent and likes him personally can become another way of getting his first Broadway production. Robert Randolph's first big musical hit, *Bye Bye Birdie*, came about through a contact in summer stock. He then went on to do many successful Broadway shows.

Some highly acclaimed out-of-town productions have been brought to Broadway with the original designers and directors. A recent example is David Storey's *The Changing Room*. After being favorably received at New Haven's Long Wharf Theatre, it moved to the Morosco Theatre in New York on March 6, 1973, with the same cast as well as director Michael Rudman and designers David Jenkins (scenery), Whitney Blausen (costumes), and Ronald Wallace (lighting).

A show can also come from Off Broadway to Broadway with the original designers. During the span of two seasons, the prolific Joseph Papp brought *That Championship Season* and *Sticks and Bones*, both designed by Santo Loquasto, from his downtown Public Theatre up to Broadway, and two other hits, Shakespeare's comedy *Much Ado About Nothing* and the musical version of *Two Gentlemen of Verona*, both designed by Ming Cho Lee, from the New York Shakespeare Festival in Central Park. Among a roster of other productions which began Off Broadway and then had respectable runs on the "Great White Way" are *Grease*, designed by Douglas W. Schmidt, *Oh! Calcutta!*, designed by James Tilton, and a revival of Leonard Bernstein's *Candide* (from the Chelsea Theatre Center, Brooklyn), designed by Eugene Lee.

No matter how a designer gets a Broadway show, it is important to his career that the production be a hit. A long run can give enormous exposure, and his name and work will be remembered by the public and the industry. This has been proved again and again in the theatre.

Who can remember the names of the designer, director, actors, and writers of most shows that have been "flops"? Like the shows, their names tend to be forgotten. But even with a failure, an exception can occur when a powerful drama critic singles out the work of the stage designer and gives him a rave notice in his review. *The New York Times'* critic, Clive Barnes, seemingly carries the most weight with the ticket-buying public and the trade, and he may devote a paragraph to the designers in an enthusiastic notice, commenting on their triumphs in the production. Not only can this critical praise be personally gratifying to the artist, it can help establish him professionally.

Another fact of Broadway life: A collaborating team with one or more hit plays running can easily be the artists most in demand at the moment, no matter how much talent is around. Those with current successes always appear to be the ones who are the first choices of people putting new works into production. For this reason, the designer of a hit show may suddenly find himself deluged with all kinds of offers from producers, directors, or agents who are eager to represent him.

The designer's employment, like that of the other creative theatre craftsmen, can be sharply affected by the number of productions staged each season. The fewer shows produced, the less work there is to be had. This list (extracted from one published in the trade paper *Variety* in June 1974), gives an idea of the spread of the production record from the beginning of the century to 1974:

The same *Variety* summary, which started with 1899, shows that the record high for productions was the 1927–1928 season (183 new plays, 53 new musicals, 28 revivals, for a total of 264) and the record low to date was the 1970–1971 season (16 new plays, 17 new musicals, and 13 revivals—a production total of 46).

SEASON	NEW PLAYS	NEW MUSICALS	REVIVALS	TOTAL
1973–1974	21	12	15	50
			(Pre-opening flops 2)	
1963–1964	42	15	6	63
1953–1954	42	9	8	59
1943–1944	59	19	19	97
1933–1934	124	15	12	151
1923–1924	130	41	15	186
1913–1914	74	37	17	128
1903–1904	68	30	20	118

Stage design by Boris Aronson
FIDDLER ON THE ROOF
Based on the stories of Sholom Aleichem
Adapted by Joseph Styne
Directed by Jerome Robbins
Imperial Theatre, New York (1964)

Boris Aronson was asked how he solved the problems of designing two musicals as totally different as FIDDLER ON THE ROOF and COMPANY. "Fiddler on the Roof is the title of a very famous painting by Marc Chagall. Both the director and producer felt that the lightness, the playfulness of mood found in Chagall's work should be incorporated into the design. This contribution was to the atmosphere, but was not the solution to the design itself.
I reread the Sholom Aleichem stories . . . Tevye's house was described as a circle within a circle. I designed it as two revolving stages . . . one large and one small.
FIDDLER was an attempt to show the beauty of nature, growing even within poverty." — Boris Aronson

Fees and Royalties

The United Scenic Artists Union Local 829 Agreement with the League of New York Theatres and Producers, Inc., has established minimum rates for designers. Although the rate of a scenic designer for the first set on any type of production was $2400 in July of 1974, this fee (and all fees) is subject to an annual increase according to the agreement, which is reviewed every three years. Minimum rates for additional sets after the first one, unit settings, phases (scenic effects that change the original stage picture, such as projections), and bare-stage productions are also established, or the producer and the designer may agree upon the union minimum flat rate for each show. Besides settings, specific minimum rates apply to costume and lighting designs, depending on the type of production. All contracts have fringe benefits.

While the well-known designer with a great deal of experience and a name is most likely to command a higher fee than the new designer, this is not always the case. To get a show, some

59

established designers may agree to a lower fee than usual (but never below minimum) and work on a royalty basis. The weekly royalties a designer is able to negotiate on a Broadway show are strictly between him and the producer. They can vary considerably from a specific weekly royalty to a weekly percentage of the gross. The producer also agrees to pay the designer's expenses that are incurred for materials for making sketches and blueprints and all incidental expenses associated with the production. The titles to the designs and the drawings remain the property of the designer.

The Agent

Instead of having to cope with the personal business concerning a production, many well-known designers employ agents to do this for them. The primary purpose of an agent, of course, is to help obtain work and to negotiate the terms of contracts. A good agent can know the ins and outs of the business and be able to

protect the creative artist from pitfalls he may not be aware of. (A designer who is working out of town may also benefit frequently by having an agent represent him while he is away.) At the same time, while one occasionally hears that some designer gets a show because the producer knows his agent, most experienced directors usually have a designer in mind for their production.

Theatrical agents in New York City abound; one only has to leaf through a source like *Simon's Directory* to see the long list. Hard-working agents earn their 10-percent fee, and the better ones may be reluctant to sign an unknown talent. As in getting many jobs in the theatre, it is best to have someone experienced recommend or refer you when seeking one. It may be wise to sign with a reputable and established independent agent rather than a big agency. Some designers suggest that for a new designer it is advantageous to sign for three years and no more, for although one may not make that much money when first starting, by

Stage design by Boris Aronson
COMPANY
Book by George Furth
Music and lyrics by Stephen Sondheim
Directed by Harold Prince
Alvin Theatre, New York (1970)
(Photograph — Robert Galbraith)

"FIDDLER was based on short stories. COMPANY was based upon a series of vignettes about married life in New York. . . . people living in glass cages.
I designed COMPANY using no paint — Plexiglas, steel and projection. New York is a paced city . . . you don't stroll, you dodge. I created obstacles for the actors to relate to . . . forcing them to move certain ways . . . push buttons . . . elevators going up and down. . . . The city moving the man." — Boris Aronson

the end of that period he can have made a name and contacts for himself. In any case, the agent should be able to "read" a portfolio well and be familiar with what is involved in the designer's contract. Many designers prefer to use the services of an attorney to negotiate their business matters and to advise them; still others transact all of their own contracts and business themselves.

The Designer's Obligation

The stage designer of scenery, costumes, or lighting for a Broadway production renders specific services that are carefully spelled out in an agreement between the League of New York Theatres and Producers, Inc., and the United Scenic Artists Local 829:

SCOPE AND DEFINITION OF SERVICES:

This Agreement applies and is limited in its application to Scenic Designers, Costume Designers, and Lighting Designers, and Assistant Designers (hereinafter collectively called "Employees" and sometimes referred to herein as the "Designer" or "Assistant"), employed by or engaged in a theatrical production produced by the Employer. The work performed by the above-named Designers may include but is not limited to:

A. *Scenic Designer:* (designs the production and renders the following services in connection therewith):
   1. To complete either a working model of the settings to scale or to complete color sketches or color sketch models of the settings and necessary working drawings for the constructing carpenter at the reasonable discretion of the Producer or his authorized representative.
   2. To supply the contracting painter with color schemes or color sketches sufficient for the contracting painter.
   3. To design or select or approve properties required for the production, including draperies and furniture.
   4. To design and/or supervise special scenic effects for the production, including projections.
   5. To supply specifications for the constructing carpenter, to supervise the building and painting of sets and the making of properties, and, at the request of the Producer or his authorized representative, to discuss estimates for the same with contractors satisfactory to the Producer or his authorized representative, such estimates to be submitted to the Producer or his authorized representative at a specific time. If the Designer is required to participate in more than three estimating sessions of each

class extra compensation shall be paid as provided in paragraph IV (A) hereinafter [not included in extract].
   6. To be present at the initial pre-Broadway set-up and Broadway set-up days and dress rehearsals; to attend the first public performance and opening out-of-town, and the first public performance in New York and to conduct the scenic rehearsals therefor.

B. *Costume Designer:* (designs the costumes and renders the following services in connection therewith):
   1. To submit a costume plot of the production listing costume changes by scene for each character in the cast.
   2. To provide color sketches of all costumes designed for the production and any form of a visual representation for costumes selected for the production.
   3. To supply for the contracting costume shop complete color sketches or outline sketches with color samples attached, including drawings or necessary descriptions of detail and its application, sufficient for the contracting costume shop.
   4. To participate in not more than three estimating sessions with costume shops of the Producer or his authorized representative's choice for the execution of the designs if so requested. If the designer is required to obtain more than three estimates for the same costumes, extra compensation shall be paid as provided in paragraph IV (B) hereinafter [not included in extract].
   5. To be responsible for the selection and coordination of all contemporary costumes worn in the production including selection from performer's personal wardrobe where such situation arises.
   6. To be responsible for the supervision of all necessary fittings and alterations of the costumes.
   7. To design, select and/or approve all costume accessories such as headgear, gloves, footwear, hose, purses, jewelry, umbrellas, canes, fans, bouquets, etc.
   8. To supervise and/or approve hair styling and selection of wigs, hairpieces, mustaches and beards.
   9. To be present at the initial pre-Broadway and Broadway dress rehearsals and the first out-of-town and New York openings of the production.

C. *Lighting Designer:* (designs the lighting for the said production and renders the following services in connection therewith):
   1. To provide a full equipment list and light plot drawn to scale showing type and position of

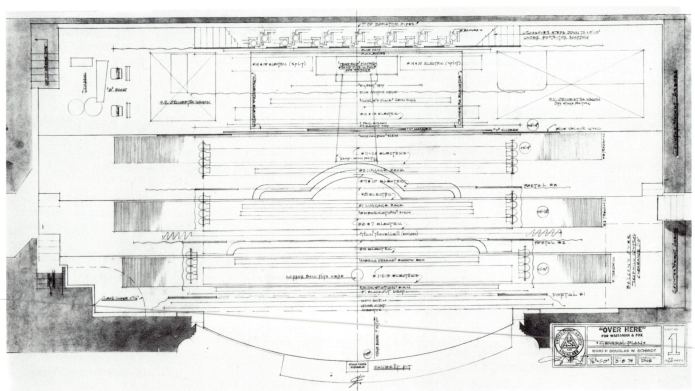

Stage designs and plan by Douglas W. Schmidt
OVER HERE!
Music and lyrics by Richard M. Sherman and Robert B. Sherman
Book by Will Holt
Musical numbers and dances staged by Patricia Birch
Directed by Tom Moore
Sam S. Shubert Theatre, New York (1974)

Schmidt's designs for the musical OVER HERE!, starring
the Andrews Sisters, unmistakably catches the mood and
period of the movie musical of the forties. The
proscenium opening was 40 feet wide by 21 feet high.
The personality photographs and logos on the arch portals
are painted on translucent muslin and framed with
aluminum.
Among the technical devices were three treadmills
approximately 3½ feet wide by 60 feet long to give the
idea of a train trip from the West Coast to the East; the
orchestra was on a large elevator upstage, 26 feet across;
rear screen projections were used.

all instruments necessary to accomplish lighting design.

2. To provide color plot and all necessary information required by contract electrician.
3. To provide control plot showing allocation of instruments for lighting control.
4. To supervise and plot special effects.
5. To supply specifications and to obtain estimates for the same for the Producer or his authorized representative from contractors satisfactory to the Producer or his authorized representative, such estimates to be submitted to the Producer or his authorized representative at a specific time. If the Designer is required to obtain more than three estimates, extra compensation shall be paid, as provided in paragraph IV (C) hereinafter [not included in extract].
6. To supervise hanging and focusing of the lighting equipment, and the setting up of all lighting cues.
7. To be present at all pre-Broadway and Broadway set-up days and dress rehearsals; to attend the first public performance and opening out-of-town, and the first public performance in New York and to conduct the lighting rehearsals therefor.

Stage design by Douglas W. Schmidt
GREASE
Book, music and lyrics by Jim Jacobs and Warren Casey
Directed by Tom Moore
Musical numbers and dances staged by Patricia Birch
Eden Theatre, New York (February 1972)
Broadhurst Theatre, New York (June 1972)

The Designer's Assistant

There are times when a designer needs to be two places at once while drafting, models, and other chores are being completed. Broadway designers hire assistants to expedite fulfillment of these obligations, and there is no doubt that one of the best ways for a new designer to learn the ropes and to gain experience is by assisting a well-known designer. This enables him to learn the many things that are done in the New York theatre and to see how a particular designer approaches them. It gives the new designer an excellent background to prepare him for working on Broadway (or anywhere, for that matter), which he cannot get in any other way. Most get the job of an assistant by being recommended by another designer, or they may get it by being interviewed with a portfolio of their work and good references. However it happens, when the assistant is being hired a busy designer expects to find someone thoroughly capable of handling the work and willing to stick with it as though it were his own production.

Setting by Tony Walton
PIPPIN (Touring Company)
Book by Roger O. Hirson
Music and lyrics by Stephen Schwartz
Directed and choreographed by Bob Fosse
Costumes by Patricia Zipprodt
Lighting by Jules Fisher
Imperial Theatre, New York (1972)
(Photograph — Friedman-Abeles)

A number of assistants have gone on to become well-established designers themselves. Nor is this method new; both Jo Mielziner and Donald Oenslager first embarked on their remarkable careers by working in the 1920s with famous theatrical designers. Oenslager worked with Robert Edmond Jones, as did Mielziner, who also was an apprentice to Joseph Urban and Lee Simonson. Since that time both Mielziner and Oenslager have themselves employed a large group of assistants who have in turn gone on to design on Broadway and are hiring their own assistants today. Ming Cho Lee, who assisted Mielziner for several years, has offered generous and invaluable help to young designers, among them Douglas W. Schmidt, David Mitchell, Marsha L. Eck, Ralph Funicello, John Scheffler, Marjorie Kellogg, Leigh Rand (Jenkins), John Kasarda, Leo Yoshimura, Miguel Romero, and Patricia Woodbridge.

Other designers work several years as assistants, and may do occasional shows of their own, but do not establish themselves independently. Some prefer this and some do not. There is no way to gauge how long a new designer may work as an assistant before going out on his own. Most assistants have worked anywhere from one to seven years. Sometimes an assistant lands his first big show at the suggestion of the designer he is working for, who may be too busy or just not want it.

An assistant can be asked to do almost anything to get a show ready. His normal job is to draft the drawings for the production and, more often than not, to work on the model. He may also help in the preparation of sketches by laying out the drawing for the painting, but most top designers do all of their finished sketches themselves. Other tasks include finding research material, obtaining all sorts of samples for car-

65

New York Shakespeare Festival

DELACORTE THEATER   CENTRAL PARK   SUMMER 1973

Produced by JOSEPH PAPP

PRESENTS

WILLIAM SHAKESPEARE'S

KING LEAR

Directed by EDWIN SHERIN

Setting by SANTO LOQUASTO
Costumes by THEONI V. ALDREDGE
Lighting by MARTIN ARONSTEIN
Music by CHARLES GROSS

Associate Producer BERNARD GERSTEN

THE CAST
(in order of speaking)

THE DESIGNER'S BILLING. Playbills of a drama and a musical, showing the appropriate billing of the designers with other collaborators of the productions.

IMPERIAL THEATRE

STUART OSTROW
presents

PIPPIN

A Musical Comedy by
ROGER O. HIRSON
Music & Lyrics by
STEPHEN SCHWARTZ

starring
(in alphabetical order)
ERIC BERRY
JILL CLAYBURGH
LELAND PALMER
IRENE RYAN
BEN VEREEN
and
JOHN RUBINSTEIN

with

CANDY BROWN	CHRISTOPHER CHADMAN	KATHRYN DOBY
GENE FOOTE	ROGER HAMILTON	RICHARD KORTHAZE
JOHN MINEO	JENNIFER NAIRN-SMITH	SHANE NICKERSON
ANN REINKING	PAUL SOLEN	PAMELA SOUSA

Scenery Designed by	*Costumes Designed by*	*Lighting Designed by*
TONY WALTON	PATRICIA ZIPPRODT	JULES FISHER

Musical Direction	*Orchestrations*	*Dance Arrangements*	*Sound Design*
STANLEY LEBOWSKY	RALPH BURNS	JOHN BERKMAN	ABE JACOB

Hair Styles by ERNEST ADLER
ORIGINAL CAST ALBUM ON MOTOWN RECORDS
Music Rights Administered by Jobete Music
Publications from the Score by Belwin Mills

Directed and Choreographed by
BOB FOSSE

---

pets, draperies, and curtains, or tracking down props and stage furniture, all of which are approved by the designer. If the same designer is also creating the lighting or costumes, an assistant can be assigned to each of these categories. Quite frequently, when the designer must attend rehearsals to see how the action of the show is developing, have conferences with the director, or remain in the studio to work, the assistant may fill in for him at the scenic shop and costume house, checking on the progress in both places. Besides working in New York City, assistants may also travel out of town to work on new productions. First-rate help is always in demand, and it is not inappropriate to note that the best and most reliable assistants are the ones who are hardly ever out of work.

According to the United Scenic Artists Local 829, assistants to the designer on legitimate theatrical productions are paid by the management on a weekly basis through the filing of an assistant contract with the union. When the designer negotiates his contract, the management and the designer agree on the length of time for which an assistant is to be hired, and it is so stated in the contract filed with the union. Such contract must also be approved by the union before any work is performed.

The Designer's Union Contract

No work of any kind can be done by a designer or assistant designer (scenery, lights, or costumes) before the contract between the designer and producer has been approved (signed and filed) by the United Scenic Artists Union Local 829, and such contract has been received by the designer.

Billing

It is always standard practice on any Broadway production to give the stage designers appropriate credit for their creative endeavors on the production, including the playbill and the many forms of advertisements for the show. The designer's billing is fully covered by the Agreement between the League of New York Theatres and Producers, Inc., and the United Scenic Artists Local 829.

The United Scenic Artists Local 829

The United Scenic Artists Union Local 829 of the International Brotherhood of Painters and

Allied Trades has jurisdiction in these fields: the legitimate theatre, opera, ballet and all its branches, motion pictures, and television. The local is an association of artists and craftsmen, formed to protect craft standards, working conditions, and wages. Chartered on June 24, 1918, the United Scenic Artists is the union to which the following belong: scenic designers, art directors for television and movies, scenic artists, costume designers, lighting designers, mural artists, and members in diorama and display. The union is composed of those members who are qualified and can work in all classifications or members who may qualify in one or more classifications and work only in these. In 1975 Ben Edwards was president of Local 829 which has a membership of around 900. There were then two business representatives, Andy Clores and Abe Kanter, and their areas of responsibility included: (Clores) television, feature and commercial motion pictures, mural art, diorama and display, and exhibition; (Kanter) legitimate theatre and all its branches such as Broadway, off Broadway, off-off Broadway, stock, repertory, regional, opera and ballet, industrial shows, and scenery-suppliers' studios. The address is: United Scenic Artists Local 829, 1540 Broadway, 15th floor, New York, N.Y. 10036. Tel.: (212) 575-5120. In Chicago, the address for Local 350 is: United Scenic Artists Local 350, 343 S. Dearborn Street, Chicago, Ill. 60604. Tel.: (312) 431-0790.

There is a reciprocal agreement between Locals 350 and 829, the International Brotherhood of Painters and Allied Trades, and Scenic Artists Local 816, I.A.T.S.E. (West Coast).

Qualifying for Membership in All Classifications of Local 829

Rigid examinations are given yearly for qualification for membership in the United Scenic Artists Union, and they usually take place in late spring. Interested persons are interviewed with samples of their work (designs, photos, and so on) beforehand, and those who become applicants are tested extensively. They may be examined to qualify in all classifications (scenic designer, costume designer, lighting designer, and scenic artist) or, if they so choose, in one or more of these categories.

An applicant who wishes to take the full exam for all classifications is formally tested in all phases of stage design and painting, ordinarily given over a four-day period on two consecutive weekends (Saturday and Sunday) in late May and/or early June. This time is selected to coincide with the end of the school term. However, the date and place can vary from year to year. Parts of the examination are given in locations where appropriate equipment and space are available. For example, in the spring of 1974, exams were given in scenic and costume design at Parsons School of Design, lighting design at the Master Theatre, and those for scenic artists at Nolan Scenery Studios. Several weeks prior to all this testing, the applicant is assigned a show to design as a "home project," which may include set designs, color elevations, working drawings, and a model; costume sketches with swatches and detailed instructions for their execution; a complete light plot showing all instruments and their uses for lighting the show; and examples of specific subjects for scene

PAINTING ON THE HOME PROJECT FOR THE SCENIC ARTISTS EXAMINATION. Young women artists, applicants for taking the scenic artists examination in the late spring of 1974, are shown working on part of the assigned home project, a 4 foot by 6 foot painting of an interior on muslin. Subjects included in the supplied line drawing are: brocade wallpaper, marble fireplace with gilt framed mirror above, carved-wooden folding screen with tapestry, metal fire screen, porcelain vase with flowers, fabric draped over screen, and flagstone hearth. Pictured: Hope Auerbach, Sue Chapman. (Photograph — Lynn Pecktal)

painting. New applicants should not underestimate the amount of time required to finish the home project.

Problems in all areas of design and painting, similar to those mentioned above, are covered on the days of the formal examination. Besides being talented, it is vital for the applicant to be well-organized with his time, techniques, and working materials so he may proceed with sufficient speed throughout the examination and finish each assigned project with ease. While the exam is comprehensive and thorough, it retains the high standards set by its members. A nonreturnable fee of $65 for registration plus $15 for each classification is required to take the full examination. For the applicants who passed, a 1974 initiation fee of $1000 was paid to the union, after which the new member was eligible to work in all classifications of Local 829.

Qualifying for Membership as a Scenic Artist

Recently, the union created a separate category for those applicants who prefer to take the examination to qualify as a scenic artist only, and they are tested at the same time of year as the applicants in the other categories, with the emphasis being placed on scene painting rather than design. A take-home project is also given to the scenic artist applicant and may consist of drawing and painting backdrops for a theatrical production; reproducing drawings in full scale; rendering realistic samples of classical ornament and architecture; creating a three-dimensional sculptured panel; making a lettering layout and painting a portrait for use on the stage. As in the exam for all classifications, time is allotted for formal testing where the applicant executes additional projects covering the various phases of scene painting. A nonreturnable fee of $65 for registration plus $15 was necessary to take this examination in 1974, and for those who passed an initiation fee of $1000 was required by the union. The scenic artist would then be eligible to paint in the areas covered by the jurisdiction of Local 829, which include the theatrical scenic studio, motion pictures, and television.

DESIGNING BEYOND BROADWAY:

Although designing Broadway productions will doubtless continue to represent a special attainment in American theatre, there are other and perhaps wider areas in which the professional designer can aspire to work—sometimes with fewer creative limitations than Broadway imposes. The pages that follow explore some of them, beginning with two unique institutions, the Metropolitan Opera and Radio City Music Hall. The role of the stage designer off Broadway and off-off Broadway in New York is examined next, then the world of summer stock (the package show and the resident summer company), the professional resident companies, and university theatre. Production photographs and stage designs suggest the great variety and tremendous vitality in evidence today beyond Broadway.

THE METROPOLITAN OPERA

Designing for the Metropolitan Opera in New York, one of the world's great houses, is in a very special category. International in many aspects, the Met actually mounts more productions by international designers than by Americans. The roster is nevertheless distinguished by any standard, with the 1974–1975 program listing Cecil Beaton, Nicola Benois, Eugene Berman, H. M. Crayon, Rolf Gérard, Peter J. Hall, Rudolf Heinrich, Charles Knode, Ming Cho Lee, Motohiro Nagasaka, Caspar Neher, John Piper, Jean-Pierre Ponnelle, David Reppa, Wolfgang Roth, Günther Schneider-Siemssen, Jan Skalicky, Josef Svoboda, George Wakhevitch, and Franco Zeffirelli. (Stage directors for the Metropolitan make a similarly impressive list and include a number whose primary achievement has been in the spoken theatre. The 1974–1975 repertory included works staged by John Dexter, August Everding, Colin Graham, Bodo Igesz, Patrick Libby, Fabrizio Melano, Nathaniel Merrill, Günther Rennert, Sandro Sequi, Patrick Tavernia, and Wolfgang Weber.)

The Metropolitan management selects the designer for each production. As in other areas of theatre, the choice of some of the notable American designers who have worked there has

Setting, costumes and visual effects by Peter Wexler
LES TROYENS by Hector Berlioz
Libretto by the composer
Staged by Nathaniel Merrill
The Metropolitan Opera, New York (1973)
(Photograph – © Beth Bergman, 1974)

Scene: The queen's closet in Part 2.
Mignon Dunn as Anna (left), Shirley
Verrett as Dido.

come about in various ways. The late Eugene Berman, who designed the settings and costumes for *Don Giovanni, Rigoletto, La Forza del Destino, Il Barbiere di Siviglia,* and *Otello,* recalled that he did his first opera (*Rigoletto*) at the Met in 1951 only after being introduced to general manager Rudolf Bing by Horace Armistead, an old friend. Berman had tried to design for the Met earlier, but his approaches to Edward Johnson, Bing's predecessor, were fruitless. Robert O'Hearn's career started at the Met when he did a production of *Don Giovanni* for the Washington Opera Society with director Nathaniel Merrill, which Mr. Bing was invited to see; about a month later Bing invited Merrill and O'Hearn to direct and design the Metropolitan's 1960 production of *L'Elisir d'Amore.* O'Hearn has since designed the sets and costumes for *Parsifal, Der Rosenkavalier, Hansel and Gretel, Die Frau ohne Schatten, Samson et Dalila, Aïda, Die Meistersinger von Nürnberg, Queen of Spades, The Marriage of Figaro,* and *Boris Godunov* (unproduced).

Desmond Heeley, the English designer, was chosen to design at the Met after he had designed the sets and costumes for *Rosencrantz and Guildenstern Are Dead* (1968) on Broadway (for which he won two Tony Awards). Bing and Herman Krawitz saw the show two weeks after it opened and invited Heeley to do the 1970 *Norma.* He also designed the sets and costumes for *Pelléas et Mélisande* in 1972.

The high proportion of international designers whose work is seen on the stage of the Metropolitan Opera is a reflection of the number of international directors engaged, since the director frequently recommends to management a designer with whom he has already worked. Star singers, too, have been known to suggest designers. They may have been very little aware of the scenic designer but remember that a specific production was highly successful in another theatre and feel particularly secure about the sets. In addition, designers who have developed careers in Europe have generally had wider opportunities than their American colleagues to design opera, more often than not working up from assignments in provincial

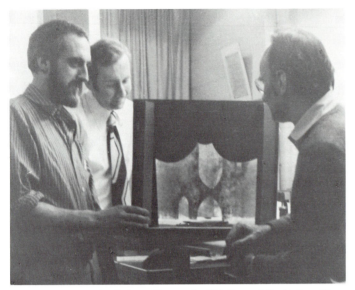

In the design office on the fifth floor of the Metropolitan Opera complex, Desmond Heeley (left) shows his model for Debussy's PELLÉAS ET MÉLISANDE to Don Jensen (center) and David Reppa, associate designer at the Met (right).
(Photograph – Lynn Pecktal)

theatres to designing productions for a major opera house. A designer who comes from Europe to do a new setting of, for instance, *La Traviata* for the Met may already have done three or four productions of it abroad in the course of his development. However, in the mid-1970s the management has begun to rely on the talents of American designers.

If the designer for an opera at the Metropolitan is not an American, the fact may put additional burdens on the resident personnel at the opera house. Because of the nature of scheduling at the Met, work on a production may be going on a year to eighteen months before performance. After an international designer presents his final production design to management for approval, he may not reappear until everything is on stage. David Reppa, associate designer on staff at the Metropolitan Opera, whose office is located with the scenic studio on the fifth floor of the opera complex at Lincoln Center, is basically the designer when the designer is not there. He must thus treat each setting as if it were his own. He develops working drawings, solves problems, and oversees the execution of the scenery. Reppa is in touch with the designers only if major problems occur. (While doing some thirty new productions during

seven years at Lincoln Center, he has not had to write a designer more than two or three times.) Going over the sketch or model, Reppa points out, is "like a doctor diagnosing a case. You look at a patient and you can sometimes tell what is the matter. You look for the problem areas. I'm not saying that problems don't arise once you get into production, but we have to solve those right away. Every designer is told by the management, usually, that regardless of the designs, we always have to make them work for our storage problems. The designers will say, 'Fine, that's your problem. I just want it to look this way.' So, if we find a problem, like breaking a piece of scenery, we have to find a way we can do it and make it work for us and look the same way for the designer."

A production conference is held to go over the entire opera. Normally, those present are the director of stage operations (Rudolph Kunter, also head electrician), the head carpenter (Steve Diaz), and head prop man (Dick Hauser), all from the stage; the heads of the various shops: the carpenter shop (Joe Volpe), prop shop (Dick Graham), and scenic shop (Stanley Cappiello), and Reppa. Management may also be represented. Since the designer and director work together before the approved designs come in, the director is not ordinarily present. The director can be on one side of the world, in fact, and the designer on the other; at the Met both usually see what is on stage for the first time when they arrive for rehearsal.

The proscenium opening of the Metropolitan stage is a 54-foot square, the same as in the demolished opera house that stood at 39th Street and Broadway. The big difference between the old proscenium and the new is one of set height. While this seldom went above 28 feet in the old house, it may be as much as 32 feet at Lincoln Center. (The stage of the new house is very deep, as was that of the famous old one; the designer's challenge in accommodating great crowds in some operas did not change when the location did.) Each designer works differently to get his designs on the big Met stage. Some make models, some do sketches; some make both, governed mostly by schedule. For his new *Tosca* in 1968, Rudolf Heinrich submitted three sketches and three ground plans in $\frac{1}{4}$-inch scale. Designers usually do ground plans in this scale because they are sent a set of $\frac{1}{4}$-inch plans when they are engaged by the Met, so when the ground plans for the opera come back, they are invariably ¼-inch. Since the stage is so large, these are relatively easy to carry around — but the Met never works from ¼-inch scale, and part of David Reppa's job is to put the plans into a larger one. On this *Tosca*, the entire drafting was taken from the sketches and ground plans without making a model. Details are all ½ inch or 1 inch to the foot, and sometimes even "full scale." Many small changes can take place at this point since the drawing in the sketch can be deceptive. There may be slight adjustments in the vanishing point or the perspective. It is simpler to make changes when working from a sketch than it is from a model. If a full model has not been submitted, there is not time to do one; only occasionally are partial models made, to check out particular set pieces.

A fairly new feature in design at the Met is the *Bauprobe*. This is standard practice in most

European opera houses, but the Metropolitan only really began to have a *Bauprobe* for the productions of *Carmen*, designed by Josef Svoboda in 1972, and *Tristan und Isolde*, designed by Günther Schneider-Siemssen (1971). A *Bauprobe* is simply a mock-up of the new set on stage with any old flats or scenery that happen to be around, once the model and ground plans have been submitted. This massive arrangement of forms on the stage allows the director and designer to check the sight lines and shapes from the auditorium. "One of the built-in problems you always have in opera that you don't have in other theatrical productions," David Reppa observes, "is being able to accommodate anywhere from a hundred fifty to two hundred people on stage at once, particularly in a Verdi opera where the chorus is there and then, two seconds later, they're gone. And fifteen minutes later, they're all back in again. It's a huge traffic problem to plan out and have

Costume (Virgins) by Desmond Heeley
NORMA by Vincenzo Bellini
Libretto by Felice Romani
Directed by Paul-Emile Deiber
The Metropolitan Opera, New York (19˙0)

Costume (Arkel) by Desmond Heeley
PELLÉAS ET MÉLISANDE by Claude Achille Debussy
Libretto by Maurice Maeterlinck
Directed by Paul-Emile Deiber
The Metropolitan Opera, New York (1972)

a place for them and yet to make a design that is interesting and holds together when they're not there.'' The *Bauprobe* is staged mainly if a designer has never worked at the Met and is not familiar with the stage and how it relates to the auditorium. Until a designer has a feeling of the auditorium and its color, he does not know what the built-in problems are, and the *Bauprobe* helps solve some of these before actual work is begun on the scenery.

Finding time to have a *Bauprobe* can be difficult, however, as there is almost always something happening on the Met stage. The Met can have a complete dress rehearsal of an opera in the morning, plus a performance at night. The first three or four weeks of the season are especially heavy. Before each opera comes into the repertory, it has a complete dress rehearsal, and it may also have had one or two stage rehearsals before that, depending on how long it has been out of repertory. An opera that was completely new at the end of

the preceding season will have other rehearsals in various parts of the building, then all elements will come together on the stage for one dress rehearsal, or perhaps one piano rehearsal and one rehearsal with orchestra. A production never goes back into the repertory without a complete dress rehearsal.

How a designer goes about conceiving a particular opera is an interesting facet of Metropolitan production. In creating sets and costumes for Debussy's *Pelléas et Mélisande* in 1972, Desmond Heeley felt himself faced with one of the most difficult assignments a designer could have. ''The first thing that came into my mind,'' he said, ''was that you cannot possibly let the curtain come down, because the minute you lower lights into a blackout, your neighbors start searching for the sweeties, they find their shoes, or they start talking. So somehow [the production] had to bridge from scene to scene, and it meant that the scene changes as such were just as important as the

Stage designs by Robert O'Hearn
DIE FRAU OHNE SCHATTEN by Richard Strauss
Libretto by Hugo von Hofmannsthal
Directed by Nathaniel Merrill
The Metropolitan Opera, New York (1966)

Emperor's Terrace, below.
The sketch of the emperor's terrace was rendered with acrylic paints. The terrace (on an elevator) lifts and goes out of sight, and the Dyer's house (below stage) comes up. The scene thus moves from a fantasy realm in the sky to a mortal earthly place below.

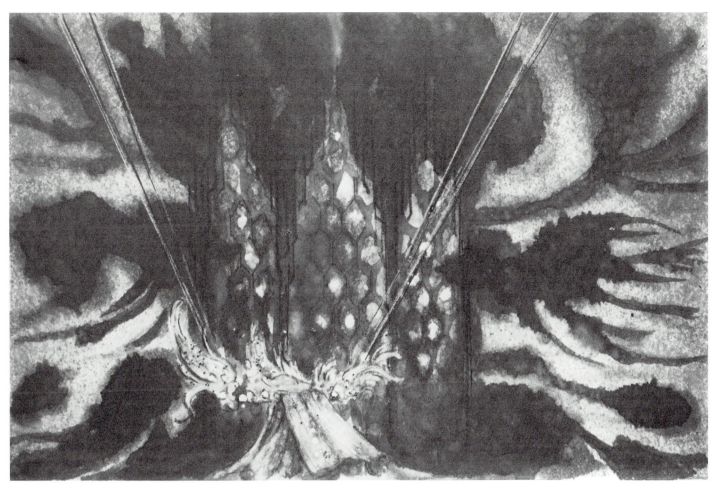

The Empress' Bedroom

The Dyer's House

The Dyer's House

sets themselves, and that one should dissolve into the other.'' In the nearly two years Heeley had to work on the opera, he designed several versions of *Pelléas,* each one becoming simpler, before he delivered the final design. *Pelléas* was directed by Paul-Emile Deiber, an actor from the Comedie-Française with whom Heeley also did *Norma* at the Met.

For *Pelléas,* Heeley listened to the music a great deal and made endless lists: ''Which is the most important section and what can I do without to make the focus rivet onto the singer? I began to think in terms of a photograph. In a photograph, sometimes you have a very short depth of field, and you can focus on a face or an eye. What's behind the eye, the ears, the back of the head, or forward of that eye? It is blurred and out-of-focus, so it rivets your attention. To me, the production is terribly passionate and very strong, very dark. The characters talk constantly about the lack of light. There's a light from a lantern, there's a light from beyond the sea, the light appears for a moment in the grotto, so it's a perpetual twilight.''

Heeley wanted to dissolve the edges of the scenery as much as possible without using projections, and he remembered an effect he had discovered by accident a few years earlier while doing a play at the National Theatre in London. Trees were being glued onto ordinary squared-off scenic netting laid flat on the floor. In the process, some of the workers spilled glue on the netting. ''When it was backlighted,'' Heeley recalled, ''it was fantastically brilliant. I've always thought it would be nice to use that, and it was an effect that was stored in the back of my mind.'' With this idea, Heeley discovered through experiments that it was possible to build architecture with solid edges that fragment and disappear into the net. ''It was a very difficult thing to bring about. Using layer after layer of netting and splashing glue on it gave an intangible quality. One could play with these back and forth until you could fool the audience, hopefully, into thinking 'Is it really there, or is it not?' It would make its own void. It was like freezing a Jackson Pollock and hanging it in midair. All of the objects were made of this stuff. It's like seeing a picture in smoke or a picture in water or milky glass. It's not the kind of transparency you have with scrim or bobbinet. In fact, they

move slightly and can make your eyes go funny, but with very careful lighting, you can achieve an extraordinary effect. I intend to further explore this technique in a different way. This is the beginning of it, I think, for me.''

When he came to the costumes for *Pelléas et Mélisande,* Heeley explained, ''The cast themselves kind of define the shapes. I like to overlay and overlay with different fabrics or by painting, by spraying, or antiquing the fabric to lose the contemporary feeling of the clothes. For instance, the Arkel costume is bridal veiling put over some funny old silver lace we found. This is put over a muslin in a way so it's laminated. It's all bumps and scratches and wrinkles. It looks like hell close-to, but when you get away from it, you can't tell what it's made of, and it has a certain mystery. This is a constant thing, particularly on clothes. I like to do a great deal to disguise and put a glaze over them.''

Robert O'Hearn is one of the few present-day American designers who has designed more than two operas for the Metropolitan Opera. He follows the American system of designing and submits working drawings along with his sketches and models. Of all the operas O'Hearn has designed for the Met, one of his favorites, Richard Strauss' *Die Frau ohne Schatten,* was the most difficult. Before making sketches, he spent almost two months analyzing the complex work with huge charts of factors for each scene: length of time, what happened in the scene shifts, symbolic meaning, color ideas, and plot developments. ''It's so involved,'' O'Hearn noted, ''because it has three different worlds—the spiritual world, the in-between world [of the Emperor and Empress], the mortal, earthy world of Borak the Dyer and his wife. Each of these had to have a different look so the audience would have some feeling of the story. I wanted it to be entirely out of the imagination.'' In the beginning he looked at pictures of Ceylon and Siamese temples, trying to think of some actual place to base the architecture on, and finally he threw that out completely: ''If I did use anything for research, the crystalline domes of the terrace of the Emperor's palace were based on microphotographs of some little crustacean in the sea. It looked vaguely like the dome of a temple with a finial on top of it. Since the whole thing was about life and fertility and

74

Costumes by Allen Charles Klein
LES CONTES D'HOFFMANN by Jacques Offenbach
Libretto by Jules Barbier and Michael Carre
Directed by Bliss Hebert
The Metropolitan Opera, New York (1973)

(Top) Spalanzani (first appearance), Chorus (Act I)
(Bottom) Chorus (Act I), Spalanzani
Klein's technique of rendering each figure with an
outstretched arm provides details of the sleeves. The
woman with dress draped over her arm shows the
details of both the undergarment and footwear.

75

being mortal or not being mortal, I wanted this feeling of nature to go through the whole production. So, many of the drops were based on this cellular and organic kind of thing."

One of O'Hearn's techniques to keep the drops from looking at all realistic was doing the painting elevations in batik, an idea that came after he saw an article on making batik pillows in a *Woman's Day* magazine in the supermarket. He suddenly realized this was what he wanted, because it was a half-accidental and a half-controlled method of painting. O'Hearn explained how he did the batik painting: "You paint wax on fabric and dye it, and put more wax on and dye it some more. But the trick that helps control it in between these stages is that you paint on it with colored inks. They remain permanent, so you can make it much more subtle and adjust the dye job. I draw out what I have in mind, and maybe paint some first, put some dye on, then hot wax, then some dye, and paint some more, so probably there were about five dye stages in the whole dyeing process. At the end, you completely cover the whole thing with melted wax and paraffin together, put it in the refrigerator so that it gets very hard, and then crunch it in your hands so that all the paraffin crackles. Then you put this in a deep color—say a very deep navy blue or a deep wine-red—and when you eventually take the wax off, there is an all-over network of these little crinkled lines. So this gave the elevations an excitement that you couldn't do by hand. Of course, the painters didn't love them, because they had to copy this work by hand."

O'Hearn's finished designs were then given to the Met scenic shop, where the painters actually caught the idea very quickly. A typical procedure was used for several scenes. There would be a translucent backdrop with a scrim in front of it. The scrim for the first scene was put on top of the backdrop, which was on the floor in the paint shop. Once the effect was painted and the scrim was taken off, the drop underneath was almost painted too. With only a little touching up, there were two copies. "When they were hung in the theatre, they were about fifteen feet apart, so the winged messenger could appear between the two," O'Hearn said. "There was a projection on the front of the scrim of almost the same thing that

was painted, and behind it on the backdrop was a spotlight. So between all of that, you really couldn't tell where it was in the air. There was no feeling of drops. You saw this glowing nebula from the air, and it was really quite wonderful. I think one of the best uses of projection is to heighten the already painted effects on scenery."

For the Metropolitan's production of *Die Frau ohne Schatten*, which drew wide praise, O'Hearn had been asked to exploit the working machinery of the new theatre, and many exciting technical effects took place in the opera. A few examples: During a scene change in full view of the audience, the terrace scene on the stage floor went up in the air while the Dyer's house on the understage came up from the basement. A big stairway that was part of the underground temple was on the revolve. The table lift was used for the harem appearance, and the mirror and some of the girls entered through a trap in the floor. For the flood effect, the Dyer's house went down, leaving a completely empty stage floor. "Unfortunately," O'Hearn explained, "you did see the stage floor come down, but it didn't seem to be objectionable since so much was going on, and there was loud music. Once it was down, you ended up with this bare stage that had a water-ripple lighting effect which we first worked out in my living room. We used pans of water with mirrors on the bottom and wiggled our hand in the water to get the ripples. The electricians rigged up a little paddle wheel to keep the water agitated. They shined a spotlight on it and the reflection in the mirror came out and it looked like the whole stage had drowned. It's quite easy to focus. The light shines down into the mirror and bounces up to where you want it. We had two of these offstage right down in the wings next to the proscenium, and these would flicker water reflections on the set. It really looked better than any optical projection."

Robert O'Hearn also designs the costumes for his productions at the Met. Management much prefers the same person to do sets and costumes, and since operas are planned so far ahead, there is adequate time. In discussing the costume designer's problems, O'Hearn recalled that the only trouble he had ever had was from a ballet girl once, and from

76

Stage design by Boris Aronson
MOURNING BECOMES ELECTRA
by Marvin David Levy
Libretto by Henry Butler
Based on a play by Eugene O'Neill
Directed by Michael Cacoyannis
The Metropolitan Opera, New York (1967)
(Photograph – Robert Galbraith)

"I wanted to emphasize the grandeur of the play, and at the same time I didn't want to lose the importance of the actor onstage. I went about this by 'cornering' the performers with my design. I imposed obstacles. An obstacle forces a performer to respond to it . . . to move around it, or in front of it. As soon as the actor responds to this obstacle there is a relation, a contrast . . . the actor becomes more visible. Cornering was a process of imposing these obstacles in areas which would frame the actor on exits and entrances, immediately bringing attention to him, emphasizing him." – Boris Aronson

a replacement who came over from Europe to sing Dalila. "She brought her own sort of clothes that had been whipped up in an attic in Budapest or some place. They were the worst looking sort of sequin jobs you've ever seen — like burlesque striptease. After all, Dalila is supposed to be a priestess, not a prostitute. We really had quite a time with that lady. We made a couple of minor compromises with her, and she finally wore our costumes."

Part of the opera costume designer's job is to enhance the physical appearance of the singers. O'Hearn says he really concentrates on "trying to make heavy ladies look slim. So I often do what I call my 'hostess gowns' for them, which tend to look a bit 1940. It's a long line, usually with a lighter panel down

the middle and a couple of long hanging drapes from each shoulder. They become a chiffon drape in the back and hide the bulk behind. Some of them come out looking remarkably well. When you can make Rita Gorr look fairly sylphlike for Dalila, it's pretty good. And Birgit Nilsson was a problem for *Aïda*. She is a big-boned lady, and to make her look like an Ethiopian slave was a little difficult. But all the top people have been wonderful and so professional about these things that I really have no problems."

There is an enormous number of costumes for each Metropolitan production, often anywhere from two hundred fifty to five hundred, and every new costume is made up in the Met's own costume shop on the second floor

77

of the opera house. The only items not built in the shop are the men's boots. Because the costumes are expected to last at least fifteen years, and because they get much hard treatment traveling back and forth from the warehouse and on tour, they are built very strongly. The costume shop is seldom working on only one show, as constant replacements are required for chorus members who don't fit the old costumes, as well as new costumes for new singers or cover singers. Both the scene shop and the costume shop work year-round, with a reduction in staff only during the summer months.

The Met has a shopper who confers with the designer to choose fabrics from stock books of fabric swatches. In addition, materials may be selected from such fabric houses as Far Eastern, Stroheim and Romann, Gladstone, and Beckenstein's. The shopper also searches for trims, buttons, and any other items needed for the costumes.

Rudolph Kuntner, director of stage operations, does the lighting for the operas at the Met; he and the director and designer usually work out the lighting for the productions together. An average of two days is allowed for lighting rehearsals of a very simple new production, but complicated operas with a great many projections take longer. After these independent rehearsals, the lighting is worked on and perfected during a couple of dress rehearsals. There is no repertory plot at the Met; every opera has its own light plot and each production is lit completely from scratch. Instruments are focused and gels changed for each performance and even between acts.

The scheduling of the subscription distribution of the operas ordinarily accounts for the number that are presented each season, and also for the number of times they are done. An individual opera may play eight or nine performances in a season, but the same opera never plays back-to-back—two performances of an individual opera in the same week are the most that will be scheduled. As many as twenty-four different operas can be kept in repertory with the new productions. This means bringing the scenery in from two storage warehouses, one at 129th Street in Manhattan and one in Maspeth, Long Island. The Met also uses other warehouses for storing props and costumes. Backdrops are rolled and wrapped

and are kept in long racks, usually at 129th St. At the beginning of the season as many as can be accommodated are brought to Lincoln Center and placed in the "drop cut," a storage space that goes down about three floors into the stage. Here backdrops are kept in a series of racks. When an opera is dismantled at night, all the old drops are put on the lift at the same time and placed in their respective slots for storage. Then the new drops for the next evening are put on the lift and brought up.

RADIO CITY MUSIC HALL

Some New Yorkers, professional theatre people and longtime residents alike, dismiss Radio City Music Hall as a gigantic movie house and tourist attraction, even though a complex and fully designed stage show is mounted there four times a day. From the designer's point of view, however, this famous "showplace of the nation" offers challenges and technical possibilities of a kind found nowhere else. The gigantic stage at Radio City Music Hall is one of the largest and best-equipped in the world, and on it productions are presented in grand style. Almost any kind of scenic effect imaginable can be created in this theatre seating 6200 people, in such presentations as "The Nativity" at Christmas; the "Glory of Easter," a big cathedral pageant; "Bolero"; "Rhapsody in Blue"; and the "Underseas Ballet." For more than twenty years the scenery for Radio City has been designed by James Stewart Morcom, who began as art director in 1950 and succeeded designers Bruno Maine, Vincent Minnelli, and Clark Robinson. Morcom, however, retired in the latter part of 1973 and was succeeded by John William Keck.

Work on a new production follows a standard sequence at the Music Hall. There is always a show onstage, one approved and in the works, and one being planned. About a month before a new show, John Keck has a preliminary production meeting with the producer, then another on the Monday preceding the Thursday opening. At these meetings, the producer can be Peter Gennaro or John Jackson. The producer usually knows beforehand what the corps of precision dancers, the Rockettes, will do. The producer, being the one who decides such things, may say, "I want to use the Rockettes in a very novel number. They're

Cutaway drawing of the Music Hall stage showing the hydraulic pistons that lift the stage by elevators. (Photograph – courtesy of Radio City Music Hall)

Setting by James Stewart Morcom
CONTRAST IN RHYTHM — Corps de Ballet
Produced by Leon Leonidoff
Costumes by Frank Spencer
Radio City Music Hall, New York (1959)
(Photograph — courtesy of Radio City Music Hall)

Much of the large scenery at the Music Hall is unframed. The ornament painted on fabric is cut out and glued to scenic netting.

going to be firecrackers for the Fourth of July and I want them in a red-white-and-blue background as simple as you can work it out." To this the designer answers, "I happen to have a red curtain, a white curtain, and a blue curtain — full curtains. I can use half of each of these and hang them up and make red, white, and blue stripes, and it wouldn't cost a cent." Whenever possible, old scenery in the storehouse is revamped to save on costs and the budget is used for a big new finale or a new set for the Rockettes, although it can be spread over the whole production. Each upcoming show nevertheless means getting the scenery ready for the Rockettes, singers, and various acts.

After the first production conference, John Keck is ready to go about designing splashy color presentations of the scenery in ½-inch scale. Working in this scale makes the finished renderings and drafting more than average size, since the stage is over 100 feet wide, with a depth of 60 feet from the curtain to the cyclorama. Even though "masking in" on the sides reduces the overall width to 70 feet, there is still a great deal of space to be filled with scenery. Backdrops, for instance, hang at 45 feet and trim at 38 feet, and are normally 85 to 90 feet wide.

In creating his set designs, John Keck uses everything from pastels to colored pencils to paints, on all kinds of paper and board, depending on the effect he is seeking. They can be sketched on tracing paper, or they can be collages of several different papers with flitter and other metallic materials glued on them.

Old designs are sometimes reworked when the scenery is coming out of storage. "If it's something I see we can change or paint over," Keck explains, "I'll take an old sketch of Minnelli's or Albert Johnson's, Bruno Maine's or Morcom's, and by the time I'm through it looks like new scenery." Once the sketches are finished, they are presented for financial approval and are shown to the heads of production departments to see what the problems might be.

If old settings are being turned into new, finding the original designs is a simple matter. An enormous collection of stage memorabilia dating back to December 27, 1932, when the Music Hall opened, includes sketches and production photographs of every show. A single design or photo can be pulled out of the files on a moment's notice, and each piece bears a number that corresponds to the actual items stored in a Bronx warehouse. An assistant,

who is not a union member, takes care of the office, the filing, and the storehouse.

Building at the Music Hall itself is restricted to construction of small scenery and props in the basement shop, where they are also painted and touched up. Newly designed scenery like big drops and big sets (or old ones being redone) is painted by a theatrical scenic studio, since there isn't room to do it at the Music Hall. Occasionally it is a problem finding a scenic studio (chosen by a bid session) willing to take the work during busy periods, because they cannot always give up the space to do drops that are 45 feet high by 90 feet wide. The studio that does the set usually supplies the scenic artists who come to the Music Hall for touch-ups. On big traditional holiday shows like those at Christmas and Easter, two painters may be needed for a week or longer, but for the average show they only come in for two or three days before the opening. These scenic

Stage design by James Stewart Morcom
TEMPLE OF THE SUN (⅜-inch scale)
Produced by John Henry Jackson
Radio City Music Hall, New York (1973)
(Photograph — Lynn Pecktal)

Costumes designed by Frank Spencer
EASTER SHOW
Bunny heads by Joe Stephen
Hats by Andy Pellicano
Radio City Music Hall, New York (1974)
(Photograph — courtesy of Radio City Music Hall)

Materials: White plush fabric over canvas body
held by hoops. Heads cast of Celastic covered
with white plush, cheeks and noses painted pink;
eye openings covered with plastic screening. Eyes
painted green, lavender, and pale blue. Hats
decorated with flowers, feathers, netting, and
sequins.

artists work in numerous places throughout the Music Hall complex — in the scene shop on the lower level, in the wings, or on the stage between stage shows. More often than not, on a day before the show changes, a prehung backdrop is let in on the stage floor for touch-up while the movie is playing. If it is not finished during the film, it is flown and then let back in after the next stage show.

The extraordinary equipment at the Music Hall provides endless technical possibilities for scenic effects. The stage is really three elevators with a 43-foot-diameter revolve cut in the center. With the elevators locked together, the revolve can turn; it can also go around while the elevators rise or sink. The orchestra is equipped to rise and move onto the stage, riding like a boxcar on wheels in a track. It can also move to the No. 3 elevator and sink to the basement and, with all three elevators locked and lowered, cross the sunken stage, go back onto its own pit elevator, then rise in the pit — making a complete round trip. To bring action out into the audience, the elevator floor of the orchestra pit comes up flush with the stage floor, forming an extension of the apron. There is also a removable runway around the orchestra pit. It can be used flush with the pit elevator or in front of the orchestra when it (the orchestra) remains in the pit. The lights are controlled from a prompt box, sunk in the floor in the first rows of the auditorium so the operators can see the stage

as the show is in action. The footlights can turn over electrically to make a flat stage.

Still other spectacular effects can be created. The steam curtain sunk in the floor downstage (parallel with the footlights) may be used to block out a scene, and rain can fall from two rain pipes into a duck cloth on the first elevator, which is depressed three inches to catch the water. Keck reports that there is rain about every two years on the great stage. The cyclorama is outfitted with lights on dimmer to give a starry sky with clouds projected; there is also a ''star drop'' of the same type of set-up as the cyclorama which can be moved up- or downstage. The gold contour house curtain (112 feet wide by 78 feet high), with thirteen lines on individual motors, forms any outline desired for a frame.

When a new production is being mounted at the Music Hall, there is very little time for the changeover from the old show to the new. Everything must be finished overnight so that the new stage show is ready to go on at noon the next day. As soon as the last show has ended and the last movie starts at 9:30 P.M. on Wednesday, the sound curtain is pulled down and old scenery is swiftly dismantled and sent to the warehouse. Shortly thereafter, new sets are being put into place and what could not be prehung is hung. All of the scenery is transferred by 4:00 A.M., ready for the lighting rehearsal, at which time the producer, designers, electricians, and stagehands go through

Setting by John William Keck
A POTPOURRI OF BUNNIES AND CHICKS —
Easter Show
Produced by Peter Gennaro
Costumes by Frank Spencer
Radio City Music Hall, New York (1974)
(Photograph — courtesy of Radio City Music Hall)

Scenery units included painted (unframed) cut leg drops with lights, framed profile chickens, and Easter basket. Translucent vacuum-formed Easter eggs were 4 feet wide, 5 feet 9 inches high, 9 inches deep. The plastic eggs were sprayed white to conceal the dancers behind them; some broke apart, opened by the dancers as though they were hatched from them. Patterns on the eggs were created by taping Roscolene gel on the inside and were revealed when the eggs were lighted from behind.

the show (without people) and light it. Then at 7:00 or 7:30 A.M., the production is put together for a complete rehearsal with the entire company (in costumes and make-up) and the orchestra. The show is rehearsed until as late as 10:30 A.M., when the house opens for the movie, and another new stage show is ready to go before the public at 12:30 P.M. on Thursday.

OFF BROADWAY

In the theatrical world, Off Broadway is as well-known as Broadway and those in the industry have long been aware that it is one of the best places to get a good start in the theatre in New York. Countless creative artists have

benefited greatly from having their work seen off Broadway and as a result have gone on to Broadway, television, and work in films. Off Broadway has been recognized for years as an area where serious productions could be done with more stress on the artistic quality than on commercial requirements; in this respect, Off Broadway has been very similar to Off-Off Broadway. Some of the most outstanding works in the modern theatre have been produced off Broadway, including new plays, classics, and revivals of shows that failed on Broadway — primarily because the first aim was to produce good theatre.

Off Broadway was once thought of mainly as an area of tiny lofts and dingy basements where exciting productions could be attempted

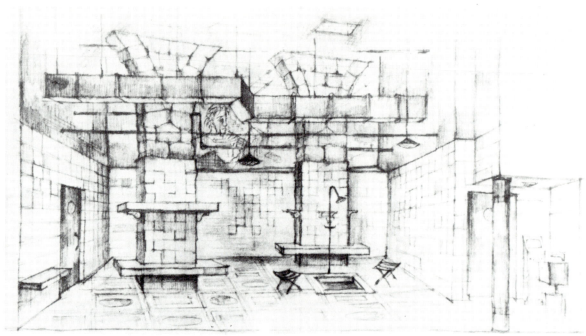

Sketch and setting by David Mitchell
STEAMBATH by Bruce Friedman
Directed by Anthony Perkins
Lighting by Jules Fisher
Truck and Warehouse Theatre, New York (1970)
(Photograph — Neil Peter Jampolis)

The effect of realism was heightened by the actual steam and water onstage in David Mitchell's Off-Broadway setting for STEAMBATH. The tiles on the walls of the setting were made of routed Masonite.

Setting and model by Elmon Webb and Virginia Dancy
LONG DAY'S JOURNEY INTO NIGHT
by Eugene O'Neill
Directed by Arvin Brown
Lighting by Ronald Wallace
Promenade Theatre, New York (1971)
(Photographs – Elmon Webb)

The action takes place in August 1912 in the
living room of the Tyrone's summer home. The
realistic interior was designed for a proscenium
stage with a shallow thrust.

without costing a great deal of money. Because of the high production costs today, however, "Off Broadway" refers more to a geographic region than to an inexpensively mounted show. In the mid-1960s, average cost of an Off-Broadway production was around $15,000; ten years later it had catapulted to far more than double that amount. A straight play off Broadway in 1974 could cost as much as $50,000 and a musical $75,000, with ticket prices approaching the Broadway range. Fortunately, not every production costs this much to stage.

Getting work off Broadway for a new designer is much the same problem as obtaining an assignment anywhere else in the theatre. Talent and preparation are vital, a good portfolio and résumé do not hurt, and prior recognition is useful. But, here as elsewhere, recommendation by a friend in the business can carry great weight, and more jobs are found through personal and professional contacts than by seeking interviews cold.

However it comes about, getting that job can launch a young designer's career. As on Broadway, an off-Broadway production that gets prime reviews and has a long run can help the designer achieve recognition and possibly new assignments. (He may also have

a chance to make some money on a hit show, because of the length of the run, and because the Off-Broadway union contract specifies royalties according to seating capacity of the theatre.) It is naturally of paramount importance that the designer establish a good working relationship with those in the trade when doing any show.

Successful off-Broadway ventures may move to Broadway, in which case the same production designer may come with them. Recent transfers from Off Broadway to Broadway include *That Championship Season, Sticks and Bones, Two Gentlemen of Verona* (from the Delacorte Theatre in Central Park), *Grease,* and *Oh! Calcutta!* A few artistic and commercial off-Broadway successes remain off Broadway. The most phenomenal example is *The Fantasticks,* in its sixteenth year at the Sullivan Street Playhouse.

Some designers do only a few shows off Broadway, but others do many before moving up to the Great White Way or elsewhere. Robin Wagner designed nearly twenty off-Broadway shows before getting his first Broadway production. At the same time, a group of very seasoned designers work both on and off Broadway, among them Ming Cho Lee, Rouben Ter-Arutunian, Raoul Pène du Bois, Peter

Setting by Kert Lundell
PAPP by Kenneth Cameron
Directed by Martin Fried
Lighting by Roger Morgan
American Place Theatre, New York (1968)
(Photograph—Frederick Rolf)

Designed to be a room in the Vatican, the setting incorporated a variety of objects, shapes, and materials, positioned in front of a black velour cyclorama.

Stage design by Don Jensen
HOW TO GET RID OF IT
Music by Mort Shuman
Lyrics by Eric Blau
Based on AMEDEE by Eugène Ionesco
Directed by Eric Blau
Astor Place Theatre, New York (1974)

Set in Greenwich Village at the present time, the scenery was designed for a proscenium opening 29 feet wide by 22 feet high; the depth of the set was 18 feet.

Larkin, Douglas W. Schmidt, William Ritman, Kert Lundell, Karl Eigsti, Ed Wittstein, Lloyd Burlingame, William Pitkin, Edward Burbridge, Wolfgang Roth, James Tilton, Santo Loquasto, Robert D. Mitchell, Robert U. Taylor, Neil Peter Jampolis, David Mitchell, and Fred Voelpel. In addition to working with a good director on a fine script, many established craftsmen also enjoy the rapport and the closeness that can come in working on an Off-Broadway production, where the pressure and hassle of the highly commercial environment is not always present.

Off Broadway has many different types of theatre and stage, classified by the number of seats in the house. There is a wide variety of size and shape, with seating arrangements and stages that vary accordingly. Well-known Off-Broadway theatres currently include the Eastside Playhouse, Cherry Lane Theatre, Provincetown Playhouse, Eden Theatre, Circle in the Square (downtown), Promenade, McAlpin Rooftop Theatre, Theatre Four, Theatre De Lys, Astor Place Theatre, Truck and Warehouse Theatre, St. Mark's Playhouse, Greenwich Mews Theatre, Jan Hus Playhouse, American Place Theatre, Gramercy Arts Theatre, Sullivan Street Playhouse, Roundabout Theatre, and Newman and Anspacher Theatres (both Public Theatre, New York Shakespeare Festival).

This list of nine active theatres gives some idea of the spread among size, stage dimensions, and location of off-Broadway houses:

THEATRE AND CAPACITY	PROSCENIUM OPENING	STAGE WIDTH	STAGE DEPTH	CEILING HEIGHT
Theatre De Lys 121 Christopher St. (299 seats)	28' 0"	40' 0"	10' 0" (plus thrust 14' 0")	15' 0"
Cherry Lane Theatre 38 Commerce St. (185 seats)	17' 6"W 11' 0"H	27' 0"	21' 0"	20' 0"
Jan Hus Playhouse 351 East 74th St. (199 seats)	28' 0"	46' 0"	20' 0"	9' 0"
Promenade Theatre 2162 Broadway, at 76th St. (299 seats)	34' 0"	49' 0"	11' 0" (plus apron 9' 0")	20' 0" (approx.)
Circle in the Square 159 Bleecker St. (299 seats)	None	16' 0"	50' 0"	17' 0"
Astor Place Theatre 434 Lafayette St. (199 seats)	None	24' 0"	18' 0"	18' 0"
American Place Theatre 111 West 46th St. (299 seats)	38' 0"	22' 0" (thrust) 52' 0" (upstage)	39' 0" (from back wall to tip of thrust)	21' 0" (playing level to bottom of catwalk)
New York Shakespeare Festival—Public Theatre:				
Newman Theatre 425 Lafayette St. (299 seats)	40' 0" (an end stage)	85' 0" (with column obstructions)	35' 0"	21' 0"
Anspacher Theatre 425 Lafayette St. (299 seats)	None (thrust stage)	23' 0"	33' 0"	Nominal 29' 0" at center (from floor to lighting grid)

Setting and lighting by Peter Harvey
THE BOYS IN THE BAND by Mart Crowley
Directed by Robert Moore
Theatre Four, New York (1968)
(Photograph — Les Carr)

"THE BOYS IN THE BAND needed a representation of an overly decorated, fashionable New York apartment, keeping within the taste of its homosexual owner. To hold the artificial look of a "decorator" interior I made a collage of interior-decoration photographs, using the necessary locations (study, living room, bedroom, etc.) in a slightly expressionistic composition. I kept the furnishings to a minimum, all in black and silver to blend with the black and white photographs of the set. There was no conventional set dressing as this was provided in the photographs; also the photographs were carefully scaled so that architectural details and furniture would be in the right proportion to the actor. The carpet was gray, masking black, and the lighting instruments were fully exposed. Costumes were, of course, in natural colors. All of this gave an effect of exposure and harshness as well as a piquant unreal-real reality to the scene." — Peter Harvey

Model by David Mitchell
HAMLET by William Shakespeare
Directed by Joseph Papp
The New York Shakespeare Festival
Anspacher Theatre, Public Theatre, New York (1967)
(Photograph — Neil Peter Jampolis)

Stage types include proscenium, open or thrust, and arena; the off Broadway designer is limited or freed by the special characteristics of the house for which he is conceiving a production. How he gets his settings built and painted depends on management preference and budget size. The scenery may be executed by one of the theatrical scenic studios as for a Broadway show (budget permitting), by one of the nonunion shops that do off-Broadway work, or by craftsmen in the theatre itself.

Off-Broadway groups have been responsible for creating artistically superlative productions for several years. Among the most notable are Joseph Papp's Public Theatre and the New York Shakespeare Festival, the Circle in the Square, the Phoenix Theatre, the American Place Theatre, the Negro Ensemble Theatre, the theatre of Richard Barr and Edward Albee, and the Living Theatre of Julian Beck and Judith Malina.

OFF-OFF BROADWAY

Any designer planning to work in the Off-Off Broadway theatre should realize that making a

living is not the dominating factor; what really counts is working in a creative environment where there is time for experimentation and learning. A vast number of writers, directors, actors, and designers work off-off Broadway just for the love of it. Most must hold other jobs to support themselves, which is one reason performances are given only on weekends. Admission may be free, or a small contribution may be required. But, since making money is not the first consideration in Off-Off Broadway theatres, they are not under the pressures of the box office or what critics say about the show to make it run. Often, as much time as needed is allowed for rehearsal, and in many cases productions open only when they are ready.

In such a climate, off-off Broadway is perhaps one of the most challenging areas in which a designer will work in the theatre, for he must be inventive and improvise with no money or very little, creating in surroundings which usually have more limitations than the stage in a local high school. Productions are staged everywhere—from intimate coffee houses to factory lofts, from garages to vacant stores and churches —and the designer may be called upon to

Stage design by Robert U. Taylor
THE JUDAS APPLAUSE by Gary Munn
Directed by Robert Kalfin
Chelsea Theatre Center
Brooklyn Academy of Music (1969)

Taylor's design is an imaginative representation of a bar in Washington where John Wilkes Booth spent time before he shot Lincoln.

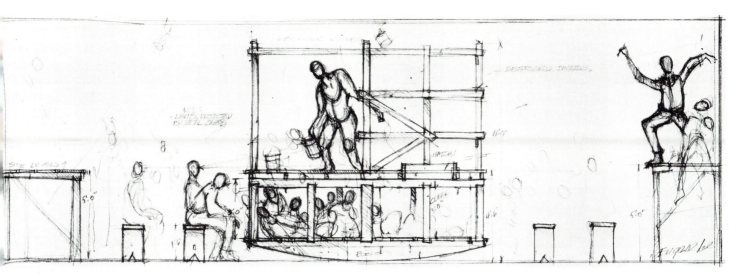

Side Elevation
Scale: ½ in. = 1 ft.

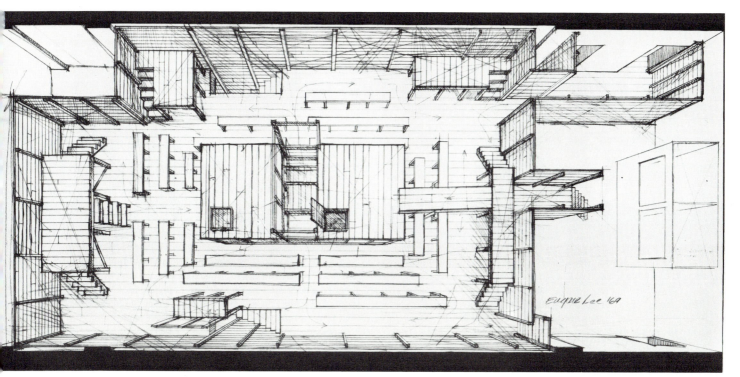

Stage designs by Eugene Lee
SLAVE SHIP by LeRoi Jones
Directed by Gilbert Moses
Chelsea Theatre Center
Brooklyn Academy of Music
Brooklyn, New York (1969)

The action of the drama takes place in the hold of a ship. The top drawing is an elevation view from one end. Below is a perspective drawing from above, indicating how the playing areas and seating arrangement of the house relate to each other.

91

devise a setting and props by scraping together whatever he can. Formal plans and drawings are minimal, with much of the work done on the spot. More often than not, help is scarce. The designer may find himself doing practically all of the work alone or with the assistance of one or two technicians. He may also have to depend on volunteers for aid in painting scenery or obtaining lighting equipment. While off-off Broadway is a great place to do imaginative designing, the designer's greatest investment is his time.

Off-Off Broadway today produces most of the shows in the New York theatre, with some five hundred presented a year. Beginning mostly in Greenwich Village, the Off-Off-Broadway theatre has spread throughout the city. There are now so many that a large number of these non-Equity productions do not get notice or reviews from the well-known drama critics, who are usually obliged to cover larger Equity productions first. There is an almost infinite variety of theatres whose offerings run the gamut from the classics to new American plays to improvised productions involving audience participation.

Two of the first and most prominent Off-Off-Broadway organizations, Joe Cino's Café Cino and Ellen Stewart's Café La Mama, were founded in the early 1960s. The prolific Ellen Stewart's La Mama is still going strong, but Café Cino ended with the death of its founder

in 1967. Among the many other recognized companies are Al Carmines' Judson Poets' Theatre, Ralph Cook's Theatre Genesis, Joseph Chaikin's Open Theatre, Charles Ludlam's Ridiculous Theatrical Company, André Gregory's Manhattan Project, the Old Reliable, the Extension, and the New York Theatre Ensemble. Several of these companies have received foundation aid and support, which has enabled them to tour.

Like Off Broadway originally, Off-Off Broadway serves as a training ground and as a showcase not available anywhere else in the city for new talent. With Off Broadway becoming more and more commercial, it is possible that noncommercial Off-Off Broadway will soon be the one area remaining for continued experimentation in the New York theatre.

SUMMER STOCK

Stock is a household word to everybody in the entertainment world and almost anyone who keeps up with the theatre. "Doing stock" is an excellent way for the young designer to get practical experience in the theatre. Many drama-school and university students find it an ideal place to work between their years of study and afterward. For some, it is also a good method of finding out if they want to continue in the theatre. It is not only the young and inexperienced who do summer stock, however;

Setting by Don Jensen
ROAR LIKE A DOVE by Lesley Storm
Directed by Robert Ellis Miller
Lighting by Alan Leach
Ogunquit Playhouse
Ogunquit, Maine (1960)
(Photograph – Edward D. Hipple)

Very detailed settings can be achieved frequently in one week-stock, as evidenced by Jensen's interior at the Ogunquit Playhouse. Some summer stock theatres such as this one have an excellent collection of furniture and props, which is invaluable to a designer.

Setting by David Jenkins
THE MISANTHROPE by Moliere
Directed by Austin Pendleton
Lighting by Richard Devin
Costumes by Ruth Wells
Williamstown Theatre
Williamstown, Massachusetts (1973)
(Photograph – Michael C. Durling)

This setting for a modern version (1960s) of Molière's MISANTHROPE was designed for a proscenium opening 32 feet wide. Three-dimensional plastic molding and ornament were applied on the flats, which were 13 feet 6 inches high. The setting was surrounded in back with black velour.

Setting by Helen Pond and Herbert Senn
SUMMER AND SMOKE by Tennessee Williams
Directed by Jeffery Hayden
Lighting by Robert Thompkins

Cape Playhouse
Dennis, Massachusetts (1973)
(Photograph – Craig of East Dennis)

a large number of seasoned craftsmen work along the "straw hat trail" and enjoy it. The scenic-designer team of Helen Pond and Herbert Senn, for example, have designed for Broadway, but they still go back each summer to design at the well-known Cape Playhouse in Dennis, Massachusetts, as they have for a number of years.

The best way for a new designer to secure a summer-theatre job, of course, is through someone who knows the producer, through a designer who has previously worked there, or by recommendation from some well-respected person in the theatre. Summer-stock producers have much to cope with in planning a season; hiring a designer, they want the assurance that they are engaging someone who will be self-sustaining through the whole season, in both talent and temperament. The salary in summer-stock companies can vary considerably, depending on the designer's experience and qualifications, although some producers have a top limit and hold the fee down to that figure. A weekly salary of $250 to $300 is considered average by some producers in the better Equity houses. For the ambitious young designer, the compensation may be much less important than the experience. Leo Shull's *Summer Theatres* contains detailed information on summer productions.

Working in stock quickly teaches a designer much about both the technical and the practical aspects of designing. He learns to organize his time carefully and to do good work fast, because everything has to be gotten together in such a short time. There is usually a week in which to get a summer package show on, and some typical resident summer stock companies will have two weeks. In this period, the designer not only designs the settings and drafts the plans, but usually also paints much or all of the scenery and supervises the props. He may have to do all of this while contending with a sparse budget. The work is made much easier if the designer has a good assistant to help draft and paint, and the services of resourceful apprentices. Anyone who has worked in stock appreciates the importance of having a talented technical director and skilled carpenters, but the summer-stock designer may have to do much of the work alone. There is always enough work for a one-setter to be finished properly in a week; with a multiset

show, life can be hectic, to say the least. (In the resident stock companies [as opposed to package shows], things may be just as busy for the costume designer.) Most dependable summer theatres have a collection of stock items—including wings, doors, stair railings, and platforms—and a wise designer lightens his load by using as much as he can from this source, although it may dampen his ambitions. Naturally, it is a different story when the time, budget, and help are plentiful.

From one's earliest recollections of designing in stock, any number of things stand out. There were the inevitable flats painted with dry colors mixed in size water which had to be washed before they could be repainted for the next show. And to disguise the cracks between the flats, a "dutchman" was made by tearing off narrow strips of muslin, dipping them in paint, and applying them wet on the join. Or perhaps a wild arrangement of smilax was found and stapled over the crack to hide it. Then, those times when it was necessary to stay up night after night to get a big show painted, plus having a week of rainy weather where nothing seemed to dry. Often no aniline dyes could be put on backdrops that had to be used for other shows, and it was completely unheard of to think of purchasing a new seamless scrim. But, while much of this has changed, today there are still those stock theatres where the designer can always learn a great deal by having to improvise and use his ingenuity.

Summer Package Shows

Package shows are cast and rehearsed (most often in New York City) before arriving at the summer theatre, and the actors only have to adjust to the new scenery and physical surroundings at each place they play. A package show may be cast with stars or may be a production with talented actors who are less well known. Over the course of ten weeks the company of actors travels to as many theatres, presenting the same show, ordinarily with a run-through on each new set prior to the opening. Before a package show goes into rehearsal, a scenic designer is hired to design the master plan(s) and elevations. Copies are sent to the resident designer in each theatre where the company is to play as a guide for designing the sets. All the usual entrances, exits, placement of furniture, and kinds of prop are noted on these copies, so the actors do not have to change the blocking and stage business from place to place.

The resident designer does not work with the director, as is normally the case, since the director is represented by an "advance man" who appears at the theatre about a week before the production is to open. This person functions as an assistant director as well as general stage manager and "all-round problem solver," and answers any questions that the scenic and lighting designers, producer, or the resident stage manager might have. The costumes travel with the show; a special item at the top of the advance man's list is a note to the set designer about the colors of the female star's clothes. (Always of the utmost importance, this is done so the colors of her costumes do not clash with or fade into the scenery. Since a star often has many changes of clothes during a show, they can easily include practically all the primary and secondary colors, and a designer may have to settle for something like a pale-gray set, just to play it safe.) There are all sorts of other notes for the designer, such as "no heavy pillows on the sofa" or "all doors must be at least seven feet to accommodate Cesar Romero's height." This kind of summer theatre is a wonderful place to get experience doing a lot of handsome interiors, and it is well worth the time and effort.

Many of the best-known and oldest summer theatres that book package shows are beautifully run, and the stage and shop facilities, including the prop rooms, are kept in immaculate order. Since most of these theatres are in resort areas, the type of show presented is geared to a vacation audience. The season can feature revivals of recent Broadway hit plays and musicals, as well as some that are very old indeed. Sometimes one or two new plays that are generally advertised as pre-Broadway tryouts are produced, but these seldom reach New York. On the whole, the playgoer usually comes to see the stars and it is not always imperative that the show be an artistic success. The management is well aware that the main concern of the audience is often who is playing rather than what is playing.

Some of the oldest and most reputable summer theatres that play package shows are the Ogunquit Playhouse (Ogunquit, Maine), the Lakewood Theatre (Skowhegan, Maine), the Cape Playhouse (Dennis, Mass.), the Falmouth Playhouse (Falmouth, Mass.), the Westport Country Playhouse (Westport, Conn.), the Pocono Playhouse (Mountainhome, Pa.), the Tappan Zee Playhouse (Nyack, N.Y.), Playhouse in the Park (Philadelphia, Pa.), the Candlewood Theatre (New Fairfield, Conn.), and the Ivoryton Playhouse (Ivoryton, Conn.).

Resident Companies

The resident summer company is composed of actors, directors, and designers who work together as a creative group on the premises. While a show is playing one week, the people in the company are getting ready for the next one. Much of the best work in good resident companies is done when the concentration is on the artistic merits of the plays themselves instead of as vehicles for a star or featured actors. Many of these summer theatres play the entire season with a resident Equity acting company, sometimes supplemented with apprentices, while others engage a star from time to time or bring in actors for certain parts. The repertoire may include all sorts of work other than the typical summer fare. A Neil Simon comedy can play back-to-back with Shakespeare or Ibsen and then be followed by a hit musical or an avant-garde piece, all of which can offer both the company and the audience a season of versatile and exciting theatrics.

The work of the stage designer can be far more appealing and inspiring in the resident summer stock company than in package shows, not only because he has a chance to do many different productions, but if he works with an imaginative director he is also not always likely to stick to the same plans or concept as the original show and can branch out on his own. In most summer theatres, there is very little time off for the designer, especially if the company plays in repertory. The scenery is kept intact for each production and cannot be reused until the show ends its run, and in many cases the designer may be expected to be on hand to check the set out each time the show returns.

A sampling of well-known resident Equity summer companies would include the Williamstown Theatre (Williamstown, Mass.), the Olney Theatre (Olney, Md.), the John Drew Theatre (East Hampton, N.Y.), the Bucks County Playhouse (New Hope, Pa.), the Totem Pole Playhouse (Fayetteville, Pa.), the Mountain

95

Playhouse (Jennerstown, Pa.), the Cecilwood Theatre (Fishkill, N.Y.), the Sharon Playhouse (Sharon, Conn.), and the Peterborough Players (Peterborough, N.H.).

In addition to summer package shows and resident summer companies, numerous other summer opportunities exist for designers with the Shakespeare festivals, music tents, and opera and dance companies.

RESIDENT PROFESSIONAL THEATRE

Some of the finest productions in current American theatre are being staged by resident or regional companies. Since the primary aim of these groups is artistic productions rather than commercial return, they usually provide an exciting atmosphere for creative work, not only for the stage designer but also for the directors and actors. Resident companies present the classics, serious modern dramas, and avant-garde plays with a sprinkling of original scripts. Offerings may be works of Shakespeare, Molière, Shaw, Chekhov, Williams, Miller,

O'Neill, Albee, Pinter, Beckett, Ionesco, or Pirandello, and occasionally the revival of a popular Broadway hit. Although there are companies that operate on a repertory basis, an overwhelming number of resident theatres do not repeat their productions, but let a single play finish its run and then go on to another. A large majority of resident theatres are non-profit organizations, supported by government aid (the National Endowment for the Arts and state arts councils), by grants (from the Ford, Rockefeller, and other foundations), by local and private contributors, and by subscription drives.

From the designer's viewpoint, many pluses exist for working in these resident companies, especially in the more reputable ones. Besides the emphasis on artistic quality and the opportunity to create with top-flight acting companies, there are other considerations. Usually more-than-adequate time is allotted for designing and executing a production. The scheduling varies with the theatre, but many allow four to six weeks to mount a production. Budgets are gen-

Setting by Douglas W. Schmidt
CAMINO REAL by Tennessee Williams
Directed by Michael Kahn

Lighting by Joe Pacitti
Cincinnati Playhouse in the Park (1968)
(Photograph — Walter Burton)

Stage design by Karl Eigsti
THE LAST MEETING OF THE KNIGHTS OF THE WHITE MAGNOLIA by Preston Jones
Directed by Alan Schneider
Kreeger Theatre
Arena Stage, Washington, D.C. (1975)

This comedy in two acts takes place in the meeting room of a rundown hotel in a small West Texas town. Designed for a semithrust stage, the perspective drawing showing both interior and exterior views was made for a stage width of 35 feet from wall to wall of the inside set. The ground plan shows not only the usual requirements, but a portion of the tongue-and-groove planking on the raked floor.

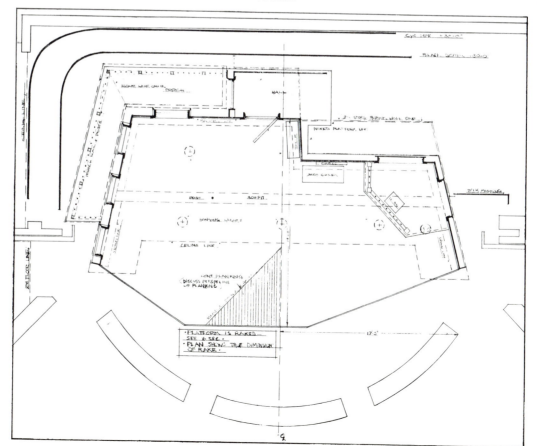

Setting by Lynn Pecktal
THE WALTZ OF THE TOREADORS by Jean Anouilh
Directed by Rocco Bufano
Lighting by Albin Aukerlund
Costumes by Peri Grenell
Barter Theatre
Abingdon, Virginia (1962)
Pictured: Georgia Bennett, Ned Beatty
(Photograph – Douglas Patterson)

A solarium setting was created by using wooden window frameworks covered from behind with pearl screening. In other scenes, the bedroom at center, was concealed by an open-framework (three-folding) unit holding Austrian curtains (made of scrim) and draperies with tiebacks.

erally good. In the best-planned companies, the technical staff and shop facilities are highly organized, and the stage is well equipped. A fair number of resident companies stage attractions in more than one theatre, and also tour.

Designers both with and without experience on Broadway work in resident theatres. For either category, the most prominent companies can be ideal for doing stimulating productions with excellent directors while earning respectable fees. Not only do these organizations offer the designer a place to experiment, he can also be assured of being employed for a reasonable period of time. Some companies hire resident designers for the entire season; others "job in" several designers. An average season is thirty-five to forty weeks, running from September through May, although some companies run shorter or longer periods and others play during the summer months.

The total number of resident theatres throughout the country has grown rapidly in recent years, offering new opportunities for employment. Many well-known companies that have been around for a long time are still going strong. Three of the earliest theatres—Robert

Porterfield's Barter Theatre in Abingdon, Virginia, established during the depression, in 1932; the Cleveland Play House, which began in 1916 and had its first professional director in 1921; and the Pittsburgh Playhouse, which was started in 1934 and became professional in 1965—have served as excellent training grounds for an impressive roster of writers, directors, actors, and designers.

Other resident companies formed later than the pioneers and still active are Nina Vance's Alley Theatre in Houston (1947); Zelda Fichandler's Arena Stage in Washington, D.C. (1950); the Milwaukee Repertory Theatre (1954), formerly the Fred Miller Theatre; and Los Angeles' Center Theatre Group (1959). Many new companies founded in the 1960s are currently thriving, among them Cincinnati's Playhouse in the Park (1960), the Tyrone Guthrie in Minneapolis (1963), the Theatre Company of Boston (1963), the Seattle Repertory (1963), Baltimore's Center Stage (1963), the Hartford Stage Company (1964), Philadelphia's Theatre of the Living Arts (1964), Providence's Trinity Square Repertory Company (1964), New Haven's Long Wharf Theatre

Model and setting by Elmon Webb and Virginia Dancy
YEGOR BULICHOV by Maxim Gorky (American premiere)
Directed by Arvin Brown
Lighting by Ronald Wallace
Long Wharf Theatre, New Haven, Connecticut (1970)
(Photographs — Elmon Webb)

Model by Gordon Micunis
THE VENETIAN TWINS
by Carlo Goldoni
Directed by Robert David Macdonald
Minnesota Theatre Company
Tyrone Guthrie Theatre (1970)
(Photograph — Gordon Micunis)

The design of the ½-inch-scale white-paper
model for the thrust-stage production of
Goldoni's THE VENETIAN TWINS was
duplicated for the actual setting except that
the center platform was removed, which
allowed the stage floor to become the street.

Setting and costumes by Gordon Micunis
THE VENETIAN TWINS by Carlo Goldoni
Directed by Robert David Macdonald
Lighting by Robert Scales
Minnesota Theatre Company
Tyrone Guthrie Theatre (1970)
(Photograph — Gordon Micunis)

Micunis designed a very pictoral proscenium
production for the thrust stage at the Guthrie
Theatre. The asymmetrical thrust served as
the street, with an entrance and exit over a
bridge going into a vomitory downstage
left and another downstage right
into a pit.

Setting by Elmon Webb and Virginia Dancy
THE ICEMAN COMETH by Eugene O'Neill
Directed by Arvin Brown
Lighting by Ronald Wallace
Long Wharf Theatre, New Haven, Connecticut (1972)
(Photograph — Elmon Webb)

(1965), the Studio Arena Theatre in Buffalo (1965, established in 1927; it had been an amateur house and school), the Los Angeles Inner City Repertory Company (1967), and the Detroit Repertory Company (1967). There have been some notable *nonresident* professional theatres, among them Ellis Rabb's Association of Producing Artists (APA) founded in 1960 and William Ball's American Conservatory Theatre (1965).

UNIVERSITY THEATRE

It is hard to imagine any university or college campus in the United States today without a theatrical production of some kind. The offering may be mounted by an extracurricular group that does one or two shows a year or it may be the work of students in a theatre-production course for academic credit. The quality of stage productions on campus ranges across a wide spectrum, but by the mid-1970s the best compared favorably with work to be seen in the commercial theatre, were acted in superbly equipped houses, and were often particularly notable for the design and lighting.

No matter where an aspiring designer begins, some experience can be gained from any organization that affords an opportunity to work in the theatre. When no formal training program is available, an ambitious designer may learn a great deal just "by doing," working with community or little theatres or even high school productions. Participating in the efforts of such groups is a good way of testing interest; some people soon decide that they are not really interested in the theatre as a career, others realize it is exactly what they want to do and

Set design and costumes by Robert U. Taylor
CORIOLANUS by William Shakespeare
Yale Drama School
New Haven, Connecticut (1967)

For the CORIOLANUS he designed at the Yale Drama School, Robert U. Taylor suggested the Roman setting by stylized columns and chose to reflect a society in the early Republic in which patricians move on elevated walkways as the poor run like rats through trenches. The costumes for the gladiator, always dressed for combat, further portray a culture in which the fighter, not the wise man, is considered the best fitted to lead. Source for the costumes was a Nick Fury comic book.

go on to train at an institution in which work and study in all phases of theatrical designing are available.

Several universities have had important theatre departments or a drama school for many years, offering degrees in design as well as in other specialties. Other schools are now expanding their theatre departments, with many offering majors for the first time. The oldest theatre schools and university theatres include the Yale Drama School (New Haven, Conn.), Carnegie-Mellon University (Pittsburgh, Pa.), Goodman School of Drama (Chicago, Ill.), Northwestern University (Evanston, Ill.), University of Iowa (Iowa City, Iowa), University of North Carolina (Chapel Hill, N.C.), University of Michigan (Ann Arbor, Mich.), San Diego State College (San Diego, Calif.), Indiana University (Bloomington, Ind.), Brigham Young University (Provo, Utah), University of Colorado (Boulder, Colo.), University of Georgia (Athens, Ga.), University of Illinois (Urbana, Ill.), and U.C.L.A. (Los Angeles, Calif.).

Students who plan to enter drama schools must always have some experience in designing beforehand—university or college, summer stock, or elsewhere—plus a facility for drawing and painting. Some institutions require a college degree for entrance, others offer undergraduate courses. Besides enrolling in a drama school to get a solid background in all-around theatre designing (sets, lights, costumes, scene painting), the student designer has a chance to take such vital courses as architecture, sculpture, fine-art painting, and drawing, which the school can offer as part of the theatre program or which can be elective courses. He may also be able to work in courses in important aspects of the humanities.

Designers study in a drama school for a multitude of reasons. Some attend because they plan definitely to design for the professional theatre, and they may or may not earn degrees; others go to get degrees so they can teach in a university where they may also design some or most of the productions. Young designers with a bit of experience study at a drama school so they can learn more about designing and how to do good presentational sketches to prepare the design portfolio they need when seeking work.

Setting by Rolf Beyer
LYSISTRATA by Aristophanes
Directed by Rod Alexander
Lighting by Bruce McMullen
Costumes by Alicia Annas
Hopkins Center Theatre
Dartmouth College

Hanover, New Hampshire (1971)
(Photograph—Al Olsen)

For this play on a timeless human theme, the designer created a futuristic missile-site setting instead of the traditional locale of ancient Athens. Rockets, missiles, and geometric shapes were constructed of such materials as plastic, stainless steel, and chromium.

Setting by Rolf Beyer
TI-JEAN AND HIS BROTHERS
by Derek Walcott
Directed by Errol Hill
Lighting by Richard Jeter
Hopkins Center Theatre
Dartmouth College
Hanover, New Hampshire
  (1971)
(Photograph—Al Olsen)

Some also realize they need to study more theatrical drafting or scene painting, both essential in the theatre and especially helpful for earning a living when they are working as assistants to a designer or painting for a theatrical studio, television studio, or the movies.

For talented designers with little experience, a drama school can give the advantage of seeing their set, costume, and lighting designs realized on the stage—along with constructive criticism and advice they will receive as part of their course of study. And, with many professional Equity companies appearing as part of the theatre program in universities today, the students have more chances than before to grow by observing and participating.

Theory and the book knowledge gained in a university are important, but the practical experience possible there is perhaps even more important. Too, contacts made during this time will be with people one sees and hears about throughout his career. There are many successful Broadway stage designers who are self-taught, some who did not even go to college, but few today would recommend that a young designer reject a chance for advanced study thoughtlessly.

A number of established designers have been or are instructors in colleges and universities, among them Ming Cho Lee and Jeanne Button at the Yale Drama School; Ben Edwards, Oliver Smith, Lloyd Burlingame, Karl Eigsti, Fred Voelpel, and Charles Rosen at New York University; Howard Bay at Brandeis University; Eldon Elder at Brooklyn College; and William and Jean Eckart at Southern Methodist University.

Outside the university framework, the non-profit Studio and Forum of Stage Design in New York City is an excellent place for a designer to enroll to take all or part of the curriculum, which includes courses in scenic design, costume design, lighting design, and scene painting. Established in 1958, the Studio is directed by Lester Polakov and the faculty includes Robert O'Hearn, Douglas W. Schmidt, Ben Edwards, Jane Greenwood, José Varona, Peggy Clark, John Gleason, Charles Levy, and Thomas Skelton.

WORKING IN OTHER AREAS

A background in the theatre prepares the designer for working in a number of related fields. Many designers work as art directors for feature motion pictures; television specials, series, and commercials; as theatre and architectural consultants, teachers, and lecturers; as designers for industrial shows, murals, displays, exhibits; and as interior designers for public rooms in hotels and restaurants, or for other commercial firms. Involvement in another creative field presents a challenge, keeps a designer busy, and the compensation can enable him to afford to work in his first love, the theatre. Lloyd Evans, for example, candidly relates that if it were not for his job as art director of the CBS-TV series *Love of Life* he would not be able to design the one or two opera productions for the New York City Opera that he has done annually for the past several years.

While some designers become involved simultaneously in dual capacities, others only do so when they are free of theatrical assignments. When you consider that there never have been enough productions on Broadway to employ all of the talented and available theatre artists, it is certainly easy to see why dedicated theatre artists very frequently choose to work outside New York City where there may be much more time and less pressure in creating a production. The emphasis can be placed on making an artistic endeavor rather than a commercial vehicle, and, also, the competition is much less severe than on Broadway.

A Conversation with ROUBEN TER-ARUTUNIAN

Born in Tiflis, Russia, on July 24, 1920, Rouben Ter-Arutunian was educated at Friedrich-Wilhelm University in Berlin, the University of Vienna in Austria, and the École des Beaux-Arts in Paris. After working in Europe, he came to the United States in 1951 and began to design for television. His first Broadway production was George Abbott's *New Girl in Town* in 1957, for which he created both the scenery and costumes. He has designed sets and costumes for a wide diversity of productions both on and off Broadway, for the American Shakespeare Company at Stratford, Connecticut, and for an impressive roster of prominent opera and dance companies. Among his awards are a Tony, an Emmy, and an Outer Circle Award. He has also been an art director for the motion pictures *The Loved One* and *Such Good Friends*. Rouben Ter-Arutunian's design credits include:

Broadway:
Goodtime Charley (1975)
All Over (1971)
The Devils (1965)
Ivanov (1965)
Arturo Ui (1963)
Advise and Consent (1960)
Redhead (1959)
New Girl in Town (1957)

Opera Companies:
Hamburg State Opera
Spoleto Festival

San Francisco Opera
Santa Fe Opera
The New York Pro Musica
New York City Opera
Teatro Alla Scala, Milan
La Fenice, Venice

Dance Companies:
New York City Ballet
American Ballet Company
Martha Graham Company
San Francisco Ballet
Joffrey Ballet

Pennsylvania Ballet
Harkness Ballet
Ballet Rambert
Royal Danish Ballet
Glen Tetley Company
Paul Taylor Company
Netherlands Dans Theatre
Alvin Ailey Dance Theatre
Stuttgart Ballet
The Royal Ballet
Royal Swedish Ballet

Model by Rouben Ter-Arutunian
GOODTIME CHARLEY
Book by Sidney Michaels

Music by Larry Grossman
Lyrics by Hal Hackady
Choreographed by Onna White

Directed by Peter Hunt
Palace Theatre, New York (1975)
(Photograph — Martha Swope)

What had the most influence on your decision to become a stage designer?

It was the Russian Ballet, which I saw in 1936, under the direction of Colonel de Basil. They toured Europe in the thirties and gave a series of performances which I saw at the age of fifteen, and it impressed me no end. They were the standard ballets of the repertory of Diaghilev. I thought it would be simply wonderful if I could do that kind of work.

I always went to the theatre as much as I possibly could, and when I finished school, I studied piano for about a year. . . . I thought I would become a concert pianist. I had been taking lessons for quite a while, and then I started to like it and tried to take it more seriously. But one doesn't quite begin a career of that kind of serious piano playing at that age. So I switched for a side that had really impressed me so much, which had given me my most beautiful impression — ballet, the beauty of the color and the beauty of the settings, the movement and music, all that combined.

Did you have much training in the arts?

I studied classical painting at the École des Beaux Arts, and I did a few productions here and there. But my serious professional life started in New York doing various commercials and soap operas at CBS television in 1951. The demands of television really were quite good exercises.

Is there a special approach that works well for you in designing a production?

If it's a play you read it, naturally, once to get acquainted with it and to see if you like it. After you have read it, you read it through again and sort out the technical requirements that are inherent to the play itself. The physical arrangements, simple exits and entrances in relation to the climaxes, and the action will give you the physical requirements of the set. Then you've got to read it again and see where the important segments of the action are, where the climaxes are, what is the general tenor of the whole piece. You radar into it. An antenna goes up with a not really quite logically definable process apart from the physical necessities! You can't design a set any way you like and superimpose it on the play, and then be surprised if it doesn't work. So you had better really very carefully read the play

and see what is required. And then, of course, you ought to get together with the director to see if he will really follow the author. There are directors who ignore the author and simply say they don't want the window there, nobody is going to go to it and open it, and they won't jump out of it. But you must be prepared and have absorbed the author precisely. And then it depends on the discretion of the director on which way you go, which way you continue.

How did you approach Edward Albee's All Over when you designed it?

I read the first page of the play, in which the set is described by Albee in a rather realistic way — a rather gloomy, masculine, dark-paneled living room with an alcove farther upstage in which the dying man is lying in bed. And it read very much like a New York brownstone at the turn of the century that has been preserved in its rather striking, powerful, and dark elegance up to today. Also, the dying man and his wife and mistress are in their seventies, and so it would be rather natural to have a room which would still be of the past or of their youth. But I didn't feel that kind of realistic setting was appropriate to the play, which to me seemed to be more comparable to a reading exercise similar to a chamber concert where the various musical instruments carried their own line. So I felt that nothing else but physical requirements of where this one sits, how much this one moves, and what is the minimum of furniture that would be needed to make it possible for the actors to play was necessary. Everybody felt the same way about it — the producer, the author, and the director. . . . We all agreed upon that approach. And the music relation has also been mentioned by various critics.

Do you use the same initial approach in designing a play that you would an opera or a ballet?

Costume designs by Rouben Ter-Arutunian
THE UNICORN, THE GORGON, AND THE MANTICORE by Gian-Carlo Menotti
Choreographed by Louis Johnson, Cincinnati (1972)
Choreographed by John Butler, Spoleto (1970)
(Photographs — Sandy Underwood)

Yes, I always try to be as precise in determining the requirements of the author. With opera it is even a little bit easier in a way, because you do have a certain time span which is imposed by the music. So it gives you a little bit less liberty, maybe, but it gives you a better support also; it works two ways. Certain things have to happen within the certain span of music, which is determined by the composer in the choice of time sequence. So these are physical requirements that you have to consider.

Does the music in opera work for you as inspiration the same way a script does in a play?

Exactly. It works for me because you do have a script. You have certain requirements that the script places upon you. But prior to that, it is really the music itself that is the final determining factor in designing for opera.

Of the three—opera, ballet, or plays— which do you prefer designing?

I prefer any one that is really challenging and of major quality because it appeals to me. I have no particular preference. Yet I find ballet more attractive to work for, because dancers by nature are far more disciplined, are far more attractive personally to work with than any other professional category on stage.

What, then, is the most important element in designing for the dance?

. . . to do that certain something that will add to the overall impression and the overall effect. . . . Then, naturally, there are the considerations of space that are basic and there's not much to say about the fact that dancers need space. You can't clutter the stage. You can't encumber them. Whatever you add or whatever you put on the stage has to help, it has to add to either the movement in a way of counterpoint, or a magnet or a focus, or simply as a mood-setting device. Whatever it is, you have to think that first it ought to be practical —practical in the way that it should not take up too much space on stage, but it should also be practical enough that the company could travel with it. It can happen that somehow you are stuck with something rather unwieldy that might look very well, but cannot be used on smaller, less well-equipped stages in smaller cities, or it just becomes too difficult to transport or handle. So that is really also a very, very important problem, apart from the esthetic one.

What ballet that you have done recently have you enjoyed?

I try to enjoy most of them, not all of them. But a more recent major production was a few years ago in Hamburg at the Hamburg State Opera with Glen Tetley. He is the major contemporary choreographer in Europe and this country, little by little, seems to have a chance to see his work. The ballet was from a score by Olivier Messiaen called *Chronochromie*. There are bird calls in the score, not only imitated, but he used real bird calls. Messiaen was quite fascinated by the sound of birds and has used them frequently in his scores. So there was a vague hint of maybe birdlike pictures, movements. Otherwise, it is a completely abstract work. The setting was a completely bare stage with a white floor, no maskings, no black velour or anything of that kind. In the more or less center of the stage was a white filigree-like sculpture of either a nest or a forest or a group of trees, which was made of shaped tubular plastic. It was a bushlike center, an assembly of dimensional shapes through which dancers moved.

Do you make a model for each show you are designing?

I always make models and I do not always make a painted sketch in terms of a pretty picture, which I find one can dispense with. The spatial relationships are far more important to present to a director and technical departments than a picture. The color sketch can, in a way, present the mood of the set and its possibility a little more appropriately than a model. Again, it depends on what kind of set it is. But still, I personally find the model more important. Of course the ideal is to do both, and very often I do both. It depends a bit on the time element and, more, it depends upon the nature of the setting.

Do you find your time is such that you need assistants?

Stage designs by Rouben Ter-Arutunian
ORPHEUS ET EURYDICE by Gluck
Directed and choreographed by George Balanchine
Hamburgische Staats Oper, Hamburg, Germany (1963)

Opposite page (left) "Le Tombeau D'Eurydice,"
(right) "L'Enfer," (left) "L'Elysee"

Absolutely! I use assistants for stage design in terms of preparing the technical drawings, which I find a little boring to do because it means to work on the set for possibly the third or fourth time. The first is the initial concept, which sometimes needn't be more than a tiny little ink or pencil sketch, or the so-called thumbnail sketch, in which all the elements of the design are already present. From there you go into a bit larger, more elaborate sketch or into the model itself. Usually, I do the model from the thumbnail sketch. And very often you do two models. One is a very rough one, where you just indicate the space for yourself and possibly the director. Then you go into a finished model, which also can be a copy of the texture, meaning it is either painted or it is a replica of the material of which the set is going to be made. (And you ought to come as close as possible to it, otherwise the model is really not much help.) During that time I like to have the assistant do drawings or sometimes help me to some degree in manual work on the model. Next comes the fourth phase, the painted sketch, so that the director and the producer have something to look at — and get acquainted with your possibly more romantic concept of the stage setting. I use the word *romantic* in terms of the way that maybe the mood is more precisely presented than in a model, where

it is not always easy to duplicate lighting effects that you want to achieve in your setting. Of course, sometimes it is really not possible to duplicate everything in the scale of your model.

By now, I have become so familiar with the physical requirements of the play, opera or ballet that I am following the action of that particular work and always relate to the figures naturally. The costumes develop more or less in a natural way — out of the flow of your acquaintance with the work. They are a sort of logical extension into the area which is occupied by the human beings, by bodies that have to be dressed in some way in order to act out the play.

You feel that you obtain more creative unity by designing both the costumes and settings?

There is no question about it. The stage designer ought to design everything that appears on stage. I'd never heard of a stage designer who didn't do costumes himself before I came to this country. Specialization is a practice that is rather standard here, but in Europe it is simply automatic that the stage designer also does costumes. It's become less automatic now, because the practice of this country has apparently influenced even European stage design in that matter. Now occasionally major stage designers do not do costumes. I think it has a little bit to do with the fact that it is very time-consuming to do

costumes — not to design them, but to have them executed. The fittings take forever and usually there is a great number of costumes. Selecting fabrics and determining patterns takes time. With the jet age, singers appear in various opera houses all over the world doing the same parts, and stage designers reproduce their stage productions more or less the same way for various houses all over Europe. The jet age prevents them from having enough time. Consequently, they are not likely to spend too much time on the minor matter of completing their visual designs with the costumes and don't do them any more.

You must also think in terms of how the scenery is going to look when it is lighted.

Oh, absolutely! Lighting is a major part of the way scenery looks. Often enough, a bad set has been made to look very well with some ingenious lighting and vice versa, and many a good set has not been helped by the insistence on the use of color on the part of the lighting designer, who has his own ideas. Sometimes .you have not been able to get together and things like that happen. But you must always think of how it will look when all comes together, and you are the only one able to have that vision. Nobody else knows what is in your mind and which way you want to be presented finally, when all these ingredients come together. But

Model of permanent set by Rouben Ter-Arutunian
American Shakespeare Festival
Stratford, Connecticut (1960)
Retained until 1962 and used for six plays
(Photograph—H. L. Kirk)

this is one of the great problems in designing: you must keep your vision, you must protect it, you must defend it, you must always remain true to your first inner sight of it.

In designing both the sets and costumes, do you have an assistant for each?

Yes. Very often I like to have the assistant on costumes find the materials and fabrics. By "materials" I mean if these costumes are to be made of something other than wool, cotton, or silk. Maybe rubber or plastic; or all kinds of strange textures that are inherent in the design can be used. So a great deal of time goes into research on that order.

The research depends on what kind of play it is. If it is an historical play in which it is decided that the costumes are called "authentic," then it is always quite comfortable to refresh your memory or to follow particular details in cutting or in the underpinnings of those costumes. In spite of the fact that you are familiar with the period—I am told one should be—you have not been required to duplicate this appearance or style, so you never have really been too closely concerned with details. Now you familiarize yourself with them, either deciding that you want to imitate them or to use details from them. Or you decide that you do not want to follow authenticity slavishly, but to adapt it somehow into our way of thinking of that period. And maybe you use a shorthand of these details. But no matter what, you still have to know what it was about before you can make this decision.

[Costume] research is always necessary in either goods, joining the material, or even with the garments themselves that are still available in collections. The Metropolitan Museum has a very impressive collection, so you ask for help there. For instance, I did a play in Vienna which takes place at the turn of the century, and I had a chance to very closely study the dresses of that

period—the cut and where the seams are and how they fall, the underneath, how they are finished, why they move the way they appear to move in the paintings, or even the photographs of that period. This is terribly helpful, and you must do that if you decide that you want it to look that way—and you must do it even if you decide it shouldn't look that way.

This is something that an assistant can do for you. The assistant may go and locate these things, but *you* must go and look at it yourself, because it is an artistic decision of major importance for your final design—how you want to approach it. That is the way I use assistants, but I have never yet had anyone to design anything for me, which I understand can also be the practice: you know, the whole chorus line is designed by an assistant. Still, the decision is for the major designer—if he wants to accept somebody else's design that is probably made under his guidance, why not? But I still don't like to have sketch artists to do my sketches and hire them to make fashionable costume sketches and present them on the pretense that they are my own.

Have you any favorite kinds of material in designing for the ballet?

I always like materials that come to life through a certain function, mostly light, of course. That, I find, gives them a certain mystery, a certain something that is not substantial and maybe that

is a personal preference. I always like certain lines that go off into perspective, into somewhere we don't know where—into a mystery. I like materials that appear and disappear or vary their appearance through a device. But I can't say that I don't like beautiful wood texture. Any kind of texture of nature is appealing to me. It still seems, more often than not, I use plastics, undoubtedly a contemporary material. Whether this is a personal preference or whether it is something that I thought was appropriate for a certain ballet or play or opera, I do not know. I hope it was a right decision.

What are the essential differences between designing for television and designing for the stage?

The design for the stage is from a fixed point of view, which is usually either in the first balcony or the orchestra center or anywhere dead center. Of course you must consider the sight lines, but the point of view doesn't change position. Whereas design for the television camera is a design in a dimension of 360 degrees (in the round), or at least three-quarters. The camera changes point of view constantly and also changes lenses, so it is a design in a relationship that changes not only in depth through the uses of different lenses, but also changes position. I've always found it terribly good to be ready in spite of the fact that the director might have told you before that without any question, a certain part of the set is never to be seen on camera. (Then, for some strange reason, the director decides that that is precisely what will be used for the scene.) It is always good to be prepared. . . .

In films, you usually prepare an entire room for the camera. When the scene is being shot, one part is removed. Either one wall is being removed, or props and furniture are being removed to make it possible for the camera crew and personnel to be in that particular area. Quarters can be cramped, but you still have the entire room and you move to the other side. You have a 360-degree setting, and this similarly is the case in television studios. I have always used the entire space, and have the background almost in 360 degrees with a small opening for the camera and a few cables which moved in that overall space. But first of all, I've always found space most attractive, particularly on the television screen. The fragment of a setting in an overall large space seems much more indicative and much more important than an overall cluttered setting.

In television, do you get what you want creatively in the lighting and do you have a certain amount of control?

It depends entirely on who cooperates with you. You have to be very careful right from the beginning to be sure that not only the camera crew but also the lighting designer and other technical personnel are really seeing eye to eye with you. Let's say you have been quite clear in establishing a particular way to proceed in lighting, which for the textures and for the materials involved in your setting are simply imperative and could not be done in any other way. But still, a lighting designer in moments of grandeur goes on in his own artistic ways. The set is being lit with you present, with every new light going up in the most inappropriate place. You see disaster developing similar to a thunderstorm that is still far away on the plain and yet it is coming: And you maybe even ask a few questions and try to remind the gentleman in charge that that isn't really what had been discussed, what is necessary, and what will give the right results, but he still knows better than you.

And, strangely enough, as costume designer also having something to do with costumes, you may sometimes discuss hair and make-up, but that really goes too far, because obviously a costume designer should stop at the neck. Then if there is a hat, go above the hair. This has been sort of standard in television and it has always been a major battle to educate people that you will only too gladly use their practical experience, but the decision of whether eyebrows are black or green is yours, not theirs. It doesn't have anything to do with professional knowledge, it is a point of view. It is the finished product that is in your mind and nobody else's. There is a relationship between a face and a costume and a set. The visual side is the responsibility of the designer.

I'm really amazed that it is all so departmentalized. A lighting designer's contribution is terribly important, a make-up man can do absolutely marvelous things, and I have had wonderful collaborators in that area. But there is a vision and a sketch, and this is the way in which you [the designer] describe how you want a certain character to look. That invention is yours and probably has come about in long discussions with the director and some-

Setting and costumes by Rouben Ter-Arutunian
COPPELIA by Leo Delibes
Book by Charles Nuitter (after E.T.A. Hoffmann)
Choreographed by George Balanchine

Lighting by Ronald Bates
New York City Ballet
New York State Theatre, Lincoln Center (1974)
(Photograph—Martha Swope)

Model by Rouben Ter-Arutunian
THE BASSARIDS by Hans Werner Henze
Libretto by W. H. Auden and Chester Kallman
Directed by Bodo Igesz

Santa Fe Opera
Santa Fe, New Mexico (1968)
(Photograph — Martha Swope)

times even the actor or singer or dancer. Everybody else is then responsible to carry that through under your supervision, to get the results that have been thought about. The more practical experience there is to get these results, the better. You'll find film to be the opposite of that; it does not give us enough artistic creation, and one does not want that.

What are the chances for a young designer aspiring to come to New York to design on Broadway?

They are waiting. There is one thing that is marvelous about this country: anyone who is new, has a new face, a new name, and has something new to offer will be given a chance. . . . The talent always wins out. Of course to keep up and re-establish yourself is another story. It's always the last job that counts, and so you'd better be good or you're out for a while until you manage to pull yourself together again and do something that is very impressive and better than the good one before. It always has to be better. And the better you are, the more difficult it is to get better, but that's the way it is.

What background is necessary for a new designer?

Experience is one way and the best, really. There's nothing better than to just get coffee and hang around, whether a person wants to design or isn't quite sure what he wants to do. What possibly may be a more secure way is to just train himself and get as much education as he can. There is such a thing as a place to study literature or history of the theatre or history of art, apart from an exercise in practical ways. It is impossible to do without painting and sculpturing. Stage design really makes use of all that in a manner in which it is subordinate to the author. And if you do not exercise, how is your sense of color ever going to be tested or how is it ever going to develop? Sculpture gives you a sense of space, a sense of dimension. If you do it yourself, immediately your eyes are opened up to different ways of understanding and seeing things. I don't think it is possible to become an accomplished stage designer without having been an art student.

Your settings have ranged from traditional painted settings to the sculptured and abstract. Do comment on this.

I don't enjoy the painted set and I think it's a very old-fashioned approach.

I do like luxury, and I don't think there is anything more luxurious than space. . . . Space and clean air are really luxuries today, and I like space on the stage, and I like clarity — clean air on the stage. To me, there is nothing more attractive on stage than an empty, organized space and maybe one symbolic fragment that summarizes the whole play or opera or ballet. That emptiness and spaciousness and cleanliness is usually as expensive as an elaborate cluttered setting, possibly even more so. The organization and the proportions that help this organization have to be so carefully calculated, and the texture that makes that emptiness has to be so carefully considered. If there is just one symbolic fragment, it has to be so precisely executed and so exclusively finished that it finally costs as much as the heavily built setting. Somehow, psychologically one does not mind spending for quantity. I do, but that is a personal preference. But generally, managers object less to paying for quantity than paying for a tiny little bit of quality. I really do like excellence, and I'd rather have very little, with that little expertly finished, than a great deal thrown together.

THREE

Developing a design

Each professional designer has his own personal way of developing a concept of stage design and carrying it through the production, and the approach may vary from one production to another. There are thus no inflexible rules as to precisely how one should or must develop a concept from idea to finished theatre design. Of course, the designer must make a visual statement that is consonant with the author's or composer's intention, and must call on all his intellectual, artistic, and mechanical resources to do so. Ultimately, his inspiration comes from the work itself. At the same time, there are certain progressive steps every designer in the commercial theatre moves through in one way or another between his first discussion of a design project and the time it is finished, ready for scenery to be constructed. We shall explore that sequence in this chapter.

Once the designer is committed to design a stage work, he becomes familiar with the material and then arranges a conference with the director to discuss the approach to the show. (If the script is an original, it may not yet be complete, and the visual concepts that develop through the exchange of ideas with the director may influence the writing of the manuscript.) On any production, the relationship between the director and designer is of paramount importance. Usually, it is the director who sets the style of approach and guides all of the elements of the production into focus while, hopefully, complying with the author's intentions.

As a good example of how a director explains to a designer what he wants, Desmond Heeley remembered vividly what Michael Benthal said in an early conference at the Old Vic when they did *Twelfth Night* together. Benthal's challenge went something like: "There are two people who are going to have a conversation between here and here, right? They can't be farther apart than that. I need a kind of perching height—that's usually about two feet six inches, a bit lower if you can make it. Nothing must come on, nothing must go off. It all wants to be kept onstage . . . a way off to her house, a way off to the sea. That's all. We can make it work like that." This simplicity of approach to a designer does not encroach on his abilities. Heeley added that Benthal "gave me the compliment of saying I

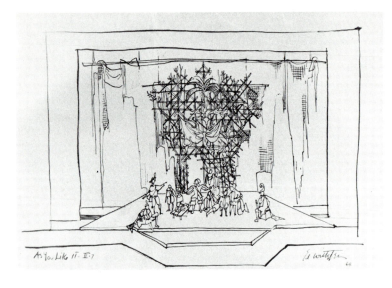

was a professional. The only thing he had to say about costumes was, 'The most important thing is that Viola has to look like a real boy. The rest of the period is up to you. If you can make her look like a real boy, that's the period we'll use. You can do the rest.' "

An experienced director who is imaginative, interesting, and visually oriented can be stimulating indeed for a designer. There are good directors who are visually oriented and can understand almost anything a designer sets out to do. There are also fine directors who cannot visualize anything except what they see in a sketch or in a model. Still other directors are unable to read either a model or a sketch, only grasping the designs when they are put on stage, but may know intuitively if they are right for their intentions in the production. Frequently, a director who cannot visualize the designs early will ask for voluminous changes. A designer must remain true to his design and not feel compelled to do something which does not come naturally; but he must also learn to compromise.

Because the personal relationship between a director and a designer should be one of total harmony, the designer must cultivate discretion and diplomacy. The interchange of sensing what the other thinks and what inspires the other is, in fact, often referred to as a "theatrical marriage." It is this kind of creative collaboration that produces a show with a unified concept and contributes greatly to the artistic success of the production. There are any number of creative teams in both the theatre and opera. The close association of producer-director Harold Prince with Boris Aronson on

Stage designs by Ed Wittstein
AS YOU LIKE IT by William Shakespeare
Directed by Stephen Porter
American Shakespeare Festival
Stratford, Connecticut (1968)

Production for a proscenium stage with a thrust.
(Top): Line drawing in ink of Act II, scene 7 — The Forest of Arden — showing the basic idea of the set onstage.

(Center): Painted sketch of Act II, scene 4 — The Forest — indicating colors and textures of the scenery, stage lighting, and actors on the set. (Photograph — Lynn Pecktal)

(Bottom): A close-up, in the scenic studio, of some of the actual scenery. The materials included wooden latticework, erosion cloth, and carved skulls. (Photograph — Ed Wittstein)

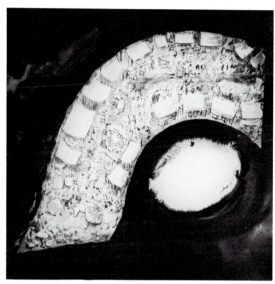

Stage designs by Lester Polakov
THE BARTERED BRIDE
Music by Bedřich Smetana
Libretto by K. Sabina
Produced and conducted by Sarah Caldwell
Opera Company of Boston (1973)

Creating several designs for this production evolved from many models and sketches. To bring the original freshness of this comic Czech opera into his design, Polakov did research in Prague at the Smetana museum and others specializing in folk art. To accommodate the many scenes and the music that demanded a flowing succession of images and textures, he devised several free-form shapes (loops made of filled scrim with thin horizontal boards, suspended on wires) on which could be projected a collage of sketches, photographs and patterns, suggesting the environment of Czech village life. Real textures and forms seen in Czechoslovakia were used in the assemblage. Photographs at bottom right and top right are projection designs.

A Little Night Music, Follies, Company, Cabaret, and *Zorba* is one example. Another is the collaboration of Tom O'Horgan with Robin Wagner on *Jesus Christ Superstar, Inner City, Lenny,* and *Hair.* At the Metropolitan Opera, Robert O'Hearn has designed almost all of his operas with director Nathaniel Merrill, while at the New York City Opera, Lloyd Evans has teamed with director Frank Corsaro for the majority of his productions.

At the first conference of the director and the designer, all general aspects of the production may be discussed and several different approaches talked over. In the close exchange of ideas between the colleagues, the visual style is determined and agreed upon, although this sometimes takes several sessions. Such matters as the playing areas, the placement of entrances and exits, the kind of furniture and props are talked over, and particular reference may be made to colors, materials, textures, or periods. The mechanical aspects of the production are also explored and discussed in detail. If the show has more than one setting, the time element in the shifts is of utmost importance, since a rapid change is always desirable. How the show will move must also be solved—by wagons, by flying, by turntables, elevators, or a combination of several means. The kind and type of theatre where the production will be mounted becomes a determining factor in the concept of the production, because the designer must design in the space he has to work with, both onstage and offstage. While all sorts of problems can be solved at the initial session, other meetings are held as the show's concept is being realized, as new ideas develop, and as sketches, plans, and models are completed. Depending on the specific production, the overall feeling of the setting, lighting, and costumes can be decided on either at one time or at individual meetings. In any event, open communication must exist throughout the developing period. (In conferences as well as in individual working out, both designer and director refer very frequently to the script.)

Naturally, the designer's role is particularly extensive when he is designing both the sets and costumes or sets and lighting. Many designers claim that in the commercial theatre there is not enough time to create in all three categories, and it is interesting to summarize the personal preferences of first-rank theatre designers. Rouben Ter-Arutunian and Raoul Pène du Bois, for instance, tend to follow the European idea of doing both sets and costumes. Jo Mielziner and Donald Oenslager (except for one show) have always done both the settings and lighting in every production they have designed, while Ben Edwards, Howard Bay, and Robert Randolph do sets and fre-

quently the lighting. Oliver Smith, Ming Cho Lee, Robin Wagner, Peter Larkin, and Boris Aronson have been highly successful in concentrating primarily on creating scenery. The names of Jules Fisher, Jean Rosenthal, Peggy Clark, Tharon Musser, Thomas Skelton, and Martin Aronstein are well known in the area of lighting design, while Theoni V. Aldredge, Patricia Zipprodt, Florence Klotz, Irene Sharaff, Jane Greenwood, Ann Roth, and Freddy Wittop are established costume designers. Whether the designer works in one or all three categories, his work on a production can be greatly increased when he is designing for a musical, because there not only is he collaborating with the director and the author but also with the choreographer, the lyricist, and the composer.

Preliminary thumbnail sketch by Douglas W. Schmidt
THE MINES OF SULFUR by Richard Rodney Bennett
Libretto by Beverley Cross
Directed by John Houseman
Juilliard School of Music
New York (1967)

Scene: An English country home. Pencil sketch on tracing paper, approximately 7 $\frac{1}{2}$ by 9 in.

THUMBNAIL SKETCHES

Small, rough thumbnail or idea sketches are the most casual and basic type of theatrical sketch. The first thumbnails are made simply as the designer starts formulating his visual ideas, to see what the possibilities are and to show what his designs will look like. A designer

[Diagram:]

Producer

Playwright
Composer
Librettist
Author

Choreographer — Musical Director — Stage Director — Scenic Designer

Lighting Designer

Costume Designer

Dancers — Singers — Actors

Preliminary sketch by Karl Eigsti
WINGS
Music, book and lyrics by Robert McLaughlin
and Peter Ryan
Directed by Robert McLaughlin
Staged musical numbers by Nora Christiansen
Eastside Playhouse, New York (1975)

This Off-Broadway musical is based on
Aristophanes' THE BIRDS.

doing either sets or costumes may make several
such sketches after conferring with the director,
but it is not unusual for the designer to draw
rough sketches as he is exchanging ideas during
the meeting. This is an easy way for him to
converse visually with the director, and often
the spontaneous thoughts and thumbnails
that come forth during this discussion are the
most effective sketches in the production.
Thumbnails are usually made with pen, pencil,
or felt-tip pen; some designers make them to
scale in $\frac{1}{8}$-inch or $\frac{1}{4}$-inch, while others do not
use any specific dimensions. These small
drawings are sometimes rendered in color,
but they can be in black and white. Working
from the tiny sketches, the designer enlarges
them into a standard scale (usually $\frac{1}{2}$-inch) and
makes changes as his inspiration evolves and
adds details wherever necessary.

RESEARCH

The successful designer uses some form of
research when he is developing his designs,
something from his earlier experience or perhaps material collected for the production at
hand. Simply looking through research material can easily refresh memory, offering many
new possibilities in the design concept. In
doing research for a specific new work, most
established designers examine a great deal of
source material, capture the essence, and then
through their own individual style and theatricality incorporate it into the stage designs.

Designer Rolf Beyer relates that Donald
Oenslager once said to his students about research: "Go to the National Geographic if you
want research material, but don't copy it. Look,
digest, and regurgitate." A student of Oenslager's had drawn a lamppost on a sketch and
Oenslager said, "That doesn't look like a lamppost." The student replied, "Well, I copied it
directly from a photograph," and Oenslager
retorted, "Never mind, you have not caught
the 'lamppostness' of a lamppost!" Beyer
summed up his own feelings about research
by saying, "It's true. You have to go beyond
copy. If you feel strongly about the play, you
have to say it to the audience. You may abstract an object. You may make it bigger,
smaller, change the color, make it more simple.
You can take that lamppost and do all sorts
of things with it—cut it out of stainless steel,
paint it pink, turn it into musical comedy—but
the audience has got to know that they are
looking at a lamppost."

It is interesting to note the direct sources
certain designers used in various productions.
Robin Wagner was inspired by material from
the Hellstrom Chronicles and patterns of insect
life when he did the sensational musical Jesus
Christ Superstar. For Neil Simon's hit comedy
The Prisoner of Second Avenue, designer
Richard Sylbert worked with photos of interiors
and exteriors of modern buildings actually
photographed on Manhattan's Second Avenue.
When Robert O'Hearn was designing the
Richard Strauss opera Die Frau ohne Schatten
for the Metropolitan Opera, he drew from
microphotographs of cells, wood fibers, and
tiny crustaceans. And for the dramatic Lincoln
Center production of Antigone, Douglas W.
Schmidt devised gigantic carved stone panels
inspired by a book of reproductions of classical
Greek ruins.

Apart from general research, definite source
material is always necessary to both the set
designer and the costume designer. Scenically,
this can be any kind of subject matter from an
antique weathervane to a piece of wrought-
iron filigree work or a Roman acanthus scroll.
For the costumer, it may be finding a figure
indicating how the fabric is draped and the
way it falls in an Empire gown, or the type of

braid detail on a Civil War general's uniform, or how costumes are constructed. In either category, research can be required for almost anything—textures, colors, shapes, and periods of history. Some designers submit the exact source of research to the scenic studio with their painter's elevations, saying, "I want it to look like this"; the same thing can happen in the costume house where the clothes for the production are being built. When this is done, the artists executing the designs have a direct communication about the work rather than having to wonder what the designer really wants and where the idea originally came from.

Every seasoned theatre designer harbors a research collection of some sort, and many are extensive and complete. The diversity ranges from splendid art books to the *National Geographic* magazine and random pages of interesting subjects clipped from such publications as *Holiday* magazine, neatly filed. A tightly organized collection is always helpful, since it allows the designer to lay his hands on what he wants immediately. The picture and costume collection in good libraries and

museums, of course, offer marvelous research opportunities.

Although one may think that research pertains only to the esthetic part of the show, there is an extraordinary amount of data needed in the technical or mechanical aspect of the production. Before a designer starts to put his design down on paper, especially if he is trying out something new or tricky, he may first seek information from a reputable scenic shop, to see if his ideas will work. The questions can cover any number of things, from whether a winch can move a particular unit of scenery up and down on a raked deck to the strength of new plastic materials for a setting and how they will take paints. As a result of the varied experience of the many craftsmen in the top-flight studios, one or another usually knows the answers or can suggest someone who does.

TRANSLATING THE DESIGNS

The realization of a scenic design in models, sketches, and drawings as discussed here would go through every step under ideal circumstances. How many steps you use is totally

Paint elevation by John Conklin
THE NUTCRACKER by Tchaikovsky
  (Act II)
Philadelphia, Pennsylvania (1972)
(Photograph—Lynn Pecktal)

Conklin created this paint elevation for a sharkstooth scrim backdrop. His research material was cut out and glued directly on the sketch to indicate the details for drawing the architecture on the backdrop. Only half the symmetrical design was rendered on the drawing because the painting was to be reversed and repeated on the opposite side.

Model by José Varona
LA TRAVIATA by Giuseppe Verdi

Libretto by Francesco Maria Piave
Netherlands Opera, Amsterdam (1974)

dependent on how busy you are and on where and how your show is being executed. In other words, if you are doing most of the work yourself, you would not necessarily need explicit plans and models. Any designer worth his salt has designed and painted at least a few brilliant productions early in his career by working with only minimal plans. Some of these may have had nothing more than rough plans and elevations drawn on $\frac{1}{4}$-inch graph paper, or even been basic ideas sketched on the back of a paper napkin. If you are designing a show in one-week stock, it would be unthinkable to do an elaborate model, painted elevations, and very detailed plans unless the season had been scheduled long in advance and you had ample time to work on the production. Remember too that you can often build, paint, and dress an actual set in the theatre in the amount of time it takes to prepare all the drawings and sketches mentioned here.

The situation, then, governs the formal planning. If you are designing a production in a repertory company or a university theatre or for Broadway and have several weeks or months in which to get it ready, with a large crew to execute the work, detailed plans and probably a model would be very necessary. Even then, you should be prepared to expect to make a few changes. There is seldom a

production in which the plans for the scenery do not undergo some kind of revision before they finally get onstage. Broadway is not excluded, only it is much more costly than elsewhere.

A pattern is not always followed as to whether the floor plan or the front elevations are designed first. While it is customary to start out with the floor plan, some designers begin with the elevations and then go to the plan. At any rate, realizing a design is always a matter of working back and forth from one to the other during the designing process, making changes until satisfactory results are obtained. It is also par for the course to do the drafting for the show before doing the model, although even this pattern varies. Often a designer will do only rough drawings, then build the model scenery (which can be measured by a scale, by calipers, or by marking the dimensions precisely on a piece of paper, and then transferring them to the drawings). However else they work, the most experienced designers start to put their designs down on tracing paper or graph paper by doing a series of rough pencil sketches to get ideas. Doing several rough pencil sketches and overlays is a better method of starting a drawing rather than trying to figure everything out on one sheet of paper and still keep it neat.

Model by David Mitchell
IL TROVATORE
   by Giuseppe Verdi
Libretto by Salvatore
   Cammarano
Prison set
Directed by Tito Capobianco
Paris Opéra
Théâtre National, Paris
   (1973)
(Photograph — Thom Lafferty)

Models versus Painted Renderings

Since the proscenium stage is the most typical, let us assume that it is the one with which we are working. Here is a comparison of the basic advantages of a model and a rendering for a proscenium production:

MODEL OF SETTING	RENDERING OF SETTING
Shows mass, form, proportions in true three-dimensional relation.	Shows mass, form, proportions in two dimensions.
Removable flat model scenery can be scaled easily for executing full-scale drawings; calipers can be used to measure three-dimensional parts.	Since presentational rendering of the setting is normally in perspective, it cannot be scaled.
Painted model parts can be used as paint elevations.	Paint elevations are usually needed in addition to presentational rendering.
A good presentation method for those who cannot paint or render well. Sometimes tiny lights (or lamps) are placed inside the model to indicate suggestive lighting ideas.	Can show painted mood and atmosphere, and the same setting can be shown in many different views with painted lighting.
Indicates clearly to the director: traffic and blocking, entrances, exits, playing areas, sight lines.	Director must also work with floor plan and elevations along with the renderings.
Normally requires more time than rendering.	Usually takes much less time than a model.
Helps solve technical problems easily.	Technical problems are solved by additional drawings.
Shows color, style, and period.	Shows color, style, and period.
Indicates scale of actor to the scenery.	Indicates scale of actor to the scenery.
Troublesome to store and transport.	Easy to store and transport.
May show actual three-dimensional textures and materials.	Textures and materials are generally simulated by painting, but materials can also be collaged on the design.

Sketches (Renderings) of the Stage Design

A typical sketch of the stage design traditionally shows the setting as it appears to the audience. Most likely, it will represent a poignant or dramatic scene from the production, which the designer renders to indicate how the setting will look under stage lighting, complete with mood, atmosphere, and depth. Those who know the beautiful set sketches of the noted

118

Stage design by Sandro
   La Ferla
THE KNACK by Ann Jellicoe
Directed by Keith Fowler
Virginia Museum Theatre
Richmond, Virginia (1970)

Scene: London, a basement
street-level apartment. The
sketch is a collage with
newspapers (floor), lace
(walls), and balsa wood
(moldings) glued on illus-
stration board. Materials
painted over with gouache
and inks.

American designers in the early part of the twentieth century, Lee Simonson, Robert Edmond Jones, Jo Mielziner, and Donald Oenslager in particular, cannot forget the highly dramatic feeling of theatricality they achieved in so many of their renderings.

Although the pattern of making a presentation sketch has not changed drastically today, some designers never make a typical sketch as such, but instead concentrate on painted models, the painter's elevations, or both. When sketches of the stage design are made, they can be rendered in full color or variations of a single color and are not normally used as the painter's elevations. However, at times designers have specified that they be utilized for such purposes. The scale of $\frac{1}{2}$ inch = 1 foot is standard for sketches, but for large musicals where several scenes are involved they are frequently drawn in a smaller scale such as $\frac{1}{4}$ inch = 1 foot.

The designer's sketch can be rendered in all sorts of painting media, including designer colors, casein, acrylic polymer plastic colors, vinyl, tempera (egg-water or egg-oil emulsion as a binder), gouache (watercolors prepared with gum), Dr. P. H. Martin's Concentrated Watercolors (transparent dyes), India ink, pastels, colored pencils, chalk, or even oil paints. Some stage designers render with a combination of these, others stick to only one medium. In every instance, the designer selects his paints and materials in terms of what works best for him and what will give the desired results.

Most designers prefer a good white illustration board or a heavy white paper to paint on. Before applying paint to the board, some designers put on a base coat or texture the surface with Liquitex Gesso, an acrylic polymer emulsion base white primer that can be thinned with water. This dries fast, and produces a nice surface for painting. Gesso is also excellent for basecoating models constructed of several different materials so they can all have the same lay-in before painting. While most colors are applied by brush, an air brush (with which controlled air pressure is used for applying paint in an atomized spray) can be very effective for creating blends and textures. Colors can also be sprayed on from an aerosol can.

Painter's Color Elevations

The painter's color elevations are made specifically by the designer for the scenic artist to paint from and indicate just what the designer wants each piece of the scenery to look like. All the colors, details, and paint treatment are rendered for the wings, backdrops, ground cloths, built units, props, and set dressing. As a rule, these elevations are shown in $\frac{1}{2}$-inch scale, but there are always exceptions. Sometimes $\frac{1}{4}$-inch is used, especially where there are very few details; if they are highly detailed, elevations may be made larger. Various notations are put on the sketches to instruct the artists: "paint molding very tight and realistically," "make lettering slick," "adjust perspective in the architecture," "make this wall slightly

PRESENTATION SKETCHES

Stage design by Allen Charles Klein
MANON by Jules Massenet
Libretto by Henri Meilhac and
Philippe Gille Act III, scene 1
Directed by Bliss Hebert
Kennedy Center, Washington, D.C. (1974)

Stage design by Frank Lopez
THE VISIT by Friedrich Duerrenmatt
Act II
The action of the play takes place in and around
the little town of Gullen, somewhere in Europe
A project (1974)
(Photograph — Frank Lopez)

Designed for a proscenium opening 36 ft. wide,
the sketch in ½-in. scale was rendered in
transparent and opaque watercolors on illustration
board.

Stage design by Eugene Berman
LA FORZA DEL DESTINO by Giuseppe Verdi
Libretto by Francesco Maria Piave
Act IV, scene 2 — A wild rocky place in
the mountains not far from the convent
Directed by Herbert Graf
The Metropolitan Opera, New York (1952)
(Courtesy of Arnold Abramson,
photograph — Mr. Abramson)

120

Stage design by Karl Eigsti
INQUEST by Donald Freed
Based on INVITATION TO AN INQUEST by Walter and Miriam Schneir
Directed by Alan Schneider
Music Box Theatre, New York (1970)

Stage design by Eugene Berman
PULCINELLA
Music by Igor Stravinsky
Choreographed by George Balanchine and
    Jerome Robbins
New York City Ballet
Stravinsky Festival
New York State Theatre, Lincoln Center (1972)
(Courtesy of John Keck; photograph—Arnold
    Abramson)

Sketch rendered with ink and watercolors.

Stage design by John Lee Beatty
COME BACK, LITTLE SHEBA by William Inge
Directed by Marshall W. Mason
Queens Playhouse
Flushing, New York (1974)

UTILIZING A THRUST STAGE. Several interior
(living room, kitchen, bedroom, and halls) and
exterior playing areas are juxtaposed to create this
simultaneous scene setting. Note how the various
areas are emphasized by using platforms and steps
of different heights.

Stage design by Karl Eigsti
BOESMAN AND LENA by Athol Fugard
Directed by John Berry
Circle in the Square Theatre, New York (1970)
(Photograph—Lynn Pecktal)

The action of this Off-Broadway drama takes place
on the mud flats of the river Swartkaps, South
Africa. The stylized sketch, rendered with acrylic
paints and Dr. Martin's transparent watercolors on
illustration board, shows various patterns made by
the crevices in the mud where the water
drains into the river. Clusters of roots and
rocks jut above the mud.

121

PAINTER'S ELEVATIONS

Paint elevation by Raoul Pène du Bois
NO, NO, NANETTE
Beach scene backdrop
Music by Vincent Youmans
Book by Otto Harbach, Frank Mandel
Lyrics by Irving Caesar, Otto Harbach
Adapted and directed by Burt Shevelove
Forty-sixth Street Theatre, New York (1971)

Paint elevations by Santo Loquasto
WHAT THE WINE-SELLERS BUY by Ron Milner
Directed by Michael Schultz
New York Shakespeare Festival
Vivian Beaumont Theatre
Lincoln Center (1974)

The painter's elevations in ½-in. scale for
both interior and exterior units were painted
directly on prints of the drafting, mounted on
illustration board.

Paint elevation by Robin Wagner (below)
JESUS CHRIST SUPERSTAR
Lyrics by Tim Rice
Music by Andrew Lloyd Webber
Directed by Tom O'Horgan
Mark Hellinger Theatre, New York (1971)

Wagner's paint elevation in ¼-in. scale for half
the bubble cyc. Hundreds of bubbles in various
sizes were drawn with pencils (using circles cut
out of ¼-in. plywood) and painted with aniline
dyes on the translucent muslin drop, 84 ft. wide
by 50 ft. high. Note the seam where the two pieces
of muslin joined was incorporated in the design as
part of the effect, the light source is indicated
from the orifice at the center of the drop.
(Photographs — Lynn Pecktal)

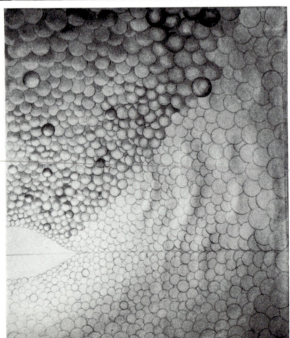

darker.'' Most designers use their elevation
drawings to transfer the outlines of the scenery
onto white illustration board (or heavy paper)
for painting. Bainbridge Board Number 80 is
one of the best and most popular, and Whatman
Board is also excellent. Both these boards take
paint and dyes beautifully, as do such other
good brands as Strathmore illustration board.

Rather than redrawing, some designers paint
directly on prints of the drafting (either blueprints or black line on white paper), which can
be submitted mounted or unmounted. When a
designer creates an elaborate color model with
removable scenery, the pieces of the model are

Model by Ben Edwards
FINISHING TOUCHES by Jean Kerr
Directed by Joseph Anthony
Plymouth Theatre, New York (1973)
(Photographs — Kenneth Pew)

WHITE PAPER MODEL IN ¼-IN. SCALE
The comedy takes place in the Cooper home in an eastern university at the present time.

MATERIALS USED:
1. Heavy white paper, white illustration board, and white glue that dries clear for constructing the proscenium opening, base, flats, ceiling pieces, and so on.
2. Pencils for making outlines of moldings, bricks, terrace stonework, and ornamental details.
3. Clear acetate on which the window and door mullions and the terrace slats were painted.
4. Soft wood and heavy white paper for creating the beams, stairway railings, bookcases, and furniture.

MODEL SIZE IN ¼-IN. SCALE. Proscenium opening: 38 ft. wide by 13 ft. 9 in. high. Height of ceiling from floor: 18 ft. Deepest part of the setting at the bookcases on the stair landing: 22 ft.
ACTUAL SIZE OF THE MODEL: 15 in. long by 6 in. high by 6 in. deep. Note the placements of the six doors and four bookcase units in the interior setting. Rear view of model shows the backing flats with window units, bookcase units, terrace wall, and latticework.

Most commercial designers keep a file of theatre plans with such information or have easy access to it through production carpenters, scenic studios, or theatre managers, but there are always instances when measurements must be taken on the physical stage to get the actual dimensions. For instance, obstructions on the stage that might interfere with the scenery may not always be noted on copies of theatre drawings, and these may have to be checked out on the spot. Among these are jogs in the upstage or offstage walls, supporting columns or posts, air-conditioning vents or air shafts, radiators and pipes, low pinrails or catwalks, or stairs.

It is also vital for the designer to have a plan and section drawing of the theatre house so that sight lines can be checked from the orchestra, mezzanine, and balcony. And, even if the set designer is not lighting the show, he must be fully aware of the limitations of the house and stage with respect to lighting and the equipment for it. He must always think of how the production will be lighted and where the instruments will hang or be positioned, and must allow space for them on his plans when he is doing the drafting and model-building. Needless to say, the set designer and lighting designer must confer back and forth when doing a show.

THE BASIC (ROUGH) MODEL

For his individual use or even for a presentation, a designer may construct a simple basic model in ¼-inch scale. These models are usually cut out of white or gray paper, with only the architectural details penciled in and without any actual thicknesses being shown. The furniture and the props are created in the same way. A rough preliminary model is frequently necessary for the designer to see how the forms, proportions, and space of a setting are working out before he gets into drafting or the detailed model. One of the quickest ways is to draw the floor plans and elevations on ¼-inch graph paper; these are then cut out and folded and pasted together. Another good method of checking on the visual elements in a setting is to make a more accurate model by working with the blueprints after the ½-inch elevations and plans have been drafted. When the prints have been mounted on illustration board, the pieces of scenery are cut out with an X-Acto knife and are glued together to form the model of the set.

No real boundary line can be established as to what constitutes a standard rough model, since they vary so much, but this information applies to most rough models:

Scale. Usually small with ¼ inch = 1 foot, but can be ⅜-inch or ½-inch, especially if a rough model is being made by cutting out the pieces of scenery from blueprints and adhering them to cardboard or illustration board.

Materials. For model scenery: very simple materials like heavy paper (white or gray), cardboard, or ¼-inch graph paper. Heavier materials are used for larger sized models. For base, proscenium, back wall, and supporting members: heavy paper or cardboard.

Indicating details. Actual color of scenery is not usually shown. Details are drawn in pencil or pen, relief and thickness on scenery and furniture not normally shown unless some important feature.

Attachment of pieces. Cut-out pieces of scenery can be attached temporarily by masking tape or rubber cement or permanently by glue.

THE DETAILED MODEL

The most impressive models, of course, are those built and painted in enormous detail, where all the scenery, furniture, and set dressing is executed in color. Ming Cho Lee and Robert Randolph are two designers who usually make models of this type for each show they design. Both concentrate on indicating almost every possible facet of detail, showing dimensional forms and textures, all thicknesses, the exact kinds of material they want, and every piece of

dressing, down to the last picture on the backing. In their model furniture, it is not unusual for them to simulate brass beds with real brass or actually to carve the turned wooden legs of a table from balsa wood. Their models are also constructed so that the different units of scenery (wings, wagon units, and drops) can be easily removed from the model of the stage itself for use by the painters. Each item is covered in the scenic studio with clear acetate to protect it from dirt and paint. In the same manner, any complicated three-dimensional pieces are available for the carpenters to build from in addition to the usual elevations and plans on the drafting. Models in this degree of exactness can also make it much easier for those planning the lighting and the costumes, and for those selecting the props.

CONSTRUCTING THE MODEL OF THE STAGE TO HOUSE THE SETTING

It is necessary to create a model shell of the stage in which to house your model settings. This structure simulates the existing stage where the production is being mounted and includes the base (stage floor), the proscenium wall with the proscenium arch, the house portal, the back wall, and any other objects required in the theatre proper, plus bracing and supporting members which hold these model pieces together. Most model shells are simply rectangular boxes with the SL and SR sides left open to permit visual access and to let light through. The top of the structure is also left open so that the scenery can be viewed from above and hanging pieces of the model setting can be lifted out. (For a single interior set with a ceiling piece, the back wall and bracing members on the side are sometimes omitted.) The rectangular-box model is the most practical structure for handling, protecting the model settings from damage, and for storage. If you are doing several shows in the same theatre, the model of the stage can be used over and over.

The Base (stage floor)

Since the base of the model must support the entire portion of the existing stage house (proscenium or other) and the model pieces of the actual designs in the production, it should be

Model by Robert U. Taylor
RAISIN
Based on Lorraine Hansberry's A RAISIN IN THE SUN
Book by Robert Nemiroff and Charlotte Zaltzberg
Music by Judd Woldin
Lyrics by Robert Brittan
Directed and choreographed by Donald McKayle
Forty-sixth Street Theatre, New York (1973)
(Photograph – Robert U. Taylor)

(Left) Taylor's complete model in ½-in. scale shown with lighting had a proscenium opening 45 ft wide by 24 ft high.
(Right) The same model for Raisin shown with the proscenium and brick wall removed. The model was made of illustration board, balsa wood, metal rods, and guaze. The actual scenery for the production was constructed of wood (platforms, levels, steps, and openwork flats), sharkstooth scrim (covering certain areas of the flats made of 1 by 3s), and steel pipes 1 in. O.D.
(Photograph – Lynn Pecktal)

made of a strong material that does not bend: ¼-inch Masonite, ¼-inch plywood, Upson board, or heavy mounting board. The size of the base can be that of the complete stage, including offstage space on the left and right, full depth from the edge of the apron to the back wall, or the full onstage space plus only the offstage space needed to realize the design. The first is often necessary when you are indicating storage of scenery offstage during a performance or when there is other mechanical involvement, such as units being moved offstage by winches. It would be impractical to indicate all the offstage space, especially if the stage floor is of extraordinary size. Exceptions can occur when the production is utilizing a thrust stage (an extension of the apron) or a raked deck that extends beyond the existing stage. Further variations in the stage floor are found in a production on an open stage (three-quarter round or full round). Because the floor plan is such a major part of the design, the base of the model often includes the first few rows of seats to show the relationship of the playing areas to the audience.

It is best to paint the base a basic color before putting any pieces on it or before transferring the ground plan. If you are using Upson board or mounting board, it should also be painted on the reverse side to prevent the board from warping. After the base has been painted and has dried, the floor plan should be laid out on it, either by transferring it from a drawing with transfer paper or by drawing it lightly and directly in pencil.

Proscenium Wall and Opening

This piece of the model structure is usually the same width as the base; the total height is determined by whatever distance you need to take care of your tallest piece of scenery (portals, backdrops, and other hanging units). The height of the proscenium wall does not normally include the full height of the grid because that, too, would add unneeded bulk to the model structure. If your proscenium opening is 36 feet by 20 feet high, in ½-inch scale it would actually be 18 inches wide by 10 inches high. Since the proscenium wall prominently frames your design, it should be made of a sturdy material and the opening should be neatly cut out. It can be built with illustration board, mounting board, mat board, or ⅛-inch Masonite. The thickness of the proscenium opening (height and width) can be created with the same material or with appropriate lengths of balsa wood, which also helps brace the proscenium wall. While proscenium openings are frequently black, they may be colored to match the proscenium wall in the actual theatre or they can be covered with fabric, flock, or some other material.

For support, lengths of illustration board or balsa wood (or other soft woods) can be cut and glued along the outer ends and top of the proscenium wall before it is attached. When ready, attach the wall by gluing it (Sobo or Elmer's Glue-All) to the base. Pins can be used to hold it firmly while the glue is drying.

Back Wall and Sides

The back wall, usually the same size as the proscenium wall, is made of like materials and is braced in the same way. Sides of the model shell may be left partially open or enclosed. They too should be braced well with lengths of illustration board or small strips of wood that are positioned perpendicular to the proscenium and to the back wall. On the top of the inner sides, flat pieces of illustration board at least an inch wide should be attached parallel to the base and glued so marks can be made to simulate the position of the rigging lines. These marks on both sides should be accurately measured and numbered so they can be easily identified. Then, when the units of hanging scenery are placed in the model, the small wooden dowels (or other supports) that extend across the top of the individual scenery can be lined up accordingly. (You do not necessarily need to indicate the rigging lines, of course, if there are no hanging units of scenery. For example, a box set may have only a house portal, ceiling unit, and masking pieces indicated on a model.)

House Equipment

Once you have completed the shell of the stage itself, the next step in building the model is to construct any house equipment you may be planning to use. This can include the house portal, masking legs and borders, cyc, or other pieces. All of these can be cut out of illustration board in the desired color—or painted—and then positioned and attached to the model of the stage according to the positions where they play.

Making and Assembling Model Scenery

The process of putting the actual model scenery together and painting it varies so much with every production that only generalized steps can be outlined. The photographs of models on the accompanying pages show how the building and painting of models require different treatment for each. Lloyd Evans' model scenery for *L'Incoronazione di Poppea* at the New York City Opera, for instance, was constructed simply out of illustration board and paper, but it was painted in elaborate detail. It was made up of a combination of pieces: cut drops, a backdrop, profiled and three-dimensional set pieces. The next model shown was designed for *Ariadne auf Naxos* by Helen Pond and Herbert Senn, also for the New York City Opera. This is an example of very intricate model building as well as detailed painting.

The steps that follow are typical in making and assembling model scenery, but the order can vary because the process is totally dependent on individual design style and the production.

1. *Laying out the scenery.* Draw the outlines of the pieces of scenery on the materials (illustration board, heavy paper, fabric, or whatever).

2. *Painting the pieces.* You may want to paint the model scenery in transparent washes as in a watercolor technique, or to do it completely in opaque colors, or use a combination of the two. If, however, a particular piece, such as a cut drop on illustration board, is being painted, it is often easier to cut it out after it is finished and then touch up the edges. But if you are making a three-dimensional unit of scenery attached to a wagon, it might be better to cut it all out and put it together, then do the painting. This is especially true if the model scenery is to be textured or have appliqués put on before it is painted. You must decide what works best for your purposes.

3. *Cutting out the pieces.* Sharp cutting tools are always desirable. X-Acto knives, mat knives, single-edge razor blades, and scissors are all good, and small manicure scissors are very helpful for cutting out intricate work from heavy paper. Implements such as snips and pliers are sometimes necessary for cutting and shaping wire and metal materials.

4. *Gluing and assembling.* Several items can be used to hold the cut-out pieces of model scenery together while the glue or cement is drying. These may be small strips of masking tape, magic transparent Scotch tape, straight pins, or push pins.

Model by Lloyd Evans
L'INCORONAZIONE DI POPPEA by Claudio
  Monteverdi
Libretto by Francesco Busenello
Directed by Gerald Freedman
New York City Opera (1973)

The opera was designed to have a proscenium opening 44 ft. wide by 29 ft. high. Both three-dimensional pieces and cut backdrops in the model were painted on illustration board.

Units of the model setting came apart so they could be covered individually with clear acetate and used as painter's elevations by scenic artists. (Photographs—Lynn Pecktal)

Model by Helen Pond and Herbert Senn
ARIADNE AUF NAXOS by Richard Strauss
Libretto by Hugo von Hofmannsthal
Directed by Sarah Caldwell
New York City Opera
New York State Theatre
Lincoln Center (1973)
(Photographs — Lynn Pecktal)

Top:
The model of the theatrical stage setting was created to play on a revolve 25 ft. in diameter. The opening of the draperies inside the proscenium of the ½-in.-scale model = 18 ft. 6 in. wide by 13 ft. 6 in. high. Overall size of the model: 11 in. high by 12¾ in. wide, excluding the projecting sconces on the sides. Disassembled pieces in the foreground are profiled wings which slide onstage and offstage in the model.
Bottom:
Rear view of the model showing decorative frameworks which also support the scenery.

String or thread can also be wrapped around objects when feasible. Since most models must be neat, apply glues sparsely, but use enough to hold the materials together well.

5. *Adding details.* Any necessary items like furniture, draperies, curtains, banners, signs, or other objects should now be cut out or carved, put together, and painted.

6. *Finishing the model.* You will find on most models that you work back and forth on cutting, gluing, assembling, and painting. In addition, new ideas usually develop which necessitate making some minor changes like adding more highlights, taking down an area that is too bright, repositioning a unit of scenery, or adding another prop.

MATERIALS FOR MAKING MODELS

Select model materials that are lightweight but strong enough to hold together well when they are glued and painted.

General Materials

For stage house and scenery: illustration board, Bristol board, chip board, or similar boards; balsa wood in various sizes and shapes (sheets, blocks, and rods).

For base: ¼-inch plywood, ¼-inch Masonite, Upson board, or heavy mounting board.

For supports and bracing: lengths of balsa wood and softwood such as pine (¼ by ½ inch), or pieces of illustration board.

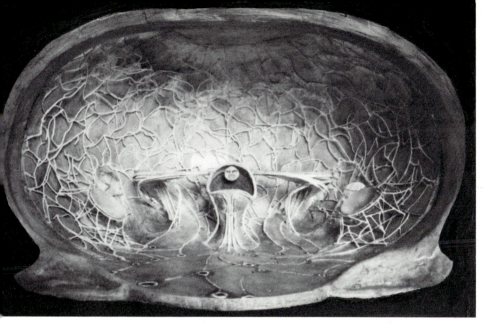

Model by Kert Lundell
BRAIN CHILD
Book by Maxine Klein
Music by Michel Legrand
Lyrics by Hal David
Directed by Maxine Klein
Forest Theatre
Philadelphia, Pennsylvania (1974)

The scene for this musical takes place inside a girl's brain. The model was created with brass rods and clear liquid acrylic which hardens and remains clear. Proscenium dimensions were 42 ft. wide by 26 ft. high, stage depth 28 ft. The width of the oval was 32 ft.

Model by Elmon Webb and Virginia Dancy
A WHISTLE IN THE DARK by Thomas
    Murphy
(American premiére)
Directed by Arvin Brown
Long Wharf Theatre, New Haven (1968)
(Photograph — Elmon Webb)

The model, in ½-in. scale, shows a setting of a council house dwelling in an English industrial town. A balsa-wood framework overhead (16 ft. above the floor) corresponds to the lighting grid of the Long Wharf Theatre. The setting is approximately 22 ft. wide.

Model by Peter Wexler
LES TROYENS by Hector Berlioz
Libretto by the composer
Directed by Nathaniel Merrill
The Metropolitan Opera, New York (1973)
(Photographs — Peter Wexler)

Views of a unit model in ¼-in. scale, Part I, LES TROYENS. Materials included wood, wire, gesso, and gold leaf.

Tools for Cutting

X-Acto knives and blades
Scissors
Single-edge razor blades
Mat knives
Cutting pliers and snips
Small saws

Glues and Cements

Elmer's Glue-All (dries transparent and hard)
Sobo Glue (dries transparent and flexible)
Rubber cement for temporary holding
Spray adhesives (Scotch and Letraset sprays)
Duco cement for glass
Plastic cement for Plexiglas (REZ-N-BOND)

For Holding Items Together While Glue Is Drying

Push pins	Transparent tape
Straight pins	Thread or string
Masking tape	Clothes pins

Papers and Fabrics for Model Scenery

PAPERS

Metallic paper	Wallpaper
Flocked paper	Paper doilies
Marbelized paper	Brown wrapping paper
Watercolor paper	Sandpaper
Charcoal and pastel paper	Graph paper
Construction paper	Tortoiseshell paper
Textured Oriental papers	Newspaper
Lace paper	Tissue paper
Rice paper	Parchment

FABRICS

Organza	Nylon
China silk	Rayon
Voile	Oilcloth
Dotted Swiss	Paisley
Lace	Satin
Muslin	Sateen
Canvas or sailcloth	Taffeta
Cheesecloth or gauze	Velveteen, velvet
Scrim	Terrycloth
Linen	Wool
Duvetyne	Bobbinet
Broadcloth	Gingham
Burlap	Chintz
Buckram	Flannel
Denim	Corduroy

Materials for Creating Sculptured Forms and Texture on Models

Styrofoam (rigid or shredded)	Foam core board ($\frac{1}{4}$ inch thick)

Display foam board ($\frac{1}{2}$ inch thick)
Foam rubber
Prestofoam
Ethafoam
Polyester fiber (like that for cushions)
Small pieces of Plexiglas and Lucite
Mylar
Clear polyethylene film
Opaque vinyl covering
Cellophane
Spackle paste
Natural and synthetic sponges
Plaster bandages (on a roll)
Aluminum foil
Sculp-metal (a medium that models like clay and hardens into a metal)
Rubber
Balsa wood
Wood shavings
Corrugated cardboard
Sawdust
Cork
Vermiculite
Pebbles
Sand
Screen wire
Brass wire and rods
Pipe cleaners
Cotton balls
Soda straws
Linoleum
Bits of cheesecloth dipped in clear liquid latex
Plasteline

Miscellaneous Items for Ornamental Details and Furniture

Paste pearls	Yarn
Seed pearls	Thread
Small ribbons	Small chains (like necklaces)
Small braids	
Sequins	Leather
Buttons	Felt
Beads	All kinds of costume jewelry
Flitter	
Con-tact plastic	Toothpicks
Balsa wood	Florist wire
Heavy white drawing paper	Dollhouse furniture ($\frac{1}{2}$-inch scale)
Small mirrors	Feathers

Paints and Materials for Finishing Models

There is an enormous variety of products that can be used to paint models. They can run the gamut from those you buy at art stores in tubes and jars to those that can be bought in cans at theatrical paint stores. Like scenery, the model is often finished in a combination of several different materials, and a number of the same paints that are applied on scenery can also be put on the model. They include:

Designer colors (opaque watercolors)	Latex
	Colored inks
Casein paint	India ink
Acrylic polymer plastic colors	Aniline dyes
	Pastels
Dr. Martin's Concentrated Watercolors	Colored pencils
	Felt-tip pens
	Tempera or poster colors
Vinyl	Oil

Model and drawings by Lynn Pecktal
SOUND AND LIGHT AT FORD'S THEATRE
Produced and directed by Charles Guggenheim
Ford's Theatre
Washington, D.C. (1970)

The architectural elements of the stage and house were influential in the design of the scenery for this production. A detailed model was made of Ford's Theatre to see how the scenery during the time of Lincoln worked in the existing theatre. This included the apron, boxes, and stage proper. The settings consisted mostly of soft pieces: two muslin backdrops, 3 canvas cut leg drops (portals), 1 scrim drop, 1 scrim show curtain, a framed profile column unit, furniture and props. The pencil drawings on Clearprint drafting paper show the scrim show curtain and cut drop portals. Prints of the drawings were mounted on illustration board. The prints were dampened slightly, then the board was sprayed with 3M Spra-ment adhesive, and the drawing was pressed into place.

Drawing of scrim eagle show curtain showing painted house draperies and valance of the Ford's Theatre. Painted (opaque) canvas draperies are glued on the sides of the scrim.

(Bottom)
Drawing of No. 2 canvas cut leg drop (soft portal), 26 by 47 ft., indicating architectural details. Painted draperies for No. 1 and No. 3 portals are shown in the center. The unframed portal was designed with cut draperies to hang without support by netting. The vanishing point for drawing the architectural elements in perspective is located on the floor line at center.

Spray paints in aerosol cans: Flat or gloss colors and metallics.
Clear Spray Fixative in aerosol cans: Plastiklear and Krylon. Besides being preservatives, they produce a glossy surface.

Applying Paints

Watercolor and oil-painting brushes in various sizes: red sables, pure white bristles, oxhair for detailed work; also assorted small scenic brushes for laying in.

Small sponges	Small paint rollers (1 inch wide)
Air brush	Aerosol cans of paint

Basecoating Models

Liquitex Gesso (acrylic polymer emulsion base), which can be thinned with water, dries rapidly,

and can be painted over immediately with casein, acrylic polymer plastic colors, tempera, and others.

Creating Texture

Liquitex modeling paste and extender (acrylic resin emulsion) can be used alone or with Gesso or Liquitex medium to create textured surfaces.

DRAFTING

Any designer who drafts his own show knows the extraordinary amount of work it takes to produce drawings that are neat and accurate. Both of these qualities are most essential for any kind of drafting, but extremely so in the theatre, where the whole show is built and assembled by what these drawings dictate; if errors have to be corrected afterward, they add to the labor and cost.

While a number of Broadway designers draft their own productions, others employ assistants solely for this job. Designers can be busy with several shows at once or they may be designing the costumes or the lighting on the same production. Since drafting requires so much time, doing his own can keep the designer from concentrating on other areas of the show. Whether the designer chooses to do sketches or a painted model for his production, the drafting is an absolute must, for it is his translation of the technical aspects of the scenery—how it is built, how it is placed on stage, how it hangs, how it moves, and how it is stored. The drafting of the designs is seen by virtually everyone connected with the show, from the director to the lighting designer, the carpenters, and the scenic artists, plus the property man, the electricians, and the stage manager.

As in model-building, before a designer can get down to drafting the show accurately, he must first acquire the exact dimensions and specifics of the stage proper, and in these terms no two Broadway theatres are alike. Additional drafting may have to be done on a hit show when it moves from one theatre to another since the sets may have to undergo extensive revamping because of variations in stages and theatre houses, but there are situations where this can be kept to a minimum. It is also necessary to know the dimensions of legitimate theatres out of town where a show is trying out or going on

tour. This alone can create a great deal of added work if the designer must make changes.

The designer may begin laying out his initial drafting in a small scale, sometimes on graph paper ($\frac{1}{4}$-inch or $\frac{1}{8}$-inch), or on regular tracing paper until the desired plans are formed sufficiently to be enlarged into the standard scale of $\frac{1}{2}$ inch = 1 foot. Often, several ideas and combinations are explored in both these plans or elevations before the final selection is made. In fact, many changes can occur throughout the whole drafting process as new ideas develop. Some designers prefer to check out their designs by making rough $\frac{1}{4}$-inch models on white paper, either before or after they have started the drafting. To do very neat drafting where a lot of details are involved, many designers work by doing a series of overlays on tracing paper or by first laying out the particular sheet in rough form, which is then retraced for the final sheet. The well-experienced designer or assistant has his own individual method for drawing with speed, accuracy, and neatness.

The majority of the drafting for a Broadway show is done in $\frac{1}{2}$-inch scale and includes the floor plans (ground plans), the designer's elevations (looking from the front), a hanging section view of the set or sets on stage, and the details—which are drawn in a scale appropriate to the complexity of the piece. The scale for these details can be 1 inch = 1 foot, $1\frac{1}{2}$ inches = 1 foot, or in a larger scale if the subject requires. Working drawings (looking from the rear of the scenery) are not done by the designer, because any good scenic shop knows how to build the scenery and how to break it down. On a large show, like a musical that has many sets, there can be anywhere from twenty to thirty sheets of drafting indicating all of the usual views necessary for constructing each set and for their placement in the theatre. Also included in the drafting may be a drawing that is made in the very small scale of $\frac{1}{8}$ inch = 1 foot, showing all of the different backdrops, scrims, or ground cloths in the production. Laid out without details, this composite drawing of the soft scenery serves as a check sheet for the scenic studio to see the total amount involved and the various sizes of each piece. It can also be used for a bid session or for a record when the studio is ordering the particular pieces to have them made up.

Setting by Ming Cho Lee
HENRY IV (Part I) by William Shakespeare
Directed by Gordon Davidson
Lighting by Martin Aronstein
Mark Taper Forum
Los Angeles, California (1973)

**DRAFTING THE DRAWINGS FOR A UNIT
SETTING**
On the following pages are the drawings
for Ming Cho Lee's unit setting, drafted in
½-in. scale. Details are drawn in 1½-in.
scale.

**PLAN OF THE STRUCTURE AND
PLATFORM** (below). Shown are the size
and position of platforms, steps, posts,
doors, walls, and boards of the raked
floor. All height dimensions are taken
from the stage floor.

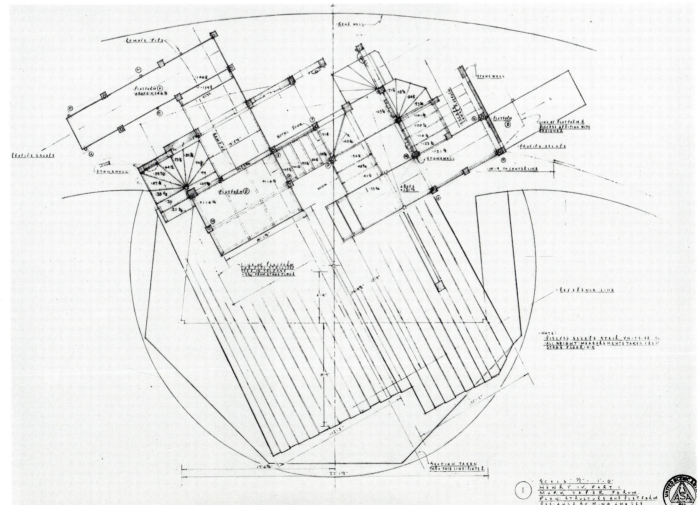

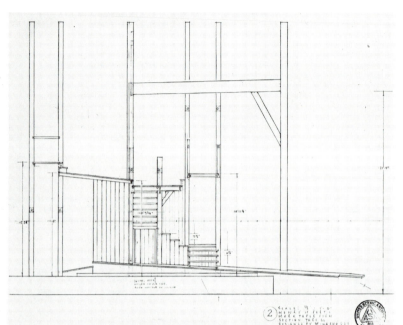

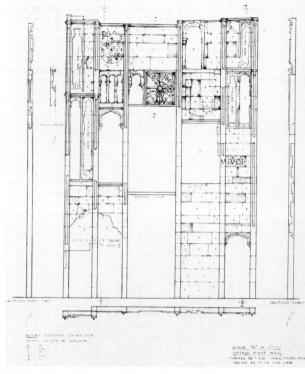

SECTION VIEW THROUGH CENTER LINE (above)
The drawing is made looking from stage right to
stage left.

ELEVATION OF UPSTAGE RIGHT WALL (above).
Numbers determine the depth of stone relief on the walls:
Number 1 — 1½ in., 2 — 3 in., 3 — 4½ in., and 4 — 6 in. Open
spaces are shown by an "X." Section views through "A"
(at left), "B" (at right), and "C" (at left of center
drawing) are drawn to show the various thicknesses at
the points indicated by the cutting lines. Pencil shading
on the drawing is done to show dimensional qualities.
ELEVATION OF UPSTAGE LEFT WALL (below). Again,
section views are drawn through "A" (at top), "B" (at
right), "C" (at left of center elevation), and "D" (below).
Wall number 3 is at the left.

**DRAWING OF THE MAIN PLATFORM WITH SECTION
VIEW** (below). The drawing indicates the layout of the
boards on the floor and the direction of the rake, boxing
line, platform framing, and existing platform. Boards at the
downstage edge range in width from 8½ to 12 in. The
rake of the floor is ¾ in. to a foot.

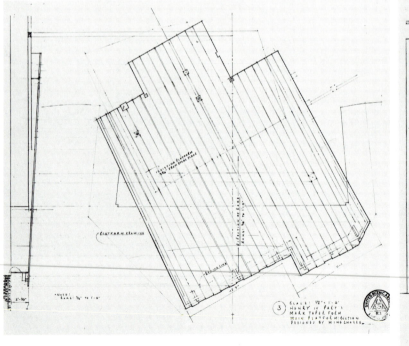

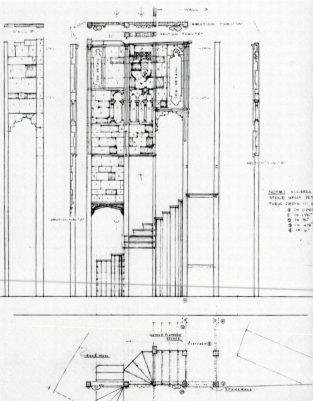

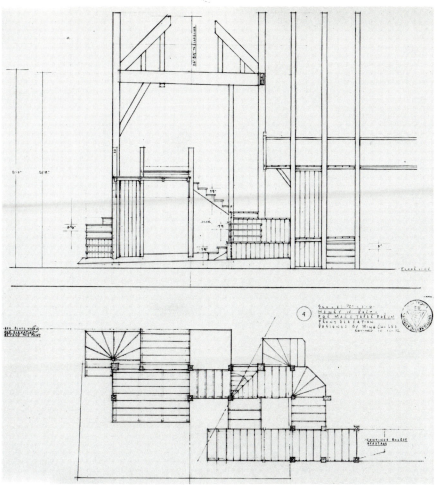

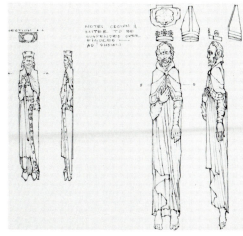

DETAILS OF STATUES (above). Three-dimensional statues on the stone walls of the setting vary in height from 4 ft. to 7 ft. (including the crowns and miters). Drawings for the statues (scale: 1½ in. equals 1 ft.) show front elevation, side elevation, and top view (to section A – A, and to section B – B).

FRONT ELEVATION OF PLATFORMS, STEPS, AND POST AND BEAM STRUCTURES (left). Risers of the steps range from 7½ to 8⅝ in. Below is the top view showing the design of the boards on the platforms and steps.

Drafting Equipment

Whether you are an established designer, a young designer starting out as a freshman in college, or a graduate student in drama school, there are certain materials and equipment needed for drafting, and those who have had a great deal of experience in drawing know the value of having good tools. You may be able to get along with minimal equipment at first, but there is almost no end to the available supplies which make drafting easier. Among objects necessary for drafting are:

CHECKLIST OF DRAFTING EQUIPMENT

Drawing board and plastic-coated drawing-board cover.
Drafting table and stool (wood or metal).
Table lamp (fluorescent, incandescent, combination).
T-square (wood, metal, plastic and wood).
Architect's triangular scale or architect's flat scale.
Drafting pencils, or lead and leadholders.
Lead pointers and pencil sharpeners.
Colored pencils.
Erasers (like Eberhard Faber) and gum eraser, and thin metal eraser shield.

Transparent plastic items:
  Triangles (30–60-degree and 45-degree) in various sizes.
  Irregular curves or French curves.
  Protractor (circular or semicircular).
  Ellipse guides.
  Other templates: triangles, hexagons, squares, diamonds, furniture, lighting instruments
  Lettering guides (for lines).
A set of drawing instruments, including compasses, dividers, bow pencil, bow pen, ruling pen, and so on.
Beam compass.
Metal straightedge.
Draftsman's duster brush.
Cleaning powder (Whisk) to use while working on drawings.
Transparent tape and tape dispenser.
Miscellaneous items: scissors, mat knife, board for cutting paper, inks, various pens, and penholders.
Other equipment for more expeditious work:
  Adjustable triangles.
  Folding parallel rulers.
  Adjustable T-squares.
  Adjustable curve rule (K&E).
  Parallel ruling straightedge.

Drafting paper:
  Rolls or pads of tracing paper (thin, regular, and heavy weight).
  Excellent paper for doing finished drawings: Albanene (K&E) or Clearprint technical paper.
  Graph paper for making rough drawings.
  Carbon transfer paper.
File cabinets for drawings (wood or metal).

Drawing Pencils and Leads

Because the weights of lines in drafting vary (heavy, medium, light), appropriate pencils are used to make them. Standard brands are Koh-I-Noor, Eagle Turquoise, and Venus. Drafting pencils and leads range in degrees of hardness from 6B (very soft) to 9H (very hard). Since the amount of pressure applied on pencils can vary with the individual using them, you can frequently make both heavy and light lines with the same pencil and therefore can get by with fewer pencils and leads than are listed below. These should be used as guides rather than requirements. Usually H, 2H, 3H, and 4H are satisfactory for doing theatrical drafting.

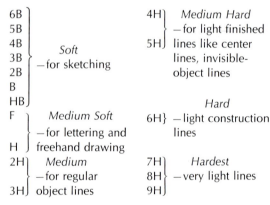

6B 5B 4B 3B 2B B HB	*Soft* —for sketching	4H 5H	*Medium Hard* —for light finished lines like center lines, invisible-object lines
F H	*Medium Soft* —for lettering and freehand drawing	6H	*Hard* —light construction lines
2H 3H	*Medium* —for regular object lines	7H 8H 9H	*Hardest* —very light lines

TYPES OF CONVENTIONAL LINE USED IN DRAFTING

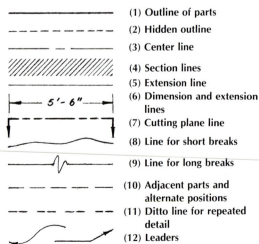

(1) **Outline of parts**
(2) **Hidden outline**
(3) **Center line**
(4) **Section lines**
(5) **Extension line**
(6) **Dimension and extension lines**
(7) **Cutting plane line**
(8) **Line for short breaks**
(9) **Line for long breaks**
(10) **Adjacent parts and alternate positions**
(11) **Ditto line for repeated detail**
(12) **Leaders**

Drawing Paper

Drawings are put on drafting paper simply so copies can be printed for the craftsmen involved with planning, building, painting, and erecting the show. Choose a drafting paper that you can work with comfortably so that your drawn lines will come out well on the blueprint. Even though good drawing paper is expensive, using it will save you time and frustration. There is nothing more agonizing than to have a drawing lead rip through the paper of a detailed work. Finding a preferred paper may mean trying out different kinds. For all practical purposes, it is wise to use thin tracing paper for rough initial work and a heavier drawing paper of better quality for the finished drafting. Theatrical drafting is rarely, if ever, done in ink unless for some specialized presentation.

Sizes of Drawings

There are no standard measurements for how large or small the overall sheets of drawings should be. The scale you are working in and the size of the production plus the type of existing stage house normally determine these. However, the larger the drawings, the more costly it becomes to have copies made and the more cumbersome they are to handle while executing the show. (That is also why it is not a good idea to leave a lot of unused space on drawings.) While it is nice to have all the drawings the same size, especially if the blueprints (or black-and-white prints) are to be stapled together along one side to form a set, this is not always possible and is not always expected. Average-size drawings can be anywhere from 18 to 24 inches or 24 to 36 inches. It works well to cut the paper from the roll a bit larger than the intended size in case you must draw another view or if the edges get torn. A good way to prevent tearing is to place a continuous border of masking tape around the extreme edges of the paper. Then position the bottom of the tape-bordered paper parallel to the bottom of the drafting board and, using additional small pieces of tape, attach the corners of the paper to the board. This keeps the drawing from getting torn when working over it with drafting instruments or when lifting up two of the corners of the paper to slide rough drawings under to be traced. The bottom edge (preferably) or one other edge should remain positioned at all times so the paper does not have to be lined up with the straightedge each time a rough drawing is to be traced. After the drawing is finished, the continuous strips of tape on the edges of the paper can be removed by gently peeling them back or by trimming them off with a mat knife.

Borders and Title Blocks

Borders, heavy lines drawn $\frac{1}{4}$ to $\frac{1}{2}$ inch from the edge of the drafting paper around each sheet of drafting, dress up the appearance of the drawing, but they are optional. Every sheet of drafting should have a title block in the lower-right-hand corner that gives the following information:

1. Name of the show.
2. Act and scene.
3. Name of theatre, company, or producer.
4. Name of particular drawing.
5. Scale in which the drawing is done.
6. Designer's name.
7. Date of drawing.
8. Revision dates.
9. Number of sheet (prominent). If total is 12 sheets, it can be labeled 5 of 12, 8 of 12, etc.
10. Union stamp (if any) and signature.

These title blocks (about $2\frac{1}{2}$ by 4 inches) can be drawn in pencil each time or put on with a permanent rubber stamp which can be purchased from a firm like the American Stamp Manufacturing Co., Inc., 121 Fulton St., New York, N.Y., 10038. Tel.: (212) 227-1877.

Lettering

Besides the drawings themselves and the dimensions, the most conspicuous aspect of the sheet of drafting is the lettering. While neatness and accuracy are essential in drafting, the lettering alone can make the drafting appear sloppy or slick. Freehand-lettering ability comes naturally for some designers but is difficult for others. Although mechanical aids like Leroy lettering sets are good to practice with, they are painfully slow for theatrical drafting work. Practice is the only solution to achieve better lettering.

Light parallel guidelines are usually necessary in all drafting to produce neat consistency of lettering. You can learn to judge the spacing for these by eye as well as the size of the lettering and not have to rely on measuring them or using a lettering guide each time. As a rule, lettering is kept as small as possible (no less than $\frac{1}{8}$ inch high) but clearly legible, and is normally laid out in a line parallel to the

top and bottom of the sheet. Sizes and type (caps and upper and lower case) vary according to the purpose. For example, for headings like Plan and Elevation, you would use bold capitals, whereas for general notes you would use upper and lower case.

Labels

Labels appear on all drawings to identify each piece of scenery properly. They may be thought of in two categories. *General* labels include many items, among them views of drawings (Elevations, Plans, and Sections) or overall headings (Drawing Room Furniture, Ballroom Draperies, Garden Foliage). *Specific* labels refer to the actual piece—Act 1 Show Portal, Act 3 Fountain, or SL Alcove Backing. In turn, the same label is put on the scenery as it is built so the painters and stagehands can easily know which piece they are working with. Whenever it applies, flats are labeled in the sequence in which they play. In an interior box set, they are labeled by either letters or numerals, starting on stage right. These can be A, B, C, etc., or 1, 2, 3, etc., and continue upstage and then to stage left. They may also be indicated by R1, R2, R3, etc., for the stage-right wall, L1, L2, L3, etc., for the stage-left wall, and C1, C2, C3, etc., for the center wall. The selection is entirely up to the designer. Wing and border sets are labeled similarly, starting downstage and working upstage. In every instance, groups of labels should be consistent in size, boldness, and clarity.

Notes

Like labels, notes can be general or specific. Notes printed on the drafting often say a lot more than can be shown in drawings. They can function as a clarification on a drawing where there might be doubt about some aspect of its execution or material or to emphasize an important point, or to indicate something totally new. However used, they refer to an idea on the drawings which should be noticed immediately by those reading it. These examples are typical: "Plexi windows are beaded and painted," "Provide 2-in. leather cushion for window seat," "Designer will select door hardware for all paneled doors," "All woodwork to be three-dimensional unless otherwise noted," and "Curtains hang in 100% fullness."

Dimensions

Next in importance to the drawings themselves, dimensions are an indispensable feature in drafting. They save an enormous amount of time for the carpenters building the scenery and the scenic artists drawing it. Dimensions are given for size and for location. They can be drawn in several ways, but these basic rules apply:

1. They should be positioned outside the outline of a drawing whenever possible. This is done by using extension lines, which should start just clear of the outline and go past the dimension line. The dimension line, parallel to the outline of the drawing, is a light line with a narrow arrowhead $\frac{1}{8}$ inch long on each end which touches the extension lines (or the outline when it is not on the outside). Dimension lines may be broken in the center to allow the dimension to be placed, or may be continuous and the dimension put above it.

2. The standard method for dimensioning is in inches and feet. Inches are shown by ″ and feet by ′ with a dash between the two. Anything over 12 inches is labeled in feet. Typical examples: $0'-8''$, $12'-0''$, $30'-6''$.

3. When a space is too small for a dimension, it is placed nearby with a leader (see p. 140) pointing to the particular space.

4. Dimensions are placed on a drawing so they read horizontally from left to right on the sheet, or so they read from the right-hand side of the sheet.

5. A series of dimensions may be staggered in order to avoid confusion.

6. On ground plans, heights of platforms and steps above stage level are often given by +6, +12, +18, etc., those below the stage by -6, -12, -18, etc.

7. A center line or the outline of a drawing should never be used as a dimension line per se.

8. Dimensions for circles are given in radius dimensions by using a radius line going from the center (indicated by +) to the outline of the circle. The dimension line starts a bit beyond the center and has an arrowhead on the end which touches the circle. The dimension itself is positioned above the line (or the line can be broken and the dimension inserted) with an *R* placed after the numbers. The diameter of a circle can also be shown as a note with a leader pointing to and touching the circle with a *D* placed after the numbers.

9. The same dimension is not usually repeated on different views of an object.

10. If a dimension line is placed within a sectioned area, the section lines should not go over the number.

Ground Plan

A ground plan, the most important single drawing of a setting, is the view of the scenery from above as it is placed on the floor of the stage. It indicates where all of the scenery and furniture plays in the existing stage structure and includes any house equipment being used. This view is drawn as a horizontal section whereby a cutting line arbitrarily goes through the flats at some point but is above such units as platforms, steps, and furniture. A ground plan is usually drawn in the scale $\frac{1}{2}$ inch = 1 foot. Different types of line are used on the drafting to denote the stage structure, the scenery positioned on the floor, and the pieces that hang or are placed above the floor. (See Types of Line.) Before you really start putting the plans on paper, two lines should be drawn:

1. The downstage *set line* of the stage—shown by a light broken line which goes from the right return to the left return (or the proscenium line or the portal line or the curtain line). The set line can vary with the theatre.

2. The *center line* of the proscenium opening—downstage to upstage, shown by a center line.

These two lines are used as guides to relate to and measure from when putting all the other lines on the drawing, and this standard method is not only the most accurate way to draw a floor plan, but the same procedure is also followed precisely when the set is erected in the theatre. The floor plan of the actual stage should be drawn first, then the scenery, and finally the furniture.

CHECKLIST FOR A GROUND PLAN

The Stage

The proscenium opening

The apron

All walls around the stage indicating maximum measurements, exits, entrances, doors, stairs, obstructions (jogs, columns), and the pinrail.

The pinrail above the stage floor (either SL or SR) should show the position of the rigging lines, starting downstage and working upstage to the back wall, with the applicable hanging scenery drawn and labeled on each. Although lighting plots are usually made on separate drawings, light pipes and border lights can be denoted for clarity and for allowing space, especially if there is a great deal of scenery in the flies.

House Equipment

House curtain, traveler, house portal, tormentors, teasers, right and left returns, legs and borders for masking, cyclorama, or plaster cyc.

Scenery Units

Show curtain, act curtains, back-up drops for gauzes, show portals, flats, set pieces (profiled and three-dimensional), ground rows, backings, backdrops, cut drops, leg drops, free-form hanging pieces, platforms, decks, wagon units, revolves, ramps, steps, periaktoi, and sliding screens.

Also drawn lines indicating the position of ceiling pieces, ground cloths, rugs, tracking slots for winches, jackknife stages, and any traps in the floor that may be used in the production.

Furniture and Props

All furniture in the normal playing position, plus any other position it may be changed to for another scene; position of any special props; position of lamps (on furniture, on walls, or hanging overhead).

Dimensions of the scenery shown on the ground plan do not always need to be extensive, because the individual measurements of each piece are shown in detail on the front elevations. It is important, however, to show such measurements as overall widths and depths, particularly those for locating specific points like the corners of an interior set which are needed for positioning the scenery when building it and setting it up in 'he theatre. The amount of dimensioning varies with the production and its needs. A ground plan is ordinarily made for each set, but sometimes the plan of another set in the show is indicated by light broken lines on the same drawing. This may be done to represent the different depths of the sets or to define where pieces change for certain scenes in a unit setting.

Front Elevations

While the ground plan reveals how everything looks from above, the front elevations indicate how each piece of scenery looks from the front. Every piece of scenery is shown in a flat stretched-out view that is dimensioned sufficiently for the carpenter to build it or for the scenic artist to draw it. As far as actual placement of the overall drawings on the sheet of drafting paper is concerned, there are only generalized patterns to follow, because each show is different. As a rule, it is advisable to

think of the drawings on a sheet as a group of patterns which form an attractive overall design. Normally the ground plan and the hanging section view are centered on separate sheets of drafting paper, but the front elevations and details vary tremendously and are laid out and grouped on the sheet according to production demands. Every designer develops his own way of planning these drawings.

For wing-and-border productions, standard procedure is to begin with the first scene and show the first downstage and most prominent piece of scenery, then work upstage and proceed with the smaller units. This method is repeated for each setting. On traditional box sets, the pattern is to start with the stage-right return and draw each piece of scenery in the order in which it plays, continuing on to the stage left return. Each drawing should be clearly labeled.

Pieces of scenery on the front elevations can be indicated with space allotted between each piece or by only a line separating them; this depends on the type of set. Sometimes flats are shown in groups, like the various flats that make up the stage-left wall, the stage-right wall, and the center wall. Besides showing the front elevations themselves, other views in $\frac{1}{2}$-inch scale (like the plan, top view, end view, and section view) often accompany the various pieces on the front elevations. The number of views needed is determined by

DESIGNING MULTIPLE MOVING SETTINGS FOR A MUSICAL (following pages).

Sketches, models, and drafting by Robert Randolph
APPLAUSE
Book by Betty Comden and Adolph Green
Based on the film ALL ABOUT EVE and
  original short story by Mary Orr
Music by Charles Strouse
Lyrics by Lee Adams
Directed and choreographed by Ron Field
Palace Theatre, New York (1970)
(Photographs — Robert Randolph)

Robert Randolph's thumbnail sketches, detailed models, elevations and plans illustrate the technical problems involved in a production where the scenery must change rapidly and smoothly. Primarily, the scenery was changed by wagon units moved by winches (guides in the portable deck), by ¾-inch plates on metal domes, and by flying units in and out. On the following pages are shown thumbnail sketches, models, and drafting for four scenes from APPLAUSE.

THUMBNAIL SKETCHES (top four):
Dressing room, Joe Allen's,
Margo's bedroom, Connecticut house

MODELS (three):
Connecticut house (above left)
Joe Allen's (above right)
Backstage (left)

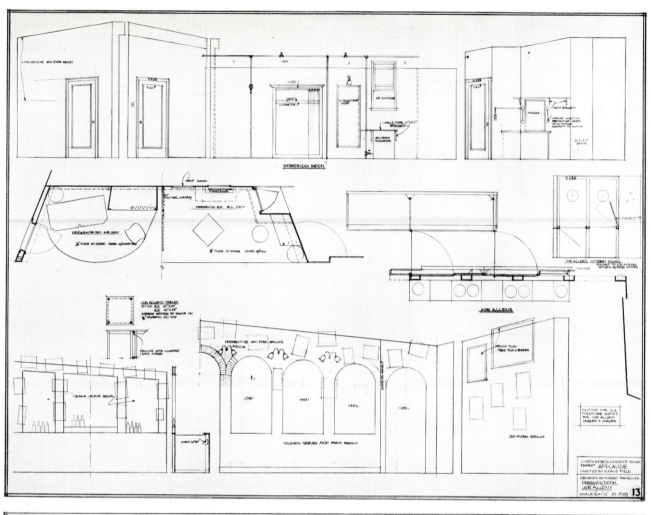

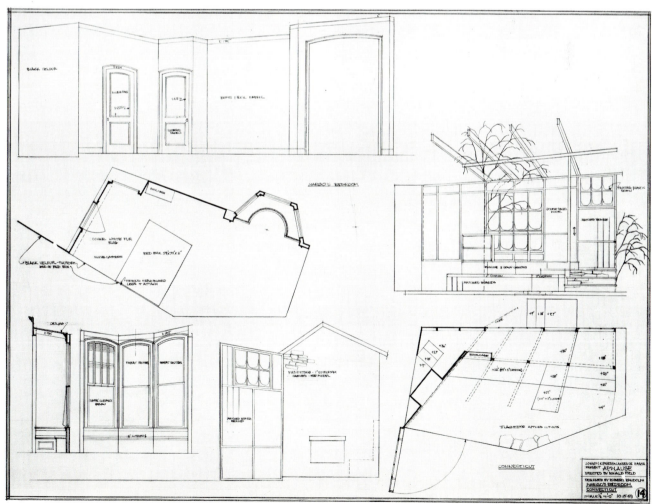

The plans for APPLAUSE at the Palace Theatre shown greatly reduced. Note the outlines where sets go offstage for storage.

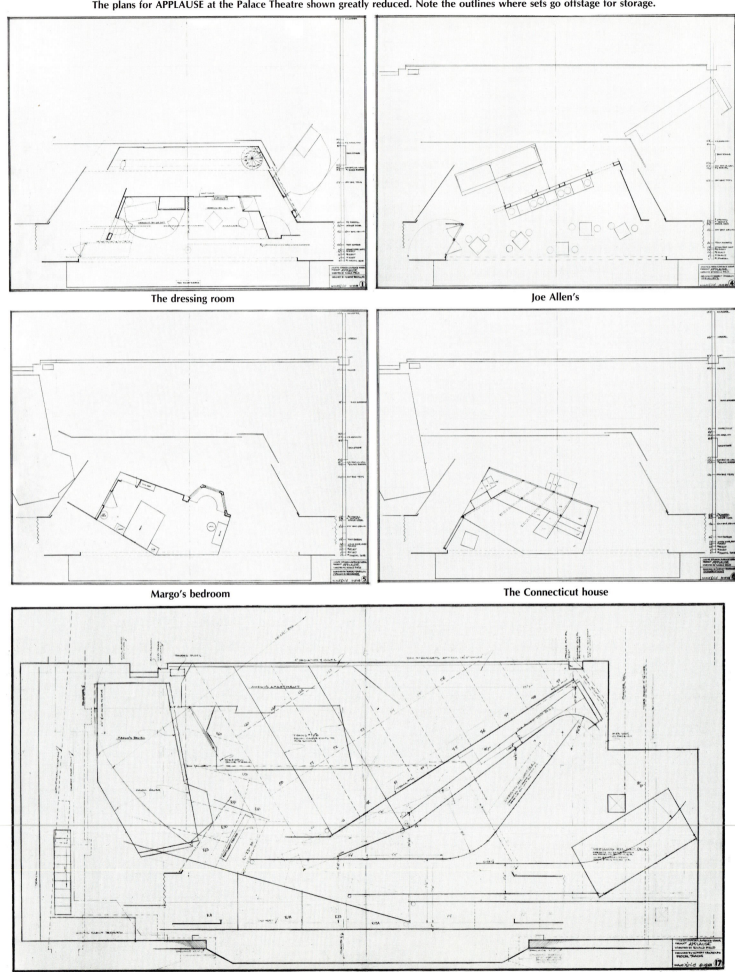

The dressing room

Joe Allen's

Margo's bedroom

The Connecticut house

Drawing showing portable deck and floor guides for APPLAUSE

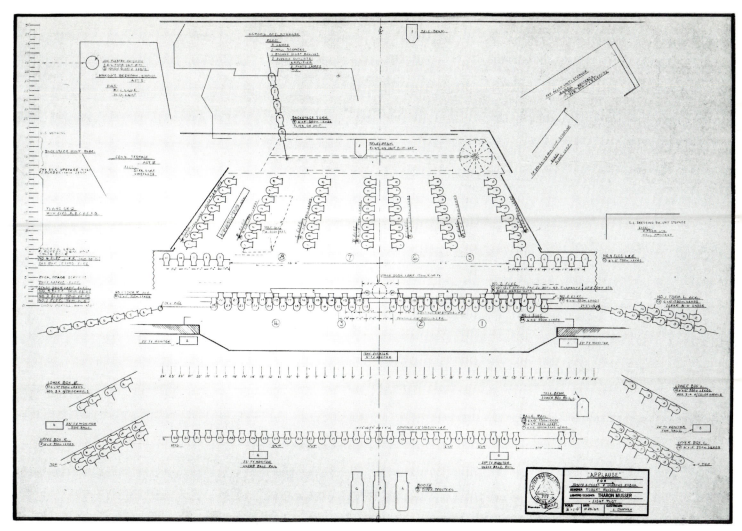

Tharon Musser's ½-in.-scale light plot for APPLAUSE, showing type and location of instruments in the house and on stage. Besides the plot, an instrument schedule (a board hook up) was made for the production's electricians to execute the lighting and for cost estimates of equipment (rental or purchase). This schedule indicates the type, area covered or use, location, color, wattage, outlet, dimmer, ganging, and any other necessary data for each instrument. A cue sheet indicating when each circuit is working, its intensity level, and the amount of time it works was made for running the show.

Instruments shown on the light plot include:

Balcony rail: (28) 6″ x 12″ 750 w. Lekos, (4) 6″ x 9″ 750 w. Lekos, (1) 6″ x 12″ 1000 w. Leko with iris

Upper boxes left and right: (12) 6″ x 12″ 750 w. Lekos

Lower boxes left and right: (4) 6″ x 12″ 750 w. Lekos, Nos. 3 and 4 with color wheels

No. 1 torm right (20′ high): (8) 6″ x 12″ 750 w. Lekos

No. 1 torm left (20′ high): (12) 6″ x 12″ 750 w. Lekos (clear 8′ under)

Show portal trim: 18′

No. 1 electric pipe (trim—21′—0″): (24) 6″ x 12″ 750 w. Lekos

No. 2 electric pipe (trim—22′,—0″): (22) 6″ x 12″ 750 w. Lekos

No. 3 electric pipe (trim—23′—0″): (2) 10′—15 lt. strips—PAR 56—300 w. SP filaments, up and down stage

No. 4 electric pipes left and right (trim—30′0″): (11) 6″ x 12″ 750 w. Lekos

Flying grid with electric pipes A, B, C, D, E, F, G:

A electric pipe: (8) 6″ x 12″ 750 w. Lekos, units Nos. 1, 2, 4—iris

B through G electric pipes: (8) 6″ x 12″ 750 w. Lekos

Backstage torm (flies on unit): (5) 6″ x 9″ 500 w. Lekos

Footlight trough (SR): (1) 5′ backing strip—60 w.

Stage door lamp (DS Center): 150 w. R—40 FL

On theatre gridiron: C.B.S. type unit with (5) 1000 w. quartz lamps

Margo's bedroom—storage (SR)—Act I—electrics: bed lamp, desk lamp

Connecticut house—storage (SR)—Act II—electrics: sofa lamp, fireplace

Margo's apartment—storage (US Right)—electrics: 3 lamps, 2 wall sconces, 1 stained-glass shelf, 2 duplex outlets (amplifier, TV flood lights)

Joe Allen's unit—storage (UP Left)—electrics: 3 wall brackets, 1 bar strip—3 circuits

SR Dressing room unit—storage (DS Left)—electric: floor lamp

SL Dressing room unit—storage (DS Left)—electrics: mirror lights, wall bracket

Lights on Gay Bar ceiling (flies)

23″ TV monitors: Nos. 1 and 2 (SL and SR, front of proscenium) Nos. 3 and 4 (for balcony) Nos. 5 and 6 (under balcony rail)

5″ TV monitor: Tony elevator

"In terms of the number of units and switchboards used, APPLAUSE was the smallest major musical I have lighted. The only side lighting was down left and right by the first tormentors. Dancers love side lighting and this could have been tricky with a choreographer-director. But we fell in love with Randy's [Robert Randolph] backstage set and made the lighting work with it. It was one of the best backstage sets I have seen. Because of the ceiling piece, all emphasis was down light instead of side light. The lighting design was controlled essentially by the backstage design."

—Tharon Musser

what it takes to completely show the shapes of the scenery. On a single front elevation drawing, applied dimensional detail and painted detail are differentiated by notes with arrows. A designer also draws the position of such objects as sconces, paintings, and valances so the carpenter will know where and how to construct wood for their attachment on the flats.

Details

While detailed drawings can be shown for certain objects in $\frac{1}{2}$-inch scale, it is often necessary to do them in a larger scale to define clearly what you have in mind. Details can involve any subject, but these are the most common in the execution of scenery:

1. Built pieces that are to be applied directly on scenery (cornices, baseboards, chair rails, panel moldings, cartouches).
2. Fully built pieces that attach to scenic units (newel posts, balusters, handrail volutes, finials, brackets).
3. Built pieces that are to be flat cut-out profiles (latticework, grillwork, foliage, trees).
4. Independent pieces like furniture and props (chandeliers, throne chairs, console tables, picture frames, statuary).
5. Soft pieces of scenery that are to be cut out of the material without building (banners, flags, draperies, tapestries).

Sometimes only a front view and plan are needed; for soft scenery (no. 5), where there is no building, only the front elevation is necessary. But details which are really complicated may call for a front view and plan, plus an end (or side) view, top view, and section views at several points. What drawings are required depends on the object. If you are drawing a piece of molding on a front elevation in $\frac{1}{2}$-inch scale, and it is a standard item at a company like the Maxwell Lumber Co. in New York City (which has a catalog of moldings), it would only be necessary to put a note with an arrow on the drawings giving the call number of the molding that you want. For instance, at Maxwell's this could apply: a base molding—M214 ($1\frac{1}{8}$ x $2\frac{1}{4}$); a nose-and-cove molding —M226 ($1\frac{3}{8}$ x $2\frac{1}{4}$); a crown molding—M254 ($\frac{3}{4}$ x $3\frac{5}{8}$); or a panel molding—M199 ($\frac{7}{16}$ x $1\frac{3}{8}$). If the molding is a combination of several

pieces, you perhaps would draw a section view in full scale to show an example of what is desired.

Details can be shown on separate sheets of drafting or on sheets of the $\frac{1}{2}$-inch front elevation. They should always be dimensioned sufficiently and prominently marked in the applicable scale. Common scales for details are 1 inch = 1 foot, $1\frac{1}{2}$ inches = 1 foot, 2 inches = 1 foot, 3 inches = 1 foot, and full scale.

Hanging Section View

The hanging section view, also usually in $\frac{1}{2}$-inch scale, is especially vital if you are doing a production with several sets and have a lot of hanging scenery in the flies. It is a vertical section view of the scenery as it plays onstage, with an imaginary cutting line slicing through the setting at the center line. The drawing of the hanging section can be shown as it appears from the center looking toward stage right, or from the center looking toward stage left, whichever view shows the scenery most advantageously. Generally, the furniture is not shown on the hanging section view, because it would only make it more detailed and confusing. However, if certain pieces of furniture have a special function, they can be included. Because the hanging section view denotes how the various units of scenery relate to each other vertically, this is an essential drawing for checking the sight lines from out in the audience. This lets you see that each piece of hanging scenery (portals, borders, cut drops, etc.) masks the next piece hanging behind it, all the way to the farthest unit upstage. The extreme sight lines are solved simply on this section view by drawing very light lines from a point in the center of the front row of the orchestra to the bottom edge of each unit of hanging scenery. This point represents the average eye level of a seated person and is about 3 feet 6 inches to 3 feet 8 inches from the floor of the orchestra.

A section view also is a must for the lighting designer to plan the position of his instruments between the different pieces of scenery. He can see the exact height they should hang to be out of sight and plan how the light instruments can be directed to focus on the playing areas and scenery. Once a show goes into production, the craftsmen frequently work back and forth from the ground plan to the hanging section view to see how the scenery goes together on stage. Since the hanging section drawing is primarily for this purpose instead of building, it is usually kept free of a lot of dimensions.

Working Drawings from the Rear

A set of rear-view drawings showing the carpenters in the scenic shop how to build settings from behind is not done by the scenic designer. Experienced scenic shops are adept at constructing scenery and do not expect the designer to provide such drawings. Instead, the scenic shop (head carpenter or draftsman) does rear-view working drawings for the carpenters by using the designer's ½-inch front elevations, etc., and by conferring with the designer for anything out of the ordinary. Sizes and positions of such items as rails, toggles, braces, supports, hardware, breaks in the scenery, and other details pertaining to construction are designated by the shop draftsman on the drawings. Only when there is an unusually complex problem does the designer normally do working drawings from behind.

Rear-view drawings of the designer's scenery in repertory, regional, or stock companies are usually done by the technical director or production carpenter. This is not to say, however, that a young designer should not know how to do rear-view drawings, because such ability is a must in order to be knowledgeable and practical in designing, and undoubtedly is a part of the classwork in design-drafting classes in a drama school or a university theatre.

Getting Everything on the Drafting

A good way to make sure that all the essentials and details have been included on the drafting is to imagine that the show is going to be executed without your being around and that consequently everything pertaining to the production must be included on the drawings.

For both the experienced and the inexperienced draftsman, a good and practical book for reference is French and Vierck, *Fundamentals of Engineering Drawing and Graphic Technology*, 3d ed. (New York: McGraw-Hill, 1972).

SELECTING A SCENIC STUDIO FOR BUILDING AND PAINTING A SHOW

Once a scenic designer has finished the designs and drawings for a commercial production and they have been approved by the direc-

**CREATING DIFFERENT SCENES
BY LIGHTING A UNIT SETTING (following pages).**

Setting by Eugene Lee
Lighting by Roger Morgan
BROTHER TO DRAGONS by Robert Penn Warren
Directed by Adrian Hall
Costumes by Franne Lee
Trinity Square Repertory Company
Wilbur Theatre, Boston (1974)
(Photographs — William L. Smith)

Shown are Roger Morgan's lighting plot and lighting section, and photographs of scenes on stage. Morgan used a minimum number of light sources. Instruments included: 5000-watt Fresnels, 2000-watt scoops, 750-watt Lekos, 1000-watt incandescent bulbs (three work lights in cages), and 2-by-4 fluorescent lamps (2 tubes, 4 ft. long).
Black velour surrounded Eugene Lee's unit set on three sides and no attempt was made to mask lighting instruments overhead. Many variations were achieved with minimal props (carried on by the actors) and changes of lighting. Additional instruments in the first photograph are from other productions in the repertory.

PHOTOGRAPHS
1. Work lights at a rehearsal. The large units in the foreground are Colortran 2000-watt scoops. Three large 5000-watt Fresnels can be seen in the rear. Note the three hanging practical lamps in cages used for the hurricane effect. The fluorescent fixture hangs just above canopy at center.
2. Lighting for the final scene. Two 5000-watt Fresnels backlighting through the canopy slats, create the patterns on the floor.
3. There are three lights on in this cue. The group of actors (apple bobbers) are seen in the light of a 5000-watt Fresnel. The two 6-in. Lekos are used to light the downstage area. Each Leko is positioned on a box boom (in the house). The Leko mounted on the house left boom is focused on the actress (stage left), and the other Leko on the house right box boom is focused on stage right.
4. For the keel boat scene at night, a single 5000-watt Fresnel at center from behind (dark blue) casts shadows on the slats. A single Leko from front lights the actors (family). The kerosene lamp on the table is real and the actor in back carries a torch.
5. The scene is lighted by one 2000-watt Berkey Colortran scoop.

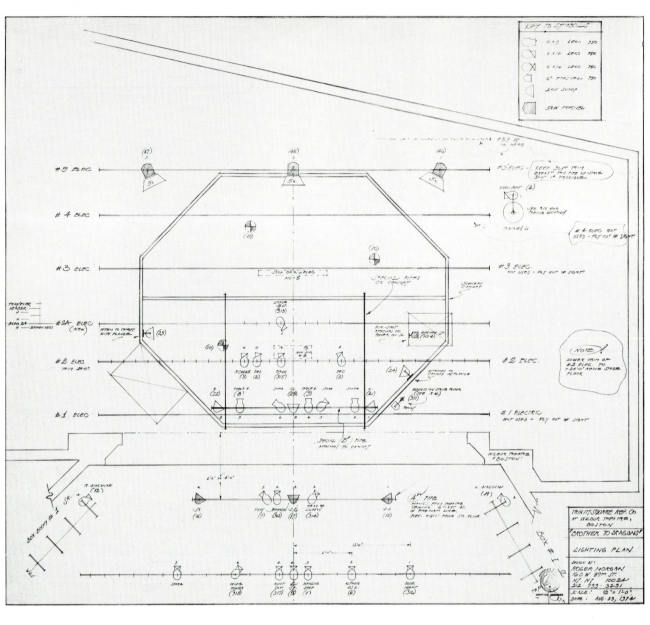

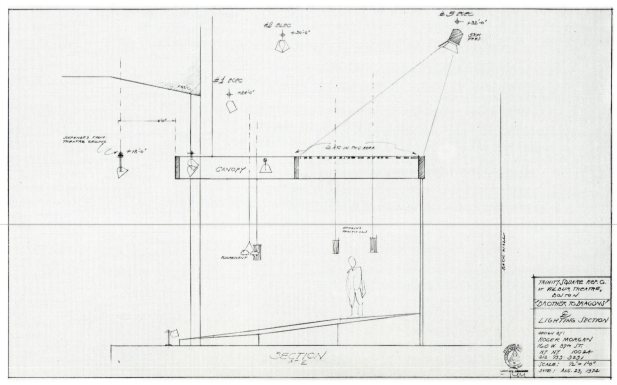

tor and producer, a theatrical scenic studio must be selected to build and paint the scenery. This is achieved initially by arranging a "bid session" which is called by the producer who has placed the designer under contract. The bidding can be held at his office or at the designer's studio; the main purpose is to find out how much it will cost to execute the scenery and which union shop will do it. Although several studios may be invited to attend, it is general practice to invite at least three shops to a bid session. In this way, the producer can get a good idea of what the average cost will be for the show. A studio may be represented by the owners, head scenic artist, and head building carpenter, but practice varies with each shop.

At the bid session, the designer gives a full presentation of the production, going over the designs and sketches, explaining them at length, along with the drafting and detailed drawings. A full set of drawings for the show is expected from the designer. While the colored sketches and model (often painted) are also presented at the same time to the studio heads who are bidding on the show, it is imperative that the drafting accompany them so the exact details can be clarified and discussed explicitly. A studio cannot give a complete estimate without knowing exact specifications of each particular piece. Sometimes a designer will stamp "For Estimate Only" on the drawings for a bid session. This can mean the director may not be in total agreement and there may be changes, or the designer may not have fully decided on certain parts of the scenery and may want to get an idea of how much they will cost.

It is often the practice for a studio head to give an individual breakdown of just how much each piece of scenery is going to cost the producer, not only for a portal, a platform unit, but also for drops, scrims, or built props. If something has to be cut from the production, the designer and producer can easily tell just how much money they will be saving. Frequently a designer has to cut portions of scenery to stay within the budget, and some designers always plan on this happening. By the same method, the designer can also get an idea of the cost when he wants to add a similar unit of scenery, since he already knows the figures. And when the designer is still working on

finishing a portion of the show, it can be figured separately as it comes in.

During the bid session, particular reference is made by the designer as to how the settings are to be constructed and painted, what materials are needed for special effects, how the units are to move and store, and any other pressing problems which might have to be solved. The scenery-studio contractor goes over all aspects of the presentation, asking pertinent questions. He is ordinarily supplied with a full set of the designer's drawings to take with him so he can go over the details to complete his estimate, in which materials, labor, overhead, and profit are considerations when figuring the show. After a day or two, the contractors call in their bids to the producer.

While it is considered standard for the studio offering the lowest bid to get the construction contract, this does not always happen, for several reasons. The designer, especially if he is well established, may prefer to take the show to a specific studio that he knows well and where he particularly likes to work. On the other hand, the producer may favor a studio he himself has done business with many times before, and the designer may have no choice but to agree. Too, the desired studio may already be heavily committed with other productions and unable to meet the deadline for delivery date. There have been situations where a show is split between two or divided among three studios as a result of lack of time. Whenever the studio has been selected, a contract is signed between the producer and the head of the studio. This contract, which has been in use for many years, specifies that the studio be paid one-third of the total amount on signing, one-third when the work is half-way completed, and the remaining one-third when the show is delivered.

In the next chapter we shall examine what takes place in the theatrical scenic studio after the contract is signed and the designer's relationship with the studio.

Model by Oliver Smith
INDIANS by Arthur Kopit
Directed by Gene Frankel
Brooks Atkinson Theatre
New York (1969)
(Photograph—Martha Swope)

A Conversation with OLIVER SMITH

Oliver Smith resides in a townhouse in Brooklyn Heights facing the Manhattan skyline. This conversation with him took place between classes at New York University School of the Arts, where he is an instructor in rendering and oversees senior design tutorials. Smith was born in Waupun, Wisconsin, in 1918, and his first professional production was for the ballet *Rodeo* at the Metropolitan Opera in 1942. One of the theatre's most prolific designers for musical comedy, drama, opera, and the ballet, he has designed the settings for some three hundred stage productions. He has also been co-producer of a good number of these, as well as a co-director for the American Ballet Theatre. He has designed several films and has received numerous awards: The New York Drama Critics' Awards (5), Tony Awards (5), the Donaldson Awards (4), and the Sam S. Shubert Award for Achievement in the Theatre. Among the Broadway productions Oliver Smith has designed settings for are:

All Over Town (1974)
The Women (1973)
Last of the Red Hot Lovers (1969)
Indians (1969)
Plaza Suite (1968)
Cactus Flower (1965)
The Odd Couple (1965)
Hello, Dolly! (1964)
Dylan (1964)

Barefoot in the Park (1963)
The Night of the Iguana (1961)
Camelot (1960)
The Unsinkable Molly Brown (1960)
Becket (1960)
The Sound of Music (1959)
Flower Drum Song (1958)
Time Remembered (1957)
West Side Story (1957)

A Clearing in the Woods (1957)
Auntie Mame (1956)
My Fair Lady (1956)
In the Summer House (1953)
Paint Your Wagon (1951)
Gentlemen Prefer Blondes (1949)
Brigadoon (1947)
Billion Dollar Baby (1945)
On the Town (1944)

How did you become interested in scenic design originally—how did you start out?

I'm what I call a self-taught scenic designer—I never studied it at a university. I studied architecture at Pennsylvania State College and had done scene design in college as an extra-curricular activity. And in the middle of my architectural courses, I decided to switch to a more liberal arts course, and actually studied to go to the Yale School of Drama to write plays. I had no intention of designing scenery whatsoever. I finished my four years and had my B.A.; however, my family decided they wouldn't finance me at Yale unless I worked in New York for a year, then I could go to Yale after I had supported myself for a year. They had very stern ideas about that. So I came to New York and became interested in theatre, in design, and became successful enough that I never thought of going to Yale to write plays or to study design. My beginning in New York was helped a great deal by a cousin of mine named Paul Bowles, a writer. He introduced me to William Saroyan, who gave me my first job. It was a play I designed, and I wasn't even in the union.

But my first production that I took credit for was a ballet, presented by the Ballet Russe, called *Saratoga*. It was done at the Metropolitan Opera House, which was a marvelous break to have as a first exposure. I would say the first success I had was *Rodeo* for Agnes de Mille and that was followed by *Fancy Free* by Jerome Robbins and Leonard Bernstein. My beginnings in scene design are really through the ballet, and I've been involved in the ballet ever since.

How do you begin designing a play or a musical?

What I do is read the material, listen to the score if it is a musical, and if it's present, read the script. And then I do a lot of thinking. I don't draw a line, I just brood—concentrate. I might make tiny sketches on envelopes or pieces of paper, just as idea sketches, but not anything I plan to use particularly. If it is a project that requires research, I do a thorough research and collect a large body of it, which I study carefully. Then when I start to work, I put the research all away, forget it. I mean, it has to be absorbed subconsciously unless I'm using some very specific detail that's required or suggested by the author.

Then, I approach plays or musicals from two different ways. One way can evolve entirely from floor plan. I think that's because I have an architectural background and I think in terms of floor plan. And I think a beautiful floor plan makes for a beautiful design, as it does in any building. The interrelation of spaces which is determined by a floor plan gives the set a special quality. And it actually does a lot of work for the director in terms of staging—how to get people on and get them off. That's really what it's all about. Then, while I'm doing a floor plan, in my mind I'm visualizing how it looks. So by the time I've finished floor plans, an elevation is a relatively easy thing for me to do, because it's all designed. It's a simultaneous action. But since I don't have four hands, I can't draw the elevations the same time I'm doing the floor plans. But I work very rapidly on the elevations.

What do you put the elevations on?

Paper, Bristol board—it can be a variety of materials. I usually draw them in quarter-inch scale. They're small because that's the scale in which I can work very rapidly. Once that scheme or those ideas are approved, I enlarge them into half-inch elevations. Now that is one way of approaching it. An-

Setting by Oliver Smith
HELLO, DOLLY!
Book by Michael Stewart. Music and lyrics by Jerry Herman
Based on THE MATCHMAKER by Thornton Wilder
Costumes by Freddy Wittop

Lighting by Jean Rosenthal
Directed and Choreographed by Gower Champion
St. James Theatre, New York (1964)
Pearl Bailey Company (1967)
(Photograph—Friedman-Abeles)

Setting by Oliver Smith
CAMELOT
Book and lyrics by Alan Jay Lerner
Music by Frederick Loewe
Staged by Moss Hart

Choreography and musical numbers by Hanya Holm
Costumes by Adrian, Tony Duquette
Lighting by Feder
Majestic Theatre, New York (1960)
(Photograph—Friedman Abeles)

other way is to get some sort of elevation which is appealing in composition, mood, and atmosphere. And at the same time one is doing that elevation, you are automatically, in your head, doing a floor plan. It's just a reverse action. I have done many productions that way too. In a multiscene musical where you have a great many scenes, often it's one set which starts a train of thinking going, and then everything else interrelates to it. In *My Fair Lady*, for example, the study scene is the one that keyed the whole show. That was the first scene I did, and from working on that I evolved the rest of the show. In *West Side Story*, I'd say the rumble scene was the determining scene. And *West Side Story* is a show that I designed twice. I designed a whole scheme and was ready to put it in the shops, but at the last minute, I had a brainstorm, threw it all out, and redid it all in about eight days. I had spent maybe three months' work on it, so it wasn't as if the vocabulary was new.

What was the reason for changing the design?

I just had a brainstorm! I thought I could do something I liked better. I often do that. I'm perfectly capable of throwing something out at the last minute and starting over. I don't believe designers should save every scrap of paper that they work on. I like a great amount of productivity in designing and not getting wedded to one idea.

When you make thumbnail sketches, do you make several or do you hit it the first time?

It's a variable thing. I think it depends also on how much one is involved in the material. Once you have done over three hundred shows, there are certain shows you love and certain shows you are doing to be a professional. You can't love three hundred shows.

Do you also build models?

Very rarely. Certain scenes, certain productions have evolved in the designs from models. *Night of the Iguana, Dylan,* and *Indians* are three productions

that evolved from model form rather than painted elevations. They were largely attempts to be sculptural in feeling, rather than as enlarged paintings. I feel that scenic design breaks up into many different styles or forms. I feel there is the form of enlarged easel painting, which is often connected with the ballet. Or the form of romantic realism, which is again related to painting. I think the current vogue is sculptural. Most of these designs are realized through models rather than the painted elevations. And I believe there will be a return to the painted style. Those things are simply cycles that we go through. I don't think that any one form is the ultimate form of designing a set. It can be realized in many different styles. I'm not one who has a set esthetic. I like to work in many different styles.

I do believe that there are certain cardinal rules or guidelines which apply to all expert scenic design. In other words, I think that the purpose of the designer is to service the director and

Setting by Oliver Smith
THE NIGHT OF THE IGUANA
by Tennessee Williams
Directed by Frank Corsaro
Costumes by Noel Taylor

Lighting by Jean Rosenthal
Royale Theatre, New York (1961)
Pictured: Alan Webb, Bette Davis, Patrick
    O'Neal, Margaret Leighton
(Photograph — Friedman-Abeles)

the playwright and the composer, and not to show off as an easel painter. Therefore, I think the best sets are often the simplest, least fussy, and least distracting. The purpose is to see the performance and not to be the star of the show, usually. Sometimes there are exceptions to that.

How did you go about designing Leonard Bernstein's Mass *for the Kennedy Center in Washington?*

That is an example of a set which grew from elevation, not floor plan. When I talked to Gordon Davidson, the director, we discussed the general needs and approach to the *Mass*. It was a little difficult since the *Mass* was being written the same time it was being designed. But we anticipated what Lenny [Bernstein] was going to do. I made about a hundred twenty small thumbnail sketches and Mr. Davidson picked twenty to twenty-five, then we narrowed it down to about eight, then three, two, and finally one. You could do the *Mass* in any number of ways. It's a very rich, complicated piece. I feel the material also tremendously affects the design.

When I'm working as a designer, I try to empty my mind of all ideas before I associate myself with the material so that I don't do any preconceived ideas. And out of that material, something affects my subconscious, and that triggers something, which later, somehow or other, seeps through the conscious mind and something begins to come out. I believe the subconscious is

extremely important in scenic design. Many times, for example, when one is confronted with an extraordinary, complicated problem, I often think about it before I go to sleep. Instead of counting sheep, I design scenery. Then at a certain point, I go to sleep, and in the morning I wake up and rise quite early and it's all solved. One of the interesting things about work is that when I was young and a beginner in this profession, I worked mostly at night, because it was quiet and I enjoyed the solitude. And I used to start around eight-thirty or nine in the evening and work until six in the morning. Now my entire work schedule has changed. I get up at six and work till twelve or one and I finish for the day. I think maybe it has to do with growing older — younger people like to stay up all night and older people like to go to bed.

Can you describe the set you did select for the Mass *and why?*

The design that was finally selected was the simplest, and perhaps the least interpretive. It was simply an abstract solution for handling two hundred twenty musicians on stage — to get them off and on in an attractive and functional manner. It did not try to make a religious comment. At one time I had the feeling that there could be a very interesting solution which combined the ritual of both the Catholic church and the Hebrew religion. But it got a little too complex, and I felt it was better to let Lenny's score say what was to be

said, which was complex enough, rather than to pile on more and more complexity. And I think that was under the direction of Gordon Davidson again. It was the way he saw the piece.

Another interesting problem about the *Mass*: it was a dedicatory piece for the Kennedy Center, so therefore I wanted to do a setting which seemed to grow out of the auditorium itself, and not be just a stage sitting there. I didn't want to do a setting which would be like a graduation exercise with a lot of potted palms. I wanted something which had some color and form and emotion, and at the same time was religiously abstract. The floor plan did take the shape of the Roman cross, but a great point was not made of this.

Did the coloring have anything to do with the concept?

No. The auditorium was red, so I decided to use red. Plus the fact it's also a color I am very partial to. I enjoy the use of color in scenic design. To me, it has great visual and psychological value. Whereas at the moment, we are in a period of theatre where we don't use color much. It's not fashionable. The fashionable current design is a negation of color in which lighting and form supply the same emotional need. And I think there will be a great return to the use of color. It's a phase or cycle.

All the current sculptural scenery was done in the twenties and thirties in Russia, anyway. There's nothing new about any of it. I feel it's done very expertly and I enjoy it. I like it, but I don't feel it's the ultimate and that it's eternal. One of the things about scenery is that you have to remember when the show closes, it all gets burned on the ash heap, and it's not something which is preserved in a museum for immortality. It's a thing that exists in a moment. I think scenery, therefore, often reflects the exact historical period in which it is created, as well as what it's interpreting. In other words, it exists in a double time sense. For example, we are now in a period of great social unrest and social change and social revolution. Our serious productions reflect that. I think it's a natural reflection of the serious artist to his time, just as that exists in painting and that exists in architecture. You have today what is called the "brutal style of architecture." It is very sculptural, very strong, full

156

of dynamics. And it's not suave, it's not noncommittal. It makes a tremendous statement. The works of Breuer and Rudolph are examples. I think that you find much contemporary scenery in the same way.

In designing musical comedy, do you have some favorite productions?

Oh, yes, we all have our favorites. They don't necessarily coincide with the most popular. I would say my favorite production was *West Side Story*. Second would be *My Fair Lady*, and the third *Hello, Dolly!* . . . On the other hand, I might have done certain failures which I liked enormously too, and which I think were just as well designed, and sometimes better than the ones you get Tonys for. Tonys are usually selected for popularity, not for artistic creativeness.

When you started out to design Dolly, did you have a particular feeling in mind?

No. I had to do something where there was too much scenery to get onto a stage which was too small. It was first a technical solution of the use of space. I would say the scenic elevations were a rather joyous comment on a period and style which I have always enjoyed and liked. Therefore, I used the vocabulary I've been acquiring for probably thirty years. I didn't have to do any research. I could just sit down and draw it very quickly.

You seem to have a light and charming approach to all your musicals.

Firstly, I think musical comedy, generally, is created as entertainment. They're not supposed to be lectures or moral—you're not in church. And I feel the reason people go to musicals is that they want to have a delightful time. I don't take a terribly pseudo-profound view of what they're looking at. I think that the thing to do is to entertain them visually, just like they're being entertained aurally. My idea of being entertained visually is bright, lively, attractive colors, attractive forms, and not trying to impose a quasiserious philosophic approach. Also in musicals, since the emphasis is very often on speed rather than profundity, it is extremely important that scenes change rapidly and attractively. It's how they get on and off stage that makes for the overall design. The design is not something to be looked at just as a static

Stage designs by Oliver Smith
LA TRAVIATA by Giuseppe Verdi
Libretto by Francesco Maria Piave
Act II and Act III (below)

Directed by Tyrone Guthrie
The Metropolitan Opera, New York (1957)
(Photographs—Louis Mélançon, courtesy of Opera News)

thing in itself like you would look at a painting in a gallery. It's really part of the choreography.

What about plays?

Now I think plays are quite different. They are very serious in nature, and the more interesting plays often are serious and disturbing. Musicals are rarely disturbing. Perhaps *West Side Story* has a certain social comment to make. But

West Side Story is also rather operatic in its form, rather than operetta. And the musical stage takes its form from operetta, vaudeville, and opera. Sometimes a certain musical will have an emphasis in one direction more than in another. Now *West Side Story* I would consider opera. *My Fair Lady, The Sound of Music,* and *Camelot* would be operetta. Those were all musicals which I

enjoyed doing. I have no disdain about operetta. I like operetta just as I like Offenbach and Strauss. And I feel there is a certain snobbism about opera which will vanish.

You have also designed operas for the Metropolitan Opera.

Designing for opera is a form I also like very much. I don't want to limit it to just the Metropolitan Opera productions, because that is a special way of designing. You design something for the Met in one way or with one set of problems. Then working with Sarah Caldwell at the Boston Opera is another set of problems, but equally fascinating and often more creative. The smaller repertory companies, not the New York City Opera, often have more to say than the Metropolitan, which is the final Valhalla for all designers! But I don't think it necessarily brings out their best work. Often their best work is done for smaller regional companies, where the director and the amount of rehearsal time and the whole acting dynamics of the opera are much more emphasized than just a lot of musical pincushions who are out there singing.

To get to the Met—it was an exciting event because I was working with a very gifted director named Tyrone Guthrie. And he taught many people how to direct opera. Peter Brook was one of the people he helped teach. Guthrie was one of the foremost directors in the world of opera—an extraordinary human being. So anything one did with him was always an exciting adventure, an exciting exploration—you never knew where you were going to end. *Traviata* was something we did rather quickly and enjoyed. I don't think of it as a profound piece of design. I think it was effective, attractive, better than average, but not the world's greatest, necessarily.

Did you do this opera in a certain style?

Yes, it was a romantic evocation of the period. The most interesting thing was in the third act—an enormous staircase which Dr. Guthrie wanted and [Rudolf] Bing didn't want. And we built this staircase in many sections. One of the problems was that the staircase was twenty feet high, and the shop in which it was built only had an eight-foot ceiling. So it had to be built in a great many sections and put together.

And when Mr. Bing first saw the stair on stage, I think he was rather appalled. It was also complicated by the fact that [Renata] Tebaldi, who was singing the lead, refused to go up more than two steps on this twenty-foot staircase. So it was kind of wasted until [Maria] Callas used it with great aplomb later when she did the role.

The other production I did at the Met was *Martha,* an unfortunate opera. I did it out of sheer desire to work at the Met, and to work with another great opera director, Carl Ebert, who at one time employed Mr. Bing as his assistant. Ebert worked in Europe—Germany—at the time of the Nazi takeover, and established Glyndebourne. And I spent fascinating moments with Ebert in Berlin working on *Martha,* which he detested as much as I did. It was an example of two artists working together, hoping to do something better some day together, such as *Don Giovanni* or a more serious piece which Bing had promised us and never fulfilled.

You are a co-director of the American Ballet Theatre. How did this come about?

Lucia Chase is the founder of it. I became co-director with Miss Chase in 1945 when she decided that she would assume a directorship if she didn't have to do it alone. The idea was that we would do it for several years, and then find another person to do it and we would retire. And what happened was, I guess we enjoyed what we were doing and enjoyed working together. It was a very happy collaboration, and we're still directing thirty years later.

About that time I also had worked with very actively engaged choreographers, some of whom emerged from the *corps de ballet* of Ballet Theatre—Jerome Robbins was one, Michael Kidd was another, Herbert Ross was a dancer. I would also include Agnes de Mille in this group. This was the beginning of American choreography in the United States. And out of that emerged a whole school of what we call American choreography. Before that, it was totally dominated by the Europeans—[George] Balanchine, [Leonid] Massine, [Frederick] Ashton. Also, we were beginning to go into a period of choreographic directors; so many of these choreographers became directors for musicals. I think one of the reasons I

did so many musicals was because these were friends of mine, with whom I had worked in the ballet, who became suddenly very important in musical direction on Broadway. I suggested to Jerry [Robbins], for example, that Lenny Bernstein do the music for *Fancy Free,* and in that sense helped produce that ballet. And then out of that, we did our first Broadway show together—*On the Town,* which was successful in the original form, not the revival.

And you employ designers?

Oh, yes, I've introduced many designers to the ballet. In costume design, I introduced Freddy Wittop, who had never done a ballet. I've used many of our American designers, which for the record is well known, and in the discovery of designers, I suppose some have been European as well. I've used certain painters like Rico Lebrun. [Eugene] Berman, of course, had already been a very famous designer—in theatre designing—before I used him. It was also my idea to commission Chagall to do *The Firebird* originally, which the Ballet Theatre did, and I think it was his first big ballet production. [Robert] O'Hearn and [William] Pitkin are two examples of designers who did their first ballet [for us]. I feel [ballet] is a wonderful starting point for any designer, because it requires imagination, one does not have too much money, and one has to make up in talent what one lacks in the luxury of budget.

As an instructor in stage design, what do you feel are the problems that confront the students today?

I don't think of the students as a collective body, but I think of them as a series of individuals. And I find that each individual has separate questions and separate problems and separate enthusiasms. I don't feel there are many set rules. There have to be certain basic rules which one learns to apply, and when you really get skillful, then you can break all the rules. But you don't break them before you know what you're breaking. All I can do is lay down the basic rules which I have learned over a long period of time and in many productions, and then show how they have been broken very successfully. But they don't have any one problem—some are concerned with space, some are concerned with style, some are concerned

Setting by Oliver Smith
MY FAIR LADY
Book and lyrics by Alan Jay Lerner

Music by Frederick Loewe
Adapted from Bernard Shaw's PYGMALION
Staged by Moss Hart

Lighting by Feder
Mark Hellinger Theatre, New York (1956)
(Photograph — Friedman-Abeles)

with just the mechanics, and others are concerned with conception. It varies with the individual student.

Does the future of the aspiring young designer lie on Broadway or elsewhere?

Today, since it has become increasingly competitive, and it's not just Broadway, we have to think of theatre design as Off Broadway and regional theatre. And the regional theatre has developed enormously in the last five years in America, and it's going to continue to develop so that many of the finest designs in the future will not necessarily be done on Broadway. They'll be done in regional theatres and in these large cultural centers which dot our country like so many thumbtacks, and which are very good. I think the serious young students are more interested in that world than they are in Broadway — they may not make as much money, they may also make much more. But it's where they can express their serious, creative side rather than something which is trying to please a producer who's usually culturally uninformed and, generally, directors who aren't culturally too informed. I find the whole theatre scene has changed enormously, of course, from the time I first started. Thirty years later, it's quite different.

Were the directors more informed when you first started out?

I think there always have been a certain number of very well-informed and talented directors. I would say about ten percent. Ninety percent have cer-

tain facilities, but a rather limited vocabulary. That's how I would boil it down. You can do a scenic design with an idiot, but you can't do really a beautiful scenic design. I feel that my best work has always been where I was collaborating with a serious and gifted director.

Did you enjoy the motion-picture medium as much as the theatre?

No. But I enjoyed working in it for the various personalities that were involved. It was interesting to work with producers such as Sam Goldwyn and Arthur Freed and Dory Schary. I worked with remarkable directors in movies and I was very fortunate. I designed *The Bandwagon, Oklahoma!, Guys and Dolls,* and *Porgy and Bess.* But I found designing for the movies, in the end, too conditioned by the cameraman and by the director, who are the people that have power, visually, in a picture. The designer has very little to say. Also it was the time when pictures were doing the type of scenery which I enjoy designing that no longer exists. And in the current vogue of pictures, it's the selection of site. Many of the pictures are shot on location, and I'm not interested, you know, in arranging a lot of ashtrays for a cameraman.

You prefer the theatre?

Yes. And working in the theatre, you work rapidly. In other words, you work under enormous pressure which is concentrated over a period of about ten weeks. And to work on a big-budget picture requires over a year. I find that

it is very hard to keep peak interest for a year, because when you shoot a picture of that type, what you usually get on film is about a minute and a half a day, maybe two minutes a day. It's like piecing together an enormous mosaic rather than seeing it all in one wallop as you do in the theatre. I think people are attracted to one form or the other. Many directors today much prefer working in films than the stage.

What about designing for television?

I have no interest in designing for television. I think it's ghastly and very little of it is worth looking at. I don't think that a screen as small as it is can register very interesting scenic detail. At least in the movies it's an enlarged scale, but when you look at a small miniature form, I don't feel it can do the scenic designer justice. It isn't that I have any disdain for my colleagues in television design; I don't mean to imply that at all. I just don't think you can get anything in a space that's twelve by fifteen inches to look like anything, particularly when you've got to have a close-up of the star, thousands of dancers, and so forth — it's just a lot of dots moving around. I have never seen any original design on television that hasn't been done better in the theatre first. And the most interesting designs are the commercials where they have animated forms and have nothing to do with the people. But I've never seen an original piece of design for television that is superior to the theatre, or equal to it. The theatre is where the action is.

FOUR

The theatrical scenic studio

The scenic studio is where the designer's scenery is built and painted. Once the designs are completed and a bid session is held to determine which scenic studio will do the scenery, the designer's sketches, models, and drafting are submitted so that the scenery can be executed. Although today the designer creates the stage designs in his own studio, in the early days this work was done in the model room located in the scenic studio proper; the painting of scenery was frequently done in one building, the construction in another. Today, both departments are generally housed under one roof, often on the same floor. Even though new paints and plastic materials and equipment such as the Hudson spray tank are being used in the modern scenic studio, the nature of the business remains the same and almost the same amount of work must be done by hand by the scenic artists as in years past.

Because there were many more Broadway productions during the early part of the century, more scenic artists were employed than today. The peak number of Broadway shows was produced in the 1920s and 1930s. In the ten-year period from 1920 to 1930, the number of productions ranged from 152 to 264 in a season; from 1930 to 1940, 91 to 207; from 1960 to 1970, 48 to 74. In the 1973–74 season, there was a total of 50 productions.

While much of the painting in the scenic studios years back was done vertically on the paint frame, the horizontal method of painting scenery on the floor is used extensively in the commercial studio today. The older generation of designers and scenic artists recalls a great number of scenic studios in the New York area that had paint frames. From some years after the turn of the century and into the fifties, many well-known theatrical scenic studios appeared, among them H. Robert Law, Dodge and Castle, Gates and Morange, Platzer and Emens, the Hippodrome, Unit and Wicks, Ackerman, Holak, Ernest Grau, Cleon Throckmorton, Shubert, New York Studios, Lee Lash, Ward and Harvey, Kaj Velden, Louis Kennel, Triangle, Imperial, Alliance, Rakeman, and McDonald-Stevens. During this time and later, several prominent scenic artists operated their own studios. Joseph Urban (1872–1933), the noted scenic artist and designer, came from Europe to work for the Boston Opera Company in 1911, and later went to work at the Metropolitan Opera. He is given credit for bringing to the

Exterior units by Marsha Louis Eck for LUCIA DI LAMMERMOOR (1969) at the New York City Opera assembled as they will play so painting surfaces can be matched and blended. Artificial vines are fastened on specified areas.

(Right) Another view of the round-platform unit for LUCIA, showing front of crumbling ruins. (Photographs — Arnold Abramson)

(Below right) John Pitts working on Ming Cho Lee's sharkstooth-scrim backdrop for the New York City Opera's IDOMENEO (1975). (Photograph — Lynn Pecktal)

To construct Lloyd Evans' prop horse for DON GIOVANNI (1972) at the New York City Opera so it could be mounted by a singer, the armature was of metal pipe with ¾-in. plywood attached, on which blocks of Styrofoam were bonded. The carved Styrofoam was covered with right-side-up velour pieces saturated in scenic dope. Forming cloth shaped the smaller areas. Sculpture was finished with casein paints. For storage, the head was removable. (Photograph — Stephen Shapiro)

United States the method of painting on the floor rather than on a paint frame. Then there was Robert Bergman, long remembered for his famous "Bergman Bath," who painted on Lee Simonson's first setting as well as many of his later ones, and also painted shows for Jo Mielziner and Donald Oenslager. Some of the other very fine scenic artists were Bradford Ashworth, who worked for Bergman and later had his own studio, Walter Harvey of Ward and Harvey, Horace Armistead and Leon Warren of Center Studios, Gus Wimazal of Triangle, and Eugene Dunkel of Dunkel Studio.

In sharp contrast to earlier years, there are fewer theatrical scenic studios in existence today in New York, and they do all of the building and painting for Broadway shows, operas, and ballets, including the national touring companies and the bus-and-truck productions. The two major shops are Feller Scenery Studios, run by Peter Feller, and Nolan Scenery Studios, operated by Arnold Abramson and Charles Bender, who succeeded Willie Nolan. In charge of the other studios are Francis Messmore (Messmore and Damon), William Hart (Hart Scenic Studios), Jim Hamilton (Design Associates), Leo Meyer (Atlas Scenic Studios), Mario Beritto (Lincoln Scenic), Herb Legar (Variety Scenic), and Harry Widlicka (Theatrical Equipment Corp.).

See appendix for addresses of theatrical scenic studios in the New York City area. While it is impossible to list other scenic studios throughout the United States and Canada, these can be found in Simon's Directory, also listed in the appendix.

Although the following requirements can apply to studio space generally, they are vital when looking for facilities to paint scenery horizontally:

1. A large area of unobstructed floor space, preferably a softwood floor so drops can be stapled or tacked down easily. It should be level, without depressions that would cause the paint and water to collect.
2. Good lighting. Even though there may be an abundance of natural light, good consistent artificial illumination is absolutely essential.
3. Overall interior height must be sufficient for the erection of full stage settings when they are being built.
4. Proper ventilation and heat, adequate electrical power, sufficient water, and good access for loading and unloading.

5. A catwalk or overhead gallery for viewing the scenery from a distance is helpful, but a tall stepladder can be used. (Sometimes the designer or artist looks at the work through a reducing glass, a double concave lens that diminishes the appearance of size.)

Finding a building complex that meets these requirements and does not have a staggering rental and maintenance fee can be a problem. Many scenic studios are housed in structures resembling large warehouses, former factories, skating rinks, or commercial plants. Most of the New York scenic studios have chosen locations in areas fairly remote from Broadway. They are scattered in many places—the Bronx, Brooklyn, Queens, Long Island, New Jersey, and Connecticut. Only two theatrical studios remain in Manhattan proper. The Metroplitan Opera Scenic Studio at Lincoln Center is, of course, not a commercial studio.

DEPARTMENTS OF THE SCENIC STUDIO

A typical scenic studio consists of two main departments—building and painting. The *building* department includes the carpenter shop (where flat construction, built work, and covering are done), the iron shop, the machine shop, and the electric shop. The *painting* department is not subdivided. To take care of production work in both departments, one can easily see the advantage in having extraordinarily large areas of work space, especially when a studio is building two, three, or four separate productions at the same time. Tight organization is required for housing equipment and storing materials, for having convenient areas to work in, and for finding enough free space in which to put all of the newly built scenery.

SCENIC STUDIO CREWS

In the New York theatrical scenic studios, crews consist mainly of members of the United Scenic Artists Local 829 and the International Alliance of Theatrical Stage Employees (IATSE). Sometimes members of the Brotherhood of Carpenters (outside construction) are employed as extra help in the scenic shop when there are not enough IATSE men available. The basic crew at each studio varies widely. In the larger shops, fifteen to twenty persons may comprise the list of regulars, with the count possibly

George Jenkins' architectural units constructed of stock pieces of commercially stamped woodwork, set up for painting, for 13 DAUGHTERS (1961), a musical (locale Hawaii, late nineteenth century).
(Photograph — Munro Gabler)

shops in New York also execute other work in related fields. This can include the building and painting of scenery and props for industrial shows, display work, exhibits, or Off Broadway (whenever the production budget will allow it). A theatrical studio may also do the scenery and props for a television show or a television commercial or for a movie. On a smaller scale, work can be contracted for a mural in a restaurant, a backdrop for a commercial photographer's studio, a job for an individual in business, like constructing and painting cabinets for an office, or a personal job for someone's apartment, such as a decorative canopy for a terrace.

One of the big problems for any scenic studio is being able to acquire enough work to keep its scenic artists and carpenters employed year round so that the key men and regular crew are not lost. This is often difficult for a studio to accomplish and still make money. The slow period or "slack season" in a studio is usually considered to be anywhere from April to July, but it is never constant and can always vary from year to year, according to the number of shows being produced in a particular season. It also varies with how much other work is being scheduled at that time.

going to fifty or sixty or more during very busy periods. The best scenic studios have always retained a nucleus of talented craftsmen who have many years of technical experience in the theatrical industry.

THE COST OF SCENERY PRODUCTIONS

With the rising costs of production in the 1970s, the scenery for an average one-set show can start anywhere between $18,000 and $20,000, and for a musical it can be in the vicinity of $50,000 to $150,000. Naturally, these figures vary with the individual designs, and the time it takes to execute the scenery has a great deal of bearing on a production's cost. A show built and painted in a period of three or four weeks can often make it necessary for the shop to put in much overtime so that the scenery can be finished properly on schedule, whereas a show planned over a much longer period can cut the cost of labor considerably. Unfortunately, this is not the way it ordinarily happens.

OTHER TYPES OF WORK DONE IN THE SCENIC STUDIO

Aside from doing the scenery for the Broadway theatre, national companies, bus-and-truck companies, operas, and ballets, the scenic

STARTING WORK ON A SHOW

Since subsequent chapters deal specifically with detailed methods and techniques of cre-

The demon Pazuzu, slightly taller than a man, was created for William Peter Blatty's THE EXORCIST film (1973). Art director: William Malley. Styrofoam glued on a wooden armature was covered after carving with pieces of velour dipped in scenic dope and painted with water-base paints.
(Photograph — Arnold Abramson)

ating scenery, this section is a short introduction. (The index will show where fuller discussion of particular subjects can be found.)

When beginning on a new show, it is standard practice for the painting department in the scenic studio to start painting backdrops on the floor while the carpentry shop is in the early stages of building the scenery. Not only does this give the artists work, it also gets the backdrops out of the way before the space is needed for painting the framed and built units. During this period, pounce drawings are also made (for both building and painting purposes) as necessary for the show. The more floor space a shop has, of course, the more drops can be painted at one time. A large area is especially advantageous when doing a big musical with a great many backdrops. Nolan Scenery Studios, for example, has a huge area of unobstructed wooden floor space, and in an area 80 by 110 feet crews can easily staple down a large cyc on the floor or lay down four average backdrops (28 by 48 feet) simultaneously.

This kind of space is also ideal when framed scenery is being laid flat on the floor for painting. After it is built and covered by the carpenters, it is delivered to the scenic artists' department for painting. Here all the surfaces are prepared for painting. They are cleaned, dusted, sanded, or whatever is necessary before priming (the very first coat) is applied. Once they have been primed, pieces of scenery are then laid out on the floor in their proper playing sequence (especially for an interior box set) for drawing and painting.

THE CHARGEMAN IN THE THEATRICAL STUDIO

A chargeman in the theatrical scenic studio is just what the name implies. He is the head painter in charge of all the painting on a show, and he picks and hires the scenic artists who work for him. Not only is it his responsibility to oversee every aspect of the painting on the scenery, he is also expected to make final decisions on any elements of a setting that may require artistic supervision in either building or materials, according to the designer's preferences. In order for the chargeman to know precisely what the designer wants, the details of the stage design are fully discussed by them. Then the chargeman delegates the work to his men or women. While the charge-

man is in the position of taking credit for a job well done in the studio, he also must take the blame if something goes wrong and the designer is not pleased. The chargeman's role is demanding and challenging, because accurate decisions must be made quickly. In some studios the chargeman also represents the shop by participating in the bid sessions to figure the cost of scenery for shows.

THE SCENIC ARTISTS

All scenic artists who paint in a theatrical scenic studio in New York City are members of the United Scenic Artists Local 829. In most cases, scenic artists who have worked regularly for some years in a theatrical studio are members qualifying in all classifications of the union, meaning that they can also work as scenic designers, costume designers, or lighting designers. But many of them prefer working in a studio, although some design as well when shows are available. The choice to work regularly as a scenic artist offers security with continuous compensation, plus such accompanying benefits as vacation pay and health insurance. This position differs from that of a freelance designer, where the nature of the theatrical industry is such that he or she may be busy one day and not be doing anything the next.

In the larger New York scenic studios, around five or six artists are employed with regularity over the year. These key men are fine craftsmen with years of experience, and most of them tend to remain at the same studio. Like the designer, a good scenic artist has to be knowledgeable and capable in numerous areas of his craft. Besides being adept at drawing and painting, he must be familiar with all sorts of subjects—from architecture to sculpture and from furniture to fabrics. Although in years past scenic studios could include such specific categories for the artists as "lay-out," "lay-in," and "detail men," today the artists are expected to work in any of these areas.

Working Day

According to the union's standards, a normal day's work for the scenic artist is six and a half hours, and that period of time is strictly followed. Anything over six and a half hours becomes overtime, which is double-time pay, and the same applies to any work on Saturday,

Sunday, or holidays. During the course of a day, an artist in the studio may find himself working on one specific job or on many. It is not at all out of the ordinary to jump back and forth among several pieces of work so that time is not wasted. Instead of waiting for the wet paint to dry on a particular surface, the painter will move on to something else and then go back to the first piece later. In the afternoon it is customary to prepare scenery so that it is thoroughly dry and ready to be worked on the next morning. Typical examples include starching a backdrop or priming new flats.

Wearing Apparel

As far as work clothes are concerned, there is no special wearing apparel required in the scenic studio. The scenic artist selects his or her clothes for comfort and practicality, and they are also geared according to the different seasons. Since scenic studios are not air-conditioned (only the Metropolitan Opera studio is) because of the horrendous cost, the temperature can be extremely hot in the summer and very chilly in the winter. For precautionary measures on scenery, it has always been a habit for the painter to wear shoes that have leather soles instead of rubber or a similar material; leather soles do not track dirt on scenery (especially backdrops) anywhere near as much as the other types. For instance, while walking and working on an expensive seamless muslin backdrop that is to be translucent on stage, more than average care must be taken. An artist may put a brown paper bag on each foot and attach it at the ankles with masking tape so that the soles of his shoes do not mess up the painting that is not yet dry on the backdrop. Or he may remove his shoes and work in his stocking feet if the backdrop has dried. All of these precautions prevent unnecessary accidents, thereby saving time and labor in production costs.

Hiring Extra Scenic Artists

When a studio becomes very busy on a show, extra scenic artists are hired as the work demands. They may be called to come in and work for one day or several or for weeks. Working as added help is a splendid way for an artist to become a regular in the scenic studio when there is an opening. During this stint a new artist can demonstrate his talents and how he actually functions on the job. In hiring

extra painters, the chargeman (head artist) may telephone the union office to find out the availability of union members who have placed their names on "the list" simply for that purpose. The same list of men and women can also serve to supply scenic artists for other media, such as motion pictures or television (features or commercials). While checking with the union is the most direct source for getting painters, the chargeman may hire an available union scenic artist by contacting him personally, or the member can make a direct contact with a studio.

Shop Men

Each scenic studio usually employs one or two shop men. Once referred to as "paint boys" in the old days of the studio, shop men are industrial members within the scenic artists' classification and perform a number of tasks in helping the artists, but do not do their work. An examination is not required to become a shop man; however, an initiation fee and monthly dues must be paid to the union according to that category. In their duties, shop men take care of brushes and buckets, keep Hudson spray tanks and hand spray guns clean, place units of built scenery on the floor for painting, tack backdrops down on the floor and take them up, help the scenic artists snap lines, and generally assist as needed. Shop men also go on errands for the studio to pick up sketches and drafting from designers and go out to purchase special supplies for the studio as well as pack the touch-up kit and take it to the theatre. Many young painters and designers have gained a wealth of experience from the early training they received by first working as shop men in a theatrical scenic studio where they were able to observe and learn, thereby enabling them to go on their own after passing the United Scenic Artists examination. At present this does not tend to be a common practice.

THE DESIGNER'S CONFERENCE WITH THE SCENIC STUDIO

Soon after the shop has been designated to do the show, the designer meets with the heads of the scenic studio departments to go over the particulars of the scenery. This meeting can take place almost immediately after the

In the drafting room, Nolan's Scenery Studios, Oliver Smith (left) confers with Charles Bender, head carpenter, on building plans of a new show. (Photograph — Arnold Abramson)

selection of the shop or whenever the designer is ready with his work. Many times the director has changed his mind on a number of things since the bid session and adjustments must be made on the drafting. The drafting may be sent to the studio first so the building can be started, then the painted sketches follow. When he is ready, most likely the designer will bring his original tracings (or sepia copies of them) to the shop, where in turn several copies of blueprints will be made for the designer, the shop office, and for building and painting departments. But he can also bring drawings he has had printed elsewhere.

Many of the details may have been generally talked over at the bid session, but they are now thoroughly discussed in depth and the real problems are studied both esthetically and mechanically. The set designer describes the overall picture he wants to the shop heads and then elaborates on the specifics, mentioning what he most prefers, and inquires how these effects can be best executed. More often than not, a designer should expect to make some changes in his design because of cost or practicality. The experienced designer is aware of the benefits that can be obtained from a good scenic studio with a backlog of knowledge gleaned from the many shows they have done over a period of years.

During the conference, the studio may think of ways to cut down the running costs of manpower in the theatre by the manner in which the scenery is built. Often a smaller number of men can be required to move units by the way they are planned to "break." In some cases, to save on stagehands, it may be better to have

an electric winch instead of a hand winch. Sometimes a show will use manually operated winches out of town and, if the show is a hit in New York, then have them converted to electrical winches to save money on the number of stagehands employed. Frequently, a producer or the general manager will help make these decisions. Also to help cut costs, a scenic shop may suggest materials that are less expensive (and often lighter-weight) which will give the designer the effect he wants. Since a reliable shop is fully acquainted with the legitimate theatres in New York and the tryout theatres out of town, the designer can be further assured that his scenery will work properly. The scenic studio knows the data concerning each particular theatre — the height, width, and depth of the stage, the kind of grid, the available storage space, and the limitations of each. It is well known that an exceptional scenic studio can make a designer's work look good, while the studio's reputation is also on the line, especially to the trade.

MAKING WORKING DRAWINGS FOR CONSTRUCTION

Although a designer may be considered a fine technician who does very accurate drawings, a reputable scenic shop will ordinarily check over all his dimensions and the specifications on his drawings to make sure that each piece of scenery will work. This is always done before the work is started on a production, because the scenic shop is completely responsible for seeing that the scenery works properly. Any questions or problems which might arise are then solved with the designer and the studio.

Working drawings are made by the shop draftsman, who traces over the designer's drawings, and they are done mainly to show the carpenters where the "breaks" are to occur in the scenery, both for practicality (so the pieces are not too large to handle or move) and for visual purposes (so the breaks come in the least obvious places). These working drawings may also indicate the kind of covering on the units, the type of stiffeners, the hanging hardware, and sometimes the hinging hardware. On platform units, the placement and description of casters or legs may also be designated. Working drawings are normally made in ½-inch scale, the same scale as the designer's plans and elevations, and they are drawn looking at the front of the scenery. An exception to this may be a ceiling piece (of average size). It is sometimes drawn looking from the back (above), because it is traced from the working ground plan to see if it fits properly. Although making working drawings from the front is contradictory to what is usually taught in school, it is done for two reasons: it is more practical to trace the working drawings off the designer's drawings, and it is less confusing for the carpenters to build scenery when all the drawings are indicated in the same way. In any case, drawings should always be clearly labeled "front view" or "back view." Occasionally, a ground plan may be done in 1-inch or 1½-inch scale, where the detail is such that more accurate measurements can be obtained by working in a larger scale. A working drawing does not have to be made for every piece of scenery. This is generally determined by the size and complexity of the unit.

FURTHER VISITS TO THE SHOP DURING BUILDING

Once the show is under way in the shop, the designer pays periodic visits to view the scenery in its building process to see if everything is working out as planned. It is his prerogative to make sure that the shop is interpreting his drawings properly, to answer any questions about its construction, or to make any changes he deems necessary. In essence, it is a general viewing of the actual scenery in its full scale for the first time. The designer is there to express his approval or disapproval, and he does. He may wish to make minor adjustments in his design by adding a new shape on a profile piece or by changing a material that will give a heavier texture on the scenery, or any number of other things. If the designer desires major changes that increase the cost, they are subject to approval by the producer or general manager.

The number of visits the designer makes to the scenic studio varies widely with the show and with the individual designer. Some make only one or two visits during the show's execution, while others may appear almost daily. It is rare indeed when a designer is not present at least once, but that has happened, simply because he knew and trusted the workmanship of that shop. Sometimes when a designer is too busy, an assistant may come to the shop as his representative. This can happen when the designer is doing either the lighting or the costumes for the same show, or when he may be working on other productions which require him to be at rehearsals or other places.

Depending on the type of production, the built scenery is usually set up in the shop to see that everything goes together as planned. It can be the whole set (especially if it is an interior) or segments of it. When the building of the show has progressed that far, the designer is notified by the shop when the set will be assembled so he can come in and view it. And on some productions, the director of the show will bring his cast of actors and actresses to the scenic studio to become acquainted with the set while it is up, and they may even rehearse on it after the shop has closed for the day.

The designer also normally comes in to see the scenery after it has been painted and goes over it in the same fashion as he did with the building. A few minor changes can take place here too, or the scenery may be fine the way it is. A designer may wish to have stacks of newly painted scenery opened up to look at, and occasionally finished backdrops are unfolded and laid out on the floor for him to examine. Since the larger shops have pipes available for hanging drops, a backdrop or special piece may be flown so that it can be viewed in its normal vertical position. And, while it rarely happens, a few designers prefer to have the complete set erected in the shop after it has been painted so they can see how everything looks together. Because it costs extra labor to do, such an arrangement is usually known beforehand and is included in the bid session. If the scenic designer is not doing the lighting on the show, the lighting designer may also come in to look at the finished building and painting so he or she is aware of all the particular elements of the set.

In the very early days of the scenic studio in New York, the stage designer worked on the same premises as the scenic artists. His headquarters in the studio were known as the "model room," where he designed the scenery which was then created and painted under one roof. Only recently this method of working

(Left) Three-dimensional wooden cornice, decorated with stencil painting, from Lloyd Evans' scenery for Johann Strauss' DIE FLEDERMAUS (1974) at the New York City Opera.

(Right) Stage carpenter Munro Gabler turning wooden balusters on a lathe.

(Left) Eugene Berman's painted rolling units, draped with scenic netting, for PULCINELLA (1972).

(Right) Lloyd Evans' profile chandelier for DON GIOVANNI (1972) at the New York City Opera consisted of a front and back profile painted on two flat surfaces of ¾-in. plywood spaced 4 in. apart. The electrified candles held 30 tiny bulbs. Real chains were attached to the unit for effect but not support.

(Left) Raoul Pène du Bois' framed canvas portal for Act I of NO, NO, NANETTE (1971), national company. Constructed from carpenter's working drawings, extra ¼-in. plywood was allowed along the edges for drawing the final design. When primed with whiting and glue size, 2-ft. squares were snapped in charcoal; drawing was laid out directly on portal. After painting, white areas, marked with Xs, were cut away with a Sabre saw.

(Right) Looking down from a ladder on a portion of Lloyd Evans' moody backdrop for SUMMER AND SMOKE (1972), designed for the New York City Opera. Used as a translucency, it was made of muslin with opaque trees laid in after the sky (in oval washes) and architecture had been finished.
Photographs—Lynn Pecktal)

168

(Left) Window backing of city buildings in perspective, painted on folding flats, for Robert Randolph's scenery in NO HARD FEELINGS (1973).

(Right) Rouben Ter-Arutunian's setting of sculptural shapes for the Joffrey Ballet's THE RELATIVITY OF ICARUS (1974) was constructed of ⅛-in. mirrored Plexiglas on a framework of wood and metal. The canvas-covered oval platform was painted with aluminum paint (bronze powder mixed with lacquer).

(Left) Pieces of dark-gray flexible polyurethane foam, carved with an electric knife, were adhered with vinyl adhesive to a painted cut muslin leg for the scenery in SEBASTIAN (1974) designed by Sandro La Ferla for the Harkness Ballet. Finished sculpture, approximately 1½ in. thick, was painted with vinyl and casein paints.

(Right) Ornament cut from ¾-in. plywood for Lloyd Evans' stairway railing in DIE FLEDERMAUS (1974). A basic pounce was used first, then ornament was added by painting shapes on the wood with black vinyl to fit the angles and to give strength. Unpainted wood was cut away.

(Left) Scenery for three productions being executed at the same time. (Top right) A scrim drop for Ming Cho Lee's 1975 IDOMENEO setting for the New York City Opera. (Below right) Drawing for a unit in Raoul Pène du Bois' setting for DOCTOR JAZZ (1975); (left) graining is applied with aniline dyes on a wing laid in with dry pigment colors and glue size on Robert Randolph's scenery for WE INTERRUPT THIS PROGRAM . . . (1975).

(Right) Various types of carpet and rug cut and nailed onto David Mitchell's castered, contoured platforms were sprayed with aniline dyes, then textured with latex and vinyl paint for BORIS GODUNOV (1974), Cincinnati Opera and Canadian Opera.

169

The wooden bridge Lloyd Evans designed to enhance Butterfly's first entrance in MADAMA BUTTERFLY (1967) at the New York City Opera. Distinctive features include routed edges on plywood railings, Styrofoam ready for carving adhered to the top of newel posts, contoured section pieces under railings covered with forming cloth (before ragging), and bracing structures under the wooden bridge disguised by profiles of rustic shapes.

Precise full-scale charcoal drawings on brown Kraft paper, perforated with a pounce wheel, were made by scenic artists so a carpenter could duplicate Jo Mielziner's doors and stairway unit for DON'T DRINK THE WATER (1966), Woody Allen's comedy (locale: an American Embassy behind the Iron Curtain).
The ornamental stair railing, shown separated from the stairs, was made of ¾-in. plywood. Edges were routed and dimension relief added to the face by applying scenic dope squeezed from a plastic ketchup container.

Three-dimensional doors with real panel molding had painted molding and ornament within the panels. Outside straight and curved molding was created with a router. Overdoor design was cut out of plywood. (Photographs—Munro Gabler)

was repeated when Eugene Berman came from Rome to design the Balanchine–Robbins ballet *Pulcinella* for the Stravinsky Festival at Lincoln Center in 1972. As always, Berman designed both the sets and costumes. His scenery for the ballet was built and painted at Nolan Studios, where an office was turned into a model room for him to use during the execution of the production. For several weeks before the ballet's première, Berman spent the mornings sketching, designing, and painting numerous ¼-inch set models while an assistant put them together and drafted drawings. As each design was drafted and approved, it was given to the carpenter shop for building and then to the scenic department for painting. In the afternoons, Berman worked in a similar fashion at Karinska's, where the costumes for the production were executed.

LOADING THE SHOW

Before a show is taken from the shop, a great deal of planning is done to make sure that the scenery is going to work properly in the theatres where it is to be housed. About a week or so prior to the "load-out," the production carpenter (hired by the producer) for the specific show meets with the shop heads in the scenic studio to go over the mechanics of the scenery, inspecting how the different units are built and how they fit together so he will be able to organize them knowledgeably in the theatre. He may be accompanied by an assistant or other stagehands. The designer is sometimes present for these meetings and sometimes not. In his planning, the production carpenter tends to do a number of things. He may make up his own personal hanging plot according to the existing conditions (flylines, storage, and so on) in the particular stage house. In addition, he may have suggestions for the shop about little things that will help make the show run better. His duties further include figuring how many trucks will be needed to haul the scenery and how many individual canvas covers are required to wrap around each piece of scenery so that it is protected from damage during traveling. In all, the production carpenter may make several stops at the scenic studio as well as being there to organize the scenery on the day or days it loads out.

Over the same period of time, other production heads are usually in attendance at the

170

shop. The head prop man (often with an assistant) is there to check out the props and get them all together. He may do special work on the props and then pack them for moving. Quite often props such as furniture, set dressing, or hand props are sent to the studio only because the show needs to have a drop-off point for them. This way they will all be in one place and taken out with the rest of the show. The head electrician may also make visits to the shop, especially when the lights are an integral part of the setting. His tasks in the scenic studio are similar to those of the other production heads.

Anyone who has ever worked in a scenic studio is well aware of the familiar expression "the truck is here." That is the time when a real rush is on to get all of the scenery finished, and there is always a lot of scurrying about in both the carpentry and painting departments. Theatrical union truckers (members of the Teamsters' Union) are employed by the producer to transport the scenery to the theatre, either in or out of town. Pieces of scenery are dismantled, wrapped, and loaded. The shop carpenters are responsible for taking the scenery to the truck, where the truckers pack it. Once the scenery has reached the theatre, it is unloaded by the stagehands and set up on stage.

WORKING AT THE THEATRE

During the time the show is being assembled and put together in the theatre, a carpenter from the scenic shop is present to make sure that the scenery is working properly and to solve any problems pertaining to it. The set designer can be on hand at various times while the scenery is being set up or can come in after it has been almost finished. From here on until the show opens in New York or elsewhere, the designer is busy getting the remainder of the set dressing and props completed and putting finishing touches on his work.

Since this is the first chance to see everything in its place onstage, there are usually pleasant surprises along with a few minor disappointments. It is always exciting for the designer to watch a run-through out front with the director, seeing the actors in make-up on the set with lights, costumes, and props for the first time, but invariably changes must be made. After discussing with the director problems that may be either visual or physical, the

designer can decide to have a touch-up call for scenic artists to make repairs or changes in the painting as well as to have the house crew of carpenters in the theatre make adjustments in the construction of settings or props.

If the set designer is also designing the lighting, he must allow time for checking out positioned instruments, focusing them with the electricians, and making necessary adjustments in the lighting. He must also set specific light levels and light cues with the director and run the cues with the electricians. In addition, if he has designed the costumes, he must make any needed changes or alterations in them. All of these aspects of the final work can involve numerous conferences with the director and sometimes the producer.

GOING ON A TOUCH-UP

Whenever scenic artists go to the theatre with paints and brushes to make adjustments on the painted scenery, the task is most aptly referred to as "going on a touch-up." It is usual procedure for the studio that originally painted the show to send its own scenic artists to the theatre, but this is not a set rule. Touch-ups are necessary on every kind of production, including plays, musical comedies, ballets, and operas, for any of several reasons. Chiefly they are requested for making changes in the design and painting of a new show before opening; touching up scenery which has been damaged during loading, unloading, set-up, or in the playing of the show; repainting (touching up) settings of long-running hit shows, or those in operas or ballets that have been kept in repertory for some years.

While the majority of touch-ups take place in New York City, scenic artists also travel to such tryout towns as New Haven or Philadelphia when trouble has occurred with the scenery. Touch-up jobs are always unpredictable. No matter where they happen, the experience can be interesting for the painters, or it may be hectic and chaotic. Quite often, if a new show is being well received by the public and there are only minor repairs to be made on the scenery, the general atmosphere backstage can be calm and casual. This is an ideal situation for painting on a touch-up, because there is time to finish all the repairs on the scenery and props with ease instead of having to rush ahead frantically. In contrast,

GOING ON A TOUCH-UP IN THE THEATRE. Scenic artist Fred Jacoby touching up three-dimensional molding on the ceiling of William Ritman's set for 6 RMS RIV VU (1972) at the Helen Hayes Theatre.

some producers expect miracles within the six and a half hours of regular time and keep the artists working at a very fast pace to avoid having them go into overtime (double-time) pay.

A touch-up is ordinarily called by the designer and okayed by the producer or general manager. It is an established regulation that when scenic artists go on a touch-up for a Broadway show, the house crew for that particular theatre is also called. This can include the production carpenter (in charge of all the house crew), the house carpenter, the head electrician, the head prop man, and additional stage hands as needed. They move the scenery during the touch-up, turn on the lights or whatever, and at the same time make repairs and adjustments in the stage setting or lighting under the designer's supervision. The stage manager and other responsible people may also be present. But foremost, the scenic designer or his assistant always appears at the touch-up to give exact instructions to the scenic artists. Usually two artists work together on a job, with one designated the chargeman and the other the second man, according to union policy.

When a great deal of change is being made in a show, as many as four or five scenic artists can work in the theatre at once. Before the musical comedy *Irene,* starring Debbie Reynolds, opened Broadway's newest legitimate house, the Minskoff Theatre at Broadway and 45th Street March 13, 1973, a big call was scheduled to touch-up Raoul Pène du Bois' scenery. Since the preceding December 16, when the musical opened its first tryout engagement in Toronto and then played Philadelphia and Washington, the show had undergone replacement of the director, first Sir John Gielgud and then Gower Champion, and consequently changes occurred in the settings. On March 9, a few days before the opening

at the Minskoff in New York, four scenic artists, assisted by a shop man, worked a full day and into overtime to get the scenery in shape, repainting parts and retouching original pieces that had been damaged during the trouping. While the touch-up was in progress, newly designed backdrops and framed portals created by du Bois were delivered to the theatre from the scenic studio.

On other shows, where only a couple of artists are called, all the painting may be expected to be finished in a single morning. During this time there may be a light rehearsal for light cues or for focusing new instruments while the artists paint in semidarkness as wagons of scenery are being rolled off and on stage. Sometimes scenic artists paint pieces in the wings while a full rehearsal is in progress on stage—a typical situation when a new show is opening or an old one is returning to the repertory of an opera or a ballet. There are also touch-ups that are more of a repaint job than a mere touch-up. The designer may have miscalculated some of the colors or shapes of the design and want changes made simply because things do not work. Occasions have arisen where a whole interior (or set pieces in a musical comedy, for that matter) must be almost completely repainted before the opening. Just as frequently, rewrites in the script and directorial changes from the original concept, especially on a new play, can necessitate changes in the scenery without having anything to do with the designer's initial approach.

Before the scenic artists actually start to work on a touch-up, all brushes and colors are well organized in a convenient spot where the light is good. Usually this is along the edge of the apron or downstage in the wings. Brown Kraft paper is laid on the floor, on which containers are placed and colors are mixed. When a specific color has to be matched and a sizable amount is needed (more than just a few brushfuls that can be taken from the containers and palletted on the brown paper), the scenic artist quickly makes a sample of the desired color on a piece of newspaper or other paper. A lighted match is held close to the painted sample to speed the drying and the dry sample is then held up to the surface being matched. When it appears to be satisfactory, the artist proceeds to mix a batch of the color in a container. To save time running back and forth, several general colors (whether for walls

Show curtain by Eugene Berman
DANSES CONCERTANTES
Music by Igor Stravinsky
Choreography by George Balanchine
Ballet Russe de Monte Carlo, New York (1944)

Not every touch-up takes place at the theatre. In 1972, at Nolan Scenery Studios, designer Eugene Berman was permitted (with a scenic artist standing by) to touch up the original show curtain he designed for Stravinsky's ballet in 1944. (Photographs—Arnold Abramson)

and woodwork or foliage and rocks) are mixed in quart-size tin cans and placed in a cardboard carton with brushes so they can be carried around the set. This keeps them within easy reach and from being overturned. The paints are applied by brush or sponge, depending on the nature of the work. Frequently, the colors are stippled or dabbed on the scenery, or they are thinned down with water and glazed over the painted surface with a brush. In addition, a touch-up can include spraying the offstage side of a rolled ceiling with warm water in a Hudson spray tank to tighten up the loose canvas, or getting rid of marks or spots on framed scenery covered with velour by using sticks of pastels from a full box included in the touch-up kit. (Best results on the velour are achieved when the pastels are applied under the actual stage lighting for the scene, not the work lights.)

The Touch-Up Kit

Paints, brushes, and all other equipment likely to be needed for scenic work at the theatre are packed in a large case known as the touch-up kit. A scenic studio maintains at least two complete kits, which are always kept fully stocked. Additional materials are added according to the nature of the work to be done on the particular production. On some shows, original colors are saved and labeled so they can be taken to the touch-up.

STANDARD EQUIPMENT IN A TOUCH-UP KIT

1. *Brushes:*
   All sizes of liners and lay-in brushes, usually two of each.
2. *Paints:*
   Caseins—A 1-qt. container of all the standard colors, plus 1 gal. black, 1 gal. white.
   Vinyl—1 gal. of clear gloss vinyl.
   Bronze powdered colors—A 1-lb. container of gold, silver, and copper (clear gloss vinyl serves as the binder).
3. *Dyes:*
   Powdered aniline dyes in assorted colors.
4. *Containers:*
   A 5-gal. bucket for water, several 1-gal. pails. Small tin cans in various sizes.
5. *Brown Kraft paper:*
   A roll 3 ft. wide and approximately 20 ft. long.
6. *A roll of masking tape.*
7. *Clean rags.*
8. *2 yardsticks.*
9. *Razor blades.*
10. *Sponges*—natural and synthetic.
11. *Paint-can openers.*
12. *Paint sticks*—for stirring.
13. *A can of clear spray fixative.*
14. *Charcoal sticks and a snapline.*
15. *Sticks of white chalk.*
16. *Regular pencils.*

These supplementary items can also be included:
1. Hudson spray tank.
2. Spray gun and compressor.
3. Paint rollers and tray.
4. Box of pastels for touching up velour scenery.
5. Any special paints or equipment.

173

TOURING COMPANIES

National Road Company

The national road company is essentially a show that has been successful on Broadway and then tours the country. In scenic production, the road company is usually very close to the original design. It can be the same or it can be somewhat cut down, according to how detailed it is, for moving and traveling. Many times a complete new touring set is built in the scenic shop to go on the road while the original show is still playing. In other cases, the original set may go on tour after the engagement has terminated in New York. So that the scenery will fit on the various stages where the show is to play, an average set of measurements (width, depth, height) is taken of the different theatres. National road companies can play in large cities anywhere from four to six weeks or much longer, depending on the success of the show. The scenery is transported by truck (trains have generally become a thing of the past for moving scenery) while the actors travel by plane, train, or bus. On some big hit musicals which are designed to have a portable deck to accommodate tracking devices in the floor and so on, a heavy scenic show may have two identical decks to save time in setting up the scenery. While still playing an engagement with one deck, the other is sent to the next theatre so when the remaining scenery arrives, it is ready for set-up.

A Bus-and-Truck Company

A bus-and-truck company is a simplified version of a Broadway show in which the scenery is cut down to a bare minimum. It can play a week here, a week and a half there, or even split weeks. Because the bus-and-truck company is booked for such short engagements, the scenery is usually redesigned to be as flexible as possible, making it easy to set up and take down in a short span of time. Some shows may be almost all soft, with only a few framed or built pieces. The actors generally travel by bus and the scenery, props, electrics, and costumes are often geared to fit into one or two trucks.

THE METROPOLITAN OPERA SCENIC STUDIO

One of the unique features of the Metropolitan Opera scenic studio is that it is housed in the opera house proper. Situated in the vast Lincoln Center complex in New York, the Met studio on the fifth floor is unlike the commercial scenic studio in that the scenery created there is for Met productions only. Not only are the stage settings built and painted there, but the costumes, props, and lighting are also realized on the same premises. This offers a splendid opportunity for the artists working at the Met to observe an opera being put together in all of its creative processes. They can observe the early formative stages through to the finished work as it appears dramatically on the stage.

Russian-born Vladmir Odinokov, for many years head scenic artist in charge of supervising the painting at the Metropolitan Studio, has often been known to improvise new methods of painting along with original names to go with them. A term he is known to use periodically is *to spuddle,* which is said to be a cross between spattering and puddling. Members of his crew point out that this is achieved by "spattering artistically and violently." During the course of looking over the work his painters are doing on the scenery for an opera, another well-known saying attributed to Odinokov is "Paint like an artist, not like a slave." As in many other theatrical organizations, the scenic artists at the Met become almost family-oriented. Approximately six to eight artists are employed on a regular basis in the paint shop, but when the work becomes very busy, other painters are added. In a rush period, as many as fifteen may be working at the Metropolitan scenic studio.

Painting on the Floor

The Met scenic studio on the fifth floor rear of the opera house consists of two large unobstructed rooms where the scenery is painted on the floor. The largest of these, the main room, is 60 feet wide by 68 feet long and is approximately 10 feet high. In a diagonal direction southeast of this room is another sizable area 29 feet wide by 70 feet long. In both spaces, soft scenery (backdrops, legs, borders, and ground cloths), framed scenery (wings and set pieces), and platforms are painted on the floor, with drops and ground cloths usually executed in the larger room. An average drop at the Met can be 45 feet high by 68 feet wide, while a cyc for a production like Strauss' *Salome,* designed by Rudolf Heinrich, is 130 feet wide by 60 feet high. If a drop is larger than the floor areas, it is necessary to take "bites" in it. This involves stapling down as much of the drop as possible for painting, then folding up the remaining end. Care is taken when stapling through the drop where the end is folded so that the fabric is not damaged. After that portion of the drop stapled to the floor has been painted (or touched up) to the end where it is folded, the staples are removed and the rest of the drop is put down for painting.

Painting on the Frame

In addition to floor painting, the Met studio has two paint frames for upright painting, the only ones currently used full-time in the city. Situated east of the main painting room, the paint frames are housed in a gallery that begins on the fourth floor and extends through the sixth. They hang parallel to each other, face to face. Between the frames are two bridges where the scenic artists work. The lower bridge is located on the fourth floor and the second one is directly above it on the sixth floor. Each bridge is about 10 feet wide. If an artist is working on the bottom portion of a backdrop, he uses the lower bridge, and for the top part he

goes to the upper bridge. The front paint frame is 67 feet 4 inches wide by 57 feet high, whereas the back frame is 72 feet wide by 43 feet 11 inches high. Both frames work electrically, and to move them up or down, you only have to push a button to move the scenery in the desired direction. A stop button is used in order to change directions. A 3-foot-high chain guard is permanently attached on either side of the bridge to prevent the painters from getting too close to the edges while working.

Several stagehands are needed to put a backdrop on the paint frame. A backdrop is stapled on the paint frame by first attaching the top, then the bottom, and finally the sides. The edges of fabric are attached to the wooden frame with an air-pressure stapler (like the Senco stapler) using $\frac{5}{8}$-inch staples. Once the top is fastened, the backdrop is pulled down taut and checked to see where the bottom falls. If it is shorter than the bottom of the frame and does not meet the wood, a wooden batten can be nailed onto the frame at the bottom parallel to the top, depending on the size of the drop. A vertical wooden batten can also be attached

Painting is done on both paint frame and floor at the Metropolitan Opera Scenic Studio. Edward Haynes, Madeleine McEvoy, and Joe Gerson outline mortar between stones on scenery for Franco Zeffirelli's OTELLO.

Working on the lower bridge between the Metropolitan Opera's two paint frames, scenic artist Walter Klech checks the painting to be touched up on a backdrop for LA FILLE DU RÉGIMENT designed by Anna Anni. A chain guard on either side of the bridge keeps the scenic artists from getting too close to the open wells in which the paint frames move.

Scenic artist Robert Winkler uses a special lacquer to paint patterns on slides for the grotto scene in Debussy's PELLÉAS ET MÉLISANDE (1972), designed by Desmond Heeley. The slides are made of pyrex-type glass to withstand the high-intensity heat of a 10,000-watt projector.

Vladimir Odinokov adjusts projector for drawing on drop mounted on paint frame. (Photographs — Lynn Pecktal)

to one side of the paint frame if the width of the drop does not meet the frame on the side. Sometimes at the Met when there is a problem of getting a linen backdrop stretched to meet the edges of the paint frame, it is solved by wetting about 15 feet of the sides with water applied from a Hudson tank. Then the drop is stretched while wet and stapled. Besides backdrops, borders are also placed on the paint frame when a rush is on.

Two, three, or four scenic artists may work on a drop simultaneously when it is on the frame. The paint is applied on the material with brushes, sponges, and the Hudson tank. Sponges are ideal for painting textures on the framed drop as well as for painting scrims or bobbinets on the frame. Because there is no surface to back the drop when it is on a frame, the fabric must be hit harder with the bristles of the brush than if it were being painted on the floor. The colors are mixed on a table pallette that moves on casters and also holds the paints and brushes.

Paints, Fabrics, and Materials

Newly designed productions at the Met can remain in repertory from ten to twenty years; considering that the stage settings are repeatedly put up, taken down, packed, and hauled away to storage in the repertory situation, the fabrics and materials for the scenery are selected with that in mind. Instead of canvas, bleached and unbleached linen serve as the most durable fabrics for covering wings and for making backdrops. Muslin, of course, is utilized for translucencies, and scrim and bobbinet for gauzes. Either linen or velour may be used for wings and borders. An average wing at the Met can be 5 feet 9 inches wide by 28 feet high, while a border may be 68 feet wide by 21 high. Like the commercial scenic studio, the Met shop works with many different paints, including casein, aniline dyes, vinyl, and latex. Latex paint is regarded as holding up well on the scenery at the Met. Frequently, thin latex is put on both linen backdrops and heavy duck ground cloths.

At the Metropolitan Opera scenic studio, all sorts of plastics go into making the scenery. Styrofoam, Ethafoam, and Prestofoam (a flexible plastic) are employed for cutting out and carving three-dimensional objects. Pieces of theatrical gauze are then applied over them as a covering before painting. For creating textures in heavy relief, large units of scenery have been molded and cast in fiberglass, as was the case for Verdi's *Otello* (designed by Franco Zeffirelli) and Beethoven's *Fidelio* (designed by Boris Aronson). The Met has its own facilities for doing fiber glass work on the fourth floor where the carpenter shop and welding shop are located. A well-known source used by the Metropolitan Opera scenic studio for obtaining unusual plastic materials and other scenic supplies is Alfred Haussmann (2 Hamburg 70, Tonndorfer Hauptstrasse 79, West Germany).

Drawing

For drawing on paper pounces or directly on the surface of the scenery, the Met uses 3-foot squares as a standard grid for ordinary drawing, and for detailed drawings both 1-foot and 2-foot squares. On certain occasions a special projector designed by scenic artist Vladimir Odinokov is used to reproduce the exact drawing of a stage design onto a vertically framed backdrop. The projector, mounted on a castered table, is operated on the bridge between paint frames. A very short angle of projection is obtained by using a mirror positioned on a 45-degree angle in front of the projector, which enables it to function at a distance of only six feet. In addition to the movable table, the projector itself is equipped so that it can be easily pushed back and forth horizontally whenever focusing. This was created and used for execution of Marc Chagall's settings for Mozart's *The Magic Flute*.

Initially, both the design and the backdrop are marked off in squares. The design is gridded in $1\frac{1}{2}$-inch squares (for the scale $\frac{1}{2}$ inch $= 1$ foot), while the backdrop is done in 3-foot squares. When ready to use, the squared-off design is turned upside down and placed against a piece of framed glass attached vertically to the table. Positioned directly in front of this is the projector. When it is turned on, a light shines on the scaled design, reflecting it through the lens to the mirror which corrects the image and projects it onto the gridded surface. Here, the artist draws the projected image with a charcoal stick, working on one square at a time until the backdrop is finished. The light in the projector is regulated by a rheostat conveniently placed on one side of the table.

Pertinent facts about the Metropolitan Opera stage appear in *The Official Guide to the Metropolitan Opera House* by Herman E. Krawitz, available at Lincoln Center.

A Conversation with BEN EDWARDS

Ben Edwards talked about theatre and his experience in the lower-Manhattan townhouse in which he lives and maintains a studio. A native of Alabama, Edwards studied at the Feagin School in New York and received his theatrical training in several stock companies prior to his Broadway debut designing Dorothy Thompson's *Another Sun* in 1940. In addition to designing sets, he has created the lighting and costumes for many shows. Besides Broadway, he has designed productions for the New York City Center, the Minnesota Theatre Company, Buffalo's Studio Arena, Kennedy Center, Washington, D.C., the American Shakespeare Festival at Stratford, Connecticut, and Margaret Webster's Shakespearean Company. Ben Edwards' film designs include *Lovers and Other Strangers, Last of the Red Hot Lovers,* and *Class of '44,* plus several television specials, among which are *A House without a Christmas Tree, A Thanksgiving Treasure,* and *Look Homeward, Angel.* He teaches design classes at the Lester Polakov Studio of Design and New York University. He is married to Jane Greenwood, the costume designer. Currently he is president of the United Scenic Artists (membership numbers around 900). Below is a partial list of his Broadway productions:

A Moon for the Misbegotten (1973)	*Purlie Victorious* (1961)	*The Waltz of the Toreadors* (1957)
Finishing Touches (1973)	*Big Fish, Little Fish* (1961)	*The Ponder Heart* (1956)
Hay Fever (1970)	*Face of a Hero* (1960)	*Sing Me No Lullaby* (1954)
Purlie (1970)	*Heartbreak House* (1959)	*Anastasia* (1954)
More Stately Mansions (1967)	*The Disenchanted* (1958)	*The Remarkable Mr. Pennypacker*
The Ballad of the Sad Café (1963)	*Jane Eyre* (1958)	(1954)
The Aspern Papers (1962)	*A Touch of the Poet* (1958)	*The Time of the Cuckoo* (1952)
A Shot in the Dark (1961)	*Dark at the Top of the Stairs* (1957)	*Diamond Lil* (1949)

Setting and lighting by Ben Edwards
A MOON FOR THE MISBEGOTTEN by Eugene O'Neill
Costumes by Jane Greenwood
Directed by José Quintero

Morosco Theatre, New York (1973)
Pictured: Colleen Dewhurst,
    Jason Robards
(Photograph — Martha Swope)

Where did you study when you first came to New York?

I came on a scholarship to a theatre school, the Feagin School of Dramatic Art. At that time it was up on 57th Street between Eighth and Ninth Avenue. That building housed the Blackfriars Theatre after the Feagin School moved. It is now torn down. (Stillman's Gym was up on the top floor, so when we used to go to school, Primo Carnera and that group of boxers would always be on the elevators.) It was a theatre school, but there wasn't much accent on scene design. It was like the American Academy. There were only two schools of that type in New York at the time. Oh, there were some private coaches that had schools, and except for the American Academy, they were mostly all run by women. If you look at the old *Theatre Arts* magazines of the thirties, you will see ads for all those dramatic coaches. Many of them were from the South — ladies who came up, studied drama in Europe, then suddenly settled down to the teaching and coaching world. I always teased Bob Whitehead about one, the Elizabeth B. Grimble School, which he attended about the same time I was at the Feagin School. Lucy Feagin came from Alabama and founded Feagin School in 1915 in a studio in Carnegie Hall. She had gone over and studied with John Gielgud's aunt who, I believe, was a sister or cousin of Ellen Terry's [Gordon Craig's mother]. She came from Union Springs, my home town, and that's how I happened to go there.

Had you gone away to school before you came to New York?

No, I had only gone to high school. I came here when I was seventeen, went to the Feagin School and did scenery for the plays there. I built most of the scenery myself with the help of the students and a handyman-janitor. They had a shop in the school. Dr. Milton Smith, head of the drama department at Columbia University, gave a lecture course at the Feagin School in scene design. I did a lot of work with him, and used to go up to Columbia and talk with him. I was more interested in designing than acting.

What did you do during the summers?

I met a teacher named Grace Mills, who directed plays at Feagin School, and she said, "You should go to the Barter Theatre this summer." So I saw

Robert Porterfield and went down for the summer as the designer. It was in the mid-thirties, the third season of the Barter. Then I came back and went to the Feagin School the final year. During that year, I also went to another school on certain days, the Florence Kane School of Art at Radio City. I studied drafting with Emeline Roche, a superb drafting teacher. At that time she was doing all the drafting and model-making for Aline Bernstein. She had also worked with Norman Bel Geddes when he was doing *The Miracle* up at the Century Theatre. There were six of us in the theatre school for drafting, and that's where I met Lester Polakov.

I got a job doing scenery the following summer in Falmouth, Massachusetts, where we got room and board and all of fifteen dollars a week. I was asked to go to the Mohawk Festival up in New York state, which Charles Coburn was doing, and I remember I went over to see him in the National Arts Club in Gramercy Park, and we talked about it, but it paid no money, only room and board. I was getting fifteen dollars at the other, but I went back to see Coburn and I remember he said to me, "Son, you must learn in your life never to vacillate." I've been told the person who went to the Festival that summer when I went to Falmouth was Oliver Smith.

You did several seasons of stock before you designed in New York City?

Yes. The next thing I did was with a director named Charles Hopkins, who had been quite a well-known theatrical producer in New York before the Depression. He had done *Mrs. Moonlight* and several A. A. Milne plays in New York, and had been a very wealthy man in real estate. At this time, he was getting together a group for the Federal Theatre in Roslyn, Long Island, and I was asked to go out there with him. Then, because they thought the work we were doing out there was worthy of getting into New York, we were invited to do a repertory of several plays for a limited engagement at the Maxine Elliot Theatre. We did Shakespeare's *Coriolanus*, George Bernard Shaw's *Pygmalion*, a thing called *No More Peace* by one of the German playwrights, and *Captain Jinks of the Horse Marines*.

Do you count that as your New York debut?

Not really. The Federal Theatre certainly was where I met a lot of New York theatre people. Abe Feder was with me on lighting, and Jeanie Rosenthal was Abe's assistant. I left the Federal Theatre before it was finally dissolved by Congress and went to a theatre in Marblehead, Massachusetts, for several years. This was before summer theatres had package deals. We used a star system of sorts, but they were original productions. I know we did a revival of *The Yellow Jacket* which was most interesting. Alexander Woollcott, Harpo Marx, and Fay Wray were in the cast. We also did *The Emperor Jones* with Paul Robeson. But really, my first Broadway job was an unsuccessful play called *Another Sun* by Dorothy Thompson, the columnist. It had to do with the German refugees and their adjustments to New York City.

Just how do you go about designing a show? Is there a certain way that works best for you?

Well, I try not to think about the scenery too much when I read the play. I try to think of the play itself and what it is saying and, somehow, have the scenery evolve from the play. If you don't get a lot from the script, it's a very difficult job to design it. Unless a play has something to say, all you can do is "that room" they ask for. It's very hard to design when the playwright is just pot-boiling and writing junk that he hopes to make a fortune on. For a bad play you sometimes do something that's very attractive, but you don't feel any great satisfaction. I think I'd really rather try and interpret the play than just do some interior decorating that dazzles the eye. The reviews of a lot of plays say "the whole evening was a disaster, but the scenery was just beautiful." There's something wrong about this. If the whole evening is something of a disaster, well, the scenery ought to be a disaster, too.

What plays that you have designed are your favorites?

It's very hard to say. I don't think I've ever had a play where the set was a failure unless the whole operation was a failure. And then it seems that one thing piled on top of another — you weren't happy with the set, the play didn't work, the direction didn't work: nothing worked. Of course, I adore *Waltz of the Toreadors*. That play was very successful.

**Stage design by Ben Edwards
A TOUCH OF THE POET by
Eugene O'Neill**

**Directed by Harold Clurman
Helen Hayes Theatre, New York
(1958)**

It got rave reviews and was doing very well. Then Ralph Richardson got ill and an understudy played it a while. Ralph finally went back to England, and the play had to be closed. But it went on the road, and strangely enough, even though it was an Anouilh play, it made money on the road. We used the same set, and I don't think there were any changes. It toured for a full season all over the United States. I've liked a lot of plays I've done. Although it is not one of his greatest plays, I enjoyed O'Neill's *A Touch of the Poet.* I don't think it was a completely successful play, but it had some quality in it. O'Neill knew what he was writing about and what he was trying to say. That was even true in the other O'Neill play I did more recently, *More Stately Mansions,* which wasn't finished by O'Neill. It was dragged out of his manuscripts after he was dead. You knew what you were trying to do with it because you understood what he was trying to say, and that was a great help. It's the first time I had worked with José Quintero. He is a wonderful director, and I enjoyed working with him tremendously. Recently we worked on *A Moon for the Misbegotten,* which was most rewarding and a huge success.

You have also worked with Elia Kazan and Harold Clurman.

They are marvelous directors, and they both know what a play is about and what they are driving at. And when you work with them, there is no question about what the play means. *Dark at the Top of the Stairs* is the most successful

one I did with Kazan, but I also did *Sundown Beach,* a play that was originally produced for the Actors Studio. It was the initial appearance of many of the actors and actresses from the studio and also the first real emergence of Julie Harris. Cloris Leachman was also in it, and Maureen Stapleton was a walk-on. I've done many plays with Harold. The first play I did with him was *The Time of the Cuckoo* with Shirley Booth, the last play at the Empire Theatre. Then I did *A Touch of the Poet, A Shot in the Dark,* a revival of Shaw's *Heartbreak House,* and *The Waltz of the Toreadors* and several others.

How about Purlie? *You designed both the play and the musical.*

Howard da Silva directed the first *Purlie.* The strong influence and the most help to me was the author, Ozzie Davis, who is black. I had had a lot of disagreements in the musical and in the play. It was the scene where the old Captain and Gitlow, I think he's called [both in the musical and the play], have that great confrontation which is a wild kind of comedy, an exaggeration that Ozzie had intentionally set up. I decided to put it in front of a minstrel poster. I never could have done it without Ozzie. There was no real fuss, but the director and producer feared that the stereotype minstrel poster would offend blacks. I had remembered those posters from childhood (where the black boy is jumping over the fence with the dog biting his pants as he is stealing the watermelon). Ozzie Davis stood by me.

He said it was exactly what it ought to be. I ran into the same thing when Ozzie wasn't around while I was working on the musical of *Purlie.* We had to tone it down before the cast arrived. I felt it unnecessary, but certainly I had no desire to offend.

Who directed the musical?

The producer of the original, Philip Rose, a very charming man. The musical wouldn't have gotten on if it hadn't been for Phil. I don't know how we ever opened, as there was no money. Somehow he managed to scratch and scrape and we opened. It was the same way getting it on the road. It's been on the road and has done very well.

Do you think that a good scenic studio can make your show look better?

Yes, of course it can. A paint elevation by a designer is not a final thing—it's the key and a beginning. The painters are the "artists" in the scene studio. That's why they go into the craft. And when they are finished, their painting should look like the designer's sketch but which has gone through some interpretations in order to achieve this. If a shop doesn't have good scenic artists, there is little I can do. It's a matter of cooperation, the relationship with the scene painters and the designer. You can't overwork the painting by repainting over and over or it is ruined. Gus Wimazal at the old Triangle Studio was one of the great scene painters of the world. He always said, "I'll find an accidental way to do that."

Of the two, which do you prefer work-

179

ing in—motion pictures or television?

I don't have any preference. I enjoy working in movies very much, and in TV, too. Theatre is much harder. I say much harder, but it is also much more rewarding. If you do a set that you feel is successful, there it is, and it works! The relationship (and working *in* the theatre) between directors, designers, and the other people is far closer and more precise than in movies and television. There's a time and money element in all movies and all television that doesn't leave room for real collaboration. The cost while you are taping or shooting in television is so enormous. There's not enough time to really work on shots and on angles. It's the same in movies, too. Movies now are made on very tight budgets. I think years ago in the movies, there were sketches for every frame. You look at *The Thief of Bagdad* which William Cameron Menzies designed for Douglas Fairbanks [Sr.], and that was a "designed movie," there's no doubt about it. Every frame and everything in the design was thought out.

When you're working as an art director in movies, do you make a lot of rough sketches?

No. There's no time for that any more. You talk about it. Sometimes you do have a set sketch of some sort, but it's just for scenes. It has nothing to do with the frame. After all, a movie is what you see on each frame, the composition, and what effect you are getting. That is part of the art of movies. I don't think it's done at all now from a designer's approach. I really think that it's an accidental thing. What you do is be sure that everything looks the way it should so whatever the camera does, the background and the atmosphere are going to be right—with a good cinematographer and director.

It could be planned and thought out in more detail.

Yes, but that would take another four weeks of preproduction and would cost another fifteen or twenty thousand dollars which they don't want to spend. They have a budget and a shooting schedule and they really mean to stick to it. Some go over it, of course, but that depends on the director and his relationship with the producer. Directors want as much as you can give them. They're very cooperative. It's the system and the set-up now. No one has any time. The clock is ticking, and every time the clock ticks ten minutes, it's five thousand dollars, so you're fighting the clock.

Do you have assistants?

Yes, you have assistants, one or two— one mostly. And you work with all of them—the builders, the painters, the same as in television and the theatre. There are drawings to build by, and you are there on the scene seeing that everything is done.

When you designed the television specials All the Way Home *and* Harvey *and* Look Homeward, Angel, *how long did you spend on each?*

Oh, about seven to eight weeks.

Would you consider working on them similar to designing in movies?

Yes, but the shooting and camera work on them is quite different. Movies use one camera. Oh, there are occasions when they throw in several cameras for a scene. If there is a car burning up or something expensive, they put several cameras on so they are sure they will not have to retake it, because it's terribly expensive. But for just the average shot, they do a set-up and relight each set-up. Therefore, it's much more painstaking. Television cannot do that. They do it to a certain extent, but it has to be done very quickly—the relighting—and they use at least three cameras—ready, moving, cutting. In other words, they do not usually do the set-ups as in a movie. They don't move that one camera to another shot and then take scene after scene after scene. In movies, they do only two pages of the script or four pages at the most a day. With all those cameras in television, they generally do

Stage design by Ben Edwards
THE WALTZ OF THE
TOREADORS by Jean Anouilh

Directed by Harold Clurman
Coronet Theatre, New York (1957)

Setting by Ben Edwards
PURLIE
Book by Ossie Davis, Philip Rose,
    and Peter Udell
Based on the play PURLIE VICTORIOUS
    by Ossie Davis

Music by Gary Geld
Lyrics by Peter Udell
Directed by Philip Rose
Lighting by Thomas Skelton
Broadway Theatre, New York (1970)
(Photograph—Friedman-Abeles)

a third of a whole script in a day.

Do you enjoy working on one more than the other?

Well, I prefer movies only because I prefer their camera. There is a certain distortion in a television camera, however good. The movie camera is much sharper and the lighting is much more painstaking. You can imagine if you're lighting a scene and you've got cameras from three angles, the lighting has got to be much more general than for each movie set-up. That means, when you move that movie camera you relight, and it takes half an hour or an hour for each set-up. As I said, we only do two to four pages of a script a day. If you've ever looked at a script, that's not a lot of pages.

How far in advance do you start on a movie?

Well, it depends, two or three weeks, that's all. It's pretty much of a ratrace. I think years ago in Hollywood, they used to start months in advance and do all that business of models and everything else.

You have to be ready to find locations for exteriors or interiors.

They do a lot of location work, but you also have to work on those locations and quite often change things. On *Lovers and Other Strangers* and *The Last of the Red Hot Lovers*, I would say that eighty percent of both of those movies was done on sets in the studio and not on location. In *The Last of the Red Hot Lovers*, all the interiors were built in the studio except for a few shots in a couple of diners and some street scenes which we did on location. In *Lovers and Other Strangers*, we did the wedding scene in a ballroom out in a Tarrytown motel. But we changed the decoration and did that whole ballroom all over. It was a big square ugly room. We put in canopies, grillwork, tables, all kinds of things. It was a big overhaul job.

All we were doing, in a funny sense, was using the room as a studio. I've often wondered if we had been in a large Hollywood studio, if it wouldn't have been just as cheap to have built

the set. For a night scene, which we were shooting during the day, we had to put black tarpaulins thirty feet outside the windows so we could black it all out when we wanted to. And we put artificial trees outside with the real trees and landscaped them. It was a huge operation, not just going there and shooting on location at all. We did use the actual motel hallways in Tarrytown. We'd take a shot of actors walking into the room, the real room, we'd cut, and then the room was copied in a studio.

How did you happen to go into teaching scene design at Lester Polakov's School of Design and at New York University?

I was asked to do it, and I feel one should do those things. I've been doing it several years at Lester's, but I only do one or two courses there a year, like five weeks of critique. Sometimes I think of myself when I first came here at seventeen years of age—all of the excitement and staying up night after night in those summer theatres. I used to stay up three nights every week paint-

Stage design by Ben Edwards
PURLIE — Big Bethel, a country church in south Georgia
Book by Ozzie Davis, Philip Rose, and Peter Udell
Based on the play PURLIE VICTORIOUS by Ozzie Davis

Music by Gary Geld
Lyrics by Peter Udell
Directed by Philip Rose
Broadway Theatre, New York (1970)

ing, because I wanted the scenery to look right.

Is practical experience the best thing for students who are starting out in stage design?

Well, I couldn't completely say that. An educational background combined with a theatrical background, I think, would make it a little easier. But I think if you have talent, it "outs" no matter what you do or where you go. I really wish I had gone to Harvard, Yale, or Princeton. I would have liked to have been in Dr. Baker's class at Harvard and Yale. I suppose everyone would like to have lived through all the periods of history, to have been an apprentice to da Vinci or Michelangelo. That's what it all adds up to, doesn't it? I always feel that the problem with Scott Fitzgerald's writing is that he never made the football team at Princeton. I don't feel that I have any blight of that sort. But, I would have liked to have experienced it. I don't feel that I have missed anything by not going to the University of Alabama. But I wouldn't have minded going to one of the Ivy League schools at their very peak. I wouldn't particularly want to go to them now. I spent a lot of time

on the periphery of them when I first came here, and theirs was a very charming world.

Do you have any particular thoughts about the stage or designing in the theatre at the present?

Well, I don't think it's any different from what it has always been. The theatre is in a bit of a shaky position, but we'll come out of it. Designing is in a silly stage. I think it's faddist. I don't think we have very many good plays, so it is very hard today. In the shows you see, I don't feel any interpretation or analysis of the play. It's just people doing flashy things, and it all seems very glad and wonderful. But there's no real innovation. The scenery reminds me of everything I did in the Federal Theatre, or the theatre of Russia in the twenties and thirties. The whole recycling in the last ten or fifteen years — the Brechtian concept — was going on in the thirties. I don't find any difference.

What about the prospects for a young designer today?

It seems better than it ever was. There are not as many plays being done, and that's unfortunate. But I think a designer has a much fairer chance of getting a start than when I came along because

the whole trend today is youth. It wasn't then; it was very entrenched. Not intentionally so, but it was. Today everyone is hoping for something new. Everyone is looking for a gimmick, but I think their work is going to be pretty limited if they don't move on from what they are doing.

Is there a designer who has had a great influence on your own work in the theatre?

Robert Edmond Jones' *The Iceman Cometh* summed up what theatre design is all about. It stated in scenery the exact purpose of the play. It was one of the great sets. In the waterfront bar, he captured the atmosphere of a Third Avenue bar as seen by Eugene O'Neill. There were not even any bottles used except when they were pulled out from under the counter. The bottles were important only when the actor needed them. When the actor, Dudley Digges, moved through the room, you knew it was as O'Neill meant it to be. And that's what design is about — the set conveyed what O'Neill meant. You have to try for that. You have to have that same point of view. In musicals you also need that same point of view visually, even if the emphasis is on fun.

FIVE
Drawing the scenery

If you had the chance to visit a scenic studio during a busy period when a lot of drawings were being made, you would realize that a scenic artist must have a wide background in the techniques of drawing. Since theatre design covers such a large range of subjects, there are daily confrontations with all types of problems in both freehand and mechanical drawing. One assignment in freehand sketching can involve making such drawings as portraits, figures, foliage, landscapes, or classical ornament. Another job may require the use of mechanical drawing with tools in executing detailed architectural settings, including interior and exterior scenes. More often than not, the subject of a design calls for a combination of the freehand and the mechanical. In any case, the importance of doing good drawings can never be overemphasized, because no matter how well an object or design is painted, it will not look right unless the drawing is skillfully executed. In the scenic studio, drawing can be thought of in three general categories: as drawings for painting, as drawings for building, and as drawings for both building and painting.

As a well-rounded draftsman, the scenic artist must be exact in duplicating the drawings on the designer's drafting from $\frac{1}{2}$-inch scale (usually) to full scale on brown Kraft paper. When the scenic artist, for example, is called upon to make detailed drawings to show all the necessary information for building a three-dimensional object (trees, statues, curved stairways, etc.), the precise form of the object is represented by drawing two or more views, using the principles of orthographic projection. Views may include the plan (or sometimes top view), front elevation, side elevation, sections, and details. All drawings have appropriate dimensions and notes indicated for building and are perforated wherever necessary with a pounce wheel so the lines can be transferred to the surface by rubbing a bag of charcoal over the holes in the brown paper. Occasionally, an object is shown pictorially by making a simple isometric or oblique drawing to let the carpenters know what it will look like when the different views are assembled.

For a production where there is an unusually shaped prop (in plane or curved surfaces) that needs drawings for construction, the scenic artist must know how to find the true lengths of the lines that form the three-dimensional

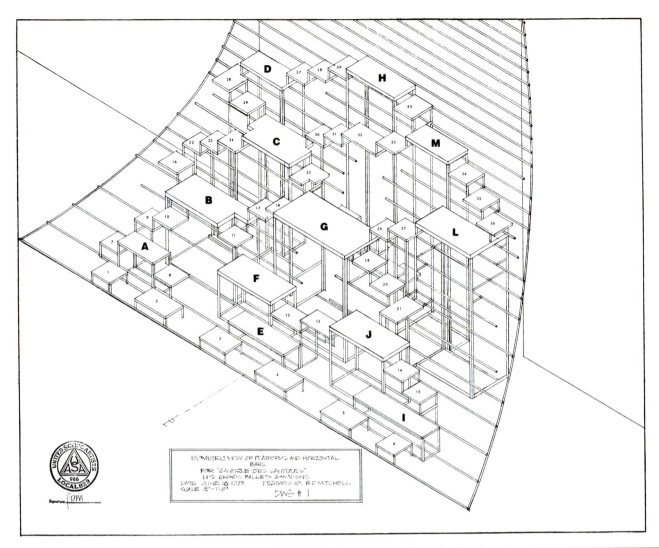

ISOMETRIC VIEW OF PLATFORMS AND HORIZONTAL
BARS
FOR "CANTIQUE DES CANTIQUES"
LES GRANDS BALLETS CANADIENS
DATE JUNE 18, 1973   DESIGNED BY R. D. MITCHELL
SCALE ½"=1'-0"
DWG # 1

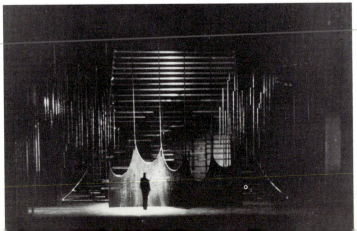

Isometric drawing and model scenery by Robert D. Mitchell
Ballet-oratorio CANTIQUE DES CANTIQUES
Choreographed by Fernand Nault
Les Grands Ballets Canadiens, Montreal (1974)
(Photographs—Robert D. Mitchell)

**DRAWING AN ISOMETRIC VIEW FOR CONSTRUCTING
SCENERY.** Mitchell's ½-in.-scale isometric view of platforms and
horizontal bars shows fronts, sides, and tops of platforms in one
view, simplifying any complexity resulting from looking at three
separate drawings. The unit was designed to symbolize a
mountain. The platform heights produced a crisscross pattern for
the movement of actors, singers, and dancers. DIMENSIONS:
proscenium opening—44 ft. wide by 24 high; curved horizontal
bar unit—38 ft. wide at base; highest platform approximately
17 ft. MATERIALS: horizontal bars 1-in.-diameter metal, painted
brass; top quarter of bars real brass; vertical platform supports
2-in.-square metal rods. Tops of platforms: expanded metal mesh
to allow lights to shine through.

Photographs of lighted model show platforms and horizontal bars
combined with hanging scenery units:

(Left) Vertical bars of 1½-in. O.D. brass pipe sleeves with
pipes inside form an irregular bottom. The sleeves hung stationary as a
group, but pipes inside moved when the unit was let in.

(Right) Large square unit of mirrors (26 by 26 ft.) behind mountain
was made of 2-by-2-ft. mirror squares, each tilted at an angle to the
large square.

(Bottom, left) Sculptured unit in front of mountain was a framework of
½- and ¾-in. O.D. steel on which assorted mirror shapes were attached.

(Bottom, right) Black translucent contoured China-silk curtain with
weights at bottom.

object and make development drawings to
show the precise layout of each surface. To
cite an example, when Willa Kim designed
Ontogeny for the American Ballet Theatre in
1970, she devised a large egglike prop in
which a dancer was supposed to stand. Designed to be just over six feet, the egg was to
be made so that it retained its natural form,
yet when a supporting cable at the top was
pulled it would collapse and could be pulled
upward as a tall narrow shape. The egg (a
little more than half round) was specified to be
made in seven petal-shaped vertical gores with
heavy piano wire serving as the curved supports on the edges of each gore. To create this
object in full scale, full-size drawings were
first made of the plan and elevation, then from
these two views points were figured and projected to form a third drawing which showed
the flat, stretched-out true shape of a single
gore. In turn, all of the gores of scrim were
cut from this pattern.

A working knowledge of all the rules of
perspective is also essential in scenic work,
including the commonly used linear types,
one-point perspective (also called parallel
perspective) and two-point perspective (angular perspective). Three-point perspective
(oblique perspective) is not frequently used.

If the scenic artist is laying out a drawing in
perspective from the designer's work (sketch
or drafting), an overlay of tracing paper is
usually put over it so the artist can determine
the vanishing points and draw all the lines
which come from them. Vanishing points in
the design may be located in several different
places. Once all of these have been plotted
on the overlay, it is gridded off in squares.
This insures more accuracy in laying out the
actual full-scale perspective of the design;
furthermore, there usually is not sufficient space
in the studio to measure and locate all of the
points with snaplines. By doing this first on
the tracing, the perspective lines can easily
be found by measuring from the grid lines.
When a perspective design is meant to be
drawn in a loose and casual line style, it is
much better to draw fairly accurate lines on
the pounce drawing (or directly on the surface
material) and then achieve the desired loose-
ness when doing the inking and the painting.

As far as perspective is concerned, an artist
will frequently draw (freehand or mechanically)
directly on a surface by judging the perspective lines by eye, according to the design. Such
drawings can be made for arches, valances,
window mullions, doors, or bookcase shelves
and can be drawn in charcoal on the wood
or plywood that has been allotted by the carpenters. This usually happens while the setting
is being assembled in the building process
and the drawing is done by this method because there is not time to do a full-scale perspective drawing on brown paper or because
the drawing is simple. It should also be mentioned that an interior box setting designed
to be in perspective normally has a horizon
line that is positioned 5½ feet above the floor,
the average height of a man's eye. This measurement is less, of course, for settings on a raked
stage.

Good material to study on perspective includes:
Bibiena, Giuseppe Galli. *Architectural and Per-
spective Designs.* New York: Dover Publications,
1964.
Brooks, Walter (ed.). *The Art of Perspective Drawing.*
The Grumbacher Library. New York: Western
Publishing Company, Inc., 1968.
de Vries, Jan Vredeman. *Perspective.* New York:
Dover Publications, 1968.
Norton, Dora Miriam. *Freehand Perspective.* New
York: Bell Publishing Company, 1970.
White, Gwen. *Perspective—A Guide for Artists,
Architects and Designers.* New York: Watson-
Guptill Publications, 1972.

Stage designs by Jo Mielziner
GUYS AND DOLLS – The Crap Game
Based on a story and characters by Damon
   Runyon
Book by Jo Swerling and Abe Burrows
Music and lyrics by Frank Loesser
Staged by George S. Kaufman
Forty-sixth Street Theatre, New York (1950)
(Photographs – Peter A. Juley and Son)

Perspective is evident in all three of Jo
Mielziner's sketches for GUYS AND DOLLS:
the sketch of the underground crap-game
scene, the translucent backdrop with
opaque painting on the back (second
sketch), and the framed hanger positioned
in front of the backdrop.

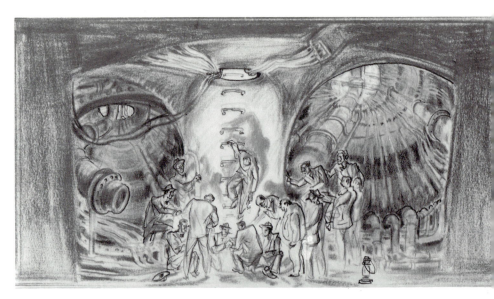

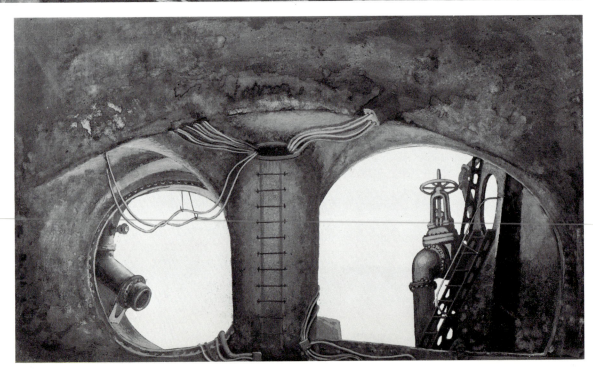

Stage design by Allen Charles Klein
MANON by Jules Massenet
Libretto by Henri Meilhac and Philippe Gille
Act IV, scene 2
Directed by Bliss Hebert
Kennedy Center, Washington, D.C. (1974)

Stage design by Lester Polakov
THE PURPLE DUST by Sean O'Casey
Directed by Philip Burton
Cherry Lane Theatre
New York (1956)
Scene: a Tudor mansion in Ireland. Note
illusion of depth gained by use of perspective.

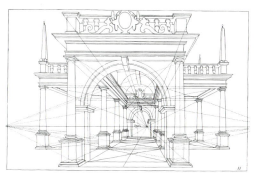

A perspective drawing of an
architectural setting illustrates the
use of three vanishing points.
From "Perspective" by Jan
Vredman de Vries, Dover
Publications, Inc., 1968.

PERSPECTIVE
DESIGNS

Comparative Greek and Roman Orders of Architecture

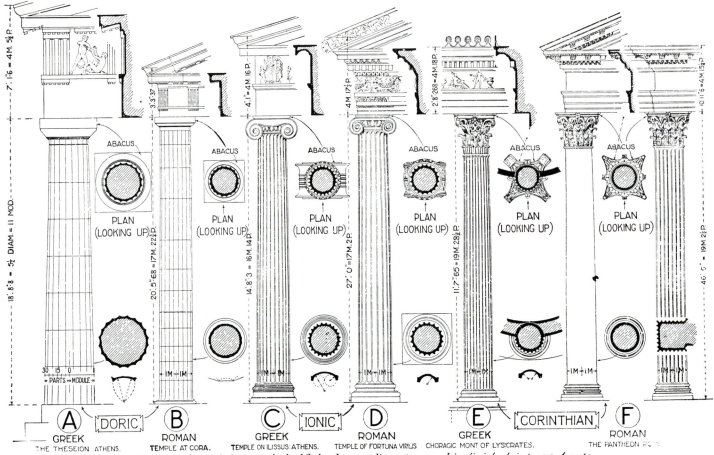

NOTE.— A module equals half the lower diameter and is divided into 30 parts

DRAWING AND PAINTING FLUTES ON A PILASTER AND A COLUMN. To create painted pilasters and columns with flutes, the drawing must be executed with special care. Particular attention should be given to proportions of moldings, flutes, and flat members of the pilaster. These samples, made by Fred Jacoby, were drawn and painted on brown Kraft paper which served as the base color for the painting. At left, the pilaster was painted with light coming from the left. Opaque colors were mixed for painting light, shade, and shadow. Proper application of these is what makes the pilaster look three-dimensional.

To draw the correct spacing of flutes in the column, a simple section (black line) drawing of half the diameter was made and the flutes projected vertically through these points to form the front elevation of the column. The light also comes from the left. Washes of aniline dye colors were brushed on the right and, to a lesser degree, on the left to make the column appear round.

Orders (above and opposite page) from A HISTORY OF ARCHITECTURE ON THE COMPARATIVE METHOD by Sir Banister Fletcher. 16th edition. Charles Scribner's Sons, 1954. By permission of the University of London.

Comparative Proportions of the Orders After Sir W. Chambers

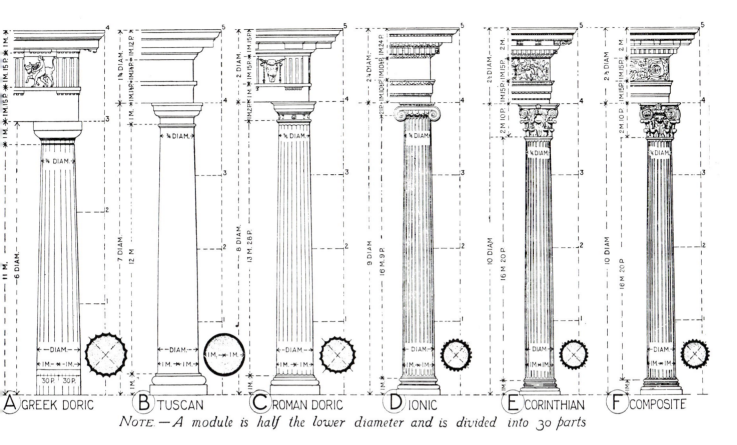

A GREEK DORIC B TUSCAN C ROMAN DORIC D IONIC E CORINTHIAN F COMPOSITE

NOTE.—*A module is half the lower diameter and is divided into 30 parts*

THE FIVE ORDERS OF ARCHITECTURE

Every theatre designer and scenic artist is expected to be familiar with the orders of architecture. Whether it be modern architecture or theatre architecture, interior designing or furniture designing, these orders have had a powerful influence down through the ages. The Roman architect and engineer Vitruvius, who lived in the first century B.C., set up specific standard proportions on the Greek orders, defining the Doric, Ionic, and Corinthian. His work *De Architectura*, available in ten volumes, is a detailed exposition on all types of Greek buildings. Much later on, the proportions of Vitruvius were revived by Giacomo Barocchio Vignola (1507–1573), the Italian architect, who included the Roman, Tuscan, and Composite. Vignola wrote *The Five Orders of Architecture*, which was used extensively during the Renaissance and afterward. For modern-day use, the orders of architecture are classified thus:

Three Greek	*Five Roman*	
Doric	Tuscan	Corinthian
Ionic	Doric	Composite
Corinthian	Ionic	

An order is made up of a column (base, shaft, and capital) and entablature (architrave, frieze, and cornice). Each order varies as to proportions, ornament, molding, and detail, with the capital of the column being the most characteristic feature in each one.

On this subject, these books are recommended:

Fletcher, Banister. *A History of Architecture on the Comparative Method.* New York: Charles Scribner's Sons, 1958.

Mansbridge, John. *Graphic History of Architecture.* New York: The Viking Press, 1967.

Robb, David, and J. J. Garrison. *Art In the Western World,* 3rd ed. New York: Harper and Row, Publishers, 1953.

CHECKLIST OF GENERAL DRAWING TECHNIQUES USED IN THE SCENIC STUDIO

Although it is almost impossible to compile a complete list of the numerous drawing techniques in scenic work, those below represent a general coverage of what the well-rounded scenic artist must be able to do, assuming that he already has a good basic background in the overall aspects of freehand, mechanical, and architectural drawing. Large-scale drawings

189

done in the scenic studio usually must be more exact than the designer's drafted drawings, and oversized mechanical tools are needed. In many cases, it should be remembered that those methods below concern not only drawing from flat straight-on views like plan, front elevation, side, top, and section, but also drawing from perspective sketches. The following are commonly used:

1. Drawing a circular arc tangent to two lines.
2. Constructing ellipses (by several methods), both freehand and mechanically.
3. Constructing hexagons, pentagons, and stars, first starting with circles.
4. Dividing a straight line in several equal parts by projecting an angled line (from one end) which has been marked off in equal measurements and then projecting parallel lines (starting by joining the two ends with a line) from the latter to the given line. Example: finding the equal spacings of treads on the plan of a stairway.
5. Developing the true-shape views of curved or unusually shaped surfaces.
6. Doing lettering of all types.
7. Drawing volutes for Ionic capitals on columns or for railings on the ends of stairways.
8. Making front elevations, section views, and perspective drawings of various classical moldings.
9. Making freehand drawings of animals, figures, and portraits.
10. Doing freehand drawings of trees, foliage, and ornament.
11. Drawing various kinds of arches.
12. Transferring a line of marked measurements proportionally to a smaller or larger line (area), as in drawing moldings in perspective.
13. Constructing real vanishing points for drawing architecture by using snaplines coming from an actual point, and also by simulating similar lines coming from an imaginary vanishing point when only a top and bottom line are given, whereby the angle between is divided into half to produce another line, and then the two halves are divided in half, and so on. This method is often used to simulate guidelines for believable stage-perspective drawings, since there is not always space enough in the scenic studio to have the actual vanishing points to work with.

DRAWING EQUIPMENT FOR LAYOUTS ON THE WORK TABLE

Basic drawing equipment and materials are needed for table work, and these items are for making small pounce drawings, squaring off sketches, drawing overlays, doing lettering on signs, and laying out patterns for stencils:

1. Roll of clear acetate, 2 ft. wide, for covering and protecting sketches, as well as marking off grids.
2. Ball-point pens for marking grids on the acetate.
3. Large clear plastic triangles, 30°–60° and 45°.
4. Writing pencils.
5. T-square, approximately 42" long.
6. Black and red wax marking pencils.
7. Steel straightedges, 3-ft. and 6-ft., for measuring (marking dimensions) and drawing.
8. Beveled wooden straightedges, 4 ft. and 6 ft. long, for drawing and for using as a guide when pricking straight lines.
9. Triangular architect's scale.
10. Metric scale.
11. Clear plastic protractor.
12. Compasses, small and large, approximately 6 in. and 2 ft. long.

BASIC GEOMETRICAL DRAWINGS COMMONLY USED IN THE SCENIC STUDIO (below)

DRAWING A REGULAR PENTAGON IN A CIRCLE
Drafting instruments or a plastic template can be used to draw a pentagon or hexagon on the drafting board, but such equipment is inadequate for large geometrical drawings.

Steps of Execution (first and second drawings):
1. Draw circle.
2. Draw diameter AB.
3. Draw perpendicular diameter CD.
4. Bisect EB to get midpoint F.
5. Using FC as radius, draw arc CG.
6. With C as center and CG as radius, draw arc through circle at H.
7. Straight line HC becomes one equal side of the pentagon.
8. Find the remaining four sides by marking off distance around the circle.

DRAWING A STAR IN A PENTAGON. A star made by drawing straight lines from the five points.

DRAWING A HEXAGON IN A CIRCLE. Using the circle with diameter AB and perpendicular diameter CD and the same radius, make arcs intersect the circumference. Join these points and the center points of the radius (AB) to make the hexagon.

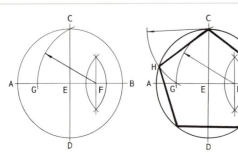
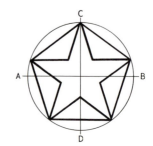
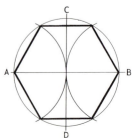

13. Large scissors.
14. Mat knife and X-Acto knives.
15. Single-edge razor blades.
16. Pounce wheels.
17. Velour-covered (face down) table for perforating pounces.
18. Charcoal sticks, regular and jumbo sizes.
19. Charcoal sharpener (medium grit sandpaper glued on an angle inside a cigar box).
20. Charcoal pounce bags for table use.
21. Clear Krylon spray fixative.
22. Brown Kraft paper, 3 ft. and 6 ft. wide, for making drawings and cutting patterns.
23. Roll of tracing paper, 42 in. wide, for overlays.
24. Masking tape, 1 in. and 2 in. wide.
25. Sheets of stencil paper.

into feet and inches), 6-, 8-, and 12-ft. lengths.
2. A 6-ft. right angle for drawing perpendiculars.
3. Large wooden compass, approximately 4 ft. long.
4. Bamboo drawing stick to hold sticks of charcoal or chalk.
5. Charcoal pounce bag with a long handle.
6. White sticks of chalk for dark surfaces.
7. Snaplines, 50- and 100-ft.
8. Linen string for drawing large circles and ellipses.
9. A length of $\frac{1}{16}$-in.-diameter aircraft cable (with a loop on one end to put on a driven nail) for drawing extremely large circles.
10. Heavy cotton or nylon thread (black and white) for squaring off backdrops.
11. Hammer, assorted nails, and tacks for holding threads and snaplines.
12. Weights (containers of unopened paint) to hold large pounces in place while in use.
13. Long thin laths, 12- to 16-ft., for drawing large curves.
14. A large piece of velour for perforating pounces on the floor.
15. Transfer screen for making repeats of a drawing.
16. Feather duster and flogger for dusting off charcoal and dirt.
17. Steel tapes, 50-ft. and 100-ft.
18. Brown Kraft paper, 3 ft. and 6 ft. wide, for drawing pounces.
19. Masking tape 1 in. and 2 in. wide.
20. Clear Krylon spray fixative.
21. Felt-tip pens.

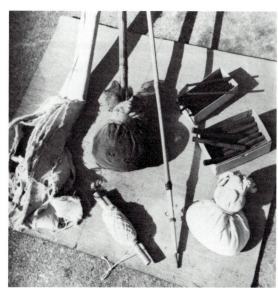

BASIC EQUIPMENT FOR DRAWING AND POUNCING (Clockwise from left): (1) Flogger made of canvas strips attached to a wooden handle. Used to beat dust and charcoal off surfaces. (2) Charcoal pounce bag on a bamboo handle. (3) Bamboo drawing stick. Charcoal stick in the split end is held with a heavy-duty rubber band. Bent wire inserted in the splits forces charcoal stick out as it is used. (4) Regular charcoal sticks. (5) Jumbo charcoal sticks. (6) White pounce bag. (7) 100-ft. snap line, rubbed with a stick of charcoal or chalk. (Photograph—Lynn Pecktal)

DRAWING EQUIPMENT FOR LAYOUTS ON THE FLOOR

Although some of these items are used for both table and floor work, additional equipment is necessary for floor layouts (freehand cartooning and mechanical drawing) on large pieces of scenery and for drawing big pounces which are large enough to cover full stage backdrops:

1. Straightedges with long handles (and divided

The Floor Straightedge with a Long Handle

The straightedge with a long handle is a device that is constantly needed for drawing and painting lines as well as for measuring while standing. It is very simple to construct. Made of lightweight seasoned wood, the straightedge is normally 1 by 4 inches in lengths of 6, 8, and 12 feet. The bottom edges are beveled to keep the paint from smudging and running under them; when you are painting lines, the straightedge should be tilted slightly also to help prevent this.

On the top surfaces of these straightedges, marks are made by lightly scoring the wood with a saw to denote specifically: each foot, each 6 inches, and, on either end, the first 12 inches. For clarity, it is very helpful if the 6-inch marks are scored with a broken line. To make these marks stand out more distinctively, straightedges are painted white or a very light color.

The long vertical handle, which is 3 feet 4 inches in length, is attached and centered on

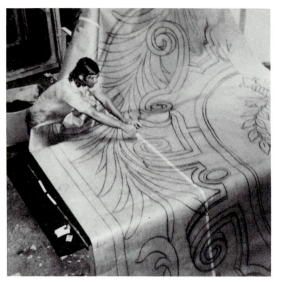

the straightedge so that the straightedge is balanced perfectly when it is lifted by the handle. To make the handle easy to manipulate, the end should be neatly rounded off with a plane, then sanded. Sometimes the handle (at the bottom) is constructed with a hinge at the bottom to allow it to fold parallel with the edge for traveling. A light sanding is occasionally necessary to remove the dried and caked paint from the edges of the straightedge.

The Lightweight Wooden Hand Straightedge

One of the best kinds of wood to use for making a hand straightedge is seasoned Philippine wood. This lightweight wood makes it easy to hold in the hand while working, and it also retains its shape well. Used primarily for lining with a brush, the straightedge is also needed for table work when straight lines are to be laid out on a drawing. Standard sizes for scenic work are: 3 inches wide by 4 feet or 6 feet long by $\frac{5}{16}$ inch thick. This straightedge is also beveled on each side (and sanded) to keep the paint from running under it and to make the brush move easily while it is guided along the edge. A hole should be made in one end of the straightedge so that it can be hung vertically in storage to keep it from warping.

Charcoal

Charcoal is an indispensable material for producing drawings and sketches on numerous surfaces. One of its main assets is that it can be easily dusted off. For drawing, charcoal sticks can be held by hand or in a bamboo drawing stick. They are used with regularity for drawing on paper pounces, backdrops, wings, ground cloths, and wooden set pieces, as well as for marking measurements and for rubbing on snaplines to create straight lines. Charcoal lines should not be snapped on unstarched muslin intended for translucencies as they do not always dust out. (If lines are needed in a translucency, it is best to stretch heavy cotton or nylon thread over the stretched-out fabric and attach them with carpet tacks.) For scenic work, two sizes of charcoal are ordinarily used. Made by M. Grumbacher, Inc., these are: Regular ($\frac{1}{4}$ inch diameter by 6 inches long) with fifty sticks to a box, and Jumbo ($\frac{1}{2}$ inch diameter by 6 inches long) with twenty-five sticks in a box. Powered charcoal is also a standard item in the studio. It is purchased by

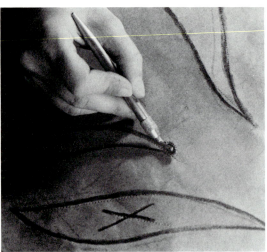

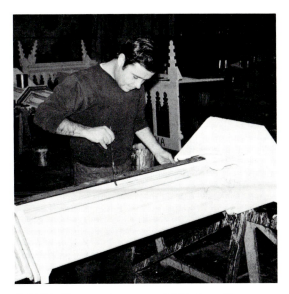

(Left) Working on velour-covered table top with nap face down, scenic artist Ken Calender with a pounce wheel perforates a charcoal drawing on brown paper for Carl Toms' scrim panel for the New York City Opera's I PURITANI (1973).

A close-up of a pounce wheel showing the perforations made in brown Kraft paper by pushing it over the drawn charcoal designs. (Photograph — Kenneth Pew)

(Third) Charcoal bag rubbed over perforated holes in brown-paper pounce to transfer drawing to canvas for painting. Unopened gallon paint cans are placed on corners of pounce to keep it from moving.

(Fourth) Scenic artists Ken Calender and Ben Kasazkow use straightedges to paint straight lines while touching up Donald Oenslager's scenery for THE MIKADO (1959) at the New York City Opera.

(Above) Robert Motley paints thin lines on Ming Cho Lee's set piece for MARIA STUARDA (1972) at the New York City Opera by stroking a lining brush against a hand straightedge.
(Photographs — Lynn Pecktal)

the pound, and its sole use is to make pounce bags, which are rubbed over the surface of a perforated drawing to transfer designs and patterns.

Like a pencil, a charcoal stick needs to be sharpened often when you are drawing with it, and this is done by shaping the end of the stick like a flat chisel. A handy charcoal sharpener that is easy to construct can be made out of a cigar box. A sheet of sandpaper is glued to the top of the box, and the front of the lid is merely pushed down into the box, positioning the sandpapered surface at an angle. Then as the charcoal sticks are sharpened, the excess charcoal is collected in the box, and it is later used as extra charcoal for filling pounce bags. Or you can make another kind of charcoal sharpener by removing the lid of the cigar box and stretching and attaching a piece of screen wire across the top.

White Chalk

Although white-chalk sticks are needed less frequently than charcoal, they nevertheless are staple items for drawing and rubbing on the snaplines that are going to be put on dark surfaces. These chalk sticks are the same as those used in schools, and come packaged in boxes containing 144 sticks. Colored chalk is occasionally utilized to define more clearly and separate lines of drawings that might be overlapping each other on a full-scale elevation or plan.

The Bamboo Drawing Stick

To make it unnecessary to bend over while drawing on the floor, a long lightweight bamboo stick is used as a standard holder for the sticks of charcoal. The typical bamboo stick is about 3 feet long. However, in order to produce better control in both drawing and painting, many scenic artists prefer being able to hold the very end of the bamboo handle when they are working. The length of the stick, of course, varies with the height of the person, and for that reason, bamboo sticks are frequently cut to size for each individual. The diameter of the bamboo stick is selected according to the size of the charcoal being used, and the charcoal may be either $\frac{1}{2}$ inch or $\frac{1}{4}$ inch in diameter. The bamboo is hollowed out on one end, then splits are made in it by sawing, which allows the end to open slightly so the charcoal stick can be easily inserted. By sawing parallel to the length of the bamboo, at least four splits 5 inches long should be put in the end to accommodate a 6-inch charcoal stick. A heavy-duty rubber band is then wrapped around the end of the split bamboo to hold the charcoal securely. A piece of heavy wire is quite helpful to force the charcoal through the stick as it is being used. The wire can be bent in an S shape and inserted through two opposite splits in the bamboo before the charcoal is put in. Several different sizes of bamboo sticks are used to hold the brushes while painting, and many of these are attached firmly with masking tape for work in the scenic studio.

The Snapline

A snapline, also called a chalkline, is one of the most effective ways to obtain a straight line with accuracy and speed. It is made of a twisted cotton cord that is usually white. Average lengths of snaplines are 50 and 100

DRAWING FULL-SCALE ORNAMENT AND MOLDING ON BROWN KRAFT PAPER. Classical ornament and molding were drawn full-scale on brown Kraft paper to make these presentation drawings for an architectural setting. The objects were highlighted with sticks of white chalk and shaded with sticks of charcoal to give a three-dimensional appearance. In the first photograph, notice the side view of the lion's head and the ornament, and the sections of moldings which indicate thicknesses of materials for building.

feet. A snapline is stored by winding it criss-cross around a wooden stick in a manner similar to winding up string on a kite. On the loose end of the line, a 3-inch loop is tied so two fingers can hold it when it is in use.

The line is normally snapped by two artists. With both beginning on the same end, one person holds the loop as the other stretches it taut and rubs the desired length of line consistently and generously with a stick of charcoal or chalk. Both artists should wrap the ends of the line around their fingers a couple of times to ensure a firm hold. When ready, the line is held on the two desired marks, stretched tightly, and one person reaches out, picks the line up, and snaps it. For snapping very long lines such as those for gridding off a backdrop on the floor, a third person may snap the line from the middle to give a more distinctive line on the surface. (This is especially necessary if the floor is uneven.) Sometimes this third person also snaps it from the middle by placing his foot on the taut line and then snapping each half separately. A carpenter's snapline (in a case) is not used, for practical reasons: It requires a great deal more time to rewind in the case when it is to be replenished, and it takes even longer for snapping a number of lines at once. Also, you do not obtain the same kind of consistency by using it as you do when the charcoal stick or chalk stick is hand-rubbed on the line.

There are various other ways in which one person alone can snap lines on horizontal surfaces. The opposite end of a line can be anchored by placing a 2-pound weight on it or by putting the loop around a nail driven into the floor. Both of these methods also work nicely when you are establishing the vanishing points on large perspective layouts or when you are drawing big circles, arcs, or ellipses. For doing similar work on the paint frame, a safety pin is a good device to fasten to the end loop for holding the opposite end on the fabric.

Although they are not currently used much in the scenic studio, a bow snapline and a pole snapline are other useful devices when one person is working alone and needs to snap shorter lines on vertical or horizontal surfaces. Both of these implements are made of wood and each has a snapline stretched and fastened to its extreme ends. Lengths for the bow and pole can be anywhere from 6 to 10 feet. The shape of the bow is very much like one used in archery. The pole is a flat piece of wood with two 1-foot extensions of wood fastened perpendicularly to the pole on each end. Basically, it is constructed like a jog with one stile removed, whereby the snapline takes the place of the stile.

Pounce Wheels

The pounce wheel is a most essential item whenever a pounce drawing on brown paper is to be perforated. This small pricking wheel is run over the lines of the design, leaving small holes so the drawing can be transferred onto a surface (fabric, wood, or whatever) by rubbing a bag of powdered charcoal over the paper. These little metal wheels are made in different sizes with metal or wooden handles and they are selected according to the intricacy or simplicity of the drawing. The smallest-size wheel, for instance, is ideal for pricking minute ornament detail. Often the wheel is guided along a metal or wooden straightedge, especially when very straight lines are required in architectural drawings or on large lettering pounces. Whenever you are pricking, the pressure of the hand on the pounce wheel should always be controlled. If too much pressure is applied while perforating the paper, tearing will result, and if the wheel is pressed down too lightly, the pricking will not be successful for transferring the designs.

As a work area, a tabletop covered with a piece of velour placed face down is best for pricking the paper pounce. A sheet of 4-by-8-foot plywood ($\frac{3}{4}$ inch thick) laid on two folding work horses is good to use for a table, because it can be easily stored after use.

Swivel-type pounce wheels with aluminum handles can be purchased in various sizes. The following are stocked by Flax Art Stores (Chicago, New York, Los Angeles, San Francisco):

No. 9: $\frac{1}{4}$-in. dia.—21 teeth per in.
No. 10: $\frac{1}{4}$-in. dia.—15 teeth per in.
No. 11: $\frac{5}{16}$-in. dia.—15 teeth per in. (beveled on one side to follow lines more easily)
No. 12: $\frac{7}{16}$-in. dia.—15 teeth per in.
No. 50: 1-in. dia.—15 teeth per in.

Stock Paper Products

Brown Kraft paper. Widths of 3- and 6-foot brown paper are standard sizes for studio work. These come on a large roll and are maintained on a horizontal metal rack which is moved on casters. Used chiefly for the drawing of all kinds of pounces, the brown paper is also used for keeping scenery clean, for wrapping drops and other scenery, and for mixing paint which is taken from the palette of containers with a brush and put directly on paper when laid on the floor.

Gray bogus paper. This large roll of heavy-weight paper comes 58 inches wide, and it too is kept on a similar metal rack. An indispensable product, gray paper is put down on the floor under backdrops and scrims to absorb the water when painting and to form a smooth working surface. It is very effective as a masking paper, and is also used for wrapping and packing scenery.

Wax paper. A white wax paper which is made in a 48-inch-wide roll is laid under scrims and openwork scenery to keep them from sticking to the floor when applying latex mixtures, or when using glues or the like. It is sometimes needed for tracing off designs with a grease pencil and for masking.

Stencil paper. Heavy oiled stencil paper is manufactured in 3- and 4-foot-wide rolls, and also in oiled sheets 18 by 24 and 24 by 36 inches.

Tracing paper. Standard tracing paper is generally necessary for transferring small designs and for doing overlay drawings on drafting or sketches. Common sizes for scenic work are 36-inch and 42-inch rolls.

DRAWING A FULL-SCALE DETAILED POUNCE ON BROWN PAPER. Drawing with a stick of charcoal on brown Kraft paper that has been marked off in 1-ft. squares, scenic artist Ethel Green duplicates a majestic lion in full scale from Carl Toms' ½-in.-scale paint elevation for I PURITANI (1973) at the New York City Opera. (Photograph—Lynn Pecktal)

With the designer's sketch nearby, scenic artist Paul Goranson draws a figure to go on Marc Chagall's backdrop for the New York City Ballet's THE FIREBIRD (1969). (Photograph—Arnold Abramson)

DRAWING AND USING A POUNCE

For many years, scenic artists have used the method of drawing a pounce to reproduce a full-scale drawing of the designer's sketch. Although the most common scale for the designer's sketch is $\frac{1}{2}$ inch = 1 foot, it can also be $\frac{1}{4}$-inch, $\frac{3}{4}$-inch, 1-inch, or any number of scales. The actual sizes and the uses of the pounce can vary just as much. The pounce may be as large as a full-stage backdrop or scrim, or it can be a small one just for an individual piece of ornament. Paper pounces are needed for making repeats of patterns, or they may serve as a "one-shot deal." They may

Stage designs by Nicola Benois
TCHAIKOVSKY'S SUITE NO. 3
Choreographed by George Balanchine

New York City Ballet
New York State Theatre, Lincoln Center (1970)
(Photographs — Arnold Abramson)

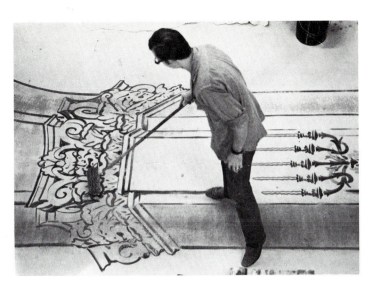

FULL-SCALE POUNCE DRAWINGS. Full-scale charcoal drawings on brown Kraft paper is standard preparation for detailed drawing on scenery. The photographs illustrate how scenic artists draw and enlarge ornament from the designer's sketches.

Opposite page (top left) This ballroom setting consisted of linen cut leg drops and cut backdrops, designed to hang as soft units without framing; architectural ornament, moldings, draperies, and wall sconces painted on flat surfaces; only the chandeliers (flat profiles) were framed and supported by wood.

(Top right) Designer's detailed sketch of a composition capital for the pilasters, executed with charcoal and gold paint on tracing paper.

(Center, left) The full-scale drawing of capitals for a group of pilasters in perspective for stage left, reversed and repeated for stage right, made after covering sketch with a grid of squares on clear acetate, with comparable squares in full scale snapped in charcoal on brown paper. Each form of ornament, molding, and flat members of pilasters drawn was outlined with a neat single line to precisely define each form. Every line of finished drawing was perforated with a pounce wheel to transfer design to the linen surface.

(Center, right) Final lines drawn on a wall-sconce pounce after

lightly sketching its shape. At left, under charcoal bag, is a perforated pounce drawing on tracing paper of a single candle and holder, used for repeats. At right is sketch of sconce.

(Bottom) Close-ups of inked capitals of the pilasters. Inking is usually done to save the drawing when designs are overpainted, but in this case it functioned as part of the complete work and was applied after the linen was laid in with the base color. The quality of the painted lines was varied by solid and broken lines, increasing and decreasing widths of the brush strokes, lightening the original sepia inking color (caseins and aniline dyes) with water, and dry brushing.

ABOVE (top left) Textured patterns of semitransparent colors were put on by pushing a thick paint roller over inked pilasters.

(Top right) The same treatment of drawing, inking, and painting was followed on other architectural elements at top of cut drop.

(Above left) Designer's detailed sketch of ornamental panel.

(Center) Brown-paper pounce of panel. Guidelines for molding were laid out first, then ornamentation was drawn with charcoal.

(Right) Panel (in reverse) after linen drop was basecoated, perforated drawing of panel pounced on drop with charcoal, charcoal design inked, and background of inner center panel partially painted. (Scenery drawn and painted by John Keck)

be made for painting, for building, or for both.

A short cut can be taken when working on a design that is symmetrical, for you only need to fold a piece of paper and draw half of the pounce. Then, when it is perforated with the pounce wheel, the tiny spikes go through both layers of paper. But a pounce drawing obviously is not necessary for every piece of scenery, and this is determined by the type of design and the methods of execution. Drawing or "cartooning" is often done on the scenery itself.

Squaring off the Sketch

The first thing to do when you are drawing a pounce is to cover the designer's color sketch (elevation) with a sheet of clear acetate to protect it from paint and dirt and to draw grid lines on it with a grease pencil (china marker) or ball-point pen. Then, to find the vertical center, the bottom of the sketch should be very carefully measured, divided accurately in half, and marked. On this mark, place a triangle and draw the vertical center line perpendicular to the bottom. This line should then be labeled with a large CL so that it is easily identified.

In reproducing the design to full scale, the sketch is divided into a series of squares to provide a grid to work from. Once the center line is constructed, vertical parallel lines are drawn left and right of the center line, and horizontal parallel lines are made, always working from the bottom of the sketch to the top. The vertical lines are numbered, beginning from the center line (CL) and going to the left (1, 2, 3, 4, and so on), and from the center line to the right (1, 2, 3, 4, and so on). The horizontal lines are numbered from the bottom line, which is zero, then 1, 2, 3, 4, etc.

The size of the squares, of course, is determined by the complexity of the sketch. One- and 2-foot squares are best for drawings that are very detailed in design, like architecture and ornament. For foliage drops, ground cloths, and the like, 3- and 4-foot squares are used, and even 6-foot squares are sometimes laid out for drawing clouds on a sky drop. Not every drawing has to be squared off for drawing a pounce. A very small and simple design may require no more than the center line, the width measurement, and the height measurement.

For drawings requiring a larger size of brown paper than the standard 3-foot or 6-foot widths, strips of these are fastened together with masking tape. If the design happens to be for a typical backdrop in a Broadway production, it can be around 28 feet high by 48 feet wide, and for this pounce the necessary strips of brown paper are measured off and cut from the roll. Then, when they are accurately laid out on the floor, they are taped together temporarily to hold the paper together while drawing, and the small pieces of tape are later cut for easier handling when the pounce is being perforated.

The same method is used for squaring off the full-size paper as it is for the squaring off of the sketch. Using the 6-foot right angle (framing square), a line is constructed perpendicular to one of the outside edges of the paper for the bottom (or side) line. From this line, measure and mark off the grid lines on all four sides with a straightedge. A snapline (with charcoal) is used to make the grid lines through these marks (as mentioned, when you are snapping lines, more accuracy and speed can be obtained when two persons on either side of the snapline hold it tightly and a third person lifts up the line and snaps it from the center).

Perforating the Paper with the Pounce Wheel

After the charcoal drawing of the pounce has been completed, it is ready to be perforated with a pounce wheel. So that the scenic artist does not have to struggle with this very sizable piece of paper, the masking tape holding it together is cut and the individual strips are rolled up, and then each is pricked separately on the velour-covered pounce table. This method is not always used for pricking such a large pounce, however. When a real rush is on in the studio, the strips of paper are attached with long continuous pieces of masking tape and the pounce is laid out on top of a stock velour backdrop (already stretched out on the floor) so that several artists can work rapidly and prick the drawing at one time.

Sanding the Holes on the Back

As soon as the perforations with the pounce wheel have been finished, the paper (in strips or in one big piece) can be turned over and rubbed lightly with a piece of medium-grade sandpaper to make certain that all the holes are fully opened. This allows the powdered charcoal always to come through the holes when it is pounced on the actual scenery. If you are working with strips, they should be reassembled in their appropriate sequence and held together with long pieces of tape, so the charcoal dusting does not leave an unwanted straight line of charcoal on the fabric when the pounce is being used.

Making the Charcoal Pounce Bag

The charcoal pounce bag, which is rubbed over the holes of the pounce to transfer the lines of the design to the scenery, is made up in the scenic studio. It is created by beginning with about twelve 16-inch squares of cheesecloth that are neatly stacked in layers and by then pouring $\frac{1}{2}$ pound of powdered charcoal into the center of the squares. Once this is done, the four corners are picked up and held securely while they are bound and wrapped tightly together with masking tape. If a long handle is needed (to use when standing), it is inserted just before the taping, then it is all securely fastened. A white pounce bag can be made of dry whiting in the same manner for applying lines on dark scenery.

Preserving Charcoal Lines

Depending on the design, lines pounced in charcoal are not always inked, and to keep them from rubbing off while work is being done, they are sprayed with a fixative. Any excess charcoal should be lightly dusted off with a feather duster or flogger before the fixative is applied. Crystal-clear acrylic (Krylon and Plastiklear) that comes in spray cans is good for holding charcoal lines on paper pounces and also on surfaces (whenever applicable) that are to be painted. This spray fixative is frequently put on all kinds of paper pounces, including lettering, portraits, or architecture. For large areas of fabric that are sketched in charcoal but do not get inked (like foliage drawn on a backdrop or stonework on a ground cloth), a fixative of glue size, using the proportions of one part priming size to four parts water, can be sprayed over it lightly with a Hudson spray tank.

Inking the Lines

Inking the lines retains the pounced (or drawn) charcoal lines, and the kind of paint and color selected for this is determined by the particular design. The inking is ordinarily applied with a small lining brush dipped in colors of aniline dye, casein, vinyl, or latex. Felt-tip pens are much used for inking, because they bleed through when water-base colors are laid in over them, as do aniline dyes that are mixed in thin clear shellac (thinned with alcohol).

199

A perforated pounce drawing is often repeated on the same piece of scenery. On Lloyd Evans' backdrop for the opera SUMMER AND SMOKE (1972), a brown-paper pounce (same dimensions as backdrop) was made and design transferred on a muslin drop by rubbing a bag of powdered charcoal over perforated holes.

To save time, the dark lay-in color was brushed on the whole area to be opaqued, instead of cutting around the inner details. When this had dried, the drawing of architecture was repounced with bag of white-powdered chalk. Later, the windowpanes were cut out and a large piece of linen scrim glued behind windows. Sky was translucent. (Photograph — Arnold Abramson)

DRAWING WITH ANILINE DYE

After sketching a drawing lightly with charcoal on brown paper, aniline dye (put on with a lining brush) is very good for drawing a more definite and improved line. The outer edges of this painted line are then usually perforated with the pounce wheel. The dye itself is used

DRAWING AN ORNAMENT POUNCE ON BROWN PAPER WITH ANILINE DYE. These ornament patterns were made for David Mitchell's scrim backdrop in BORIS GODUNOV (1974), Cincinnati Summer Opera and the Canadian Opera. Patterns were painted with aniline dye without binder on brown paper after preliminary drawing had been done with charcoal, using a grid of 1-ft. squares. Besides achieving smooth-flowing strokes with a brush on brown paper, another advantage was that the ornament's two outside lines could be made at one time. The ornament pounce was perforated and the patterns were transferred to the scrim surface. (Photograph — Lynn Pecktal)

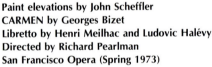

Paint elevations by John Scheffler
CARMEN by Georges Bizet
Libretto by Henri Meilhac and Ludovic Halévy
Directed by Richard Pearlman
San Francisco Opera (Spring 1973)

Panels and ceiling pieces for Acts I and II. Scheffler's

linear designs were drawn with pen and ink. (Ink was purchased by the gallon.) Designs, drawn with large magic markers with tips 1-in. and ¾-in. wide, were reproduced on framed primed canvas panels. Panels hung in front of a burlap background, suspended by ⅛-in. airplane cables. Some panels had ceiling pieces angled forward.

without a binder to avoid wrinkling the paper when it dries.

Drawing details of a pounce with dye is often done for objects like window mullions, elaborate iron grillwork, period chandeliers, and wall sconces. By using this method, only skeleton outlines and rough sketching need to be made, because the final lines (two outside edges) are painted with aniline dye by a single stroke-width of the brush. Lining brushes for this vary in size from ½ inch to 2 inches. Both wood and iron construction may be built on top of this actual dye drawing, or it can be perforated and used for repeats in both painting and building as needed.

This technique of drawing with the brush is also most useful if you are cartooning the profile edges on foliage borders and for profile pieces that are in the process of being built. In these cases, a dye or opaque color (in sharp

contrast to the final painting or surface material) is used for drawing the profile directly on the wing or the wood, and it is a general rule for the carpenters to cut away all of the material on the outer side of this inked (or painted) line, including the line itself.

DRAWING FREEHAND CURVES WITH THIN LATHS OR CHAINS

If very large curves and ovals are to be drawn in full scale, they are not always constructed mechanically. Sufficient floor space, large instruments, and all the time it takes to figure such dimensions are not always available. But there are two techniques which are most helpful in drawing a "full" large curve or oval. Both are used after the points of intersection for the curve have been obtained. They can be achieved by scaling the measurements from the drafting and transferring them to the full-scale surface, or by working from an overlay of gridded squares. In either, all such points should be clearly marked with an X.

The first and most often-used method is bending a long flexible lath to pass through or over these marked points of intersection, and this wooden lath is generally $\frac{1}{4}$ inch by 1 inch wide and from 12 to 16 feet long. Placement and bending of the lath to make it pass through each point is much easier and faster if two people work together, because both can hold and deposit weights on it at the same time. Unopened one-quart cans of paint, which are usually plentiful in the studio, work very well for weights.

The curved lath should always flow freely and not have awkward or wavy bends in the curving. Once the lath is set to your satisfaction, take a drawing stick with charcoal in it and draw along the curved lath. The process of the lath serving as a drawing guide is similar to using an adjustable curve ruler in drafting. You may find that some of the marked points will have to be altered slightly, but it is much better to have a "full" curve than to follow each mark religiously.

Drawing with the chain, the second method, applies to a much greater curve. It may be for making a large oval for a cut drop or drawing massive drapery swags for a show curtain. As a drawing guide, a long piece of link chain works beautifully. While the chain may be any length, it should be at least 30 feet or so long. This method requires two people, and it is also used after the points of intersection (X marks) have been made on the drawing surface.

To set the chain in place for a large oval, first stretch it out on the floor. A person on one end should remain stationary throughout and tightly hold that end of the chain on the floor. The person on the opposite end should lift his end up in the air while pulling slowly to make it taut, and then he should let the chain come down carefully into place at the stationary end. As this is being done, the chain is slowly swung in the direction of the marked points until it hits on each marked X. When it is all set, take a bamboo drawing stick with charcoal in it and draw the oval lightly, making sure the chain does not move. If you are working vertically on a paint frame, long lengths of hemp or other rope can be used in the same way when large full curves are needed for drawing enormous sweeps of drapery. In this case, the rope can be nailed

on each end so it hangs naturally in the desired shape.

THE TRANSFER SCREEN

If a large design is drawn out on a piece of scenery (either backdrop or framed unit) and is to be repeated, a transfer screen works well. Constructed like an ordinary flat, the framing of the transfer screen is about 6 by 6 feet overall and it has linen scrim tacked and glued on the face. A standard device in the scenic studio, the screen is stored so that it does not get torn.

When using the transfer screen, lay the flat side (with the scrim) on top of the design to be repeated. The design can be easily seen through the open fabric. Then, working on the scrim, take a stick of charcoal and trace over the lines of the design to be copied. The charcoal lines will remain on the scrim. When you have finished, lift the screen and place it on the new area where it is to be repeated. Again, draw over the same lines on the linen scrim with the charcoal, and the charcoal will go through the fabric onto the new surface. A transfer screen also serves well when quite a few repeats are to be made, as the original lines will stay on the linen until they are dusted off.

For a single repeat, another method of using the screen is to take a corn broom and sweep over the lines which have been traced on the scrim, thereby transferring the lines onto a new

USING THE TRANSFER SCREEN. Linen scrim attached to a wooden frame, is a great time-saving device for tracing large designs to be repeated. Lloyd Evans' inked designs on canvas border for L'INCORONAZIONE DI POPPEA (1973). Transfer screen is laid on work to be repeated and traced over with charcoal, which remains on the linen scrim. Screen is then laid in position (here, turned over and reversed) and drawing is transferred through onto the fabric by drawing with charcoal on the same outlines. Drawn designs on linen scrim can also be transferred by brushing scrim with a corn broom. (Photograph – Lynn Pecktal)

surface. At the same time, the screen may be reversed when it is repeated. If you are copying a much larger design than will fit on the screen, the design can be transferred by dividing it into sections and then doing them one by one.

LETTERING

Hardly a show comes along without having some kind of lettering in it, whether for hand props, set dressing, or the scenery proper. Both the designer and the scenic artist are expected to have a reasonable knowledge of lettering and how it is created. While the scenic artist may not have to perform with the skill and speed of a professional letterer, his work should appear as if it has been done by one.

Lettering research is invaluable to either the artist or designer, and both rely upon it when drawing and painting lettering, except for the most familiar kind. Since there are so many styles of lettering, it would be difficult to retain all the details of each type face that is inevitably used in theatre design. Many designers have books on lettering and leaf through them when selecting types of printing for a show. On his design elevation, a designer may specify the type and color of lettering by notation or by rendering two or three letters as an example, whereas others do it in complete detail. Sometimes the copy for lettering is put on the drafting with a note for coloring. And although the layout may seem to be correct when it is drawn in the small size of ½-inch scale, it often has to be adjusted when it is blown up to full scale. Any designer knows this and expects the scenic artist to make the lettering look professional, but one should always realize that good lettering requires time, since it must be laid out mechanically and must be neat and exact.

In doing good lettering, it is necessary to have a knowledge of the shapes and proportions, the order and direction of the strokes, and the spacing (composition). And, of course, it is essential that uniformity be maintained.

Shaping Letters

Single-stroke vertical lettering (roman) and single-stroke inclined lettering (italic) are two basic types of lettering. When shaping letters, it is standard to make the upper part of some letters (and numbers) slightly smaller than the lower part, so they do not appear topheavy. These are: B, E, F, H, K, S, X, and Z as well as the numbers 2, 3, and 8. In B, E, F, and H the

MODERN ROMAN LETTERS*

center horizontal stroke is *raised* a bit above center. For K, S, X, and Z (and 2, 3, 8), the width of the upper part is *reduced* slightly. The vertical or inclined strokes are always made from the top to the bottom and the horizontal strokes from the left to the right.

Proportions

Like so many aspects of lettering, proportions are judged a great deal by the "trained eye," which comes with practice and experience. This can mean how one part of a letter is proportioned to another part of the same letter. One may say, "On that letter, the bottom is out of proportion with the top." Or it can also mean how the proportion of one letter relates to the proportions of another letter.

The proportion and shapes of lettering naturally vary with the layout. While the standard way of laying out letters is termed normal, letters may be compressed (decreasing the widths) or extended (increasing the widths). This is done correspondingly on the spaces between the lettering. When *large capitals* are

* Warren J. Luzadder, *Fundamentals of ENGINEERING DRAWING*, rev. ed. © 1946. Reprinted by permission of Prentice-Hall, Inc. Englewood Cliffs, N. J.

GOTHIC LETTERS*

being combined with *small capitals* to form words, a common standard proportion can be used: the small capitals should be $\frac{4}{5}$ the height of the large cap.

Spacing the Letters

Spacing out all the letters appropriately is equally important for the shaping and proportions of lettering. Good lettering which has been irregularly spaced tends to look strange. In scenic terminology, the space between letters is frequently called the "sand," or the weight between the letters. One artist might casually comment to another, "You need more sand between those two letters" or "There's too much sand between the cap and the lower case."

By studying the letters in the alphabet, many variations in the shape of the letters are revealed. Because of the nature of their shape, some letters are placed closer to other letters and some letters are placed farther apart. For instance, the letters L and T can be spaced closer together than a G and an O. Rather than trying to follow a set rule, the trained eye is always the best judge for spacing, and this becomes easy and obvious through experience. One should think of the lettering and spacing as a design.

LAYING OUT THE LETTERING

In the scenic studio, all but the simplest lettering is laid out to full scale on brown paper so a

perforated pounce can be made, rather than putting it directly on the surface where it is to be painted. The same kind of pattern is made for letters that are to be cut out of wood or metal. As in drafting, *guidelines* are drawn lightly for any lettering, since they are vital for keeping the lettering uniform. When capitals are being made, a *base line* (bottom) and *cap line* (top) are needed. If lower-case lettering is also being used, two more guidelines are drawn. These are called the *waist line* (for the top of the lower case) and the *drop line* (for the bottom of the lower case letters, like *g* and *y*). The heights of the lower-case letters are normally two-thirds the height of the capital letter. For example, if a capital letter is 6 inches high, the lower-case would be 4 inches high. The measurement from the base line to the drop line is the same as the measurement from the waist line to the cap line or, in this case, 2 inches. While guidelines are generally straight and parallel, they can also be constructed in perspective or have curved layouts, depending on the design.

For *inclined* lettering (capitals or lower case), guidelines are also made. In order that uniformity be retained in the slanted lines, "slope" or direction lines are drawn lightly as guides for the inclined letters. When one is doing large inclined letters, it is very helpful to construct an angled template out of heavy paper or cardboard. This is good to keep the angles of the slope line consistent by lining up the bottom of the template on a straightedge.

After all the guidelines have been laid out on the brown paper, the lettering to be executed is sketched in roughly and lightly with a stick of charcoal. A single skeleton stroke is drawn first, regardless of the type face involved, letting one know how to judge the proportions and the spacing. And sometimes, when a word must fit into a given width or height, the first letter of the word is drawn, then the last, and the artist works toward the center from either end, thereby finding out whether the letters in the word should be compressed or extended.

Continuing on, the outlines of the letters are neatly shaped and sketched in next, working over the basic single strokes. If this is a kind of lettering that is to be done mechanically, like Gothic capitals (as opposed to a type such as an advertising script), a straightedge and a compass are normally used to finish the drawing, especially when the lettering is sizable (anywhere from 6 to 18 inches in height). Other types of lettering may be laid out completely freehand. A fast and frequent method of laying

LETTERING ON A BACKDROP
Robin Wagner's translucent, seamless muslin backdrop (30 ft. high by 48 wide) for the musical SEESAW (1973) required both freehand and mechanical lettering. (Photographs—Lynn Pecktal)

Steps of Execution:

1. Backdrop stapled on floor over gray bogus-paper and starched.
2. 2-ft. squares snapped lightly in charcoal for laying out drawing.
3. Signs and lettering drawn freehand and with straightedges.
4. Hot paraffin wax was brushed on muslin to mask small lights around signs (to be translucent) before painting.
5. Signs and letters painted with aniline dyes (transparent), then black background of casein and latex paint (opaque) cut in around details.
6. Wax masking the dots was carefully scraped off with dull knives.

out a type like old English text or advertising script is to paint the letters freehand with a color made of aniline dye (using no size), just after the shapes have been sketched in roughly with charcoal on the brown paper. Nice full curved shapes can be made with brushfuls of dye on the paper, and the contrast of the dye on the paper makes it easier to visualize how all of the lettering looks together. For this, a brush is selected which has bristles wide enough to cover the body of the letters in single strokes. Then the outer line of each painted letter is perforated with a pounce wheel. And, quite logically, the more accurately the letters are laid out on the paper pounce, the less corrections there are during the finished painting.

In designs where the letters are large and must be repeated several times in the copy, a separate pounce is often made for each letter, and the actual spacing of the letters and words is done when they are transferred onto the backdrop or flat with the charcoal bag. And if there is a need, it is very easy to change the spacing of a letter by merely dusting it off, then re-pouncing it with the charcoal. Before painting

lettering, it is generally necessary to dust off the excess charcoal on the pounced surface.

PAINTING LETTERING

In laying out good lettering, one learns to paint it precisely and neatly through practice and experience. In the scenic studio, lettering is painted both freehand and with a straight-edge, and all kinds of water-base paints are normally used. These are selected according to the surface they are going on and which will produce the best results for the job. Any color should be thinned enough to spread evenly and smoothly with the brush.

For small lettering work, regular lettering brushes are ideal, and some scenic artists buy their own lettering brushes and take care of them, whereas others use those belonging to the studio. Among these are Grumbacher's red sable lettering brushes, which have straight sharp edges, and sign Fitches that have white bristles and square chiseled edges. But for painting large lettering, the usual scenic lining brushes work beautifully. On big letters, the outer edges are "cut in" first, then the center areas are filled in.

For quick lettering reference, one of the best sources is the Letraset (instant lettering) catalog, available at good art-supply stores. It contains an extraordinary amount of data on complete alphabets, type styles, line borders, illustrations of art sheets, architects' symbols and patterns, electronic symbols, and many others.

CARVING LETTERING. (Left) Tombstone facing for a movie prop made of display foam and foam core. Lettering drawn on ½-in. display foam. Raised beveled letters "Giovanni Pollari" cut out of ¼-in. thick foam core with an X-Acto knife and glued on; the remaining copy was cut into display foam. (Photograph—Lynn Pecktal)

USING SIGNS TO DEFINE SPECIFIC LOCALES.
A sign Robin Wagner devised for THE GREAT WHITE HOPE (1968) was cut out of ¼-in. plywood and held tiny lights; turkey wire, collaged with bits of fabric and paper textured with paint, formed up-stage background. (Photograph—Arnold Abramson)

A Conversation with ROBERT RANDOLPH

Robert Randolph, born in 1926 in Centerville, Iowa, was educated at the State University of Iowa and was an instructor in architecture there and an architectural and industrial designer before coming to New York. His first assignment on Broadway was designing the scenery and costumes for *The Saint of Bleecker Street* in 1954. He then went on to become an established designer, doing the scenery for the hit musical *Bye Bye Birdie* in 1960. Since that time, he has created the settings for around fifty Broadway productions, most notably for musicals and plays, and has also done the lighting for a large number of them. In addition, he has designed *The King and I* at the Dorothy Chandler Pavilion and *Porgy and Bess* at the Ahmanson Theatre, both in Los Angeles. Robert Randolph has been art director for many television shows and for several years has designed the scenery for the annual television Tony Awards presentation in New York. Among his Broadway design credits are:

We Interrupt this Program . . . (1975)
Gypsy (1974)
Words and Music (1974)
Good Evening (1973)
Applause (1970)
Golden Rainbow (1968)
Henry, Sweet Henry (1967)
Sherry (1967)

Sweet Charity (1966)
Walking Happy (1966)
It's a Bird, It's a Plane,
    It's Superman (1966)
Skyscraper (1965)
Anya (1965)
Funny Girl (1964)
Any Wednesday (1964)

Foxy (1964)
Sophie (1963)
Little Me (1962)
Bravo Giovanni (1962)
Calculated Risk (1962)
How to Succeed in Business
    without Really Trying (1961)
Bye Bye Birdie (1960)

Stage designs by Robert Randolph
GYPSY
Book by Arthur Laurents
Music by Jule Styne
Lyrics by Stephen Sondheim
Directed by Arthur Laurents
Winter Garden Theatre, New York
(1974)

Setting and lighting by Robert
  Randolph
SKYSCRAPER
Book by Peter Stone
Based on DREAM GIRL by Elmer Rice
Music by James Van Heusen
Lyrics by Sammy Cahn

Directed by Cy Feuer
Dances and musical numbers staged
  by Michael Kidd
Costumes by Theoni V. Aldredge
Lunt-Fontanne Theatre, New York
  (1965)
(Photograph — Friedman-Abeles)

When did you first become interested in the theatre? Did you design shows in high school and college?

I did them all over. I went to the University of Iowa to get an architectural degree, not a theatre degree. I got my master's in fine arts there, and at the same time I took all the theatre courses and everything about theatre design. I also wrote the book and lyrics for a lot of musicals while I was there, and I directed and designed three of them. Then I taught architecture there three years before I came to New York.

How did you go about getting your first job in the theatre?

I wrote to my high school dramatic coach — who had come to New York — and asked him how I should go about better preparing myself for coming to New York. Then he wrote a big letter telling me not to come. He said that it was too difficult, the competition was too great, and that you can starve for years before you get anywhere, but if you really want to come, here's what you should do. He gave me a list of summer stock theatres in the East where I could apply. So I wrote twenty-one letters, and by June first of that summer, I hadn't received any replies. I had to make a decision about what I was going to do, and after I had agreed to teach that summer at the University of Iowa, I

started getting letters. Out of the twenty-one, I got nineteen offers. So I blew it for that summer. But just as summer school was ending, the Salt Creek Summer Theatre in Chicago did call me. I went there and worked for a month at the end of their season, and then went back to school. During the following year I agreed to go to the Lakewood Theatre in Skowhegan, Maine, for the summer. This was one of the offers I had gotten and I kept in contact with them particularly because it was one of the best theatres. One person I met was Clayre Ribner, and she became a friend of mine. I went back to Iowa for my last year at the college. Then I came East the following year to do summer stock at Somer's Point in Atlantic City, N.J. We did musicals, and I spent the summer there and then I came to New York.

Whom did you contact in New York?

I only knew this one person in New York — Clayre Ribner — besides the people I worked with in stock. The first day I was here I called Clayre and she said, "We're doing a show in our office [Michael Abbott], *Late Love*. The designer is Stewart Chaney, and he is doing three Broadway shows and he needs someone to help him get props. I mentioned your name and asked him if he wanted to see you and he said, 'Send him over tomorrow.'" And I went over and

got the job. It was the second day I was in New York and I was assisting on three Broadway shows — *Late Love, A Girl Can Tell,* and *Sherlock Holmes.* It was phenomenal luck.

I took the union exam the following spring and got in. Then I worked for Ben Edwards on fourteen productions and with George Jenkins on about twelve. *Two for the Seesaw* and *Happiest Millionaire* were a couple of his shows. I did seven with Boris Aronson. For the next seven years, I assisted. After a while you get calls from everybody. When you assist well you always work, and you make a good living at it too. During that time I assisted on about sixty shows. But I worked all year round to do it. That includes automobile shows and things like industrials.

Bye Bye Birdie was the first big show of your own.

Yes. I met Ed Padula the second year I went to Atlantic City to do stock. He was the director there and we did twelve musicals together. We always said we'd do a show in New York. Well, he had this script called *Let's Go Steady* that was getting nowhere here for two years. The score was written and then Gower Champion came in and agreed to do it. He got Mike Stewart to rewrite the book, and it was called *Bye Bye Birdie,* and I did it. From then on, it was sort of like a fairy tale. *How to Succeed* followed that, *Bravo Giovanni, Little Me,* and right on down. Since I first worked with Feuer and Martin, I've done every show of theirs.

When you are beginning work on a production such as a big musical, how do you approach it?

First of all, I have strong opinions about what a show is about, what theatre is about. Every play and musical is an entity in itself. You have to approach each project as a different one. A great many people feel that designers have a style or a certain way of doing a show. They talk about so-and-so is right for this show because we want it to look like the way he does a show. I don't like that because I don't think that's a way to approach a show. I think the idea is that each show has its own personality, not only in the way it is written and the way it sounds, but also in the way it should look. And every script you look at, you look at as a blank first. You can't say, "Oh I'll do such-and-such with this show." It evolves into a style, into a place. When you're most successful doing that is when the show becomes a success, too. And that is because everybody works together to the same point of view and the same goal. You can't have a rubber stamp and stamp out things. You can't stamp out a musical script, music, or any of that. When it becomes reminiscent and "looks like," "sounds like," it will be mediocre. Now that, as a general thing, is how I work. That's my approach and that's the way it works. It's a growing thing. It's an exchange because you are creating for the first time.

In summer stock, or when you do any community theatre or college theatre, you generally have a script that has already been proven, unless you are doing a new script. If you're doing a revival, that's different—you are not faced with making the script as well as the sets work because it is a totally different kettle of fish. You are creating something for the first time. Now that *How to Succeed* has been a famous hit and people do it, they can do it almost any way, but all the problems of the set have already been worked out. In other words, when they say they move from one scene to another, we've already done the groundwork. That's not to say you can't be creative reproducing a new set of designs. Unless you're going to change

it all around and rewrite the script; then you've got another problem. But I think a designer should be part of the creative end of it—he has to be.

Then it is essential to have several long meetings with the director.

I think the meetings are the most important thing because not until you begin to think alike can you really work together. You know where you are going. But not only thinking alike—it's the invention of new ideas that come up. That's the creative part of it. I think a person like Bob Fosse is one of the best directors in the business. It's fun for him to come over. We sit and have a cup of coffee and we talk about everything except the play [or the musical]. But we are both leading each other into other conversation along the way, because we have thoughts. Sooner or later, we bend the conversation into an abstract thought. Maybe it's a poster we saw or a picture or a painting or an idea, maybe it was a movie or a piece of music or a concert we went to. It seems to have no relevance to what the musical is about, but it generates an idea about the musi-

cal. And before you know it, we've arrived at some new approach as to what the show is about. In *Sweet Charity*, we worked for about three months on concept. The first concept was a good one. But all of a sudden one day, I had the model nearly done; we looked at it, and a lot of things like drops and wings were flying in and out. It was all done in a very dripping watercolor style where it was just color flowing in and out. But the drops and the legs were solid, and that couldn't happen, because it would interrupt what was going on on stage. It was a big dance show, so we had a lot of space. Everything was done off the floor.

The thought occurred to both of us at the same time—that was wrong. So I just turned to him and said, "Okay, it's out. I have another idea. We'll do it all with light, and no paint." So he went away, and I went out and bought bicycle lamps. I built a light frame of little lights and made a cyc, because I do everything in models. And by changing the colors and the positions of all these things, I painted with light the same thing that I had painted on the drops before because

Scenery and lighting by Robert Randolph
GOLDEN RAINBOW
Book by Ernest Kinoy
Based on the play A HOLE IN THE
HEAD by Arnold Schulman
Music and lyrics by Walter Marks

Directed by Arthur Storch
Choreography by Tom Panko
Costumes by Alvin Colt
Sam S. Shubert Theatre, New York
(1968)
(Photograph—Friedman-Abeles)

the look was right—the movement was wrong. So, therefore, we had a cyc that stayed there, and only the lights changed and blended to make these different shapes. The only thing we needed was the line that was on the drawing, which we did in wire. Now when a piece of wire flew in, you hardly noticed it until all of a sudden it was there.

How long did you spend from the time you first started working on Sweet Charity *until it opened?*

Oh, at least nine months. Most musicals that take that long are done by people who really plan that far ahead—like Feuer and Martin. When anybody plans that long to do a show, they're doing it with a great deal of care. They know what they are doing. They aren't throwing a show together to get it on stage. If it takes longer to develop something, people like that will delay it. They are very successful too, in everything they do. Hal Prince is the same way. He develops a show over a long period. Because it takes that long to generate the thing. Even *Applause* took a long time. I guess we started on it before the script was written. Ron Field and I had long talks and long developments. Scenes evolved from our talks that eventually became the script. Things developed like who was this woman and where did she go? What bar did she go to? Did she go

to the party afterwards? And all these things became part of the script later on.

That isn't really the usual way of working, is it?

Well, as I say, I don't find it unusual. I have worked on productions where a finished script was handed me, and I was told this is the way the show is going to be done, without any relationship to a contribution from me before it was written. But somehow, eventually, those scripts are the ones that get changed the most. All of a sudden, this doesn't work, that doesn't work, the scene doesn't work. Maybe if it had all been worked out earlier, it would have saved some of that trouble. In almost every show I have ever done that was a hit, the amount of changing out of town was practically zero.

Do you build models for every show that you do?

Yes. First of all, there's a great thought period of making small sketches—idea sketches, I call them. What I try to avoid in these is a concept of color and style of painting or any of that. What they really serve as is an idea of where you are, or where you are about to go, or whatever. The look is secondary at that point, because those quick sketches take fifteen minutes or so. The idea may take three days. You go through a series of those, which gives the director or writer

(or whomever you are working with) an idea of how you're thinking. It's something to relate to. Some of the most successful sketches are the simplest. They just tell you in a couple of glances what that whole thing is. From that point, when you start making decisions about the way the show's evolving, then you get into bigger and more firm things. My opinion about sketches is this: a sketch will never tell you exactly what happens on stage, because it is a two-dimensional thing, unless you have a photographic rendering, which would take forever to do. But that is not the purpose of a sketch. It is to get you to a certain point with the director. Then you must get into a model to find out the dimension, because the director is directing in three-dimension, not in two. You'll never know what it looks like until it is in a model. And I make my models in total detail so that when you are through, there are no questions. Whenever we go out of town with a show, nobody is surprised at what is up there, because they've seen it before in miniature.

That's why you put all the detailed furniture and props in your models?

Everything! And the color and the style, because I think you're dealing in a design, not a sketch. A sketch will never tell you that. There's a freedom about a sketch which can be very lovely in itself, but it is not the scenery. Because all of a sudden, you're dealing with hard things—things with shape and dimension—totally different. So I think an important item, too, is that because of that, you have to think in terms other than just paint. To achieve certain concepts, you have to find new ways of doing things. Many people say you approach a design without any restrictions—anything can be worked out or accomplished. That's true, up to a certain point. In many cases, a totally free imagination can conceive fantastic vision, but I don't think it always works. When you have a totally free imagination, you imagine some ethereal "setting look" and then you try to find ways to make that happen. You try to achieve something that you have imagined in space. There's no relationship to anything, and you try to achieve it. The way it is finally achieved may be less than the imagination. I think one works better, sometimes, if you know limitations.

In other words, you have limitations

Setting and lighting by Robert Randolph
HOW TO SUCCEED IN BUSINESS
WITHOUT REALLY TRYING
Book by Abe Burrows, Jack Weinstock, and
   Willie Gilbert
Based on the book by Shepherd Mead
Music and lyrics by Frank Loesser

Choreography by Hugh Lambert
Costumes by Robert Fletcher
Musical staging by Bob Fosse
Directed by Abe Burrows
Forty-sixth Street Theatre, New York (1961)
Pictured: Robert Morse and company
(Photograph—Friedman-Abeles)

Setting by Robert Randolph
BYE BYE BIRDIE
Book by Michael Stewart
Music by Charles Strouse
Lyrics by Lee Adams
Costumes by Miles White

Lighting by Peggy Clark
Directed and choreographed by Gower
   Champion
Sam S. Shubert Theatre, New York (1961)
(Photograph — Friedman-Abeles)

of the theatre size, the length the scene plays in the show — do you mean all this?

Yes. I'm speaking mainly of mechanics, of materials, of how much material can do. If you had an unlimited budget, you could probably do fantastic things. But if you don't and if you recognize the limitations to what you're doing and know them so that they become tools to your imagination, sometimes you can achieve even more by being limited. Sometimes the limitations of the stage will make you think in entirely different ways from the very beginning. I'm thinking of flies and all that. That goes for everything as far as the physical limitations of the theatre. I think there are limitations of what materials are, too, what they are made for. I don't think you can make materials do something they weren't made for. Whenever I use a new material, I must know exactly what it is going to do or I won't use it. You can use any fabric or any material you want, but you've got to know its property, what it can do and what it can't do before you ever get it on stage.

You always work your shows out very well mechanically so that you know how they work in all respects.

That's right. They are whole, not pieces of shows. You work on every aspect of it. It isn't handed over to someone else to figure out this and to figure out that. I have a great deal of respect for Pete Feller [Feller Scenery Studio], and I have a great deal of respect for Willie Nolan [head of Nolan Scenery Studios who died]. They are not too unlike. They're both brilliant. The thing I like about both of them is that you can match wits with them. In other words, Willie would never squelch an idea of mine. We argued a lot, violently. He almost kicked me out of the shop on *Bravo Giovanni,* my third show. Cesare Siepe, who played Giovanni, had to dig this tunnel very fast, hit the side of a wall which collapsed to reveal a tomb there. We did the digging in a speeded-up version with a lobsterscope to make a flickering light, which was new in those days, but no more. That's the gist of the scene.

So I went to Willie and I explained this wall and how I wanted it to work. I had designed this thing that folded up. Willie had an idea for a brick wall that collapsed that he had done a long time before. And I said, "But it isn't a brick wall, it's the wall of a tunnel that the man is digging." He kept saying, "But I've got this great idea for a brick wall to collapse by pulling one pin." I said, "No, I don't want a brick wall. You've got to do it my way." And we fought back and forth. He wanted to use this idea so badly. He finally got mad at me and said, "Oh, then you do it yourself! I'll give you one carpenter, and you go build it yourself." I said, "Thank you very much," and I left the shop. The next day I came in with a one-inch model. You couldn't do it in half-inch scale because the pieces would be too tiny. I had brought it in before to show him, and he said it wouldn't work. The tunnel was painted like it had circular ridges, which gave it a tubular effect. These rings were actually pieces all put together in irregular shapes, because Giovanni had to walk into this tomb after the wall collapsed. It couldn't be bulk. It had to be something so that when it collapsed, it went down to something like two inches high. So the carpenter and I drew out all the pieces on three-quarter-inch plywood. And they folded like accordians. They were all hinged at the bottom, but they hung at the top from one pin. When one pin was let go, the others collapsed in sequence. Now, to get it to collapse was a difficult thing, because you had to make it fold in two directions — one on the surface and one behind it.

I got an inner tube, cut it up (you know, like you did when you made rubber guns as a kid), and made springs out of the strips that would lay flat under the material, which was all covered with painted velour. When I got this all together, I showed it to Willie, and he thought it was marvelous. From that day on, he never questioned anything I ever did. So we had a good time talking about things. We matched wits about it.

Getting this unit of scenery to work was your invention.

Right. I think you invent a little as you go along. I think that stage scenery and all the effects of it are a growing thing. Each show will have something new in it — some problem that the other show didn't have. So it's not a process of learning tricks of the trade. It's a process of inventing tricks of the trade as you go along. The basic tools are minor compared to what you really have to do. For instance, the whole system of plates and pulling props on small nothings I did a long time ago when I was an assistant. I was told they wouldn't work by everyone in the business. Every carpenter said "Impossible!" when I put a chair on a piece of plywood and said, "I want that chair to go out to center stage." On one show I did it because we had wagons that went on and off. It had a fin that came up out of the floor, and I said, "Take the wagon off and leave that fin sticking out." It had bolts and everything sticking in it. Then I said, "Now take this chair and put a slot in that quarter-inch plywood and we'll put domes under it and sit that slot over the fin and take that chair out there." They said, "It won't work," but it did. The fin went down the track to the cable and the winch turned and the chair went out to center stage with no stagehand. And that was the beginning of all that plate business. It was done on a show called *Tenderloin*, which I worked on with Cecil Beaton. From then on, it just grew to many other things. In *Applause*, almost every big set had rugs on three-quarter-inch plywood plates which carried all of the furniture, because that show had more "playable" props than most musicals. Each set was almost complete, because it showed what the woman was like in all of her possessions. That was done on plates, not wagons. In New York it was all done by electric winch, but in the road company, it was all pushed on and off on the same plates. Two men could push the entire set.

You have also designed the lights on a number of your shows.

All except a few. I think lighting is an integral part of the sets, especially on a show like *Charity. Sweet Charity* is lights. It's really antiscenery. It doesn't have scenery in the usual sense. It has a lot of lighting effects that become scenery, and that never could have been achieved if I hadn't been the lighting designer also. I think about lighting in conjunction with the scenery when I am designing. It's almost part of it. It isn't as though I could hand it over to someone and say, "I want effects like this and do what you can." I can't do that. I prefer to do it myself. I find it easier. The first show I did it for was *How to Succeed.*

I know the basic rules of lighting, and the system of doing it is my own; it's everybody's own. If there were one way to light, then everything would look the same, wouldn't it? But since there are no rules you have to follow, you can do almost anything you want to achieve what you want. There is nothing that says you have to do it this way or that way. I don't light scenery; I light people. If you're successful in lighting people, the scenery will take

care of itself. It's really more important to light the people. There are some times when you must light the drops properly, or certain pieces, to get effects and depth and definition.

Do you prefer designing musicals to designing plays?

Yes, unless it is an unusual play like a *JB*. In other words, plays are not generally written with the freedom that a musical is. I prefer a drama or a play that breaks out of a box set. A comedy can break out, too, and be a fun set. But most of them are written for box sets. And the reason they are not quite as exciting is that there are not as many people involved and the problems are reduced because there are no mechanics if it's a single set. There is not as much exchange because in a play there is one man writing and he sets the stage for you. In a musical there is the insertion of music, dances, and everything else begins to multiply until it becomes a much more complex problem and much more fun.

When you designed the television series "That's Life," did you find the methods different from those of the theatre?

Absolutely. Because you are doing a show a week that isn't even written on the first day of the week, and you have to have the scenery by Friday. It's all done sort of by faith. The writers say they want a certain set and they have faith in you that you can deliver a set that will be workable for them by Friday. There is no time to fool with concepts or anything. The concept of what scenery we were going to use was already worked out when we did our first few shows. I had total freedom in color. I think they were the most colorful sets on television at that time, because there was no stopping. There was no realism at all. We had a very light, bright feeling for color television. I did 125 sets in twenty-six weeks. It averaged about five a week.

Did you have assistants to do the working drawings?

No, I did those myself. I find very few people who can draw as fast as I can and as well as I can. Sometimes it takes me longer to explain to an assistant what to do than for me to draw it myself. If I have completely organized the show up to the point of models, I can

draw it out in about four days. It's very hard work. I am always up at 7:00 A.M. and I always work until at least midnight if it's that kind of schedule. You know, sometimes you're not working at all.

If a young potential designer wants to design on Broadway, what do you feel is necessary as a background?

I think experience and experimentation. In other words, when I went through stock, I used it as an experiment, trying out new things. You're working with plays that have already been done, so it's pretty set what you are going to design. How can you do it in a new way? So it really becomes not only an experience that you get along the way, but it's got to be an experiment. It's tuning up your creativity, because I think you have to learn patterns of designing. You have to discipline yourself into thinking and creating—learning to create, learning to use what you have in your own little head to become a designer. It isn't a mechanical thing where you sit down and do it. But I think it takes developing your sense of invention, imagination, and creativity.

Do you believe in practical experience as opposed to school?

No. I think school is good, too. I think everybody must have that background. I like drama schools. But I think the drama school gives you a certain amount of knowledge to stow away in your head, and I think summer stock gives you a certain amount of experience doing things, and should also give you experience in inventing. It should also give you a new way of learning, because you're always learning, and you're always asking questions. You're never finished. The most successful thing, and I don't think anybody has written this book, is if a book could teach a person how to think, not how to do, but how to think, how to discipline themselves into thinking thought patterns which bring about the creativity, the creation. I think it is developing a creativity that will come out. In other words, not approaching the problem as a mechanical problem, but in a thought-pattern way. It sparks you to thinking different ways. And it takes discipline. It can make you a successful designer. But that isn't the only element you have to consider, because luck has a lot to do with it!

SIX

Scenic painting techniques

The importance to a scenic designer of being able to paint well can never be overemphasized, for in addition to designing the show, he must know exactly how he wants the set painted in order to have his design fully realized. Some of the theatre's most distinguished designers have long advocated that designing for the theatre goes hand in hand with painting for the theatre. For example, just a few months before his death in December 1972, Eugene Berman, the celebrated neoromantic stage designer, stated: "I think that to be a good stage designer, one should have a flair for the theatre and be a good painter. To me, a stage designer who is not a good painter is not a good stage designer." Although Berman set high standards for himself and also expected them of his contemporaries in the craft, he was nonetheless a master of both design and painting, never falling short of his goals, which he always attacked with endless enthusiasm. For him, designing and painting were pure pleasure—and inseparable.

Most designers have painted on their own sets at some point in their careers, and many still count on painting them no matter whether they are designing at a university, in regional theatre, for summer stock, or for Off Broadway. Besides enjoying painting and the creativity it offers, designers frequently cannot obtain the help of reliable scenic artists, and the simplest way to get the painting done on a production as they want it is to do it themselves. But a designer doing a Broadway show in New York, including opera and ballet (or wherever union regulations do not permit), does not paint on his own show. Therefore, the designer must accurately translate his designs through models, sketches, and drawings so they can be submitted to the scenic studio for execution.

Once the scenic shop has been chosen, the set designer discusses all his designs in great detail with the chargeman who is the head of the painting department in the studio. The designer may say, "I want the sketch for this exterior backdrop to be taken literally and painted like it is—very realistically," or "Do this translucent muslin sky drop with aniline dyes so that it will be as brilliant as possible," or "The three-dimensional ornament detail on the interior set should have bright metallic gold highlights brushed on it." If the chargeman has worked with the particular designer

These photographs show how effective realistically painted scenery can be on flat units with profiled edges. The painted ground row of a city view for Ralph Alswang's setting in FUN CITY (1972) achieved considerable depth by placing specific emphasis on foreground, middle, and distance tones. Designed to play outside the windows of a single interior set, the ground row was constructed with a framework of 1-by-3 wood covered with canvas; the profiled edges were ¼-in. plywood.

Interior architecture, molding, furniture, and props on this folding arch unit are good examples of realistic scenic painting. Note that the painting on Robert Randolph's set for BRAVO GIOVANNI (1962) was done with the light source coming from the window on the left. (Photograph — Munro Gabler)

This unit, designed by Herbert Senn and Helen Pond for ARIADNE AUF NAXOS (1973) at the New York City Opera, was made of flat profile pieces cut from ¼-in. plywood, covered with canvas and painted. The pieces were placed in front of and behind a small platform seat 36 in. high. The seat back was also ¼-in. plywood. (Top & bottom photograph — Lynn Pecktal)

several times before, he may know almost immediately what he wants and what he prefers, just by looking at his sketches and talking with him. After the meeting between the two is finished, it is the chargeman's responsibility to indicate to each of his scenic artists what is involved in duplicating the painting (always interpreting the designer's style) of each piece of scenery and how he expects it to be carried out. In doing this, much of the selection of paints and materials is left up to the chargeman, unless otherwise specified by the designer.

The production design and the individual effects it demands serve as a guide for the selection of paints on the scenery. The practicality, the durability, and the drying time of a medium are always considered, while the painting is done by long-practiced methods to insure the most effective and easiest way in which the settings can be finished. As a rule, scenery is painted broadly so that it reads well from a distance. During the progress of the painting, the designer usually visits the scenic studio to see how everything is going and to make any changes he feels are necessary.

THE STANDARD STEPS OF PREPARING AND PAINTING SCENERY

New scenery may undergo these steps of preparation and painting:

1. *Priming*
2. *Base coat* (local color or lay-in color)
3. *Finished painting* (or overpainting)
4. *Backpainting* (or opaquing)

The most typical examples of new scenery that are involved in these steps are those covered with cotton canvas, including plain wings and

flats, window flats, door flats, arch flats, fireplace flats, ground rows, ceiling pieces, profile set pieces, or dimensional set pieces and platforms. These basic processes for painting canvas-covered scenery can nevertheless vary a great deal according to the individual piece and the production.

While these steps are customary for canvas flats in an interior or exterior setting, they may not be the same when some other fabric is used to cover the units. For instance, many of the units mentioned above could be covered with white velour and finished in one step by spraying over them in dye, and not need any priming or base coat. Velour, of course, must not be primed, as this will mat the nap and destroy the effect of the velour. Sharkstooth scrim is another example of a fabric that could be finished in one shot. On other flats, decorative fabrics are used where there is no real painting to speak of except perhaps spraying lightly to age them a bit. For these, the woodwork is usually not painted on the patterned fabric, but instead is built as a separate piece and painted and then fastened by bolting onto the face of the covered flat. And even on some of the units that are covered with canvas there can be variations. A canvas-covered ceiling piece can be finished in one shot, when the priming and the base coat are put on as one. Or a platform unit (also covered with canvas) is sometimes completed with only one step of painting. Both of the latter examples may or may not require overpainting. Because they are described in detail wherever they apply, the priming and base coat are discussed here generally to give an introduction to the logical sequence for the basic scenic painting techniques. The finished painting (overpainting) on scenery which involves the basic techniques follows.

Priming

Priming, the necessary coating for a surface before the base coat and final coats of paints and dyes are applied, is necessary to keep the colors from sinking into the surface. Priming is used on several materials. To cite a few examples: On the usual canvas flats, the priming (can be caseins or dry whiting and dry pigment colors mixed with glue size) fills up the fabric and makes it dry taut. Priming for canvas is most often done in white or pale colors, but it can be any color required by the design of the scenery. On plywood or new wood, the

BRUSHING THE FIRST COAT ON NEW CANVAS FLATS. A stippling brush, attached to a long handle, is used to spread broad areas of priming quickly over new canvas-covered flats.

priming (can be opaque shellac in the desired color) fills up and seals the surface of the wood. On a translucent muslin backdrop, the priming (liquid starch) covers the fabric with a transparent glaze to produce a smooth painting surface and makes it stretch tight. The material that you are using and the individual effect that you are creating dictate what paint (shellac, starch, etc.) and color should be chosen for the priming.

Base Coat (local color or lay-in)

The *base,* which is the undertone for the finished painting, can be chosen according to the lightest tone on the sketch, the middle tone, or the darkest tone. While it is generally the lightest tone for most work, the selection is really controlled by the dominance of the particular colors on the sketch and the end result sought. As examples, for the lightest tone, it might be a background for a wallpaper pattern that gets stenciled with several colors; for the middle tone, it might be architecture that gets light and dark tones brushed on it; and for the darkest tone, it might be draperies that get light and middle tones modeled over them. This does not mean, however, that only one color must always be used. If you are base-coating foliage, you can easily blend two or three different colors (like greens and blues, etc.) together.

Finished painting (overpainting)

A multitude of techniques and paints can be a part of the finished painting on scenery, and these are discussed throughout the book wherever they apply.

Backpainting (opaquing)

Portions of translucent muslin backdrops that are to be opaque and canvas flats to be opaque are painted last by the scenic artists. Also, it is standard for the backs of such scenery units as plywood flats (covered with canvas, linen, velour, etc.), platforms, three-dimensional pieces (rocks, trees, etc.) to be backpainted with a flame-retardant paint, or paint with a flame-retardant solution mixed in it by the

Stretched on the floor in playing order is one of Oliver Smith's interior settings for THE WOMEN (1973). MATERIALS: Flats: 1-by-3 wooden frames covered with ⅛-in. plywood. Fabric: Bleached nubby linen covering the hard flats. Woodwork: Three-dimensional wooden cornices, panel moldings, door facings, chair rails, and baseboards, all bolted to the flats. Paints and dyes: Aniline dyes sprayed on fabric-covered walls (no priming), stripes painted with casein paints and dyes; woodwork laid in with opaque shellac colors, details painted with vinyl paints. Mirrors (foreground): Mylar.

carpenters. Usually it is black or gray. This can be done before or after the units are painted by the scenic artists, depending on the particular production and the time involved.

BASIC SCENIC PAINTING TECHNIQUES

The experienced artist works intuitively to achieve the effects he wants and therefore does not always analyze each technique before or while painting. Every artist has his own way of painting scenery, and the choice of what methods are applicable for executing the finished painting is left to his discretion. Since painting is a matter of constantly experimenting with new ideas, these basic techniques should serve as guides for the beginner and not suppress his ability to work freely as an artist.

It should also be noted that many of these basic scenic painting techniques can be and are combined with each other to obtain the final effect on painted scenery. Except where an already colored fabric or material is designated as the base coat, the scenery is first laid in or primed with the basic color or colors before these techniques are used. For scenic work, textures are usually applied in a bold and exaggerated fashion on the surfaces so they read well from a distance. Otherwise, they can appear as mere flat surfaces when viewed from the audience.

The most accepted ways of *finishing scenery* and *applying painted textures* are by using the brush (glazing, scumbling or dry-brushing, combing, stippling, spattering, dotting), using the paint roller, using a feather duster, using a sponge, using a paint stamp, puddling, spraying, and bathing (the transparent bath). As a process for texturing, some methods (like rag-rolling) that are time-consuming and messy have long been replaced by the paint roller in conjunction with implements such as the feather duster or flogger. Wherever it applies, the painting implement itself is discussed with the painting technique to avoid repetition.

Because the technique of lining is a lengthy process which extends from flat painted molding (on flat surfaces) into the area of painting three-dimensionally built molding, it is discussed on pages 332–335. Other kinds of scene painting included in this chapter are stencils, drapery, ornament, marble, and foliage.

Using the Brush

The brush can be manipulated in all sorts of ways to achieve texturing with the paint or dyes. While the processes below reflect the commonly used methods of applying the paint by brush, there can be endless variations of these just by the way the brush is handled. These are determined by (1) the type of brush and the quantity of paint in it and (2) the direc-

A number of painting techniques was employed in creating texture on Ming Cho Lee's canvas-framed wall and window unit for the New York City Opera's MARIA STUARDA (1972). After the unit had been primed and drawn out, it was laid in with several colors, then textured by puddling, spattering, spraying, and scumbling. All Gothic window details and stonework on walls were painted on flat surfaces except the applied piece at the bottom right, a three-dimensional strip of molding painted to match the flat work.
(Photographs—Lynn Pecktal)

tion and versatility of the stroke. Whether you are using the flat of the brush or the side of the brush, the strokes can be straight, curved or swirled, wavy, zigzagged, crosshatched in the shape of an X, or twisted. Feathering the end of the stroke by letting the brush stroke fade out lightly, gradually, and smoothly adds variety.

GLAZING

Glazing is the technique of covering a painted surface (or parts of it) with a thin layer of *transparent* color which modifies its tone. It is normally a darker color applied over a lighter color. Glazes add interest and variation to the effect. A glaze can be put on almost any piece of scenery. To name but a few, you can apply glazes over painted molding and ornament to serve as shadows and second shadows, or over painted tree trunks and branches where the glaze functions as a shade color, or generally over painted marble to add transparent veins. Whenever you are applying a glaze, the smoothness or roughness of the surface should be considered. Usually, it is a smooth surface.

Aniline dyes and caseins (thinned with water) are popularly used for making glazes. Aniline dyes in particular are outstanding for painting single glazes or multiple glazes because they do not normally need a binder, and therefore thinning them with water does not weaken a binder. But you can make a glaze with vinyl, latex, acrylic, shellac, varnish, lacquer, or oil. Years ago in the scenic studio, oil paint was highly favored for making glazes for woodwork. Although it is not used that much today, it is still a good paint for glazing wood graining on built woodwork and molding that has been basecoated. Oil paints can easily be thinned with turpentine or mineral spirits to form a thin transparent glaze. Japan colors can be thinned with the same, although some varnish should be added as a binder. While glazes are applied mostly by brush, they can be put on by sponging, spattering, spraying, or by paint roller.

SCUMBLING OR DRY-BRUSHING

Scumbling involves using a very dry brush to give texture to the painted (or laid-in) surface which is modified by brushing lightly over portions of it with an *opaque* or *semiopaque* color. Bear in mind that part of the underpainting should show through when you are scumbling. In other words, enough of the surface should be left to produce appropriate contrast. Scumbling can be achieved with one

or more colors (applied over one another or blended together), but the entire surface underneath should never be covered. The term *scumbling* is often mistakenly referred to as wet blending (two or more colors) over the entire surface, but wet blending is just what the term implies; it is not scumbling in the true sense.

There is really not a clear distinction between scumbling and dry-brushing. Usually scumbling, in scenic terms, denotes the application of paint with a brush by sparsely dabbing or smudging over painted surfaces in sporadic patterns as in texturing stonework or modeling clouds: dry-brushing refers more to the application of specific patterns (on a painted surface) such as graining woodwork or shingles.

COMBING

Horizontal or vertical *combing* is executed with a large priming brush (attached to a long handle) on both flats and backdrops to create striated patterns. A smaller brush may also be used, depending upon the effect desired and the size of the scenery. The colors should always be thin enough to flow easily from the brush. The purpose of combing can be to break up plain surfaces, simulate wooden boards, texture over painted tapestries, or produce contrast on stenciled wallpaper (before and after the stencil is applied). For stenciling, the surface can first be combed horizontally

COMBING FLATS
To give this twofold backing unit striated patterns before a wallpaper design is stenciled on the canvas, it is combed horizontally with a contrasting color. Horizontal lines are snapped lightly in charcoal for guides. Each time, one continuous stroke is made across the framed canvas flats by starting swiftly, then gradually slowing down at the end as the paint in the brush becomes exhausted. (Photograph — Lynn Pecktal)

with dyes or semiopaque colors before the stencil is put on, and then combed afterward either horizontally or vertically. This takes away the stenciled look and makes it look like fabric. To create another effect, a plaid pattern is easily achieved on a laid-in background by combing in both directions. Here one or two colors (transparent or semiopaque) may be applied on the surface. Combing should always be done in one long continuous straight line without stopping. If you are combing a large piece of scenery like a backdrop, you must use a full brush of color so there is enough paint to spread over the entire area. It is important to start off fast with the brush following you at a low angle to the surface, then slow down gradually while raising the brush to a vertical position to allow the remaining color to come from the brush. Usually it is best to try to walk backward so you can watch the stroke as it appears and adjust your speed accordingly.

STIPPLING

In the traditional use *stippling*, which has the advantage of not leaving the usual brush marks, produces a uniform texture of small dots or specks somewhat similar to sponging, except it is more subtle. However, the effect can be varied by the way the brush is turned and by the amount of pressure used in applying the color. Stippling is created by having very little paint in the brush and by holding the bristles perpendicular to the surface and working the bristles in an up-and-down motion. Although the stippling brush is made just for this purpose, any number of other stiff-bristle brushes can be used. You can stipple with a sponge, a wad of paper, or a crumpled rag.

SPATTERING

The ever-popular *spatter* can be put on scenery to develop a smooth and even texture or a rough and random texture. All kinds of paint are applied on both wet and dry surfaces. Spattering is often applied on the base coat while it is wet in combination with brushing or the paint roller so a great deal of texture is achieved before the overpainting is begun. A heavy spatter can be obtained with the brush by dipping a large lay-in brush in the color and then slapping the ferrule against the palm of your hand; a fine spattering results when you hit the tips of the bristles against the palm. A more extensive form of spattering is produced with the brush by generously showering and splashing a very thin paint or aniline dye over the surface. While spattering is done to give a general texture and to blend areas of color, it is also sometimes done specifically with several colors so the surface can take on different appearances under different lights.

DOTTING

Dotting, also referred to as *pointillage*, is a more specialized type of texture and is usually dependent on the designer's style. It involves making small individual dots (ranging from $\frac{3}{8}$- to $\frac{3}{4}$-inch diameter) at random with a lining brush, applied on the scenery after it is laid in with the basic colors. Enormous contrast can be achieved by using dots of various colors and by the space allowed between dots.

Using the Paint Roller

For fast coverage on large flat surfaces, smooth or rough, the paint roller is the most practical applicator for painting wooden stage floors, portable Masonite decks and ramps, and other solidly built platforms. It is also excellent for creating a multitude of textures on drops, flats, and set pieces. The painting surface of the latter units can be canvas, muslin, burlap, or velour. You can obtain many variations with the paint roller, depending on the thickness of the roller cover, the amount of paint in it, and the pressure used when working with it. A narrow roller (2 inches wide) is most useful for making thin irregularly shaped lines by bearing down on one side of the roller, while a wide roller (6 to 8 inches wide) with little color in it and applied without much force is ideal for creating rough and bloblike textures. These techniques, for instance, were used to create stonework texture on the black velour-covered flats designed by William Ritman for a road company of *Sleuth*. In smaller areas, the roller works well for putting paint on the edges of flats, the edges of profile pieces, or for painting metal pipes. All sorts of paint (caseins, aniline dyes, vinyl, and latex) as well as white glue and rubber cement can be applied on scenery with the paint roller.

The paint roller is manufactured in a wide array of sizes and types. It comes with cores of wood, plastic, or metal. Roller covers in many degrees of thickness and width (1 to 18 inches) are made of plastic foam, mohair, dynel, knit wool, or lambskin, and are selected for the kind of texture needed. The thick lambskin roller cover in particular is outstanding for

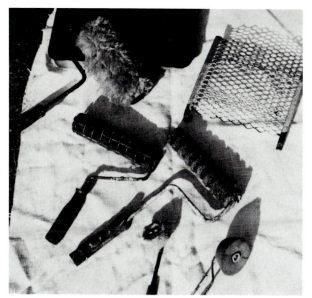

PAINT ROLLERS AND EQUIPMENT
(Top) Paint roller with thick lambskin cover resting on a paint tray. Metal bucket grid for rolling off excess paint. (Middle) Heavy turkey wire wrapped around a roller cover to produce a series of squares. Paint roller with portions of the cover cut away to form parallel lines. (Bottom) 1-in. paint roller. Paint roller for getting into corners and making thin lines. (Photograph—Lynn Pecktal)

absorbing and holding the paint, and it produces a heavily textured surface. For special effects, parts of a thick roller may be cut away with a razor blade so the remaining material on the roller forms abstract patterns or such conventional designs as stripes, dots, and squares. A series of 1-inch squares is easily formed by tightly clamping a piece of turkey wire around the roller cover.

Wooden handles and aluminum extension poles in assorted lengths are attached to the paint roller for working on floors and walls. Necessary equipment for the roller includes the paint tray to hold the color and the metal bucket grid, a most functional device which hangs on the rim inside a large bucket so that the excess paint can be drained out before the paint roller is used. Besides the standard type of roller, special kinds are made for getting into corners, and others for making sharp straight edges on moldings, doors, and windows.

Using a Feather Duster

The household feather duster made of turkey feathers provides an extremely fast method of applying either a uniform or a varied texture on large areas of scenery that are laid flat on the floor. The feather duster should have an extended handle so that it can be easily manipulated while you are standing. It is used by dipping the feathers into a large pail of thin paint or dye, letting the excess drain off slightly in the container, then applying the color on the surface by holding the feather duster vertically and working it in an up-and-down motion while twirling it gently between strokes. The feather duster can be used for texturing on almost any kind of material or fabric that is a flat surface. It may be used for applying texture with dyes on a velour cut drop, vinyl or latex on a Masonite deck, or casein on canvas-covered flats. A feather duster was used to put texture on the walls of Richard Sylbert's modern interior setting for *The Prisoner of Second Avenue*. After the canvas-covered flats were primed white (dry whiting mixed with priming size), the local color (a pale beige) was brushed on, then they were feather-dusted with a cooler color (one shade darker) and also with a warmer color (one shade lighter). This was done to give texture to the flats, since one flat color seldom lights well.

Using a Sponge

Both large natural sponges and synthetic flat sponges (household variety) provide a wide assortment of uses in the scenic studio. The natural sponges are perhaps the most versatile. These porous and pliable structures, which grow in irregular shapes, are excellent for painting on almost any kind of surface by dabbing the paint on to create texture (even or uneven), or by rubbing one or more colors together to make a blend. For texturing, the sponge is usually cut in half so the flat side can be used directly on the scenery; for added variety, it should be rotated slightly during application. When a sponge is attached to a long bamboo handle with wire, it is a good implement for applying aniline dye washes and thin caseins on backdrops of muslin, canvas, scrim, or velour. For stencil painting, the sponge readily absorbs the color and holds it well while it is being applied. Painting on vertical surfaces or ceilings can be effectively done with a sponge, especially if in the theatre proper.

The flat or rectangular synthetic sponges also come in handy. They produce a smaller texture than the natural sponge and are good for making textures that are to have sharp edges. In addition, a flat synthetic sponge mop works well for smoothing out wet areas of aniline dyes on a muslin backdrop. Besides their functions in painting, sponges are used for wiping up colors and for cleaning surfaces.

Using the Paint Stamp

This is an ideal painting method for applying

specifically shaped patterns or textures where random placement is desired, especially on large flat pieces like backdrops, legs, and borders which are tacked out on the floor. These may be such standard fabrics as muslin, canvas, velour, scrim, and monk's cloth. This technique can also be good for painting on flat surfaces of wood or Masonite. Instead of painting the patterns one by one with a brush, a long-handled stamp is used to do the repeats. In effect, paint-stamping is like using a large rubber stamp. Not only is it convenient, but it also permits the artist to work with considerable speed and variety. The paint stamp shown in the photograph at right was made up for a backdrop Ming Cho Lee designed for the Tudor chamber in *Roberto Devereux* at the New York City Opera. It was dipped in metallic gold paint (bronzing powders mixed with clear vinyl as a binder) and stamped on natural monk's cloth that was sprayed beforehand.

The actual device is simple to make. A typical paint stamp is constructed with a piece of $\frac{3}{4}$-inch plywood 12 inches square (or larger or smaller as needed). The particular pattern is cut out of an absorbent material like sponge, foam rubber, or heavy pile carpet adhered to one side of the plywood square. On the reverse side, a 3-foot wooden dowel handle is centered and attached perpendicularly. All sorts of pattern can be used: leaves in different sizes, irregular pebble shapes, a fleur-de-lis pattern, tile designs, or abstract shapes. For the best job, the paint should be tested on the surface with the selected material (sponge or whatever) for making up the stamp. For instance, heavy pile carpet might give better results when using vinyl paints or bronzing colors on canvas, whereas a sponge would work well for putting dyes on scrim.

When the stamp is made and is ready to use, you merely dip it into a low flat pan of paint or dye and then vertically stamp it on the surface. Although it depends upon the effect, it is sometimes preferable first to stamp out the excess color on a piece of paper before applying it on the scenery. A great deal of variety can be obtained by the amount of color in the stamp, the pressure put on it during application (heavily, lightly, or by fading out), and the random placement of the design.

Puddling

Puddling is simply the pouring together of two or more colors (aniline dyes, caseins, vinyls, latex, etc.) on a flat surface and letting them run together without benefit of any real labored blending. Brushes can be dipped into the paints and loaded with color, then dribbled casually onto the surface. Colors may also be spattered over the wet surface immediately afterward. Puddling works especially well for laying in the background for foliage and crumbling plaster and for painting marble and stonework.

Spraying

Both the hand spray gun and the Hudson spray tank can be used on scenery for creating textures (spattering or variegated spraying that is hazy and cloudy), for spraying flat solid colors, for spraying wet blends, or for spraying preservatives over scenery and props. The hand spray gun tends to be used mainly on small areas where a very smooth spray with good control is desired, whereas the Hudson spray tank is utilized for large areas where a more generous spray is needed. Both are splendid for the speedy application of paints and dyes. These implements are discussed in detail in Painting Equipment (pp. 270–271) and in individual processes.

The Transparent Bath

For the final process on newly painted scenery, the transparent bath is applied on the surface to antique it slightly and to give it texture (referred to as "giving it a bath"). The thin color or colors such as aniline dyes or caseins can be put on by hand-spattering with a large lay-in brush or by spraying with the Hudson tank. A transparent bath is best applied when the scenery is laid out flat on the floor. The process may be optional, of course, depending on the design. Robert Bergman, the well-known scenic artist who had his own studio earlier in the century, is often given credit for the types of bath he devised to tone down scenery. A particular bath of his consisted of mixing powdered aluminum with heavy size, which was thinned with water and then spattered on the freshly painted scenery to produce a very transparent spatter.

SPECIFIC KINDS OF SCENE PAINTING

Stencils

Almost everyone is familiar with the technique of stencil painting and how it is done. A stencil is a very fast and convenient device for repeating consistent patterns and designs onto a surface by painting. There are literally hundreds of subjects that can be made into stencils of various sizes. Those most commonly used for scenery are:

Wallpaper and wallcoverings	Egg-and-dart molding
Floral	Beading
Paisley	Guilloche
Damask	Greek key
Interlacing ornament	Dentils
Checks and cross patterns	Flutes
Decorative strips	Rosettes
Geometric designs	Medallions
Animal and bird designs	Scrolls
Bamboo	Fleurs-de-lis
Pressed-metal squares	Capital decor
Painted tile	*Geometric forms*
Abstract designs	Dots
Ornamental and architectural motifs	Squares
	Diamonds
	Triangles
	Stars

The largest stencils can range from 2 by 2 feet to 3 by 4 feet and are those utlized for wallpaper and wallcoverings, floors, ceilings, draperies, and curtains. Smaller stencils like bands, borders, ornament, and classic motifs are made for decorating cornices, panels, moldings, baseboards, columns and capitals, fireplaces, doors, folding screens, furniture, and props.

Draperies and curtains	*Brick*
Tassels	Regular
Fringe	End brick
Rope	Checkerboard
Ribbons	*Parquet floors*
Bows	Herringbone
Natural objects	Checkerboard
Flowers	*Other*
Leaves	Letters
Fruit	Numbers
Garlands	Tiny windows
Wreaths	Hinges
Snowflakes	Sunbursts
Pebbles	Spearheads

(Left to right) Stock stencils: Herringbone pattern for parquet or brick, checkerboard parquet, and common brick patterns; rope, borders, fringe, molding, and lettering stencils. Large damask pattern on stencil paper, 36 by 54 in. Lace stencil (4 ft. 6 in. by 12 ft. 6 in.) of fabric-backed vinyl made by Jack Bates for John Keck's setting in The Easter Show (1974), Radio City Music Hall.

Three stencils were required to make the floral wallpaper at right. Note the four diamond-shaped inner guides cut in the corners of the actual design (18 by 20 in.), and the research taken from a magazine.

(Above, left) Four copies of the stencil (20 by 25 in.) designed by Ming Cho Lee for the scrim panels in the New York City Opera's MARIA STUARDA (1972) being made with a Cut-awl machine. (Left) Textured bricks were stenciled with casein paint on black velour wings for Robert Randolph's APPLAUSE (1970). (Photographs — Lynn Pecktal)

Raoul Pène du Bois' wallpaper design in Act I for NO, NO, NANETTE (1970). After stenciling the pattern, artists Stanley Cappiello and Jack Hughes painted details at random on the flowers, leaves, swags, and geometrical designs. Because of the design's overall diagonal direction, a brown-paper pounce was used for the guide rather than snap lines. (Photographs — Lynn Pecktal)

A SINGLE STENCIL MAY BE:

Applied to connect continuously to another in a straight or curved line (beading or bands).

A design that is repeated on all four sides (wallpaper or brick).

Placed at random (flowers and snowflakes).

MULTIPLE STENCILS FOR ONE DESIGN MAY BE:

A set of two, three, four, or five stencils (the same size overall) with different openings cut in each, utilizing one or more colors on the individual stencil (an Art Deco stencil for draperies or wallcoverings). Two or more stencils (the same overall size) having different openings cut in each to represent modeling a three-dimensional object like shapes for light, highlight, shadow, cutting line (tassels, ropes, egg-and-dart molding).

LAYING OUT A DETAILED STENCIL

The initial step in planning a detailed stencil is to make sure that it is accurately drawn and well proportioned, because this is what determines the success of the job. While many stencils (like tassels, stars, and fleurs-de-lis) are simple to make, others are complicated in design and require a more detailed layout. Let us suppose that you are making a stencil for a damask wallpaper pattern and have already researched it and are sure of what design you want. To start, you should do a preliminary

drawing so the layout for cutting can be figured exactly. The drawing is usually put on brown paper (or sometimes tracing paper) which can easily be perforated with the pounce wheel and then transferred to the actual stencil paper by rubbing a bag of charcoal over it. Regular pencils are good for drawing the layout, and black and red wax pencils can be used to make any corrections.

In doing the layout, you should allow at least four inches of paper around the perimeter of the design. For example, if the actual design is 24 inches by 30, the total dimensions of the brown paper for the layout and for the stencil would be 32 inches by 38. The perimeters for drawing a wallpaper stencil are generally laid out in squares or rectangles, and it is very important that all the corners be exactly 90 degrees. When you have drawn the rectangle or square, construct two center lines (a vertical and a horizontal) so that you have four smaller rectangles or squares. By working from the center lines, the design will be centered properly on the stencil, and if the design is a symmetrical one, you will only have to draw half of it, then

(Left) Only two stencils were needed to paint this pressed-metal ceiling pattern for Douglas W. Schmidt's bar set in THE TIME OF YOUR LIFE (1969) at Lincoln Center. A trial sample with the darkest color stenciled last (bottom, first photograph). The final pattern with the lightest color stenciled last (bottom, second photograph). Note the totally different effect achieved in this reversal. (Photographs — Arnold Abramson)

Steps of Execution:

1. Canvas primed and base-coated, guideline squares snapped.
2. The first stencil of quarter circles (top, left photograph) painted with a sponge to form the textured background for the circles.
3. Paint brushed on through the second stencil (center, left photograph), applying a darker color to serve as the thicknesses or shade color of the pressed-metal patterns.
4. For the third stenciling, the same stencil was used with a lighter color, but the stencil was slid down consistently ¼ in. from the original charcoal guidelines to produce thickness.

Raoul Pène du Bois' painted ballroom stencil design for IRENE (1973)

fold the paper and perforate both halves at the same time. Or the pattern you are making may be such that only a quarter of it must be drawn, then it can be reversed and repeated as needed. Since a damask pattern has a great many small details, the design being copied and enlarged is usually gridded off in squares, and comparable squares in the desired scale are drawn on the full-scale brown paper layout. This makes it much quicker and easier to draw the stencil design.

PLANNING THE TIES AND JOININGS

When drawing the design, it is essential to have sufficient ties to hold the open design together. These can be planned so that they are visually pleasing, but they must not be too narrow or the stencil may tear and fall apart during use. Ties should not be less than $\frac{3}{16}$ inch in width, and $\frac{1}{4}$ inch is really better if it is a large stencil. The joinings (where one inner edge on a stencil meets the next inner edge during a repeat) must also be thought out well so they match neatly. After all the drawing has been completed, perforate it with the pounce wheel. Then, using the charcoal pounce bag, try out the design by repeating it a few times on a larger piece of paper to see just how the stencil joinings (at the top, bottom, and sides) work when the stencil is repeated. The continuous flow of the design from one repeat to another is what really counts, especially on a damask pattern. You should not be able to see that a square or rectangular shape has been painted, but instead an overall interlocking pattern. If alterations are necessary, they can be made before the design is transferred to the stencil paper.

CUTTING OUTER GUIDES

Guides (V-shaped notches) are necessary for placing the stencil on the snapped lines of the painting surface. To obtain guides, extend all of the drawn lines of the perimeter to meet the edges of the stencil paper. Where each line meets the edge, cut out a V-shaped notch. There will be a total of eight. For applying paint through a large complicated stencil as for damask, where the designs must be precisely matched on the repeats, lines are normally snapped on the painting surface both horizontally and vertically to make doubly certain that the stencil does not slip during application of the paint.

CUTTING INNER GUIDES

Although this is optional when lines have been snapped in both directions, further accuracy can be assured by marking an inner set of small guides in the corners of the design proper. These four openings are intended for painting as well as being guides, and they are ordinarily worked into the design in the shape of a circle, a diamond, or a square. Usually they are no more than $\frac{1}{2}$ inch in overall dimension. Assume that circles have been used as inner guides on the damask stencil on which you are working. By having these shapes in the corners, the last two (already painted) circles on the surface must always match the first two cut circles on the stencil as it is being placed for another repeat. In this manner an artist can tell how accurately the stencil is going on the surface (either backdrop or framed flat), particularly when the second row of stenciling has been started and there are three small circle guides on the stencil that must match the three just-painted circles.

CUTTING STENCILS

Stencils are made of oiled stencil paper which comes in rolls (3 by 4 feet) or in sheets (18 by 24 inches and 2 by 3 feet). A stencil can be cut by hand with an X-Acto knife, a stencil knife, or a single-edge razor blade, but with these instruments it is difficult to cut more than one stencil at a time. While a single copy may be adequate for a simple stencil, a detailed pattern like damask should have at least four copies cut just to be on the practical side. Having duplicates allows you to alternate when the first one becomes too wet or is damaged and also enables other painters to work with an identical copy of the stencil simultaneously. Furthermore, stencils are kept in stock for reuse, and an original copy is retained as a pattern for cutting a new set. Many designers doing Broadway shows come into the scenic studio during the execution of the scenery to pick out stencils from a huge stock collection that has been saved over the years.

The best way to cut four stencils at once is with a Cut-awl machine, a small power saw with a vertical cutting blade. It is very effective for minute and detailed cutting and can easily cut through several layers of stencil paper. The tabletop on which you are working should have a sheet of Upson board laid on it so that when you are operating the Cut-awl the vertical blade can be set to cut slightly into the surface of the Upson, thereby neatly going through all four pieces of the stencil paper. After you have selected the size of stencil paper to fit your design, cut four pieces alike. Then, if you have not done so, transfer the design or draw it directly onto the top sheet. When ready, attach the stack of four pieces of stencil paper with a carpet tack in each corner to keep them in place while cutting. On a large stencil it helps to have additional tacks in some of the center areas, and these areas can be cut last, ensuring a secure hold on the stack. With both hands guiding the Cut-awl, cut out the stencil openings by running the blade through the drawn lines of the design.

Before a newly cut stencil is ready to use, shellac (clear white or orange) is brushed on each side and then it is hung vertically to dry. This coating acts as additional protection to the oiled stencil paper and makes it easy to remove the paint afterward with a sponge and warm water. Stencils that get a lot of use are sometimes made of sheets of aluminum or brass.

STENCIL PAINTING

You can apply paint through the stencil openings onto the surface by brushes, sponges, spray guns, or by paint rollers. The largeness or smallness of the openings in the stencil plus the type of surface (soft or hard) and the kind of paint usually indicate which paint applicator to use. As examples, you may apply paint by:

Brushing aniline dye color (with Methocel added) through a floral stencil on a sharkstooth scrim drop.
Brushing casein paint through a lettering stencil on a muslin backdrop.
Paint-rolling casein paint through a brick stencil on a black-velour flat.
Sponging gold metallic paint (bronze powder) through a rosette stencil on a wooden staircase.
Spraying transparent lacquer through a sunburst stencil on a Plexiglas panel.

Stencil brushes or other stiff-bristled brushes work best for painting on stencils, and best results are obtained by using only a little paint in the brush at one time. The brush is generally held vertically and manipulated in an up-and-down motion similar to stippling with a brush. The bristles of the brush can also be worked back and forth over the stencil. You may also want to use other paint applicators. Natural round sponges work well on hard surfaces to produce a nice open texture. Hand spray guns (with the stencil placed vertically) are effective whenever a small number of repeats is being painted, but repeated spraying on the same stencil often causes the paint to run. Paint rollers with thick roller covers are good for creating texture on stencils that have large openings.

TEXTURING THE BACKGROUND BEFORE STENCILING

In stencil painting, several ideas are worked into the process so that the finished painting does not appear to be merely "stenciled." A superior stenciling job on large areas of scenery is one in which the audience is not really sure that a stencil has been used. A more interesting contrast can be achieved in the paint job of a stenciled surface if the background is varied by texturing before the stenciling is begun. For instance, a flat that is to get a wallpaper stencil is often combed over the lay-in color with a different value (darker or lighter) of the same color, applied very thinly. The direction of the combing can be horizontal or vertical, depending on the effect sought. Then, after the lines have been snapped on the surface for the stencil guides to be placed, the flat is ready for stenciling.

You can also repeat the process of combing with thin transparent colors (thin caseins or aniline dyes, in this case) after the stenciling has been finished to produce a woven-fabric effect on the patterned surface, thus taking away the mechanical "stenciled look" and giving it added texture. But combing before and after stenciling can really vary. You may want to comb it horizontally both times or vertically both times, in opposite directions, or only comb it once in one direction.

On other backgrounds, like those for a brick stencil, the lay-in can be casually brushed on the flat or built set piece with perhaps a pale gray and a medium gray for the mortar color, and when the bricks are stenciled, several colors like red, brown, and tan can be brushed, sponged, or rolled on. Still other backgrounds can be textured before stenciling by feather-dusting or by spraying. It is up to you and the effect you want to achieve.

FREEHAND PAINTING ON SEPARATE STENCILED AREAS

On large detailed stenciled jobs, separate areas of a pattern are sometimes painted freehand with a brush during or after the stenciling. It may be creating shades and shadows with a transparent color or adding lights and highlights in an opaque color, or just glazing over certain areas to break up a specific design. A great deal of this kind of painting over the stenciling designs took place on the elaborately stenciled ballroom walls of *Irene* and on the interior scenery of *No, No, Nanette*, both designed by Raoul Pène du Bois.

In addition to freehand painting on a stenciled surface, you may want to give it a transparent bath as the final painting process. Using aniline dye or thin casein, the surface can be spattered by slapping brushfuls of color against your palm or by spattering the color with a Hudson tank that has little air pressure in it.

Silk-Screening

As a stenciling technique, silk-screening is seldom used for theatrical scenery in the average studio, because of the time and cost involved in making the template as well as the fact that there are a limited number of materials and surfaces on which it is effective. Regular stencils can usually be cut with stencil paper and already used during the time it takes to prepare a good silk screen. An exception to this was the colorful show curtain for *How Now, Dow Jones,* designed by Oliver Smith, on which many stock exchange listings in small type face were superimposed on a painted background. By using one silk screen with a section of stock quotations on it (letters and numbers were a maximum of $1\frac{1}{2}$ inches high), literally thousands of copies of the type face were repeated on the canvas backdrop, laid flat on the floor. The silk screen itself was made up by a commercial firm, using a photographic process. Oil paint was pressed through the mesh of the silk by a squeegee (a neoprene blade in a wooden handle). The overall screen, including the wooden frame, measured 3 feet 5 inches wide by 5 feet 5 inches long and required two painters to shift it to the next area. Turpentine on a cloth was used for cleaning the oil paint from the screen.

Information and supplies for silk-screening may be obtained from Flax's Artists Stores in Chicago, Los Angeles, New York, and San Francisco, and from Arthur Brown & Bro., Inc. in New York. A good book on the subject is *Screen Painting* by J. I. Biegeleisen (New York: Watson-Guptill Publications, 1971), a contemporary guide to the technique of screen printing for artists, designers, and craftsmen.

Painting Draperies

Painted draperies appear with great frequency on backdrops, cut drops, show curtains, flats, and profiled set pieces. The painting surfaces may be such materials as muslin, canvas, white velour, linen, and white sharkstooth scrim. Some of the scenery in the following recently staged productions display but a few examples of painted drapery: in musicals—the music-room walls of *Irene,* designed by Raoul Pène du Bois, and the show curtain of *A Little Night*

Music, designed by Boris Aronson; in opera— the cut drops of *l'Incoronazione di Poppea,* designed by Lloyd Evans, and the show curtain, cut drop, and set pieces of *The Young Lord,* designed by Helen Pond and Herbert Senn (both productions for the New York City Opera); and in the ballet—the backdrops, show curtain, and hanging pieces of *Pulcinella,* designed by Eugene Berman.

Although the painting of drapery for a production varies enormously with the style and treatment of the designer, it is usually painted in a realistic fashion on a flat surface. Perhaps the most typical painted drapery in theatrical productions is the heavy velour baroque drapery that is often red, green, or gold and includes swags, jabots, and festoons that are elaborately decorated with painted fringe, tassels, braid, borders, or bands. Invariably, long sweeps of the elegantly painted drapery are embellished with painted tiebacks of heavy gold rope or with rosettes or other classical ornament.

Drapery is "modeled" in a way that is similar to painting molding or ornament. In all of these you use lights, highlights, and shade. But in painting drapery, you should think of "the drawing" in the drapery, and always concentrate on how the fabric hangs and how the line of the drapery flows. This quite naturally depends on what kind of fabric the draperies are supposed to be made of and whether the material is soft and lightweight or stiff and heavy. For instance, if you are painting drapery to simulate a soft material like chiffon, you know that it will hang in small folds when it is gathered, draped, and tied back, and if the bottom edge of the fabric touches the floor, it will fall gracefully in a pile. If you are painting a stiff material such as velour, it will have large irregular folds when draped and will "break" where the bottom edge rests on the floor. So the nature of the fabric and the manner in which it is draped have a great deal to do with how the drapery is drawn and painted.

LAYING OUT THE DRAWING FOR DRAPERY

There are two approaches to laying out the drawing for drapery. You can draw the outline, including the lines for the sweeps, in charcoal before the local color is applied, and then ink it so the drawing will show through. Or you can draw the drapery with charcoal after the local color has been laid in. Usually, the outline of the drapery is drawn first, then it is laid in with the local color. When dry, the details are lightly

Backdrop design by Robert D. Mitchell
IN RETROSPECT
Choreographed by Robert Rodham
Pennsylvania Ballet
Walnut Street Theatre
Philadelphia, Pennsylvania (1973)
(Photograph—Robert D. Mitchell)

PAINTING DRAPERY ON A TRANSLUCENT MUSLIN BACKDROP
Steps of Execution:
1. Backdrop stapled on floor over gray bogus paper and starched.
2. A black thread grid of 2-ft. squares stretched across drop; drawing was done lightly with charcoal.
3. All middle tones were laid in first on the drapery, saving natural muslin color for lightest tones.
4. Dark accents painted.
5. Thin transparent washes brushed over parts of the draperies, the sky, and remaining details.

sketched in charcoal and the drapery is painted.

The drawing for drapery is executed by both freehand sketching and with the aid of drawing implements. If you are drawing massive swags and sweeps of drapery on the scenery or on a large paper pounce drawing laid on the floor, you can use a long thin wooden lath (around $\frac{1}{4}$ by 1 inch by 16 to 20 feet) or a long length of steel coil chain to make nice full sweeps. Both are used as guides for drawing the charcoal line. The wooden lath is kept in the desired position by putting weights on each end, while the chain is only weighted on one end and then swung into place on the floor. Also, sizable lengths of

hemp rope can be utilized for making large sweeps if you are working on a vertical paint frame. One end of the rope is attached by a nail, and after the sweep is shaped with it, the other end is fastened with a nail. If rope is unavailable, you can use a chain on the paint frame.

PAINTING DRAPERY ON CANVAS OR MUSLIN
Assuming that the drapery is to be painted on canvas or muslin and is not being treated as a translucency, the local color is generally mixed in casein paints, or it can be dry pigment colors mixed with size water. This local color (or lay-in) should be mixed so that it is the actual color of the draperies. For modeling the drap-

PAINTING DRAPERY ON A SHARKSTOOTH SCRIM
Lloyd Burlingame designed this sharkstooth-scrim backdrop of painted drapery for AÏDA (1973) at the Cincinnati Opera.
Steps of Execution:
1. Scrim stapled squarely on the floor after laying gray bogus paper.
2. Starting at center, 2-ft. measurements were marked in charcoal on the bottom and top edges of the scrim and along the sides.
3. Drawing done in charcoal.
4. Vertical folds in the drapery defined by applying long continuous brush strokes.
5. Scrim drop laid in (left) by spraying aniline dye colors bottom to top and vice versa.
6. Painting finished (right) with aniline dyes, thin casein paints, and metallic silver (bronze powder and clear gloss vinyl) used on details and for spattering. (Photographs—Lynn Pecktal)

eries, you will then need to mix darker and lighter colors of the local color. You should mix two darks (a color darker than the lay-in, and a color darker than that). Next, mix two lights (a color lighter than the lay-in, and a color lighter than that for the highlight color).

As in painting ornament or molding, the direction the light is coming from should always be considered and determined before starting to paint. This is usually obvious from looking at the designer's paint sketch, but if it isn't, you as the painter should decide where the light is coming from. Usually light coming down from the left or right, or down from the center paints best, but it can also come up from below (left, center, or right), depending on the individual setting.

After the light source has been determined, start overpainting on the local color of the draperies by brushing on the first dark color and take this color through, establishing all areas. When you have finished painting with this, go next to the first light color and also take it through. You should always keep in mind that at least a third or more of the applied local color should be left unpainted (or saved) after these colors have been put on so the modeled quality of the drapery is not lost. Now, put in the darkest color (the accent) within the area of the dark. Continue the painting by brushing on the lightest color (the highlight) within the area of the light. Sometimes the darks may be mixed in aniline dyes to give added "punch" to the folds in the drapery. Dyes are also used for creating cut-velvet patterns and decorative borders which are applied by brush when all of the drapery has been modeled. Any details on the drapery like fringe, tassels, ropes, braid, or ornament are laid in and modeled the same way as in painting the drapery.

In the scenic studio, it is normal procedure for the painter to take one color through the whole area of drapery at one time, then repeat the process until all the colors have been applied. Not only does this work well when two or three painters are working together on a unit of scenery, but it tends to produce a consistency that is desirable for seeing the overall progress of the painting. When the drapery has been finished, it is ordinarily given a thin transparent bath by spattering it either with a large brush or with a Hudson tank containing little pressure.

PAINTING DRAPERIES ON WHITE VELOUR

If the drapery is being painted on a white-velour backdrop or on flats covered in white velour (normally laid on the floor), the lay-in color is mixed in aniline dye and is sprayed on the fabric. This can be done with a hand spray gun or a Hudson spray tank, depending on the size and effect desired, but the nozzle of either should be directed to follow the sweeps in the drapery.

On white velour, the local color for the lay-in should be the lightest color ("the light"), because it is like painting a watercolor—the light must be saved, and then the darks are worked into it. When you are spraying the light color on, you should leave some lighter areas to serve as highlights. Ordinarily, two other colors are mixed for painting on white velour. These are the medium and the dark; they are also mixed with dyes but are applied with a brush. Occasionally, a hand spray gun is used to tone the folds of the painted drapery. Again, the finished work may be given a bath. When you are painting drapery on white sharkstooth scrim, the same methods as for white velour can be used.

PAINTING DRAPERIES IN THE WET

Draperies are also effectively painted by doing them in the wet. This too, depends upon the desired effect, and sometimes it is a personal preference. Painting in the wet is usually done where the areas of the drapery can be conveniently reached by the artist, and where they are not so large that they cannot be controlled while they are wet. Some scenic artists like this method best when a smooth blending of the colors is required. It is usually necessary to work fast with the colors as they are applied so an even blending is obtained. If you are painting on muslin or canvas, liquid starch can be added to the casein colors to retard their drying time, allowing you to obtain a better blend. A separate brush is used for each color, and a clean brush with water can be used for blending.

For painting draperies on a translucent muslin backdrop, liquid starch is also good to mix with the aniline dyes; it produces an excellent translucency and, again, keeps the areas wet enough to blend well. Thin caseins are most frequently used when the muslin is not to be a translucency. Furthermore, aniline dyes may be worked over any of the above-mentioned techniques to give added richness.

Egg and dart   **Rosette**

Wrought iron strap hinge— 14th century

Wrought iron
strap hinge—16th
century

Ornamental border and fringe, painted on the muslin show curtain for
THE YOUNG LORD (1973), designed by Helen Pond and Herbert Senn
for the New York City Opera. (Right)

Steps of Execution:

1. Drop stapled on floor over gray bogus paper and starched.
2. Horizontal guidelines snapped in charcoal. Perforated brown-paper
   drawings of the ornaments transferred to muslin surface.
3. Ornament inked with felt-tip pens.
4. Local colors laid in. Background behind fringe stenciled on.
5. Light, shade, and shadow colors brushed on ornament and fringe.
   (Photograph—Lynn Pecktal)

Upper part of
wrought iron
trammel hook—
18th century

Wrought iron pilaster—
17th century

Wrought iron bracket candlestick—
18th century

Painting Ornament

No matter whether you are painting a panel
of *trompe-l'oeil* ornament or a Corinthian capital, it is absolutely essential that a good drawing
be made first, and this alone can often take
more time to execute than the painting itself.
When you are doing ornament of any complexity, either of a realistic nature or in a loose style,
an accurate drawing should be made on brown
Kraft paper and perforated with the pounce
wheel. Initially, the design being copied is
gridded off in squares, and then comparable
squares are made on the paper in the designated
scale. Once this is done, lightly sketch in guidelines to define the outline and proportions of the
ornament before you actually start to draw it.
Whenever drawing classic or realistic ornament,
best results are generally achieved by having
some source material within easy reach. Two of
the standbys for ornament research are the
Handbook of Ornament by Franz Sales Meyer
and the *Styles of Ornament* by Alexander Speltz.

Realistic ornament is painted and modeled
like molding or other three-dimensional objects and the colors for the light, the shade, and
the shadow are mixed accordingly. Once the
local color has been laid in, the perforated
pattern of ornament is pounced on the painting
surface with the charcoal bag and inked. If a
lot of ornament is being painted, the colors are
"taken through" and brushed on one at a time
as in a production line. Next, the highlight and
the cutting-line colors are applied in the same
way. Then the ornament is finished as desired
by applying transparent glazing or by bathing it.

Painting Marble

Marble painting (or "marbleizing") is an interesting way of creating patterns on various parts
of a stage setting. It can appear on almost any
kind of scenery—drops, wings, ground cloths,
or furniture—but frequently it is painted for very
elegant and luxurious sets. There are numerous
kinds and colors of marble. Some of the popular
ones are sienna and travertine (a light brown)
and Carrara (a pure white), which come from
Italy, Egyptian red, serpentine (mainly yellow-
ish-green and green), rose marble, fossiliferous,
and black-and-gold marble.

Whenever marble is to be painted, it is always
helpful to have a research sample to see just
what the specific pattern looks like so you can
either copy or interpret it. This is usually a piece
of marbleized paper or a photo of a marble object. The designer may furnish the research, or
if the scenic studio knows what he prefers, it is
painted accordingly, using his color elevation
instead of a sample. In marbleizing, the painting is really never done twice in the same way,
because marble patterns vary considerably.
There can be many different sizes and shapes
within the patterns. One designer may want the
marble bright, prominently veined, with small
shapes and another mellow and subtle with
large shapes.

In painting marble, it is important to concentrate on the direction, the flow of the veins,

Wrought iron transom grill, foliate scrolls enriched with
repoussé details—17th century

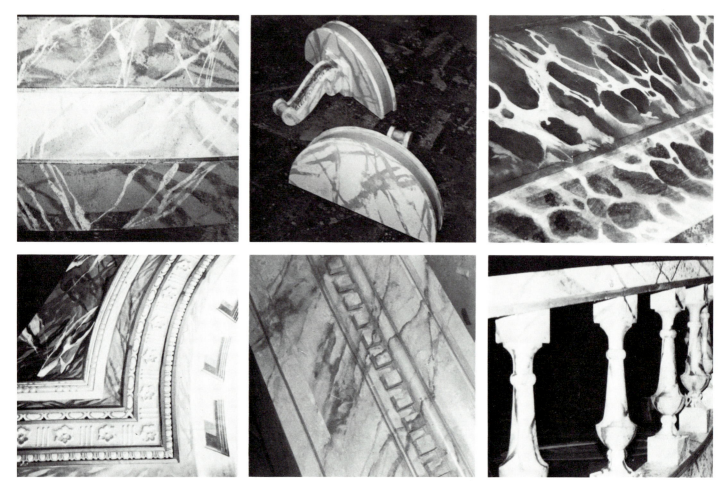

EXAMPLES OF PAINTING MARBLE
Top (left) Light and dark marble patterns in vinyl paint are brushed over an oil-paint background on Oliver Smith's bathtub for THE WOMEN (1973). (Center) Console tables for the same show are basecoated in opaque shellac with light and dark marble patterns also painted in vinyl paint. (Right) Shown before the final marble overpainting are the columns (on muslin) for Sandro La Ferla's setting of Menotti's SEBASTIAN (1974), presented by the Harkness Ballet. Below (left) Marbleizing on Lloyd Evans' canvas cut drop for L'INCORONAZIONE DI POPPEA (1973) done with aniline dyes and casein paints over a background laid in with casein paint. (Center) A wooden unit with three-dimensional molding and dentils marbleized by using oil paints thinned with turpentine over a local color of opaque shellac. (Right) The curved marbleized balustrade unit for Oliver Smith's stairs in SLEEPING BEAUTY (1974) for the American Ballet Theatre. The three-dimensional wooden balusters were turned on a lathe. (Photographs—Lynn Pecktal)

and the variety of the overall pattern. Marble must always be painted broadly to "read" from a distance. It is usually advisable to emphasize the direction of marble in one piece. If the marble is to be in more than a single piece, the direction should be shifted where the pieces are joined, just as they would be in wood graining on paneling.

You can use a number of paints to create marble. The most common are caseins, vinyls, aniline dyes, and dry scenic colors. A few years ago, some scenic artists preferred working in oil paints thinned with turpentine or benzine. That medium is still used occasionally, but mainly for props. The kind of paint should be selected by how well it works on the particular surface and how well it works for you. Marble is ordinarily painted with a brush or with a sponge. Both natural round sponges and synthetic rectangular sponges are very useful.

While there are many techniques in which marble can be painted, two methods are generally used: (1) a series of transparent glazes and (2) doing most of the marble painting "in the wet." In either of these, the surface must be laid in first with a color that is mixed close to the general tone of the marble's color. Casein paint or vinyl paint can be used for laying in muslin and canvas surfaces, while an opaque shellac is good for plywood (to seal the surface) or for metal. After the lay-in has been applied, it should be left to dry.

PAINTING MARBLE IN A SERIES OF GLAZES

If the marbleizing is being done with a series of thin transparent glazes, opaque colors (again, caseins or vinyls) can be thinned with water to make the glazes. Usually three or four colors are used to paint the marble, but this really depends on the sample or sketch. Water should be added to the colors for lightening them rather than using white. These are applied by *building up* the colors, starting with colors that are darker than the background (lay-in). After several tones have been put on, you may want to put on a color lighter than the background, applying it in the shape of the marble's veins. Once all of the marble painting has dried, you can go back over it again with the original glazes to give added depth. Aniline dyes can also be used, but they should have a bit of clear vinyl added to them for holding well on the surface. Marbleizing with transparent glazes is most useful for drops and large areas where the layers of color are hard to control.

PAINTING MARBLE "IN THE WET"

Painting marble "in the wet" is an alternate method that is effective for areas which can be easily controlled or can be reached, like a tabletop or a panel. For the background, two basic tones of the desired color can be blended together; again, these should be applied with direction according to the sample. Then, while the background is wet, take the veining colors (a dark and a light, or two darks or two lights) and trail them through the wet lay-in either with the tip of a soft brush or the edge of a flat sponge, varying the width of the lines, recrossing and intersecting them. While the painting is damp, spatter the surface, allowing it to run a bit so the brush marks are diffused. When the marbleizing has dried, it can be finished with a clear varnish (either high or low luster) or with a clear vinyl.

Creating a Painted Tortoiseshell Effect

The painted tortoiseshell effect has long been a favorite pattern among decorators. This spotty variegated coloration of yellow and brown and sometimes other colors is derived from the shell of the hawksbill turtle. The tortoiseshell effect is usually applied on such props as tables, bookcases, and decorative panels. The following process is typical of how the tortoiseshell effect is created scenically. Like marble painting, it is standard practice for the designer to submit a sample to go by, and you should always consult that.

Since such props are usually made of wood or the like, the lay-in color can be mixed in an opaque shellac by mixing dry scenic colors in Haeuser's white Enamelac. The background color may be a beige or a golden brown, and sometimes two coats are needed for a good

finish. When this has dried, it should be spattered rather generously with a bright gold or Roman gold. These golds are normally made by mixing bronze colors in clear white shellac (or orange shellac, if a warmer gold is desired). The spattering of gold should be applied with large spots of color, so it reads well from the stage, but it should not be done so heavily that it gets rid of all the background color. After drying, the surface can be given more variety by lightly spraying it with a haze of gold or brass from an aerosol can. Also, the surface is sometimes spattered very frugally with black casein or black vinyl.

The surface is ready to be antiqued once it is thoroughly dry and "tarry." Black asphaltum is ideal for this. It is black in solid form, but becomes a brownish-black when thinned with turpentine. It is best to brush a mixture of asphaltum and turpentine over the whole surface and leave it to dry overnight. The next morning, the painted asphaltum surface can be spattered with turpentine or lacquer thinner to give it a spotty variegated surface. Once the finished work is completely dry, a preservative can be applied; this can be a coat of low-luster varnish or a coat of clear vinyl.

PAINTED MARBLE PAPER

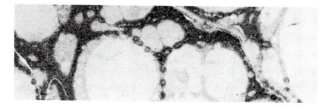

TORTOISESHELL PAPER
Sheets of both can be purchased for making design collages, covering small stage props, or research in painting.

Foliage

In doing a stage setting that is to be predominately foliage, a designer may indicate the specific kind of treatment he prefers either by rendering it in meticulous detail or by submitting a general sketch to show the drawing and the colors along with a particular piece of research that he wants the foliage to look like. Whether it is realistic (the most difficult to do well) or highly stylized foliage, it is always essential that the painters in the scenic studio know precisely what the designer wants and expects. The exact style of how the foliage is to be executed in the scenic studio is clarified between the designer and the head painter (chargeman) before work begins. Source material for trees and foliage can be selected by the designer from the works of any number of great painters like Fragonard, Guardi, Constable, Turner, or Watteau or it can even be a copy of foliage torn out of a commercial magazine.

TYPES OF FOLIAGE

The representation of foliage as scenery on stage (both realistic and stylized) takes many forms. While foliage can be found in any theatrical production, it is most prevalent in the opera and ballet. Foliage may be generally thought of in the following categories, and frequently the setting is a combination of several:

Unframed (soft) units (can be folded or rolled)	*Framed*
Backdrops	Wings and borders
Cut drops	Ground rows
Legs and borders	Profiled set pieces
Hanging panels or irregularly shaped hanging pieces	*Three-dimensional built units*
	Half round
	Three-quarter round
	Full round

Three-dimensional units can be trees, hedges, or shrubs, may have leaves, vines, plants, or flowers.

PAINTING FOLIAGE ON A TRANSLUCENT BACKDROP

Although today some designers tend to look upon realistically painted foliage as unfashionable, there are productions such as *Swan Lake* and *Giselle* that have almost always demanded that the foliage be done in a traditional style of painting where the set is basically made up of legs, borders, and backdrops. More often than not, backdrops are designated translucent.

Before painting foliage on a backdrop of translucent muslin, several steps of preparation must be carried out. You should:

1. Lay gray bogus paper on the floor.
2. Tack (staple) the backdrop down after accurately snapping lines for all four sides.
3. Starch drop in the usual manner and let dry.
4. Place black cotton threads across the backdrop to form a grid of 3-foot squares (sometimes 2-foot if there is a lot of detail) for drawing. Attach threads with carpet tacks (off the muslin).
5. Cover the designer's color sketch with clear acetate and grid it off in comparable squares.
6. Draw or cartoon the sketch on the backdrop.

The black threads perform beautifully as a grid for drawing, because snapping the lines in charcoal would show on the finished translucent muslin backdrop. It must be emphasized that the drawing for the painting should be done as carefully as possible, because it has just as much importance as the painting. On a translucent backdrop, the drawing is always executed very lightly with a stick of charcoal in a bamboo holder. When you have an area of foliage against the sky, for instance, the charcoal line should be dotted rather than continuously drawn. In this manner, the drawing shows less. After you have completed all of the drawing that is needed for painting on the translucent muslin backdrop, rip off the threads and dust the backdrop thoroughly with a feather duster or flogger before applying any color.

MIXING THE COLORS AND GETTING EQUIPMENT READY

For a translucent backdrop, the colors are mixed in aniline dyes and thin casein colors. While observing the designer's color sketch, remember to concentrate on the distant, middle distant, and foreground tones when you are mixing these. You should always test the mixed colors on a piece of fabric identical to the backdrop to see how they look after drying. When ready, the containers of aniline dyes and thin caseins can be conveniently arranged on a low wooden paint dolly, along with a large bucket of clear water for thinning the colors and for rinsing the brushes. For paletting the colors, which are taken from the containers with brushes, pieces of brown Kraft paper are laid nearby on the floor.

LAYING IN THE COLORS

Start work at the top of the backdrop and lay in the sky colors first. Very often these colors are sprayed on with Hudson tanks, then worked over in the wet (or when dry) with a long-handled brush or a sponge attached to a long handle. Next, do any other areas of painting that appear behind the foliage, like hills or fields or meadows. Since you are painting a translucency, no opaque or white paint should be used for the light colors. Instead, a watercolor technique is used, whereby the light areas (the muslin itself) are saved and washed over later.

When starting to do the foliage, first apply the far-distant and palest tones of foliage, the middle tones next, and then the foreground. Foliage is laid in to suggest various masses or clumps of leaves rather than painting individual leaves. Remember that the lay-in on a given area must be the lightest value on that area, for once it becomes darker, it cannot be lightened again. Casual brushing and the spontaneous application of foliage always gives better results than laboring over it. Interesting patterns can be created by having irregular patches of sky breaking through the foliage, and good contrast can be obtained by silhouetting one group of leaves against another.

Liquid starch (like that for starching the backdrop) is ideal for mixing in with the colors (both aniline dyes and thin caseins) to thicken them, to make them flow easily on the fabric with the brush, and to keep colors wet longer for working. By adding starch to the color, you can produce a thickness for working that is somewhat like painting in oil or in a finger-painting medium.

Many scenic artists contend that the best way to do well-painted foliage is to acquire dexterity with the brush by making continuous groups of strokes, which is somewhat like practicing handwriting by using the Palmer penmanship method. For the beginner, the best way to learn this is by repeatedly doing it. Usually the $2\frac{1}{2}$-to-3-inch Fitch brush (on a long handle) is the most desirable brush for painting leaves. The particular characteristics of the kind of tree or foliage being painted should always be considered: What is the general shape of the masses of foliage? How do they relate to the limbs and the trunk of the tree? What kind of texture does the bark have—smooth or rough?

When all of the areas have been laid in, accents and details of leaves can be painted at random while complying with the sketch. Tree-trunks and branches are laid in next, and these are modeled with light and shade, including any shadow that may be applicable. Then the particular texture or details of the bark are finished. If there are other items on the backdrop such as rocks, vines, or ferns, they are treated in the same manner. A thin transparent bath of dyes (or very thin caseins), which may be one or several colors, is usually spattered on the drop. And even during the lay-in and painting on the backdrop, the artist may spatter frequently, adding texture to the surface.

PAINTING FOLIAGE ON AN OPAQUE BACKDROP

When you are doing a foliage backdrop that is opaque, the same techniques are used as on a translucency, except the lay-in colors are the middle tones which can be worked up with opaque lighter tones and accents (both dark and light). The basic difference in doing a translucent drop and an opaque drop, then, is this: On a *translucency*, you start with the light values and work down to the dark values. For an *opaque drop*, you begin with the middle values and work down to get the darkest values and work up to get the lightest values. By putting the darks on first, you sometimes discover that you don't need as many lights as you thought.

BLEACHING AREAS PAINTED WITH ANILINE DYES

While it is better to save the "lights" (light colors) on any translucency, there are occasions when a color will dry darker than expected. This can be lightened by the use of chlorine bleach (Clorox), although it is not highly recommended unless it is absolutely imperative. A solution of $\frac{1}{3}$ bleach to $\frac{2}{3}$ water, or $\frac{1}{2}$ bleach to $\frac{1}{2}$ water (no stronger), can be applied on the muslin with a piece of rag or a brush, by spraying, or by spattering. Too much bleach, of course, can weaken the fabric or make a hole. It should *never* be used on silk.

1 part BLEACH (Clorox) to 2 parts WATER	SOLUTION FOR BLEACHING AREAS PAINTED WITH ANILINE DYES

As an alternative, it is possible to use some thin opaque light leaves over the darkly painted area. Naturally, these will become dark when the drop is backlighted on stage. But usually the front and back lighting are balanced enough for this to work. Sometimes, when it is impossible to save all the "lights," thin opaque leaves may be added for sparkle.

LIGHTENING THIN CASEINS ON A TRANSLUCENCY

If thin casein colors have been used where areas have become too dark, they may be lightened by first brushing clean warm water over the area to soften the paint. Then the fabric is rubbed gently with a sponge or clean cloth. The warm water melts the starch underneath the color and makes the paint lift off more easily. The point here is to take the paint off the surface as much as possible, rather than rub it in. Since the casein has not penetrated the fabric, it can be carefully lifted off, whereas dyes go through both the starch and the fabric.

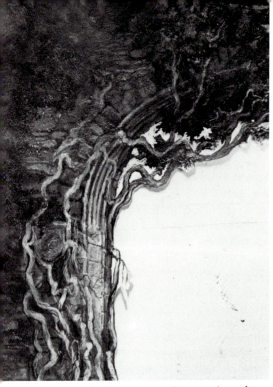

Foliage collage by Ed Wittstein
THE MERCHANT OF VENICE
American Shakespeare Festival
Stratford, Conn. (1967)

Collage in ½-in. scale. Materials: Acetate, modeling paste (Liquitex), metallic papers and colors —gold, silver, lead, bronze, and copper.

Paint elevation (partial view, ½-in. scale) of a cut leg drop and a dimensionally built tree unit by Marsha Louis Eck
LUCIA DI LAMMERMOOR, New York City Opera (1969)

Howard Bay's trees for MILK AND HONEY (1961), were made by cutting out an open framework of wood and adhering Styrofoam to it for carving by a soldering gun with a wire loop. Once shaped, the surfaces were brushed with dope and each was wrapped in 1-in.-square scenic netting to help hold the Styrofoam together and to provide extra texture. On the outside edge of the profiled foliage, loofa sponges (also called vegetable sponges) were tacked along each wooden frame, then trees were painted.
(Photograph — Munro Gabler)

Outlines of foliage pieces, shaped by a framework of ⅜-in.-round iron, were covered with silk glued on the metal with a white synthetic resin glue. The fabric was trimmed on the edges with a single-edge razor blade.
(Photograph — Munro Gabler)

Outdoor-indoor carpet was used to make the stylized foliage for William Pitkin's trees in COMEDY (1972). A bunch of leaves (about 12 in. long) was cut at once by stacking layers of carpet between two pieces of ¼-in. plywood, nailing them together, then sawing the outside edges with a bandsaw and the inner openings with a Sabre saw. The stems of the leaves were taped around limbs built of iron tubing which were then covered with narrow strips of velour saturated in scenic dope. When dry, units were finished by painting.

(Right) A section of the framed foliage border for Ben Edwards' setting in A MOON FOR THE MISBEGOTTEN (1973). Limbs, cut out of ¾-in. plywood covered with black velour, were supported on the back by galvanized hardware cloth (wire mesh). The linen scrim for the leaves was dye-painted first, then cut out and glued on the wire and wooden limbs with white synthetic resin glue.

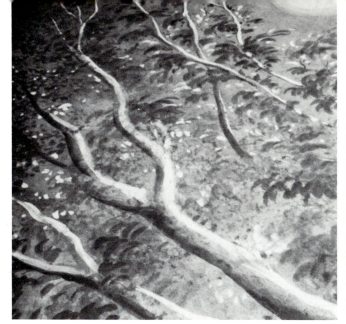

David Walker's foliage drop on muslin used as a translucency for the Joffrey Ballet's production of THE DREAM (1973). (Photographs — Lynn Pecktal)

Steps of Execution:

1. Muslin drop stapled squarely on the floor over gray bogus paper.
2. Background primed with colored starch, sprayed on, then brushed.
3. 2-ft. squares snapped lightly; tree trunks and branches drawn very lightly with charcoal.
4. The same painted by brush, using thin casein paints and aniline dyes; leaves painted with a 3-in. Fitch brush, also using caseins and dyes. Note the crisp, clean-cut strokes.
5. Random dark foliage patterns in aniline dyes applied with a paint stamp (right). Paint stamp created by using a piece of foam rubber (4 in. thick) adhered to a round wooden back with handle. Foam was then shredded by hand to make the desired patterns.

Foliage painted on muslin, cut out, adhered with white flexible glue, to scenic netting for support. The light leaves were made of burlap and glued on at points to add texture and dimension. Designed by Helen Pond and Herbert Senn for the New York City Opera's THE YOUNG LORD (1973).

(Left) For TWELFTH NIGHT (1972) Douglas W. Schmidt designed four potted shrubs. The framework for each was a wooden core (attached to the pot) around which chicken wire was shaped. John Keck and Bill Moore are shown stapling on leaves cut out of heavy white buckram and metallic paper. The shrubs were spray-painted with aniline dyes.

(Right) Viewed from the rear, one of Schmidt's hanging foliage units for TWELFTH NIGHT. Groups of leaves cut out of buckram were stapled onto a profiled leafy background of expanded-mesh wire bolted to supports of flat iron ¾ in. wide by ¼ in. thick.
(Photographs — Arnold Abramson)

Material of all kinds formed a collage of textured foliage on scenic netting for Ming Cho Lee's design in SUSANNAH (1971) at the New York City Opera. Branches cut from velour and leaves made of sharkstooth scrim, scraps of lace, burlap, and velour, plus chunks of carved foam rubber (4 in. thick) were adhered with white flexible glue on a large piece of irregularly cut netting, then painted with caseins, aniline dyes, and thin vinyls while laid flat on the floor.
(Photographs — Lynn Pecktal)

OPAQUING THE BACK OF A FOLIAGE DROP

In many instances, certain parts of a translucent foliage drop may be opaqued after the front painting has been finished. So that the scenic artists will have an outline on the rear of the backdrop when it is turned over for the opaquing, those areas are often lightly inked right after the drawing has been done on the starched muslin. Felt-tipped pens or light-colored aniline dyes (mixed in a solution of $\frac{1}{3}$ shellac to $\frac{2}{3}$ alcohol) will go through the muslin and show on the back. If the front painting is to be light and delicate, the inked line for the outline of foliage should be a dotted instead of a continuous line. In this way, it will show less.

For backpainting the areas that are to be opaque, latex paint is generally used, because when it dries, it is flexible and easily allows the backdrop to be folded or rolled. Also, latex paint tends to remain on the surface of the fabric and not go through unless it is rubbed too hard. It should be thinned with water to work well, but not made so thin that it does not cover. A test should be made with the latex paint applied on a sample of the starched muslin to see if the paint is penetrating the other side of the fabric, then adjust accordingly by making it thicker or thinner. That is why the opaquing color is often mixed in a neutral gray (or in a color appropriate to that on the front), so that if a bit of it shows through, the front painting is not ruined.

The outer edges of large areas are ''cut in'' with a $2\frac{1}{2}$-to-3-inch brush, then they are filled in with a lay-in brush. When there is no specified opaquing on the very bottom of a translucent drop (and no ground row to mask it), it is usually sprayed on the back with opaque paint to mask any lighting equipment on the floor and to diffuse the canvas pocket for the batten. This spraying may be applied in an 18-to-24-inch width, depending on the design, but it is put on heavily at the bottom and ''lost off'' at the top with a fine spray. Opaquing is also frequently sprayed on the rear of a backdrop to disguise any horizontal seams. The most common method of hiding the seams on a sky drop is to design and draw long linear clouds which completely cover the seams and, at the same time, vary the overall shape of the clouds so it is not obvious as to what has been done.

OPAQUING PARTS OF A TRANSLUCENT FOLIAGE DROP ON THE FRONT

To eliminate or to reinforce backpainting, a translucent foliage drop may be painted and opaqued at the same time on the face instead of having to turn it over later to opaque the parts on the back. For instance, various parts on the face of the drop, like the sky and distant foliage, can be painted to be translucent with aniline dyes on the starched muslin drop, and the foreground trees and foliage can be painted with opaque colors. Also, for painting groups of translucent leaves on the face, hot paraffin wax can be brushed on in the desired shapes, then opaque and semiopaque colors can be brushed over the waxed leaves. This keeps you from having to cut around the leaves with the brush. After painting, the wax is scraped off the muslin with an implement such as a kitchen knife.

PAINTING FOLIAGE LEGS AND BORDERS

Foliage legs and borders are made of canvas (sometimes linen) and are usually designed to hang soft, especially if they are for an opera or ballet playing in repertory, because this makes them much easier to handle, transport, and store. When a full set of borders and legs is laid out on the floor, it can take up quite a bit of space in the scenic studio. For instance, standard sizes of legs and borders at the New York City Ballet Company are: *Legs*—10 feet wide (plus or minus) by 40 feet high. *Borders*—15 feet high by 60 feet wide. *Backdrops*—40 feet high by 60 feet wide (maximum). At the New York City Opera, backdrops are a maximum size of 36 feet high by 60 feet wide.

In the theatrical studio, borders and legs are stapled on the floor as backdrops are and are prepared for painting in the same way. When space permits, it is ideal to arrange the legs and borders as they will play on stage; however, since space is usually limited, borders are instead placed parallel to each other in their proper playing sequence, as are the legs. Depending on the design, the drawing on them may be done either before or after the canvas is starched. Since they are not translucent, squares for drawing are snapped in charcoal. After the drawing is finished, it is sometimes inked with a felt-tipped pen or with thin anilines. For the lay-in, the regular mixture of starch is used. When the nature of the sketch is such that the starch can be tinted with casein colors, time can be saved by starching and laying in the color all at once. Often three or four separate colors are mixed in the starch and are applied by one artist using the different colors in Hudson tanks, while a second painter brushes and blends the sprayed areas. If the legs and borders are made of linen, they can also be starched or they may be sprayed with weak size water (20 parts water to 1 part size) mainly to tighten the fabric. But this depends solely on the intended effects.

Ordinarily, there are at least three sets of legs and borders in a production, and frequently there are four. In painting, the back set (upstage legs and border) should relate to the backdrop in value and color, and usually as the legs and borders progress forward (downstage), they become more detailed and have greater contrast, often possessing a deeper all-over value.

CUTTING AND NETTING

The inside leafy onstage edges on the canvas legs and borders are not cut until after the painting has been finished. The profiling is drawn on the canvas by the scenic artist with a bright contrasting color like orange or red, indicating to the carpenters who trim it that all the fabric on the unpainted side of the line is to be cut away. Sometimes cut legs and borders must be adhered to scenic netting (1-inch squares) for the cut edges to hang properly. To do this, of course, requires turning the piece of scenery over and placing it face-down. If a very detailed cut drop is being cut and netted, it is far simpler to turn it over first, cut it from the back, and then apply the netting also from the back. So that the carpenters can see where to cut the line from the back, a line is inked with a lining brush before the piece is turned. For inking, an aniline dye color (soluble in alcohol) mixed with $\frac{1}{3}$ shellac to $\frac{2}{3}$ alcohol easily penetrates through to the back of the fabric. Therefore, any intricate patterns on the cut foliage drop retain their shapes and do not have to be moved before the netting is applied.

Scenic netting is available in 30-foot widths. Before the netting is put on, it is usually dyed either dark blue or black, which shows much less on stage than if it were a light color. The netting should always be laid out and adhered correctly in order for the cut foliage to hang just right. On foliage legs, borders, or cut drops (or when "netting" any type of soft cut scenery, for that matter), the horizontal and vertical threads of the netting must always be placed parallel with the top and bottom of the finished fabric as well as parallel with the extreme sides of the piece it is going on.

When you are doing a cut drop that is to have a large piece of netting applied and the drop is put face-down on the floor, an outline is snapped in charcoal on the back of the fabric according to the size of the netting; this is usually rectangular. The netting should be figured so that it overlaps all the extreme inner cut edges of the fabric by at least a foot. In other words, if the maximum cut opening is 28 feet high by 40 feet wide, the piece of netting should be 30 feet high by 42 feet wide.

Along this snapped rectangular line, place carpet tacks about every six inches (on all four sides) and hammer them into the floor just enough to hold. The straight edges of the netting are stretched on the tacks like lace curtains being hooked on stretchers to dry. Always make sure that the netting is hooked on the tacks so that a row of squares is in the same line. Although the netting is made in inch squares, it may be a little less when it is stretched out, and it should not be pulled so tightly that it becomes a struggle to get it hooked. The best way to test it is by feel. After it is in place, reach out in a central area and lift up a portion of the net, then let it fall. If it seems too taut, it has been stretched too much and should be adjusted accordingly by snapping new lines for the tacks on one or two sides or releasing one side by one or two lines of squares. When hooked in place on the tacks, all four outer edges of the netting should be brushed with flexible white glue (like Sobo) to adhere the netting to the back of the drop. Next, brush the white glue around the inner cut edge of the drop to hold it onto the netting. When the glue has thoroughly dried, remove the carpet tacks and take the netted cut drop off the floor.

APPLYING CUT LEAVES ON LEGS, BORDERS, AND CUT DROPS

To give a piece of painted scenery a more dimensional look, some designers favor applying cut fabric foliage on the unframed canvas so that it is flexible and still can be folded. When Marsha Eck designed *Lucia di Lammermoor* for the New York City Opera, for example, both leaves and vines of fabric were attached to the leg and border drops after they were painted. Leaves of several shapes (single and clusters) about 7 to 9 inches long were cut out of pieces of linen scrim that had been painted beforehand. These were applied at random, spanning a width of 4 or 5 feet from the inside

David Walker's muslin backdrop for THE DREAM (1973), designed for the Joffrey Ballet, painted and ready to be turned over for cutting the openings and gluing sharkstooth scrim on the back for support. (Photograph – Lynn Pecktal)

Steps of Execution:

1. Muslin backdrop stapled over gray bogus paper; 2-ft. squares snapped.
2. Charcoal drawing inked with aniline dye (mixed with shellac and alcohol); mixture goes through fabric and shows on the back for cutting. Trees and foliage laid in with colors mixed with starch.
3. Pieces of black scrim adhered to tree trunks with white glue to create textures. Overpainting with casein paints and aniline dyes using brushes and paint rollers.
4. Staples removed, drop turned over and stapled face down.
5. Openings (natural muslin) cut out with razor blades, then painted sharkstooth scrim adhered on the back with white flexible glue.
6. When dry, drop turned over and stapled again on the face. Leaves of muslin, scrim, and opaque latex adhered to the foliage.
7. Remaining painting finished by brushing. Drop sprayed lightly to soften painting.

leafy edge, and 3M Spray Adhesive 77 was used to attach the scrim leaves to the painted canvas foliage. The adhesive was first sprayed on the particular area of canvas, then on the leaf itself, and the leaf was pressed into place. Only the tips of the leaves were actually fastened, permitting them to hang freely. In the same production of *Lucia,* dimensional vines and tree roots were simulated on the cut drops by putting on pieces of cheesecloth and sharkstooth scrim (1 foot wide and up to 3 feet long), which had been dipped in clear undiluted latex (Slomon's), then twisted into the desired shape and pressed onto the painted surface. After the applied pieces were dry, they were painted with vinyls and caseins.

UNFRAMED HANGING FOLIAGE PANELS

Besides the conventional type of hanging foliage pieces (legs, borders, and backdrops), other kinds can also be used. When Lloyd Evans created the forest in the mythical kingdom of *Pelléas and Mélisande* for the New York City Opera, he designed several unframed panels of linen scrim that hung in front of a painted backdrop as well as built set pieces. On these were applied many opaque patterns of trees and branches, cut out of black iron-on fabric. The scrim panels were first tacked out on the floor, and the painting was done on the sky and background. Detailed pounces were drawn and perforated, and used twice: once for transferring the patterns onto the iron-on fabric for cutting (by rubbing a bag of white chalk powder over the holes) and then for the placement of these pieces on the linen scrim (by dusting the holes with a regular charcoal bag) and for painting. A hot iron, like the household variety, was used to press the cut shapes of iron-on fabric onto the linen scrim. The placement of the tree patterns was also designed to hide the vertical seams in the

scrim. Once the appliqués were finished, the remaining foliage details on the panels were painted with caseins and dyes. Through the use of flexible lighting on stage, much depth and illusion was achieved by silhouetting the applied trees in front of the painted backdrop.

For *Susannah,* also at the City Opera, Ming Cho Lee designed a very interesting soft hanging foliage piece whereby he utilized a wide variety of applied fabrics and materials on netting to give an effect of heavy textures. To hold all of the soft profile branches and foliage in place, a large piece of scenic netting (1-inch squares) was used. This was cut in an irregular foliagelike shape and was supported at the top by gluing it to a duck canvas border cut in leafy profile. All sorts of materials were cut out and collaged on the netting. The large background shapes were formed of opera net, and these were put on first with flexible white glue. Then velour was used extensively for cutting out the branches. Next, varied leaves cut from burlap, sharkstooth scrim, lace, and velour were attached to the netting, also with flexible white glue. And in addition, sculptured clumps of foliage were carved out of foam rubber (4 inches thick) and were applied at random to create more dimension and contrast. After it was all put together, the piece was sprayed, brushed, and spattered with caseins, thin vinyls, and dyes.

DIMENSIONAL FOLIAGE UNITS AND TREES

In designing the Lincoln Center production of *Twelfth Night,* Douglas W. Schmidt made effective use of hanging foliage pieces and potted shrubs. Three large fragmented flat shapes of expanded mesh wire were supported from behind with a network of metal constructed with pieces of flat iron, $\frac{3}{4}$ inch wide by $\frac{1}{4}$ inch thick. These flat units were hung vertically for attaching the leaves on them. Many different shapes

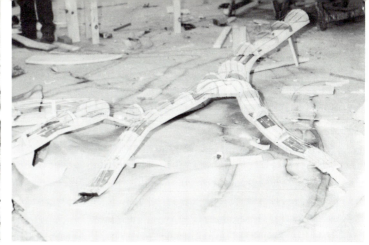

CONSTRUCTING TREES

(Top, left) For KING LEAR (1965) at the American Shakespeare Festival in Stratford, Conn., Will Steven Armstrong devised groups of leaning trees emanating from wooden platforms. The trees were constructed of metal pipe (1¾-, 1½-, and 1¼-in.) and wrapped with reeds.
(Above) Part of the ¾-round tree in Oliver Smith's setting for the musical PRETTYBELLE (1971), built directly on a full-scale charcoal drawing on brown paper. Because the limbs were designed to be in several planes, the back profiles of ¾-in. wood were joined securely at the breaks with ¼-in. flat iron pieces, bent and welded into shape. Contoured sections were cut out of ¾-in. wood to make the three-dimensional forms and positioned and nailed in place. Heavy flexible wire (running with the limbs) was then attached, after which the limbs were covered with forming cloth and strips of velour.
(Left) Douglas W. Schmidt's tree for THE MERRY WIVES OF WINDSOR (1971) at Stratford, Conn., was constructed in ¾ round and was finished by ragging with 6-in.-wide strips of torn velour. The ragging was done over a framework of wood covered with chicken wire.
(Left) The bottom unit of Lloyd Evans' tree for MADAMA BUTTERFLY (1967) at the New York City Opera after ragging (scraps of fabric dipped in scenic dope) has been applied over a framework covered with chicken wire.
(Below) The framework of ¾-in. plywood, braced by wooden stiffeners, is partially covered with chicken wire.
(Below, center) The tree for CAMELOT (1960), designed by Oliver Smith, was constructed in a series of flat plywood profiles with routed edges. The foliage was created with aluminum window screening, taped around the edges. More opaque pearl screen at the top of the stairs hid the actor playing King Arthur. Iron bracing pieces (¼ in. by 2 and ⅛ in. by 1½) were attached on the back of the cutout limbs.
(Right) A three-dimensional tree designed by Lloyd Evans for PELLÉAS ET MÉLISANDE (1970) at the New York City Opera. The trunk and limbs were evolved by ragging on a wooden framework covered with forming cloth.
(Photographs—Munro Gabler)

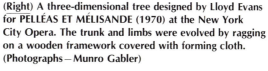

of leaves were cut from heavy white buckram (on a 30-inch-wide roll), and from thick sheets of metallic silver paper. With both of these materials, the cut shapes of the leaves ranged from patterns of one, two, three to many. The silver leaves were freely cut by using scissors without benefit of drawing.

A fast and frequently used method for cutting out the buckram leaves was employed. It involved cutting a stack of several layers of leaves at one time. As many as twenty pieces of the buckram, measuring 20 by 30 inches, were folded (or cut) and placed neatly in a stack which was then sandwiched between two pieces of $\frac{1}{4}$-inch plywood of identical size. These were nailed tightly together. On one side of the plywood, the patterns of the leaves were drawn with a black grease pencil (china marker). When the drawing was finished, the stack was given to a carpenter who used a band saw to cut along the drawing right through the wood and fabric, thereby producing many leaves. Not only is this a fast method, but the leaves are cut with a clean line. Besides buckram, several other fabrics like scrim, canvas, muslin, and felt can be used as well.

The buckram and opaque metallic leaves were fastened to the expanded mesh wire by using a staple gun. Before attaching the metallic paper leaves, each leaf was pleated along its spine, adding more dimension to the clustered foliage. More variety was obtained in the many overlays of foliage by interspersing leafy shapes of thin silver gauze and silver bobbinet.

For painting, the pieces of foliage were laid flat on the floor. Lavender and gray colors were mixed in aniline dyes, using clear vinyl as a binder. These colors were sponged and spattered generously on the foliage, and while the vinyl colors were still wet, silver flitter was sprinkled sparsely over the leaves. When the foliage units were hung in the theatre, interesting effects were created by backlighting.

Half-round floral sculptures designed by Raoul Pène du Bois for NO, NO, NANETTE (1971). Mounds under flowers were Styrofoam, as were containers, which were turned on a lathe. Flowers were pieces of fabric dipped in dope and pressed onto mounds while wet. Leaves were cut from heavy felt, dipped in dope, and applied the same way. After drying, all pieces were painted with water-base paints.
(Photograph—Lynn Pecktal)

Also in this production of *Twelfth Night,* four potted shrubs were constructed that had the same type of leaves. On each, the overall shape was oval, rising to a point that made it a total height of 5 feet. The shrubs were modeled with chicken wire, supported by a central wooden core that was attached inside the pot, which was made of turned wood. All four pots were shaped like low Japanese lanterns, 18 inches in height by 24 inches in diameter. After the leaves were stapled to the chicken wire, a certain amount of space was also left in this foliage to allow the lights to play through it.

FLOWERS AND PLANTS

Every kind of flower and plant imaginable is used on the stage. Whether they are real or made of plastic, fabric, paper, wax, or straw, they are widely employed for decorative set dressing and are often combined with other scenic materials to embellish three-dimensional pieces. Besides lending a dash of color to brighten a set as well as to add atmosphere and mood, flowers and plants can be representative of the locale of a production and indicate the season of the year. They may also be specified in the script as a focal point of the set dressing or as hand props in the form of cut flowers and bouquets.

While it is a luxury to be able to use real flowers and plants on a set, they are only practical for very short runs since they require special care to hold up well on stage and are short-lived even if they have good light, fresh air, and proper watering. For these reasons, artificial flowers and plants are ordinarily substituted. But unless artificial flowers and plants are of the most expensive variety, they usually have to be hand-shaped and appropriately arranged to appear natural and effective. Much of the time they also have to be painted or dye-sprayed to give them interest, to take away that flat commercial look, and to make them read well from the audience. All sorts of painting treatment can be applied. Some years ago, for example, when Howard Bay designed the opera *Natalya Petrovna* for the New York City Opera, he made use of many artificial plants in containers placed outside large windows and doors in a solarium setting. These plants were heavily spattered with metallic gold and silver paint (bronzing powders mixed in clear gloss vinyl), giving the foliage a glittering textured appearance under stage lighting like dew- or moisture-laden leaves.

Flowers

Roses	Azaleas	Crepe Myrtles	Marigolds	Day lilies	Lilacs
Chrysanthemums	Dwarf dahlias	Poinsettias	Snapdragons	Asters	Geraniums
Gladioli	Oriental poppies	Anemones	Carnations	Narcissi	Peonies
Tulips	Forsythia	Hydrangeas	Zinnias	Hyacinths	Spirea
Daffodils	Irises	Shasta daisies	Sunflowers	Larkspur	Hollyhocks

Plants and Trees, Trailing Vines

Palms	Lemon trees	Dracaena marginatas	Grape ivy	Corn plants (Dracaenas)
Ferns	Mimosa trees	Yucca trees	Philodendron plants	Cactuses
Scheffleras	Orange trees	Rubber plants	Trailing roses	Mother-in-law's tongues
Begonias	Aralia trees	Rhododendron plants	Grape vines	English ivy
Pine branches	Spider plants	Magnolia leaves	Wisteria	Cherry blossoms
Holly branches	Split philodendrons	Dogwood blossoms	Wandering Jew	Apple blossoms

Containers and Holders

Pots and crocks	Vases and urns	Plant stands: wood,	Soup tureens
Window and porch boxes	Flower carts	wicker, wrought iron, wire, brass	Wall planters
Standing and hanging baskets	Jardinières and compotes	Table bowls and wall bowls	Redwood planters
Tin canisters	Pitchers	Barrels	Birdcage planters

Dried Arrangements

Preserved wheat	Cockscombs	Baby's breath	Flying grass	German statice
Eucalyptus leaves	Rabbit's foot	Yarrow flowers	Star flowers	Bittersweet
Cattails	Rye grass	Bachelor buttons	Queen Anne's lace	Money plant

Specific Settings Utilizing Flowers and Plants

Gardens (simple and formal)	Terraces	Conservatories	Dining rooms	Trellises
Window gardens	Fountains	Parlors	Bedrooms	Balconies
Patios	Greenhouses	Libraries	Gazebos	Halls

General Locations for Flowers and Plants

On tables, desks, and bars	On windowsills	By stairways	In dry sinks	On wrought-iron grillwork
On shelves and in bookcases	In corners	In wall niches	On wooden latticework	Hanging from ceilings

PAINTING ARTIFICIAL FLOWERS AND PLANTS

If you want to paint plastic flowers and plants to vary their colors, acrylic spray paints (transparent and opaque) in aerosol cans can be applied, or aniline dye colors mixed with clear gloss vinyl can be brushed on them. For paper or straw flowers, casein paints can be thinned with water and brushed on.

POPULAR FLOWERS AND PLANTS FOR STAGE USE

For shows being produced in a repertory or stock company, it is possible to build up a large collection of artificial flowers and plants, combining and rearranging them differently for each production. When not in use, they should be stored in the prop room with dust covers to keep them clean. Miscellaneous equipment needed for creating arrangements are florist's wire, floral tape, scissors, tin snips, and pliers. Many of the flowers and plants above can be purchased in plastic or other imitative materials to serve as potted plants, cut flowers, or those that are supposed to be growing naturally from the ground.

There is a multitude of miscellaneous items that can be combined with dried arrangements or real flowers to produce color and contrast in design. Among these are fruit and vegetables, pine cones, tree limbs, candles, driftwood, ribbons, dried moss, peacock feathers, Indian corn.

PLACES OF PURCHASE

The sources of flowers and plants are numerous, depending on the need and the budget: floral shops, greenhouses, five-and-dime stores, department stores, hobby and craft shops, variety stores, supermarkets, and display houses.

Artificial flowers and plants can be obtained by the gross from display houses. These can be used for making garlands, wreaths, and nosegays; forming foliage on limbs; covering trellises, picket fences, and walls; creating shrubs, boxwood, and hedges by attaching foliage over a base of formed chicken wire. While such items as vines, potted arrangements, and garlands can be bought already made up, they are much more expensive. In New York City two well-known sources of artificial flowers and plants are Decorative Plant Corp. and Modern Artificial Flowers & Displays.

SUGGESTED REFERENCE:

Time-Life Encyclopedia of Gardening, an excellent series of twelve volumes published by Time, Inc., with beautiful illustrations; includes Flowering House Plants, Flowering Shrubs, Foliage House Plants, Roses, Evergreens, Lawns and Ground Covers, Bulbs, Annuals, Perennials, Vegetables and Fruits, Trees, and Landscape Gardening.

A Conversation with MING CHO LEE

Ming Cho Lee was born in Shanghai on October 30, 1930, and educated at Occidental College and UCLA. His first Broadway show was *The Moon Besieged* in 1962, and since that time he has designed many productions both on and off Broadway. He has been the principal designer for Joseph Papp's New York Shakespeare Festival and has designed sets for the New York City Opera, the Juilliard Opera Theatre, the Metropolitan Opera, the San Francisco Opera, Los Angeles Center Theatre Group, the Peabody Arts Theatre of the Peabody Institute, Baltimore, the Arena Stage, and the dance companies of Martha Graham, Alvin Ailey, José Limón, Gerald Arpino, and Robert Joffrey. Ming Cho Lee has received two Maharam Awards, for *Electra* and *Ergo,* and the Drama Desk Award for *Invitation to a Beheading.* He designed the opera *Ariodante,* one of three productions that opened the Kennedy Center in Washington, D.C. in 1971. Currently, Ming Cho Lee is the instructor in scenic design at the Yale Drama School. Among his credits are:

Broadway:
Much Ado About Nothing (1972)
Two Gentlemen of Verona (1971)
Billy (1969)
Little Murders (1967)
A Time for Singing (1966)
Slapstick Tragedy (1966)
Mother Courage (1963)
 The Metropolitan Opera:
Boris Godunov (1974)
 Juilliard Opera Theatre:
La Bohème (1972)
The Rake's Progress (1970)

New York Shakespeare Festival:
Peer Gynt (1969)
Henry IV (1968)
Comedy of Errors (1967)
Hair (1967)
Richard III (1966)
Love's Labour's Lost (1965)
Hamlet (1964)
Electra (1964)
 New York City Opera:
Maria Stuarda (1972)
Roberto Devereux (1970)
Faust (1968)

Le Coq d'Or (1967)
Don Rodrigo (1966)
Julius Caesar (1966)
 Martha Graham Company:
Myth of a Voyage (1973)
The Witch of Endor (1965)
A Look at Lightning (1962)
 San Francisco Opera:
La Favorita (1973)
St. Matthew Passion (1973)
 Arena Stage, Washington:
Our Town (1972)
Inherit the Wind (1973)

Model by Ming Cho Lee
BORIS GODUNOV by Modest Moussorgsky
Libretto by the composer
The courtyard in front of the Novodievichy
monastery near Moscow (Act I, scene 1)
Staged by August Everding
The Metropolitan Opera, New York (1974)
(Photograph — Nathan Rabin)

Did you start out in school with an art background?

Yes. I had some training in Chinese landscape painting, but I have forgotten much of it. My mother thought it was a good idea. However, I got tired of it and I didn't think it was the sort of thing to do during my teen-age years. I felt soccer was much more important, so I gave it up after two years. Then I came here and went to Occidental College, where I was in the art department. I took a year of oil painting and I was not very good at it. It seems that I was allergic to turpentine! But I took four years of watercolor and was marvelous at that because I had this Chinese landscape painting background. I also studied a year of graphics and two years of figure drawing, and I joined the speech department because I wanted to work in the theatre.

Was there anything in particular that influenced you to go into theatre work?

There were several reasons. When I was in Shanghai, I saw a great deal of theatre, especially during the Japanese Occupation period. There was also quite a bit of opera in Shanghai. Seeing a lot of opera made a big impression on me. I was between twelve and sixteen when I saw *Rigoletto,* my first opera. Then for a year I was in Hong Kong, where one of my uncles owned a movie studio; but he subsequently went bankrupt because of the movies. I found movie-making terribly fascinating. I always wanted to somehow get involved with either theatre or motion pictures. The thing that stopped me from getting into theatre right away at Occidental was that the theatre was part of the speech department and at that time I had great difficulty with my English, so that was a real obstacle. During one of the summers, I went to the University of Southern California and took quite a few courses in motion pictures and realized that motion pictures was not what I wanted. It's too specialized. Everything is divided into jobs for experts. I discovered that unless you are a director or a cameraman, you are not doing much designing in motion pictures.

Another reason was my difficulties in my oil painting classes. Back then, the New York school of abstraction was very popular, and it was difficult for me to understand abstraction. I simply couldn't figure out what was so interesting about it even though

now I design a lot of abstract sets. Also, I was frightened by the fact that painters are supposed to have this great big piece of canvas and just create. In set designing, at least you rely on a script. There is something you grab onto first. Therefore, I joined the speech department at Occidental in my junior year. Jumping from being an art student to set designing was definitely simpler.

Did you come to New York after graduation?

No. I went to UCLA and I was there for a year in the theatre department. But in those days, UCLA really did not have a design program to fit me, and I was discovering that I was designing and painting most of the shows. In fact, halfway through, I realized that I was the best designer there and I said, "What the hell?" At that time, Eddie Kook (who was president of Century Lighting Co.) always gave a talk to the graduate students every summer. A professor there, Eddie Hern, suggested to Eddie Kook that perhaps UCLA was a dead end for me and that maybe I should come to New York and what should I do when I got there? Eddie Kook said for me to call him at Century Lighting when I got to New York, and I did just that. He asked me to come and show him my work. He looked at my portfolio of some sets I had done at UCLA and called Jo Mielziner and made an appointment for me. When Jo saw my portfolio he said, "There is really something here. Your painting is very good, you have a good feeling about designing, but your drafting is horrible and you really don't know what is going on. If you don't mind some cleaning-up work and just being around doing research and occasionally doing some drafting, come and work for me if you want to." So I went to work for Jo in October of 1954. He was doing *Silk Stockings* and *Cat on a Hot Tin Roof.*

Whom did you work with at Mielziner's?

John Harvey was the associate designer and Warren Clymer was number-two man. The first thing Warren said was, "Okay, follow me! I have to look for props." But as the show got more in a rush, he couldn't go look for them and it was up to me. Leo Herbert, the prop man, had suggested that we use a Polaroid to photograph what we found, but since I was very bad with that camera, I decided I would simply

measure the props very carefully and do drawings of them.

My first real drafting job was to draft quarter-inch plans of *Silk Stockings* for each scene as it finally ended up in Philadelphia. Then I did a bar in *Cat on a Hot Tin Roof* that was very important. A portion of the bar lifted up and it was all catty-cornered on a raked platform. Joe Lynn, the prop man on that show, said we would have to build it because we would never find it. And I drew the bar so accurately that he was able to build it straight from the drawing and it worked, which was a marvelous compliment.

After *Cat on a Hot Tin Roof* was a hit, Jo Mielziner went on vacation. John Harvey and I did quite a bit of drawing for the road and bus-and-truck for *Can-Can.* If there were three drops, or three cut drops, we had to combine them into one. Then John also went on vacation and I studied for the union exam at Jo's studio, took the exam, and passed. This was in 1955.

Where did you go after you passed the exam?

I went to the Grist Mill Playhouse, a summer theatre in Andover, New Jersey, as the designer. After two shows, I was fired because I was designing much too elaborate settings. I did *Guys and Dolls,* got marvelous reviews, but killed the theatre. I called Jo, and he said, "Come and work for me." I stayed with him until 1958 and assisted on *Pipe Dream, Middle of the Night, Happy Hunting, Gypsy, The Lark,* and *Suzy Wong.* I also worked for other people, but when they did not have jobs and Jo did, I would go back to him. I worked for George Jenkins on a show called *Too Late the Phalarope* and for Rouben Ter-Arutunian on his first Broadway show, *New Girl in Town.* Then Boris Aronson saw some of my work and he decided that I should assist him.

What was your first off-Broadway show?

The Infernal Machine at the Phoenix on Second Avenue. Herbert Berghof directed that with June Havoc and John Kerr. The set was a bit heavy and operatic-looking, but Brooks Atkinson liked it so much that his review was a review about the set, which did not endear me with Herbert Berghof. At that time, I also designed the off-Broadway production of *The Crucible* with Word Baker as director and Pat Zipprodt as the costume designer. But halfway through it, they changed theatres and the circumstances became very complicated. They didn't have the money to do any of the set, including just a wooden floor. I got so mad that I withdrew my credit, and the show was a hit and ran for two years. That was a lesson. I have never withdrawn credit on any show since then.

How did you begin to design operas?

I knew Tharon Musser from when she lighted *The Infernal Machine.* Through her I got tied in with an impresario-conductor called Laszlo Halasz, who was going to produce a series of operas at Peabody Institute of Music in Baltimore, Maryland. He insisted that Tharon do the lighting for Peabody, but by that time she had become well known and was very busy and she said, "Why don't you get Ming?" So I went to Peabody and I did all the set designing and the lighting for the operas. It was also during this time that I was assisting Boris, or Jo, or whomever.

In the beginning of 1961, I was out of a job except for designing at Peabody, which didn't pay very much. From the middle of January until May I could not earn a living in the theatre, and it was a disaster. The spring season was already under way and Pete [Feller] and Arnold [Abramson] had enough painters at the scenic studios and the designers had hired their assistants. Then Bob Randolph called me about being an assistant to him. I only assisted him one day, because at the same time I got a call to be the resident designer at the San Francisco Opera. They had asked Rouben Ter-Arutunian to do a new opera called *Blood Moon* and Kurt Herbert Adler of the San Francisco Opera asked if I would assist Rouben for two weeks in New York before coming to San Francisco. Robert Randolph was very understanding about the whole thing.

Had you applied to the San Francisco Opera?

No. Jo Mielziner suggested me to Kurt Herbert Adler. In fact, I got quite a lot of things from Jo Mielziner.

Your first Broadway show followed very closely after this, didn't it?

Suddenly everything starts happening. I moved my family out to San Francisco and was with the San Francisco Opera for a season, from May to December 1961. While I was there, again Jo couldn't do a show and he sent the script to me. The producer was interested, so I took the plane to New York, saw the producer and Lloyd Richards, the director whom I had met before. All at once I got a Broadway show called *The Moon Besieged* while I was in San Francisco! Because of that, I moved my family back to New York and practically used up all the savings I had earned in San Francisco.

After I came back, Martha Graham needed a designer. For some reason, her secretary at that time was an old friend of Laszlo Halasz. So I found myself designing a set on Broadway for Martha Graham called *A Look at Lightning* before *The Moon Besieged* opened.

Again at that time, Hilmar Sallee, the company manager for Joseph Papp's Shakespeare in the Park, knew that I was back, and since Eldon Elder had gone to Stratford, Connecticut, to design, Hilmar suggested me for the job. So I went to see Joe Papp and I started designing the opening show at the Delacorte Theatre in 1962 and was his principal designer until 1973.

Is there some particular way in which you form a concept for a show?

A different show, a different idea gets formed. I would say first of all, I don't like to analyze scripts too much in detail before I start designing. Unlike all those people who read a script three dozen times, I generally read the script once just to get an impact from which I will try to form some kind of visual concept. Sometimes I make sure that I don't read the script again until I have some idea of how it should look, because it frightens me to get too involved with specifics. I always design for the total play and let the specifics fit in. The total play demands some kind of expression through materials, and this is something I always first ask a director —whether he sees this particular production of *Macbeth* in the middle of a lot of stone walls or stone panels, or should it be metallic patterns? Each kind of material would give a different production of *Macbeth*. And then, I would make the choice as to whether it is a realistic play that requires very literal settings or if it's a play that requires a nonliteral approach and essentially you present it on a platform—you create a framework on which to hang your visual statement. I usually prefer a nonliteral approach. Then I would check that through with the director. I would say I rely on directors a great deal. The director has a lot to do with it, you can't deny that.

Assuming that the basic choices have been made between you and the director, do you always build a model?

Yes, that we have to do, absolutely for every show. The director today

Model by Ming Cho Lee
THE GNADIGES FRAULEIN by Tennessee Williams
Directed by Alan Schneider

Longacre Theatre, New York (1966)
(Photograph—Nathan Rabin)

Setting by Ming Cho Lee
ROBERTO DEVEREUX by
  Gaetano Donizetti
Libretto
  by S. Cammarano
Directed
  by Tito Capobianco
Lighting
  by Hans Sondheimer
Costumes by José Varona
New York City Opera
New York State Theatre
  (1970)
(Photograph — Fred Fehl)

will never give his approval unless the design is in the model form. It is strictly a safety for both the director and the designer. Sometimes the model also becomes a design approach to a kind of production as opposed to a sketch. When you build a model, you approach things differently. You deal with the volume, the space, the mass, and the void. For example, sketching is a waste of time designing for Martha Graham. And sometimes for her, instead of starting out with a little sketch to show what I want to do, I will start out with a little model. Since most of her work demands a setting that is sculptured and spatial in nature, it is much simpler and more direct to make a model. However, model-building does take time and for most of the productions it is not very practical to use the model approach as the initial step in designing. So then there is an equal kind of emphasis on sketching and model-building.

Do you depend on the music to set the mood when designing an opera?

Yes. And to set the weight of the production—how heavy, how light, how opaque, or how transparent the work is. For dance, of course, it is something else. I listen to the music and I may then design a piece of sculpture or something that a dancer can use or go through. Quite often the music determines the type of material one uses for that piece of sculpture, whether it's a very linear kind of work that is full of pipes and forms, or whether it is a piece of granite. I also happen to do a lot of musical comedy. And again, there are

songs, and that determines a good deal as to what kind of set it should be.

In terms of designing, which do you prefer—opera, Broadway, Shakespeare, or the dance?

Designing for the dance, of course, is the most enjoyable because it is designing in its purest sense. You are designing a visual statement in a space that is compatible to a human form moving, expressing a theme, and that is pure set designing and that is most enjoyable. It is totally nonliteral because dance itself is nonliteral. It is theatre expressed through movement; therefore, if your form is compatible to the movement, you have achieved the impact of the piece of work. Opera and Shakespeare are next, because the scale of the work is larger and one is dealing either with music or with poetry. In terms of Shakespeare, you are designing for masterpieces of theatre. The scope of the work is much more encompassing and deals with a whole era of society and it demands design that is equally exciting. For example, I think *King Lear* is perhaps the ultimate statement of man and nature, and to design a production of *King Lear,* that's really something. Design for opera pretty much has the same kind of excitement even if you are designing *Bohème,* which is a realistic opera and provides a lot of problems. One is still designing for that high C of Rodolfo's aria. That's a musical statement, and you design a visual statement that is compatible to that musical statement and to that weight. As for Broadway, I have found musical

comedy more enjoyable to work on than a living-room—drawing-room comedy. I mean, I can't imagine the boredom one has to go through designing *Red Hot Lovers.* You've got to have the icebox in a certain place and the bourbon has to be bourbon, otherwise the play falls apart. Set designing is reduced to problem-solving, and that is boring.

Which of the New York City Opera's productions has been the most exciting in your experience?

Actually, the first one was the most exciting, and that was *Don Rodrigo,* an opera about Spain. I always felt that Spain is full of white, great big stone sculpture and walls, and golden sky and mosaics—and that is pretty much what I did. The set consisted of a raked platform surrounded by a gold mosaic sky, tall lean statues on gold pipes lining both sides of the platform; pieces of white carved stone wall came in for specific scenes. I think it had a real look. It is something that the Met hasn't done and the City Opera had never done. It was the first show that opened the New York City Opera at the State Theatre at Lincoln Center, and also the first production I did with Tito Capobianco as director, and in some ways I feel it's a very significant production for both of us. I have done many operas with Tito: *Julius Caesar, Le Coq d'Or, Bomarzo, Roberto Devereux,* and *Maria Stuarda.* Then at Juilliard, we did *Barber of Seville, Rake's Progress,* and *Il Giuramento* and the *Boris Godunov* in Baltimore. I think one thing Tito does

Setting by Ming Cho Lee
LA FAVORITA by Gaetano Donizetti
Libretto by A. Royer and G. Vaëz
Directed by Paul-Emile Deiber

Lighting by Robert Brand
Costumes by Jane Greenwood
San Francisco Opera (1973)
(Photograph – Carolyn Mason Jones)

that is very good for me is that he forces me to design sets in the style that is not easy for me. For example, in *Le Coq d'Or*, he demanded a lot of color, and I tend to be a very neutral-tone kind of designer, although my set painting is always full of a lot of transparent washes. Overall it is a very neutral thing so the people and the costumes can stand out. In *Coq d'Or*, he felt the set should be colorful and the costumes should be white. So he forced me to use a lot of strong colors. Designing for Tito is a challenge most of the time. Now we have done so many things together that we understand each other, to a point, very well. And we are very worried about a sense of routine beginning to creep in. Everything is happening too easy. It's what Tito calls "ham and eggs." If I finish something and I don't like it or if he doesn't like it, I'll throw it away. And we'll just keep on, because we've got to, otherwise we become just "ham and eggs."

Do you find that budget is one of the biggest problems in designing?

It is always a problem, but it's not the biggest. In fact, I have never designed a show that did not have a severe budget problem. For example, for both New York City Opera and New York Shakespeare Festival, I have a vague idea of what they can afford. They may tell me in loose terms. The main thing is one should not initially conceive anything so extravagant that it will be impossible for them. I think I am very good at cutting, as I know where I can cut. Sometimes I will cut something major if I can live without it and it doesn't destroy

the overall concept. Or I can usually cut out a lot of detail or be able to find out from Nolan's or Feller's that certain things are going to cost a lot of money. I would just make an adjustment or add a piece of support, so suddenly you don't have a huge cantilever or something unreasonable.

You have gone into theatre-consulting work. In contrast to stage design, is it as interesting to you?

Yes. I was the co-designer with architect Giorgio Cavaglieri for Joe Papp's Public Theatre. I think the two theatres there are very exciting theatres. Each has a personality and special quality. The Anspacher Theatre has a very severe mechanical thrust stage in the middle of a neoclassic room with its Corinthian colonnade and all its ornament. It creates a kind of tension that is very special. The Newman Theatre with its bare brick wall and catwalk is strictly a functional theatre that is very direct and honest. I was partly functioning as a client, because I had been Joe Papp's designer since 1962 and was in a much stronger position talking to an architect.

Now, as a theatre consultant to an architect as I was for the State University of New York at Purchase, it's different. Then it depends on how well you work with the architect, and I get along very well with Ed Barnes. Then you have a client that is the State University that has a faculty of theatre, dance, and music. And this I found difficult, because you're dealing with clients through the architect. The complication is unbelievable. It's interesting, but less satisfying, because everything becomes

a little bit neutralized when there are so many people involved. There is a committee that is the client and you know that essentially you have to please them. And if they mention a problem that you don't think is a problem or you think should be solved later rather than doing the work now and pinning it down so they have no room to move, you suddenly realize the millions of bad theatres being designed are not totally the fault of the architect, but may be the fault of the client. It's a new experience for me, and it pays well. For an architectural theatre consultant, the fee is twenty-five dollars an hour minimum. It supports my theatre projects.

When you designed Julius Caesar *in Germany, how did your production experiences compare to those here?*

Julius Caesar was a marvelous experience in Hamburg. First of all, they treat their designers as if they are human beings, and the same thing with the directors. The whole system is different. The American designer here is expected to do his design execution. We build models, do the drafting, and all the color elevations, and then give it to a shop. European houses are used to executing a set from a sketch. They have their own design staff and design technicians to execute it. It's like the Met and David Reppa's position as associate designer. The Met is set up in a European fashion so, for example, Franco Zeffirelli is not worrying about whether a step is one foot by six inches and so forth, and he is not worrying about whether the perspective is right or whether he is building models, since that is taken care of. And in Europe, the pride of a house is how well they can execute the designer's concept and the sketch. So if you go there with enough of the design execution, they think you are the greatest. And the minute they agree they will do certain things, they go out of their way, because that's their pride. It's a good credit, although they don't pay well. It's a huge expense for them to hire American designers, because they have to pay transportation and expenses.

How much time did they have to build and paint it?

I would say at least three to four months, and they demand that. We never have that much time here. How could we afford it? If a shop worked on one show for three months, they would have to close. We use a lot of vac-form materials here, but they don't. They didn't use Styrofoam for the capitals. They made them by hand-carving wood. The ironwork was like we did here; however, we redesigned the second act with more circular things, and it was much better looking. The painting was much tighter, but that doesn't mean that tighter painting is better painting. And there was very little dye used on *Julius Caesar*, and there was not the kind of "bathing" we do here. They have a lot more time. When Tito got there, he rehearsed on the painted set for three weeks.

What is your approach in teaching scenic design at the Yale Drama School?

I think in teaching there are two goals. One is that you try to maintain or to stimulate an attitude toward designing for the theatre—a personal attitude and a personal way of expressing, a personal handwriting. That's very important and it is something you can't teach. You can only stimulate and sometimes you can destroy it very easily and you have to be very careful about it. If someone has a way of doing things, and you say three times, "Well, it won't work," later he is not going to do it and you have destroyed it. You have to be able to see it from their point of view. If their point of view is so outrageous, then you have a long discussion with them.

The other part of teaching is the necessary skill, the technique, and the organization that goes into being a designer. Now that can be taught. They have to have some basic skill before they will be accepted at Yale. Sketching is definitely important and that involves finished sketches as well. Sometimes, I will try to make sure they can do a rough sketch that is readable in order to communicate the show to the director. Building models is also important, because there are sets that are sculptural and really can't be sketched.

What else do you feel is essential for a potential designer coming to New York?

I don't think that is the part that school can offer. It's a final step that I think is missing, and that is to come in town and to actually work for another designer and to know what really goes into it like I did when I was working for Jo [Mielziner]. I feel there is an obligation there. If Jo hadn't taken me in, I wouldn't

have known where to begin. You need someone to give you that step. Each year I take on someone new, either from Yale or people who come in to see me, because I feel I owe that much to Jo Mielziner and I want to keep on. The first one was Doug Schmidt, who worked for me for two years and then went on his own, then David Mitchell worked for me about two and a half years. In fact, I'd get them shows at Juilliard to design. Marsha Eck, Marge Kellogg, Ralph Funicello, and Leigh Rand also worked for me. Sometimes they left school because they felt there wasn't anywhere they could get the training for New York. And I will keep on doing it as long as Local 829 cannot set up a design-apprentice program. I will always have one assistant designer throughout the year, because I have enough nonunion-jurisdiction work and architectural work.

Do you feel the chances are good for a young designer on Broadway today?

I would say it's better now, although there are fewer jobs. Working in the theatre is changing a little bit, and I think it's better. When I started, a designer was mostly hired by a producer, and if you had designed a good show, you would have an "in" with a producer. The relationship between the

producer and the designer is very, very important because the producer does the hiring. Sometimes a really big-name director might pick a designer. Generally, when a director is hired, a producer will go down a list of names with him or her and say, "This is my preference."

In the last few years, more and more shows on Broadway have come out of regional theatre, or had tryouts there, or are coming out of Shakespeare in the Park or from Long Wharf. And those organizations are using a lot of unknown directors who have a preference for a designer they have worked with. There are a lot of directors who would be frightened to death working with Jo Mielziner. In fact, there are directors who are frightened working with me, because they have been working with my students and suddenly they are going to work with a teacher. The working relationship becomes a mess, and they prefer working with people of their own level, good or bad, and try to get something out of each other and put on a show. What happens is, more and more Broadway shows are coming out through these situations; therefore, more and more productions are having new designers. So the chances are better, even though there are less shows.

Model by Ming Cho Lee
DON RODRIGO by Alberto Ginastera
Libretto by Alejandro Casona
Directed by Tito Capobianco

New York City Opera
New York State Theatre (1966)
(Photograph — Fred Fehl)

SEVEN

Paints, binders, glues, and equipment

The painting of scenery involves the use of a combination of many different paints and materials. Naturally, not every paint and material in this book is needed for painting every production. It is up to you to decide just what you need for your individual shows. You may find that you can achieve similar painting effects by using one of several paints like casein, vinyl, latex, or other water-base paints. The latter paints, plus aniline dyes, are those most frequently used for painting scenery at the present. There are also many other scenic paints and materials discussed in this chapter.

Your decision to select a particular paint can rest on numerous factors. It may be because it is the paint you are most familiar with, or the paint that is on hand where you are working, or one that has been chosen by someone else as the best to use, or it may be that the choice of paint is controlled by its cost. Your selection should always be governed by what you feel works best for you and for the effects you want to create. What one designer and artist prefers does not always appeal to another. Other vital points of consideration in picking out paint are its appropriateness to the surface on which it is to be applied, its drying time, its durability, its practicality (ease to work with), and its versatility.

The paints and materials discussed are those being used in the scenic studios in the 1970s and the sources indicated herein are based on those available in the New York City area. In a text of this nature, it would be impossible to list every available source. While many theatre companies and university drama departments order supplies from New York City, in many cases comparable materials and paints can be obtained locally at reliable paint stores and hardware stores around the country. Name brands and preferred paints are stated as a means of identity and clarification. Because they change so frequently and vary so much, prices of items are not always quoted. You should consider the following to help determine your order for paints and supplies:

1. How many productions are being done?
2. What do you already have in stock and what needs to be replenished?
3. What new materials are being used?
4. What is the budget?
5. Can extra paints and supplies be used on the next productions?

Scenic artist Fred Jacoby checking a
paint sample on canvas against Donald
Oenslager's portal design for THE
MIKADO at the New York City Opera—
a touch-up several years after the opening.

For Eugene Berman's city backdrop in the
ballet PULCINELLA (1972), an identical
piece of muslin 6 ft. square was starched
like the drop and a small portion of the
design was painted on it with casein paints
and aniline dyes. A strong light was placed
behind and above the translucent muslin
sample so the designer could see how the
sky appeared with the opaque buildings.
(Photographs—Lynn Pecktal)

6. Do you have available storage for paints?

It is always advisable to order more paint
than is necessary, simply because if more is
needed, the cost of having it rushed to you can
become very expensive. The addresses and
telephone numbers of sources for purchasing
paints and materials in this chapter, as well
as others in the book, can be found in the
appendix.

MIXING PAINTS

Opaque Colors

Since casein is one of the most popular paints
for scenic work, let us assume that this is the
paint being discussed in this section. Whenever you are mixing paints to match a specific
opaque color on the designer's sketch, it is
always best to start out by making samples
before going ahead and mixing the required

amount of paint needed. Even the most experienced painter makes samples, and it is
not uncommon for him to have to make two
or three before being satisfied.

For samples you need a small container
such as an 8-ounce can or a metal paint lid
in which to mix the paints. To blend the colors
together, a scenic brush such as a 2-inch liner
works nicely for fast mxing, and it also enables
you to dip easily into the different containers
of color and add them as needed. Start out by
placing a small amount of the pure color or
colors into the selected container and use the
brush to blend each color well as it is added.
The fact that casein colors dry lighter than they
appear when wet should be taken into consideration when you are arriving at your color.
While you are mixing, remember the proportions and each color that is added to the mixture so these can be duplicated later in greater
quantity.

247

Once the colors are blended into one, and it appears to be the color you want, brush it onto a small piece of paper or muslin, then put it aside for a few minutes to dry. If fast drying is a must, you can place it near open heat. After the sample has completely dried, put it directly on the color being matched in the sketch to see how it looks. It may be just right, or perhaps it has to be made a little lighter or darker, or warmer or cooler. If the color sample needs any changing, adjust it, make another sample, and let it dry. When satisfactory results are obtained, proceed with mixing the full amount of color needed by utilizing the same colors and proportions employed in the correct sample. By using this method, an enormous amount of paint and time can be saved.

When you are mixing a light color, it is always better to start with white, because if this is not done, it may take much more white to lighten the color than is anticipated, and then it will be necessary to discard some of the color in order not to mix a great deal more than is actually needed.

Transparent Colors

If you are mixing colors that are to be used as washes and they are to be built up over each other (as a watercolor painting would be), the colors should be mixed by lightening them with water instead of putting any white in them. In this way, if they are glazed over, the thin pure colors will go darker with successive washes, whereas a color with white mixed in it will tend to go lighter. Also, if the color has white in it, it tends to cover the other color rather than add to it.

Generally, when you are mixing colors, there are instances where each value has to be mixed in a specific color. For example, this is

PAINTS AND DYES

Casein Paint

Form: paste
Thinner: water
Uses:

Casein colors are preferred today for doing "finished work" in the commercial scenic studio, long ago having replaced dry pigment colors. They are easier, faster, and less troublesome to prepare and use (no heating the glue for size), and are more permanent. Casein colors come in a wide range of brilliant colors, and they have superior tinting strength. One coat of casein paint usually covers the surface and it dries fast (in about 40 minutes), producing a flat and durable finish. Since casein colors cover and hold well, they may easily be painted over with several layers of color, including glazes of aniline dyes and washes of thin caseins, without fear of lifting or rubbing up. Flats can be repainted many times with casein paint.

Besides being excellent for creating the *finished work* (the final painting), casein paint is also good for the *base color* (the lay-in or local color) which is applied after the canvas surface has been primed. Casein can even be used for *priming,*

instead of the traditional priming made with dry whiting and glue size, but casein does not tighten up the canvas on framed units as well as the ground gelatine glue contained in dry whiting priming. At the same time, it becomes far more expensive to prime with casein than with dry whiting when a lot of scenery has to be primed.

For *overpainting,* casein colors are most often applied on canvas flats and backdrops (after priming), on muslin backdrops (after starching), on set pieces covered in muslin and canvas (after priming), and on wood (after priming). Also, thin caseins are put on backdrops and other soft pieces of sharkstooth scrim, linen scrim, and bobbinet (all without priming). Like dry colors, caseins dry lighter than when wet.

To prepare:

Mix
2 parts CASEIN PASTE COLOR
to
1 part WATER

Casein colors are easy to prepare for painting. They are manufactured in paste form (with binder included) and only need to have water added before they are ready for application. This is ordinarily done by adding 2 quarts of water to each gallon of the casein paste color (or 1 part water to 2 parts paste). Casein paste and water should always be mixed well. While these may be stirred by hand with a wooden stick or metal paddle, an electric hand mixer is recommended for "breaking up" the color faster and more thoroughly, especially if a great deal of paint is being prepared at one time. It is always easier if this is done before intermixing the different casein colors.

Adding Other Colors:
Aniline dye, vinyl, latex, and other water paints are frequently mixed with casein colors to obtain a particular color.

WORKING CONSISTENCY
FOR CASEIN PAINTS

required for painting panels of molding on canvas-covered interior flats. Besides the local color for the wood, you would need individual colors to make the light, highlight, shade, shadow, and cutting line. Yet in other cases of color mixing, it is another matter. A typical example is a muslin backdrop designed to have a turbulent sky and clouds painted with washes of several colors. After closely observing the sketch, you may find that four or five of the purest colors can be mixed and many of the other colors on the sketch can be obtained by merely crossing these with one another when painting, or by lightening them with water while painting.

Mixing colors other than casein, it is important to remember that the strength of colors often varies with the brand of paint and that some paints dry lighter than when wet, some dry darker, and some dry close to the wet color. This is another reason why a sample of the color or colors being mixed should always be made beforehand. It is also wise to read the labels on containers to become familiar with the individual characteristics of a paint.

Any young designer or painter usually has some experience in mixing colors or has easy access to such information because of the numerous books available on the subject. For the young designer or artist starting out in the theatre, the best way to learn how to mix colors (after learning the basic fundamentals) is to take a sketch box of paints and paper (or canvas) and go out-of-doors to practice sketching and painting. Study the way sunlight hits subjects, where it makes highlights, and how it casts shadows on objects. The learning experience of on-the-spot painting where you mix and palette your own colors according to what you see in nature cannot be beaten.

Application:
Casein paints are applied in a number of ways, including brush, paint roller, Hudson spray tank, spray gun, and sponge. If desired, caseins can be put on scenery as opaque colors, as semiopaque colors, or as transparent colors just by thinning them with water.

Popular Brands for Theatrical Work:
Iddings Casein
Luminall Fresco Colors
Para-Casein Paste Paint
Placo Caseins
Gothic Casein Fresco Paints

Casein colors can be purchased at the following companies in New York City or at comparable paint stores around the country: S. Wolf's Sons (or Playhouse Colors), M. Epstein's Son, Inc., Gothic Color Co., Theatrical Production Service, and Paramount Theatrical Supplies.

Iddings Casein Colors:

White	Red
Lemon yellow	Dark red
Golden yellow	Magenta
Orange	Purple
Bright red	Yellow ochre

Burnt sienna
Raw sienna
Raw umber
Burnt umber
Brown
Cerulean blue
Turquoise blue

Ultramarine blue
Navy blue
Emerald green
Chrome oxide green
Dark green
Black

Luminall Casein Colors:
White
Primrose yellow (Cad. yel. lt.)
New golden yellow (Hansa yel.)
Orange (Dinitraniline orange)
Bright red (Toluidine red)
Deep red (Alizarine red)
Indian red
Yellow ochre
Raw sienna
Burnt sienna
Burnt umber
Raw umber
Blue (Ultramarine blue)
New deep blue
Turquoise blue (Phthalocyanine bl.)
Bright green (Phthalocyanine gr.)
Yellow green (Ch. oxide green)
TV magenta
TV violet
Black (Carbon black)

Ordering Highly Intense Casein Colors:
Very concentrated brilliant casein colors can be ordered from a company like S. Wolf's Sons. They also will match a specific color in casein according to your sample.

Available quantities:
Casein paint comes in quart, gallon, and 5-gallon containers. Although the gallon container is the size most used in the scenic studio, it is more practical to buy a 5-gallon container of white, since it is needed more often than the other caseins. The quart sizes are ideal for taking paints to the theatre for touch-ups or for use when only a small amount of scenery is being painted.

Storage:
If cans of casein have been opened and are not in use, they should be properly stored to prevent the paste color from drying out. This is achieved by pouring about a pint of water on top of the remaining casein paste in the can and then tightly replacing the lid.

Vinyl Paint

Form: liquid
Thinner: water
Uses:

Because of its durability, its fast drying time (around 30 minutes), and its ability to cover surfaces with one coat, vinyl paint is outstanding for scenic work. In addition, it does not have an offensive odor. This premixed paint can be used for both interior and exterior surfaces, including wood, Masonite, canvas (painted or unpainted), plastic, wallboard, and metal. For painting scenery, vinyl paint is good for all of these. Vinyl colors come in a flat or gloss finish. They are not as intense as casein colors or dry pigment colors, but they can be strengthened by adding aniline dyes or casein colors.

Flat and gloss vinyl colors can be applied full strength as they come from the container, or they can be thinned with water to the desired working consistency. For instance, on surfaces that get a lot of wear and tear like portable stage decks with Masonite tops, stage floors covered with inlaid linoleum, or wooden platforms, vinyl colors are put on full strength. A semigloss finish for portable decks and floors is often obtained by mixing one part gloss vinyl with one part flat vinyl (see Painting Floors, p. 350), and it is also put on without thinning, using a paint roller that has a thick roller cover. For other surfaces, like canvas- or muslin-covered set pieces or wooden props, the vinyl colors would be thinned with water to a normal working consistency so they go on easily yet cover the surface well.

Thinning really depends on the surface you are working on, plus the effect you are creating. Frequently, vinyl colors are applied very thinly. For example, vinyl glazes are brushed over three-dimensional woodwork (which has been undercoated with two coats of colored

Aniline Dyes

Form: powder and crystals
Soluble in: water (also obtainable are dyes that dissolve in alcohol or oil and lacquer)
Uses:

These water-soluble dyes produce brilliant transparent colors which make them ideally suited for painting translucent muslin backdrops and cycs, and they are outstanding for painting on scrim and velour (especially velour in light and neutral colors). Aniline dyes also perform beautifully on raw wood, letting the natural grain of the wood show through. Sometimes a full stage setting of canvas-covered flats (after priming) is completely painted and finished in dyes. Aniline dyes are excellent for glazing colors, for bath colors (both spraying and brushing), for inking, for dyeing draperies and fabrics, and for mixing with water-base colors to enhance brilliance.

To mix:
Since certain dye colors are needed constantly in the scenic studio, a standard set of concentrated colors is mixed and kept in airtight containers (1-gallon glass jugs with screw tops). These containers of liquid dyes stay on the mixing table and are used "to work from" when mixing specific colors, rather than just pouring the powdered dye into a larger container of water. Keeping these on hand produces easier control when mixing dyes as well as saves time. To mix concentrated dye, dissolve:

---

1 teaspoon of *POWDERED DYE*
into
1 quart of *BOILING-HOT WATER*
while stirring

—CONCENTRATED LIQUID DYE

A small amount of vinegar or alcohol helps dissolve the dye, but it is not necessary if the water is boiling hot (212 degrees F.). When dyes are mixed too strongly, they crystallize and their effect is lost. For example, blue mixed too strongly can go to a red metallic color, and purple to a greenish color. To obtain a very dark color in dye on a painting surface such as muslin or canvas, it is best to do it in two "shots" rather than try to get what you want the first time. Also, if you are mixing and matching a specific color in the dye, you should always make samples of it on the identical fabric to be painted, because dyes can dry differently on each fabric.

Binders: When desired, a liquid binder (starch, Methocel, glue size, clear

opaque shellac) to give the appearance of grained wood. Or thin vinyl glazes can be brushed and sponged over such metal surfaces (also primed in opaque shellac) as grillwork or scaffolding units to make them appear old and to give them texture.

Besides vinyl colors, clear liquid vinyls (flat and gloss) have numerous uses in scenic work. Both are applied as preservatives on other water paints to keep them from rubbing off and to waterproof them, and they are also used as binders for dyes, paints, and bronze powders.

A popular brand for theatrical work is called Flo-Paint.

Available colors in Flo-Paint (in 1-gallon containers):

Super Vinyl Flat		*Super Vinyl Gloss*	
Raw umber	Golden yellow	Raw umber	Medium blue
Burnt umber	Orange	Burnt umber	Dark blue
Raw sienna	Bright red	Raw sienna	Medium yellow
Burnt sienna	Navy blue	Burnt sienna	Orange
Ch. oxide green	Silver gray	Medium green	Red
Emerald green	Ivory	Light green	Battleship gray
Dark green	Hi-hiding white	Deep green	Cream
Lemon yellow	Heat resisting white	Light yellow	Black
Magenta	Matte finish (Krom-O-	Magenta	
Ultramarine blue	Key) blue		
Cerulean blue	Black		

Clear gloss vinyl and clear flat vinyl are also available in gallon containers.

Vinyl colors can be purchased at: Flo-Paint, Inc., Gothic Color Co., S. Wolf's Sons (or Playhouse Colors), M. Epstein's Son.

---

vinyl, white flexible glue, or dextrine) can be added to the liquid aniline dyes to prevent spreading or bleeding on the painting surface.

Aniline dyes may be purchased from Fezandie and Sperrle, Inc., Gothic Color Co., Theatre Production Service, Paramount Theatrical Supplies, Bachmeier and Co., Inc., S. Wolf's Sons or Playhouse Colors, and M. Epstein's Son, Inc.

Some companies sell aniline dyes by the ounce or by the pound, others by the pound only. Dyes can cost $3 to $10 per pound, depending on the color and its solubility in water, alcohol, or oil. Whenever looking over lists to order dyes, remember that firms do not use the same names for identical or similar colors, and in choosing colors it is advisable to select a basic set of aniline dyes.

Aniline dyes sprayed over areas masked by sawdust to create designs on Robert D. Mitchell's translucent muslin backdrop for THE LOTTERY (1974).

Steps of Execution:

1. Backdrop stapled over gray bogus paper.
2. Backdrop starched with blue-tinted starch.
3. Drawing done lightly in charcoal.
4. (Left) Working on a few areas at a time, sawdust arranged by hand and brush by Robert Motley to mask various areas; black aniline dye sprayed onto muslin.
5. (Center) After dye on muslin and sawdust dried, sawdust was removed and backdrop sprayed, using Hudson tank. Process repeated until desired effect achieved.
6. (Right) After masking and spraying a second time, sawdust was swept up.
(Photographs — Lynn Pecktal)

Aniline Dyes Soluble in Alcohol, Oil, and Water
Although water-soluble dyes are the most popular for scenic work, aniline dyes are also made to dissolve in alcohol only, water and alcohol, and oil. These are designated:

A only — alcohol
O — oil
W — water
W&A — water and alcohol

The following information is from Fezandie & Sperrle, Inc., distributors of Fezan Aniline Colors:

Solutions and Solubility Code

Alcohol-soluble:
To dissolve alcohol-soluble colors, add directly to the alcohol. Use two ounces to one gallon of denatured alcohol. Stir thoroughly.

Oil-soluble:
Oil-soluble colors are dissolved in warm oil, waxes, benzol, stearic acid, oleic and fatty acids, lacquers and lacquer thinners. Suggestion: heat the oil or wax to *below* the boiling point, and then add the dry powdered color. Stir until color is thoroughly dissolved. Use two ounces of color to one gallon of solution.

Water-soluble:
To dissolve water-soluble colors, dissolve the color in boiling hot water, stirring until color is completely dissolved. Use four ounces of dry color to the gallon. The solution should be filtered to ensure complete solubility.

If the occasion arises, a company like Bachmeier will make up a specific color in dyes and match your submitted sample.

A Basic List of Aniline Dyes
The following list, selected from Baco Anilines of Bachmeier and Co., is a good basic palette of dyes to have on hand:

Indian yellow	Bismark brown
Lemon yellow	Emerald green
Raw sienna	Jade green
Orange	Moss green
Eosine	Patent blue
Rose Bengal	Celestial blue
Scarlet	Ultramarine blue
Ox blood red	Violet
Van Dyke brown	Black

Most aniline dye colors are compatible with each other and can be freely intermixed. However, some colors may react negatively and crystallize in the pail. In this case, approach the color you are attempting to get with a different combination of the basic colors. For instance, Bismark brown is sometimes difficult to use with other dye colors, but a similar brown can be made with orange and black and then this color will have less tendency to crystallize.

Latex Paint

Form: liquid or paste
Thinner: water
Uses:

Latex paint is known for its flexibility, toughness, and durability. In great part, its popularity has been a result of the extended range of colors developed in the last few years. Latex itself means any emulsion in water of finely divided particles of synthetic rubber or plastic. Latex covers in one coat and touches up reasonably well because it does not redissolve itself. It is favored for painting wooden floors and platforms, Masonite decks, and canvas-covered units. The flexibility of latex makes it ideal for backpainting portions of translucent muslin backdrops, and it can also be thinned with water to paint ground cloths. Latex dries fast (in about 30 to 45 minutes) and can be washed, if so desired, after it has thoroughly dried (24 hours). Both alkyd-latex paint (Satin Luminall) and vinyl-acrylic latex paint are used for scenic work. Alkyd-latex tends to be more scrubbable than vinyl-acrylic latex.

Vinyl-acrylic latex is used extensively for painting concrete floors (or the like) in television and motion picture studios. Any stains such as coffee can be killed beforehand by spraying with silver paint in an aerosol can. A shiny surface is sometimes applied over the dry latex paint by spraying it with liquid Johnson Glo-Coat Wax in a Hudson tank, but the wax should always be strained before it is poured into the tank.

To prepare:
Latex comes in a ready-to-use consistency and in paste form. Vinyl-acrylic latex (a polyvinyl acetate and acrylic mix) comes ready to use. Alkyd-latex flat wall paint (Satin Luminall) is concentrated. It is thinned to a working consistency by using 1 quart of water to 1 gallon of paint.

Popular Brands of Latex Paint:
Wolf paints   Red Devil paints
Satin Luminall paints   Peerless paints
Muralo paints

Wolf Vinyl-Acrylic Latex Colors:
Wolf Video Latex Colors, which are pure and vivid, are used in theatre, television, and display. They are non-bleeding (except magenta), are easily recoated, and are ready to use. These latex colors come in flat and semigloss (available colors denoted by *). Also

Acrylic Polymer Plastic Colors

Form: paste or heavy liquid
Thinner: water
Uses:

Acrylic colors, which are used extensively for graphic arts and easel painting, are extremely versatile, but—because of their expense—are usually confined to use for small areas of decorative work on scenery. Acrylic colors can be applied on almost any surface: Plexiglas, Lucite, and other acrylic sheets; cellophane, glass, plastic foam, wood, Masonite, cardboard, canvas, muslin, leather, foil, plastic sheeting, ceramics, stone, plaster, and metal. They are splendid for painting models and renderings.

Acrylic colors are tough, permanent, flexible, and quick-drying. After drying, they are water-insoluble and can be painted and glazed over right away. These emulsion-based paints can be used from the tube or jar to produce heavy areas of impasto, or can be thinned with water for watercolor techniques. Thinly applied colors dry fast; heavily applied colors take much longer.

These features are helping to make acrylic colors even more popular with scenic and costume designers.

Use of Mediums:
Different effects can be had by the use of mediums. They can be obtained to speed drying, slow drying, modify consistency, be a thinner and a final varnish, and produce a gloss or matte finish.

Gesso:
Gesso, a white liquid primer with the same base as acrylic colors, is excellent for basecoating models and creating a textured surface, if so desired, at the same time. When dry, it can be painted over with acrylic colors, caseins, or oil.

Dry Pigment Colors

Form: powder
Binder: glue size (also see pp. 254-256)
Uses:

While dry pigment colors have been generally replaced in the scenic studio by such premixed water-base paints as casein, vinyl, and latex for finished painting, they are still used for making priming, lay-in coats, for opaquing, and for making scenic dope. Dry pigment colors can also be added to these paints to obtain a particular color.

Mixing Dry Pigment Colors:
Whenever you are mixing dry pigment colors, you should bear in mind that these three parts are involved:

> Pigment—*Color*
> Binder—*Glue*
> Medium—*Water*

The pigment (color) is combined with a binder (glue), which is mixed in a liquid medium (water). The water puts these in working form, making it possible for the paint to be applied on the surface of the scenery, and when the water dries, the glue binds the pigment to the surface. The mixture of glue and water together is called *size.* Gelatine glue (also referred to as ground scenic glue) has long been the commonly used glue. See specific proportions and data for mixing size under Glues and Binders, pages 272-274

Mixing a Specific Color:
Dry pigment colors can be mixed with each other in dry powder form to make

252

scenic flat white and scenic semigloss white. Clear finishes: latex gloss clear and latex flat clear.

Scenic bright yellow*	Accent brown*	Video magenta (not nonbleeding)
Video yellow light	Scenic raw umber	Video green*
Video yellow medium	Accent black*	Accent green*
Scenic yellow ochre	Video orange*	Scenic bright turquoise
Scenic raw sienna	Scenic deep orange	Accent blue*
Scenic burnt sienna	Accent red*	Video violet*
Scenic burnt umber	Scenic bright red*	Chrome key blue

Clear latex (flat and gloss) is used in similar capacities as clear vinyl. It serves as a preservative coating on painted scenery and as a binder for bronze powders and aniline dyes (See Clear Vinyl, p. 257). Wolf's brand of clear gloss latex is called L Additive.

Satin Luminall Latex:
These bright *scenic accent colors* are available in paste form:

Dutch yellow	Tropic green
Blue velvet	Red velvet
Orient brown	*also* White

Adding Other Colors:
Aniline dyes, tinting colors, caseins, or other water-base paints can be added to latex paint to obtain a particular color.

Popular Brands:
Liquitex colors
Hyplar (Grumbacher)
Weber
New Temp (Utrecht Linens)
Aquatic

Application:
By brush, roller, or sponge.

Source:
Acrylic polymer plastic colors can be purchased at art stores. They are available in countless colors and come in tubes and jars in 2-ounce, 8-ounce, pint, quart, and gallon quantities.

the desired color and then mixed with the glue size, or the dry colors can be put in and mixed directly in the glue size. For the beginner, the first method is perhaps best, while the second approach is usually taken by the seasoned scenic artist, but it may also be a matter of personal preference.

If you are going to make a sizable amount of a color, it is always practical to mix only a small amount first and make a sample to see how it looks after it dries. Brush the color on the

Application:
Latex is put on by brush, paint roller, Hudson spray tank, spray gun, or sponge.

Sources:
Latex paint can be obtained in New York from S. Wolf's Sons (or Playhouse Colors), M. Epstein's Son, Inc., and at comparable paint stores around the country. The paints listed above are available in gallon containers. Satin Luminall White is available in 5-gallon containers.

Paint elevation of opaque trees on a gauze drop by Helen Pond and Herbert Senn for THE YOUNG LORD (1973), New York City Opera. (Below) View of finished drop on floor. (Photographs — Lynn Pecktal)

Steps of Execution:

1. Gauze drop stapled on floor over wax paper.
2. Gauze sprayed with aniline dye and casein paint.
3. Grid for drawing snapped in white chalk.
4. Drawing done with white chalk sticks.
5. Opaque painting of trees, fence, and details done with 1 part latex paint to 1 part clear concentrated latex, undiluted, using brushes.

Dry Pigment Colors

actual material on which you are going to apply it. Then, when satisfied, mix what you need. Experience teaches one to judge how much color to mix. It is much wiser to mix more than enough paint than to have to rematch the color. Extra paint can always be used for touch-ups and for opaquing (by mixing other colors with it).

Dry pigment colors require a larger amount of size than does dry whiting, and some dry pigment colors need more size than others. If you need 2 gallons of mixed dry whiting, for instance, you would use approximately 1½ gallons of size to 2 gallons of dry whiting. To avoid lumps when mixing dry pigment colors either with each other or with the dry whiting, sift them into the prepared glue size while stirring thoroughly rather than the other way around.

Available Dry Pigment Colors:
The following dry pigment colors can be obtained by the pound from the Gothic Color Company.
* The asterisk denotes a basic list of dry pigment colors and a basic list of aniline dyes of comparable colors, placed at the end of this section.

YELLOW

Milori yellow light—A very strong, brilliant cool yellow of primrose hue.
Milori yellow medium—A strong brilliant straight yellow similar to spectrum hue.
*Chrome yellow light**—A cool yellow, lemon shade.
*Chrome yellow medium**—Warm yellow, golden shade.
English Dutch pink—A rich neutralized yellow with a greenish cast.
Milori yellow orange—A brilliant yellow orange.

ORANGE

*French orange mineral**—A very brilliant orange with a slight red cast.
Chelsea vermilion—A brilliant rich red orange, strong and permanent.
*English vermilion**—A bright red orange or geranium red.
American vermilion—A deep red orange.

RED

Bulletin red—A brilliant red with a red orange cast, almost a spectrum red.
Turkey red lake—A rich blood-red hue, nearest to spectrum red that can be obtained.
Light maroon—A rich neutralized red.
English Venetian red—Valuable terracotta shade, a richer red than burnt sienna.
*Dark maroon**—A deep, rich neutralized red, darker in value.
*Magenta lake**—A deep vibrant bluish red, very intense.

*Solterino lake**—A brilliant red violet; slight rise in value; extends into beautiful pinks of great brilliance.

VIOLET

Purple lake—A rich violet with red cast.
*Violet lake**—A cool violet, very strong.
Royal purple—Intense spectrum violet.
Purple lake No. 133—Similar to the violet lake, but warmer in tone.

BLUE

*French ultramarine blue**—A warm rich blue. Slight red content.
American ultramarine blue—A warm blue similar to French, but less intense.
French cobalt blue—A spectrum blue slightly raised in value.
*Italian blue**—A very intense brilliant blue green or turquoise; frequently referred to as Urban blue; excellent sky and water tone.
Prussian blue—A deep green blue lowered in value.
*Celestial blue**—A dark turquoise; blue green lowered in value; excellent night-sky quality.

GREEN

Chrome green light—Straight green, less brilliant than emerald green.
*Emerald green**—A spectrum green, very brilliant.

Dry Pigment Colors—Mixing

Mixing Priming by Using Dry Whiting
When you are priming (the first coat) on new canvas and are using dry whiting (a white chalk) and size water, these proportions are used:

1 part *HOT CONCENTRATED GLUE*
to
10 parts *HOT WATER*

— **PRIMING SIZE**

1 part *PRIMING SIZE*
to
1 part *DRY WHITING*

— **PRIMING**
(First coat for new canvas)

Dry whiting is used when a white priming is needed on new canvas scenery. It can be tinted with dry colors or with premixed water-base paints to create a desired color for priming.

Mixing Priming by Using Dry Pigment Colors
If priming is being done with dry pigment colors like the earth colors, to hold well they need a stronger binder than the dry whiting. Black, for instance, needs a stronger size than the average pigment; always make a test with the pigment colors and glue size you are using. Mix a small batch, using specific

Chrome green medium—Straight green, slightly neutralized.

Chrome green dark*—A dark straight green, highly neutralized.

Hanover green—An imported bright warm green, excellent for foliage tones.

Saphite green—A warm green similar to Hanover green.

Malachite green*—A rich deep cool green, excellent for dark foliage.

Royal green lake—A warm deep rich blue-green tone, very strong.

EARTH COLORS AND NEUTRALS

French yellow ochre—A neutralized yellow, tan, or buff shade.

Golden ochre—A rich neutralized yellow, more transparent than French.

Burnt Turkey umber—A rich deep brown or walnut tone.

Raw Turkey umber—A greenish brown or olive; a delicate neutral shade.

Italian burnt sienna*—A rich reddish brown or brick color.

Italian raw sienna*—A rich yellow brown or tan.

Imported Van Dyke brown*—A very deep rich brown, excellent for wood tone.

English Venetian red—An inexpensive neutralized red, terracotta shade.

Ivory black*—A very rich black, slightly transparent.

Hercules black—A brilliant jet black, permanent and powerful.

Permanent white (zinc white)—A pure white of great permanence for highlight.

Lithopone—Comes in white powder form, gives opacity to priming.

Dry whiting—A white chalk, not a pigment.

Available Wet Pigments:

Wet pigments or pulp colors are also available in certain colors at the Gothic Color Company. Packaged in 5-gallon containers, wet pigments come in paste form and must have the glue binder added whenever used.

They are:

Hoyt's yellow lake—A rich transparent yellow similar to gamboge.

Turkey red lake—The same as in the dry pigment.

Solferino lake—The same as in the dry pigment.

Antwerp blue—Pulp Prussian blue, very intense.

Emerald green—The same as in the dry pigment.

Brown lake—A pulp brown, similar to Van Dyke.

Basic Lists of Dry Pigment Colors and Aniline Dyes:

(1) A basic list of dry pigment colors (indicated in list above by an asterisk), and (2) a basic list of aniline dyes of comparable colors:

Dry Pigment Color	Aniline Dye Color
Chrome yellow light	Lemon yellow
Chrome medium yellow	Indian yellow
French orange mineral	Orange
English vermilion	Scarlet
Dark maroon	Ox blood red
Magenta lake	Eosine
Solferino lake	Rose Bengal
Violet lake	Violet
French ultramarine blue	Ultramarine blue

Dry Pigment Color	Aniline Dye Color
Italian blue	Patent blue
Celestial blue	Celestial blue
Emerald green	Emerald green
Chrome green dark	Moss green
Malachite green	Jade green
Italian burnt sienna	Bismark brown
Italian raw sienna	Raw sienna
Imported Van Dyke brown	Van Dyke brown
Ivory black	Black

---

proportions, and then brush some of the mixture on the surface to be primed to see how it holds after it has dried. If it does not come off when you rub your hand over it, it is fine. If it does, the amount of glue in the size needs to be increased. The proportions on this page are ordinarily used for making the priming with dry pigment colors.

1 part *HOT CONCENTRATED GLUE*

to

8 parts *HOT WATER*

— SIZE
(For priming with dry pigment colors only)

2 parts *DRY PIGMENT COLOR*

to

3 parts *SIZE*

— PRIMING WITH DRY PIGMENT COLORS

Priming with Other Paints:

Some painters use casein (white or colors) for priming and thin it with water or with glue size (10 parts water to 1 of glue). The glue size added to the casein makes it hold better on the surface; this is important, since it is the first coat. Latex paint and vinyl paint (thinned with water) can also be used for priming. But all of these paints are more costly for priming than dry whiting

255

Dry Pigment Colors — Mixing

and dry pigment colors mixed with glue. Furthermore, there is nothing better for tightening new canvas than the scenic glue used in these.

Mixing Dry Pigment Colors to Do the Finished Painting

When it is necessary to do the finished (final) painting with dry pigment colors, they can be mixed with a working size in these proportions:

1 part *HOT CONCENTRATED GLUE*

to

15 parts *HOT WATER*

— **WORKING SIZE**
(For finished painting using dry colors)

1 part *WORKING SIZE*

to

1 part *DRY PIGMENT COLORS*

— **DOING FINISHED PAINTING WITH DRY PIGMENT COLORS**

Other Binders for Dry Pigment Colors and Dry Whiting:

As alternate binders, flexible rubber glue, clear liquid gloss vinyl (or flat), white synthetic resin glue, and carpenter's glue can be used as binders for dry pigment colors and for dry whiting.

1 part *LIQUID FLEXIBLE GLUE*

to

8 parts *WATER*

— **WORKING SIZE FOR DRY PIGMENT COLORS**

Alternate Glues Selected from Specific Companies:

Polyvinyl flexible cold water glue (Gothic Color Co.)
Available in liquid or solid form. Mix 1 part glue to 4 parts water.

Polyvinyl glue (Paramount Theatrical Supplies)
Available in liquid form. Mix 1 part glue to 1-2 parts water.

Carpenter's glue (Gothic Color Co.)
Available by the pound in granulated form. Although carpenter's glue is less expensive than gelatine glue, it does not possess the high qualities of

1 part *CLEAR FLAT OR GLOSS VINYL*

to

4 parts *WATER*

— **WORKING SIZE FOR DRY PIGMENT COLORS**

1 part *WHITE SYNTHETIC RESIN GLUE*

to

10 parts *WATER*

— **WORKING SIZE FOR DRY PIGMENT COLORS**

gelatine glue. Carpenter's glue requires soaking in water (1 to 2 hours), then heating in a double boiler until thoroughly dissolved. A strong glue, it is usually mixed with water in the proportion of 1 part concentrated glue to 16 parts water.

Sources:
Dry pigment colors and glues can be obtained from Theatrical Production Service, Gothic Color Co., S. Wolf's Sons or Playhouse Colors, Paramount Theatrical Supplies, and M. Epstein's Son.

Oil Paint

Form: liquid
Thinner: turpentine or mineral spirits
Uses:

Since it does not dry as fast and cannot be combined with all the techniques of water-base paints, oil paint has a limited use for theatrical work. It is used occasionally as a durable paint on wooden or metal objects that are going to get a lot of wear and tear or may be exposed to the weather. Oil

paint can also be thinned with turpentine to make glazes for graining over three-dimensional molding that has been first primed and basecoated with opaque shellac. Sometimes oil paint is applied over stains (aniline dyes, etc.) on old scenery so the stains will not bleed through the final painting.

Popular Brands:
Benjamin Moore   Pratt and Lambert
Sherwin-Williams

Application:
Oil paint can be put on by brush, sponge, paint roller, or by spraying.

Availability:
Oil paint comes in many colors and in gloss, semigloss, or flat finish.

Source:
Easily obtainable at paint stores in half-pints, pints, quarts, and gallons.

Tinting Colors

Scenic-Art, Concentrated Tinting Colors: Scenic-Art concentrated tinting colors are manufactured to mix with all scenic and artist's paints, including alkyd-latex-polyvinyl acrylic and oil-base. Made in numerous colors, they are available in easy-to-use plastic squeeze bottles with a tipped top. Not only are they handy for tinting in the scenic studio, but they are also good for painting in theatres or television rental studios, which do not always keep a complete set of colors in stock. This particular brand of tinting colors is made for M. Epstein's Son.

Japan Coach Colors for Tinting: These well-known flat coach colors are still used for tinting oil paint, and were long used for tinting before oil stains were developed. They should be thinned by first beating the color and then slowly adding the turpentine until a brushing consistency is obtained. In addition, mineral spirits can also be used for thinning. Japan colors may be used to tint lacquers, and when this is done, the Japan color is thinned first with lacquer thinner, then the lacquer is added. One popular brand is Ronan Superfine Japan Colors.

Moore's Universal Tinting Colors: Another brand, Moore's tinting colors, is made in a soft paste form and can be added to all types of paints—alkyd, latex, PVA, acrylic, resin emulsion, and oil. Available in cans or tubes and in a wide selection of colors, they are never to be used as a paint by themselves, but only for tinting purposes. As much as a half-pint of these tinting colors can be added to a gallon of paint. They should be added slowly to the paint while stirring vigorously.

PRIMERS, PRESERVATIVES, AND BINDERS

Clear Liquid Vinyl

Form: liquid
Thinner: water
Uses:

Clear preservatives or protective coatings to keep paints from rubbing off and to waterproof them, and as binders to hold paints, dyes, and bronze powders.

Preservative or protective coatings:
Both flat and gloss clear liquid vinyl are applied on scenery after the painting has been finished. These are usually canvas-covered set pieces like stair units, double doors, cornices (primed with scene paint and painted in casein), or three-dimensional woodwork pieces that are not covered, such as paneled wainscoting, overmantles, fireplaces, baseboards, and chair rails (primed with two coats of opaque shellac as an undertone and then glazed over with thin colors in oils), or they can be prop portraits and murals (canvas stretched on wooden frames, primed with scene paint and painted in casein or aniline dyes). Clear vinyl is highly favored because it enriches the surface and gives it a shiny finish. Both flat and gloss vinyl dry relatively fast—in about 30 minutes. Appearing white when wet, the clear vinyls dry clear and make the painted colors on the surface dry a bit darker.

A sample of the clear vinyl solution should be tried on the actual surface to make sure that it dries completely clear instead of milky. If the temperature in the area where you are working is too cold, it can cause the clear vinyl to dry cloudy or milky. Application is usually by brushing or spraying.

If using clear vinyl (either flat or gloss) as a preservative, it is best to apply two thin coats rather than a heavy one. Clear vinyl is mixed with water in these proportions:

1 part *CLEAR LIQUID VINYL*

to

1 part *WATER*

—**CLEAR VINYL PRESERVATIVE FOR PAINTED SCENERY**

Binders:
Both gloss and flat clear vinyl are good binders for aniline dyes when painting on primed canvas, starched muslin, or wood (either primed or raw). To make a working size to be mixed with the liquid dyes, use:

1 part *CLEAR VINYL*
(flat or gloss)

to

8 parts *WATER*
(including the water used for the liquid dyes)

—**WORKING SIZE FOR LIQUID ANILINE DYES (for painting on canvas, muslin, wood)**

Gloss and flat clear vinyl are also effective for transparent dye painting on sheets of Plexiglas, Lucite, or Acrylite which may be used for making such items as stained-glass windows, signs, and profile chandelier globes. Furthermore, they can be applied on glass surfaces like windowpanes, mirrors, bottles, and lamps. For holding well on plastic or glass, the clear vinyls are put on in a heavier working consistency. (See formula for mixing on the following page.)

Clear Liquid Vinyl

> 3 parts *CLEAR VINYL*
> (flat or gloss)
>
> to
>
> 1 part *WATER*
> (including the water used
> for the liquid dyes)

— TRANSPARENT DYE
PAINTING ON PLASTIC
OR GLASS SURFACES

Panels of stained glass for Ben Edwards' oriel window in Jean Kerr's FINISHING TOUCHES (1973) painted with vinyl paint on $\frac{1}{16}$-in.-thick sheets of translucent fiber glass. The drawing for each panel was laid out on brown paper, fiber glass placed over it, and outlines traced in opaque vinyl paint. Leaves, flowers, and figure were painted in transparent aniline dyes mixed with clear gloss vinyl.

Orange and Clear White Shellac

Form: liquid
Thinner: denatured alcohol
Uses:

Besides being a durable finish for floors, furniture, and wood in commercial firms and at home, both orange shellac and clear white shellac are a must in the theatrical studio. Like Haeuser's flat white (opaque) Enamelac, these transparent shellacs are vital for *priming* and *sealing* the surface of many materials before the finished painting is applied. Among these materials are new wood, plywood, veneer, Masonite, metal, and wallboard. Shellacs may also be painted on glass or plastic surfaces, as well as on canvas after it has been primed with a water-base paint.

Adding Colors:
Orange shellac and clear white shellac can be applied as transparent coats, or can be made into specific colors with dry pigment colors and become opaque. Opaque shellac is most frequently used to make *undertone colors* for wood or metal scenery which can then be glazed over with thin caseins, vinyls, or oils. Or the opaque shellac can even be applied as the *final coat* itself. If it is preferred that the shellacs remain transparent, aniline dyes (those soluble in alcohol) can be added to them, selecting whichever shellac (orange or white) that applies to the color being made. When adding either aniline dyes or dry pigments to shellac, it is best to first dissolve the dyes or dry pigments in alcohol, then mix them with the shellac.

Dry whiting (a pure white chalk) should never be mixed with shellac, for it will only emulsify and become totally unworkable. If you need white shellac, Haeuser's white Enamelac is ideal, but if that is unavailable, lithopone (a white pigment) can be first mixed with alcohol, then added to the shellac. For tinting,

Transom windows designed by David Guthrie for THE PAJAMA GAME (revival, 1973). Made of translucent Plexiglas, leading, and checkerboard designs painted with alcohol-soluble dyes mixed with clear white shellac.

Stain (oil paint thinned with turpentine) is applied on a three-dimensional wooden piece, laid flat on workhorses, painted earlier with two coats of opaque shellac (Haeuser's white Enamelac tinted with dry pigment colors). Graining is created by using very little stain in the brush. At rear is a double-door unit treated similarly. (Photographs— Lynn Pecktal)

As a binder for bronze powders, clear gloss vinyl is excellent for holding them on almost any surface, including canvas, muslin, wood, metal, and plastics. (See Bronze Powders, p. 262, for mixing the binder with the metallic powder.) Application is by brush or sponge. Use:

2 parts *CLEAR GLOSS VINYL*	
to	— **LIQUID VINYL BINDER FOR BRONZE POWDERS**
1 part *WATER*	

Alternate Binders:
Clear flat or gloss vinyl may be mixed with water and used as an alternate binder for dry pigment colors. (See Dry Pigment Colors, p. 256.) Mix:

1 part *CLEAR FLAT or GLOSS VINYL*	
with	— **WORKING SIZE FOR DRY PIGMENT COLORS**
4 parts *WATER*	

Clear gloss vinyl (full strength) can also be brushed on a surface and used as an alternate binder for imitation gold leaf (Dutch metal and bronze leaf), and as a binder for flitter or mica dust, or flock. Whenever any of these materials are being adhered, the clear gloss vinyl should be brushed on the surface in small areas so that it does not dry out before they are put on.

One popular brand of clear vinyl for theatrical work is Flo-Paint. Clear gloss or clear flat vinyl are available in gallon containers. Vinyl colors also come in gallon pails.

Universal tinting colors can be mixed with the shellacs.

Other Uses:
Inking. Aniline dye added to shellac thinned with alcohol is great for making an inking color to use on canvas or muslin backdrops. After it is brushed on with a thin lining brush, the thin shellac color soaks through the fabrics so that it can be seen on the reverse side. The inked line applied on the front is especially useful when cutting out portions of cut drops from the rear and also when backpainting parts of a backdrop.

Preservatives. Both orange and clear white shellac function as preservatives and protective coatings on painted scenery and props like floors, woodwork, and furniture.

Alternate binder for bronze powders. Shellac can be used as an alternate binder for bronze powders if you are in a pinch, but it can dull the luster of the colors.

Application:
Drying extremely fast, shellacs require quick brushing (or rolling) when being put on, and it is usually necessary to thin or cut them with denatured alcohol before application. They can also be applied by spraying. For ordinary scenic work, one quart of shellac can be thinned with one pint of denatured alcohol.

1 qt. of *SHELLAC* (orange or clear white)	
to	— **SHELLAC CUT WITH ALCOHOL FOR ORDINARY WORK**
1 pt. of *DENATURED ALCOHOL*	

If new woodwork is to get two coats of shellac, the first one should be used full strength to seal the surface well, while the second can be thinned. Before and during use, all shellacs should be stirred constantly, and the containers should not be left uncovered after the work is finished. If brushes have been left in shellac, they are cleaned with alcohol.

Thinning Shellac in Commercial Mixtures:
The most widely used shellac consists of 4 or 5 pounds of shellac gum dissolved in each gallon of pure alcohol. These mixtures are called a "4-pound cut" and a "5-pound cut" respectively, and they should be thinned with de-

natured alcohol to lighter cuts for most work. For example, on regular floors, shellac should not be applied heavier than a 2-pound cut, using 2 coats for a good job. You should always read the label on the shellac container to identify the cut of shellac.

To convert shellac	use alcohol
5-lb. cut to 3-lb. cut	$\frac{7}{8}$ pt. to 1 qt. shel.
5-lb. cut to 2-lb. cut	1 qt. to 1 qt. shel.
5-lb. cut to 1-lb. cut	$\frac{2}{3}$ gal. to 1 qt. shel.
4-lb. cut to 3-lb. cut	$\frac{1}{2}$ pt. to 1 qt. shel.
4-lb. cut to 2-lb. cut	$\frac{3}{4}$ qt. to 1 qt. shel.
4-lb. cut to 1-lb. cut	2 qts. to 1 qt. shel.

Availability: Both orange and clear white shellac can be obtained at paint stores in pints, quarts, gallons, and 5-gallon containers. When purchasing shellac, it is advisable not to stock it more than a few months ahead, because it can become old and then may not dry.

259

Haeuser's Flat White Enamelac (pigment shellac)

Form: liquid
Thinner: denatured alcohol
Uses:

As a *primer,* Enamelac is applied on new wood to seal the surface and get rid of knotholes and any staining. It is extremely good for killing the grain on plywood, old wallpaper patterns, or old colors that are to be repainted, plus any number of stains or bleeding, including oil, aniline, varnish, and grease. If stains are severe, a second coat may be needed. It can be used as a *sealer* for plaster, porous wallboard, and cement surfaces. For metalwork, Enamelac can be applied both as a *primer* and as a *final coat* on cast iron, steel, aluminum, tin, and sheet metal.

Adding Colors:
Although opaque white Enamelac comes ready to use, dry pigments or aniline dyes (or tinting colors) are often mixed with it to make *undertone* colors for woodwork and metalwork, and also for the finished *second coat.* When dry pigments or dyes (those soluble in alcohol) are being added, they should be dissolved first in denatured alcohol, then mixed with Enamelac. Undertone colors can be glazed over with vinyl, oil, casein, or aniline dyes (with a vinyl binder or the like).

Application:
Before being applied, Enamelac should be stirred thoroughly and all surfaces to be painted should be completely

dry and clean. Under normal temperatures, Enamelac dries very fast (about 15 minutes) and can be recoated in 45 minutes to an hour. Thinning is not necessary, but if desired, use denatured alcohol. It is usually applied with a brush, but can also be sprayed on or rolled on with a mohair paint roller. For cleaning brushes and equipment, use alcohol or household ammonia and water.

Availability:
1-gallon containers at paint stores.

Additional information is available from Haeuser Shellac Co.

SPECIAL PAINTS, FINISHES, AND MATERIALS

Lacquer

Form: liquid
Thinner: lacquer thinner
Uses:

In scenic work, lacquer is reserved mainly for *specialty finishes,* and is used primarily for transparent or opaque painting on such surfaces as Plexiglas, Acrylite, Lucite, Mylar, plastic tubing, chrome sheets, glass, or metal. Lacquer is also used to create a very polished

and lustrous *protective coating* on wood or the like, but it should not be applied over an oil-paint finish since the lacquer thinner will blister and remove the oil paint. Lacquer has excellent holding power and dries extremely fast, and is waterproof, weatherproof, and heatproof. In considering lacquer, remember that it can become quite costly if large areas of scenery are to be painted, and that both lacquer and lacquer thin-

ner are highly flammable.

Available Lacquers:
Lacquer is available in transparent and opaque colors as well as clear, and these may be obtained in a gloss or flat finish.

Application:
Since lacquer sets up so fast, application by spraying is usually more desirable than by brushing. Or, if the size of the

Minwax — Wood-Finishing Products

Uses:

Minwax, the trade name for a line of wood-finishing products, is unique for application on floors, paneling, trim, and furniture. Made in *transparent colors* and in *masking colors,* these products quickly penetrate the new wood and give the surface a rich wax finish. The transparent colors are used to "bring out" the natural graining of the wood to which it is applied, while the masking colors minimize the wood variations. The masking colors, however, are not recommended for floors.

Available Colors in Minwax Products:

Transparent colors
Ebony
Provincial (formerly light oak)
Natural
Dark walnut
Golden oak
Jacobean (very dark brown)
Puritan pine

Masking colors

Cherry	Red mahogany
Special walnut	Fruitwood
Driftwood	Early American
Colonial maple	Ipswich pine

All of the above colors may be intermixed, and Natural is added to make any of the colors lighter.

To apply Minwax on new wood, use a brush or cloth. Allow it to stand a few minutes after it is put on so the finish can fully penetrate the wood. Then wipe off the excess with a clean cloth, rubbing with the grain. When a second coat is needed, allow the Minwax to dry overnight between coats. If desired, a varnish may be applied for a high-gloss finish.

Other Minwax finishes: an antique oil finish, which is a hard finish offering more protection; Minwax waxes in paste or liquid form, for cleaning and polishing; and a Minwax exterior wood finish.

Clear Varnish

Form: liquid
Thinner: turpentine or mineral spirits
Uses:

Available in flat, semigloss, or gloss finish, clear varnish is used as one of the most permanent preservatives on painted woodwork, floors, Masonite-covered platforms, and furniture. It is not used on rubber-based paint. Clear varnish can be tinted with oil colors, Japan colors, or with oil-soluble dyes. Application is usually by brush. Also see Fabulon, a clear plastic-resin coating, page 351.

Sources:
Paint and hardware stores. It comes in pints, quarts, and gallons.

Aniline dyes (soluble in lacquer) were mixed with clear lacquer to make the translucent colors for the plastic panes in this fan-shaped window. Dimensional leading was created by squeezing a mixture of 1 part latex paint and 1 part pure clear latex out of a plastic ketchup bottle onto the painted panes.
(Photograph—Lynn Pecktal)

object permits, it can be dipped in the lacquer.

Adding Aniline Dye Colors to Clear Lacquer
Clear lacquer which comes in cans is easily colored with aniline dyes (those soluble in lacquer) for transparent painting. A good method of mixing dye with lacquer is to first pour a small amount of clear lacquer into a container,

add a pinch of aniline dye, then stir. The mixture can be thinned with lacquer thinner to lighten the color and also to make it work better on the particular surface. For general thinning use:

8 parts *LACQUER*	**1 gal.** *LACQUER*	
to	OR	to
1 part *LACQUER THINNER*	**1 pt.** *LACQUER THINNER*	—**TO THIN LACQUER**

Available Quantities:
Lacquer may be purchased in pints, quarts, and gallons at paint stores.

Bronze Powders

Form: powder
Binders: clear liquid vinyl, clear liquid latex, regular bronzing liquid (like a varnish), banana oil (lacquer bronzing liquid), dextrine, and shellac.

Uses:

Bronze powders are used to create decorative metallic finishes on both scenery (soft and hard) and props, and are usually applied on such materials as canvas, muslin, wood, metal, and plastic. Among their scenic uses, bronze colors are ideally suited for numerous jobs: painting and stenciling patterns on backdrops and flats, painting the

trim and molding of wooden paneling and picture frames, coating sculptured Styrofoam capitals of columns (after covering and priming), laying-in iron grillwork units and metal chandeliers, or just highlighting items like fringe, tassels, finials, and statues. Bronze powders are made in several colors and may be intermixed. The most popular ones are gold and aluminum (for silver). A list selected from Playhouse Colors includes:
Brilliant pale gold
Dark gold
Green gold
Roman gold
Aluminum

Light copper
Dark copper
Brass
Other metallic colors are available on request

Bronze powders must be mixed in liquid form with a binder before they are ready for application.

Binders:
Clear gloss liquid vinyl and *clear gloss liquid latex* are two excellent binders that hold well, dry quickly, and come ready-mixed. The following proportions are mixed to make a liquid binder for bronze powders:

Bronze Powders

LIQUID BINDER FOR BRONZE POWDERS

To mix the bronze powder with the liquid binder, first pour the powder into the selected container. Then pour the binder *into* the bronze powder, *not* the powder into the liquid, and stir constantly while doing so. This method causes the powder to mix much faster and makes it easier to mix the bronze powder in paste form. To this add more of the liquid binder to obtain the desired painting consistency. The bronze powder paste should be thinned so that it works well with the brush, sponge, or roller, but it must be thick enough to cover the surface well. Mix only as much bronze powder as you need at one time, because it will thicken after several hours and become completely unusable.

Alternate Binders:

Regular bronzing liquid (like a varnish) is another good binder for bronze powders. It can be thinned with mineral spirits. *Banana oil* (lacquer bronzing liquid) is also a great binder, and it can be thinned with lacquer thinner. Banana oil is used when a more matte finish and a faster drying time are desired, whereas bronzing liquid is used when a more gloss finish and longer drying time are preferred. Both bronzing liquid and banana oil are helpful when excessive flameproofing in the fabric has caused the gold colors to tarnish and turn green from the use of dextrine or other water-based binders. This can be remedied by allowing the colors to dry and then applying new gold bronzing colors that have been mixed with bronzing liquid or banana oil. On fabrics such as linen or velour, it is often necessary to shellac the areas where the bronzing powders (gold, silver, or other) are to be applied and then put on the metallic colors. Al-

Gold Leaf, Aluminum Leaf, and Decorative Effects

Dutch metal and bronze leaf are well-known names for an imitation gold leaf, and they come in various shades. For imitating silver, aluminum leaf is used, and there are also leaves available in copper. They come in tissue-paper books that are approximately 5½ inches square with 25 leaves in a book and cost 85 cents. Unlike the handling of 23-karat gold leaf of Medieval and Renaissance times, these imitation leaves are used today for theatrical scenery in a more temporary way to cut the high cost and the lengthy time that the traditional gilding process would involve.

Applying Imitation Gold Leaf to New Wood:

Assume that the new wood to be gilded with imitation gold leaf (Dutch metal) is a length of ogee molding that is to be applied on scenery. To prepare the surface for the Dutch metal, the wood should first be cleaned, sanded lightly, and dusted. Then, with a brush, give it a first coat of pure orange shellac (without adding any alcohol). When it has dried, sand the wood (again lightly) and dust off the surface. The shellac works well for this, because it remains non-absorbent after sanding and dries very fast. When ready, apply a second coat of orange shellac. This coat can be cut with alcohol by using one part alcohol to one part orange shellac. For every quart of this shellac mixture, ¼ pound of gold bronzing powder may be added (and stirred well), in case the leaf does not cover every small crack or fault. The second coat should be allowed to dry for at least an hour, and then with a coarse cloth give the wood a good rubbing down, always going with the grain.

Oil gold size is the adhesive for adhering the Dutch metal to the wood. A favorite brand, Hastings, comes in two kinds. One is Hastings Oil Gold Size, which is ready for gilding within 10 to 12 hours, and it stays tacky for many hours afterward. The other is Hastings Quick Drying Gold Size, and it is ready for the leaf within 1 to 3 hours. Because of its speed in drying, this latter size is most suitable for scenic work. The drying time may vary, of course, according to the temperature or weather conditions.

Before application, the gold size is poured out of its container into a can or bucket and is stirred thoroughly. It should be applied in the same way as the shellac, by brushing it out evenly and working at a rather fast pace. The proper tackiness of this varnish is most important for good adherence, and it must be tested often to find out just when it is ready to take the leaf. This is achieved by simply placing a finger on the varnished surface; if it feels sticky to the touch but does not come off on the finger, it is the right degree of tackiness and is ready for the leaf at once.

The next step is referred to as "laying the leaf." Because they are extremely fragile, gold leaves must be left between the pages of the tissue book while this is happening. However, when working on small areas, such as moldings, these books are sometimes cut in half laterally for easier handling. When ready, start at the front of the book and open to the first leaf. Spread the book open so that one hand holds the front cover and the other the sheets of gold leaf in the tissue. Gently place the leaf onto the tacky surface. By pressing it down very lightly, the leaf is released from its protecting tissue. Continue holding the

though this is a double process, it is necessary in order to keep them from sinking into the fabric and to have a lustrous finish.

Dextrine, which comes in powder form, should be dissolved in hot water, then heated in a double boiler until it becomes boiling hot and clear. Use 1 part dextrine powder to 3 parts water. When it is cool, thin the dextrine solution with water for the working consistency before mixing it with the bronze powder. Make sure that the solution is cold before it is applied on the surface, since the flameproofing can come through and make the gold turn green and lose its luster. Because of the time and effort it takes to prepare dextrine, it is easier to use clear liquid vinyl or clear liquid latex, especially since they are usually on hand.

Orange shellac and clear white shellac can be used as binders for bronze powders, but they tend to dull the colors. The shellacs are thinned with denatured alcohol if necessary.

Using Johnson Paste Wax to Hold Bronze Powders on Props:
Regular Johnson paste wax, which is used to polish floors, works beautifully to hold metallic bronze powders on certain props after they are painted. These may be wooden items, like picture frames or molding, or carved Styrofoam sculpture that has been smoothly covered. Such dry bronze powders as gold, silver, copper, and others serve as metallic highlights to enhance the painted prop. The paste wax and bronze powders together work particularly well on sculpture or relief because you can give the raised parts a slight polish and leave the undercuts dull. This can be used instead of the more costly metallic wax finishes like Treasure Gold.

Application:
Place a pile of bronze powders (one or more colors) on a piece of paper and dip a soft cloth into the container of paste wax. After rubbing the cloth in the wax, rub it into the metallic powders, then apply the mixture to the surface as desired with the saturated cloth.

Source:
Bronze powders and binders can be purchased at S. Wolf's Sons or Playhouse Colors, Theatrical Production Service, M. Epstein's Son, Paramount Theatrical Supplies, and Gothic Color Co.

book like this, turning to a new leaf as needed, always overlapping the edge of the next leaf just enough to catch the edge of the last one. Go on with this until the wood is fully covered with the Dutch metal.

When finished, clean up all the overhanging pieces and extra imitation leaf and, at the same time, firmly press the applied leaves down to make certain that they are holding well. This cleaning process is called "skewing" and is done by rubbing over the applied metal leaf with a soft brush, a piece of folded cheesecloth, or a good size piece of absorbent cotton. The soft brush is excellent on molding or intricate details. Any obvious cracks or unleafed areas should be covered with additional leafing. In theatrical work, sometimes a bronzing powder (of a similar gold color) is dry-brushed over the still tacky surface to cover the small places where the gold leaf did not take. A thorough dusting is always needed to get rid of the excess dry bronzing powder.

A clear preservative like varnish or lacquer is generally brushed over the finished gold leafing for protection and to prevent fast tarnishing. Any desired antiquing or aging should be put on before the preservative.

Using Aluminum Leaf for Other Colors:
Aluminum leaf does not tarnish or turn as much as other imitation leaves. If a gold leaf is not available, an even more brilliant gold may be obtained by first applying aluminum leaf, and when dry, glazing over it with lemon yellow or Indian yellow aniline dye, using clear vinyl in the dye as a binder. For that matter, any color of aniline dye can be used as a transparent glaze over the applied aluminum leaf to obtain a brilliant color, again with clear vinyl as a binder.

Genuine Gold Leaf:
The process of gilding with genuine gold leaf goes back to the paintings and murals of European art. This genuine 23-karat gold is highly inert, permanent, and does not tarnish or change color. It is made in metallic leaves, held in tissue-paper books measuring $3\frac{1}{2}$ inches by $3\frac{1}{2}$ inches with 25 leaves to the book. The labor to make real gold leaf adds greatly to its cost. It comes in the following karats: $23\frac{1}{2}$K—deep rich gold, $18\frac{1}{2}$K—lemon, 16K—pale gold. It is also available in ribbon form, and other special sizes are made for industrial use. It is the most fragile of the materials, and to do expert gilding requires much practice. An excellent reference book on detail gilding is *The Artist's Handbook of Material and Technique* by Ralph Mayer, 3d ed. New York: The Viking Press 1970.

Treasure Gold:
These metallic wax finishes are for retouching gold leaf or for decorating furniture, frames, and lamps. Treasure Gold wax pastes fill up the small holes and cracks, and dry fast to give a permanent nontarnishing finish. All colors are applied with the finger or a soft cloth, then are buffed to a lustrous permanent finish. They apply easily to wood, plastic, leather, metals, and ceramics, and the following colors are made in 1-ounce jars: Treasure Gold, Florentine, Renaissance, White Fire, Brass, Pewter, Silver, and Copper. It is especially helpful to have these items on hand in a repertory or stock company.

(Right)
Gold metallic paint (bronze powders mixed with banana oil) applied on canvas using a brush or paint roller over a stencil of fishnet (1½-in. squares) created textures of metallic squares on legs and borders for David Mitchell's BORIS GODUNOV (1974), Cincinnati Summer Opera and the Canadian Opera.

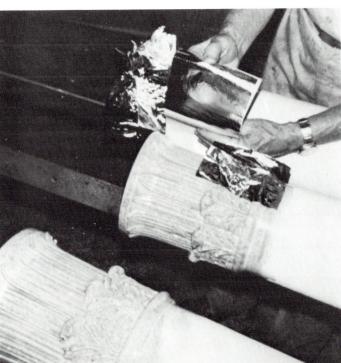

(Left, top, center, bottom)
APPLYING GOLD LEAF ON COLUMNS
Steps of Execution:
1. Two coats of shellac brushed on capitals.
2. Hastings Quick Drying Gold Size, brushed on and allowed to stand 1 to 3 hours.
3. After size dried to proper tackiness, a leaf was put on with one hand, while the leaf-tissue book was held with the other.
4. Book was opened to another leaf and process repeated until capital was covered.
5. Semiadhered sheets of gold leaf were pressed into contours of capital with a soft-bristled brush and excess leaf brushed away. Note leafed capitals in the background.
6. Protective coat of clear varnish was applied.

(Right)
Two sizes of sequin were set with a hot glue gun on the sharkstooth-scrim surface of Oliver Smith's flower trees for the American Ballet Theatre's production of SLEEPING BEAUTY (1974).

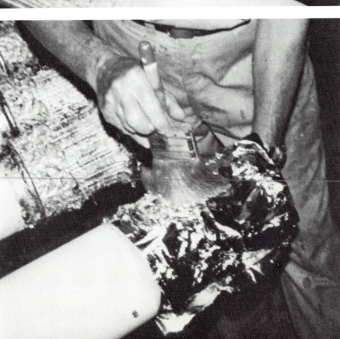

(Below)
The same basic process is used to put gold leaf on a picture frame, but the tissue book is cut in half. To do a neat job and cover all contours, two leaves are put on at once, one over the other. (Photographs—Lynn Pecktal)

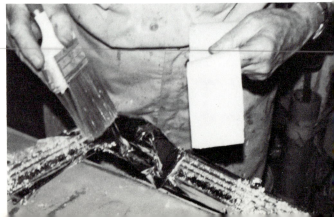

CREATING DESIGNS WITH LARGE SEQUINS SEWED ON SCENIC NETTING

Setting, costumes, and lighting
  by Ed Wittstein
CREATION OF THE WORLD
  BALLET
Choreography by Todd
  Bolender
Cologne, Germany (1964)
(Photograph — Ed Wittstein)

Silver sequins, fifty-cent-piece size, sewed on scenic netting to form glittering designs on backdrop. The framed black-velour ground row had patterns of lights in different circuits.

(Right)
Sequins on a flat profile chandelier about 6 ft. wide, created for Nicola Benois' set for TCHAIKOVSKY'S SUITE NO. 3 (1970), New York City Ballet.

(Below)
Full-scale drawing on brown paper outlines chandelier made of two $\frac{3}{4}$-in. plywood profile pieces covered with linen scrim. Back row of lights, part of the main profile piece, was covered by two layers of linen scrim for more opacity. Front row of globes, on a separate profile piece, was blocked away to make room for bulbs positioned behind. Frosted profile globes of clear Lucite were sanded on back to diffuse light.
(Photograph — Arnold Abramson)

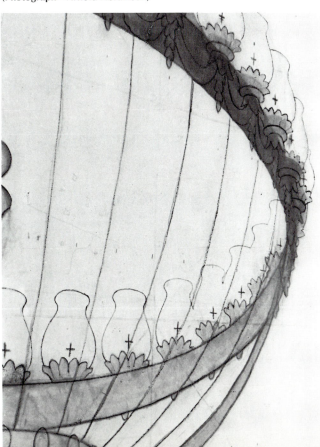

One-in. iridescent mother-of-pearl sequins glued on the painted linen scrim with Duco cement (sequins were first folded for faceted effect).

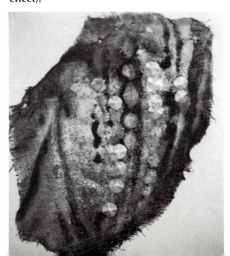

Decorative Effects

Treasure Jewels:
Treasure jewels are metallic colors that are used the same way as Treasure Gold. They come in several colors including: Emerald, Onyxite, Rose Quartz, Yellow Diamond, Spanish Topaz, Indigo, Sapphire, Aquamarine, Olive Bronze, Green Amber, Pink Quartz, and Ruby.

Flitter (Glitter):
These bright shiny glass or metallic particles are put on all sorts of decorative work to add sparkle and to create a dazzling effect on scenery and props. Flitter can be applied to enhance painted stars,

snow, ice, lettering, or ornament. It is widely used in display and at showplaces like Radio City Music Hall. Flitter is available in jars or by the pound, and is made in several colors, including silver, gold, green, multicolor, red, blue, magenta, aqua, diamond dust, or white. Binders for flitter can be white synthetic resin glues, clear vinyl, or clear latex. It always works best to brush the binder on in small areas, then sift the flitter over the wet areas as fast as possible before the binder dries.

Mica Dust:
Mica dust, made of rock, is also effective for creating a softer sparkling on stone walls or rocks and for enhancing snow scenery (flat painted or three-dimensional). It is applied like flitter.

Sequins, Beads, Spangles, and Other Items:
There is an assortment of small decorative items that can be used to produce a flashy appearance on scenery and costumes, especially for musicals, revues, and ballets. The items listed (those with holes) can be sewn on

OTHER SPECIAL PAINTS AND PRODUCTS

Fluorescent and Luminous Paints

Fluorescent paints glow in the dark under ultraviolet blacklight. Luminous paints glow in the dark after exposure to strong light. Of the two, the luminous paints are very limited for the stage, both in the time they will keep glowing and in the choice of obtainable colors. Therefore, for theatrical work, the fluo-

rescent UV colors are put to best use. While these are specialty paints and may not be involved that much in the commercial theatre, many startling and dramatic effects can be achieved with them in a variety of stage productions. In the spectacular *Underseas Ballet* production at Radio City Music Hall,

for instance, fluorescent paints are used extensively on scenery and costumes.

Fluorescent water-color paints (tempera and poster paints) are the ones most used on scenery, and these can be purchased under several trade names: Day-Glo, Daybrite, Glo-Brite, Rich-Glo, and Color-Glo. These paints are

Felt-Tip Pens and Markers

Felt-tip pens are very useful for drawing, inking, labeling, sketching, marking, and lettering. They are used on a variety of surfaces: paper, plastics, wood, metal, fabrics, and glass. Felt-tip pens are available in a wide range of transparent colors (and some opaque) and are waterproof, fast-drying, and can be blended. Popular brands include Flomaster, Design Art Markers, Dri Mark, Magic Marker, Ad Markers, Niji Markers, and Pental pens. Collectively, they have come to be known as felt-tip pens although the point may not be felt; they come in many point styles: round, round with pointed tip, round with chisel tip, wedge, square, and T-shaped square. Extra ink and cleanser (for thinning and cleaning) are also available for certain brands. Felt-tip pens can easily be obtained at art, stationery, and paint stores, hobby shops, and five-and-ten-cent stores.

Brilliant fluorescent watercolor paints (Day-Glo) highlighted the painted Buddha designed by Miguel Romero for MORE THAN YOU DESERVE (1973) at Joseph Papp's Off-Broadway Public Theatre. The Buddha, a flat profile unit of canvas on wooden framing with 1½-in. carved relief added to eyebrows, eyes, nose, and mouth, was 8 ft. 6 in. wide by 9 ft. 6 in. high. (Photographs – Lynn Pecktal)

fabric with a needle and thread or glued on with Duco Cement. Besides such scenery as backdrops, show curtains, draperies, gauzes, and pieces of scenic netting, they can be adhered to objects of wood, plastic, or metal with the appropriate glues and adhesives. A hot (electric) glue gun which uses an epoxy glue (inserted cartridges) is extremely fast for attaching small objects of plastic or glass to fabric or wood. These listed items can be opaque, clear, metallic, iridescent, or mirrored and come in many sizes and colors. They are available at LeeWards, Elgin, Ill.

60120, or at other similar companies. It is always practical to write for a catalog. Included are the following:

Loose sequins
Sequin cords
Sequin swirls
Bugle beads
Large seed beads
Faceted beads
Pony beads
Aurora beads
Barrel beads
Lentil beads
Ferris-wheel beads
Paillettes

Sunray spangles
Cartwheel spangles
Oval spangles
Fish spangles
Snowflake spangles
Faceted starburst spangles
Faceted daisy spangles
Faceted topaz spangles
Assorted fancy spangles
Flat back rhinestones
Rhinestone snowflakes
Crystal snowflakes
Filagree daisies
Filagree carnations
Mirrored rounds, squares, rectangles, diamonds, fish

much more brilliant than ordinary colors in daylight and they also glow in the dark under ultraviolet light. They work best when applied over a white surface. Fluorescent paints are also available in a number of media, including oils and lacquers.

A well-known source for fluorescent and luminous products is the Stroblite Co., New York, which offers an enormous selection of colors and media and UV blacklight equipment. A portion of their products includes transparent UV lacquers, opaque UV paints, and UV temperas. Their Stroblite "invisible" UV colors come in UV vinyl latex paint (using water as a thinner) and UV Bulletin paints (using mineral spirits as a thinner). These appear white or off-white in normal light but become radiant colors under blacklight. These ultraviolet products are also available: chalks, crayons and pencils, satins by the yard, ribbons, make-up, and so on.

Spray Paints

Spray paints, which come in aerosol cans, are handy to have around. They are great for achieving a fast, smooth coverage on props and small pieces of scenery like picture frames, chandeliers, sconces, metal pipes, grillwork, screen wire, signs, lamp bases, and furniture. Variegated patterns can be easily obtained by spraying two or more colors over each other. Krylon spray paints are one of the most popular brands. These enamel colors come in flat or gloss finish and dry fast. They are waterproof and weatherproof. The following Krylon spray paints are available in 16.2-ounce cans:

Antique ivory	Brass
Baby blue	Bright copper
Baby pink	Bright gold

Bright silver	Hunter green
Champion blue	International orange
Cherry red	O.D. khaki
Chrome yellow	Leather brown
Dove gray	Light gray
Flat black	Machine gray
Flat white	Pastel yellow
Glossy black	Regal blue
Glossy white	Surf green

Con-Tact Plastic

Con-Tact plastic is a familiar item with almost everyone, and although it is generally called Con-Tact paper, it is actually a vinyl plastic. Popular for decorating in both houses and apartments, this self-adhesive plastic is a frequent covering material in theatrical work for small props and stage dressing. Among assets: it may be used to simulate marble on the tops of tables and commodes; as decor in a modern kitchen setting; for applying lettering on signs or Plexiglas windows; and to protect the surface on a piece of furniture. Con-Tact can enhance the appearance of a borrowed or rented prop that cannot be painted. The particular pieces are cut and applied, then removed after the prop has been used.

Con-Tact, which is washable and waterproof, is available in an extensive range of patterns or solid colors; it comes 18 inches wide, and is sold by the yard or in rolls of 25 yards. The many different patterns include florals, mod designs, woodgrains, marble, and brick. Con-Tact is also manufactured in these lines: Flock, Burlap, Polished Patent, Quiltsoft, Foil, and Cushion-All.

267

Fabspray

For upholstered stage furniture such as sofas, chairs, and footstools, Fabspray is exceptionally good for giving new life to old and faded fabrics, often saving the time and cost of having to reupholster them. Manufactured in many colors, it comes in a spray can, making it simple to put on. Fabspray may be used to brighten up the original color of the fabric or to change the color completely. Best results are obtained by choosing a color close to the original or a darker color in the same family. A test should be made on a sample of the material before spraying is started, as certain fabrics sometimes require a second spraying, especially if the color being put on is lighter than the existing one.

When an evenly applied spraying is the aim rather than a variegated one, it is best to spray consistently (but not too heavily) over the whole area. When dry, go over it again, repeating this until satisfaction is achieved. This method works much better than trying to get it all covered the first time. For work on other stage props, Fabspray is utilized for various painting effects on draperies and rugs, including toning, aging, or "taking down" the color.

Fabspray also makes a vinyl spray for plastic, leatherette, and vinyl surfaces. It, too, comes in several colors and is applied in the same way.

Flame-Retardant Solution

The fire department in New York City and the fire laws in many states require that all scenery to be used in the theatre be treated with a flame-retardant. Firemen in some cities test scenery by holding a match under the edge of the fabric for ten seconds and if it just smokes and burns itself out, it is considered O.K. Although fabrics like canvas and muslin can be bought already treated with a flame-retardant, there are times when it must be done in the scenic studio. Ammonium sulfamate by DuPont (obtainable from S. Wolf's Sons in Manhattan) is dissolved with warm water to make the solution below (left).

Stir and pour into the spray tank. Then spray on the back of the canvas flats or on the back of backdrops after they have been painted. Many artists prefer spraying a drop or piece of scenery *after* it has been painted, simply because the flame-retardant solution applied before painting can sometimes change the colors when they are put on.

Dissolve
10 lbs. of *AMMONIUM SULFAMATE*
in
5 gals. of *WARM WATER*

—FLAME-RETARDANT SOLUTION

When the above is unavailable, a flame-retardant solution can be mixed by using the following (right):

Dissolve
4 lbs. of *BORAX*
4 lbs. of *SAL AMMONIAC*
in
3 gals. of *WARM WATER*

—FLAME-RETARDANT SOLUTION

PAINT BRUSHES AND PAINTING EQUIPMENT

Paint Brushes

Brushes that are used for painting scenery are created especially for the craft, and the old saying that an artist is no better than his tools is true. Whenever you are purchasing brushes, good scenic brushes of fine quality should be selected, for they produce painting of high caliber and are also easier to work with. In addition, they last much longer than inexpensive brushes, provided they are maintained and cleaned with special care; naturally, they are more expensive. The bristles in scenic brushes are the most important element, and better brushes have bristles set thicker at the ferrule. Russian brushes are far superior, as they have long and very full bristles with split (flagged) ends that allow them to hold a good supply of paint and to perform ideally, smoothly spreading the paint over the surface. Chinese bristles are also excellent in this category, as are other brushes which have all pure natural bristles. Because natural-bristle brushes hold more paint than nylon-bristle brushes, they are preferred for scenic work. However, if natural bristles are unavailable, some nylon bristles are made so they have split or flagged ends, and these can be substituted.

Although many scenic brushes are made with long handles, they may have even more extended handles put on them for painting on the floor so the artists can work freely while standing. For this, bamboo sticks (in various diameters and lengths) are split on one end to allow the brush to be easily inserted, and heavy-duty rubber bands hold the brush in place. Sometimes the split-bamboo handles are also taped with masking tape around the brush handles. While the use of specific brushes is standard for some techniques like starching or priming, others are usually chosen according to the personal preference of the artist.

SCENIC BRUSHES (left to right):
4-in. lay-in brush, 3-in. Fitch, 2½-in. Fitch, 1½-in. Fitch, 1-in. liner, ¾-in. liner, ½-in. liner, ⅜-in. liner, ¼-in. liner

SCENIC BRUSHES ATTACHED TO LONG HANDLES (below)
(Top) Dutch primer 7½ by 2½ in. with 5-in. bristles, made by Hanlon and Goodman, used as a combing brush. Stippling brush 9 by 3½ in. with 3-in. bristles, used for priming.
(Bottom) 5-in. lay-in brush. Stippling brush 12 by 3 in. with 3-in. bristles, used for starching.

SPONGES (top, right)
(Top) Synthetic sponge mop. Natural sponge wired and taped to bamboo handle.
(Bottom) Synthetic hand sponge. Natural sponges.

SPECIAL PAINTING IMPLEMENTS (below, right)
(Top) Turkey-feather duster. Foliage paint stamp, 10-in. diameter, made of 4-in. foam rubber.
(Bottom) Poster brush, with bristles cut away, used for combing. Pound brush attached to a long handle, bristles tied in five bunches. Used for creating textures, the brush is manipulated up and down as in stippling. Process is called schlepitchka.
(Photographs—Lynn Pecktal)

Lining Brushes

Small Liners. As the name implies, these brushes are for lining with a straight-edge when painting molding, inking, or for freehand painting on very small areas with intricate details. They have long handles and are made with both black and white bristles in widths of ¼, ½, ¾, and 1 inch. Angular liners (liners made with the bristles cut on a sharp angle) are sometimes used.

Large Liners. Larger liners are necessary for details of a greater size and are utilized in similar capacities as the small liners. They are also available in pure bristles of black and white, and come in the following widths: 1¼-inch, 1½-inch, 1¾-inch, 2-inch, 2½-inch, and 3-inch.

Fitch Brushes (also called Foliage and Decorating brushes): These well-known brushes are excellent all-purpose brushes not only for wide lining but also for doing finished work, especially when a sharp stroked edge is desired. Fitches have long white natural bristles that fan out from tapered ferrules. They come in numerous sizes: 1-inch, 1¼-inch, 1½-inch, 1¾-inch, 2-inch, 2¼-inch, 2½-inch, 2¾-inch, and 3-inch. The 3-inch size is the one that tends to be most used.

Lay-in Brushes

Typical lay-in brushes come in widths of 3, 4, and 5 inches. They are designed to hold a good deal of paint and their long bristles make them very efficient for smoothing it out with long strokes. Their foremost use is for laying in the base or local color on canvas and woodwork. Lay-in brushes are also needed for blending colors and for finished painting. The best grades of lay-in brushes are those made of all natural bristle.

Priming Brushes

Brushes for priming scenery are the largest ones used, since it is necessary that they hold a lot of color and spread it quickly over a wide surface.

Dutch Priming Brushes. A Dutch primer is a superior brush containing a mixture of 70 percent natural bristle and 30 percent horsehair. It is quite effective for "combing" over coats of paint after they have been laid in. The Dutch primers vary in size from 5½ to 7 inches wide.

Flat Priming Brushes. This is a less expensive primer which comes 7 inches wide and has a mixture of bristle and horsehair.

Other Brushes — Cleaners and Thinners

Stippling Brushes
Although the original use of the stippling brush was to stipple a surface after painting it to give a uniform texture, it is ordinarily used as a primer. For floor work, a very long-angled handle, at least 5 feet long, is added. Made in various sizes, a typical stippling brush has stiff bristles that are set in a wooden block measuring 3½ by 9 inches by 2 inches thick. The construction of the brush enables the painter to cover large areas easily with speed. A larger stippling brush, 3 by 12 inches with 3-inch bristles, is excellent for starching backdrops; it also must have a long handle attached to it.

Stencil Brushes
To apply the paint through the stencil, a specific brush is made just for the purpose. It is a short, round brush with stiff black bristles which comes in various diameters and lengths. Other brushes like Fitches are also used for stencil work.

Fan Top Grainers
This is a special brush for creating and simulating wood graining on scenery. The best grainers have pure white bristles and are available in widths of 2, 2½, and 3 inches.

Lettering Brushes
Most scenic artists have their own individual lettering brushes and maintain them. The best lettering brushes are those with red sable bristles, which are available in many sizes. Sign Fitches (such as sign-writers use) with white bristles are also good, and they range from ¼ inch, ½ inch, ¾ inch, to 1 inch.

Brushes Used for Shellac, Lacquer, and Oil
Rather than use the good brushes that are kept for scenic painting with water paints, specific and less costly brushes like trim and sash brushes are set aside for shellac, lacquer, and oil. Old Fitches are also used. Like all other brushes, these must be cleaned immediately after use. While real-bristle brushes are usually preferred for painting scenery, the scenic studio has some brushes with bristles of nylon that are frequently used for applying vinyl and latex paints.

Diluents for Thinning Products and for Cleaning Brushes

Product:	Thin with:
Acrylic paint	Water
Casein paint	Water
Enamel paint	Turpentine or mineral spirits
Enamelac (opaque white shellac)	Denatured alcohol
Japan colors	Turpentine or mineral spirits
Lacquer	Lacquer thinner
Latex paint	Water
Oil paint	Turpentine or mineral spirits
Rubber cement	Rubber-cement thinner
Shellac (clear white or orange)	Denatured alcohol
Varnish	Turpentine or mineral spirits
Vinyl paint	Water

Hudson Compressor Sprayer

The best-known and most popular brand of spray tanks is the Hudson spray compressor. Used originally for gardens, homes, and farms to spray insecticides and fungicides, it has come to be widely recognized for the application of paints, aniline dyes, starch, and flameproofing in painting scenery. The Hudson is very easy to operate and offers great speed. It is available in actual-capacity sizes of 2, 3, and 4 gallons. The most practical Hudson is the large-size tank (actual capacity 4 gallons), which holds around 3½ gallons of paint and still allows space for the needed air pressure. It (as well as the smaller sizes) has a cover handle at the top for opening and closing. The pump is separate, staying inside the tank during filling and emptying. To build up normal air pressure in the tank, the pump should be given around 30 full hand pumps after the lid has been fastened securely. The Hudson tank provides a fine or heavy spray just by a hand turn of the nozzle, and a large spattering is easily created by reducing the air pressure in the tank. Although the tank is normally used as it is, the cover of the Hudson can be remodeled so it can be operated by an air-compressor unit with a rubber hose.

For best results in scenic painting, the preferred nozzle in the scenic studio is the long straight one that does not turn (instead of the Roto Spray nozzle) and this can be obtained where the Hudsons are purchased. Proper cleaning of the spray tank and all its parts is always of the utmost importance because clogging will surely occur when paint is not washed out of it after spraying. Paints, aniline dyes, starch, and flameproof solution should also be strained through a piece of screen wire, cheesecloth, or fine bobbinet before they are poured in the tank. The latter two work best when they are wet first.

The Hudson compressor sprayer is made by the H. D. Hudson Manufacturing Co. in Chicago and there are sales and service offices in principal cities.

The Hudson spray tank is invaluable for painting scenery, starching backdrops, and spraying flameproofing solution. (Photograph – Arnold Abramson)

In using the spray gun, best results are gained by several light coats sprayed on and allowed to dry between coats. (Photograph – Lynn Pecktal)

Paint Spray Gun

For painting surfaces where good control and a fine spraying is desired, the spray gun (attached to an air compressor with a rubber hose) is very useful. Although it tends to be restricted to spraying relatively small areas, you can achieve faster and smoother blends with it than with a paint brush. You may want to use the spray gun to tone clouds subtly on a muslin backdrop or to spray shadows around painted ornament (masked out by gray paper) on a canvas flat, or to apply a smooth (or variegated) finish on plastics and metals. The spray gun is also effective for spraying items like louvered shutters, which are awkward to paint with a brush. Furthermore, certain kinds of simple stencils that do not have many repeats can be placed vertically and easily sprayed, although steady spraying on the same stencil without cleaning usually makes the paint run.

All types of water-base paints, aniline dyes, lacquers, shellacs, and varnishes can be applied with the paint spray gun. In all cases, the paints should be mixed thin enough to provide easy spraying, and they should always be strained so that the gun does not become clogged. Proper maintenance and immediate cleaning of the spray gun are also of paramount importance to produce good performance.

If you are ordering a spray gun, you may want to look at a catalog from one of two companies listed below. A good lightweight spray gun for scenic work is the Binks model 8, an internal atomizing pressure-fed gun that is easily operated by one hand. The gun and cup cover (in one piece) are constructed of nickel-plated aluminum and the aluminum cup holds 1 quart. This bleeder-type gun (no air valve) can be used with compressors as small as $\frac{1}{4}$ horsepower or from regulated air lines where the pressure does not exceed 40 pounds. The spray can be varied by several nozzles: the fan-spray nozzle that produces a flat spray, the round spray nozzle, and the slotted angle nozzle, which has a 45-degree angle for floor or ceiling spraying.

In the scenic studio, a large compressor has ten to twelve rubber-hose outlets spaced conveniently throughout the work area. These outlets hang vertically from the ceiling, stopping a little over 6 feet from the floor. By utilizing these, a shorter hose can be used on the spray gun and easily attached to the overhead outlet. Whenever a spray gun is needed for touching up paint in the theatre, a small portable compressor unit with a rubber hose is transported from the studio. Two manufacturers of spray guns long used for scenic work are Binks and DeVilbiss.

Other painting equipment such as the paint roller, feather duster, paint stamp, and sponges are discussed in the preceding chapter.

Paint Carrier

Whenever scenic artists work on a backdrop or other large piece of scenery laid on the floor, it is standard procedure to put the containers of paint in a "paint carrier." This prevents the pails of color from being accidentally overturned on the scenery and also makes it very convenient to lift or move the paint while working. Made of wood, the carrier is basically a low box with a tall rectangular handle; typical measurements include: a 24-inch square bottom of $\frac{3}{8}$-inch plywood with sides that are 1 by 3 inches. The handle, constructed of 1-by-2-inch lumber, has the two arms attached and centered on opposite sides of the box, and its overall height is 32 inches. For holding long-handled brushes and drawing sticks in the carrier, four metal guards are placed near the top of the two arms. Three-prong glides (of steel) are fastened to the bottom of the box on each corner to keep it from resting directly on the surface of the scenery. These hold it above any wet painting and eliminate potential damage to the fabric when it is being moved.

Heavy-Duty Hammer Tacker

The long-handled stapler is most sensible to use for tacking down soft scenery on the floor to hold it in place while working on it. It is used like a hammer and provides a fast way of attaching all types of backdrops or other fabrics (both large and small) to the floor. Squared-off straight lines are laid out to form a perimeter that will accommodate the exact size of the piece being tacked down. Then the edges of the fabric are placed neatly on the snapped lines and carefully tacked with the hammer tacker. It is always wise not to pound the staples too hard into the floor because of the extra time required when taking them out. The spacing of the staples varies with the type of fabric. For instance, staples placed on a scrim (a very open-weave cotton fabric that stretches easily) may be placed as close

Equipment for Mixing and Painting

Since there are so many types of paint used daily in a paint shop, extra containers are always needed, and they are often obtained from commercial firms or restaurants. When opening a new gallon container of paint, it is often practical to make holes in the grooved rim by hammering a 3-inch long common nail into the metal so that the excess paint will drain into the container. These are basic items needed for mixing and painting in the scenic studio:

1. 20-gal. galvanized metal containers with handles
2. 5-gal. buckets
3. 14- and 16-qt. galvanized buckets
4. 5-gal. plastic buckets for mixing and containing aniline dye colors
5. 1-gal. buckets
6. 8-oz. tin containers
7. 1-gal. glass jugs with screw-on tops for storing aniline dyes
8. Sizable tables for mixing colors

Safety Precautions

Safety precautions regarding products used in scenic work should never be taken lightly. The most sensible thing one can do is always read the labels on the products and carefully follow the warning instructions when using them. Some general safety precautions are:

1. Maintain good ventilation in the scenic shop.
2. Avoid having direct skin contact with harmful products and breathing toxic vapors. Appropriate respirators should be worn on the face when you are involved over prolonged periods with the application of lacquer and polyester resin, the mixing and pouring of polyurethane foam, and in the use of other similar products. Also, the mouth, the nose, and eyes (covered with goggles) should be protected when putting on flock with a flocking gun, grinding Styrofoam surfaces, or sanding surfaces covered with fiber glass.
3. Items such as rags that have been saturated or soaked with turpentine should not be piled in a heap because of the danger of spontaneous combustion.
4. Keep flammable solvents and dilutants away from heat and be cautious about smoking when handling and using them.

SCENERY GLUES AND BINDERS

The glues in this section range from the ready-to-use white synthetic resin glues to the standard scenic glue that must be prepared by heating. Binders, adhesives, cements, and all types of glues that are needed for painting and creating scenery are listed with formulas wherever applicable. Even though premixed paints with a binder included have come into their own, various theatrical companies and scenic studios still use gelatine glue for making size for priming and for making scenic dope, because it is the most economical and also because it dries faster than the white glues. For this reason, formulas for these glues and alternates have been included. It is up to you to make the selection you prefer.

Hot concentrated gelatine glue, taken with a dipper from a metal pail on the glue stove, is poured into a pail of hot water to make glue size (binder) to be mixed with dry pigment colors and/or dry whiting. Wooden lid for the glue pail has a notch so wooden stirring paddle can remain in pail at all times.

Gelatine Glue (Scenic Glue)

Form: granulated
Soluble in: water
Uses:

The normal binder for dry pigment colors and dry whiting, gelatine glue is a high-quality animal glue sold by the pound. It requires preparation ahead of time before it is ready to use. After the glue is completely dissolved in water and heated, it is ready to be thinned with more water according to specific proportions to make the binding for priming size, priming, working size, and dope. For the best possible results in mixing the glue, follow exact proportions. This eliminates inconsistencies in binding and the time needed to experiment and test for proper strength when mixing.

272

together as 2 inches, whereas a ground cloth (a plain-weave fabric of heavy cotton which does not stretch easily) may have them from 4 to 6 inches apart. At any rate, their placement is controlled by the number needed to hold the fabric's edge to the straight line.

Staples remain tacked to the floor until the painting is finished and dried, and are removed by lifting with a regular staple lifter.

The Arrow Fastener Company manufactures a hammer tacker that uses T 50 staples made in these sizes: $\frac{1}{4}$, $\frac{5}{16}$, $\frac{3}{8}$, and $\frac{1}{2}$ inch. The $\frac{3}{8}$-inch size, packaged in boxes of 5000, is good for scenic work. This is long enough to hold the fabric to the wooden floor, yet short enough to allow easy removal.

---

9. Metal mixing paddles and wooden paint sticks for stirring
10. Large wooden paddles (for stirring starch, size)
11. Gas or electric burners for heating hot water (for size, dope, and starch)
12. Glue stove (or glue pot) for heating glue
13. Metal strainers and pieces of cheesecloth (for straining)
14. Large deep sinks with hot and cold running water
15. Electric drill with paint-stirring attachment (for breaking up colors)
16. Low wooden dolly for holding containers of color

Storage for Paints
1. Wooden bins or barrels for dry colors, dry whiting, and scenic glue
2. Shelves for all unopened paints (casein, vinyl, latex)
3. Metal cabinets for special paints (shellac, varnish, lacquer) and solvents.

Available Protective Items:
The following can be obtained from S. Wolf's Sons in New York City:
Respirators and Mask:
Heavy-duty paint respirator (C-251) — to protect against organic vapors, paint, enamel, and lacquer mists.
Chemical cartridge respirator (MA3C) — used in low concentration of vapors and gases.
Respirator (RA-110) — dust respirator.

Paint spray respirator dual filtration (MSP-505) — a chemical respirator for protection against organic vapors and paint, enamel, and lacquer mists, and dust.
3M Brand filter mask — an inexpensive paper mask which protects against non-toxic dusts, spray particles, and powders.
Goggles:
G570: 50mm clear hardened lens.

G551: all plastic (can be worn over regular glasses).
Gloves:
Canvas — to protect hands when painting with shellac, oil paint, etc., and when working with chicken wire, forming cloth, etc.
Rubber heavy-duty and rubber acid-resistant — to protect hands from aniline dyes, Celastic activator solution (Methyl-ethyl-ketone), etc.

Mixing Priming Size, Priming, and Working Size
To prepare the glue, soak one part of the dry granulated gelatine glue (ground scenic glue) in one part water for one hour. Then place it in the double boiler and heat until the glue is thoroughly dissolved (left).

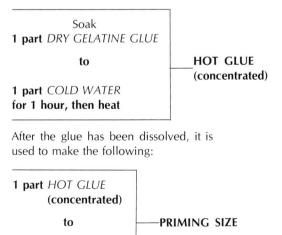

After the glue has been dissolved, it is used to make the following:

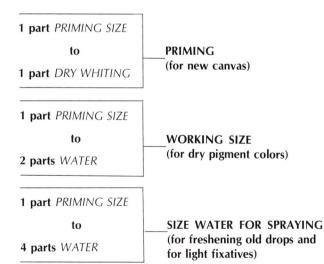

273

Gelatine Glue (Scenic Glue)

Whenever you are mixing any glues to hold dry pigment colors or dry whiting and are not familiar with them, you should automatically test the glue size you have made to see that it is strong enough to bind the pigments (or whiting) to the surface properly. The most accepted way of doing this is by putting your finger and thumb into the glue size and then pressing them together for a few moments. If they feel sticky and hold together slightly just as you begin to separate them, the glue size is strong enough. This test by feeling comes with experience. You will soon find that you can easily judge when the glue size is too strong and needs more hot water (if the finger and thumb adhere very fast) or when the glue size is too weak (if the finger and thumb do not hold well at all). It is always wise to do a final test by mixing a small amount of the glue size with the pigments (or whiting) and making a sample by brushing it on the surface to see how it holds after drying.

Alternate Glues:
See Dry Pigment Colors, page 256, for data on other glues.

Source:
Paint stores that stock theatrical supplies.

Flexible Glue

Form: slab or cake
Soluble in: water
Uses:

Flexible rubber glue is most practical to use as a binder with dry pigment colors for painting on backdrops or ceiling pieces that are to be rolled or folded because it stays flexible after drying. While this is its main function, it also can be used as a binder with dry colors for painting flats and wings.

To prepare:
The flexible glue must be dissolved first before it is ready to be mixed with water to make the working size for the dry colors. To do this, place one slab of flexible glue (weight 8 pounds) in a double boiler containing 2 quarts of water and let it soak for one hour. Then heat in the double boiler until it is dissolved. When ready, mix with hot water in the proportions below:

> **Soak**
> **1 slab of** *FLEXIBLE GLUE* **(wt. 8 lbs.)**
> **in**
> **2 quarts of** *WATER* **for 1 hr.**
> **Then heat until dissolved**

——LIQUID FLEXIBLE GLUE

> **Mix**
> **1 part** *LIQUID FLEXIBLE GLUE*
> **with**
> **8 parts** *HOT WATER*

——WORKING SIZE (to mix with dry colors)

Available at:
S. Wolf's Sons or Playhouse Colors, Gothic Color Company, Paramount Theatrical Supplies, Theatre Production Service, and M. Epstein's Son, Inc.

Methocel (100 CPS)

Form: powder
Soluble in: water
Uses:

This versatile water-soluble gum is a clear binder used for paints and aniline dyes (to keep them from running and bleeding) on such fabrics as scrim, China silk, Bengaline, satin, and translucent muslin.

To mix:
When mixing it initially with water, the Methocel powder is best dissolved by first putting the required amount being used in hot water ($\frac{1}{3}$ to $\frac{1}{2}$ of the *total* amount of water) while stirring. After it has been allowed to set briefly, the rest of the water to be added should be cold water which should also be stirred.

> **1 part** *METHOCEL POWDER*
> **to**
> **10 parts** *WATER*

——METHOCEL IN CONCENTRATED LIQUID FORM

These proportions are used to make a concentrated batch of Methocel:

A concentrated batch of the liquid Methocel is kept in a container on the mixing table, and from this, it is readily mixed as needed with paints or aniline dyes. Sometimes a general sizing of Methocel is sprayed on the China silk or satin (once it is tacked on the floor) before the paint (also mixed with Methocel) is brushed on.

Starch (Argo *Gloss* Laundry Starch)

Form: lumpy powder
Soluble in: water
Uses:

Starch is the best *primer* for creating a transparent glazing on muslin backdrops or the like (especially those that are to be translucent), and it is applied before painting them with aniline dyes, thin caseins, and other water-base paints (see Starching a Backdrop, p. 299). Starched muslin keeps the colors from running and soaking into the fabric and produces an excellent taut surface to paint on. But you must use *gloss* laundry starch, because non-gloss doesn't dry clear.

As a *binder*, liquid starch is mixed with aniline dyes to prevent running and it is used as an added *binder* for thin caseins, making them flow easily on the fabric. When liquid starch is added to dyes and casein colors, it also keeps them wet longer for working and is great for doing wet watercolor techniques. For instance, you can use starch with the colors when painting foliage or when graining wood with aniline dyes. Very heavy liquid starch is ideal for painting stained-glass windows.

To prepare regular starch:
Before the powdered starch is ready to use, it must be put in liquid form. To mix:

1. Dissolve a 1-pound box of Argo gloss starch (packaged in a blue box) in $\frac{1}{2}$ gallon of cold water.
2. Slowly pour this $\frac{1}{2}$ gallon of dissolved starch into 3 gallons of *boiling* water while stirring it thoroughly.
3. Put the mixture aside to cool before using.
4. Always strain well through cheesecloth before application.

Dissolve
1 lb. box of powdered *ARGO GLOSS STARCH*

in

$\frac{1}{2}$ gal. of *WATER* **(cold)**

then pour into

3 gals. of *BOILING WATER*
(making a total 3$\frac{1}{2}$ gals. liquid starch)

— **REGULAR LIQUID STARCH (for starching muslin backdrops)**

To prepare heavy starch:
For stained-glass windows on translucent muslin, very heavy starch is made, then it is mixed with liquid aniline dyes for painting. (See Painting Stained-Glass Windows, p. 308).

Dissolve
1 lb. of powdered *ARGO GLOSS STARCH*

in

$\frac{1}{2}$ gal. of *WATER* **(cold)**

then pour into

1 gal. of *BOILING WATER*
(making a total 1$\frac{1}{2}$ gals. liquid starch)

— **HEAVY STARCH FOR STAINED GLASS WINDOWS (on muslin)**

For other work, liquid starch can be thinned with water as needed; for painting surfaces where more strength is desired, glue size or clear vinyl can be added accordingly as is necessary.

Availability: Grocery stores and supermarkets.

---

1 part *CONCENTRATED METHOCEL*

to

10 parts *WATER*

— **FOR A GENERAL SIZING ON CHINA SILK (or similar fabrics) BY SPRAYING**

$\frac{1}{2}$ pint *CONCENTRATED METHOCEL*

to

1 gallon of *COLOR*

— **FOR MIXING WITH PAINT (or dyes) TO PREVENT RUNNING**

Source: Dow Chemical Co. Available at S. Wolf's Sons, New York City.

White Synthetic Resin Glues

(hard-drying)

Form: liquid
Thinner: water
Uses:

For all-purpose wood binding, white synthetic resin glues are outstanding. These creamy white glues dry transparent and hard, and are used as well for gluing Masonite, pressed wood, chip core, and other composition materials to wood. White resin glues can be used for adhering canvas, muslin, scrim, burlap, and Eros cloth to wood (or to each other, when flexibility does not matter). They are also good for gluing light-stock posters and large photograph

White Synthetic Resin Glues (hard-drying)

blow-ups to a solid backing like plywood or Masonite. Application can be by brush or paint roller.

Alternate binder for making dope for ragging:
Although as a binder for dope, white synthetic resin glues are more expensive and take longer to dry than gelatine glue (scenic glue), they can be thinned with water and mixed with dry whiting to make ragging dope for sculpture work. See proportions for mixing dope by using white synthetic resin glue and water with whiting in the section Applied Textures, page 281.

Popular brands of white synthetic resin glues:
The following can be purchased in 5-gallon containers:
Bergenbond

Hewhold
Dunn's Woodhesive
Mend-All
Elmer's Glue-All

Elmer's Glue-All can be purchased in art stores, paint stores, hobby shops, and hardware stores. It is available in plastic squeeze bottles: $1\frac{1}{4}$ ounce, 4 ounce, 8 ounce, and in pints, quarts, and gallons.

White Synthetic Resin Glues (flexible-drying)

Form: liquid
Thinner: water
Uses:

Because they dry flexible and clear, certain glues are best for gluing together fabrics and materials which must be rolled or folded, or must hang flexibly on stage. One of the most-used is *Sobo*, a thin, extremely clear white resin glue that dries flexible. It and similar glues can be used for gluing back the edges of painted cut drops, legs, and borders, and for gluing muslin and canvas appliqués onto scenic netting (1-inch squares) and bobbinet. It is also good for adhering decorative cut-out fabrics on costumes and upholstery fabrics on stage furniture. Sobo is not used for plastic. Another white glue is *Quik* (a heavier glue than Sobo), which also dries clear and flexible. It can glue plastics to a porous surface like vinyl, Mylar, foil, styrene to wood, fabrics, paper. Sobo glue and Quik glue are applied on the surface by the easy-to-use plastic squeeze bottles or by brush. Both of these flexible glues are great to have on hand for making models with paper and cardboard.

Availability:
Both can be purchased at art stores, paint stores, hobby shops, and hardware stores. Sobo comes in plastic squeeze bottles, 2-, 4-, 8-, and 16-ounce and 1-gallon sizes. Quik comes in plastic squeeze bottles, 4- and 8-ounce and 1- and 5-gallon sizes. The larger quantities of each can be obtained from the source below.

Source: Slomon's Labs (see p. 400).

Clear Liquid Latex (concentrated)

Form: liquid
Thinner: water
Uses:

Pure concentrated rubber latex (like Slomon's Latex) is outstanding as a *binder* and as an *adhesive*. It is a creamy liquid that dries a clear yellowish off-white and, most important, it dries extremely flexible.

As a Binder:
As a flexible binder, it is mixed without thinning with casein paste color (also without thinning) to create a heavy rubberlike opaque mixture that is used for squeezing drawings and designs on soft pieces of scenery that fold. Common materials are sharkstooth scrim, linen scrim, bobbinet, and buckram. The applied drawings of this mixture can be of numerous objects: leaves and all kinds of foliage, treetrunks and limbs, thin window mullions, details of banners, crests and flags, roof tiles and shingles, boards and bricks, flowers, patterns of lacework, signs and letters, human and animal figures, grillwork, and ornaments of all descriptions.

Framed or skeletonized pieces of scenery (metal or wood) can also be covered with the aforementioned materials, plus screen wire, and then have designs applied on them by using the latex-and-casein mixture. The concentrated latex and casein paste color (in the desired color) are mixed together in equal parts. After stirring thoroughly, the mixture becomes very thick.

Mix

1 part *PURE CLEAR LATEX* **(undiluted)**

With

1 part *CASEIN PASTE COLOR* **(undiluted)**

MIXTURE FOR APPLYING OPAQUE LATEX DESIGNS ON SCRIM (or other gauzes)

Application:
The mixture is applied on the material by using plastic squeeze bottles (like mustard or ketchup bottles) or by using wax-paper cones. You can put it on by following a pounced drawing of the designs or by doing it freehand.

As an Adhesive:
The clear concentrated latex functions beautifully as an adhesive for attaching pieces of sharkstooth scrim and cheesecloth to fabric which folds. These pieces are sometimes added at random on an already painted backdrop or cut drop to produce a three-dimensional raised effect, most typically for emphasizing vines, treetrunks, roots, or clumps of hanging moss. Leaves can also be cut out of the same fabrics and applied on soft scenery by attaching them only at one end so they hang freely. In addi-

276

Clear Liquid Latex (concentrated)

tion, the concentrated latex works well when you are creating sculptured objects. It is used to hold the fabrics (scrim and cheesecloth) on an armature shaped with wire or it can be useful for supplementing thicknesses and textures on existing items such as grapevines and artificial plants. At the same time, it can function to strengthen these and similar objects.

Application:
Full-strength latex is used for adhering dimensional shapes and flat pieces and for doing sculpture. For best results, the pieces of fabric are dipped into the latex, then removed and pressed into the desired shapes on the surface. This can be achieved by gathering, twisting, and curving the sticky pieces as well as by folding and overlapping them. You may

apply the latex with a brush, but bear in mind that the latex begins to dry quickly and therefore the wet pieces should be positioned as soon as possible. After the pieces of fabric have been adhered with the latex, they may be painted with water-base paints.

Source of Supply: Paint stores that stock theatrical paints.

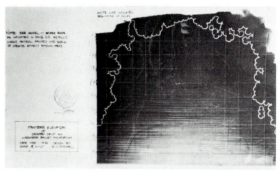

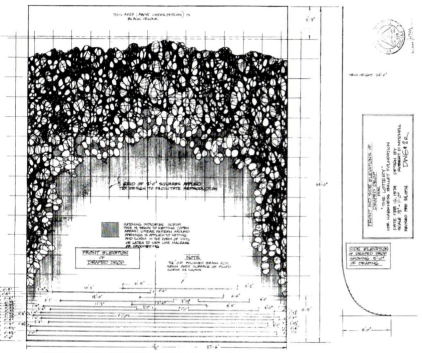

GLUING CUT SHARKSTOOTH SCRIM TO SCENIC NETTING AND APPLYING OPAQUE DESIGNS

Drafting and paint elevation is Robert D. Mitchell's backdrop design (27 ft. 6 in. by 34 ft. high) for the Harkness Ballet's THE LOTTERY (1974).

Steps of Execution:

1. Charcoal drawing on brown paper was perforated.
2. Sharkstooth scrim stapled on floor over gray bogus paper and dye-sprayed with Hudson tank.
3. Staples removed, scrim drop turned over and stapled face-down on strips of white wax paper taped together.
4. Drawings of shapes cut out and transferred to scrim by placing pounce face down and rubbing charcoal bags over perforations.
5. Openings cut out with scissors and razor blades.
6. To support the holes cut in scrim, 1-in. square scenic netting was stretched over back to hold netting in place for gluing to scrim.
7. (Right center) The stretched scenic netting, held down by metal scraps, is adhered to the scrim with white synthetic flexible glue (dries transparent) applied by scenic artist Ken Calender.
8. (Bottom) Latex drawings ($\frac{1}{4}$ to $\frac{1}{2}$ in. wide) are put on with a plastic squeeze bottle after the scrim, still on wax paper, has been adhered to the scenic netting and turned over. For maximum holding and flexibility, the latex mixture was made with 1 part clear concentrated latex (heavy) to 1 part black latex paint (undiluted).
9. A cut black velour border with webbing was attached across the top of the finished scrim drop and its irregularly cut edges were glued on the scrim. (Photographs—Lynn Pecktal)

Prop steer skulls, for the Reno set in THE WOMEN (1973) designed by Oliver Smith, were made by dipping pieces of cheesecloth into pure clear latex (Slomon's) and adhering them to forms shaped of forming cloth (flexible wire, woven but not welded) attached to wooden bases. Water-base paints were later applied. (Photograph—Lynn Pecktal)

A collage of old newspapers, pictures, and painted signs was adhered with wallpaper paste to the leaning, rough-hewn wooden walls of Ben Edwards' Southern shack for PURLIE (1970). Aniline dyes were applied on both wood and papered walls for painting and antiquing. The old movie poster above the fireplace of Jack Hoxie in ''Via Pony Express'' was painted on canvas with caseins before being adhered. (Photograph—Munro Gabler)

Wheat Paste

Form: powder
Soluble in: water
Uses:

Wheat paste is standard for adhering wallpaper and for sizing an asbestos curtain before painting. The same proportions for mixing are used for both.

To mix:
Pour 1 pound of dry powdered wheat paste into 2½ quarts of warm or cold water while stirring thoroughly to dissolve it and to get rid of any lumps. For a large quantity, increase the amounts of paste and water in the same proportions. Application of the paste on wall-paper and the asbestos curtain is done by brush. (See Hanging Wallpaper, p. 341, and Sizing an Asbestos Curtain, p. 310.)

Pour
1 lb. of dry powdered *WHEAT PASTE*

into

2½ qts. of warm or cold *WATER*

--- MIXED WALLPAPER PASTE

Sources: Paint and hardware stores.

Other products for adhering wallpaper:
Glutoline Wallpaper Paste
A powdered paste mixed with water for hanging wallpaper and wall coverings that stain easily.

Wonder-wall Adhesive
A ready-mixed adhesive (can be thinned with water) for adhering wallpaper and fabric-backed vinyl films to wall surfaces.

Dextrine

Form: powder
Soluble in: water
Uses:

This yellowish-white (or white) powder has long been the traditional binder for bronze powders but has now been replaced by clear gloss liquid vinyl as the standard binder. Dextrine can also be used as a binder with aniline dyes to keep them from running.

To prepare:
1. Slowly dissolve 1 part dextrine powder in 3 parts hot or cold water while stirring thoroughly.
2. Then heat in a double boiler until the mixture becomes boiling hot and clear.
3. When cool, thin with water for the desired working consistency before mixing it with the bronze powders. When dextrine is mixed with metallic gold, it should never be applied hot on flameproofed fabric as it can cause the gold to turn green.

Availability:
Dextrine is sold by the pound at theatrical paint stores.

Other Adhesives and Cements

Duco Cement (Du Pont):
A transparent waterproof flexible cement for adhering small items like glass jewels and sequins on fabrics (muslin, canvas, scrim, etc.). Available in tubes.

Dow Corning Silicone Adhesive:
An unusually strong silicone rubber product for repairing props, glass, ceramics, lamps, crystal, figurines, and ashtrays. Available in tubes.

Weldwood Contact Cement:
A cement for bonding formica and other laminated plastics. Available in pints, quarts, and gallons.

Mastic No. 11 (Dow Chemical):
Ideal for bonding rigid plastic foams to each other or to other firm surfaces. It can be used to bond most plastic foam materials, wood, metal, ceramic, gypsum products, masonry, and concrete to themselves or to each other. It is strong, waterproof, flexible, and sets fast. Available in 1- and 5-gallon containers.

Rubber Cement:
For mounting sketches, photographs, and drawings, and also for making models, collages, and photomontages. Since water-soluble glues can swell the paper, rubber cement works well because it does not contain water and surfaces adhered with it stay flat. It can be used as an alternate binder for gluing back the edges of muslin cut drops instead of waiting for the usual white flexible glue to dry (see Backdrops). Available in 4 ounce, ½ pint, quart, gallon.

Spray Adhesives:
Both 3M Scotch Spra-Ment Adhesive and 3M Spray Adhesive 77 (clear) are excellent adhesives for mounting photographs, renderings, and collages. They bond cardboard, cloth, paper, plastic sheeting, and foam rubber to each other or to like surfaces. Available in 11-ounce spray cans.

Plastic Adhesives and Products from the Schwartz Chemical Co., Inc.:

Adhesives:
REZ-N-GLUE (the all-purpose cement)
REZ-N-BOND (for bonding Lucite, Plexiglas, and polystyrene)
VC-1 and VC-2 (vinyl cement)
ACETATE CEMENT (for bonding cellulose acetate to cellulose acetate and cellulose nitrate to cellulose nitrate

Cleaners and Polishers:
POLY-KLEEN (for polystyrene)
REZ-N-KLEEN (for Lucite and Plexiglas)
REZ-N-POLISH (for acrylics)

Metallizing Products:
Metallizing dyes, base, and top coats

Dyes:
REZ-N-DYE (for dip-dyeing of plastics)

Coatings:
REZ-N-LAC-A (for cellulose acetate)
REZ-N-LAC-B (for butyrate)
REZ-N-LAC-C (for methyl styrene)
REZ-N-LAC-S (for polystyrene)
REZ-N-LAC-V (for vinyls)
REZ-N-LAC-MM (for acrylics)

Equipment for Preparing Glue

The Glue Stove
Since scenic glues are still an economical and practical feature in the theatrical scenic studio, a glue stove is utilized every day to heat large amounts of scenic glue and to keep it hot. It is basically a large version of a double boiler constructed in the studio iron shop from galvanized metal. The stove is table height, and measures 5 feet wide by 18 inches deep. The top part of the stove, which holds the water, is shaped like a long metal box and is 10 inches deep. It is supported by metal legs on the corners. Four circular openings cut in the top hold the selected sizes of the glue pails. As an example, a 16-quart pail needs an opening that is 11 inches in diameter. These openings hold the pails in place and keep them from touching the bottom of the metal container; gas burners beneath this container supply the heat.

The glue pails (with handles) should be of galvanized metal. A standard 16-quart pail can be purchased that is made of extra-heavy steel and is double-dipped. Wooden covers, cut to fit on them, help keep the glue hot, and wooden paddles remain in the buckets so the glue can be stirred well before using. A notch cut out of the wooden cover lets the handle of the paddle protrude.

Separate from the paint department, the carpentry shop also maintains a glue stove, which is necessary for preparing the glue that is used when the scenery is covered with canvas (see formula for mixing, p. 285).

The Electric Glue Pot
An electric glue pot is ideal for heating small quantities of scenic glue and water. Controlled by a thermostat, it turns off automatically and the glue is not allowed to burn. Electric pots are adjusted at 140°F. to 150°F., or sometimes they can be adjusted at 100°F. to 175°F. These portable glue pots can be purchased in 1-, 2-, 4-, and 8-quart sizes, and a removable inner container for the glue comes with the pot.

Using Two Pails for a Double Boiler
If a glue pot or a glue stove is unavailable, two metal pails may be used as a double boiler. This keeps the glue mixture (scenic glue and water) from being placed directly on the heating unit; for without the two pails it would surely burn. One pail (with water) is placed on the burner, and inside this, the second pail (which holds the scenic glue and water) is positioned on a brick or similar object to keep the second pail at a secure height. Such a method of heating the glue naturally requires that the water pail be watched fairly closely so that more water can be added.

The Stove for Heating Water
In addition to having a glue stove, it is imperative to have a regular stove for heating a sufficient supply of water, essential for preparing hot size and hot starch. A 20-gallon-capacity galvanized metal container is always kept in reserve on the stove; when hot water is needed for any purpose, it is taken from this. Size water is also stored on the stove, usually mixed in a 5-gallon bucket. By having these ready to use, a great deal of time is saved. In addition,

Equipment for Preparing Glue

cold water is kept ready in a large container (20-gallon) nearby on the floor. A typical stove in the scenic studio has at least three gas burners, and it measures 4 feet 6 inches long by 1 foot 3 inches deep by 10 inches high.

Dippers
Dippers are always needed for measuring and for taking liquids from containers. They are extremely useful when straining paints or starch, and at least six of these are kept on hand in the studio. The dipper is made with an ordinary quart tin can easily obtained from restaurants or other commercial establishments. A long handle of wood (2 feet by 2 inches by ¾ inch) is attached to it, positioned horizontally and flush with the rim, and the top of the ¾-inch thickness is in the same plane with the rim. For more support, the handle can be cut from a larger piece of wood and a triangular shape can be added on the end where it attaches. Nails are used to fasten the handle to the can and, to make the dipper more sturdy, a length of flexible wire is often wrapped around the can in a couple of places, then attached to the handle.

APPLIED TEXTURES

Scenic Dope

In scenic work, dope is a standard mixture made in the studio to be applied as texture on scenery. This section discusses how it is mixed (also with an alternate binder), and its basic uses: as a texture, as a glue, and as a lay-in color; the many different kinds of materials that are used with dope; and how the effects are created with it. Other texture materials that can be purchased commercially are also discussed. In the text, whenever scenic dope is made with scenic glue it is from S. Wolf's Sons, and the dry whiting is Yorkshire, imported from England, also available at S. Wolf's.

Dope, also known as "guck" or "gook," has long been a standard mixture applied on scenery to create texture. It is prepared in the scenic studio by using these ingredients: hot concentrated gelatine glue (scenic glue), hot water, and dry whiting. The mixture is often tinted with dry pigment colors or premixed water-base colors to make the desired color. While the hot glue is still considered the best binder for mixing dope, a white synthetic resin glue can be substituted. However, white glue does not dry as fast as gelatine glue and it is more expensive. It also does not produce the same quality of texturing when mixed with the dry whiting as does the gelatine glue. Other textures that can be purchased commercially are included at the end of this section.

Mixing Dope
When you are getting ready to use dope, the first step is to dissolve and melt the dry gelatine glue in hot water to make hot concentrated glue. This is done by soaking one part *dry gelatine glue* (scenic glue) in one part *water* for one hour in the double boiler. It should be heated until it is completely dissolved. Then, when you use the hot concentrated glue, it must be taken directly from the double boiler (glue pot). Scenic dope is generally prepared in three consistencies: heavy, medium, and light. The exact proportions for mixing dope are listed below and you should consult these for the kind of dope you need. It is very important that the glue and the water be hot whenever mixing dope.

1. Start by pouring the measured parts of hot water into the bucket selected for mixing. A 5-gallon metal bucket is the best container for mixing and holding a large amount of dope.
2. Then pour the measured hot glue into the hot water while stirring.
3. Next, *slowly pour* in the measured dry whiting, leaving it *unstirred*. Let this soak for at least ten minutes. This allows the liquid to soak into the

Proportions for Mixing Standard Dope with Gelatine Glue

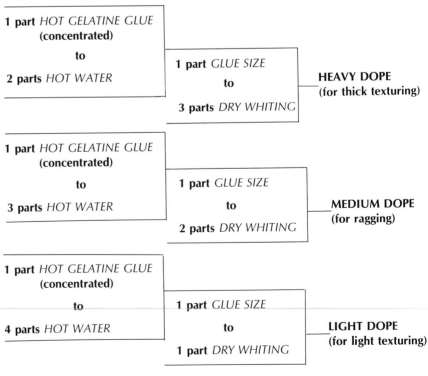

1 part *HOT GELATINE GLUE* (concentrated) **to** **2 parts** *HOT WATER*	**1 part** *GLUE SIZE* **to** **3 parts** *DRY WHITING* → **HEAVY DOPE** (for thick texturing)
1 part *HOT GELATINE GLUE* (concentrated) **to** **3 parts** *HOT WATER*	**1 part** *GLUE SIZE* **to** **2 parts** *DRY WHITING* → **MEDIUM DOPE** (for ragging)
1 part *HOT GELATINE GLUE* (concentrated) **to** **4 parts** *HOT WATER*	**1 part** *GLUE SIZE* **to** **1 part** *DRY WHITING* → **LIGHT DOPE** (for light texturing)

280

(Left)
Bombed façades in Robin Wagner's FULL CIRCLE (1973). Basic units were constructed of galvanized mesh wire on wooden framing, using scraps of canvas, muslin, sharkstooth scrim, linen scrim, Ozite rug padding, erosion cloth, and several weights of burlap to form bricks and crumbling plaster attached with scenic dope.

(Right)
Scenic dope is brushed on irregularly shaped carpet, then glued to surface of prop volcano created with framework of wood and wire mesh covered by ragging with scenic dope.

whiting, thus preventing a lumpy mixture when it is stirred.

4. When ready, thoroughly stir the mixture with a heavy mixing paddle, reaching deep into the bottom of the container to get to all the whiting. The dope should always be used when it is hot or warm, never when it is cold. If this happens, reheat the mixture by putting the pail of dope in a larger container of hot water.

Using White Synthetic Resin Glue as an Alternate Binder
A white synthetic resin glue (which dries transparent) like Hewhold, Bergenbond, or Elmer's Glue-All can be substituted if gelatine glue is unavailable. This kind of glue naturally does not require heating, nor does the water. Otherwise, the same steps can be followed as listed above. Although the white glues have similar holding properties, the proportions below are those for Hewhold glue. When you are using different name brands, it never hurts to mix a small batch of dope and try it on the surface to see if the particular glue is strong enough to hold it.

Proportions for Mixing Dope with White Synthetic Resin Glue

1 part *WHITE SYNTHETIC RESIN GLUE*
to
3 parts *WATER*
— GLUE SIZE

The glue size is then mixed with dry whiting to obtain the desired consistency:

1 part *GLUE SIZE*
to
4 parts *DRY WHITING*
— **HEAVY DOPE** (for thick texturing)

1 part *GLUE SIZE*
to
3 parts *DRY WHITING*
— **MEDIUM DOPE** (for ragging)

1 part *GLUE SIZE*
to
2 parts *DRY WHITING*
— **LIGHT DOPE** (for light texturing)

This $\frac{1}{4}$-in. plywood profile garland of flowers (about 28 in. wide) was made as a preliminary sample for Rouben Ter-Arutunian's scenery in COPPELIA (1974) for the New York City Ballet. Three-dimensional relief was created before painting by squeezing scenic dope from a wax-paper cone.
(Photographs — Lynn Pecktal)

281

Scenic Dope

The Basic Uses of Dope

While it may primarily be used by itself as a *texture,* dope functions as a *glue* for adhering assorted fabrics and materials to a surface. Furthermore, whenever it is tinted with a color and applied generally over a surface, it is utilized as a *lay-in* color. But in any of these three uses (texture, glue, or lay-in), the surface of the applied dope is almost always finished by being painted.

Dope for Texture

A brush (like a lay-in, an old Fitch, or a trim brush) ordinarily serves for putting the dope on the surface of the scenery. The type and direction of the brushing, of course, depends upon the kind of scenery which is being executed. The dope can be dabbed on with the bristles held vertically, or the brush may be dragged back and forth, then the dope may be patted here and there with the brush. Various implements such as steel graining combs, putty knives, wire brushes, and whisk brooms are often worked over the applied dope while it is still wet to give it the desired textured details. Once the applied dope has set for a few minutes, a brush full of the mixed dope can be dragged over it to achieve even more depth of texture. On surfaces of wood, plywood, or veneer (which may or may not be covered with canvas) dope is excellent for creating these textures: wood grain-

ing on boards and beams, brick and mortar, stone walls and flagstone, and also finishes on carved sculpture of all kinds. For any of these, the dope can be white, or it can be in a color (one or more) chosen as the local color. The final painting over the dope surface may be applied with several water-base paints.

Dope for Gluing

Gluing fabric or materials on scenery with dope is done to help hold it together, to protect it while in use, and to enhance its dimension by providing added surface texture. When pieces of fabric, such as linen scrim, sharkstooth scrim, flannel, muslin, canvas, or cheesecloth, are dipped into the dope and are used to cover a unit of scenery, it is referrred to as "ragging." Ragging takes place on solidly backed flats, set pieces, or platforms which can have appliqués of various materials. It also can be put on forms of wire and metal. The fabrics for ragging are selected according to the desired effect and are cut into sizes that are appropriate for the scale and the intricateness of the particular unit of scenery. Typical-size pieces of fabric can be 6 by 6 inches, 6 by 12 inches, or 12 by 12 inches. They are applied by hand-dipping each piece into the dope, or by first brushing the dope on the surface, placing the piece of fabric on it and then smoothing it out with the

brush. Extra dope can always be brushed over the covered fabric surface to give it more variation.

Glue Ragging on Carved Scenery

Large-scale scenery carved of Styrofoam, such as an elaborate coat of arms or a smaller piece like a cupid garden statue, is covered with pieces of lightweight fabric so the carved details are not lost. Cheesecloth and linen scrim are superior materials for this and the technique of covering with these is similar to that of papier-mâché. If you prefer a heavier fabric, pieces of flannel are also good.

Glue Ragging on Set Pieces Made of Wire and Wood

For three-dimensional set units like rocks, treetrunks, stumps, logs, or ground rows, glue ragging is achieved with a heavier-weight fabric. Since the basic structure is normally made of wooden framing and ribs covered with chicken wire (steel wires twisted together to form flexible hexagons), forming cloth (wire that is woven but not welded), or welded steel fabric (1-inch-by-1-inch mesh), heavy fabric is needed to conceal the outlines of the wire underneath and to give it "body." Pieces of heavy canvas and duck are standard for this work. Torn pieces of old velour work splendidly, especially if you are creating a draped or pleated effect with the

Paintings and frames are often constructed as one, the frame formed by a combination of molding and decorative edging of ¼-in. plywood. Relief ornamentation is added by shaping small fragments of cheesecloth dipped in hot dope. Dope is also brushed across molding and, while still wet, a steel comb is dragged across it to create texture.

More decorative relief is added to the picture frame by squeezing on a mixture of heavy dope from a large wax-paper cone. After frame is completely dry it is painted with water-base paints. (Photographs — Arnold Abramson)

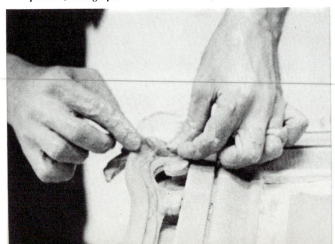

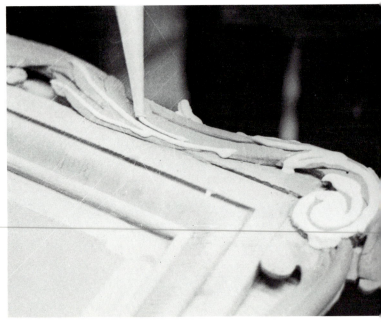

fabric. Sometimes, long strips of cotton padding (like that used for upholstery) are stuffed under large wet velour pleats to hold them in shape while the fabric dries, and the cotton remains as part of the object. Again, the fabric should always be cut or torn into workable sizes, then dipped into the dope and applied. Further texturing can be done over the covered set unit by adding torn scraps of rug padding, cut-out shapes of pile carpet, shredded plastic foam, bits of sharkstooth scrim, or scenic netting (1-inch squares), and they are put on in the same way. Still more variations in the texturing can be obtained by brushing on areas of dope, then sprinkling cork pebbles or sawdust on them while wet.

Glue Ragging of Dimensional Textures on Wooden Surfaces

Framed scenery, covered with plywood most often has appliqués of several materials put on it before it is ready for covering with a fabric and dope. Numerous materials are used, selected according to weight, durability, and effect. Large chunks of Styrofoam, pieces of Celotex panels, or slabs of foam rubber may be shaped to represent almost any kind of architectural surface material, whether decayed wood, crumbling stonework, or cracked plaster. Flexible rods of Ethafoam are also good, especially for creating molding or ornament. The stage sets, of course, that allow an enormous range in dimensional textures are those found in operas where the locales are in a state of ruin or disrepair.

For other surfaces in lower relief like brick, tilework, or wooden shingles, materials such as foam core board ($\frac{1}{4}$ inch thick), display foam board ($\frac{1}{2}$ inch thick), and Ozite rug padding work extremely well. All of these are cut out in the required shape, placed at random on the wooden scenery, and are then held to it with hot dope and tacks or staples. Mastic No. 11 is great for bonding large pieces of Styrofoam to the wood. To provide more contrast, heavy fabrics like erosion cloth and plasterer's burlap can be cut in various sizes and added to the already covered surfaces. Scraps of sharkstooth scrim and felt may be combined with these, and all of them are applied with the dope.

Creating Textures on Wooden Set Pieces with Dope and Various Paints

To obtain as much irregularity and contrast as possible in creating a textured surface, a combination of several paints, dope, and aniline dyes was applied on the three-dimensional scenery for the opera *Maria Stuarda,* designed by Ming Cho Lee. Both flat and three-dimensional set pieces were constructed of wood, which were designed with appliqués of wooden molding and ornamental cut-outs. To prepare the surfaces for the desired painting effect, the raw wood on all of these units was given a base coat of white, utilizing white dope (medium consistency) and two kinds of white paint. Instead of using a standard lay-in for the new wood (like shellac), paints were chosen that would easily take washes of aniline dyes.

First, a base coat of white casein was brushed on the wooden pieces. When this had dried, a batch of white dope (dry whiting, hot glue, and hot water) was mixed, and while this was still hot, it was applied at random by brushing it over the various surfaces of the wood to add a three-dimensional texture. Afterward, details of the panels and ornamentation were drawn and inked, using a thin vinyl color put on with a lining brush. Then white latex was dry-brushed and smeared over certain areas, also at random, while avoiding the inked outlines. The overall finished painting was achieved by spraying these surfaces with transparent dyes in a Hudson tank. Many interesting variations were obtained just by spraying dyes over these different white base coats. The dyes applied on the white casein and white dope dried darker, while the same dyes sprayed on white latex (and vinyl as well) dried lighter.

Robert Motley applying cutout pieces of Ozite rug padding on stone-fireplace unit of Oliver Smith's set for THE WOMEN (1973), working with the designer's sketch (left of center). Stones were drawn in charcoal on plywood and pieces of rug padding were cut out and glued on with hot scenic glue rather than dope. The whole surface was covered with linen scrim and painted.

Ming Cho Lee's units of scenery for the New York City Opera's MARIA STUARDA (1972), finished with a combination of several paints, dope, and aniline dyes.
(Photographs – Lynn Pecktal)

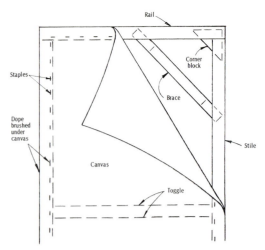

STAPLING AND GLUING CANVAS TO THE FRAME OF A FLAT

1. Canvas should exceed all edges of flat by 1 in.
2. Lay canvas on face of wooden frame. With hammer tacker (stapler) put a staple in each of the four corners, positioning each staple $\frac{1}{2}$ in. from inner edge of the 1-by-3 wood. Stretch canvas taut but not overly tight; when priming is applied, canvas will tighten sufficiently.
3. Continue stapling on rails, next on stiles, keeping staples $\frac{1}{2}$ in. from inner edges, spaced 3 to 4 in. apart.
4. When all sides are stapled, lift canvas flaps and brush dope on framing. Press canvas down tightly by hand, making sure small wrinkles (bird's eyes) caused by staples are stretched out. Canvas is not glued to toggles or braces.
5. Trim off excess canvas evenly with outer edge, using mat knife or razor blade.
6. Let dope dry thoroughly before priming canvas.

Abstract patterns cut from Ozite rug padding fastened to turkey wire, designed by Will Steven Armstrong for KING LEAR (1965) at the American Shakespeare Festival, Stratford, Conn. Supported by a framework of iron pipes, the rigid wire was bent by hand; cut pieces of rug padding were then attached with scenic dope. Dope was brushed over outer surfaces to give rough textures and to make them firm when dry.

Lloyd Evans' twofold arch unit for RIGOLETTO (1969) at the New York City Opera. Masses of raveled erosion cloth and burlap were adhered to this unit, on both front and back, where stone and mortar cutouts were made in the plywood. (Below) Raveled fragments of erosion cloth, various kinds of burlap, and scenic netting were glued to the three-dimensional RIGOLETTO scenery with scenic dope and tinted with dry pigment colors. (Photographs — Arnold Abramson)

Backdrop design by Lloyd Burlingame
AÏDA by Giuseppe Verdi
Libretto by Antonio Ghislanzoni
Directed by James de Blasis
Cincinnati Opera Company (1973)
(Photographs — Lynn Pecktal)

PAINTING LARGE FIGURES ON A MUSLIN BACKDROP (30 ft. high by 48 ft. wide). Source of light came from the urns below the figures.

STEPS OF EXECUTION:
1. Drop stapled on the floor over gray bogus paper.
2. Basic drawing done with charcoal. Pounces made of each figure in perspective (ranging in height from 23 to 14 ft.).
3. Drawing inked with felt-tip pens.

4. Backdrop starched.

5. Casein and aniline dye colors were laid in with Hudson spray tanks and sponge mops.

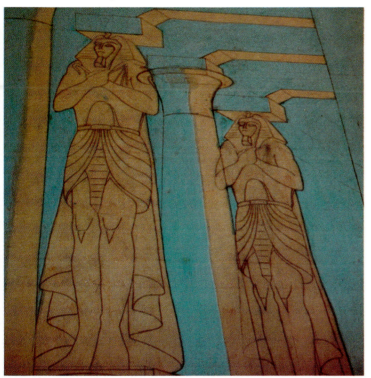

6. Details finished with caseins and dyes.

7. Details showing spattered textures.

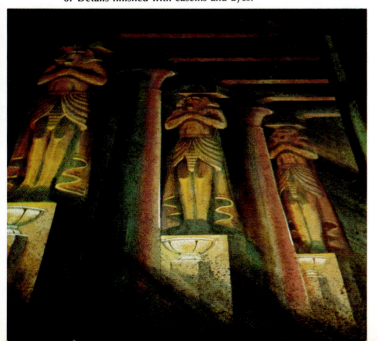

A wall of logs carved out of 2-in. Styrofoam, adhered to plywood, covered with patches of sharkstooth scrim dipped in scenic dope.

Roughhewn dimensional post shaped with 4-in. Styrofoam, also covered with pieces of scrim.

PAINTING ROUGHLY GRAINED WOOD (four views)
Roughly painted grained wood (on flat and three-dimensional surfaces) for the Reno setting in THE WOMEN (1973), designed by Oliver Smith. All primed with scene paint, overpainting and details with casein paint and aniline dyes. Techniques included wet blending, dry brushing, spattering, and glazing.

Face of bar unit, canvas on plywood. Boards drawn and inked, then primed and overpainted.

A flat door, also canvas on plywood; same execution as bar unit. Note the dye-painted shadows under the cross boards.

PAINTING AND GRAINING THREE-DIMENSIONAL WOOD (below)
Four lengths of baseboard, shown in order of execution, were for Robin Wagner's interior set in FULL CIRCLE (1973). The graining simulated a stained oak finish.
ORDER OF TEXTURING AND PAINTING (left to right)
(1) New raw wood. (2) Rough texture made with scenic dope, brushed and dragged over the raw wood, leaving some holidays. (3) Undertone color (opaque shellac) brushed over applied dope. (4) Oil stain graining color brushed on sparsely. Graining first done with same brush, pushing bristles forward and against wet stain. Next, graining combs with rubber teeth (shown center) are dragged through the still-wet stain.

(Right) The same process was used for Wagner's three-dimensional door, except here a coat of low-luster varnish (final step) has been applied. Graining patterns were also created by rubbing the wet oil stain with a soft cloth wrapped around the forefinger and by drawing with a black wax pencil before the stain was applied. (Photographs—Lynn Pecktal)

Stenciled pattern, painted on linen, for Oliver Smith's interior in THE WOMEN (1973). More than one color was used on each of several small stencils (8 by 8 in.)

Sample of painted molding, panel, and baluster on canvas for Lloyd Evans' woodwork in the setting for ALBERT HERRING (1971) at the New York City Opera (see p. 334).

Casein paints and aniline dyes were used for overpainting on this James Stewart Morcom design for VIVA MEXICO (1973) at Radio City Music Hall. Scumbling and spattering was done with brushes and texture created with paint rollers after the canvas had been laid in and primed with casein paint.

A heavy painted texture is created on a muslin backdrop by dipping a large brush into a pail of aniline dye color and generously spattering and dribbling over the surface. A design by Lloyd Burlingame for AÏDA (1973) at the Cincinnati Opera Company.

Vacuum-formed plastic bricks were stapled on hard flats and painted with vinyl paint for Marjorie Kellogg's setting in THE KILLDEER (1974) at the Estelle R. Newman Theatre, the Public Theatre, New York. (Photographs—Lynn Pecktal)

A partial view of one of Robin Wagner's upstage set pieces for FULL CIRCLE (1973), showing painted bricks on canvas.
STEPS OF EXECUTION:
(1) Canvas primed white. (2) Then basecoated with mortar color. (3) Brick colors stenciled on. (4) Texture applied on bricks by brushing on scenic dope. (5) Details and shadows painted. (6) More texturing created by spattering with paints and dyes.

Setting and costumes by Sandro La Ferla
LE COQ D'OR by Nikolai Rimsky-Korsakov
Directed by Gian-Carlo Menotti
Teatro Verdi, Trieste, Italy (1974)
Painted textured rugs suggest Oriental opulence.

Creating Textures in Designs

Stage design by Lynn Pecktal
STREET SCENE by Elmer Rice
Yale Drama School
New Haven, Connecticut (1959)
A variety of materials was used to
create textures in this collage
(see p. 124).

Setting by Sandro La Ferla
THE GREAT DIVIDE
   by William Vaughn Moody
Act II
Directed by Keith Fowler
Virginia Museum Theatre
Richmond, Virginia (1970)

Dope for Gluing Canvas

Dope for Gluing Canvas to the Frame of the Flat

A precise formula should always be used when mixing dope for gluing the canvas on the wooden frame, for two reasons: the glue mixture (dope) must be strong enough for proper adherence, and the dry whiting has to be in the proper proportion to keep the glue from staining through the canvas to the face. Any bad glue stains can become extremely obvious and appear after the canvas is painted. The dope can also be used for adhering canvas onto solid wooden set pieces. A standard formula is used for mixing this dope:

> **1 part** *HOT GELATINE GLUE*
> **1 part** *HOT WATER*
> **3 parts** *DRY WHITING*

DOPE FOR GLUING CANVAS ON THE FRAME OF THE FLAT

The hot glue should be thoroughly dissolved in the hot water. Stir well. Then slowly pour the dry whiting into the glue mixture while continuing to stir. Since this mixture should be used while hot, it is kept on the stove and always reheated whenever reusing.

When a rush is on to paint flats that have had the edges glued with the dope (and stapled) and are not yet fully dry, a handful of dry whiting can be rubbed over these areas (usually 3-inch widths of 1-by-3 boards) before the fabric is primed so the still-wet glue does not let stains come through when the priming and finished painting are applied.

OTHER TEXTURES

Latex Texture Paint (Wolf-Tex)

Besides "scenic dope," there are various other materials that can be bought and used as applied textures on scenery. Among the most popular are Perltex, Dutch Kalsomine, and latex texture paint (Wolf-Tex).

Wolf-Tex, a very thick white latex texture paint, is a product of S. Wolf's Sons and comes ready to use in a gallon container. It is a good substitute for scenic dope if texturing on a hard surface is needed, but it is more expensive. Latex texture paint can be put on woodwork or solid interior walls without a primer and dries with a flat white finish in about 30 minutes. It is excellent for camouflaging seams, cracks, nailheads, joints, and other defects on a surface. The paint may also be tinted with a water-base color if desired or it can be painted afterward.

Application:
Thick latex texture paint should be applied with a large lay-in brush, and texturing must take place while the paint is soft. After the paint has set for a few minutes, an overall texture can be made by using a spackle knife, a graining comb, a paint roller, or a whisk broom to create the intended effect.

Thinning:
If thinning is necessary for a very light texture, you can add 1 pint of water to 1 gallon of the latex texture paint.

Dutch Kalsomine

Similar effects can be created with Dutch Kalsomine, which comes in powdered form. When it is mixed with water, it creates a thick mixture for making textures on hard surfaces. A heavy texture on built woodwork, for instance, may be made with the kalsomine to simulate many coats of old peeling paint or a wood that has irregular and rough graining. Other textures of kalsomine can give the effect of swirl-finished plaster, heavy stucco, or the like.

To Mix:
Add enough warm water to the dry kalsomine to make a smooth paste. Allow it to stand a few minutes before adding additional water so that it spreads nicely when brushed. It should always be used heavy, with just enough water added to make it work easily. For every 5 pounds of powder, use about 3½ pints of water.

Application:
By brush. Steel graining combs or spackle knives can also be worked over it while it is wet. Once the kalsomine is applied, it can be painted over, or it may be tinted beforehand with a water-base color to achieve a specific effect.

Perltex

Perltex is the trade name of a powdered paint additive that produces a painted sand float or light-textured finish on hard surfaces like wooden covered wings and set pieces and platforms.

To mix:
Add 2 pounds of this powdered substance to every 5 gallons of paint to obtain a normal sand float finish. Or for a heavier sand texture, the amount of Perltex can be increased. But for mixing smaller amounts like a gallon, a 6-ounce bag or box of Perltex can be used. The Perltex should be poured into the paint while stirring thoroughly, and it should be stirred as well when it is being put on.

Application:
By brush or mohair roller.

A Conversation with RAOUL PÈNE DU BOIS

A native New Yorker, Raoul Pène du Bois started designing for the theatre in his early youth as a stopgap until he became a painter. At sixteen, he designed a few costumes for the last of *The Garrick Gaieties,* then went on to design for various revues, including a Shubert version of the *Ziegfeld Follies, Thumbs Up,* and *Life Begins at 8:40.* In 1935, at the instigation of John Murray Anderson, he designed the sets and costumes for *Jumbo,* a Billy Rose production that was the last show to play at the Hippodrome. Over the following years he designed a great many musicals, revues, ballets, night-club shows, operettas, Broadway plays, and a group of films for Paramount. He did the sets and costumes for non-Broadway shows such as *The Aquacades* in 1939, *A Night in Venice* (first production at Jones Beach), Fort Worth Fiestas, and various ice shows. Raoul Pène du Bois has won nominations for almost all theatre and film awards and is the holder of the Donaldson and the New York Drama Critics Award and two Tony Awards, one for the sets for *Wonderful Town,* the other for the costumes for *No, No, Nanette.* His uncle, Guy Pène du Bois, was an important painter of the twenties and his cousin, William Pène du Bois, is a writer and illustrator of children's books. Among his better known productions are:

Sets and costumes:
Doctor Jazz (1975)
Irene (1973)
No, No, Nanette (1971)
Ziegfeld Follies (1957, 1956, 1938)
Bells Are Ringing (1956)
Plain and Fancy (1955)
Wonderful Town (1953)
Call Me Madam (1950)
Lend an Ear (1948)
Two for the Show (1940)

Panama Hattie (1940)
Dubarry Was a Lady (1939)
One for the Money (1939)

Costumes:
Gypsy (1974, 1959)
Music Man (1957)
Carmen Jones (1943)
Too Many Girls (1939)
Leave It to Me (1939)
Two Bouquets (1938)

Ballets (S & C)
The Haydn Concerto—New York City Ballet (1968)
Jeux—New York City Ballet (1966)
Ghost Town—Ballet Russe de Monte Carlo (1939)

Films (S & C)
Kitty (1945)
Bring on the Girls (1945)
Lady in the Dark (1944)

Frenchman's Creek costumes (1944)
Louisiana Purchase (1941)

Setting and costumes by Raoul Pène du Bois
IRENE
Book by Hugh Wheeler
From an adaptation by Harry Rigby
Based on the original play by James Montgomery

Musical numbers staged by Peter Gennaro
Lighting by David F. Segal
Minskoff Theatre, New York (1973)
Pictured: Jane Powell and company
(Photograph—Martha Swope)

Where did you get your training for the theatre?

I would say that anything I know about it I learned by working in it. I never really studied theatre design at all. I expected to be a painter, but it didn't work out that way. One doesn't always do what one plans to do. Because I wanted to paint, I was enrolled in an art school for about six months, but I seldom attended classes. I must say in retrospect, it was an ideal situation. I never went to classes and nobody seemed to notice. Later, my uncle had an art school where I showed up intermittently. He had a rather disparaging attitude toward it. I remember his saying, "If they have any talent, they don't need you; and if they haven't any talent, no one can help them." If you want to be a composer, painter, or designer, you must start when you are a child and be working when you are quite young. If you go to college to study art, by the time you emerge, you are really too old. I got my first job doing costumes when I was in grammar school. I was offered a scholarship to Yale, but it seemed a waste of time, because I was already working in the theatre, and anyway, I could not afford it. A scholarship does not include living expenses, and in the midst of the Depression, I had to earn money. The theatre seemed a good way of doing it.

One of the first people I met in the theatre was Lee Simonson and his wife, Caroline Hancock. I was around fifteen or sixteen at the time. I had written a play about Dante Rossetti and Eleanor Siddal that rather interested them, and I had also designed the sets and costumes for it. Because of this they wrote letters of introduction for me to most of the people I first started out with in the theatre.

Did your uncle [Guy Pène du Bois] have a great influence on your work?

I suppose so in that he existed. From the time I was ten until I was quite established in the theatre, he was in France. An example, in a sense, is that he was a friend of Robert Edmond Jones, although he did not introduce us. When I first met Jones he was extremely amicable knowing I was Guy's nephew. It put us on a friendly basis that probably couldn't have happened under other circumstances. I thought James Reynolds was one of the great designers, although his style had little influence on me. My work is actually a reaction against the sort of thing he did. To a great extent, his work was based on exaggeration. I try to preserve the silhouette, the color, and the texture of a place or period out of the reality of the scene. I don't like to see actors overwhelmed by the exaggeration of their costumes or to make nonsense of the epoch or locale.

I like to think I have been most influenced by George Barbier, Charles Martin, Boutet de Monvel, Christian Bérard, and numerous French fashion artists of the eighteenth and nineteenth centuries such as Gabriel de Saint-Aubin, Maurice Leloir, and Jules David.

How do you approach starting work on a production?

The difficulty, an occupational hazard of the theatre, is to stall for as much time as you can get. They would like to rush you into doing sketches before you know what's being aimed at and before they know either. Discovering what a show is all about takes time and thought. When it all becomes clear, it sometimes goes very quickly. If there is a completed script, you often see the entire production the first time you read it. If not, then I often feel I shouldn't do it. Frequently how I see it is not how the director wants it and not how it finally happens.

Are there any particular directors you have especially enjoyed working with?

Enjoyed is perhaps not the exact word. Sometimes there may be quite a clash between what I would like and what the director wants. What one looks and hopes for is a director who will at least respectfully listen to your ideas and then add to them or completely alter them, but in a way that makes it possible to do a good job, a director who contributes ideas that make it possible to achieve something you can view with pride and one who helps make the show a hit and not a disaster. Such directors would make quite a long list and in retrospect, I would find I had left out many who should be included. Those who come at once to mind are John Murray Anderson, Hazzard Short, Jerry Robbins, Gower Champion, Donald Saddler, Morton Da Costa, Helen Tamiris, Bob Alton, Jack Cole, and John Taras.

Do you prefer doing both sets and costumes?

Yes, because it is so much easier to

Costumes by Raoul Pène du Bois
IRENE
Minskoff Theatre, New York (1973)

achieve a coordinated effect and a greater impact on the audience. Of course, it is possible to work very effectively in collaboration with another designer, but that depends on who the designer is. *Gypsy* with Jo Mielziner, *Music Man* and *Carmen Jones* with Howard Bay, and *Bring on the Girls* with Albert Johnson are all outstanding examples of how successful this collaboration can be.

Do you make models in black-and-white or color?

I might do either of the two. Both the subject and the time would be strong elements in deciding that. My sketches could be done in any one of a number of things—watercolor, gouache, pen and ink, or tempera. The subject and the style I am hoping to project would dictate that choice.

You have been complimented for having an extraordinary color sense. Is that intuitive or did you study it?

In a way, everything one does must be the subject of study, but it is intuitive too. I have no color theories other than the few that are obvious to any artist— warm colors advance and cold colors recede, and black makes an empty space. Every other rule you could make about color is one that would be broken the very next time you started to work.

In designing No, No, Nanette, *did you spend a great deal of time on it?*

When it happened, it was done in quite a rush, although I had been turning it over in my mind for years. I had suggested it to Harry Rigby some fifteen years ago. My original idea was to revive a series of old musicals in a unit set with the same group of players. The musical is America's original art form and there are so many to be done that

have been neglected. However, I couldn't arouse much interest in the idea. Then Harry asked if I could suggest something that Mrs. [Cyma] Rubin might be interested in producing. Again I suggested that at least *No, No, Nanette* be tried, as Vincent Youmans has always been a great enthusiasm of mine. Almost alone she saw the possibility and had the courage to do it. Still, it is to be regretted that it was not projected as the first of a series. It would have made further revivals possible without it seeming to be an attempt to cash in on *Nanette's* success.

How was the period and style of No, No, Nanette *decided?*

It had originally opened in 1925 and, as with most plays, comes directly out of its epoch. It would be completely falsified if it were done in any other period. But of course, it was not a replica of the original production. I tried, rather, to capture what a modern audience would think a musical of that time would be like.

What I attempt to do is absorb the atmosphere of the era before I start

working on the sketches so that I can design the production as though it were actually the present. No matter how modern you want to be with what you use, it should still grow from the epoch, otherwise you simply make nonsense.

Do you have assistants to help you on both the sets and costumes?

Yes. Of course if the show is very large or very rushed, they in turn will need assistants. Primarily I use Mason Arvold to assist on sets and David Toser to assist on costumes.

Your costumes for Nanette *received wide acclaim. Did you give permission for them to be copied commercially?*

Yes, rather to my surprise they sought permission to copy the sweaters and paid for it! That is the exception, I am afraid. Usually if anything has a fashion influence, it is just ripped off and nothing can be done about it. That is also true about decor ideas as well as costumes. For instance, *One for the Money* that I designed the sets for in 1939 was a show that had a strong influence on decorations of its period.

Setting and costumes by Raoul Pène du Bois
DOCTOR JAZZ
Book by Paul Carter Harrison and Buster Davis
Music and lyrics (mostly) by Buster Davis

Directed and choreographed by Donald McKayle
Lighting by Feder
Winter Garden Theatre, New York (1975)
(Photograph—Martha Swope)

Setting and costumes by Raoul Pène du Bois
NO, NO, NANETTE
Book by Otto Harbach and Frank Mandel
Music by Vincent Youmans
Lyrics by Irving Caesar and Otto Harbach
Adapted and directed by Burt Shevelove
Dances and musical numbers staged by
  Donald Saddler
Lighting by Jules Fisher
Production supervised by Busby Berkeley
Forty-sixth Street Theatre, New York (1971)
(Photograph — Friedman-Abeles)

289   Costumes by Raoul Pène du Bois
       NO, NO, NANETTE
       Forty-sixth Street Theatre, New York (1971)
       (Photographs — Lynn Pecktal)

The rather stark architectural sets were done entirely in all white or in all black with one color accent in some scenes. There was a night-club scene with what then would have been very smart. It had banquettes tufted in black ciré satin and the set had a glass floor through which most of the light came. Nobody ever thought it was black. At times it would look green to some, while others would see it as a copper set or describe it as iridescent.

Was that because of the way it was lighted?

Yes, I'm sure it was. The scenic production was a canvas for Murray Anderson's lighting which is unequalled to this day. Many directors lit their own shows back then. I have also worked with Hazzard Short, a director who achieved breathtaking effects.

You have also designed for ballets.

Yes, and I find that very interesting. It is rather like writing verse in a traditional meter. You have to fit your ideas into this predetermined form. There are only certain kinds of costumes that dancers can dance in and the center of the stage has to be kept open unless some object or construction has been choreographed into the ballet. In addi-

tion, the set must be light and virtually collapsible in order to facilitate transportation and to set up very quickly for the many widely spaced single performances.

Do you have any favorites among the shows you have designed?

All with very few exceptions, for one reason or another. Certainly *Dubarry Was a Lady, One for the Money, Lend an Ear, Wonderful Town,* and *Carmen Jones* were, although for the latter production I only designed the costumes. *No, No, Nanette* must be included too, even though it risks overshadowing everything else I have done. I suppose the costumes for *Gypsy* should be mentioned. After that show opened I left for France and stayed for six years.

What did you do there?

In theory I was painting. In practice I did nothing. I don't mean I was sitting and staring into space, but I was so enraptured with France that I didn't do the work I thought I would do.

In another phase of your work, you have designed sets and costumes for motion pictures. What films did you do in Hollywood?

I thought the best ones were *Lady in the Dark, Frenchman's Creek,* and

Kitty. Others had their moments, but unfortunately I never had the opportunity to do a great cinema so that all the designs were to a large extent wasted. I went to Hollywood under the best possible auspices. It couldn't happen again. I had done *Panama Hattie* and *Dubarry Was a Lady* with Buddy de Sylva, who was a great friend. When he went to Paramount as the executive director he brought me out there. I thought that designing for films would bring a kind of permanence to my work that the theatre lacked, but I was wrong. Unless films are masterpieces, they very soon fade from memory. However, it is surprising when years later one meets people who remember exactly some scene, effect, or costume from the most fugitive theatre production. In Hollywood I had a clause in my contract that said I could go back to New York and do one show every year. I didn't want to sever all connections with the theatre. But as so often happens in Hollywood, Buddy de Sylva had a row with the studio and left. So not wanting to stay under those circumstances, I bought my contract off and left, too.

Setting by Raoul Pène du Bois
JOHN MURRAY ANDERSON'S ALMANAC
"The Nightingale and the Rose"
Staged by John Murray Anderson
Music and lyrics by Richard Adler,
  Jerry Ross, et al
Sketches directed
  by Cyril Ritchard
Dances and musical numbers staged
  by Donald Saddler
Costumes by Thomas Becher
Imperial Theatre, New York (1953)
(Photograph — Roderick MacArthur)

EIGHT

Backdrops, gauzes, and fabrics

BACKDROPS

Next to the flat, the backdrop is the best-known scenic item to theatre craftsmen and audience alike. That large piece of material, serving as a background of painted scenes or simple washes of color, is still as much a part of the theatrical stage setting as ever. Known in the British theatre as "backcloths," backdrops today are not only made of canvas and muslin but include a wide assortment of fabrics. They are usually painted, but can be designed to be left as they are (velour, China silk, or decoratively figured fabrics). Backdrops can be made up in great variety.

Besides making a handsome sketch for the backdrop, the designer must be aware of a number of factors that involve both visual and technical aspects: how the fabric will fall, how it will take paint, how it will look under stage lighting, whether the fabric should be lightweight or heavy, what is the most practical and durable material, and what the cost is going to be. A designer doing a production may list the specifications for the backdrop on the drafting or on the sketch, although these are sometimes related verbally to the scenic studio head. Specifics noted for a backdrop include:

1. Type of drop.
2. Size—height and width.
3. Kind of fabric.
4. Placement of seams.
5. Hanging instructions for playing and storing.
6. Any special information for putting the drop together.
7. The painting.

Standard Types of Drops, Legs, and Borders

Regular backdrop (made to be folded or rolled; may be translucent or nontranslucent)

Cyclorama (the curved drop at the back of the stage)

Gauze drop (sharkstooth scrim, linen scrim, bobbinet, opera net)

Cut drop (supported with or without scenic netting or with one of the gauzes)

Cut leg drop or cut portal drop

Border (cut or straight)

Leg (cut or straight)

Traveler (in two pieces—opening from center and closing from both sides of the stage, or a one-way traveler in one piece going off and on from one side of the stage)

Roller drops (must have horizontal seams and not be hemmed on the sides)

Setting and costumes by Lloyd Evans
PELLÉAS ET MÉLISANDE by Claude Debussy
Libretto by Maurice Maeterlinck
Directed by Frank Corsaro
Lighting by Hans Sondheimer
New York City Opera (1970)
Pictured: Patricia Brooks and André Jobin
(Photograph — © Beth Bergman 1974)

Linen-scrim panels with applied opaque trees hang in front
of a translucent muslin backdrop of painted trees and foliage.
The tree trunks and limbs on the linen-scrim panels were
cut out of black iron-on fabric and pressed on. Initially,
full-scale drawings on brown paper were perforated with a
pounce wheel, and the tree shapes were transferred onto the
fabric for cutting by rubbing a bag of dry whiting over the
holes. The same pounces were used in transferring the drawings
onto the linen scrim for placement of the iron-on pieces.

Settings and lighting by Neil Peter Jampolis
LA FORZA DEL DESTINO by Giuseppe Verdi
Libretto by Francesco Maria Piave
Directed by Bodo Igesz
Costumes by Suzanne Mess
Houston Grand Opera Company (1973)
(Photograph — Neil Peter Jampolis)

A draped V-shaped cyclorama was used simultaneously
as a translucency and as a front projection surface and remained
in place throughout the opera. The latticelike patterns in
the bottom photograph were created by using slides in
two Xenon projectors. Each slide was made of two strips
of gauze bandage placed between two pieces of glass.

Scenery, lighting, costumes, and choreography by Alwin Nikolais
TENT — Nikolais Dance Theatre
University of South Florida (Première), Tampa, Florida (1968)
(Photographs — above and right: Chimera Photo; center: Brynn Manley)

A large piece of grayish-white, nylonlike fabric (30 by 30 ft.), essentially circular, is used as both a prop and a backdrop. With an opening cut in the center and seven slits around the sides, it is suspended on three battens spaced 10 ft. apart. A scrim hangs upstage (above). The fabric is lowered. Color patterns are created on it by using Kodak Carousel projectors (center). Dancers in costumes (unitards with Mylar strips) perform on the dropped fabric. Projected color patterns hit dancers, fabric, and scrim (right).

Stage design by Peter Harvey   Provincetown Playhouse
MUZEEKA by John Guare   New York (1968)
Directed by Melvin Bernhardt   (Photograph — Les Carr)

The design below was executed as a dimensional backdrop with built-out sections in colored plastic and many perforations of different shapes. The backdrop was covered with wrinkled brown paper and brightly painted. To change the appearance it was lighted from the front, sides, and rear.

Organza was used to make up the four multicolored cut drops that formed a setting for the Joffrey Ballet's SACRED GROVE (1972), below. Designed by Robert Yodice from a concept by Ming Cho Lee, each drop was sewed together with vertical seams, using 4-ft. widths of the sheer white fabric. The drops were placed on the floor for drawing and dye painting, the many random-shaped openings were cut out; then flexible white glue, thinned with water, was brushed around the openings to help retain shape and to keep edges from raveling. Strings of small beaded weights were adhered to the bottom edges of the very irregularly cut drops. (Photograph — Lynn Pecktal)

All of these can hang soft (be unframed), but sometimes they are framed. Besides variety in fabrics, there are many possible working conditions with every production. For instance, a backdrop may also be a traveler (with or without fullness), and a two-piece traveler can have rings on the back to function as a tableau curtain. If a backdrop has enough fullness, it can also be a contour curtain.

Size of Backdrops

Every backdrop varies with the individual production, but it is interesting to compare the average sizes of drops for several categories:

28 ft. by 48 ft.—a Broadway play or musical
36 ft. by 60 ft.—the New York City Opera
40 ft. by 60 ft.—the New York City Ballet
45 ft. by 68 ft.—the Metropolitan Opera
45 ft. by 90 ft.—Radio City Music Hall

Fabrics and Materials for Drops

A vast number of materials can be used for backdrops. Among the standard and most conventional scenic fabrics are muslin, canvas, linen, velour, sharkstooth scrim, linen scrim, bobbinet, and opera net. The fabrics may be flameproofed before they are delivered to the scenic studio or by the scenic artists once they are there. Backdrops can also be made of such materials as China silk, satin, Bengaline, duvetyne, flannel, corduroy, chiffon, monk's

cloth, burlap, erosion cloth, cellophane, scenic netting, and plastic materials, among others. As a rule, most of these materials come in more than one weight.

Placement of Seams

Placement of seams (horizontal or vertical) on a backdrop is affected by the nature of the fabric and the way the fabric falls, and also by the ways the seams can be disguised in the design. Travelers must have vertical seams so that when they go off and gather, the seams do not pile up. Listed here are the most commonly used backdrop fabrics and the placement of seams under normal conditions:

Horizontal seams	Bobbinet
Muslin	Opera net
(for both translucent	*Vertical seams*
and nontranslucent)	Velour
Cotton canvas	(because of the nap)
Linen canvas	Duvetyne
Sharkstooth scrim	Linen scrim
(comes in 30-ft.	(either way when
widths which deter-	hiding seams)
mines height)	Silk, satin, organza,
Linen scrim	bengaline
(either way when	(for show curtains,
hiding seams)	draperies for the set,
	and travelers)

Muslin and canvas backdrops hang best when each side is "tapered in" 6 inches at the bottom. The seams on a translucent muslin drop show much less when lighted from behind if the seams are narrow and stitched only $\frac{1}{4}$ inch from the selvage edges, retaining the same strength. The same is true of scrims.

Hanging Instructions for Playing and Storage

Notations on the designer's drafting indicate exactly where and how a backdrop is to play (including storage instructions, if any). For anything out of the ordinary, more elaborate and detailed specifications are listed, sometimes including a drawing if the rigging is complex. For a simple backdrop in a musical, one automatically knows that it will have tie-lines at the top so that it can be tied on a pipe and that it will most likely fly in and out during the show, playing and storing on the same set of lines. A backdrop in a play (also tied on a pipe) that backs up a one-setter will probably not move during the action and will play and store on the same pipe.

Scenery and lighting
 by Rouben Ter-Arutunian
THE NUTCRACKER by P. Tchaikovsky
Choreography by George Balanchine

Costumes by Karinska
New York City Ballet
New York State Theatre (1964)
(Photograph—Martha Swope)

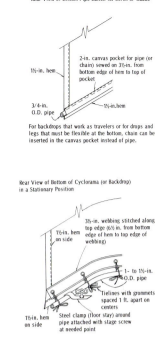

1½-in. hem

2-in. canvas pocket for pipe (or chain) sewed on 3½-in. from bottom edge of hem to top of pocket

3/4-in. O.D. pipe

1½-in. hem

For backdrops that work as travelers or for drops and legs that must be flexible at the bottom, chain can be inserted in the canvas pocket instead of pipe.

Rear View of Bottom of Cyclorama (or Backdrop) in a Stationary Position

3½-in. webbing stitched along top edge (6½ in. from bottom edge of hem to top edge of webbing)

1½-in. hem on side

1- to 1½-in. O.D. pipe

Tielines with grommets spaced 1 ft. apart on centers

1½-in. hem on side

Steel clamp (floor stay) around pipe attached with stage screw at needed point

Rear View of Backdrop That Rolls on a Wooden Batten

4-in. sandwich batten

Backdrop glued between battens joined by screws

Cut edge

3-in. sandwich batten

1½-in. skirt (selvage edge or hem)

Backdrop can have horizontal seams or have no seams. Skirt is optional.

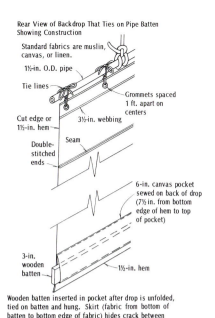

Rear View of Backdrop That Ties on Pipe Batten Showing Construction

Standard fabrics are muslin, canvas, or linen.

1½-in. O.D. pipe

Tie lines

Grommets spaced 1 ft. apart on centers

Cut edge or 1½-in. hem

3½-in. webbing

Seam

Double-stitched ends

6-in. canvas pocket sewed on back of drop (7½ in. from bottom edge of hem to top of pocket)

3-in. wooden batten

1½-in. hem

Wooden batten inserted in pocket after drop is unfolded, tied on batten and hung. Skirt (fabric from bottom of batten to bottom edge of fabric) hides crack between the drop and the floor.

Construction of an Average Backdrop

An average backdrop of canvas or non-translucent muslin, normally folded for traveling to the theatre and for storage, is referred to as a "folded drop." You may work with widths of 6-foot fabric (5 feet 9 inches flameproofed) and, starting with the first width at the bottom, make horizontal seams. After all the widths have been sewed, a 1- to 1½-inch hem is sewed around the edges. Next, webbing is sewed on the top, then grommets are placed 1 foot apart and tielines are added for holding the drop on the pipe. Behind the fabric on the bottom a pocket is attached for the pipe or wooden batten. This pocket is a folded piece of canvas that spans the entire bottom of the drop. For a wooden batten, it is ordinarily 6 inches wide when finished; or to hold a 1½-inch pipe, 3 inches when finished. In either case, the bottom of the pocket should be placed 1½ inches above the lower edge of the backdrop, which means that the actual stitching is $7\frac{1}{2}$ or $4\frac{1}{2}$ inches from the bottom edge of the drop. The extended material on the front of the backdrop is called the skirt, and this extra 1½ inches below the pocket serves to hide any crack between the drop and the floor, especially if there are any uneven areas on the stage. A scrim can have a similar pocket for a wooden batten or pipe or, if it opens as a traveler, a chain or weights. To prevent interfering with the transparent effect, a scrim pocket should be very narrow.

For a typical translucent muslin drop, wide widths of muslin (9, 15, 19, or 34 feet before flameproofing) are used; any seams are positioned horizontally. Smaller widths of muslin

are sometimes needed to finish out the top. The translucent muslin backdrop that is to be rolled instead of folded comes sewed together but unhemmed. After the drop is painted, a double wooden batten the width of the backdrop is sandwiched on both the bottom and the top. The muslin fabric is attached firmly between the double batten by screwing the two pieces of wood together from the back. The bottom of the double batten can have a skirt, made by extending the bottom of the muslin through the double batten so that the selvage extends 3 inches below. The two sides of the backdrop are then cut straight (by first snapping lines) and left unhemmed so the fabric does not pick up when rolled on the battens. Not all translucent muslin drops are rolled. Those to be folded are made up with normal widths of wide seamless muslin, are hemmed, and have webbing, grommets, and tielines at the top and pockets and skirts at the bottom.

Figuring Fullness on a Backdrop or Draperies

Fullness in the fabric of backdrops, travelers, draperies, or curtains lights well and gives a rich appearance on stage. Percentages of fullness range from a great deal to very slight. If you want a slight imperceptible ripple (in a flat muslin drop hung as a traveler without a batten in the bottom), 25-percent fullness is enough to ease the fabric so it hangs straight and does not noticeably distort the painting. Much more fullness would be required for something like China silk draperies, which need as much as 100 to 125 percent. Everything depends on the weight of the fabric and the intended effect. (The amount of fullness can also sometimes depend on the budget allotted for the fabric.) Other average percentages of fullness for items like a front house curtain and a valence are 75 percent, while a cyclorama, masking legs, and borders made in fullness would be 50 or 60 percent.

If you are planning to have a traveler, backdrop, curtain, or draperies made up so they are in fullness, always add the percentage of fullness desired to the original finished size. The following table indicates the amount of material to be added. For a cloth to be sewn up and finished at an overall width of 50 feet when hanging in the theatre, you would need:

25% fullness: 62½' wide	100% fullness: 100' wide
50'	50'
12½' (25% of 50')	50' (100% of 50')
62½' total	100' total
50% fullness: 75' wide	150% fullness: 125' wide
50'	50'
25' (50% of 50')	75' (150% of 50')
75' total	125' total
75% fullness: 87½' wide	200% fullness: 150' wide
50'	50'
37½' (75% of 50')	100' (200% of 50')
87½' total	150' total

Getting Backdrops Put Together

The studio head or the designer relays all specifications of backdrops to a theatrical drapery house, where they are made up according to the designer's wishes. When finished, the newly sewn drops are delivered to the scenic studio for painting and remain there until they are ready to go to the theatre. When there is something special about the drop, however, like sewing on large sequins or long fringe after the painting is finished, it is returned to the drapery house to have the details applied. For something unusual like this, the drapery house may be furnished a blueprint by the designer as well as the studio, and the designer may also confer with the drapery house on details. The designer, the scenic studio, and the drapery house must actually work out the execution of the drop together, all aiming for the designer's intended effect.

There is a close working relationship between a theatrical drapery house and a scenic studio. Props built in the studio or shopped for by the designer, such as chairs, sofas, poufs, and window cornices, are often sent to the drapery house for upholstering or covering. A representative from the drapery house can also come to the scenic shop to measure built arches before making up Victorian draw draperies, or to hang and fit sheer gauze curtains on an enormous four-poster bed, or to attach workable Austrian draw-drapes in a huge window opening.

Placement of Backdrops for Painting

The two traditional ways of painting backdrops are horizontal painting (on the floor) and vertical painting (on the paint frame). In the 1970s, the commercial scenic studios that paint Broadway shows execute them extensively by the floor-painting method, which has been the custom in Europe for many years. The Metropolitan Opera scenic studio has two paint frames for vertical painting, and the artists there work on frames as well as on the floor (see pp. 174-176).

HORIZONTAL PAINTING ON THE FLOOR

The dominance of floor-painting came about because of the difficulty in finding buildings with the necessary height to accommodate the vertical paint frame and its mechanics, plus the cost of the space. And since the scenic shops today build and paint the scenery for several shows at once on the same premises, having a great deal of floor space is a primary consideration. While vertical painting some years ago was initiated to save floor space in scenic shops located in small buildings with three or four floors or upstage in theatres, horizontal painting has been adopted today where the floor space doubles for either building or painting. Even so, finding enough space has forced many of the commercial New York scenic shops to locate outside of Manhattan.

Painting on the floor offers several advantages: More backdrops can be placed on the floor at one time and more painters can work on them than on a paint frame, making the whole process faster. Drawing and painting can be controlled on the floor with greater ease, because the scenery is on a flat solid surface instead of a vertical paint frame, where there is nothing to back up the fabric when the paint is being applied. Consequently, the paint does not run when it is being put on a horizontal surface. Techniques such as starching, dye-blending, bathing, and stenciling can be handled with more consistency and freedom on a horizontal plane. It is also simpler to manage a very large full-size pounce drawing when it is transferred on a horizontal backdrop by rubbing a charcoal bag over the small perforated holes.

There are relatively few disadvantages to painting on the floor. One is keeping the scenery clean and undamaged from walking on it while it is being painted, something that requires constant attention. You must be concerned that you do not spill paint, drop brushes, or snag holes (in scrim or bobbinet especially). If an elaborately painted drop is to remain on the floor for several days, it is best to cover it with polyethylene film to keep dust and dirt from collecting on it, especially if the carpenter shop is nearby. Walking on framed scenery that is laid flat on the floor can present minor problems. Some units, like velour-covered flats, can be painted vertically on the paint frame without the need to worry about stepping on the rails and toggles, which causes the fabric to be pressed down and show in the most unlikely places.

VERTICAL PAINTING ON THE PAINT FRAME

Vertical painting is done by mounting the backdrops or framed scenery on a large wooden paint frame that raises and lowers into a well in the floor. These moving paint frames are normally large enough to hold a full-stage backdrop; smaller drops require appropriate wooden battens temporarily attached at the top and side (or bottom and side) of the paint frame to accommodate the specific scenery piece. As in painting on the floor, all drops must be stapled squarely on the large open framework of wood to attain proper results. A bottom edge of the paint frame extends forward to hold flats or profile pieces fastened onto the frame for painting.

In the past, the prime reason for working on the paint frame in the city was that it saved space, since large areas of floor space were often unobtainable. A typical studio that housed paint frames was in a building 25 feet wide by 100 feet long and 60 feet high. Within this space, the structure could handle as many as six hanging paint frames, all of which moved up and down through the slots in the floors. The paint bridge, where the painters worked, was on the third floor, and it was on this level that the painters raised and lowered the frames as needed when they were working on them. The frames, hung on counterweighted lines, could be operated by hand line or a reversible electric motor.

Today, a paint frame may still be found near the upstage wall in some legitimate theatres, but these are rarely used, except on the most special occasions. A number of university and drama schools nevertheless continue to make good use of the paint frame with great satisfaction. Although it is not used with any degree of frequency in the commercial scenic studio, the boomerang, a multilevel platform unit that enables painters to work on scenery placed vertically, is still a good device when the paint frame does not lower, or the scenery is fastened to a wall or hangs on a batten. Moved on casters, this working unit has steps for access and space on it for the paints, brushes, and water.

Selecting Space for Painting a Backdrop

While designers in many universities today have spacious scene shops equipped with working paint frames in excellent condition, others must paint backdrops on the floor wherever and whenever the space becomes available. For them the work area may be the floor of the shop when scenery for the show is not being constructed, or even the floor of the stage proper when it is free. Thus the available facilities are often the determining factor in whether the designer paints vertically on a paint frame or horizontally on the floor.

Floor space for painting a backdrop should be large enough for the width and height of the drop plus about 4 feet for workspace (including a place for paints and equipment) at the bottom and sides once the drop is tacked down on the floor. Although the size of a backdrop varies with every production, a typical translucent muslin backdrop might be like the one Robin Wagner designed for the "This Is My City" scene in the musical Seesaw at the Uris Theatre, which was 30 feet high by 48 feet wide. That would mean that at least 4 feet of space should be added onto the bottom and sides of the drop, as the total area needed would be 34 by 56 feet. Even though it is useful to have space at the top, the top of the backdrop can always be tacked close to a wall when cramped for space.

In preparing and painting backdrops, remember: Gray bogus paper is put under the drop mainly to absorb the water in the starch and the paint after it has been applied on the backdrop, to allow evenness in drying, and to keep the fabric clean while it is being worked on. While brown Kraft paper can be used, it does not absorb water as well as the gray bogus paper and crinkles under the drop when wet.

Wax paper (in 4-foot widths) is placed *under* scrims, scenic netting, muslin cut drops, and the like only when a material is being glued onto them or when a paint mixture is being applied that will go through the fabrics and cause them to stick to the usual gray bogus paper. For instance, wax paper is put under a scrim if muslin cutouts are being adhered to it with a white flexible glue. Wax paper is also used under a scrim if designs are being painted or squeezed on with a thick latex mixture (like one part clear latex to one part undiluted casein paste).

Clear plastic (large pieces of polyethylene film) is usually placed *on top* of backdrops to protect them from dust, dirt, and water when they are not being worked on. Plastic is not normally put under drops because it does not allow air to get under the drop to dry the paint, especially thick latex on sharkstooth scrim.

Stapling the Backdrop on the Floor

As in so many other processes in the scenic studio, a drop is put down on the floor by following specific routines. The first order of business is finding available space in which the backdrop will go and making certain there is suitable work space around the edges. The floor is swept clean of any dirt and debris, and the area where the drop is to be stapled is covered completely with paper.

A commercial heavy gray bogus paper, 58 inches wide, is one of the best for covering the floor. It can be obtained from the Gilshire Corp., 220 Fifth Avenue, New York, N.Y., 10001, (212) MU 6-4864. Not only does this paper keep the drop clean when it is being painted, it also absorbs the water in the paints and starch and allows evenness in the drop's drying. Maintained on a movable metal rack, the roll of heavy paper is stretched out on the floor in long strips parallel to the top of the drop with an arbitrary overlap of 4 to 6 inches. To keep them firmly positioned, short pieces of masking tape are placed randomly along the edges of the paper. A particular point to remember: the gray bogus paper has a rough side and a smooth side. The rough side is the more absorbent and it is always placed "up" to prevent irregularities in the drying of the muslin, canvas, or scrim.

The new drop is taken from the package and opened up. Packed so that it opens in a vertical accordion pleat, the folded drop is positioned

to one side of where it will eventually go so it can be spread out easily. These steps are used for tacking a drop on the floor in a scenic studio, after the outline of a large rectangle or square is created by snapping lines for accurately tacking down the muslin, canvas, or scrim.

STEPS FOR STAPLING A BACKDROP ON THE FLOOR

Once the top of the backdrop has been stapled, this is a process of working back and forth on the bottom and the sides.

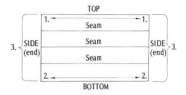

DIAGRAM FOR STAPLING OR TACKING A BACKDROP (horizontal seams) ON THE FLOOR FOR PAINTING.

ORDER OF STAPLING:
1. TOP (with or without webbing, grommets, and tielines). Corners first, center next, then spaces between.
2. BOTTOM (with or without a batten pocket and skirt). Corners first, center next, then spaces between.
3. SIDES (hemmed or unhemmed). Center seams first, other seams next, then spaces between. If seamless, centers first, then spaces between.

Top: Snap a long charcoal line where the top of the drop will be placed. Then open up the backdrop and place the top edge, with or without webbing, along this line. With two people spreading the drop over the floor (one on each corner of a side, top and bottom), walk the drop horizontally across the floor with the leading edge lifted high to get air under it. Then staple the top edge exactly along the snapped line with a staple hammer. The top edge should be pulled taut, then relaxed to lie naturally, and tacked precisely on the line. An irregularly tacked top will produce wrinkles when the drop is hung in the theatre. Working toward the bottom, stretch the drop out evenly.

Bottom: On the bottom of the drop, at the *center*, hold the edge of the fabric and pull it down as far as possible, then relax it and put a mark on the floor. This is the proper way of determining the exact height of the drop, since all drops vary some when they are sewed together. Only after the top has been tacked should the height measurement be taken. Measure this height with a steel tape, placing the tape on the very top edge and going to the

298

bottom mark. Next, carry this measurement across the bottom to the extreme left, and mark, then to the extreme right, and mark. Snap another charcoal line through these two marks, which will be parallel to the top of the drop.

Sides: To obtain accurate lines for the sides of the drop, place a 6-foot right angle at the top of the drop on the extreme of both sides and put marks to snap lines for the sides. If a right angle of this size is not available, use a large compass to bisect the top line for constructing a perpendicular line down to the bottom. Snap a line through each of these two sets of marks, thus completing the outer (perimeter) lines for tacking the drop.

Bottom: First tack right and left bottom corners. Because of the gathering effect of the sewing-machine stitching, the bottom hem (sewn on soft material) and the top (on rigid webbing) may differ. Usually the bottom will be the shorter. If so, center the bottom hem within the snapped lines, giving a tapered effect on each side. Then, tack at center and continue dividing these areas into halves. Staples (⅜-inch staples are standard for scenic work) should be no farther than 2 to 3 inches apart. For scrims, they are tacked closer together than on muslin or canvas. Any minor wrinkles in the muslin or canvas will stretch out when the fabric is wet.

Sides: The sides are always the last to be tacked. Tack the seams first. If the drop is seamless, begin tacking halfway up the side, then keep dividing the remainder into halves until finished. This is best done by two people pulling and tacking simultaneously at each edge at the same height. If the drop cannot be pulled exactly to the snapped lines, try to center the fabric equally from each side. (This is also a result of the gathering effect from the machine stitching, which is greatest when a single seam is sewn in the middle of the drop.) The drop is now ready for starching and/or painting.

CHECKING THE SQUARENESS

To double-check the squareness of a drop tacked on the floor, measure diagonally from the left top corner to the bottom right corner, then from the lower left corner to the upper right corner with a 100-foot tape. The two diagonal measurements should be equal, but they can be within an inch or two of each other and still be accurate enough.

Starching the Backdrop

The familiar process of "starching the backdrop" is the application of size preparation on the new muslin before it is painted. The size is a primer of transparent glazing; the starch gives body to the fabric and allows it to retain flexibility for rolling or folding. Once the muslin is wet with the liquid starch, the wrinkles shrink and the fabric dries taut. Most important, the starching keeps the paint to be applied from running and soaking into the fabric and also makes an excellent surface for painting with dyes, caseins, and other water paints.

The liquid starch is applied by two painters, and since this must be a continuous process to work well, it is done without interruption. With a Hudson spray tank, one person sprays the starch on the muslin backdrop as the other brushes it over the surface with a large brush with a long handle attached. In the scenic studio, a stippling brush is used.

PRIMING A MUSLIN BORDER WITH STARCH
As a primer for new muslin, liquid starch is sprayed onto a muslin border with a Hudson tank and smoothed out on the fabric with a stippling brush on a long handle. The same method is used for starching muslin backdrops. (Photograph—Arnold Abramson)

Mixing the Starch

Accurate proportions are required to mix hot starch properly. First, dissolve a pound box of Argo gloss laundry starch (blue box) in a half-gallon of cold water. Slowly pour this half-gallon of dissolved starch into 3 gallons of *boiling* water while stirring thoroughly. Put the mixture aside to cool before using. The proportions for making starch are:

1-lb. box of powdered *ARGO GLOSS STARCH* dissolved in $\frac{1}{2}$ gal. cold water and poured

into

3 gals. of *BOILING WATER* (making a total 3$\frac{1}{2}$ gals. liquid starch)

Always mix a little more starch than is actually needed; there is nothing more aggravating than lacking another gallon, and it is not expensive. An average drop (28 feet by 48 feet) requires around 14 gallons of starch—figuring that 3$\frac{1}{2}$ to 4 Hudson spray tankfuls of starch are needed and that each tank holds approximately 3$\frac{1}{2}$ gallons. The simplest way to estimate this is to allow 10 gallons of starch for every 1000 square feet of fabric.

For mixing large amounts of starch at one time, a galvanized 20-gallon-capacity barrel is ideal. These metal barrels are sold commercially for garbage cans and can be purchased at hardware stores. They are most practical for heating great quantities of water, and the handles on either side provide a good means for lifting. A wooden paddle approximately 3$\frac{1}{2}$ feet long is kept on hand to stir the boiling starch. Very often, the readied starch is tinted with a color applicable to the backdrop design.

THE STARCH BRUSH

A large brush is necessary, since the applied starch dries fairly fast and a big area must be covered quickly. An excellent starch brush is a stippling brush measuring 3 inches by 12 inches at the base. By attaching a long handle (5 feet 6 inches) on an angle of 65 degrees, the painter can reach over a wider distance than usual when brushing the wet starch without stepping in it. This feature on the brush, of course, is created in the scenic studio. If a stippling brush is unavailable, a professional window-cleaner's brush can be substituted.

FILLING THE TANK

The Hudson spray tank should be thoroughly washed out and cleaned before it is used for starching. When the tank is being filled, it is imperative to strain the liquid starch to get rid of the inevitable starch lumps or the sprayer is likely to clog. Use a household wire strainer with a layer or two of wet cheesecloth inside.

A No. 16 Hudson tank normally holds 3$\frac{1}{2}$ gallons of starch. When this amount is poured into the tank and the top is put on, around thirty hand pumps are necessary to build up proper air pressure for spraying. Both the tank and the nozzle of the sprayer should be tested before beginning work by spraying starch from the tank to see if it is coming out consistently. The nozzle can be directed so that the starch sprays into an empty bucket while you are adjusting the nozzle to produce a good heavy spray. Generally, the nozzle is closed, then adjusted for spraying by hand-turning it one and a half turns. In starching a backdrop, two Hudson spray tanks should be available, which eliminates having to wait for a tank to be refilled, since the paint boy can have the second tank filled, pumped, and always ready. It is also useful to have a small round castered dolly on which the tank may be rolled back and forth across the backdrop when spraying.

SPRAYING AND BRUSHING THE STARCH

Before starching is begun, the backdrop is given a general dusting to remove any dirt, lint, or strings from the muslin. And, since the painters must walk directly on the fabric when starching or painting, they normally clean the bottom of their shoes by rubbing them with a piece of cloth placed on the floor for that purpose.

Starching is always begun at the top of the backdrop. Working as a team, two painters walk horizontally across the drop as the first painter sprays a width of the wet starch, making sure that it is within easy reach of the painter who is brushing it. This width of applied starch is ordinarily about 2$\frac{1}{2}$ feet, but it varies with the individual's reach. The nozzle of the tank is held about 15 inches from the drop as it is sprayed and twirled in a clockwise direction, distributing the liquid starch quickly and evenly. As the painter doing the brushing follows closely behind the sprayer, he holds the starch brush with both hands, one positioned high and the other low. Brushing is done without pressure to avoid pushing the starch through the muslin, which would cause the fabric to stick to the paper or leave unwanted streaks.

SMOOTHING OUT THE WET STARCH

When the painter first brushes the starch to spread it, he makes either a horizontal zigzag stroke or a horizontal figure-eight stroke. Either provides a speedy and continuous movement of the brush. The second brushing of the starch is the more important aspect. Called "smoothing out," the wet width of starch is uniformly smoothed out by manipulating the brush in one long continuous straight line across the backdrop, always holding the bristles of the brush as vertical as possible. This procedure is repeated until the casual brush strokes in each width are brushed out, then the team continues starching the rest of the drop the same way, allowing at least a 6-inch overlap of indivudual widths of starch.

Starch is applied on a new muslin backdrop that may be planned for either a translucency or a nontranslucency. And, although a good smoothing job on any starched backdrop is essential, it is even more vital on the backdrop intended as a translucency, for this is the factor that really counts when it is to be backlighted on stage. On a translucent sky backdrop designed to have smoothly painted blends of color across it, for example, a well-brushed starch job is an absolute must. Understandably, not every drop is smoothed out the same way. The designer's sketch usually controls the direction of the final brushing. Sometimes, for both translucent and nontranslucent drops, the starching is both brushed on and smoothed out diagonally simply because the sketch has painted light rays shining across an architectural structure. For another translucency, like a drop being painted with a turbulent and murky sky, the starch may not even be smoothed out at all, but be left with the initial casual brush strokes.

DRYING THE BACKDROP

If possible, schedule the starching of a backdrop near the end of the day, leaving it to dry overnight rather than tying up floor space for a full day waiting for it. Whenever time pressure does not permit this, large portable fans are used in the scenic studio to speed up the drying process. Mounted low on the floor with casters, the fans are easily aimed in any direction where a steady flow of air is needed.

There are also occasions when it is absolutely necessary to put air under newly starched muslin for drying, particularly for a translucency, because the fabric being used is thin and the brushed starch has soaked through to the gray paper. This situation is always quite

obvious and often happens when thin muslin (120 weave) is used. Anyone who has had the unhappy experience of having to peel tiny pieces of gray paper from the back of a muslin translucency knows the boredom and time involved. When this seems likely to occur in the scenic studio, air is put underneath the drop to keep the starched muslin from sticking to the paper.

PUTTING AIR UNDER THE WET DROP

Putting air underneath a newly starched backdrop is accomplished easily by untacking a 6-foot length on each side of the drop and inserting two wooden triangular braces just under the edges of the fabric. These braces are designed solely for this use and are made of 1-by-3-inch wood placed on the flat. They are approximately 5 feet at the base and 6 inches high at the center (obtuse) angle.

The bases of the two triangular braces are nailed lightly to the floor, and the muslin edges are temporarily stapled on the tops. These braces provide two openings, an intake and an output for the air being circulated under the drop. The intake should be positioned at the top of one side where the starching is begun, the output on the bottom of the opposite side. An air-compressor hose (or a low-mounted

Air is put under a wet, newly starched backdrop of muslin when it appears likely that the wet starch will go through the fabric and the muslin may stick to the gray bogus paper when it dries. A triangular wooden unit like the one in the foreground was put under a side (top) of a wet backdrop after starching, another placed on the opposite side (bottom) of the drop to let the air out. The staples were lifted out, triangular brace nailed lightly to the floor, and edge of the wet muslin stapled to the wooden brace so an electric fan could provide air under the wet drop.
(Photograph—Lynn Pecktal)

electric fan) is used to circulate the air under the wet drop by directing it through the opening at the top. This airing, which only takes a few minutes, dries the muslin and paper enough so they do not stick together.

Watch the drop closely during the airing, since wet muslin stretches fast and there is danger of ripping. Since the ingoing air makes the center area of the fabric rise off the floor, it should not be allowed to rise higher than 18 inches. After the air has been under for a few minutes and you see that the fabric has dried enough, remove the wooden triangular braces and restaple the edges of the muslin (still wet with starch) in their original position so the backdrop can stretch taut while drying completely.

Laying Out the Drawing on a Translucent Drop

The detailed drawing for the painting on a translucent muslin backdrop can be made in one of two ways. For a drop of average proportions, it may be by making a full pounce on brown paper, perforating it, and transferring it to the muslin surface by dusting it with a charcoal bag, or the actual drawing may be done directly on the fabric with a charcoal drawing stick while standing. The latter is usually the procedure when time is short. When a big rush is on in the scenic studio, several scenic artists

A 2-ft. grid of heavy black cotton threads was stretched across Lloyd Evans' translucent muslin backdrop for DIE FLEDERMAUS (1974) at the New York City Opera. The buildings were drawn with charcoal; drawings of the figures were made on a brown-paper perforated pounce placed on the thread grid, rubbed with charcoal, and then all drawings were inked with a felt-tip pen. (Photograph — Lynn Pecktal)

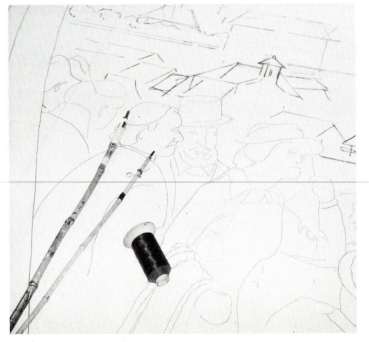

can draw on a backdrop at the same time by taking a tracing or blueprint of the sketch and cutting it into sections so each artist has one to work from.

Except for some special reason, direct drawing on the translucent muslin (stretched on the floor) is always done after the backdrop has been starched, because the charcoal will dust off more easily then, especially if one needs to make a change in the drawing. If the drawing is made lightly on the unstarched muslin, it can also often be obliterated when the wet starch is brushed across it, especially when the charcoal drawing has been purposely kept very light to avoid spoiling translucent fabric.

Before drawing is started on the backdrop, the usual grid lines or squaring off must be done. These lines, executed in full scale, are in the exact proportion to the grid lines on the designer's sketch or tracing, and are generally 2-foot squares. While these lines are ordinarily snapped with a line rubbed with charcoal for nontranslucent drops, they would remain on the translucent muslin and appear when the backdrop is lighted in the theatre. To prevent this, a grid for drawing is constructed by using black cotton thread from a large spool. The spool is easily held in one hand while unwinding it with the other hand. First, find the vertical center line. Measure the very bottom of the backdrop, divide the measurement in half, and mark it. On this mark, place the large 6-foot right-angle framing square so you can construct an accurate vertical center line from the bottom to the top. You will need another person to hold a snapline taut against the side of the framing square to extend and mark the center line precisely at the top of the backdrop. After this has been done, mark off the remaining lines (up and down and across) in 2-foot intervals on the four edges of the drop. At each marked station, just off the edge of the fabric, hammer large carpet tacks lightly into the floor around the entire perimeter of the backdrop.

When this is done, start at the top of the drop (either the right or left side), and tie the thread to the first tack, then go across the drop to the next tack, wrapping two or three times around each tack. Without cutting the thread, repeat until a complete grid is formed over the backdrop horizontally and vertically. By not cutting the cotton line, you do not have to stop and tie each one, and a great deal of time will be saved. Caution must be exercised when working and walking on top of the threads, since they break easily if you catch them with your shoes.

Once the drawing in charcoal on the backdrop has been finished, the threads are removed and the drawing is dusted lightly before painting is begun. The technique of stretching cotton lines over a surface is also good when you are drawing on drops of velour, China silk, or similar fabrics where lines snapped in charcoal or chalk would remain even after extensive dusting. White lines are used on dark fabrics. Sometimes threads are also placed at random across a translucent drop to guide the direction of the painting. The lines are so thin you can easily paint over them.

When there is really time on a production to do full-size perforated drawings on brown paper for each piece of scenery, these can have added value if the show is a hit and the same pounces are used for the road companies. For the smash-hit musical *Hello, Dolly!*, designed by Oliver Smith, all of the brown-paper pounces (including the many drawings for the translucent drops and built pieces) from the original New York production were saved intact at the scenic studio and were used time and again for the many touring companies.

Dye-Spraying Sky Backdrops

Sky backdrops designed with blends and horizontal washes of color have long been effectively painted with aniline dyes sprayed on with Hudson tanks. These sky drops are painted on such typical scenic fabrics as muslin, canvas, and scrim. The preparation before painting is of extreme importance. For any drop, the usual strips of gray paper are laid down on the floor before it is tacked out; these should extend past the size of the drop by at least 2 or 3 feet, including enough space to walk above the top and below the bottom of the drop. The extra gray paper around the edge of the drop absorbs the water when you are spraying past the fabric with dye as well as when starching. As noted, all backdrops should be stapled squarely on the floor. In the preparation, remember that starching is done for backdrops of muslin or canvas but never for scrim.

Before you begin working, cover the color sketch of the backdrop with clear plastic to protect it from paint and dirt. This also allows you to use a china marker on the plastic covering to mark the areas where the different colors of horizontal blends change on the sketch. You may make a grid for these on the sketch, or you

may wish to use a scale and simply measure up from the bottom to each mark. Measure and mark these off proportionally in full scale, drawing them in charcoal along the extreme edges of the backdrop. After this, mix the necessary colors you will need (following those on the sketch) and strain them. Each color should be poured into a separate Hudson tank. Depending on the design, this can mean having three, four, or five tanks. The availability of several tanks is essential for satisfactory results; in this process there is no time to wash them out and pour in new colors. The filled tanks, already pumped, can be placed conveniently along one side of the tacked drop. So that you are assured of a good, ample spray from the Hudson tanks, the nozzles must be tested before painting. You can adjust them while spraying into an empty bucket or their original mixing containers. On the usual sky backdrop, the colors go from dark at the top to light at the bottom, and all the

DYE-SPRAYING BLENDS ON A BACKDROP
Doing horizontal blends in aniline dyes on a translucent muslin backdrop requires fast and accurate work. Walking rapidly back and forth parallel to the bottom of the drop, Fred Jacoby applies dye color with a Hudson spray tank on this 90-ft.-wide cyc for Ming Cho Lee's set for LA BOHÈME (1972) at the Juilliard School of Music.

Steps of Execution:
1. Backdrop stapled over gray bogus paper and starched.
2. Several colors mixed in aniline dyes, following the sketch, and poured into as many Hudson spray tanks.
3. Also according to the sketch, locations of the different horizontal blends marked in charcoal along both ends of the drop.
4. Starting at the top, blends created by spraying one color over another in the wet.
(Photograph—Lynn Pecktal)

spraying is done by starting at the top and walking laterally back and forth across the drop, adding wet widths of dyes until you reach the bottom. Once the painting has started, you must keep a steady pace with the spraying and blending of the colors while they are as wet as possible to produce the most desirable results.

For a very smooth overall blend on a sky drop, it also works well to change the standard routine and start at the bottom of the drop with the lightest color, so that you add deeper colors each time. In doing this, the area of overlap is already damp with the lighter color. You continue spraying with the next deeper color, the next deeper color, and so on. By working in this manner, the colors being sprayed on are added rather than subtracted, and there is less likelihood of unfortunate edges drying in. After the painted blends have dried, check the results to see if the drop needs additional spraying.

Painting a Translucent Muslin Exterior Backdrop with Sky and Architectural Detail

Assuming that the backdrop on the floor has been starched and the drawing laid out, the first thing to do in this job is to mix the colors for the sky. On a translucency, they are usually mixed in aniline dyes. The samples of the mixed colors should be tried out on the extreme side edge of the drop to see how they dry on the fabric. One learns through experience the quantity of dyes to mix, but it is always better to mix more than needed instead of having to go back later to match a certain color.

After you have mixed the colors and each one has been strained, pour each pail of dye into an individual Hudson spray tank. Then, observing the designer's paint elevation constantly, spray and blend the sky areas wherever the colors are applicable. Even though this procedure is considered a laying-in for the sky, it often may be almost finished, with only minor overpainting needed by blending the colors while spraying them in the wet. To finish the sky details, a natural round sponge attached to a long handle or a flat sponge floor mop instead of a brush works exceptionally well. Both hold a lot of color and make the overpainting go faster and easier.

In the meantime, while you are waiting for the sky areas to dry, the local colors for the architecture and any other details can be mixed. These lay-in colors are also usually in aniline

PAINTING BUILDINGS ON A TRANSLUCENT MUSLIN DROP
Douglas W. Schmidt's translucent muslin drop for the Lincoln

dyes or thin caseins and are premixed for the sizable areas on the backdrop; the very small areas that do not require a great deal of color are mixed directly from a palette of pure colors. The palette is ideally situated on a low dolly with swivel casters and should be large enough to hold all of the pails of mixed local color plus a complete set of standard casein colors and a large bucket of clean water for mixing with the colors and for washing the brushes. Fresh water, of course, is needed periodically.

During the painting, lay pieces of heavy brown paper on the translucent drop to protect the work areas. Additional strips of brown paper can be placed on the floor near the palette for mixing brushfuls of color and water. In the scenic studio, all brushwork except the fine detail is normally done while standing, using long-handled brushes. So that you can follow the designer's color sketch as accurately as possible, it may be held in one hand while working, or placed on a floor easel if more than one scenic artist is painting.

In working on a drop like this, where you are painting on a background of natural muslin and

304

Center Repertory Company's THE TIME OF YOUR LIFE (1969) required very detailed painting to produce work of photographic quality.

Steps of Execution:

1. Backdrop stapled over gray bogus paper and starched.
2. 2-ft. squares snapped lightly in charcoal for laying out the drawing.
3. Drawing in charcoal inked before any painting started.
4. Drop painted in a series of washes using five values. The darkest color, a brownish-black (opaque) mixed first; from this, four other values were let down with water without using any white paint.
5. The finished backdrop given a bath of large spattering with one of the four lighter tones to create a grainy-photographic look. This technique of creating a very large but open spatter is also effective when painting scenery to resemble a sepia print or parchment, where a brownish or amber color is preferred.

(Opposite page) Paul Goranson and Betty Matta laying in areas of a building after the charcoal drawing has been inked. (Left) Finished buildings on the backdrop. John Keck at center. (Above) Robert Winkler and Keck. (Photographs — Arnold Abramson)

mixing colors from a palette of paints with the brush, it is often difficult to judge the various colors and values to keep them from becoming too pale after drying. The light background areas of the unpainted muslin can be deceptive when you are estimating and applying paletted colors. For this reason it is always good to get the whole drop laid in as quickly as possible, for only then can you see the relationship of the different colors and values. If there is a problem with the colors becoming too light, mix colors independently in containers, let the samples dry, match them accurately against those on the sketch, and ignore the unpainted muslin background for the moment.

After the sky has dried sufficiently, start painting on the architecture, beginning at the top of the backdrop and working downward. First lay in the palest distance tones by brushing. Then, still continuing downward, brush into the middle tones. When painting on such a drop, it is wise to alternate in different areas so that work is not always being done in a wet spot. When the lay-in colors have dried, go back and apply the details, the highlights, and the dark

accents, continuing until the backdrop is finished. If it is in keeping with the design, the newly painted surface may be given a "bath," a common practice for applying texture, for diffusing the brush strokes, and for pulling it together. Ordinarily the bath is made of an aniline dye color or a very thin opaque color thinned with water and applied by the Hudson tank or by spattering the drop by hand with a large brush. When the tank is being used for this, it should have an open nozzle and low pressure. If the brush is preferred, a large spattering is easily obtained by one hand hitting the ferrule of the brush against the open palm of the other hand. A fine spattering can also be achieved with a big brush by striking the tip of the bristles against the palm in the same way.

Basecoating (Laying in) the Local Colors on any Backdrop that Folds

For laying in flexible base colors on new backdrops of muslin, canvas, or linen, the size formula (p. 306) can be used to mix with casein colors. Ingredients can be reduced in proportion for smaller amounts.

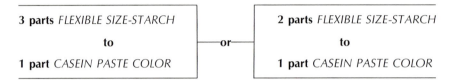

| 1 qt. *FLEXIBLE GLUE* (concentrated liquid) |
| 16 qts. *HOT WATER* |
| **with** |
| 14 qts. *LIQUID STARCH* (1 lb. box of Argo gloss starch dissolved in $3\frac{1}{2}$ gals. of boiling hot water) |

— **FLEXIBLE SIZE-STARCH**

Enough casein paste color is added to this flexible size-starch mixture to cover the fabric.

The casein paste color is usually thinned with the size-starch in these proportions:

| **3 parts** *FLEXIBLE SIZE-STARCH* |
| **to** |
| **1 part** *CASEIN PASTE COLOR* |

—or—

| **2 parts** *FLEXIBLE SIZE-STARCH* |
| **to** |
| **1 part** *CASEIN PASTE COLOR* |

After this lay-in is brushed on the fabric, it is normally overpainted with casein paints or aniline dyes, depending on the subject matter.

Handling a Backdrop in the Scenic Studio

Although the scenic artist is not expected to handle the backdrop in the theatre, he must nevertheless know how to get it ready to travel to the theatre after all of the painting has been finished. This requires being able to roll and fold a backdrop. It is also necessary to be able to turn a backdrop in the scenic studio if work is to be done on the back.

TURNING A BACKDROP

Turning a backdrop on the floor is very simple and is necessary whenever the painting on the front has been finished and work needs to be done on the back. Typical examples of work on the rear are opaquing and applying fabrics like scrim on cut-out portions of the backdrop.

Two people are needed to turn a backdrop, and they work from one end of the drop to the other. Although you may begin at either end, let us assume that the starting end is on the right. One person is stationed at the top right corner and another on the bottom right corner. To start, both pick up their respective corners and walk laterally toward the opposite (left) end of the drop while raising the fabric high in the air. Both continue walking until two-thirds of the total width of the backdrop is folded on top of the remaining third. Still together and without losing a pace, they turn and reverse direction, folding one-third of the total fabric back over the second layer and then dropping it. At this point, the folded drop in a section view should appear as a flattened figure S.

Now, working from the unmoved left end, with one person at the top and the other at the bottom, the two reach under the fold at the left and pick up the two corners, again lifting high over the previous folded portions, and walk laterally to the original starting line with this end, where it is dropped. Finally, both return to the left, find the two remaining corners, and stretch out the rest of the backdrop, straightening the fabric until it is in its original location, except that now the backdrop is turned over.

ROLLING A BACKDROP

A drop that is to be rolled normally has a wooden sandwich batten attached to the top and usually one at the bottom. The sides are never hemmed, since the extra layers of fabric (muslin or canvas) would pick up additional thickness as the fabric is rolled. Most often a rolled drop is a muslin translucency where the creases from folding would harm the painting

TURNING A PAINTED BACKDROP TO DO OPAQUING, CUTTING, AND GLUING OR CUTTING AND NETTING

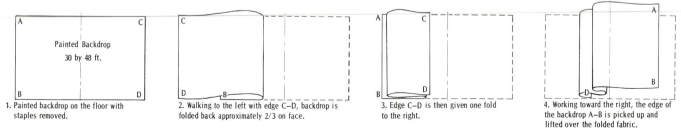

1. Painted backdrop on the floor with staples removed.

2. Walking to the left with edge C–D, backdrop is folded back approximately 2/3 on face.

3. Edge C–D is then given one fold to the right.

4. Working toward the right, the edge of the backdrop A–B is picked up and lifted over the folded fabric.

FOLDING A BACKDROP (MUSLIN, CANVAS, LINEN, OR SCRIM) FOR TRAVELING OR STORAGE

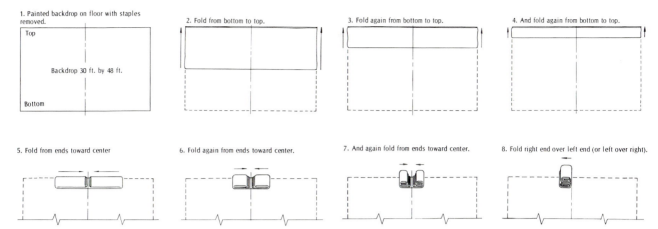

1. Painted backdrop on floor with staples removed.

Top

Backdrop 30 ft. by 48 ft.

Bottom

2. Fold from bottom to top.

3. Fold again from bottom to top.

4. And fold again from bottom to top.

5. Fold from ends toward center

6. Fold again from ends toward center.

7. And again fold from ends toward center.

8. Fold right end over left end (or left over right).

or fabric of a backdrop. The same preliminaries are followed for getting a drop ready to be rolled as for folding one. In this case, however, the wooden battens at top and bottom are attached after the drop has been painted and the staples have been removed.

To roll an average-size drop requires at least four or five people. Again, it is a process of working from the bottom to the top. The people rolling are spaced equidistant to each other on the floor at the bottom of the drop. It is imperative that all start together and roll the batten as a team, always working consistently, for if the fabric is rolled too tightly or too loosely, it will become irregular on the batten and wrinkle. The best approach is to let the fabric roll naturally.

The degree of straightness in rolling the drop can be judged by looking at the seams and seeing where they appear each time on the roll. If the fabric is seamless, it must be judged by eye. If the fabric is obviously becoming too tight on one end or in the middle, cut a strip of gray paper and place it on the drop while rolling to add bulk at the problem area.

To loosen the fabric on a certain part of the wooden batten while rolling, give the roll a few bounces slightly forward by lifting the batten a few inches off the floor and then dropping it. To tighten the fabric while rolling, increase the

grip of the hands and pull the batten toward you as the rolling continues. If neither of these methods corrects the irregularity, have everyone unroll the drop a bit and start rerolling at the point the trouble began.

A drop is considered well rolled when the top is parallel with the inside bottom batten. After rolling the drop, you can cut 2-inch-wide muslin strips and tie them at necessary intervals to keep it in place, but these should never bind and squeeze the fabric, or heavy wrinkles and puckers will form. For protection, an appropriate cover of canvas or polyethylene film is tied around the rolled drop for traveling and for storage.

FOLDING A BACKDROP

Finished backdrops on the floor are either folded or rolled for travel to the theatre and for storage when they are not in use. A standard backdrop that is to be folded normally has tie-lines at the top, a batten pocket and skirt at the bottom, and is usually hemmed on the sides. After the painting has been finished and is thoroughly dry, the staples removed, and the union label stenciled in a lower corner on the back, pertinent information is marked on the backdrop. This includes the name of the production, the act it plays in, and the center-line (CL) mark; all should appear on the front of the drop at the top.

A backdrop is always folded from bottom to top. For an average-size drop, this task is handled by three people, with one stationed on either end and one in the center. The person in the center must walk directly on the face of the painted drop during the folding. Starting at the bottom, the edge of the drop is picked up and

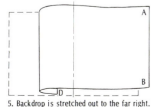

5. Backdrop is stretched out to the far right.

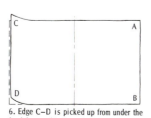

6. Edge C–D is picked up from under the backdrop and is stretched to the left until the backdrop is in place.

lifted simultaneously by all three to get air under the fabric while they walk together toward the top of the drop. As this is happening, the two people on each end pull outward to keep the fabric as tight as possible. Just before reaching the top, the fabric is lowered and the bottom edge is placed even with the top of the webbing. The whole technique of folding involves speed and good coordination on the part of everyone.

After the air has come out from under the folded half, any wrinkles should be stretched out so the fabric is perfectly flat. The folding from bottom to top is repeated until the fabric is decreased to a width of approximately 3 feet, although this dimension will vary with the height of the individual drop.

Now the direction of folding changes. Each end of the already-folded portion is picked up and folded into the center with a space of at least 1 foot left between the ends when they are folded inward. Folding is continued until the last fold on each side of the center space is around 3 feet. One of these halves is then folded over on top of the other, and the drop is ready to be wrapped and labeled. When it is opened at the theatre by the stagehands, the top of the backdrop is opened first; the tielines and marked center line are easily accessible so they do not have to open up the whole drop and lose time.

Painting Stained-Glass Windows on Translucent Muslin

For stained-glass windows that are to be on translucent muslin, colors are prepared in aniline dyes mixed with very heavy starch. The starch gives the windows an excellent translucent quality when they are backlighted. The aniline dye powder should be mixed first in concentrated liquid form, using the proportions:

Dissolve **1 teaspoon of powdered** ANILINE DYE **in** **1 qt. of** BOILING WATER	**CONCENTRATED LIQUID DYE**

Stir thoroughly and use mixtures of concentrated dyes to make the desired colors with the heavy starch. The starch is mixed in these proportions:

Dissolve **1 lb. of powdered** ARGO GLOSS STARCH **in ½ gal. water and then pour** **into** **1 gal. of** BOILING WATER **(making a total 1½ gals. of liquid starch)**	**HEAVY STARCH FOR STAINED GLASS**

Do not pour the 1-pound box of starch directly into the boiling water. Instead, dissolve the 1-pound box in ½ gallon cold water for easy mixing, then pour this into the gallon of boiling water. Stir well, then mix with the aniline dyes.

The stained-glass colors on the muslin may be built up heavily, but allow time for complete drying before painting the opaque mullions, leading, and other window detail around them. If these windows are to be painted on a backdrop that has already been completely starched, they may be effectively painted with the same starch-and-dye mixture. A framed window may be painted front and back, very heavily, thus achieving the effect of thick, irregular glass. On a drop that must fold or roll, the texture must be painted in without the actual build-up of starch on the surface.

Masking Out Small Areas in Liquid Wax

Very small areas on a muslin backdrop (tiny windows in buildings, designs formed by dots, stars in a night sky) that are to be translucent may be coated with hot wax to mask them out so they will not take the paint or dye when it is

A dull kitchen knife was used to scrape the paraffin wax off the windows of a city building on Robin Wagner's muslin backdrop for the musical SEESAW (1973). The wax, applied hot on the muslin with a brush, was put on to mask out the windows when painting and to allow them to be translucent when lighted on stage. (Photograph—Lynn Pecktal)

applied over them. The wax works beautifully when there are numerous small areas on a backdrop. This technique was used on Robin Wagner's backdrops for the 1973 musical production of *Seesaw*. Hot wax masked out the lightbulb dots around the painted electric signs on one drop and the many windows in the buildings on another city backdrop.

If the translucent areas are to get specific colors rather than the natural muslin color, these should be painted before the wax is applied. Paraffin wax is used for this process. It is melted in a pail and placed in a second larger pail containing boiling water. The liquid wax should remain in this double-pail arrangement while working, even though this necessitates emptying the water when it gets cold and replacing it with hot water so the wax is always kept liquid. The wax is then brushed on the surface with a small brush.

When all the waxing is set, it is left on the muslin fabric while the rest of the area is painted. This may be achieved by spraying or brushing with caseins or dyes, depending on the designer's intended effect. After the painting has dried, the wax is ready to be scraped off the muslin with a single-edge razor blade or a dull kitchen knife held horizontally with the blade perpendicular to the surface so it does not damage the fabric. The residue can be removed by broom or heavy-duty vacuum.

Masking for Translucent Clouds on a Sky Backdrop

If a sketch indicates translucent clouds on a muslin sky backdrop, they are ordinarily masked out so the sky colors (usually in aniline dyes, sometimes thin caseins) can be sprayed over them. The maskings are made of heavy gray bogus paper and cut out with scissors to fit the shapes of the particular clouds. Allow at least 2 inches of space from the edge of the gray paper to the outline of the clouds, lightly sketched in charcoal. Then place small metal weights near the edge of the paper to hold the maskings while the sky is being sprayed.

To keep the clouds from having a "hard edge" around them, sawdust can be generously sprinkled around the outside edge of the paper masking to form an irregularly shaped line. The idea here is to draw artistically with the sawdust the way the clouds are shaped on the design. The line of sawdust should be about 4 inches wide so that it overlaps the paper well yet goes onto the muslin. Since the color does not penetrate the sawdust, the outer edge should be varied as much as possible by sprinkling the sawdust both lightly and heavily.

When you are ready to paint, start at the top of the tacked-out drop and walk back and forth horizontally across the floor while spraying on the color or colors. Continue working downward and horizontally until the painting is finished. After the drop and the sawdust have dried, the areas of sawdust can be swept up with a broom or a commercial vacuum cleaner. Then you may apply painted detail and toning on the translucent clouds with a brush, a hand spray gun and compressor, or a natural round sponge wired to a long handle.

Priming a Reflector Drop

In the theatre, a reflector (bounce) drop is a white backdrop hung upstage of a translucent backdrop. It is normally made of canvas and is usually similar in size to the translucency. When lighting instruments are properly focused on the reflector drop, an even wash of light is bounced onto the rear of the translucency.

A white priming is used to paint this new canvas backdrop, and it is sprayed and brushed on the fabric in the same manner in which a backdrop is starched, but it does not have to be smoothed out. The backdrop is first tacked out on the floor; then, beginning at the top, two painters (one spraying and the other brushing) walk back and forth horizontally until the painting is finished. It is completely primed in "one shot."

So that the priming does not crack when the drop is folded or rolled, flexible slab glue dissolved in water is used for the dry whiting. To mix the priming for the reflector drop, use these proportions:

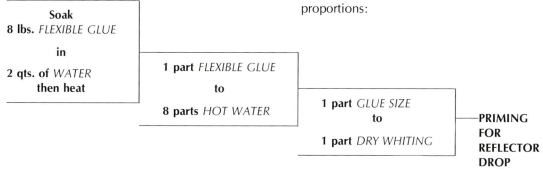

Sizing an Asbestos Curtain

Always size an asbestos curtain before painting; otherwise it absorbs paint as it is being applied like an ink blotter. This curtain, which is extremely heavy, hangs downstage in the smoke pocket against the proscenium wall, and in case of fire on stage is used to separate the stage area from the house. This curtain is also lowered when the theatre is not in use.

Occasionally the asbestos curtain is painted or decorated with designs. Both this and the sizing may sometimes be done in the theatre in which it is hanging. In this case, scaffolding and ladders must be set up so the painters can reach the height of the curtain. When the curtain is sized and painted in the scenic studio, it is executed on the floor like a regular backdrop. Common wallpaper paste, mixed with water in the same proportions as those for hanging paper, is used as a sizing to coat the asbestos before painting.

A large priming brush is good for applying the mixed paste over the surface of the curtain,

and the brush is worked in all directions to smooth it out. When this sizing has thoroughly dried, it is ready to be painted.

Pour	WALLPAPER
1 lb. of dry powdered *WHEAT PASTE*	PASTE
into	FOR SIZING
2½ qts. of warm or cold *WATER*	ASBESTOS CURTAIN

Gluing Back the Edges of a Cut Drop with Rubber Cement

When time is short and one cannot wait for white flexible glue to dry, rubber cement is effective for gluing back the edges of the muslin fabric on a cut drop or separate legs or borders designed to hang without benefit of scenic netting or one of the gauzes. Whether the openings are to be cut out of a drop of painted architecture or out of draperies, 2 inches of excess fabric should be allowed around the line of these openings, so they can be folded back and

Setting by John Conklin
BEATRIX CENCI by Alberto Ginastera
Libretto by William Shand and Alberto Gerri
Directed by Gerald Freedman

Costumes by Theoni V. Aldredge
Lighting by Hans Sondheimer
New York City Opera, New York State Theatre (1973)
(Photograph – © 1974 Beth Bergman)

The action takes place behind a sharkstooth scrim with roots painted on the front.

glued to keep them from curling when they hang on stage. The cutting with scissors can be done on the front of the drop (or when it is turned, on the back side), since an inked line must bleed through onto the reverse so one can see just where to fold back and press down the fabric. The inking on the front may be put on with a felt-tip pen or by brushing on a line with a thin mixture of aniline dye and shellac.

Once the painting on the muslin cut drop is finished and the unwanted fabric has been cut away, the drop is turned over on the back so the gluing can begin. The 2-inch width of the fabric being turned back must be slashed perpendicular to the line with the scissors to let the muslin fold neatly, taking the shape of the profile around the desired openings. To make certain

that the fabric holds, two applications of full-strength rubber cement are put on, both on the fabric being folded back and the fabric under it. For application, the rubber cement is poured from its container into a paint tray and is put on rapidly with a 4-inch-long paint roller. After the first coat of rubber cement is applied, the second application is put on the same way, just before the slashed pieces are ready to be pressed firmly into place. If there are any sharply cut corners in the profile of the cut openings that might cause the material to tear easily during handling, they should be strengthened on the back with a diagonal patch before the 2-inch excess of fabric is pressed down. This is done by gluing a 2-by-6-inch strip of canvas close to the corner on an angle, then the tabs.

Setting by Lynn Pecktal (below)
CAT ON A HOT TIN ROOF by Tennessee Williams
Directed by Don Weightman
Lighting by Albin Aukerlund
Costumes by Marianna Elliott
Barter Theatre, Abingdon, Virginia (1959)
Pictured: Mitchell Ryan, Marcie Hubert
(Photograph – Douglas Patterson)

The set consisted of three framed portals with gauze draperies, an upstage gauze drop with muslin appliqués (shutters, columns, and balusters), and a muslin backdrop painted with aniline dyes. A series of platform units (upstage), a chandelier, and furniture completed the setting.

Stage design by Sandro La Ferla
SEBASTIAN
Music by Gian-Carlo Menotti
Choreography by Vincente Nebrada
Harkness Ballet
Harkness Theatre, New York (1974)

La Ferla's setting had details painted on a sharkstooth scrim hanging upstage of cut leg drops.

DESIGNS USING GAUZES

GAUZES

The Gauze Family

The gauze family—sharkstooth scrim, linen scrim, bobbinet, opera net, and cheesecloth—has long been popular in every type of theatrical production, from ballet to opera and from drama to musical comedy. Gauzes have numerous uses. The appearance and success of the gauze drop onstage depends on the tight control of the stage lighting. A scrim appears opaque or solid when it is lighted on a sharp angle from the front, and when lights are brought up behind, it becomes transparent. A scene in the theatre is often played in front of a scrim (which can be anything from a show curtain to an abstractly painted drop), then the lights cross-fade to introduce a complete new scene behind it, after which the gauze flies out. A scene can also take place in front of a scrim drop while another vignette is tightly lighted behind it. Usually it is necessary to hang a dark or black drop (of velour, duvetyne, or duck) behind the scrim when it

Sharkstooth Scrim

The most prominent fabric in the gauze family is the sharkstooth scrim. It is woven with a vertical rectangular or ladder pattern and is made in widths of 30 feet (varies from 28 to 29 feet or more). When the full width is used, the selvage edges become the top and bottom edges of the backdrop. Standard colors are white, black, and sky-blue. While this medium-weight fabric is one of the most expensive gauzes, it is usually the ideal one to use because it provides both excellent opacity and transparency and hangs extremely well. It also takes dyes and opaque colors nicely. Besides functioning as an unframed drop, scrim is used as a covering material for various framed units where a transparent effect is desired. They may be units like foliage, banners, flags, signs, or abstract designs that have an

Linen Scrim (Linen Gauze or Theatrical Gauze)

Linen scrim is a closely woven lightweight fabric that comes in a natural linen color. It is made in widths of 6, 12, and 15 feet and offers more transparency than sharkstooth scrim, but the size of the linen widths sometimes limits its use. Linen scrim is most often used for hanging gauze panels or for full-size drops where the appearance of the seams do not hinder the design visually. More often than not, these seams are artistically disguised by the designer to include opaque designs such as ironed-on appliqués, squeezed-on latex patterns, or applied details cut out

Bobbinet

A very lightweight gauze of hexagonal mesh, bobbinet comes in widths of 30 feet; the size of the mesh varies. The large-size mesh is similar to mosquito netting. Weiss bobbinet (I. Weiss & Sons) is a fine mesh and comes 218 inches wide. Bobbinet is the most fragile of the gauzes and requires very delicate handling to prevent its being torn. It gives maximum transparency when lighted from behind, but the surface opacity is secondary. Bobbinet is frequently used

Scenic Netting

Scenic netting is made in a natural mesh of 1-inch squares and comes in widths of 30 feet. Very much like fishnet, it is standard for supporting cut drops or independent cut-out designs. These designs are usually flat painted trees, foliage, architecture, and drapery cut from muslin or cotton canvas duck. They are especially effective in the ballet and opera, both for realistic and stylized designs. Many other kinds and shapes of lightweight fabrics can also be cut out and applied to netting. On stage, the netting may be designed to hang in a large rectangular or square piece, or it

Opera Net

Opera net, a heavy open fabric, has a large rectangular woven mesh and is quite strong. Made in a natural color, the height ranges from 24 feet to 29 feet 6 inches, and the length is usually made up in 20 to 24 yards, thus creating greater waste and making it more expensive than other gauzes. The effect created by opera net is not vastly different from that of sharkstooth scrim.

Paint elevation for a scrim show curtain by John Scheffler
LA PÉRICHOLE by Jacques Offenbach
Directed by James de Blasis
Houston Grand Opera Company (1974)

A rendering in $\frac{1}{4}$-in. scale for a scrim (60 by 30 ft.), designed so that the scene behind could be introduced by bleeding through with light. Monogram on the curtain is of Don Andres, Viceroy of Peru around the turn of the century.

is on stage to keep the front lighting from hitting the setting directly in back of it; this back-up drop is flown out just before the fade-through of the scrim.

For sheer mood, ranging from the romantic to the mysterious, whole scenes are sometimes dramatically lighted and played behind a dark scrim or bobbinet drop, especially in opera. At the same time, this highly theatrical effect can be heightened by the use of moving light projections on the gauze. In other instances, painted scrims or bobbinets can be hung in front of a backdrop or cyc to give the illusion of great depth, provide an atmospheric feeling of mist and fog, or just create a stage picture that is in very soft focus. Both sharkstooth and linen scrim are used extensively for hanging panels, curtains, and banners as well as for covering materials on many framed units.

outline of metal or wood to which the scrim is adhered, usually with a white synthetic glue. Other uses of scrim include supporting cut drops and as a covering material for sculptured scenery. Although sharkstooth scrim is normally 28 to 29 feet or more for the 30-foot width, I. Weiss and Sons in New York employs a technique that enables them to double the height with a practically invisible joint. In other words, you could have a sharkstooth scrim that is 56 feet high (greater or less), depending on the design requirements. As a surface material for texture on flats, sharkstooth scrim is sometimes put on over new canvas-covered flats. The scrim is wrapped around all four edges (stiles and rails) and stapled on the back. Both the scrim and canvas on the face are painted at one time.

of muslin or canvas. The seams may hang either horizontally or vertically. Like sharkstooth scrim, small cut pieces of linen scrim are frequently used as a covering material on Styrofoam sculpture, plywood appliqués, and the like. Linen scrim, if not ordered bleached or sprayed beforehand with a light and thin opaque color, can limit the use of pale aniline dye colors. This gauze fabric may also be purchased in colors in 50-inch widths.

to create an illusion of distance in front of a sky drop and also for supporting lightweight fabric appliqués, either as a full-size drop or as a cut drop. For covering scenery like built window units, bobbinet may have lettering or ornament cut out of iron-on fabric affixed to it. Occasionally a piece of black bobbinet is stretched over a borrowed or rented painting to subdue its brightness. Bobbinet comes in white, black, and sky-blue.

can be cut in a very irregular shape. Netting should always be cut vertically and horizontally along the lines of the mesh so it will hang properly. Netting can also function as a purely decorative element instead of as a support for anything. It is sometimes dyed and used as a material for making see-through draperies. Pieces of netting in various sizes are frequently glued on three-dimensional trees, rocks, and sculpture to produce more texture and body. To further enhance this texture, a thick mixture of scenic dope is brushed over the applied netting, then it is painted.

Cheesecloth

Because cheesecloth is not a practical or durable fabric for large areas of scenery, its theatrical use is limited. This loose and open-weave fabric easily snags and does not hold its shape. Cheesecloth can be purchased bleached and unbleached in bolts of 3-foot width; pieces are used mostly for straining paint and liquid starch, for making pounce bags, and for covering sculpture (Styrofoam, plaster, and so on) with finely shaped details that are not to be obliterated.

Fine bobbinet

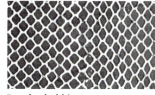
Regular bobbinet

Linen scrim

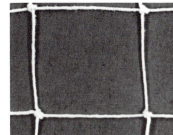
Scenic netting

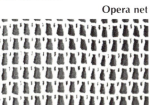
Opera net

Cheesecloth

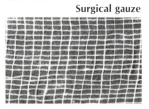
Surgical gauze

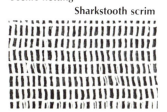
Sharkstooth scrim

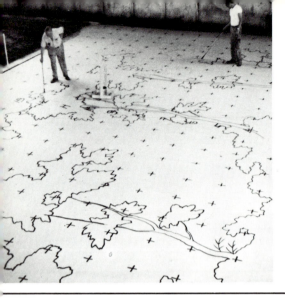

The grid and outlines of David Walker's foliage design for the Joffrey Ballet's THE DREAM (1973) were laid out on gray bogus paper before stapling the scrim backdrop (30 by 48 ft.) on it for painting.

Steps of Execution:
1. Sketch in $\frac{1}{2}$-in. scale was covered with acetate and marked off in 2-ft. squares.
2. 2-ft. squares in full scale snapped in charcoal and numbered on gray paper.
3. Charcoal drawing and Xs denoting squares (left) were inked with black paint to be seen through the scrim.
4. Scrim drop stapled over gray paper, trees and foliage painted (right). (Photographs – Lynn Pecktal)

Drawing on Paper under the Scrim

One of the easiest and most practical ways to lay out the drawing on a scrim drop for painting is to draw on the gray paper laid on the floor before the scrim is put on top of it. Although the heavy gray paper is used primarily to keep the fabric clean and to absorb the water in the paint, it also serves as a drawing surface, since the drawn lines can easily be seen through the scrim. Once the long strips of paper are laid, place small pieces of masking tape at random along the edges to hold them together. Then mark off the large area of paper in 2-foot squares.

The drawing on the gray paper is done first in charcoal (held in a long bamboo stick), and the drawn lines can be improved if necessary when they are permanently inked. For inking under the scrim, use black paint to make the drawing clearly visible when the scrim is tacked over it. (This should be a black vinyl or latex paint that holds well on

Tacking down a Scrim

A sharkstooth scrim is tacked on the floor for painting in the same manner as other backdrops; here too the top with the webbing is always attached first. Once this is done, the most important single feature in tacking a scrim is to make certain that the rectangular patterns of the fabric are stretched out vertically in a straight line. The way a sharkstooth scrim is stretched out on the floor for painting in the scenic studio is the way it will hang after it is in the theatre. Always tack down a scrim without excessive stretching. Like a muslin or canvas backdrop, the height measurement for the bottom line of the scrim is found by measuring at center from the already-tacked top down to the loose bottom. The bottom should be stretched and pulled down with both hands, again at center, allowed to be relaxed and lie naturally flat, then marked at the bottom. The height measurement is now taken with the tape measure from the very top of the scrim to this bottom mark. This procedure is used because scrim always varies when

Pouncing on Scrims

Placement of the brown-paper pounce on a full-size scrim drop is located by matching the center line of the pounce with the center line of the scrim. You do not start from either end, because drops can vary in width when they are made up. The bottom of the perforated pounce should always be even with the bottom of the scrim, and weights are essential to keep the paper pounce from moving when you are walking on it to dust the charcoal bag over the perforated designs. Gallon cans of unopened paint can be placed on each corner.

Stenciling on a Scrim

Applying painted patterns with a stencil to scrim is done as on other scenic fabrics, whether unframed backdrops or framed wings. For scrim, the paint should be thin enough to work well on the material, and a natural sponge is one of the best applicators. While a brush can be used, if the paint fills the holes and dries in them they appear as opaque blobs when lighted from behind.

Ironing Appliqués on Scrim

Iron-on fabric is generally applied after the scrim has been painted, and proper positioning of the cutout appliqués sometimes necessitates repouncing of the drawing. All of the iron-on fabric should be cut out at one time and or-

Spraying Scrim with White Latex Paint

White latex paint sprayed lightly on a new scrim already tacked on the floor works nicely if the scrim is to have intricate and detailed designs painted on it. The flexible latex holds the shape of the scrim after it dries and produces an excellent base coat when aniline dyes are being used. Equally important, latex spraying puts a new paint surface on the entire fabric to eliminate the possibility of lights picking up the bare dyed areas differently from the ones painted with opaque paint. For example, a pale sky that has clouds painted in dye may need a few corrections in opaque color. When lighted, these few brush strokes may "pop out" as much lighter even though they matched in color and

John Conklin's sharkstooth scrim for the Pennsylvania Ballet's THE NUTCRACKER, Act II (1972)

Steps of Execution:

1. Scrim drop stapled on the floor over gray bogus paper.
2. Horizontal blends sprayed on with aniline dyes in tanks.
3. Design transferred to scrim with perforated paper pounce.
4. Architecture laid in and painted with casein paints, applied with very dry brushes. White oil paint, excellent to stop aniline dyes from bleeding through paint, was brushed on sparsely for lights and highlights.

---

the paper and does not bleed into the fabric when the water and color are applied on top.) This method of drawing on gray paper eliminates making and perforating a large brown-paper pounce as well as the chance of losing the pounced charcoal line during the painting. It is very helpful if the intersections

of the lines forming the 2-foot squares are marked in black with an X. These can become guides for painting while looking at the corresponding gridded squares on the color sketch. This method, of course, works best where the design does not really have a lot of details on it. It is ideal for doing a sky

with cumulus clouds, for example, or for a landscape that has simple trees and foliage. For highly detailed work the ordinary paper pounce is more appropriate.

---

it is made up into a backdrop. For instance, a scrim designed to have a height of 30 feet could really be around 29 feet 6 inches, or even 29 feet 8 inches. It is thus impossible to snap a square or rectangular perimeter beforehand and have it come out the proper size of the scrim backdrop without guessing.

If the height measurement has proved too much for the stretch of the fabric when tacking out a scrim, raise the bottom line an inch or two rather than risk a tear in the fabric or struggle to make all the sides meet the snapped lines. On a scrim, the staples are tacked much closer together than on a muslin drop, since a scrim tightens more when wet

than muslin. Linen scrim and bobbinet offer very little stretch when tacking a backdrop of either on the floor. Both should also be squared off for tacking by snapping lines on all four sides.

A pounce of half a symmetrical drop or detail repeated on the scrim requires care when dusting with the charcoal. The excess charcoal can spill off the edge of the paper onto the new scrim

and a dusty charcoal line will appear on the fabric. To avoid this, mask the sides of the pounce with additional strips of paper. If a paper pounce is to be reserved and repeated, always dust ex-

cess charcoal off well with a feather duster or flogger before turning it over.

---

ganized in piles before the ironing is started. A very hot household iron is needed to make it adhere sufficiently. When pressing, place a piece of muslin over the iron-on fabric, especially if small pieces are being put on, to pre-

vent scorching the scrim. The same basic rules apply when adhering iron-on fabric to bobbinet, but bobbinet is extremely fragile and can burn very easily. A clean metal tray (like those used for paint rollers) makes a good resting

place for the hot iron when not in use. If a piece of the iron-on fabric must be removed, run the hot iron over it and quickly lift the fabric off. You can expect the adhesive to leave a mark on the fabric and may need to paint over it.

---

value in the studio. The latex, put on with a Hudson sprayer, is thinned first with water and is mixed in these proportions:

1 part *LATEX PAINT*
to
3 parts *WATER*

WHITE LATEX TO BE SPRAYED ON A SCRIM

The mixture should be strained before pouring it into the spray tank.

315

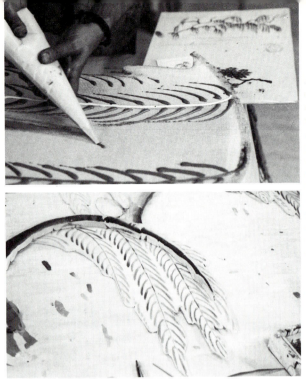

A mixture of latex and casein paint (1 part pure clear liquid latex thoroughly mixed with 1 part undiluted casein paste) is ideal for creating decorative patterns on framed or unframed scrim. This thick mixture is easily squeezed out of a wax-paper cone to draw foliage on a set piece covered with sharkstooth scrim (glued to an iron frame) designed by Oliver Smith for LOVELY LADIES, KIND GENTLEMEN (1971). Finished pieces are attached to $\frac{3}{4}$-in. plywood limbs covered with white velour and painted with dyes. (Photographs — Arnold Abramson)

A lace pattern can be used to create an ornamental design on a sharkstooth or linen scrim, especially for musicals or ballets. The design is put on a brown-paper pounce in the desired scale and transferred to the fabric surface stapled flat to the floor over wax paper. Designs are made with opaque latex squeezed from a wax-paper cone or plastic ketchup bottle. The flower at top may be 12 to 15 in. wide on actual scenery. Lace research can include Chantilly (French or Spanish), point de Sedan, rose point or point de Gaze (French), point plat de Venise, punto in aria, and gros point de Venise (Italian).

Applying Opaque Latex Drawings on Scrim by Hand

When a scrim or other gauze (soft or framed) is designed to have opaque lines drawn and applied on it, a special mixture of one part pure clear latex such as Slomon's and one part casein paste color is used. The pure clear latex holds well on the open fabric and after drying permits flexibility in folding the drawn designs on the scrim. It is thoroughly mixed with the undiluted casein color and, after it has been stirred vigorously, becomes quite thick. No water is added to the casein paste; it is always used as it comes out of the container, as is the concentrated clear latex. For stirring, an electric hand mixer is ideal.

So it will not dry out, the mixture is not made up until it is to be used. For

> **Mix**
>
> **1 part** *PURE CLEAR LATEX* **(undiluted)**
>
> **with**
>
> **1 part** *CASEIN PASTE COLOR* **(undiluted)**
>
> **stirring thoroughly until it becomes very thick**

MIXTURE FOR APPLYING OPAQUE LATEX DESIGNS ON SCRIM (or other gauzes)

the same reason, great quantities should not be mixed very far ahead. The whole success of this process is to apply the latex drawing on the fabric with consistency and evenness, making clean-cut lines, so when the scrim is lighted from behind they are neat and completely opaque. This mixture can be used for any number of designs, from enormous patterns of Venetian lace on gauze panels to a scrim show curtain with a Ronald Searle type of drawing on it, plus an abundance of other varied subjects.

For application, pour the latex mixture into a commercial plastic mustard

Gluing a Cut Drop to a Scrim

Before a cut drop is glued to a scrim that supports it when hanging, the scrim is usually painted, and in most cases the cut drop itself is also painted. Since the finished cut drop must be lifted up and turned over, then placed face down for the scrim to be adhered to the back, all the canvas (or muslin) profile edges on the drop must be completely trimmed beforehand. After the cut drop has been turned over and accurately laid out face down, its outer edges are stapled just enough to hold it in place. Then the painted scrim (also face-down) is positioned directly on top of the openings in the cut drop, and it too is stapled neatly around the four edges. All the edges on both the cut drop and the scrim (one on top of the other) should be as parallel to each other as possible.

Flexible white glue that dries clear

Dyeing Scenic Netting

The use of netting on stage ordinarily requires that the natural color be dyed. The darker the color of the netting, the more it will disappear visually when properly lighted. As a consequence, most netting is dyed either black or dark blue. To dye a piece of netting 30 feet high by 48 feet wide, a container capable of holding at least 20 gallons is needed. This may be a 20-gallon galvanized barrel or, ideally, a long metal trough that will hold the same amount of dye. The trough usually has to be specially constructed.

To mix black dye for the netting, first measure out a full quart of dry black crystals into a container. Dissolve this quart of crystals by slowly pouring it into 3 gallons of boiling water while stirring. You should then pour the 3 gallons of black aniline dye into 17 gallons of cold or warm water.

Always wear rubber gloves while dipping the netting and when removing it

Paint elevation for a backdrop by Oliver Smith
WINESBURG, OHIO
Dramatized by Christopher Sergel from the
    book by Sherwood Anderson

Staged by Joseph Anthony
National Theatre, New York (1958)
(Photograph — Arnold Abramson; sketch — collection of
    Mr. Abramson)

The Palais Royal backdrop on muslin for
IRENE (1973), designed by Raoul
Pène du Bois. Windows and lamps
were translucent, the rest opaque.

STEPS OF EXECUTION:
1. Backdrop starched after stapling
   over gray paper.
2. 2-ft. squares snapped lightly in
   charcoal for drawing.
3. Charcoal drawing inked with felt-tip
   pen.
4. Walls, molding, sidewalk, steps, and
   general areas laid in with casein
   paints. Lettering, ornament, and
   other details painted with casein
   paints and aniline dyes.
5. Windows and lamps (to be translucent)
   laid in and painted with aniline dyes.
   Portions of patterns on window
   shades were stenciled, then painted
   freehand.
6. Grillwork on railing, lamps, and
   above entrance painted last.
7. Backdrop turned over and stapled
   in place for opaquing with latex
   paint, brushing around inked window
   and lamp lines that bleed through
   the muslin.
   (Photographs — Lynn Pecktal)

Paint elevation for a backdrop by John Scheffler   Directed by Roy Lazarus
MADAMA BUTTERFLY by Giacomo Puccini   Oberlin Music Theatre
Libretto by Luigi Illica and Giuseppe Giacosa   Oberlin, Ohio (1970)

A combination of dyes and opaque paints were used
to paint this muslin backdrop (40 by 29 ft.), which had a
translucent sky. The drop was used for all three acts.

PAINTING REALISTIC FOLIAGE ON A MUSLIN BACKDROP. Carl Toms' realistic foliage drop
for I PURITANI (1973) at the New York City Opera (painted in four days).

STEPS OF EXECUTION:
1. Drop stapled on the floor over gray bogus paper.
2. In 2-ft. squares, main clumps of foliage drawn lightly in charcoal, then inked with a felt-tip pen.
3. Sky and water areas laid in with mixtures of starch and casein colors, applied with Hudson
   tanks, smoothed out by brushing. Foliage background next laid in on the sides and bottom.
   Colors were casein and aniline dyes. Order of brushing on foliage colors: (1) Middle tones (about
   four), (2) dark tones, (3) light tones. Care taken to brush dark tones behind the areas where
   light leaves would be. All dark tones were semitransparent, all light tones opaque.

PHOTOGRAPHS:
1. Applying clumps of leaves with middle tones (using a 3-in. Fitch brush) on left of the backdrop.
2. Same foliage area after it has been finished.
3-5. Views of completed foliage.
6. Close-up view of light leaves being added with a 1¼-in. detail brush.
(Painting by John Keck; photographs—Lynn Pecktal)

Paint elevations of draperies by Peter Larkin
GOLDILOCKS
Book by Walter and Jean Kerr
Music by LeRoy Anderson
Lyrics by Joan Ford, Walter and Jean Kerr
Directed by Walter Kerr
Lunt-Fontanne Theatre, New York (1958)
(Photographs — Arnold Abramson)

(Left) A linen leg, 10 ft. wide by 40 ft. high, for the ballet PULCINELLA (1972), designed by Eugene Berman.
STEPS OF EXECUTION:
(1) Linen leg stapled over gray bogus paper. (2) Leg primed with blue starch applied with a Hudson spray tank, smoothed out with a large priming brush. (3) 2-ft. squares snapped in charcoal; design then drawn with charcoal. (4) Drawing inked with black casein paint. (5) Drapery and wood painted with casein paints and aniline dyes applied by brush.

Stapled on the floor are Oliver Smith's draperies (on linen) for SLEEPING BEAUTY (1974), American Ballet Theatre.
STEPS OF EXECUTION:
(1) Medium tones (starch and casein paints) sprayed as lay-in on the linen following sweeps of drapery folds. (2) Dark tones (casein paints and aniline dyes) applied with a synthetic-sponge mop. (3) Lights and highlights (casein paints) put on with a square sponge. (4) A latex size (1 qt. heavy clear latex to 4 gals. water) was used to thin the casein paints and to make the caseins and aniline dyes hold better on the fabric. (5) Pounces drawn for tassel fringe, then painted after drapery was finished. (Photographs — Lynn Pecktal)

Stage design by Lynn Pecktal
LUCIA DI LAMMERMOOR
  by Gaetano Donizetti
Libretto by
  Salvatore Cammarano
Act III, scene 2
Directed by
  David Bamberger
Corporacion de Arte Lirico,
  Teatro Municipal
Santiago, Chile (1970)

The architectural units upstage
of the dimensional platform and
stair units were designed to be
painted on canvas, cut out, and
glued to scenic netting. A
translucent muslin drop hung
upstage.

or ketchup squeeze bottle or put it into a wax-paper cone, which you can make. In either case, the mixture is squeezed onto the fabric by hand. A wax-paper container for holding the latex mixture is made by first cutting a piece of wax paper 18 by 36 inches and giving it one fold so it becomes an 18-inch square. Assume that one of the corners of this square is to form the point of the cone and an opposite corner in a diagnoal direction is to become the top. Starting at one edge of the side of the square, roll this paper tightly into a cone shape. Use a long strip of masking tape on the outer straight edge to hold it together. Also place a piece of tape on the tip of the cone, since the desired opening on

the top is not cut until the cone is filled. Several of these cones can be made up at one time so you do not have to interrupt the application process to make new ones.

Before applying latex on the scrim, lay strips of wax paper under the fabric to prevent sticking to the surface underneath. The technique of applying the opaque latex to the fabric is very similar to that of decorating a birthday cake and is really a matter of drawing with the latex container. If the wax-paper cone is being used, fill with the latex mixture one at a time. Secure the top of the cone by pressing the edges of the top flat together and roll them down. Attach them with masking tape. The

cone must be securely taped or leakage will occur. As the latex is used, the cone is rolled down from the top. When ready, cut a hole in the tip of the paper cone with scissors. The size of this hole determines the width of the latex flow and sometimes requires experimenting before you start. While the usual widths of the squeezed latex are $\frac{1}{4}$ to $\frac{3}{4}$ inch, an allowance should be made in the cut opening, because the latex tends to widen a bit as it settles and dries on the fabric. If you are using a plastic bottle, one hand holds and guides the tip and the other hand squeezes the bottle to force the mixture out gently. This requires some practice to achieve regularity and precision.

(like Sobo) can be applied on the scrim and will soak through to the fabric of the cut drop underneath. First brush an inch width of the glue on the back of the scrim wherever the cut edges of the fabric appear under it. These cut edges are easily seen through the scrim. Sec-

ond, brush another line of glue 2 inches wide on the extreme top, extreme sides, and—whenever it applies—on the bottom. If cut pieces of muslin or canvas must be glued on the scrim from the face, wax paper should always be laid under the scrim before starting work so

it does not stick to the floor or gray paper underneath.

from the dye, to protect your hands. The netting should remain in the dye until it is well soaked. After it has soaked sufficiently, remove and hang it up to dry on a batten suspended in the air. If a batten is unavailable, the netting can be laid out on the floor and dried on top of gray paper.

1 qt. of dry *BLACK ANILINE DYE CRYSTALS*

dissolved in

3 gals. of *BOILING WATER*

then poured into

17 gals. of *COLD OR WARM WATER*

MIXING BLACK ANILINE
DYE FOR NETTING
30' BY 48'

FABRICS AND MATERIALS

Muslin

Muslin is a plain-weave cotton fabric made in widths of 6, 9, 15, 19, and 34 feet. After flameproofing, the widths become a little less—the 6-feet becomes 5 feet 9 inches, the 9-feet becomes 8 feet 6 inches, and so on. Widely used for regular backdrops and translucent backdrops (with seams and without), muslin is made in degrees of fineness, a factor that should definitely be considered when ordering; 140 muslin indicates the fabric has 70 threads

Enameling Duck

Enameling duck is the standard cotton canvas duck for covering ordinary stage flats and most set pieces with profiled edges. It is referred to by *weight in ounces* per square yard when it is ordered instead of by numbers. Eight-ounce enameling duck is the average weight used on typical scenic flats and has two-ply cotton threads running vertically (warp) and horizontally (filling). It is manufactured 6 feet wide and shrinks to about 5 feet 9 inches after flameproofing. If a much wider piece of duck is needed for covering, such as that for a two-fold or three-fold flat unit,

Duck Canvas

Duck canvas is a heavy plain-weave cotton fabric used for ground cloths. It is selected by *the numbered ducks* that denote the construction and the weight of the fabric; the smaller the number, the heavier the weight of the fabric. Number 8 duck canvas is the standard fabric for making ground cloths. In this particular canvas, there are three plys of cotton in the warp and filling, the strongest construction in ducks. Because of wear, including wagon casters

Linen Canvas

Linen canvas, a strong plain-weave fabric, is made of flax fiber. The tooth or texture can range from smooth to slubbed (irregular twisting of threads). Although this durable lustrous fabric offers a superior painting surface, it is used infrequently in the commercial theatre, mostly because of its high cost. It is made in varying widths from 36 to

Velour and Duvetyne

Velour
Velour has a heavy-pile weave and a very rich texture that absorbs light beautifully. More than any other fabric, it gives infinite depth to a background, especially when dark colors are selected. It can be obtained in several weights: 26-ounce (heavy), 24-ounce, 19-ounce, and 17-ounce (light). The 19-ounce weight is average for scenic work. This velvetlike fabric comes 54 inches wide in black and white and in numerous colors, including royal blue, sapphire blue, bright turquoise, sage green, hunter green, gold, brown, beige, gray, rust, wine, red, and purple. Velour is made primarily of cotton but is sometimes woven in mohair or wool. The cotton is used universally for theatrical scenery. Among its vast number of uses, velour functions as an excellent covering material for framed portals, flats, profiled set pieces, and three-dimensional built units. It is used often as

China Silk and Bengaline

China Silk
This soft, lightweight fabric has a plain weave and comes in widths of 36, 40, and 50 inches, depending on weight. Available in many colors, China silk is a decorative fabric for show curtains (with or without fullness), banners, flags, stylized arrangements of drapery, or free-flowing hanging patterns. For ballet or musicals, an elaborate effect of moving water can be achieved with a large piece of China silk made by sewing several widths together and then hemming it. The effect is accomplished by laying the fabric flat on the stage floor like a ground cloth and, with someone holding each of the four corners, the big piece of lightweight silk is lifted off the floor just enough so that it can be waved freely to get air under it. When you are painting on China silk, it is most helpful if Methocel (a water-soluble gum) is added to the mixed aniline dyes or thin caseins to keep them from run-

Burlap, Erosion Cloth, Monk's Cloth

Burlap
A plain woven fabric of jute in various weights, burlap is made in a natural color with widths ranging from 3 to 8 feet and can be obtained in colors in 4-foot widths. The rough-textured fabric is ideal for covering surfaces on scenery, particularly platforms and solidly backed set pieces, but it is also good for soft scenery like rustic curtains and drops. In shaping sculptured scenery, pieces of burlap are most useful when dipped in a mixture of plaster of Paris or scenic dope and applied on a framework of wire and wood.

Erosion Cloth
Erosion cloth is an extremely heavy rope cloth made of hemp that is available in 3-foot widths. It can be obtained from Dazian's or I. Weiss & Sons in New

| Muslin | Canvas | Velour | Nubby bleached linen | Monk's cloth |

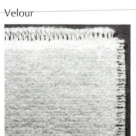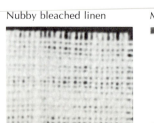

running vertically and 70 running horizontally per square inch. This is the best number to use for translucent backdrops and for taking paint well. A thinner weight is 128 muslin (64 vertical and 64 horizontal threads). Sometimes this is used when the better 140 muslin is unavailable. As a covering material for regular flats, muslin is not ordinarily used unless some translucent effect is involved.

the required widths of canvas are stitched together on the sewing machine, using face-to-face seams. This allows the whole unit to be covered with one complete piece of fabric and eliminates the need for a canvas "dutchman" or overlapping the widths on each other. The fabric should be glued on the wooden stiles on which hinges are attached to eliminate slack when the unit folds.

rolling on it, No. 8 duck has been found to be the best weight for making ground cloths. It comes 6 feet wide and, when widths of the canvas are sewed together for joining, creates fewer seams for the stage wagons to roll over. These seams between the widths of duck are stitched twice on the sewing machine by using a lap seam for strength and to keep the material flat. When a colored base is desired, the most satisfactory results are obtained by using dyed duck.

90 inches, but the most popular widths range from 48 to 72 inches. For theatrical use, it comes both natural (unbleached) and white (bleached). White linen is sometimes preferred when aniline dyes are being applied. Being so durable a fabric, the Metropolitan Opera covers most of its scenery with linen canvas as well as using it for backdrops.

an unframed material for backdrops, legs, and borders. With its ability to hang and drape well, velour is often selected as a fabric for stage draperies that serve as full settings and also for dressing individual sets. The seams are positioned vertically with the nap running down. Sometimes, however, when it is desired to have the color of the velour fabric appear darker on drops or flats, the direction of the nap is reversed and placed so that it all runs upward.

Duvetyne
Duvetyne is an inexpensive substitute for velour, but it is not as effective on stage. Made of cotton sheeting that is napped to give it a suede finish, it comes in widths of 36 and 54 inches and can be purchased in black and white and many stock colors, including blue, red, pink, wine, green, gray, brown, tan, and gold.

ning on the fabric when they are being applied. It is also a good idea to lightly spray the China silk (stretched out and stapled on the floor) before painting on it.

Bengaline
Since this ribbed fabric hangs beautifully and takes stage lighting nicely, it is a splendid material for show curtains and traveler curtains that have fullness; and also for draperies that are to be used for set dressing. It has a semilustrous finish and comes in widths from 44 to 48 inches. Bengaline is made in white, black, and a variety of colors including red, wine, blue, green, brown, gray, and gold. If you are painting on Bengaline, Methocel should be mixed with the colors as a binder to keep them from spreading on the fabric.

York City. The large, irregularly shaped threads and the very open weave make it possible to create unusually heavy textures for scenery, whether it is glued on a surface or allowed to hang loosely as panels, a backdrop, or drapery.

Monk's Cloth
Monk's cloth is a heavy cotton fabric in a basket weave (two by two threads or four by four threads) that works well for wall hangings where a tapestry appearance is desired. It also can be used for curtains and drops. Since it pulls and ravels easily, all cut edges must be finished by hemming. The natural color is frequently used for painting, but it can also be done on assorted colors of monk's cloth. Monk's cloth is available in 4-foot widths.

Repp	Coarse burlap	Regular burlap	Erosion cloth	Rug padding

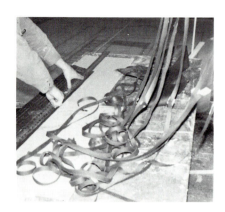

For a bus and truck company of NO, NO, NANETTE (1973), Raoul Pène du Bois' ornamental railing, originally a built unit, was cut out of iron-on fabric and pressed on a linen scrim panel already adhered to the cut backdrop. The heavy-duty iron rested on a metal paint tray.

1-in.-wide strips of iron-on fabric were cut with a single-edge razor blade and held against a metal straightedge to make mullions for windows backed with linen scrim. All guidelines on the black iron-on material were snapped in white chalk before any cutting was begun.

Iron-on Fabric

Iron-on fabric is made with a rubbery backing for easy application with a household iron and is excellent for many types of appliqués where a neat, clean outline and total opaqueness are required. Black and white iron-on fabrics are the most commonly used in the scenic studio, but almost any kind and color of fabric can be selected by the designer and sent out to have backing applied. Iron-on fabric is excellent for applying opaque designs on sharkstooth scrim, linen scrim, bobbinet, and buckram, as well as on muslin and canvas or such materials as screen wire. Sometimes the designer may choose to use iron-on appliqués of satin or ultraviolet fabrics, for example, on the face of a drop as a purely decorative element where the color and texture of the fabric itself are part of the design rather than an opaque effect.

The design to be executed is laid out or pounced either on the face or the back of the fabric, then cut out with scissors or a single-edge razor blade. If the iron-on fabric is to be painted before it is put on, the medium is usually aniline dyes or caseins, and the results are best if painting is done before the cutting. The fabric can be painted after it has been adhered, but it may have to be pressed again with the iron if it gets too wet during the painting and the edges begin to curl during drying.

A very hot iron is required to make the fabric hold to another material. To eliminate stretching the iron-on fabric out of shape when it is being applied, lift and lower the iron vertically rather than moving it back and forth as in regular ironing. Take care whenever using the hot iron on scrim and gauzes to avoid scorching. As a precaution, place a piece of muslin over the iron-on fabric to keep the iron from scorching both the iron-on fabric and the material it is going on.

Selected fabric to be coated with the rubbery backing can be sent to Peters Brothers Coating & Laminating Co., Brooklyn, N.Y., to be made up. The minimum order is a 100-yard roll, with widths of the fabric ranging from 36 to 48 inches. At least ten days should be allowed. Smaller quantities can be purchased from I. Weiss & Sons.

Other Fabrics and Materials

Satin
A smooth and glossy fabric, satin is made with a rayon or silk face and a cotton back. It is available in widths of 36, 45, and 50 inches and can be selected in numerous colors to produce lavish act curtains or stage draperies.

Filled Scrim
White scrim, similar to sharkstooth scrim, has the holes filled in and is well suited for cycloramas. It comes 28 feet 4 inches wide. Filled scrim is normally available in white, but will be dyed to order by I. Weiss & Sons in New York.

Flannel
For scenic use, cotton flannel is a good covering for carved Styrofoam sculpture and the like. The flannel is cut in pieces that are then coated with or dipped in scenic dope for application on the Styrofoam surface. With dope, flannel is also a choice material for modeling appliqués of ornament and molding on wooden panels. This soft-napped fabric ranges in widths from 36 to 54 inches.

Repp
Repp is available in chevron (herringbone), horizontal, and whalebone weave in widths of 4 feet and in various colors. It is used for front stage curtains, valances, and stage drapery sets.

Felt
Felt, a nonwoven fabric that has the advantage of not raveling, is made primarily of wool and cotton or wool and rayon or various mixtures that are matted together by heat and moisture under great pressure. Available in different weights, it is manufactured in 72-inch-wide rolls and can be bought in a multitude of colors. Because it can be easily cut, sewed, stapled, and glued, felt is ideal for making certain theatrical props and set pieces. Items such as leaves, flowers, or ornament can be attached flat to a flexible material, or they can be shaped dimensionally and fastened firmly in place on all sorts of rigidly carved scenery.

While the fabrics and materials discussed here are the standard ones for scenery, there are other specialty fabrics and materials a designer or artist may want to use, including fluorescent satin, jewel cloth, Las Vegas cloth, eyelash cloth, chiffon, corduroy, terry cloth, cellophane, lamé, fiber glass fabric, Mylar and other plastics.

For fabric sources and addresses, see pp. 400–401. Other sources for scenic fabrics and supplies in New York, the United States, and Canada can be found in Simon's Directory, published by Package Publicity Service, Inc., 1564 Broadway, New York, N.Y. 10036.

WINDOW DRAPERIES AND CURTAINS FOR STAGE SETTINGS

Designers are not expected to make their own draperies for a stage setting, but they must know the effect they want and furnish the proper instructions for execution. For Broadway productions, draperies are made by a drapery house. In stock, repertory, or Off Broadway, they are made up by the property master, an assistant, or anyone adept at sewing. While draperies for the stage do not always have to be constructed precisely as for the home, they must conform to the elegance or dowdiness called for in the production. You would have one kind of draperies for a lavish eighteenth-century drawing room, another kind for a modest country cottage, still another for a simple modern kitchen. The designer asks himself just what sort of draperies the inhabitant of the setting would have, taking into account the character and theatricality of the show. Points to think about always are scale, line, and proportion of the design, color and pattern of the fabric, how the fabric falls, and how well it reads from the audience.

The period and type of setting usually control the style of the drapery treatment. Draperies are used not only on windows but also on beds and canopies and in arches and alcoves. Though one may think of draperies primarily in realistic settings, draperies also include those arbitrarily arranged on fragmented pieces of scenery, free-form swags and jabots hanging independently on a batten, or a large backdrop of stage draperies in fullness hanging on a pipe. Draperies for the stage sometimes are designed so the shapes of the valances, cornices, or swags are executed in perspective. When having draperies made, it is valuable for the designer to be familiar with the materials that can be used:

Common Fabrics for Stage Draperies (or Curtains)

Velour	Bengaline	China silk
Velvet	Linen	Sharkstooth scrim
Brocade	Muslin	Polyester and cotton
Taffeta	Fiber glass	Dacron batiste
Satin	Monk's cloth	Corduroy
Nylon	Sailcloth	Denim
Chintz	Gingham	Duvetyne
Repp	Organdy	Damask

Making Draperies

Making draperies for settings is actually no different from executing them for the home. If you are not familiar with how draperies are constructed, it is easy to find a booklet at a Singer Sewing Center or read the *Better Homes & Gardens Sewing Book* or any other book that has information on how to make draperies. As a general rule, you will find that when making draperies best results are produced by pinning or basting the widths of fabric together before stitching on the machine; this also applies to sewing hems. It is often necessary to press seams flat with an iron after you sew them.

The Fullness of Draperies

Average fullness for draperies is 100 percent (see Backdrops), but this figure depends on the kind and weight of the fabric. For example, the more sheer the fabric, the more fullness is needed. Also, if the fabric has sizable patterns that must be matched, more fabric is required. When designing elegant draperies, a rather grand effect can be obtained on the bottom by having the drapery made a foot or so longer than the normal length and then letting it fall in a graceful pile on the floor.

Lined or Unlined Draperies

Most designers select fabric already knowing whether they want the draperies to be lined or unlined. Instead of the usual beige sateen lining, for the stage it can be other suitable fabric to make the draperies opaque so the light does not shine through, or perhaps a material to introduce a new color or pattern on the back side. The lining requires about as much fabric as do the draperies, but the bottom of the lining is always made a couple of inches shorter than the draperies so it does not hang below them.

Headings

The method by which draperies are treated at the top gives them unity and produces style and a specific design. The tops of draperies may be designed to be covered with a valance or cornice or to be left uncovered. When needed, stiffness in the top of headings is obtained by using a material such as buckram or crinoline sewed into the top hem. Among the headings that can be used for draperies are gathered fabric on rods, pinch pleats, box pleats, accordion pleats, scalloped tops, and straight tops with loops or rings.

Valance and Cornice Boxes

Valances, the horizontal treatment at the top of window draperies, are a matter of taste and period of the production, and not all windows

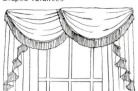

Draped valances

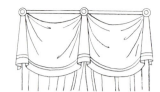

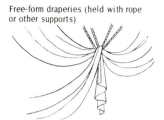

Free-form draperies (held with rope or other supports)

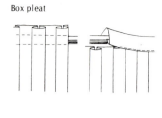

Box pleat

Cotton fringe
(in different lengths)

Chainette fringe
(2 to 38 in. long)

Banner fringe
(in different lengths)

Rayon bullion fringe
(2 to 24 in. long)

require them. Numerous shapes can be incorporated to change the horizontal line as well as increase the overall visual width and height of the actual windows or French doors. Valances can be covered in fabric to match the draperies or be in contrasting fabric. Or they can be executed with entirely different materials such as wood, felt, plaster, metal, or plastic, all designed in a variety of shapes and dimensional relief. Cornice boxes for drapery can match the architectural elements in an interior, following the treatment of the moldings and paneling. The proportion of the valance or cornice height to the drapery should be about one-eighth or 12.5 percent of the total drapery height.

Valance boxes are usually made with a framework of soft wood and covered with $\frac{1}{4}$-inch plywood or $\frac{3}{16}$-inch Masonite. The flat front of the valance box, often profiled according to the shape of the design, has a return on each end that is about 6 to 8 inches deep and a top that acts as a dust cover and stops light leaks. For stage settings, the most practical way of attaching it to the framing of the flat or window facing is by loose pin hinges. The valance box is also functional for housing the drapery rods and the hardware that holds them in place. Sometimes valance boxes are constructed only as a simple framework of wood on which to drape free-hanging swags of fabric or a flat decorative fabric shape.

Decorative Trim for Draperies

Trim comes in various materials, including cotton, silk, and rayon (solids and patterns), and metallic trims such as gold and silver are very popular for theatrical draperies. Many of the trims below can be used on other items besides draperies, among them bedspreads, bed throws, canopies, tablecloths, pillows, bolsters, cushions, tapestries, awnings, valances, lampshades, and upholstered furniture.

Fringe	Braids	Ruffles	Cordings
Ball fringe	Borders	Gimps	Appliqués
Tassel fringe	Tassels	Galoons	Sequins
Loop fringe	Roping	Laces	Beads
Bullion fringe	Ribbons	Binding tapes	Spangles

Methods of Hanging Draperies

The most usual methods of hanging draperies on the stage are similar to those used in the home:

1. Fabric hem or casing supported on wooden or metal rods.
2. Drapery hooks (drapery pins) attached to drapery and hooked on a rod.
3. Wooden, metal, or plastic rings attached to fabric and hung on rods.
4. Flat loops of fabric sewed to draperies and hung on rods.
5. Lengths of fabric draped through large rings or around other ornament.

For use strictly on the stage, the drapery can also be attached or supported by:

Webbing, grommets and tielines. For draperies that are to be tied around metal pipes or wooden battens and hung from wires and cables, webbing is sewed to the top of the drapery after the fabric has been folded back at least an inch, then grommets are attached (usually 1 foot apart on centers) and tielines are inserted. Fabric that is to have fullness or pleats is laid out accordingly and stitched to the flat webbing.

Attaching drapery with Velcro. Velcro, a nylon-tape fastener consisting of a two-part tape, is great for attaching draperies, curtains, canopies, valances, and dressing-table skirts. One part of the tape is covered with finely woven monofilaments that form permanent hooks, and the other part is covered with a pile of soft nylon loops. One tape is attached to the drapery fabric and the other is put on the surface where the drapery is to hang. For attachment, the two tapes are pressed together and the hooks stick to the loops. The tapes are separated by peeling them apart. Velcro can be put on objects by stapling, tacking, gluing, or sewing. It is also used for holding photographs and small pictures in place and for holding costume parts together until they must break away. Standard colors are black, white, and beige. A special adhesive is available for adhering Velcro.

Stapling draperies directly to the wood. This is a common practice when time is short and the budget is low. It works satisfactorily if the draperies do not

Small ball fringe

Jumbo fringe

Pompoms

Tassel fringe

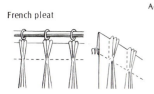
French pleat

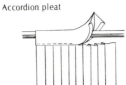
Accordion pleat

Gathered fabric on a rod; gathered heading above rod

Flat loops attached to a straight top

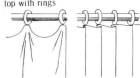
Scalloped top with rings; straight top with rings

move during the show, if damage to the fabric does not matter, or if the top of the drapery is to be covered by a valance or is not seen.

Tiebacks and Holdbacks

Draperies secured by tiebacks or holdbacks look better if these are placed at a point somewhere above or below half of the total height of the drapery. Tiebacks can be made of the same fabric or contrasting fabric, with widths varying from 2 to 4½ inches. These are usually double-faced or lined so they do not wrinkle and may be embellished with trim and cut to match the draperies and valance. Small rings are sewed on either end and attach onto hooks screwed into the woodwork. Roping, tassels, and chains may also be used. Holdbacks, rigid forms of ornament, can be medallions, sunbursts, spearheads, feathers, or leaves and can be made of metal, plaster, plastic, or wood.

Accessories Hung behind Draperies

There is a large group of accessories that can be hung behind draperies to provide contrast in color or texture in the window treatment. You will find that these items can also be used on windows without draperies:

Glass curtains or sheer curtains.
Lace curtains.
Hinged wooden louvered shutters.
Venetian blinds.
Horizontal wooden slats.
Regular window shades.
Colorful fabric shades.
Austrian curtains.
Roman shades.
Bamboo blinds.
Vertical strings of beads.

Donald Oenslager designed these ornate window valances for AVANTI (1968). Modeled in Styrofoam on a ¼-in. plywood base, using knives, a hot wire loop, and sandpaper for carving, the units were covered with pieces of muslin and scrim adhered with scenic dope. Sheets of imitation gold leaf were then applied on the surfaces by first coating them with Hastings' quick-drying gold leaf size. (Photographs—Munro Gabler)

Gimp

Materials and Equipment for Making Draperies

Fabric
Sewing machine
Needles and thread for basting
Scissors
Pins
Tape measure
Pleater tape and hooks
Velcro tape for attaching
Beaded or single weights for bottom hems (to make draperies hang better)
Rings for hanging draperies
Appropriate drapery rods and hardware
Rings and hooks for tiebacks
Necessary carpenter tools
Iron and ironing board for pressing seams open and for pressing finished draperies

Sources of Drapery Fabrics

Department stores, fabric shops, five-and-dime stores, and variety stores. In New York City, Dazian's is a well-known source for all kinds of theatrical fabrics.

A Conversation With HOWARD BAY

Howard Bay currently lives in New York and commutes to Brandeis University in Waltham, Massachusetts, where he is a professor of theatre arts. Born in Centralia, Washington, Bay was educated at the Universities of Washington and Colorado, Westminster and Marshall Colleges, and at Carnegie Institute of Technology. His Broadway debut was *Chalk Dust* in 1935, and he went on to gain prominence with his work for the Federal Theatre. He has designed the settings for more than 160 productions for the theatre, and for most of these he has also done the lighting. He has been stage director for several legitimate shows and has served as a production designer for films. Among his awards are two Tonys, a Maharan, two Donaldson awards, and a Guggenheim Fellowship. For many years, Howard Bay was president of the United Scenic Artists Union. His book *Stage Design* was published by Drama Book Specialists in 1974. He wrote the Staging and Stage Design section for *Encyclopaedia Britannica III*. Some of his Broadway credits are:

Man of La Mancha (1965)	*Two on the Aisle* (1951)	*Follow the Girls* (1944)
Toys in the Attic (1960)	*Come Back, Little Sheba* (1950)	*Ten Little Indians* (1944)
The Cool World (1960)	*The Big Knife* (1949)	*Carmen Jones* (1943)
The Music Man (1957)	*Magdalena* (1949)	*Something for the Boys* (1943)
The Desperate Hours (1955)	*As the Girls Go* (1948)	*The Corn Is Green* (1940)
The Shrike (1952)	*Show Boat* (1946)	*The Little Foxes* (1939)
The Children's Hour (1952)	*Up in Central Park* (1945)	*One Third of a Nation* (1938)
The Autumn Garden (1951)	*Deep Are the Roots* (1945)	*Power* (1937)

Setting by Howard Bay
ONE THIRD OF A NATION by Arthur Arent

Produced by The Living Newspaper
Unit of the Federal Theatre

Directed by Lem Ward
Adelphi Theatre, New York (1938)

How did you start thinking about being a scenic designer for the theatre?

Strangely enough, I always wanted to be a stage designer. And while I was in junior high school and high school, I attended art school concurrently, the Chappell in Denver. It had a grand faculty then. Before I went to college I started doing summer stock at Elitch's Gardens in Denver and elsewhere. But my real apprenticeship was on the W.P.A. Federal Theatre, where I was the star designer. The economics were reversed: labor was no object, but materials were costly. We had plenty of time for experimental work with directors and producers. I think it's better training than being dumped out of school into stock. There was and is no one to learn anything from in stock, particularly painting. The whole syndrome of banging stuff out and "making do" is just a specious kind of theatricality. That Depression theatre was a better initiation into the commercial entertainment world.

Where was this?

Here in New York. I was even on the forerunner of the Federal Theatre, which was a valuable make-work deal that sent out mobile theatres to the parks and neighborhoods. That was in 1934. Somebody gave us millions of yards of bed ticking and we used it for all of the scenery. And the scenic artists developed a good style with dyes and starches. We did the very old-fashioned thing of painting furniture and dressing on the walls. When the actual Federal Theatre came into existence, you worked in normal theatres with standard facilities.

What about directors?

Well, of course you had Orson [Welles]. I was primarily connected with the Living Newspaper and the Experimental Theatre with the old Provincetown director, James Light. Then Lem Ward was a very fine director. In fact, I did all his shows, both on the project and ultimately on Broadway. Joe Losey and Brett Warren worked on the Living Newspaper. The W.P.A. was a struggle; the economics of it got kind of rugged. And simultaneously, I started doing things like *Marching Song* for the Theatre Union. That was a left-wing theatre group that was based on trade unions and season-ticket-selling; it was left of the Group. Right after that,

Stage design by Howard Bay
MAN OF LA MANCHA by Dale Wasserman
Music by Mitch Leigh
Lyrics by Joe Darion

Choreography by Jack Cole
Book and musical staging by Albert Marre
ANTA Washington Square Theatre
New York (1965)

I did a show with Joe Losey about child labor that took place in the tobacco barns, the shade-grown tobacco of Connecticut.

Your first Broadway show came about as a result of the Federal Theatre?

Well, *Chalk Dust* was Federal Theatre. That was in 1936 and it was an interesting show, directed by Jimmy Light. Then at the Experimental Theatre, we also did a script about John Brown called *Battle Hymn,* which was directed by Vincent Sherman, who after that went on as a director for Warner's. And the Living Newspaper's *One Third of a Nation* made a large splash, and also *Power.*

Did you do the setting and the lights?

Sometimes and sometimes not. One of the Experimental shows was *Native Ground,* Virgil Geddes' midwest saga, and Abe Feder did the lighting for that one and it was a beautifully lit show. Then I did the original *Little Foxes* with Herman [Shumlin] and Lillian [Hellman]. I went to Europe in the spring of 1939, based on the money from a film I had done at the 1939 New York World's Fair with Joe Losey. Joe Losey and I put together a film project and sold it to the petroleum industries. All the petroleum industries in the world, except for Shell, got together to do a show and an exhibit and a building out at the Fair Grounds. So Joe made a grand prospectus of a stop-motion puppet film in technicolor. That's the hardest thing you could do in film, of course.

And none of us had had any experience with film! But we blithely went ahead and I wound up having not only to design the sets and puppets but to get together the physical set-up for the execution of the puppets and the sets. In fact, it was the first time that seamless latex was used—for the puppets that were all variations of little oil-drop characters. Anyway, it gave me money to go to Europe in the spring of 1939, and the Federal Theatre died simultaneously and I went into straight commercial designing.

Did you go to Europe to study or to travel?

Just to travel. The great Zürich Fair, which was done by a single board of design, was on. So having just left the dust and the beaverboard of Flushing Meadows to come on a beautifully laid-out operation was something. And that's when I first heard of Hans Erni, who had done this giant exterior mural. I came back shouting about Hans Erni, but no one had ever heard of him. Now he's gotten around a bit. He's a great draftsman.

When you approach designing a play, how do you progress?

Well, I read the script in a rather non-mechanical way, just pretending I'm a layman; I let it ooze around a bit. Then I go to research. I do a tremendous amount of hunting around if time permits; ninety-nine percent of it doesn't turn up in the final product. But I like to get the atmosphere and the period architectural detail thoroughly in mind. When the pressures of the calendar demand that I get down to business, I start with thumbnails. I always hire a very good assistant so I don't have to worry about drafting. First, the rough pencil sketches incorporating the research, and then the renderings. I always try to postpone directoral and producer approval, depending on the schedule, until I feel that I have something solid. Also, even when I am the busiest, I always do my prop and furniture chasing, the selection of draperies and fabrics, and the lighting. I must scurry around a bit and keep good help that sticks to the drafting. I have always worked that way; I never could delegate selection of key things.

Do you like to work with a model?

It depends on the complexity of the structure whether I make a model, or

whether the director needs it for the mechanics of traffic. It also depends on the plasticity of whatever you are doing.

You also do your own lighting.

I think the design of lighting and set is one indivisible creative process, and I wouldn't know how to divide it up. In the pressures of schedule, to design something and then have to backtrack and arbitrarily punch holes in the set to let the lights in would be pointless; or if you have to work with a lighting designer who has a certain rigid format of lighting. I also feel that the business of lighting has been blown up too much. It's a craft, and it's an important craft, but I think when it's separated, it tends to get exhibitionist. I've always felt that commercial theatre is so departmentalized anyway, why add to it? It tends towards the safe way of doing everything—everybody off doing their separate chores.

Do you have an assistant for lighting?

Not usually. I prefer to work directly with the production electrician. Ralph Holmes has worked with me on lots of shows, basically on drafting and assisting, rather than on lighting. Although once, I had an opening in Philadelphia and an opening in Boston the same night. So Ralph and I had to shuttle back and forth and leave notes for each other and cover it that way.

What about designing costumes?

I do costumes on occasion when I'm forced to—I don't like to. I think it's easy to do the sets and lights simultaneously, because you can schedule your time—your shopping time, and your shop-visiting time, and your drawing-board time. But fittings demand another way of working. And I discovered very early that the designers who pretend to do both sets and costumes really don't. They throw the emphasis on one or the other. Their forte is costuming or their speciality is scenery, and assistants do one or the other. Also, I don't really like to argue with an actor or an actress that green looks good or "What about the shoulder bone?" I've done costumes successfully, but only where the management couldn't hire the proper costume designer. I was forced into doing the costumes for *Carmen* out at the San Francisco Opera and into doing costumes for *La Mancha,* for instance. And many years ago, I did several operas for

Leon Barzin and the National Orchestral Association, but only because Karinska executed the clothes. And so the quality of the execution and even her assistance in the designing I sorely needed. To this day, I still am not an expert on the structure and the cutting of costumes. So I need a good assistant.

Of the more than 160 stage productions you have designed, do you have two or three you liked more than others?

No. Certain ones were fun at the time and each different. *Carmen Jones* was novel at the time it appeared; that worked out well. [Raoul Pène] du Bois did the costumes and that was fine, so ultimately, when we did *The Music Man,* I suggested du Bois and it turned out well again. In straight shows, I think it was most rewarding working on a couple of Lillian Hellman's shows. They made sense and there was a basis and a reason why you created an environment for certain people who act in a dramatically logical way. I particularly liked *The Little Foxes,* and I did the revival too with Mike Nichols at the [Vivian] Beaumont [Theatre at Lincoln Center]. I admired *Autumn Garden* very much, and *Toys in the Attic.* Also, I did a lot of interesting Victorian stuff in the early 1940s. I seem to have spells doing types of shows: social dramas, the Victorian gimcracks, and then the ga-ga musicals. I did a whole flock of the girlie shows in the 1940s war years. In fact, I ended up directing the last Bobby Clark musical, *As the Girls Go,* which is probably the last splurge of the old-time jazzy girl show.

How did your directing of that show come about?

Well, I was sort of Mike Todd's lieutenant for so many years. The first show I worked on with him was Cole Porter's *Something for the Boys* [with Ethel Merman], which he produced, and I did the sets and lighting. Somehow or other, in that period the book direction and the dance direction and the overall staging were all compartmentalized things. And the book directors were usually not that important, unless it was [George] Kaufman or [Moss] Hart or [George] Abbott—someone of that stature. We found that most of the book directors were sort of newly graduated stage managers who were nice to actors and actresses and made them feel com-

326

Stage design by Howard Bay
SHOW BOAT
Music by Jerome Kern
Book and lyrics by
  Oscar Hammerstein II
Based on the novel
  by Edna Ferber
Directed by Edward
  Greenburg
Los Angeles Civic Light
  Opera Company (1953)

fortable. So you might as well do it your-self. Also, I always wanted to work with Bobby Clark and I wanted to know how he functioned.

Did you do more work for Mike Todd?

Yes. I sort of followed him around and we made decisions about things. And then I directed and produced the over-seas USO *Up in Central Park*—I did all versions, including the film.

How much was the scenery budget for Up in Central Park?

It wasn't much in those days. I think it was roughly $30,000. The total budget of the show was only $115,000, so it returned its investment rather rapidly as it broke at a low figure. That sort of show you don't do today, al-though it was light mechanically. It was just a question of having the flies to pull up the drops, of which there were over thirty—many were translucent. How long would it take to do that strictly painty show today?

One of your greatest hits was Man of La Mancha; *there were many com-panies. Is it a favorite of yours?*

Yes, there was a plasticity in the use of the theatre. And it got away from the old-fashioned pictorialism represented by, say, *Up in Central Park* or *Showboat* or *Music Man*. It was created from the word ''go'' by the director and myself. It was painful to look at some of the road-company shows. You didn't have the stairs, you didn't have the sharp lighting, you just didn't have what you had originally.

You did Man of La Mancha *for the*

ANTA Washington Square Theatre, which no longer exists. How did you come to decide on the kind of thrust and the kind of stairs you used?

Albie [Albert Marre] and I worked it out together. In examining the previous shows in the ANTA, we didn't feel they had used the place, or the shows didn't allow them to use the theatre because they were basically standard prosce-nium shows. Or else they tried to com-promise by framing it and not by putting it out there in the midst of the people and forgetting about the background. So *La Mancha* was tailored to fit the place, even insofar as having to drill and dig and to take out the concrete [and shore up the sand] so the platter could float.

The only other version of *La Mancha* which was successful was the London production. Everyone was intrigued with the Drury Lane Theatre, and Albie and I went over to survey the situation. It's a vast place with a twenty-foot pit and an eighty-foot stage, with all those tiers of boxes running around the place. And what some people forgot is that *La Mancha* is basically an intimate show and it would rattle around and get lost in the Drury Lane. But there were very few theatres available at the time. The London half of the management hap-pened to own the Piccadilly, which no one considered because it didn't have a pit. I suggested that they tear out the stage. And after a long pause and the estimate, that's precisely what they did. In the last two weeks of the show that was playing there, they rerouted all

the utilities underneath the stage which had been there for nigh onto a hundred years. All the electrical pipe and plumb-ing and heating were rerouted. Then they closed the show and they tore out the deck. So the cyc went to the cellar, and the platter really floated. You came to the edge and then you dropped off. So even in the second balcony, you were not conscious of any bottom.

What is the most challenging and dif-ficult show you have had to design?

It was way back and I still remember it—*One Touch of Venus*. It was mainly because the director and the writers had never done a musical before and they didn't quite get the idea of the necessity of having transition scenes between the full-stage scenes, and they didn't recognize it until Boston. So we sat around the front of the house trying to invent crossovers and reprises and dance effects—stuff which would make the show flow. That's how Sono Osato was born. Agnes de Mille suggested, ''Well, you know that little Eurasian girl we have, she could do this with that,'' and that is how it all came about. So that was a tough one also because it had bulk, which was demanded by the script. I was doing *Carmen Jones* and a couple of straight shows simultaneously. In that period, from 1943 to the spring of 1946, I guess I had a record, since I had nine shows running at once.

Are we going through a phase in the theatre today in which the scenery is more three-dimensional and sculp-tural than realistically painted?

327

That happened years ago. I think the skeleton thing is sort of at the end of its era. The frankness of using stage space, recognition of the actual dimensions of stage without perspective, masking, and pretending limitless distance and depth, I'm all in favor of. Commercially, you'll always have the proscenium, and the only way you can break that is to extend out over the apron and try to minimize the frame.

What about designing films rather than the theatre?

I love films. It isn't that I care too much whether the kind of style we use in the theatre is not applicable to films, it's just that I don't think you have very much control over your product as a film art director. Also the completely designed show has been out for years anyway. I liked doing that *Midsummer Night's Dream* a few years ago. Balanchine was transplanting ballet to the film media as close as you could do it. And we shot it in twelve shooting days, with three cinemascope cameras in one studio, and we did dressing and lighting late at night and in between takes. Twelve shooting days, and on the thirteenth day I couldn't get out of bed because I had a slipped disc. It was from working and the tension and the long hours on a concrete stage. I stayed in bed for a while.

But a couple of films I did in Hollywood were styled films. One was a completely designed show, *The Exile*, with Doug Fairbanks, Jr., a cop-and-robber period piece which was done exclusively in the studio. When I went to Hollywood, it was on a two-year straight designer-director contract, merely on the cycle theory that [Vincent] Minnelli had done it. But I went at the wrong time because the studio fell apart. The Rank Empire [who owned the majority stock] disappeared and the studio became sort of a graveyard, so it wasn't the best timing in the world.

What about designing for television?

Oh, I did a great deal in the early days of TV which was more interesting in a way, because we initiated the props-and-set-pieces-against-the-cyc style. Ralph Holmes was with me and he did the lighting. Now TV is too often Grade C moviemaking—although a *Pueblo* comes along occasionally, and that was satisfying.

As an instructor at Brandeis University, can you comment on the program there and how it came about?

Nine years ago, when they built the new theatre, they decided they had better do something with it—so they imported people. And I was brought in, and I in turn brought in technical people as well as the directors. I set up the design department and the way of teaching. I initiated a graduate program in design as fast as I could. With the new plan and the new program, I got some good people—a production manager and a technician-carpenter—the best in the Boston area, and also a costume designer, Maureen Hennegan, who brought in a pro cutter. We have a good scenic artist, Robert Moody. We take in a limited number of graduate students who are carefully auditioned from undergraduate departments throughout the country. And at any given moment, we only have about fifteen or sixteen graduate students. We cram an awful lot into the MFA program. And we do not make a separation like they do at Yale or Tech or other places by having a major in design and a major in technical theatre. All the people are exposed to scenery, costumes, and lights, and then by the end of the second year, they can move off into their own special interests.

Today in the repertory theatres and the schools, there's less specialization anyway. I do no designing at school, I just teach and supervise.

What is the most important background a potential designer should get in school?

If it's physically possible the student should have a couple of years of straight drawing prior to being immersed in stage mechanics. Seldom do the schools have the good old-fashioned academic drawing. There isn't that cross-fertilization between theatre and art departments. I teach a certain amount of rendering and Moody teaches drawing, so we try and patch up those holes in their training. And occasionally, we take an applicant who hasn't done any theatre, but who has a drawing facility and an interest in doing design. Sometimes they turn out better than people who have done purely technical theatre work in their undergraduate schools.

We pick out the half-dozen or seven or eight best students that apply; their qualifications vary and that's one reason we take only a few, because we have to give them individual attention to correct their deficiencies, to get them up to a certain level. For instance, we have good luck on the people who have taken the union exam. To begin with, I don't want them to have my style which is

Stage design by Howard Bay
UP IN CENTRAL PARK
Book by Herbert and Dorothy Fields
Lyrics by Dorothy Fields

Music by Sigmund Romberg
Staged by John Kennedy
Century Theatre, New York (1945)

Setting by Howard Bay
MARCHING SONG by John Howard Lawson
Presented by the Theatre Union

Staged by Anthony Brown
Bayes Theatre
New York (1937)

not a single style anyway, so I think that they're more flexible and equipped to do a variety of productions.

How many theatres do you have at Brandeis?

We have three, so the students shuttle around and everyone gets a shot at doing scenery on the main stage, designing the lighting in the second theatre, or doing the whole thing in the third theatre. And then they do costumes, and then lighting on the big stage. The main theatre is a proscenium with a thrust. It's a flexible open theatre. The experimental theatre is an odd-shaped room, but you can juggle around the bleachers and your staging area. Even if someone basically comes for costumes, they will have to have done a set and lighting before they get out of the place. Plus

they do a thesis which is a complete portfolio of sets, costumes, and lights.

What would you suggest for practical experience after school?

Well, with employment being what it is, it's kind of academic to say apprenticeship to a designer, because there's not that much employment around. But that's ideal, of course. There are a few repertory theatres hanging on around the country, and if the ex-student could work with a good senior designer, that is valuable. Now, even with the stringent economics, school theatres are more professionally oriented. The most glaring deficiency in schools is the level of scenic painting. You know, there are almost no scenic painters teaching in America, which is kind of peculiar. Arnold Abramson goes up to

Yale one day a week, which is not very much. A resident instructor in scenic painting is very important. The first time it ever happened was when I suggested Horace Armistead to Boston University when they were setting up their program. And Horace was the first scenic artist who really stayed in a school situation and taught both design and scenic painting until he retired.

What do you think will happen in stage design in the near future?

The trend is away from the personal pictorial statement—the reflection of the artist's individual stylistic mannerisms—towards a more eclectic use of any visual data, ready-mades, lifted from anywhere. I guess you could call it theatrical collage.

NINE

Framed scenery,
decks, ground cloths,
and furniture

FRAMED SCENERY

Backdrops were discussed in the preceding chapter. We now examine other equally vital processes in the execution and painting of scenery. "Framed scenery" is simply a classification for convenience. It can be applied to canvas-covered flats, plywood-covered flats, profiled plywood pieces, ceiling pieces, and three-dimensional pieces. Some of the techniques in this chapter, such as lining and painting on velour, can also be used on backdrops. The sections on Decks and Ground Cloths describe the many ways in which floors and decks can be treated on stage and how they are finished and painted. Floor surfaces such as Masonite, plywood, wood, metal, carpet, linoleum, and canvas are discussed. The final portion of the chapter covers selecting, designing, renovating, and painting stage furniture and includes a chart of furniture dimensions.

Many books have been written on the subject of basic scenery construction, and this is an important aspect, but this chapter stresses the finishes on framed scenery and the overall scope. Interested readers unfamiliar with the techniques of building, placement on stage, rigging, storing, and running of scenery should consult the pertinent books listed in the Bibliography.

Like materials used for floor designs, materials for wall treatments can be thought of as *real* or *painted materials,* designed for either realistic or stylized settings. One example of an actual material is new raw wood stained with a transparent color to allow the natural graining to show through, but real materials can also be combined to make objects such as bricks rather than using bricks as such. They can be cut out of plywood, Masonite, and Upson board and painted, vacuum-formed with a sheet of plastic and painted, or simply painted on a flat canvas surface. In other words, the treatment of walls can be (1) actual materials designated as such, (2) a combination of materials forming three dimension objects and painted as something else, or (3) objects represented by painting on a flat surface.

When starting to plan a design, it is often helpful to survey the general scope of items used for walls as well as for roofs and ceilings. The list on page 332 may serve as a basis for getting ideas about interior and exterior treatments for scenery.

Setting by Kert Lundell
THE SUNSHINE BOYS by Neil
  Simon
Directed by Alan Arkin
Lighting by Tharon Musser
Lunt-Fontanne Theatre,
  New York (1974)
Première – Broadhurst
  Theatre, New York (1972)
(Photograph – Bruce W. Stark)

Stage design by Sandro La Ferla
THE MEDIUM by Gian-Carlo Menotti
Directed by Gian-Carlo Menotti
Conducted by Yutaka Hoshide
Yubinchokin Hall, Tokyo (1974)

Stage design by Karl Eigsti
THE HOUSE OF BLUE LEAVES by
  John Guare
Directed by Mel Shapiro
Truck and Warehouse Theatre,
  New York (1971)

Setting by Lynn Pecktal
YOU NEVER KNOW – a musical play
  by Cole Porter
Directed by Robert Moore
Lighting by Walter Dolan
Ogunquit Playhouse, Ogunquit,
  Maine (1963)
(Photograph – Edward D. Hipple)

Checklist of Finished Interior and Exterior Wall Treatments

Wood (real or painted)
Paneling and molding of various kinds
Rough-hewn planking and beams
Clapboards and wood siding
Logs
Bamboo
Commercially stamped wood panels
Cedar shingles (also for roofs)

Wallpaper and wallcoverings (real or painted)
Overall wallpaper patterns
Patterned panels with borders
Mural or scenic wallcoverings
Actual fabric (velour, canvas, scrim, burlap, decorative patterned fabrics)
Vinyl wallcoverings (solids or patterns like bath or kitchen tile)
Cork panels

Metal (real or painted)
Pressed-metal wall and ceiling patterns
Perforated metal sheets
Aluminum sheets and pipes
Iron grillwork

Stone, marble, brick, plaster, etc. (painted or simulated with three-dimensional textures)
Fieldstone
Granite
Corkstone
Smooth marble slabs for panels or trim
Marble chunks in random sizes
Marble tiles for walls (or floors)
Smooth plaster
Stucco
Various bricks laid in many patterns
Concrete walls, cinder blocks

Plastics and synthetics (actual materials)
Acrylic sheets like Plexiglas, Lucite, Acrylite for transparent, semitransparent, or translucent effects
Panels of vacuum-formed patterns
Molded patterns in fiber glass
Fiber glass corrugated panels
Insulated mineral-surfaced siding

Shingles and treatments for roofs
Wood shingles (real or painted)
Slate shingles (painted)
Tin roofing (real or painted)
Clay roof tiles (painted)
Raffia (real or painted)
Bundles of straw (real or painted)
Straw matting (real)
Metal shingles (real or painted)
Pantiles (painted)

Lining

Lining is an important feature in painting and a basic scene painting technique. It is discussed here rather than with other painting techniques because it extends into the process of painting three-dimensional molding that follows. We take a look at laying out the drawing for painting molding on an interior setting, lining the molding with lining brushes, using the lightweight wooden straightedge, using a thin flexible lath for lining curved molding, the direction of light, mixing and applying lining colors, and photographs showing how molding and paneling are painted.

Besides the illustration of painting molding by lining on a flat surface, photographs in this section show how three-dimensional molding units are textured, grained, and finished and how natural woods are painted with transparent colors to let the grain show through the colors.

LAYING OUT THE DRAWING FOR PAINTING MOLDING ON AN INTERIOR SETTING

Good proportions and exact dimensions are essential for laying out molding that paints well.

These qualities are best realized by first drawing the profile, or section, of each type of molding being used. The section view defines where each line is to be placed on the layout of the molding and makes it easier to think in terms of light, shade, and shadow when painting. Both the dimensions and proportions must be accurately scaled from the designer's drafting and placed on the scenery accordingly.

The drawing for the molding of an interior set is laid out after the canvas flats and set pieces have been primed and have dried. They should be arranged flat on the floor in the sequence in which they play on stage, with the bottoms of the flats or set pieces forming a straight line so the molding can be laid out consistently and continuously when it is being drawn and painted. Any built dimensional pieces, such as paneled doors, mantles, or pilasters, are put in their respective places on the flat scenery and their outlines marked in pencil so the areas of flat molding to be painted will match with the real, built molding. They are usually removed after marking and may be put back later to match in with the final painting.

Setting by Helen Pond and Herbert Senn
THE JOCKEY CLUB STAKES by William Douglas Home
Directed by Cyril Ritchard
Lighting by Robert Tompkins
Cape Playhouse, Dennis, Massachusetts (1973)
(Photograph—Craig of East Dennis)

Stage design by John Lee Beatty
PHILADELPHIA, HERE I COME! by Brian Friel
Directed by Lucia Victor
Professional Theatre in Residence
Queens, New York (1975)

Classical Moldings

Bead

Fillet

Fascia

Cavetto

Scotia

Cyma reversa

Cyma recta

Ovolo

Torus

Quarter round

The painted moldings that appear most often in stage interiors are baseboard, dado, chair rail, wainscot, and cornice. These may be in a set that is completely paneled in wood, or they may be combined with various kinds of wall treatment like stenciled wallpaper, painted plaster, and grass cloth. When marking off the measurements for any of these moldings or wall treatments, always start at the bottom of the flat and work upward. In this way any variations that result from irregularities in the building or joining are eliminated.

The marking is done with a thin stick of charcoal; it is started on either the extreme right or left wing and continued across the remaining units. One of the most efficient and accurate methods of marking moldings that run horizontally is to place each measurement on one long thin lath. The marked lath is then placed on the sides of each flat and held evenly at the bottom so the marks can be transferred quickly. This eliminates measuring off the feet and inches each time. A shorter lath or strip of paper can be used for marking moldings that run vertically.

For speed and accuracy, two painters work together to snap charcoal lines through the first marks. To retain these lines and have them show through after the base coat (local color) is put on, they should be inked with a felt-tip pen or lined with aniline dye. All the excess charcoal and dirt are dusted off with a flogger, then the local colors for the woodwork and the walls are applied. As a rule, the detailed painting on the walls is done first, and then the molding is ready to be lined.

LINING THE MOLDING WITH LINING BRUSHES AND LONG-HANDLED STRAIGHTEDGES

To produce effectively painted molding, it is necessary to have good lining brushes and well-kept straightedges. Long, soft-bristled lining brushes that retain their shape and hold a lot of color are ideal for painting the straight lines and come in various sizes. To line an ogee molding that is 2 inches wide, for instance, typical brush sizes can be $\frac{1}{4}$-, $\frac{1}{2}$-, and $\frac{3}{4}$-inch. Often, when painting, the scenic artist dips the lining brush into the color, drains off the excess paint on the inside of the container, and then hits the bristles flat on the floor to shape them before starting to line with the straightedge. This simple technique is used repeatedly when lining, especially thinly painted lines.

Lining brushes with long handles are made even longer by inserting them into the split ends of bamboo sticks so the painter can work with flexibility while standing. Since this is the most practical way to paint molding on scenery laid flat on the floor, it is the one most frequently used. The floor straightedge (constructed with a long handle) is utilized as well.

When lining, the scenic artist holds the brush with one hand and the handle of the straightedge with the other, placing the edge parallel with the inked lines and then tilting it back slightly to keep the color from running and smearing under it. Using the edge as a guide, the lining should always be applied with the brush by making long, even, swift strokes. This is much easier to control and manipulate when the artist holds the tip of the bamboo stick.

USING A LIGHTWEIGHT STRAIGHTEDGE

The lightweight straightedge is held in the hand for lining on vertical surfaces, but it can also be used horizontally for lining small details on the floor and for scenery laid on work horses. The proper way to hold this edge has long been traditional among experienced scenic artists. By turning the hand so the palm is facing the artist, the straightedge is placed in back of the thumb and little finger, with the remaining three fingers supporting it from behind. The hand holding the straightedge should be centered to maintain good balance when it is held parallel to the painting surface.

USING A THIN FLEXIBLE LATH FOR LINING CURVED MOLDING

For painting molding that is designed to be curved but is still a flat surface, a thin flexible

Paint elevation by
  Marsha Louis Eck
MANON by Jules Massenet
Libretto by Henri Meilhac
  and Philippe Gille
Directed by Tito Capobianco
New York City Opera (1968)
(Photograph – Kenneth Pew)

The sketch for a candlelit
evening scene indicates the
paint treatment of the moldings
and panels on the curved wall
unit 15 ft. wide by 17 ft. high
in Act II. Above each window
are faded Fragonard lunettes.

wooden lath makes an excellent straightedge. Once the lath has been positioned, it is held in place by putting weights on each end, with the aid of another artist, or both. The lath is put to equally good use for lining molding laid out on a curved surface, and is held in place the same way.

DIRECTION OF LIGHT

The direction the light is coming from is usually obvious on the designer's sketch, but it can be specified by a notation. This is a necessary question for any painter to answer before starting work. The light can be coming from a window located in the center of the set or from an overhead chandelier; in these cases, the light is painted accordingly, often changing its direction at the source so that half the light may be painted as coming from the right and half coming from the left. Light can also be from one direction only, and when the light source is not indicated, it is standard to assume that it is coming from the left and from above.

MIXING AND APPLYING THE LINING COLORS

Before painting is begun on molding, all the different lining colors should be mixed at one time and each should be tested by sample. A small (4-foot-square) paint frame can be used for this purpose, and it should be laid in with the base color. The profile (section) and front elevation of the molding to be lined are drawn on the sample base color. This elevation is where each color is tested to see how it dries, and to get the total effect of all the colors as they appear together on the piece of molding. These colors, which are variations of the base color, should have the name marked on each container so it can be easily found when it is on the floor, because many artists often work at the same time on lining molding.

When applying lining, you must constantly think in terms of whether the painting is to indicate a round, curved, or flat surface. The colors used to simulate flat members of a molding (such as the ''light'' on a bevel) have sharp-edged lines, while those for round members (such as the ''shade'' on a half-round) have ''lost-off'' edges made by dry-brushing or scumbling. *Not too much* of the base (local) color should be painted out when the lining colors are applied or the whole effect will be lost.

In the scenic studio, lining colors are normally mixed with caseins, and they work better when mixed fairly thin. These typical colors are applied in this sequence:

LINING MOLDING, PANELING, AND A BALUSTER
The sample on canvas was made for Lloyd Evans' scenery for ALBERT HERRING (1971), New York City Opera. The direction of light comes from upper left. All colors were mixed with casein paint except the local (dry pigment color and whiting mixed with priming size) and the final dye glaze.

Steps of Execution:
1. LOCAL COLOR: raw sienna and white. This also served as a primer. The molding, panel, and baluster were drawn lightly in charcoal, inked with a felt-tip pen.
2. GRAINING: burnt umber thinned with water. Wood graining then brushed on according to the sketch.
3. LIGHT: yellow ochre, raw umber, a touch of white.
4. SHADE: burnt umber, a little black.
5. SHADOW: black, a little burnt umber.
6. CUTTING LINE (thin line between the shade and shadow): pure black.
7. WARM HIGHLIGHT: orange, white.
8. COOL HIGHLIGHT: cool purple, white.
9. GLAZE: thin Van Dyke brown aniline dye on the shade side with some also on the light side.

LINING LIGHT-COLORED PANELING WITHOUT WOOD GRAINING

The panel was painted with the light coming from above left.

Steps of Execution:
1. LOCAL COLOR: white, raw umber, yellow ochre.
2. LIGHT: white, some local color, primrose yellow.
3. SHADE: raw sienna, raw umber, some local color.
4. SHADOW: raw umber, a little local color.
5. CUTTING LINE: burnt umber, a little local color.
6. HIGHLIGHT: white, a touch of lemon yellow.
7. GLAZE FOR SHADE SIDE: shade color thinned with water.
8. LIGHT GLAZE: light color thinned with water.
   (Samples – Fred Jacoby, photographs – Lynn Pecktal)

1. *The Light*

   It is best to start with the light first, because it is easier if necessary to paint out part of the light with the shade color; this, of course, is done when the two are adjacent.

2. *The Shade*

   The shade is a dark warm color and denotes that part of the molding not hit by the light source.

3. *The Shadow*

   This is a cooler color than the shade, although the shade and shadow are often close in intensity. To be transparent, the shadow is usually mixed in a thinner consistency than the other lining colors and most frequently is made with aniline dyes.

4. *The Second Shadow*

   A darker value of the shadow color, this is used to indicate the shadow caused by a second light source and is the narrower of the two shadows. If mixed in dyes, the second shadow can be made (with the shadow color) by simply going over the shadow again (with the same color), because the dye becomes darker with each brushing.

5. *The Cutting Line* or Accent

   Also known as the accent, the cutting line is the strongest color used and is always applied as a very thin line to denote the deepest divisions in the molding. This is a very dark warm color, as it is placed where the reflect color is found.

6. *The Highlight*

   The lightest color, this is applied sparsely and at random within the inner area of the light color. The highlight can be warm for an interior, cool for an exterior.

7. *The Dye Glaze*

   Brushing this thin transparent dye color over the flat painted molding takes away the "mechanical" look, and both the "light" side and the "shade" side are glazed freely. It is especially effective to start with the brush at the corners of panel molding and gradually let the stroke fade out before reaching the next corner.

Painting Three-Dimensional Woodwork with Natural Graining

A design that specifies that all built woodwork in a setting has to be painted and finished realistically involves several steps of preparation for the job to be a good one. Usually this is for an interior set like a paneled library or a formal drawing room, and a natural graining treatment is given to all the dimensionally built units (which have real molding and other applied pieces), including doors, windows, panels, cornices, and the like. The graining may also be applied on any related flat scenery where woodwork is so designated. Examples of settings that have had three-dimensional molding painted realistically are Ben Edwards' living-dining room for *Finishing Touches,* Douglas W. Schmidt's Russian period sets for *Enemies* at the Repertory Company of Lincoln Center, and Lloyd Evans' scenery for *Albert Herring* at the New York City Opera Company.

PREPARATION OF THE NEW WOOD

Before new wood can be painted, it must first be finished properly. Any cracks or holes in the wood should be filled with a prepared, hard-drying spackling putty. When this has dried, sand the areas of wood that have been spackled, using a piece of medium-grade sandpaper wrapped around a wooden block. The rough surfaces and sharp edges on the wood should also be sanded well. Before painting, thoroughly dust and brush out all small particles of wood and spackle from the sanding.

MIXING THE UNDERTONE COLOR IN SHELLAC

The new woodwork is given a base coat of shellac to seal the surface of the wood and to serve as an undertone for the graining color. Dry pigment colors are mixed with a shellac to make this undertone base. For contrast, it is usually two or three shades lighter than the

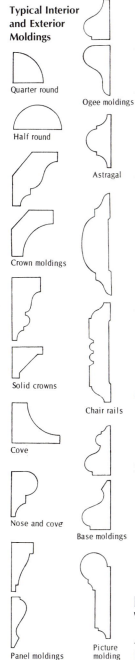

Typical Interior and Exterior Moldings

Quarter round

Half round

Crown moldings

Solid crowns

Cove

Nose and cove

Panel moldings

Ogee moldings

Astragal

Chair rails

Base moldings

Picture molding

graining color. These steps are followed for making the undertone *color:*

1. As a binder, use clear white shellac *or* orange shellac (a better binder) *or* Haeuser's white Enamelac.
2. Always pour the dry pigment colors *into* the shellac. Do this slowly while stirring vigorously. The amount of dry colors to be used for mixing into the clear white or orange shellac should be enough to make the desired color and to make the mixture completely opaque. A sample of the color should be tried on the wood before the work is started. When white is needed, use white Enamelac, which is opaque, or lithopone. *Never* add dry whiting or zinc white into the shellac, for it emulsifies and thickens it so much that it becomes unworkable.
3. Thin the mixture sparingly with denatured alcohol if necessary, but too much alcohol will make the color rub up. Typical colors used for mixing undertones for wood are:

Mahogany—Burnt sienna and white
Oak   —Yellow ochre and white
Walnut   —Yellow ochre, raw umber, and white

APPLYING THE UNDERTONE COLOR

With a pure bristle lay-in brush, apply the shellac color smoothly and swiftly, working the brush back and forth, going with the grain of the wood. Shellac dries very quickly and consequently requires fast brushing. It is normal to give the wood a *second* coat with the same undertone color. For this coat a little more of the pure clear shellac should be added to the original undertone color; this makes the graining stain easier to apply. Sand lightly between coats if necessary.

USING OIL GRAINING COLOR

An oil-stain color (put on without thinning) is superior for the graining color and is applied over the shellacked undertone. A preferred brand of oil paint is Benwood, a Benjamin Moore product that comes in a variety of wood-color stains; this and others can be purchased in good paint stores. When ready to use, the oil stain is put on sparingly over the surface with a loose-hair lay-in brush approximately 3 inches wide. Not too much area should be covered with the stain at one time, for it will start to dry before the overgraining can be done, and that must definitely be executed in "the wet." Graining with the brush in the wet stain allows the undertone color to show through.

Overgraining can be done with the same brush, but it should be very dry. To start, position the brush on the surface with the bristles pointed straight ahead, with the handle lifted slightly (as when pushing a putty knife forward). Keeping the brush in this position, push against the bristles and forward through the wet stain, while at the same time making the lines slightly wavy so that the graining simulates exactly the kind of wood it should be. It should clearly be oak graining or walnut graining or whatever; anyone unfamiliar with the grain should study a sample of the real wood beforehand. Additional brushwork is sometimes necessary to convey the details of a specific kind of grain, like the flake figure in white oak or the broken stripe in mahogany, and these are also painted over the initial graining while it is still wet.

The units of woodwork to be painted should always be placed flat on work horses or on similar objects of table height. There should also be some planning as to what gets painted first on the piece of scenery. For example, if paneling is being grained, the center of the panel should be done first, then the molding, then the stiles, and so on. Working from the center out is the easiest and simplest way to cover up where the brush starts and stops and at the same time eliminate the need to mask the ends of a board.

USING VINYL FOR THE GRAINING COLORS

Although an oil stain gives the most effective finish for graining, it requires much more drying time than water-base paints. When there is not enough time to apply oil, a substitute may be made by mixing the graining color in a vinyl color and thinning it with water as needed. While this may not produce as subtle a finish as the oil stain, it can be successful when applied over the shellacked undertone (two coats) in the same way as the oil stain. Since vinyl dries much faster than oil, one must work very quickly to achieve the desired graining effect.

PAINTING LATTICEWORK ON CANVAS
A light hand straightedge and a ¼-in. lining brush were used to finish latticework for Helen Pond's and Herbert Senn's stage unit in ARIADNE AUF NAXOS (1973) at the New York City Opera.

USING A PRESERVATIVE

For an oil-stain finish, a permanent preservative like clear varnish is normally brushed or sprayed over the grained wood. It is applied without thinning and the finish may be flat, gloss, or semigloss. When vinyl is used for the graining color, it may have a preservative of clear vinyl (flat or gloss), using the proportions of 3 parts vinyl to 1 part water. If time permits, varnish can also be brushed or sprayed on the vinyl graining.

Transparent Painting on Raw Wood to Retain the Natural Grain

In both realistic and stylized production designs there are always settings in which the raw wood is to be painted with the natural grain showing through the transparent color. These sets or pieces are usually constructed of softwoods like No. 2 common shelving pine, rough spruce crating lumber, Douglas fir, and unfinished cedar. For flooring, No. 2 pine planking is widely used.

One of the most effective and easiest ways to paint new woods is with aniline dyes mixed in water. They may be applied with a brush or, for more rapid covering, the Hudson spray tank; however the transparent dyes are put on, they speedily soak into the surface of the new wood and let the natural graining show through. Sometimes a binder like glue size is added to the mixed dyes to insure a better holding of the color and can be done by adding 1 quart of size to every 5 gallons of the liquid dye. Additional dyes or other watercolors are often worked over the initial color to simulate texture and antiquing or to vary the coloring. When a gloss finish is required, a clear varnish or clear gloss vinyl can be brushed over the dyed wood; both are good as a protective coating, especially for floors that have been painted in dyes.

Thin washes of other paints such as vinyl, casein, or latex (all thinned with water) may also be used on new woods, although they are not always as brilliant or as effective as dyes. An oil-stain color (thinned with turpentine) works well, but the longer drying time, the odor, and the added cost must be taken into consideration when using it.

A graining color mixed with vinyl paints and thinned with water is brushed on a wooden three-dimensional door primed and basecoated with opaque shellac. Oil graining color remains wet longer than vinyl, allowing more time to create graining patterns with the brush.

Steps of Execution:
1. Canvas-covered flats, backed with plywood, were primed white.
2. After priming, the local color (actual color of the lattice) was laid in over designated areas.
3. Background squares under the lattice were stenciled with the stencil at left, making any drawing unnecessary.
4. Shade color (thicknesses of the laths) was applied.
5. Shadow color brushed on. Note the cast shadows of the top laths are wider on the background than those of the bottom laths.
6. A thin cutting line was put on between the shade and shadow.
7. The light (shown brushed on) was applied last. (Photograph—Lynn Pecktal)

Velour-Covered Flats

Whenever the budget of a show allows, many designers favor velour fabric as a covering material for flats as well as for profiled set pieces and three-dimensional units. The heavy-pile fabric may be white, black, or a number of colors, and the covering of the velour is done according to a set pattern. Like soft (unframed) velour drops or hanging velour panels, the direction of the selvage edges on the fabric should be positioned vertically with the nap going down. It will be obvious if the widths of velour are not going the same way, for it will look like two different shades. When in doubt, always test the fabric by rubbing your hand over it. The velour should rub smoothly from top to bottom when the nap is correct. (When it is wished to make the color of the velour appear darker, the direction of all the fabric is reversed, with the nap going up.) When the nap on the velour goes down, it reflects more light than when it goes up.

If flats are being covered with velour, they

should be lined first with canvas duck or painted muslin, which makes the velour opaque and stops light leaks. Old backdrops are good for lining the velour, but the best solution is to use rubber-backed velour. For pieces of scenery wider than the normal width of velour, widths of fabric should be stitched together on the sewing machine before the covering is begun. Unlike canvas, velour is wrapped around all the edges of the flat except the bottom rail, which is backtacked. This keeps the fabric from being torn when it is shifted on the floor during set-up. Backtacking is common in upholstery work. It is achieved by using a standard flexible cardboard strip ($\frac{3}{8}$- or $\frac{1}{2}$-inch wide) and hammering carpet tacks in it to hold the bottom of the velour fabric and keep it in a neat straight line. Allow about an inch of fabric to be turned back. Place the bottom edge of the fabric face down (the 1-inch allowance) and then attach the flexible cardboard strip over the fabric with tacks positioned about every $1\frac{1}{2}$ to 2 inches. When you have attached the bottom edge, lift up and fold the fabric back, stretching it out toward the top of the flat. Then wrap the top edge back on the rail and tack it, then do the same on the sides (stiles). Before the final tacking, tack the fabric temporarily by putting a few tacks in the outer edges of the flat to hold the fabric taut in place.

If you are covering profile pieces with velour, the same wrapping procedure holds true for the edges, but they are wrapped around and glued on the back, not tacked. This eliminates ragged edges and raveling of the fabric. Wrapping the edges with the heavy-piled velour also serves to produce a neater and "less-seen" join when the two flats must be butted flush on the edges. This, of course, also depends on the lightness of the color and the style of painting that goes on it.

DRAWING ON VELOUR FLATS AND BACKDROPS

Once the framed units of velour are ready to be painted, they are laid out on the floor in the sequence in which they play on stage, and any drawing should be *lightly* sketched or snapped in charcoal, as it does not always dust off velour. For designs of any complexity it is best to make a perforated paper pounce. If grid lines are needed for drawing on a velour backdrop stretched out on the floor, threads should be stretched over the fabric. Often the vertical seams of the velour drop work well for grid lines. These can be measured on the actual

backdrop and then marked off with a grease pencil on the designer's sketch (covered with clear acetate) in the appropriate proportions.

PAINTING ON VELOUR FLATS AND BACKDROPS

The techniques of painting on velour flats are the same as for unframed velour backdrops. The only basic difference is the awkwardness of working over the wooden framing. In applying the color, undue pressure on the brush or roller can emphasize the position of the rails, toggles, and stiles in the flats unless special care is taken while working over them. Dyes and all kinds of paints are put on velour. When you are mixing colors, you will find that much more paint is needed for velour than for muslin or canvas. And, if color is being put on with a brush, it is always easier if the strokes are brushed with the nap instead of against it.

As noted, velour for covering flats or making up backdrops may be white, black, or one of several colors. Both flats and drops are laid out flat on the floor for painting. Depending on the production, backgrounds of velour can be sprayed with aniline dyes, and details may be caseins (as well as dyes) put on by brushing, sponging, stenciling, or paint roller. Sometimes when a very textured pattern (like stonework or rough plaster) is desired on velour, especially on a dark color like blue or black, a mixture of glue size is spattered generously over it; where it hits the nap and dries, the nap remains pressed down, producing an interesting and variegated effect on the same color. The effect can then be enhanced by texturing over it with other colors (in casein) applied by paint roller and by brush.

Metallic paints such as silver and gold bronzing colors are mixed with clear vinyl as a binder and brushed on velour, going with the nap whenever possible. If simple decorative patterns in bright colors (like borders of ornament) are to be put on dark predyed velour, it is occasionally necessary to take a brush and carefully prime the areas first with white opaque shellac (Haeuser's Enamelac) so the colors do not fade into the velour. After the shellac has dried, the colors (usually in casein) can be applied.

Flocking on Scenery

Flock, tiny fibers $\frac{1}{16}$ inch long, is applied on scenic pieces to give them a suede or velour-like finish. When a set is covered with velour, the real molding and the built wooden appli-

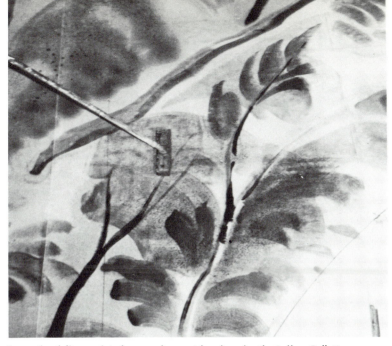

Suggestive foliage painted on a velour cut leg drop for the Joffrey Ballet's LE BEAU DANUBE (1972), based on Constantin Guys' designs. Drawing was done lightly in charcoal. Aniline dye colors were put on with a sponge mop (above) and with Hudson tanks. A 3-in. Fitch brush was used to paint details.

Flock being applied on scenery to give it a suede or velourlike finish, using a flocking gun with rubber hose attached to an air compressor. Wooden cutout was painted with black gloss vinyl as a binder to hold the black flock. Only a small amount of paint was brushed on at a time so it would still be wet when the flock was blown on.
(Photographs—Lynn Pecktal)

This basketweave pattern on Oliver Smith's velour-covered portal for LOVELY LADIES, KIND GENTLEMEN (1970) was painted with colors mixed to represent light, shade, shadow, cutting line, and glazes.

Steps of Execution:

1. The lay-in color, mixed in aniline dyes, was sprayed on the framed velour.
2. The pattern was transferred onto the surface with a perforated pounce.
3. Design inked with a felt-tip pen.
4. Painting done with a brush and a straightedge and by freehand brushing.
5. A stencil of tiny squares was used to paint the dark spaces between the strips of the woven pattern. (Photograph—Arnold Abramson)

qués are sometimes flocked with the same color so all the scenery has a consistent texture on the surface. Flocking is exceptionally good for very small cut-out pieces of wood and Masonite, where covering them with velour would be tedious and most time-consuming, especially if the fabric has to be cut and glued back on each edge. This is true in particular of such profiled wooden cutouts as fancy grillwork, thin stylized trees, skeletonlike ornament outlines, and lettering. Flocking is put neither on scenery that receives a great deal of handling nor on units that are to be walked on.

Flocking is applied over the surface immediately after a wet adhesive has been brushed on, and only small areas should be brushed on at one time. A regular flocking gun, attached to an air compressor, is superior for shooting the minute fibers onto the wet scenery. For small jobs, the flock can also be sifted over the wet areas by hand, but avoid working with it for any length of time without wearing a mask. Paper should always be laid under the piece to catch the excess flock, so it can be emptied back into its cardboard container for later use.

As a binder, undiluted vinyl paint or latex paint or a white synthetic glue is best for holding flock. It is very helpful if the adhesive is a color close to that of the flock in case any "holidays" occur in the application. Painting on flock is done in the same way as on velour. Flock can be purchased in antique brown, black, red, emerald green, silver gray, and white.

Painting a Rolled Ceiling

A ceiling piece for a setting is constructed to roll whenever its size and shape make it too large to fit into the standard opening of a theatrical transfer truck. The framing for an average ceiling consists of two long battens on which the canvas is permanently tacked and glued in place, with the stretchers and diagonal braces held to these battens by ceiling plates. The loose canvas on the two end stretchers is temporarily tacked or laced in place.

A rolled ceiling is always painted while it is assembled with the canvas stretched in place as it would be in the theatre. It is primed and basecoated at the same time. Since the canvas must be rolled for traveling, the binder for the paint must be flexible. Hot liquid starch is added to make the paint flow more freely on the canvas surface. These proportions are followed for mixing the size and paint:

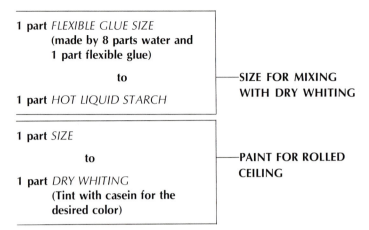

1 part *FLEXIBLE GLUE SIZE*
    (made by 8 parts water and
    1 part flexible glue)

           to

1 part *HOT LIQUID STARCH*
                        — **SIZE FOR MIXING
WITH DRY WHITING**

1 part *SIZE*

           to

1 part *DRY WHITING*
    (Tint with casein for the
    desired color)
                        — **PAINT FOR ROLLED
CEILING**

For painting, the ceiling piece is laid on the floor, and it is easier and faster when two painters work together to do this; the technique used is very similar to that for starching a backdrop. Always begin the painting on the downstage edge of the piece, applying wet widths of color parallel to the edge. These widths are ordinarily about 2 feet wide and are sprayed on by the first painter with a Hudson spray tank.

The second painter follows behind with a long-handled priming brush, spreading the color over the canvas surface, then goes back over it to smooth it out. This smoothing-out each time should be done in one continuous straight stroke parallel to the downstage edge. Continue this process until all the canvas is covered with paint. After the ceiling piece has dried, details or texturing can be applied.

So that it can roll, the ceiling is completely disassembled when it is thoroughly dry. The canvas ceiling is then given one fold with the painted side on the inside, and the battens are placed face-to-face. With these held together, the canvas is rolled on the battens. Usually two or more people are required to do the rolling, depending on the size of the ceiling. Afterward, muslin strips should be tied around the rolled ceiling to hold it together.

Opaquing the Back of a Flat

The purpose of opaquing (or backpainting) a flat is to prevent light leaks through the canvas when it is on stage, to tighten the canvas, and to cut down any possible light reflection from the back. Sometimes flats are painted on the back simply because they may show during a change of scenery on stage. When opaquing a flat, the main consideration is not to harm the finished painting on the front.

For placement and easy reach, single flats that are to be opaqued are angled vertically on their sides against a wall or similar upright

so that the canvas is never pressed against a hard surface when brushing the paint on. A two-fold or three-fold flat is positioned on the floor on its sides by "tenting" it, which allows it to stand freely as well as letting the air circulate around it to dry faster. A three-fold is tented the same way, and after the two upright flats have been opaqued, the unit is given a turn so that the third flat is angled upright; then it is backpainted. Flat set pieces with unusual shapes are set up similarly.

Once the flats have been put on their sides and are ready for opaquing, gently push the canvas away from the wooden toggle rails and braces, which are sometimes stuck to the canvas by the glue in the priming that soaks through when it is brushed on the face of the canvas. Brushing the paint under these pieces makes the overall canvas tighter and more uniform after it dries.

MIXING THE OPAQUING FOR FLATS

While opaque water-base paints such as latex or casein can be used for opaquing, dry whiting and glue size are favored in the scenic studio because they are much less expensive and because the glue size tightens up the canvas so well. To mix opaquing for flats, dry whiting and glue size are used in these proportions:

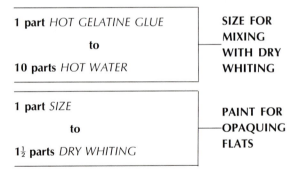

1 part *HOT GELATINE GLUE*

           to

10 parts *HOT WATER*
               **SIZE FOR
MIXING
WITH DRY
WHITING**

1 part *SIZE*

           to

1½ parts *DRY WHITING*
               **PAINT FOR
— OPAQUING
FLATS**

Mix the glue size by pouring 10 parts of hot water and 1 part of hot gelatine glue into a 5-gallon bucket while stirring. A quart can makes a good measuring container for this. When the size is ready, pour in 1½ parts of dry whiting to each part of size and stir thoroughly to dissolve lumps in the whiting.

A dry pigment color is ordinarily added to tint the opaquing; the amount depends on the specified color. The color of the opaquing on the back may be chosen because it will be seen during the action of the performance, or it may be a color selected to match the dominant color on the front of the flat in case there is a chance of the color bleeding through the canvas. Among the most typical colors for backpainting are raw-umber gray, black, dark brown, or dark blue.

APPLYING OPAQUE PAINT

With a large brush (like a 5- or 6-inch priming brush), paint the outermost edges first and then fill in the center areas. The opaquing should be put on sparsely, working the brush in all directions. At the same time, take care that the paint does not run down the front of the flat. Any runs and puddles that may have collected on the stiles and rails should be smoothed out completely so they do not soak through the canvas and cause waterspotting on the face of the painted flat.

Hanging Wallpaper

Although wallpaper is found more frequently in television and motion pictures than in the threatre, it is nevertheless put to good use in certain productions. When William Ritman designed the Riverside Drive apartment for the 1972 hit comedy 6 RMS RIV VU, he used several different patterns of real wallpaper in the foyer and on the backings. These wallpaper flats were sprayed with aniline dye colors to age them.

The wings on which the wallpaper is pasted are covered with a firm material such as veneer, plywood, or wallboard; these surfaces should always be clean and well sanded and all holes filled with spackling paste. So that the paper holds well, the new materials are basecoated with shellac (clear white or orange or Haeuser's Enamelac) before the paper is put on.

The most convenient way to hang paper is on wings standing vertically. Before starting, the height of the area being papered should be measured and an allowance of two or three inches beyond the required measurement made at the top and the bottom when the paper is being cut. A fairly large work table is necessary for cutting and applying the paste on the wallpaper—a 4-by-8-foot sheet of ¾-inch plywood laid on two work horses does very well. When you are ready, open a roll of the paper face up on the table, mark off an appropriate length, and cut it off the roll. Repeat this with a second length of paper, but before cutting butt the edges of the two lengths together and see that the patterns and joins match exactly. A bit of wallpaper is usually wasted in the cutting, but this depends on the distribution of the pattern repeats. Only with patterns such as stripes do

you avoid this. When the patterns have been matched, cut the remaining lengths accordingly. Ordinarily, a rough estimate (adding some extra) of the needed lengths of the wallpaper is made before starting.

If the wallpaper is not pretrimmed, it should be trimmed now. With the pattern side up, hold a long steel straightedge on the paper while cutting along the designated line with a sharp mat knife or razor blade. This trimming allows the edge to be butted, not overlapped.

MIXING WALLPAPER PASTE

Wheat paste, which is available at paint shops and hardware stores, is used for attaching the wallpaper to the surface. It is mixed by slowly sifting the flour paste into a pail of cold or warm water while stirring, using the proportions:

Pour 1 lb. of dry powdered WHEAT PASTE into 2½ qts. of WARM or COLD WATER	MIXED WALL-PAPER PASTE

Repeat these proportions as needed. For extra holding strength, a white synthetic glue is sometimes added after the wheat paste has been mixed. If you wish, 1 pint of white glue can be added to every 5 gallons of the mixed paste.

BRUSHING AND FOLDING THE WALLPAPER

It is customary for two artists to work together whenever wallpaper is being hung. One brushes the paste on the cut lengths of paper while the other hangs it. A special wallpaper-paste brush 6 to 8 inches wide and about 4 inches long is used for putting the paste on the paper. Once the patterned side has been placed face down, the paste should be brushed on evenly and consistently on each length.

Before the paper is handed to the artist who is hanging it, it is folded by a standard procedure. Assume the cut length of wallpaper is 9 feet. With the paste side up, take hold of the bottom and make a flat fold (paste to paste), placing this edge at a point roughly two-thirds of the total length, or 6 feet. Make a second fold with the remaining third, also with paste side to paste side, by lifting up the top edge and putting it down flat within an inch or so of where the bottom edge ends. Finally, give the larger fold two or three rolling folds, thus making the whole length easier to handle. This procedure is repeated for each piece of wallpaper being hung.

APPLYING THE WALLPAPER

The paper is folded in this manner because the short fold (top) is opened first, enabling the artist to position it immediately and then press it into place at the top of the wall while the long fold hangs down, remaining temporarily pasted together until it is ready to be opened. This method makes it convenient to handle and position the paper, especially since the artist is usually working on a ladder. Also, the folding lets the paper absorb the water in the paste readily, making it more pliable for hanging.

Setting by John Scheffler
WHO'S AFRAID OF VIRGINIA WOOLF? by Edward Albee
Directed by Garland Wright
Lighting by Marc B. Weiss
Cincinnati Playhouse in the Park (1974)
(Photographs — Sandy Underwood)

Prepasted wallpaper was put on hard flats (wooden frames covered with ¼-in. plywood).

The first length of paper must be applied very carefully, so the vertical edges hang plumb. If it is put on irregularly, the joins on the following lengths will also be out of plumb. A hand-grip smoothing brush is needed to press the wallpaper down and smooth out the wrinkles. This is done initially in the center of the paper, working from the top down. Then the paper is brushed horizontally from the center to each outer edge, again working downward. Excess paste that has gotten on the face of the paper is removed with a large natural sponge that is frequently dipped in a pail of clean warm water. At each joining, a small wooden wallpaper roller is pushed up and down the paper's edges to assure a firm hold. Finally, the extra paper at top and bottom is neatly trimmed off with a razor blade.

Similar techniques are employed for hanging wallpaper on television and motion-picture scenery. In these media, the wings are usually prepared when they are put together in a fixed position, whereas in the theatrical scenic studio the units must be prepared to disassemble for travel and set-up. In television commercials, sets are invariably designed with wings that are to be wallpapered, and newly constructed wings are merged with old ones to form a new set. Any wallpaper on the used wings is torn and scraped off, then the surface is sanded before the new paper is applied. Two-inch-wide masking tape is put on to cover the cracks, or a cloth mesh tape (2 inches wide) can also be placed over the joins of the wings by using a spackling paste (such as Dap or Muralo spackle), smoothing it with a putty knife and sanding it when dry. This mesh tape (like a buckram) is especially effective for hiding the cracks when the wings are to be painted rather than wallpapered.

GLUTOLINE WALLPAPER PASTE

Glutoline, an odorless, colorless cellulose paste, is ideal for hanging wallpaper and wall coverings that stain easily. To mix it, fill a clean bucket with cold water and pour the powder in while stirring. Follow the instructions on the box as to the amount of cold water needed; this varies with the weight of the wallpaper being hung. After 15 minutes, repeat the stirring until the mixture is of an even consistency, then apply the Glutoline like other wallpaper pastes. For vinyl wall coverings, Glutoline 77 is recommended. These products are made in Western Germany and are imported by The Henneux Company in New York.

WONDER-WALL ADHESIVE

Wonder-Wall adhesive is excellent for affixing both wallpaper and fabric-backed vinyl films to wall surfaces. Walls do not ordinarily need to be primed or sized unless they are extremely porous. If they do, they can be primed with the paste adhesive by thinning each gallon with a quart of water. This adhesive comes ready to use and should be applied uniformly to the back of the wallpaper (or vinyl) with a paper-hanger's brush or paint roller. It may be thinned with 1 pint of water to the gallon when applying on paper or lightweight vinyls. For hanging vinyl, use the same techniques as for hanging wallpaper.

If heavy-duty vinyls are being used, water should not be added to the adhesive. Remove any excess adhesive on the paper or vinyl with a sponge dipped in warm water. The equipment should also be cleaned with warm water. Wonder-Wall adhesive is made by the Lenox Wall Covering Company.

Covering Flats with Decorative Fabrics

The flats of an interior setting are now and again designed to be covered with a fabric purchased for the purpose instead of using regular canvas and painting it. While the fabrics are usually for a very elegant wall treatment in an elaborate drawing room or a salon (like a heavy brocade, a striped pattern of water-marked taffeta, or a Schumacher printed damask), they may also be much less expensive materials for dingy barroom sets and interiors. Aside from the fact that it becomes very expensive to duplicate certain patterns in great detail by painting them, the designer is often interested in the weight and texture of the cloth and how well it will absorb the stage lighting.

Covering the built wings with a decorative fabric is accomplished in a manner similar to that of covering them with velour, the main difference being one of matching and joining the patterns. Careful planning and measuring are required to do this each time, and one must take into account where the edges of the flats butt and overlap so the fabric patterns on the next wing join correctly. It is always best to work with a floor plan and to arrange the wings in the proper sequence before covering is begun. To prevent light leaks, the flats are often covered with muslin or canvas before the decorative fabric is put on.

With the selvage edge of the fabric always running vertically, attachment normally begins at the bottom of the wing, where two methods of attachment can be used. A tacking strip (similar to the one for upholstery work) is put on the back of the fabric at the bottom and held in place with tacks, making an allowance of 1 or 2 inches in the length of the fabric so it can be folded back under the tacking strip (see Velour Flats). The other method is by gluing and stapling the bottom, as when covering a regular flat. This method is used whenever a separate wooden baseboard or other applied material will cover it. In either case the fabric is wrapped around the edges and stapled on the back at the top and sides of the flat to avoid spoiling the appearance of the fabric with staples and possible glue stains on the face.

PAINTING SCENERY COVERED WITH DECORATIVE FABRICS

Most often the scenery covered with fabric is sprayed with aniline dyes (in a Hudson tank) to provide proper aging and texture for the stage. Although this is governed by the design, formal interiors may be given a subtle dye-spraying at the top, on the sides, or in the corners, adding contrast to the fabric and taking away the "new" look. Another approach is to comb the fabric with an appropriate color mixed in aniline dye, using a large brush on a long handle. This method is good whenever the design of the fabric visually "pops out" too much. For best results, the scenery should be laid flat on the floor while doing this. The direction of the combing on the flat may be vertical, horizontal, or both. If the design specifies that the interior walls are to have a dirty, worn, or faded appearance, the fabric is also sprayed or brushed with aniline dyes, and sometimes opaque water paints are used effectively along with the dye to create a diversified appearance.

Creating Three-Dimensional Details on Scenery

The stage designer is repeatedly confronted with creating three-dimensional capitals and cornices, whether the set is realistic or stylized. In either case, it is necessary to have a drawing indicating good proportions, particularly for capitals. One of the best ways to go about creating a capital is to determine the basic shape first and then proceed with the ornamentation. Capitals and cornices are shown on page 344.

Views of a classical capital — Temple of the Vengeful Mars in Rome.
(Courtesy of John Keck, photographs — Kenneth Pew)

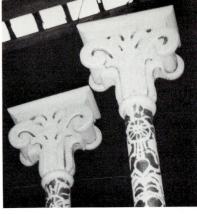

Capitals for TWELFTH NIGHT Lincoln Center Repertory Company (1972), above, designed by Douglas W. Schmidt were wood and Styrofoam atop columns of cardboard rug tubes; wooden stiffeners inside extended to top blocks of capitals. Bases were turned wood. Spiral ornaments (volutes): routed ¾-in. wood. Thicknesses between volutes: layers of Styrofoam. Profile leaves on capitals: ¼-in. plywood. Tops: wooden blocks with molding. Right: capitals on stenciled columns basecoated with vinyl paint, but not finished.

Painted capitals and columns on Lloyd Burlingame's muslin backdrop for AÏDA (1973), Cincinnati Opera Company.

Capital of flexible cardboard for Will Steven Armstrong's setting in JULIUS CAESAR (1966) at Stratford, Conn. Patterns for the volutes and leaves were drawn on brown paper, then marked on the cardboard, cut out, scored, bent, and glued onto a turned wooden base. Before painting, polyester resin was brushed on capital to make it firm and durable.
(Photograph — Munro Gabler)

A painted capital on Oliver Smith's linen cut drop for SLEEPING BEAUTY (1974), American Ballet Theatre.

Capitals built with two thicknesses of ¾-in. wood for the volutes, with routed edges. A stock piece of egg-and-dart molding forms the echinus between the spirals.

Cornice for THERE'S A GIRL IN MY SOUP (1967), designed by Hutchison Scott, was constructed completely of wood, including egg-and-dart molding on the bottom portion. The end of the cornice shows how the different pieces of wood were put together.
(Photograph — Munro Gabler)

A three-dimensional Corinthian capital made of composition ornament on a wooden shaft, available from the American Wood Column Corp., Brooklyn.

Three-dimensional leaves, below, were cut out of Ozite rug padding and glued on the curved wooden-cornice unit of Oliver Smith's set for PLAZA SUITE (1968). After scenic dope was brushed on the leaves, the whole cornice was laid in and painted with water-base paints.
(Photographs — Munro Gabler)

Douglas W. Schmidt's enormous cornice for Gorky's ENEMIES (1972), Vivian Beaumont Theatre, was constructed of an assortment of wood. The cornice was covered with canvas, laid in with a base color, then painted with colors mixed to represent light and shade. The end was covered with black velour.
(Photographs — Lynn Pecktal)

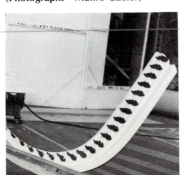

Photo Blow-Ups and Stock Posters

Whether for a prop or for set dressing, a photo blow-up (like those of movie stars) or a light-stock travel poster must inevitably be mounted for the stage. For practicality these are most often mounted on $\frac{1}{4}$-inch plywood or Masonite. The following method was used in mounting the many photo blow-ups and posters in Robert Randolph's stage designs for *Applause*, both in the settings for Joe Allen's and for the Gay Bar. To mount a photo blow-up or light-stock poster permanently, these supplies are needed: mounting board, cut to size with edges sanded; white flexible glue, such as Elmer's; 6-inch paint roller and roller tray; a clean wet flat sponge; and a large container of clean water.

Roll up the large photo and completely submerge it in a container of water large enough to contain it without bending. While this is soaking, pour the white glue into the tray and with the roller apply the glue on the mounting board. It should be put on evenly, completely covering the board's surface. Remove the photo from the water, unroll and lay it flat on clean paper just long enough for the excess water to dry off. It is easier if someone helps hold the photo during the mounting. With two people holding the four corners, the photo should be lifted and guided into place, and the helper (positioned at the top) should press his two corners into place. Continue holding the bottom of the photo in the air while the helper (working from the top downward) gradually presses down the remainder and smooths out the center of the photo with the clean wet sponge. Then, working outward from the center, smooth out the remaining edges, pressing out all air bubbles and wrinkles. The mounted print should be allowed to dry before handling.

Scenery for Marionette Theatres

The techniques for designing, building, and painting scenery for a touring marionette theatre are very much the same as those for the conventional stage, but on a much smaller scale. The reduced size, however, does not reduce the amount of time needed for planning and organizing a new production. Usually only two or three people do all the work, seeing it through from start to finish, and then go on tour with it, playing engagements in theatres, schools, and entertainment centers. One such troupe whose home base is New York is the Dragon Marionettes, a company headed by Diane Menes and her husband, Mier Menes.

They present shows in a small portable theatre with a proscenium opening that is 3 feet high by 6 feet wide and a stage depth of 2 feet 6 inches. Overall, the unit is about 10 feet wide by 8 feet high, an area large enough to mask the two people operating the show from backstage. In the tiny theatre, the scenery is designed so the overhead structures always leave adequate openings for the vertical strings to be operated with complete ease and flexibility. An average-size flat for this company is 2 feet wide by 3 feet 6 inches high; to conserve space, the flats are often double-faced with canvas and painted to play in more than one scene.

Casein colors are mixed and applied on the surface of these small flats for the priming, the laying-in, and the finished painting, and transparent aniline dyes are used to complete the details. Included in the painting are brilliant daylight fluorescent colors that appear very intense in normal light and in the dark under ultraviolet light give a magical glow to the scenery that is most effective for children's theatre. These colors can be used on almost any kind of clean surface that is first painted white.

Backdrops for the marionette productions are designed with both the visual and the practical in mind. The finished backdrops of muslin (5 feet 4 inches high by 6 feet 4 inches wide) are attached on window-shade rollers from which the ratchets have been removed and which are securely positioned in a sunken trough in the floor rather than hanging overhead. When needed during the performance, they are pulled up and hooked at the top; this keeps them taut and also provides good storage. During painting the backdrops are first tacked face-down on the floor and the back is primed with white latex paint, which gives body to the fabric yet allows it to be flexible for rolling and unrolling. When dry, the backdrop is turned over, re-tacked, and the front is primed with white casein, the same medium used in mixing the colors for the final painting.

All set pieces and props for the marionette company are constructed so they break down as much as possible for packing and traveling, since the whole show is ordinarily transported in a single panel truck or station wagon. Space must be allotted for packing the portable stage unit, the props, the lighting instruments, the sound equipment, and the marionettes themselves in addition to the miniature scenery.

A typical show may have as many as 15 marionettes in the cast. Standing 18 inches tall,

John Keck designed and painted the very small-scale scenery for the Dragon Marionettes' production of THE PEDAL CAR MYSTERY (1971) by Diane Menes. (Photographs — Lynn Pecktal)

Strung on black-nylon fishlines, far right, the marionttes as they appear on stage. (Photograph — Mier Menes)

these figures are constructed with heads of fiber glass and body parts of carved wood; a washable paint (such as acrylic or vinyl) is used for the body details. Costumes are built directly on the figures; when a change of clothing is required for the character an identical marionette is substituted, since it is impossible to change costumes with the rigging attached. The different parts of the marionettes are moved by thin black nylon fishlines, and a single figure can have as many as nine attached, all of them fastened to a wooden airplane control at the top. To keep the lines in order, the marionettes are always stored in a neatly tied, cloth bag.

DECKS AND GROUND CLOTHS
Floor Treatment

Whether designers are working with ground cloths, carpeting, portable platform decks, or a covering of ¼-inch plywood in 4-by-8-foot pieces, they are constantly seeking new ways and materials to create interesting textures and patterns for the floor. Several examples of floor treatment in well-known modern productions can be cited. When John Bury designed the raked rostrum deck for the interior setting in *Old Times,* the floor was covered with 6-inch-square Masonite tiles, using two thicknesses (⅛-inch alternating with ¼-inch) arranged in checkerboard fashion. To provide contrast, the ⅛-inch-thick tiles were reversed so the rough back side was placed face-up, and the whole deck was finished with fast-drying Fabulon (a clear plastic resin coating for floors). In designing the brownstone apartment for Neil Simon's *The Gingerbread Lady,* David Hays used Masonite in another way. Sheets of 4-by-8-foot Masonite (⁵⁄₁₆ inch thick) were laid out flat on the stage deck to form the complete floor, then parquet patterns were drawn on and cut into the Masonite by scoring with a router. After the individual boards were painted and grained in vinyl paints, a clear varnish was applied over the surface.

Plywood is another material that has long been put to good use as a floor covering for stage settings. Such a set was Carl Toms'

English country house for the New York production of *Sleuth,* in which Toms designed the floor to have patterns of slightly raised large stonework. The whole playing area of the set was first covered with sheets of ¼-inch plywood (4 by 8 feet) that functioned as a base for the applied stones. The random stones (also cut out of ¼-inch ply) were tacked on this plywood covering after their edges had been well sanded. Then vinyl paint was used for laying-in the wooden surface and also for modeling the final painting on the stone appliqués.

Santo Loquasto selected Ozite outdoor-indoor carpet to cover the raked wooden floor of his exterior sets in *What the Wine-Sellers Buy,* Ron Milner's play produced by the New York Shakespeare Festival at Lincoln Center. Designed to simulate rundown concrete sidewalks, the Ozite was cut away wherever cracks in the pavement were desired, exposing the ¾-inch plywood underneath. Textures were created on the Ozite carpeting by latex paints applied with paint rollers; latex paints were also brushed on the wooden cracks. For another Lincoln Center production, in the downstairs three-quarter-round Mitzi E. Newhouse Theatre (formerly the Forum), Loquasto designed an unusual ground treatment for *The Tempest.* Here he used several tons of golden sand that was contained on the circular stage floor by a 2-foot-high circular rim.

Metal sometimes serves as a floor covering, as in Douglas W. Schmidt's set for *Antigone* at the Repertory Company of Lincoln Center. Schmidt incorporated various shapes cut from aluminum flashing, nailed on a circular wooden deck. The deck was then painted with transparent aniline dye colors mixed in shellac.

Still another material was chosen for a company of *Man of La Mancha.* Howard Bay used a custom-made molded latex covering reinforced with burlap for the floor. It had raised patterns of molded stone and was fixed to the raked wooden deck. The surface was laid in with latex paint and texturing with vinyl paint.

Check List of Floor Treatments

In designing and painting floors, remember that they can be executed for the stage with actual or simulated materials. The designer's choice can encompass an almost unlimited field. Even more variety can be obtained by laying out the designs in perspective or on unusual angles when feasible as well as by combining materials.

The physical stage can have:	Various platforms, levels, and ramps (on flat stage floor)
A flat stage floor	Raked stage (or portable raked stage platforms on top of flat stage)
Full-stage portable deck (over flat stage floor)	

ACTUAL STAGE FLOOR MATERIALS CAN BE:

Normal *stage floor* of wood.

Ground cloth (perhaps the most common) of heavy duck canvas. Laid flat on the stage floor. Can be painted in many ways, from solid colors to varied patterns and designs.

Carpets and rugs, ranging from Ozite outdoor-indoor carpet to wool pile. Can cover full stage floor or can be area rugs, random rugs, scatter rugs, accent rugs, runners, all put on the normal stage floor or placed over a painted ground cloth. Among numerous types are Oriental, shag, flat braid, acrylic pile, straw mat.

Sheets of plywood (or cutouts of same adhered on plywood sheets). Laid flat on stage floor or made to form tops of platforms, etc. Can be left uncovered and painted or covered with such materials as canvas, burlap, erosion cloth, Ozite rug padding and painted.

Masonite sheets (or cutouts of same), scored or unscored and painted. Laid flat on stage floor or plywood sheets.

Molded latex covering. Raised latex patterns reinforced with burlap and adhered with an adhesive on sheets of plywood, then painted.

Metal sheets like aluminum or tin, usually attached to platform tops or sections of plywood instead of stage floor. Generally painted with transparent colors to retain metal quality.

Metal grating. Pieces of metal grating, perforated metal, or iron grillwork can cover openings in stage floor or openings in platforms and have lights underneath. Also translucent effects can be obtained with fiber glass panels on top of open ironwork platform tops and have lights underneath.

Tile, cork, rubber, asphalt.

FLOOR PATTERNS CAN BE PAINTED TO SIMULATE:

Wood
    Plain strip flooring
    Random width planking (with wooden pegs or butterfly wedges)
    Parquet in various patterns (checkerboard, herringbone, etc.)
    Wooden tile
Stone
    Granite (rough or polished) in square or irregular shapes
    Flagstone (shale or sandstone)
    Cobblestones
    River stones
    Coarse sand

Marble and concrete
    Marble slabs and tiles
    Terrazzo (marble chips in cement)
    Concrete (marked off in squares or rectangles)
Patterned carpets
    Painted on a ground cloth
Linoleum
    Printed patterns (stenciled)
    Linoleum tile
Tile
    Cork
    Asphalt
    Clay

Brick
    Can be painted in several patterns: herringbone, soldier courses, basketweave, concentric circles, concentric squares, etc.
Natural elements
    Grass, leaves, flowers, sand
    Water
    Rocks
Other floor patterns
    Geometric designs
    Decorative ornaments
    Abstract textures

Making a Ground Cloth

Since a ground cloth gets so much wear during the run of a production, it is only practical that it be made of a durable covering material; No. 8 duck canvas, a heavy plain-weave cotton fabric, is standard. In making up the ground cloth, the widths of canvas are sewed so that the seams run parallel with the proscenium opening. The widths are placed together with the selvage edges face to face, then stitched on the sewing machine. When the seam is sewed, the selvage edges are pressed down together in one direction and are next stitched to the canvas (on the back) on the extreme selvage edges, producing a lap seam. These flattened selvage edges are normally directed downstage when placing the ground cloth; in this way the seams show less when viewed from the audience.

The outside edges of a ground cloth can be hemmed or may have webbing stitched on the back around the edges. Tacks placed along the

(Left) Model (from above) by Santo Loquasto
SEPHARDIC SONG — Eliot Feld Ballet
Newman Theatre

New York Shakespeare Festival, Public Theatre
New York (1974)
(Photographs — Lynn Pecktal)

PAINTING NETTING PATTERNS ON A DUCK GROUND CLOTH (below)

Model dimensions: Portal opening — 36 ft. wide by 17 ft. 6 in. high. Depth of stage from front edge to bounce drop — 35 ft. Height from floor to ceiling — 21 ft. Patterns of erosion cloth were designed to be painted on a duck ground cloth with actual pieces of erosion cloth continuing around three edges (SL, SR, and UPS) suspended by ropes from battens above.

A flexible stencil (below, left) was made with a piece of erosion cloth. Various threads were pulled out and the edges tied to keep them in shape. While one scenic artist placed the erosion-cloth stencil on areas drawn on the ground cloth, another sprayed aniline dyes over the erosion cloth with a Hudson tank to create the patterns shown.

The patterns of netting (below, center) were finished by brushing on colors mixed to represent lights, shades, and shadows. Both aniline dyes and caseins were used. The overall painting was varied by spraying with aniline dye colors. Shown is a dark edge of the ground cloth.

Pieces of erosion cloth used to continue around the edges of the painted ground cloth were tacked to the floor with nails so the desired patterns could be made by cutting, tying, pulling, and wrapping the heavy threads. A length of roping supports an outer edge.

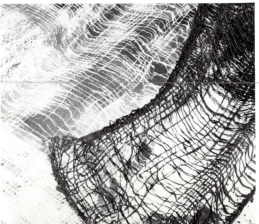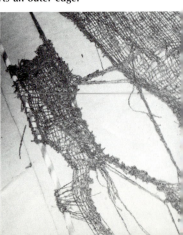

(Opposite page) Stage design by Allen Charles Klein
TOSCA by Giacomo Puccini
Libretto by Luigi Illica and Giuseppe Giacosa
Act III – Roof of the Castel Sant' Angelo
Directed by Bliss Hebert
San Diego Opera (1974)

Klein's stonework painted on the floor ties in
with the stone walls, an example of unity in a
stage design.

Setting and lighting by Sandro La Ferla
MARAT/SADE by Peter Weiss
Directed by Keith Fowler
Virginia Museum Theatre, Richmond (1969)

The setting consisted of a floor of wooden
shapes made of ¾-in. plywood covered with
aluminum sheeting extending into the
orchestra pit, tile walls of scored Masonite,
metal pipes, and showers with water
running over the floor into a trough in
the orchestra pit.

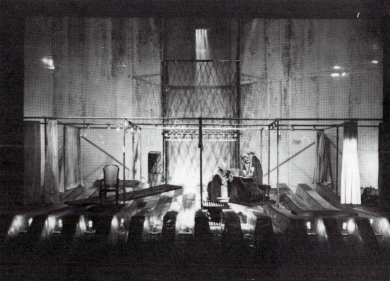

(Below) Setting by Kert Lundell
THE KID by Robert Coover
Directed by Jack Gelber
Music composed and directed by Stanley Walden
Lighting by Roger Morgan
American Place Theatre, New York (1972)
(Photograph – Lew Gluckin)

This western saloon set had a flat thrust
stage floor of planks. The setting was
approximately 38 ft. wide, 20 ft. deep,
with a trim of 20 ft. Among the materials
were black plastic panels, silver Mylar on
dimensional ornament, and crating lumber.

Examples of Painted Floor Designs

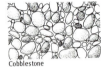

Cobblestone

Patterned carpet

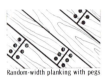

Random-width planking with pegs

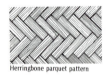

Herringbone parquet pattern

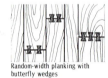

Random-width planking with butterfly wedges

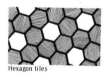

Hexagon tiles

Flagstone

Checkerboard tiles

edges hold the ground cloth in place. Overall size of the ground cloth can vary as much as the play, ballet, or opera it is used in. Sometimes they are quite sizable: a typical ground cloth for the New York City Opera at the New York State Theatre is 58 feet by 38 feet 6 inches when bound.

Painting a Ground Cloth

When a ground cloth is tacked on the floor for painting, lines are snapped and squared to form an accurately measured perimeter. Using a hammer stapler, always staple the bottom downstage edge first, beginning at the corners, then do the rest of the fabric in between, checking that this bottom edge is as straight as possible. Next, go to the upstage edge of the ground cloth and stretch the fabric (from the bottom upward) to the top line and staple the corners first, then do the remaining fabric on the top edge. Last, staple the ends.

The drawing for the painting on a floor cloth can be done either before or after putting on the lay-in colors. For these, both aniline dye and thin latex paint (thinned with water) are readily applied on ground cloths. Although a binder is not necessarily needed for the dyes, it does help make the dye hold better on the heavy duck canvas.

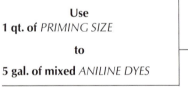

Use	DYE PAINTING
1 qt. of *PRIMING SIZE*	ON A
to	GROUND
5 gal. of mixed *ANILINE DYES*	CLOTH

An alternate binder may also be used: ½ pint of clear flat vinyl to every 5 gallons of dye. In either case, stir the mixture well, strain it, then pour it into a Hudson spray tank.

The aniline dye or thin latex paint is best applied by two painters, one spraying the color from the Hudson tank while the other brushes it over the fabric with a priming brush, using the same methods as when starching a backdrop. Working horizontally in the same direction as the seams, make sure that the seams are thoroughly brushed with the color, or a white line of unpainted fabric will be prominent when they are completely stretched open. Also, if there are any minor wrinkles appearing in the duck, they will stretch out when the fabric is wet. Overpainting on the ground cloth can be done in vinyl, latex, casein, or dye, according to the nature of the design.

Painting Full-Stage Portable Decks

Many large-scale musicals and some plays are designed to include a deck that not only covers the entire playing stage floor but often the apron and offstage areas as well. This portable deck, consisting of a series of 4-by-8-foot platforms and assorted plugs, is set up on the existing stage of the theatre where it is to play. It is ordinarily 4 to 6 inches high, with the deck top covered in ¼-inch Masonite. For each production, the deck is especially constructed to accommodate all the functions of the various pieces of stage machinery needed to move the units of scenery during the show. Most prominently cut into the tops of the platforms are the tracking slots for guiding the units that come on and go off; concealed underneath from view of the audience are such items as the metal cables from the winches that make the wagons and scenery move. To save time, big hit musicals on tour sometimes have two complete sets of decks—while one is playing, the other can be set up in the next theatre in which the show is booked.

The platforms that make up these decks are set up for painting in the scenic studio in the sequence in which they are to play on stage, and the tops and downstage front edges are normally painted with vinyl paints in the proportions of 1 part flat vinyl to 1 part gloss vinyl, without thinning.

Mix	FOR PAINTING
1 part *FLAT VINYL PAINT*	MASONITE-
With	COVERED
1 part *GLOSS VINYL PAINT*	DECKS

A vinyl-acrylic latex paint may also be used, without thinning. All these paints are used because of their durability, and they remain waterproof enough to be wet-mopped during the run of the show. For a large area of this sort, the paint is mixed in a 5-gallon bucket with a metal bucket grid placed on the rim for rolling off excess paint. Rollers on long handles are worked in all directions to put the paint on the surface. Any obvious blobs or streaks of paint should always be smoothed out well by the rollers. A heavy lambskin roller cover is preferable, since it holds an ample amount of paint and creates a heavy texture when rolling. It also makes it easier to apply paint over and into hardware on the deck surface such as countersunk screwheads and steel pivot plates.

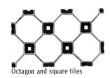
Octagon and square tiles

Squared stones

Brick Patterns for Walls
and Floors

American bond

Herringbone

Basket weave

Soldier courses

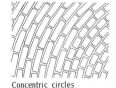
Concentric circles

If there are raw edges of wood made by cutting into the top of the deck for tracking guides, they should be painted with small brushes before the rolling. (These tracking slots are necessary, as noted, for guiding the units of scenery on and off stage and may move transversely, diagonally, or up- and downstage, depending on the production design.) By painting all of these the same color as the top of the deck, they show less, especially when viewed from the mezzanine and balcony. While many decks are of one solid color like black, gray, dark blue, or dark brown, others may involve several blends of colors or elaborately painted patterns. In this case, it is still most practical to first paint the entire deck with a color (using it as a lay-in), then apply the overpainting. If a deck is to have painted details such as tile, stonework, or greenery, it should always have a clear preservative sprayed over it for protection. This can be done by spraying or brushing with clear vinyl (flat or gloss) or with a clear varnish, which makes the finish even more durable.

Painting Rugs and Carpets

While rugs are usually rented or bought for a production, a designer occasionally specifies that a new rug (of a commercial variety) be painted with ornate and elaborate details, such as might be found in carpets of the domestic baroque or Aubusson traditions. When this is to be done, the carpet selected for painting should have a very short pile and should be made of cotton or a similar fiber in order to take water paints well. A synthetic fiber ordinarily requires the application of opaque paint, which leaves a stiff pile on the carpet when it dries and also takes an enormous amount of labor and paint. Indoor-outdoor waterproof carpet is sometimes chosen to have simple designs painted on it. Vinyl, latex, or casein may be tried, but this carpet too requires extra time and paint, and it dries with an unpleasant stiffness. Whenever possible, it is best to avoid having to paint a new carpet or rug completely for the stage.

Spraying down the colors of a rug or aging it is a different matter, for this does not require detailed painting or total absorption of the paint on the whole surface. When carpet fibers will take it, a spraying of aniline dye is easy to apply and will let the rug retain its flexibility. Thin watercolors may also be mixed in casein and put on sparingly by spraying.

Fabulon

Fabulon is a clear plastic-resin coating that is an excellent fast-drying finish for new or old wooden floors. In theatrical work, it can be applied as a gloss-finish preservative on natural and painted wooden floors and on Masonite-covered floors. It comes ready to apply and does not need stirring or thinning unless it has thickened in the open container during use. Fabulon reducer is added if thinning is necessary; it is also useful for cleaning the painting equipment. Fabulon is easily put on with a brush or with a mohair roller. (You should have clean containers and roller pans.) When working with Fabulon, good ventilation is a must; extreme caution should be exercised with this flammable mixture, and it must not be applied near fire or flame. Allow at least an hour for drying.

Painting Parquet Floors on a Ground Cloth

Instead of covering the stage floor with a rug or carpet, an interior set may have a ground cloth painted to give the appearance of patterned wood. Parquet floors, which were prominent in elegant European interiors during the eighteenth century, are invariably reproduced for both period and modern settings. For stage use, the most popular parquet patterns are the checkerboard and the herringbone designs. Although the standard strips of wood for these are 2 by 12 inches, they vary with each designer, and in the theatre the sizes are usually increased so they read better from a distance. Parquet borders of contrasting shapes are sometimes added around the outer edge of the floor to finish off large areas of parquet in a room.

The heavy duck ground cloth should be stapled securely to the floor before painting. Unlike backdrops, ground cloths are first stapled on a straight snapped line at the bottom. This is important for producing an even edge, because when it is placed on the theatre deck, this downstage edge shows the most. The upstage edge and sides of the ground cloth generally continue offstage in an interior set. After attaching the bottom, stretch the cloth out evenly toward the top upstage edge, and staple. Then continue the stretching and stapling on the sides. Snapped lines are ordinarily made for all sides although the heavy duck does not always stretch precisely to meet them.

For the lay-in color, aniline dyes or thin latex colors are splendid. Both adhere well to new duck, yet allow it to remain pliable when folded. Here again, the color should be put on by two artists, using the Hudson tank for spraying and a long-handled brush to spread it over the surface of the cloth. When the laying-in is finished and has dried, the drawing for the parquet patterns is laid out. As usual, the first order of drawing is to find the center line by measuring the bottom of the cloth. Mark this measurement with a piece of charcoal, place the 6-foot square on it, and construct a snapped center line perpendicular to the bottom.

For checkerboard parquet designs, the dimensions of the squares are marked off, working from the bottom edge and from the center line. Vertical and horizontal lines are snapped through the marks with charcoal. To avoid confusion, these squares are inked before the parquet strips are laid out, using a felt-tip pen or aniline dye applied with a lining brush. Proceed by marking off the individual parquet strips inside the squares. These go faster and more accurately when lines are snapped continuously through the squares horizontally and vertically, as in graph paper. When inking, select the charcoal lines according to the sequence needed.

After all the drawing has been inked, the individual parquet strips are ready to be painted. Usually, two or three transparent dye colors are mixed for graining the wooden strips; a 2- or 3-inch Fitch works beautifully for brushing the dyes on. Several scenic artists can paint on the parquet strips at one time, each taking a different color while graining the strips at random. When the graining is completed, the ground cloth is generally given a bath in dye to break up the consistency of the surface and to age it.

A similar procedure is followed for drawing and painting herringbone parquet floors on a ground cloth. One exception is that instead of snapping all the 45-degree lines for this pattern, a sizable perforated pounce or a stencil of the herringbone pattern is used to make the strips after parallel guidelines are constructed.

Painting Parquet Floors on Routed Masonite

Another method of creating parquet floors is by having the entire floor of the set covered with sheets of Masonite (4 feet by 8 feet by $\frac{5}{16}$ inch thick) on which the outlines of the small wooden strips are actually cut out of the Masonite, producing a three-dimensional, realistic appearance. Once all of the drawing

for the parquet strips has been laid out, a router machine with a V-groove bit can be used to cut through the drawn lines.

When painting the Masonite, a dark base coat color is effective, as this will remain on the V-shaped cut lines after the parquet strips have been painted and grained, thereby eliminating the work of having to paint lines on them later. The base coat is generally mixed with gloss vinyl or flat vinyl (or half and half) and put on with a thick paint roller. The graining colors, brushed on the individual parquet strips, are also mixed in vinyl. A clear preservative, like a one-hour varnish or Fabulon, is applied on the floor after all the painting has been finished.

Painting Inlaid Linoleum Floors

At times a designer prefers to have inlaid linoleum affixed to the tops of platforms or on a floor of plywood sheets. Linoleum may be used for such sets as a foyer, a kitchen, a dressing room, or a bath, and it is often painted like black-and-white checkerboard tile or in various colors. The tiles can be in solid colors or can have a decorative flavor with patterns made by stenciling. In most cases, vinyl paint is used on the inlaid linoleum and, when the painting is dry, a preservative of heavy clear varnish is applied. If thin transparent washes are needed, especially for painting over linoleum that has colored patterns, the colors can be made with clear lacquer and aniline dyes (soluble in lacquer). These transparent colors are then brushed or sprayed on the linoleum.

Painting Platforms and Decks Covered with Aluminum Flashing

The treatment of the floor is an integral part of any overall set design; it is even more important for an open-stage production, since there may not be much scenery other than the deck, and it is seen very closely by the arena audience from many different angles. Rather than relying on painted canvas or wooden surfaces, the resourceful designer may select a new covering material such as aluminum flashing, ordinarily utilized in house construction. This shiny metal surface is usually painted so that it is antiqued but still retains an interesting and lustrous texture. The effect is heightened when the platforms are designed to include well-defined geometric shapes on several levels.

To paint a metal surface of this kind, use a base coat of clear white shellac. Depending on the desired color or colors, orange shellac is

352

also good. The shellac is mixed with denatured alcohol in these proportions:

4 parts CLEAR WHITE SHELLAC **to** **1 part** DENATURED ALCOHOL	BASE COAT FOR ALUMINUM FLASHING

For speed and consistent texture, the shellac is put on with a thick paint roller, working it back and forth in many directions. After the shellac has dried (normally about 20 minutes), the surface is ready for the finished painting. Transparent aniline dyes are used with clear vinyl (flat or gloss) as a binder. As usual, the powdered dyes should first be mixed in boiling water, cooled, then added to the clear vinyl. These proportions are used:

3 parts CLEAR VINYL PAINT **to** **1 part** WATER (including the water in the liquid dyes)	VINYL FOR OVERPAINTING ALUMINUM FLASHING

These colors can be put on with a thick paint roller or with a brush. By using dyes in the vinyl, darker ranges of the same color can be obtained by going over them a second or third time, thus giving more contrast to the texturing. To preserve the final painting, clear white shellac is sprayed over the surface with a Hudson spray tank. The shellac should always be strained before it is poured into the tank, which should be thoroughly cleaned out with alcohol immediately after using.

FURNITURE

Selecting Furniture for the Broadway Stage

Since the appearance of furniture in a stage setting is as prominent as any of the other scenic elements, a great deal of care goes into choosing it for Broadway productions. Not only must it meet all of the visual requirements, it must be practical as well. Furniture for a setting may be acquired by renting, borrowing, buying, or by making it; stage furniture is often designed for construction in the scenic shop. When a designer goes to pick out a piece of furniture for a production, consideration for selection is based on such characteristics as style, period, shape, size, color, and whether it is functional. In tracking down furniture, the telephone often proves to be a fast way of locating a special

piece; when one appears to be a possibility, the scenic designer or an assistant goes to look at it.

The source of furniture and props varies widely with the individual designer and production in New York, but they can come from almost anywhere—Bloomingdale's, Macy's, Azuma, the Salvation Army, or even a neighborhood thrift shop—and certain galleries deal primarily in supplying pieces for theatrical shows. Some of these galleries rent furniture on a weekly basis, stipulating that if the show runs a certain length of time, the furniture is considered bought; other dealers may sell it outright. One of the oldest and most notable galleries for supplying superb antique furniture and *objets d'art* in New York is the Newel Art Galleries. Another well-known gallery that also has period furniture and other stage pieces is Encore Studio (see p. 400).

Renovating Stage Furniture

Both new and used furniture purchased for a Broadway production is delivered to the scenic shop to be altered to fit the needs of the show. This includes both pieces of furniture fine enough for any home and objects strictly for the stage. New pieces are sent mostly for painting, while the used furniture is there primarily for a general repair job, which can include anything from strengthening and bracing the legs to make them sturdy to fixing the seats so they do not sink when the actors use them on stage. Sometimes the size or shape of the furniture must be altered for the action as well as the visual effect. A section may be cut out of the center of a long dining table to make it smaller, or a Chippendale sofa may have the legs made higher, especially if it is to play on a raked stage where each leg must be added onto according to the way the piece sits on the rake.

One production for which an enormous quantity of furniture was renovated to conform with the designer's specifications was Boris Aronson's setting for Arthur Miller's drama *The Price*, which takes place in the upper storage floor of a family dwelling. Massive pieces of furniture and assorted props were stacked up and meticulously arranged on a raked deck after various legs had been added, extended or sawed off, and other alterations had been made by the carpenters.

In the scenic shop, it is not unusual to have a complete piece of furniture duplicated by carpenters to match an original piece, provided it is not a monumental and very time-consuming task. When furniture is to be painted, it is finished according to the designer's color sketch and notations, which indicate such details as the kind of fabric and upholstery materials to be used. Furniture may also be upholstered in the shop after it has been painted, or it can be sent to a drapery house for covering.

Designing Stage Furniture

There are all sorts of reasons why stage furniture is designed to be constructed for a production rather than bought or rented, and the type of production involved determines this. Furniture may be constructed because of one or more of these factors: It has to blend in with the rest of the visual elements of the designer's overall scenic concept (for example, the furniture and props throughout Eugene Berman's production of the ballet *Pulcinella*); duplicates are needed (like the matching benches in Ben Edwards' *Purlie* church scene or the pews in Oliver Smith's *Mass*); special effects or some particular action must happen with it (Jo Mielziner's desks and seats rising up and lowering into the deck of *The Prime of Miss Jean Brodie*, which were operated by a hand winch); it is impossible to find the right kind of furniture or the cost is prohibitive (items such as harpsichords, organs, or the decoratively painted baby grand piano Raoul Pène du Bois designed for *No, No, Nanette*); or it has to be practical in size or weight (four-poster beds, armoires, refrigerators, or a period stove like the one Carl Toms created for *Sleuth*).

When furniture is to be made, the designer does drawings (plans, elevations, sections, and details) that are drafted like those for the scenery, but ordinarily in a larger scale such as $1\frac{1}{2}$ inch = 1 foot or 3 inches = 1 foot, and often in more elaborate detail than for scenery. Unless drawings are made of the furniture, it may not be figured at a bid session, because there is no way for the studio head to know exactly what the designer has in mind. (For the same reason, carpeting and artificial flowers can be other items not included in the bid.)

Getting Furniture and Props Outside Broadway

Finding the right furniture and props for a show can always be a problem. While stock, repertory, and university theatres usually have a wide selection on hand, there are productions that require unique pieces. It may be necessary to buy, rent, or borrow furniture. Furniture may be purchased from the Salvation Army, Goodwill Industries, thrift shops, or other local shops and be repaired and renovated for stage use. You can usually get by with furniture on the stage you could not use close-up at home. Some companies will loan furniture for theatrical productions in exchange for program credit; others will have nothing to do with the theatre. If you are very busy working on a show, an ideal situation is to have a reliable person on props who will go out and find the furniture. Since you as the designer are responsible for approving the furniture and props for a show, it is enormously helpful if the person in charge of props can get measurements, descriptions, and take pictures with a Polaroid camera and then report back with these findings.

Touching up Scratches on Furniture

Old English furniture polish is excellent for covering scratches and nicks on furniture that is of dark or medium-dark finished wood. It should be applied over the whole surface with a soft cloth. Then, after a few minutes, the surface should be rubbed dry with a clean cloth.

Painting over Furniture without Removing the Old Finish

There is not always time to remove an old finish on furniture by using a product like Red Devil paint and varnish remover. If you wish to paint over old furniture that has been finished with an oil stain or has been varnished and has a smooth surface, you can do so with an opaque shellac. Dry pigment colors, first dissolved in denatured alcohol, can be mixed with clear white shellac, orange shellac, or Haeuser's white (opaque) Enamelac to make the desired color. You may want to mix the actual color and complete the painting in one process. Or you can mix the shellac color as an undertone and make it a bit lighter than the finished color, then grain over it with a thin color. The latter can be vinyl paint thinned with water or an oil-base paint thinned with turpentine. For durability, a preservative of clear flat or gloss varnish can be brushed over the surface.

Putting a Stain on Furniture of New Wood

Several transparent finishes can be put on new wood to allow the natural graining to show through. An oil stain such as Ox-Line can be thinned with turpentine and brushed on the new wood. The amount of turpentine added determines the lightness of the stain. You can also use Minwax products. In addition, aniline dyes can be mixed in water and applied on the raw wood. So that the dye does not run or rub off when it is exposed to water or moisture, always plan to coat it with a clear varnish. One of the best is Marvethane, a polyurethane varnish by Sherwin-Williams, which is tough, durable, and dries rapidly. It comes in gloss or satin finish and is also an excellent varnish for finishing furniture for home use. For best results on furniture, two or three coats should be applied. At least twelve hours should be allowed between coats, and when each coat is thoroughly dry, a smoother finish can be had by rubbing each coat with very fine steel wool, making sure that the surface is wiped clean each time. The surface can be enhanced by applying Johnson's paste wax and then rubbing it with a soft cloth to obtain a very glossy finish.

Filling in Holes and Cracks in Furniture

Plastic Wood (cellulose fiber filler), which comes in cans and tubes, is splendid for filling holes and cracks in furniture. It is available in several wood colors and in natural. The Plastic Wood hardens quickly and can be sanded and drilled, then painted or stained. For any large holes, the Plastic Wood should be put on in a series of layers, allowing it to dry between applications.

CONSTRUCTING AN ARMCHAIR WITH ¾-IN. PLYWOOD
A rustic armchair made of ¾-in. plywood for Lloyd Evans' setting in RIGOLETTO (1969) at the New York City Opera. Single layers are combined with double layers of wood and all edges are finished by routing. (Photograph — Arnold Abramson)

Stage design by Sandro La Ferla
THE RULING CLASS by Peter Barnes
Directed by Patrick Henry
Goodman Theatre, Chicago, Illinois (1972)

La Ferla's rendering in goauche, inks, and Conté chalk on thick illustration board is a detailed example of furniture and props arranged effectively.

For Arthur Miller's brownstone attic in THE PRICE (1967), Boris Aronson attached furniture and props as a unit for stability and to fit the raked deck. (Photograph — Munro Gabler)

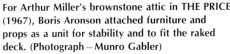

VARIOUS KINDS OF PICTURE FRAME

Average Dimensions of Furniture

The following information can be useful for drawing floor plans and front elevations, for making models, and for finding furniture (all dimensions are listed in inches):

CHAIRS	WIDTH	DEPTH	HEIGHT
Kitchen chairs	14 to 16	14 to 16	32 to 36 Seat: 17 to 18
Side chairs (ladderback)	18 to 21	16 to 20	40 to 48 Seat: 18 to 19
Wooden armchairs (not upholstered)	20 to 27	16 to 18	40 to 48 Seat: 18 to 19
Wing chairs	28 to 34	28 to 34	43 to 48 Seat: 16 to 17
Armchairs (seat and back upholstered)	26 to 30	24 to 28	36 to 48 Seat: 16 to 18
Windsor chairs (without arms)	15 to 19	15 to 18	34 to 40 Seat: 17 to 18
Windsor armchairs	19 to 22	19 to 22	34 to 42 Seat: 17 to 18
Dining-room chairs (no arms)	18 to 21	18 to 22	34 to 39 Seat: 18 to 19
Club chairs	30 to 34	34 to 38	31 to 35 Seat: 17 to 18

TABLES	WIDTH	DEPTH	HEIGHT
Oval dining-room tables	78 72	48 42	29 to 30 29 to 30
Round dining-room tables	42 dia. & 48 dia.		29 to 30
Oblong dining-room tables	66 60 58	44 40 38	29 to 30 29 to 30 29 to 30
Round pedestal tables	42 dia., 44 dia., & 48 dia.		29 to 30
Trestle tables	60 to 72	34 to 36	29 to 30
Tilt-top tables	24 dia. to 42 dia.		26 to 28
Tea tables (round or oval)	26 to 30	20	24
Square card tables	28 to 30	28 to 30	26 to 29
Library tables	60 to 84	24 to 36	24 to 30
Dressing tables	42 to 48	18 to 22	29 to 30
Occasional tables	26 to 28	26 to 28	27 to 29
Square occasional tables	24	24	27 to 29
Night tables: small large	14 to 17 17 to 24	14 to 17 17 to 24	25 to 30 25 to 30
Candle stands	12 dia. to 21 dia.		25 to 31
Serving tables	36 to 48	20 to 22	32 to 36
Consoles	38 to 48	12 to 15	28 to 30

	WIDTH	DEPTH	HEIGHT
End tables and lamp tables	15 to 25	15 to 25	20 to 24
Nest of three tables (typical sizes)	25	17	23
Tea carts	27 to 32	18 to 21	26 to 29

SOFAS	WIDTH	DEPTH	HEIGHT
Large sofas	72 to 96	32 to 42	31 to 37 Seat: 17 to 18
Medium sofas	60 to 72	30 to 42	31 to 35 Seat: 17 to 18
Small sofas	48 to 60	28 to 32	31 to 33 Seat: 16 to 18
Two-seaters and loveseats	42 to 54	24 to 33	31 to 33 Seat: 16 to 18

OTTOMANS, HASSOCKS	WIDTH	DEPTH	HEIGHT
Ottomans: large small	20 to 30 15 to 20	18 to 24 15 to 20	15 to 18 12 to 16
Round hassocks	16 to 26 dia.		12 to 16

COCKTAIL TABLES	WIDTH	DEPTH	HEIGHT
Oblong cocktail tables	36 to 54	17 to 22	15 to 17
Round cocktail tables	20 to 35 dia.		15 to 17
Butler's-tray table (open) (closed)	42 35	30 23	17 21

DESKS (typical sizes)	WIDTH	DEPTH	HEIGHT
8-drawer double-pedestal desks	43	21	30
9-drawer, secretary desks	36	19	76
7-drawer library desks	56	26	30
3-drawer desks	60	24	29

PIANOS, BENCHES, STOOLS	WIDTH	DEPTH	HEIGHT
Concert grand pianos	58 to 62	106 to 108	38 to 40
Music-room grand pianos	58 to 60	83 to 87	40
Parlor grand pianos	58 to 60	70 to 81	40
Baby grand pianos	53½ to 58	54 to 68	38 to 39
Standard upright pianos	57 to 70	23 to 26	44 to 50
Studio pianos and spinets	49 to 59	18 to 26	36 to 40
Piano benches	30 to 36	14 to 16	18 to 20
Piano stools	14 to 15 dia.		19 to 25

BUFFETS, CHINA CABINETS	WIDTH	DEPTH	HEIGHT
Buffets with china cabinets	50 to 66	18 to 20	73 to 78 Buffet: 30 to 33

Buffet with hutch (typical sizes)	47 to 48	17 to 18	69 to 70 Buffet: 30 to 33
China cabinets	32 to 44	14 to 21	62 to 74

BEDS; MATTRESSES; BOX SPRINGS*	WIDTH	LENGTH	HEIGHT
Daybeds	30, 33, 36	75	20 to 21
Twin or single beds: regular	39	75	20 to 21
extra-long	39	80	20 to 21
Double beds: regular	54	75	20 to 21
extra-long	54	80	20 to 21
Three-quarter beds	48	75	20 to 21
Queen-size beds	60	80	20 to 21
King-size beds	76 or 78	80	20 to 21

*Add extra dimensions for frame and/or headboard.

DRESSERS, CHESTS, DRY SINKS	WIDTH	LENGTH	HEIGHT
Dressers	42 to 72	19 to 20	32 to 35
Chests	32 to 40	19 to 20	35 to 55
Dry sinks	34 to 40	18 to 22	35 to 40

BENCHES, STOOLS, BARS	WIDTH	LENGTH	HEIGHT
Trestle benches	60 to 72	14	17½ to 18
Deacon's benches	42 to 60	19 to 21	33 to 39 Seat: 17 to 18
Dressing room benches	18 to 24	12 to 16	16 to 17
Hearth stool (typical size)	14 dia.		17
Bathroom stools	10 to 13 dia.		16 to 17
Bar stools	13 to 14 dia.		24 to 30
Portable bars	60 to 78	21 to 24	40

REFRIGERATORS	WIDTH	DEPTH	HEIGHT
Refrigerators: large:	28 to 34	25 to 32	57 to 66
small	20 to 24	24 to 27	50 to 57

ELECTRIC, GAS RANGES	WIDTH	DEPTH	OVERALL HEIGHT
Ranges: larges	36 to 40	25 to 27	45 to 48
small	21 to 30	25 to 27	45 to 48

TELEVISION TABLE (on casters)	WIDTH	DEPTH	OVERALL HEIGHT
Standard size	24 to 36	16	16

WALL DECOR—PICTURES, PAINTINGS, HANGING PROPS

Like draperies and lamps, paintings, prints, and other set dressing should reflect the personality and taste of the characters living in the setting and should always be selected with that in mind, although getting the desired size, color, shape, and design of objects sometimes obliges the designer to make compromises. But once they have been found, sufficient planning must always be made for framed paintings, photographs, prints, and other hanging objects so that they can be safely attached to scenery and stay in place. Any designer who has seen one of these falling during a performance knows the precautions that must be taken to prevent this.

If the flats in a show are not solid (covered with plywood), toggles or stiles should be constructed on the back to provide a firm anchor for hanging objects attached on the front of the flats. For large objects, it is always advisable to have two picture hooks on the back (which fasten into picture sockets attached to the face of the flat) so they do not shift. Paintings, photographs, and the like can also be hung on wires or cables attached to picture molding used as part of the design, or independently on a pipe batten from above. Pushpins can be used to secure small photographs or posters on soft solid surfaces like wood. Velcro is very good for attaching small items that must be removed during the show.

Checklist of Hanging Props

Paintings and watercolors (portraits, still lifes, landscapes, abstracts)
Reproductions of paintings
Etchings, engravings, lithographs, and prints
Tapestries and other fabric hangings
Murals
Silhouette figures and portraits
Glass paintings
Woodcuts
Velvet paintings
Modern silk-screen posters

Theatre and travel posters
Personality and celebrity posters
Photographs of various sorts
Maps and charts
Mirrors
Audubon prints
Musical instruments
Sports pictures
Framed needlepoint, petit point, Bargello, and other embroidery
Sconces
Wall clocks and barometers

Flags, banners, and signs
Hanging sculptures of metal, wood, glass, ceramic, plaster, and plastic
Hanging vases with foliage and flowers
Icons and crosses
Swords, shields, and coats of arms
Rifles and pistols
Calendars
Hanging china, plates, and trays
Bell pulls
Collections of keys, butterflies, dried flowers, shells, coins

A Conversation with DONALD OENSLAGER

This conversation with Donald Oenslager took place in his office-studio, located high above Broadway in the heart of Times Square. Born March 7, 1902, in Harrisburg, Pennsylvania, Oenslager was educated at Phillips Exeter Academy and Harvard. His distinguished theatrical career ranks him as one of the major stage designers of the twentieth century. From the time he made his professional debut with the ballet *Sooner and Later* in 1925, he has designed more than 250 productions for the New York theatre, including operas, musicals, ballets, and dramas. Donald Oenslager has been a consultant on theatre architecture and design for countless projects. He has lectured extensively, and his work has been represented in numerous exhibitions. In addition, he has written *Scenery, Then and Now* (1936, rev. 1966), *The Theatre of Bali* (1941), and *Stage Design — Four Centuries of Scenic Invention* (1975). Among his many awards are an honorary doctorate of fine arts, a doctorate of humane letters, and the coveted Tony Award. As Professor of Scenic Design at the Yale Drama School for four and a half decades, he has had an extraordinary influence on several generations of Broadway designers — Will Steven Armstrong, Patton Campbell, Stewart Chaney, Peggy Clark, Alvin Colt, John Conklin, William and Jean Eckart, Eldon Elder, Charles Elson, Lloyd Evans, David Hays, Peter Larkin, Sam Leve, Santo Loquasto, Jean Rosenthal, Robert U. Taylor, and Fred Voelpel, to name only a few. Some of the Broadway productions and operas for which he has designed both settings and lighting are:

Good News (1974)	*Coriolanus* (1954)	*A Doll's House* (1937)
Spofford (1967)	*Peer Gynt* (1951)	*Otello* — Metropolitan Opera
Orfeo — New York City Opera	*Years Ago* (1946)	(1937)
(1960)	*Abduction from the Seraglio* —	*You Can't Take It with You* (1936)
A Majority of One (1959)	Metropolitan Opera (1946)	*Johnny Johnson* (1936)
The Marriage-Go-Round	*Born Yesterday* (1945)	*First Lady* (1935)
(1958)	*Pygmalion* (1945)	*The Farmer Takes a Wife* (1934)
The Pleasure of His Company	*My Sister Eileen* (1940)	*Salome* — Metropolitan Opera
(1958)	*The American Way* (1939)	(1934)
Mary Stuart (1957)	*The Man Who Came to Dinner* (1939)	*Anything Goes* (1934)
Major Barbara (1956)	*Of Mice and Men* (1937)	*Girl Crazy* (1930)

Setting and costumes by Donald Oenslager
TOSCA by Giacomo Puccini
Libretto by Luigi Illica and Giuseppe Giacosa
Act I — Interior of the church of Sant'
   Andrea della Valle

Directed by Tito Capobianco
Lighting by Hans Sondheimer
New York City Opera
New York State Theatre (1966)
(Photograph — © Beth Bergman 1974)

Stage design by Donald Oenslager
DIDO AND AENEAS by Henry Purcell
Libretto by Nahum Tate
Directed by Elemer Nagy

Produced by the Yale Theatre
New Haven, Connecticut (1953)
(Photograph—Peter A. Juley and Son)

Did you study stage design at Harvard?

After a fashion. George Pierce Baker gave a course on the history of dramatic literature. But then I took courses on drawing and painting and concentrated in fine arts. Arthur Pope, who wrote *Tone Relations,* was in charge of drawing and painting in the Fine Arts Department at Harvard. One day, John Mason Brown and I and one or two others went to him and asked if he would give us a course in stage design. He was very interested in the visual theatre. He said, "All right, let's do it every Thursday afternoon from two to four. We'll make a course out of it." So four or five of us gathered together and we made sketches and models and designed productions. We talked about plays and each other's work and criticized. And that was a course which Arthur Pope gave us in my junior year at Harvard in 1922.

Then I arranged another course with him. I knew nothing about the whole

visual history of the theatre. There were no books about it. Sheldon Cheney's and Allardyce Nicholl's historical summaries were still unpublished. I asked Arthur Pope this time if I could just make up a course of my own and do research in the Widener Library and the library of the Fogg Museum and investigate the course of the evolution of the visual theatre. After doing this, I made a report at the end of the year and he gave me a grade. While at Harvard I also designed a number of plays for George Pierce Baker in his 47 Workshop and I designed many productions for the Harvard Dramatic Club. That was essentially my training—a self-training program for four years.

What happened after you finished Harvard?

I received a Sachs Traveling Fellowship, which was a very generous fellowship in the fine arts, to study the visual theatre abroad. John Mason Brown and I spent almost a year studying the theatre in England, Scandinavia, Germany, Cen-

tral Europe, and Greece. Our Baedeker was *Continental Stagecraft* by Kenneth Macgowan and Robert Edmond Jones [1923]. Bobby Jones wrote us a credo which we read nightly on the *Olympic* in the second-class bar until the paper wore thin and we had memorized it. We were very interested in observing first-hand the new movement of the theatre in Europe. That was the Symbolist theatre and the Expressionist theatre of the postwar theatre of Europe. We went to plays, operas, and ballets. We met designers, actors, directors, and technicians. All were most kind to us wherever we went. I made sketches and John wrote articles for H. T. Parker, the critic for the Boston *Transcript.* These became a record of our trip. All the time I went to museums, collections, and libraries, acquainting myself with these treasures, because I think that's invaluable for the practicing designer. I studied architecture, past and present, and began making collections of drawings and prints. The theatre we saw that

Stage design by Donald Oenslager
MAJOR BARBARA by George Bernard Shaw
Directed by Charles Laughton

Morosco Theatre, New York (1956)
(Photograph — Peter A. Juley and Son)

year and the theatre men we met gave us new horizons. Only Gordon Craig did not open his door to us, but by return note recommended that we study with an American master, George Pierce Baker. It was Professor Baker who had given us our note to Craig!

You worked with the Provincetown–Greenwich Village Theatre. How did that come about?

When I returned from abroad, I came to New York and asked Robert Edmond Jones if there were any possible place for me in the Provincetown–Greenwich Village Theatre, of which he and Eugene O'Neill and Kenneth Macgowan were the directors. I became an apprentice to him and made all of eighteen dollars a week. I shopped for samples of materials, buttons, and properties. I found costumes for the O'Neill one-act sea plays. I worked with Millia Davenport, their costume designer, sewing up costumes. That costume shop, incidentally, was above Throckmorton's scenic studio on 4th Street. You put your hand out the window and you had to be careful an elevated train wouldn't take it off. I also made certain properties for productions, too. Because apprentice salaries were slim by day, they put us to work in plays in the evening. I was in

a square dance in *Desire under the Elms* with Walter Huston. Eight of us were dancing in that little room that Bobby Jones designed. Every time I went around in the square dance, I looked at the audience and did a different dance step, thinking I was another character. That was the influence of Stanislavsky!

When did you design your first show in New York?

In 1925. Alice and Irene Lewisohn asked me to design a ballet, *Sooner and Later,* down at their Neighborhood Playhouse on Grand Street, which is now part of the Henry Street Settlement. This ballet, a dance satire, was in three parts. One was primitive dance, the second was the machine age, and the third was the world of tomorrow. We got Thomas Wilfred, who invented the "Clavilux," to project mobile rhythms of the crystalline world of tomorrow. That was the first time it was used in the theatre. It was a very early experiment in projected lighting.

What was your first Broadway show?

It was an Actor's Theatre production of a new play by John Galsworthy called *A Bit o' Love,* starring O. P. Heggie. In those years, an organization like the Actor's Theatre would put a play on for a number of special matinées just be-

cause there was genuine interest among a certain audience who came to see it. Robert Milton was the director. I did both the suggestive sets and the lights, which had to be done with strict economy.

Wasn't this about the same time you began teaching at Yale?

That very same year—1925. I had worked with George Pierce Baker at Harvard. And the year I was studying abroad, Mr. Harkness gave Yale the funds for a drama school. He had first gone to President Lowell at Harvard, offering him the funds to build a theatre and establish a theatre department, but Mr. Lowell felt it was not a propitious time to have such a department at Harvard. So Mr. Harkness went to the president of Yale, and Dean Meeks of the School of Fine Arts agreed entirely— with only one condition: that Baker would come from Harvard to head the school. Dean Meeks called Professor Baker, who said he would do it with alacrity.

Because I had worked with Baker at Harvard, he asked me if I would take on the training in visual theatre in the new Yale Drama School. I admired him enormously, and was glad to do it. The Yale Drama School opened in 1925 in

Stage design by Donald Oenslager
THE LEADING LADY by Ruth Gordon
Directed by Garson Kanin

National Theatre, New York (1948)
(Photograph—Peter A. Juley and Son)

an old house on Hillhouse Avenue while the new theatre was being built. When Dwight Wiman wanted me to design Ibsen's *Little Eyolf* in New York, Mr. Baker thought it was essential for me to remain in New Haven. At the end of that year, I said I would be pleased to continue on the condition that I would live in New York and commute to New Haven two days a week. For forty-five years I commuted twice a week, and later once a week, teaching the first-, second-, and third-year designers.

How did you arrive at what should be taught in a stage design course?

No one had ever given a professional course in stage design in this country, so I had to make one up. In the beginning, every area of the theatre except acting was taught at Yale. The Yale Corporation felt that instruction in acting should not be given in a university. I always believed that it was absolutely essential that designers know everything about the visual background of the theatre. By knowing the theatre of the past, I felt students came to learn theatre of today and tomorrow. That is why I stressed the importance of a knowledge of the background of the theatre—scenery, costumes, lighting, and technical work. I have always felt that tradition should be part of a designer's background.

It was my hope that by the end of the first-year course in design, students would discover their own talents and their own directions. To that end, I was very tough with students so that by the spring term, they would discover their own style and way of design and their personality as artists in the theatre. In the second year, assignments were varied and difficult problems, because in an effort to design his best, the student has to solve the most difficult problems quickly. By the third year, the students were on their own and responsible for major projects and productions. By the end of the third year, they were prepared to practice in the Broadway theatre or Off-Broadway theatre, or motion pictures, television, or educational theatre entirely on their own. Over those forty-five years of teaching, I tried to adapt my courses to the changing world of the theatre. I realized that teaching could be as exciting as designing. I have always thought learning to design should be as exciting as teaching it.

How do you work when you are beginning a production?

It has always been my practice that when I read a script, I think not only how it is going to look on stage, but how the actors will move in it, and how a director can use it. I first read the script for the pleasure of it, and then I read it for all the problems involved. Then I like to have a conference with the director. We go into it at great length as to approach and visual style. Then I draw up many plans on graph paper, knowing in plan how it will look visually in elevations. The director and I have additional conferences. Very rarely have we disagreed on the plan. It is not my practice to work with directors who try to design a production. Directors have to have confidence in the designer and recognize his contributions and talents. I've enjoyed working with many wonderful directors in the theatre, including George Kaufman, Moss Hart, Garson Kanin, Guthrie McClintic, and George Abbott.

You also design the lighting for your settings.

When I design a set, I light it at the same time. I never felt I could design a set unless I knew how I was going to light it. I've lighted almost every production I have designed. One exception was *Antigone,* which I designed for the Stratford Theatre [Connecticut], and there they had a resident lighting designer,

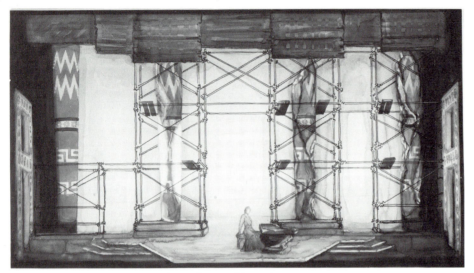

Stage design by Donald Oenslager
ANTIGONE by Jean Anouilh
Translated by Lewis Galantière
Directed by Jerome Kilty
American Shakespeare Festival
Stratford, Connecticut (1967)
(Photograph—Peter A. Juley and Son)

Paint elevation by Donald Oenslager
TOSCA by Giacomo Puccini
Libretto by Luigi Illica and Giuseppe Giacosa
Act II—Baron Scarpia's apartment in the Farnese Palace
Directed by Tito Capobianco
New York City Opera
New York State Theatre (1966)
(Photograph—Peter A. Juley and Son)

Tharon Musser. I have been interested in lighting from the very beginning. The possibilities of light at that time were wide open. Modern stage lighting was in its infancy, and I thought of lighting as a new force in the theatre. At Harvard, Stanley McCandless and I collaborated on lights when we did productions at Professor Baker's 47 Workshop.

You designed the sets and costumes for Tosca at the New York City Opera, which is in the repertory there. How did you approach the settings?

The libretto states exactly where it is set. The first act is in the church of Sant'Andrea della Valle, the second act is the Great Hall of Michelangelo's Farnese Palace, and the third act on the ramparts of the Castle of Sant'Angelo, and there it has to be! I did not want to reproduce these specific places, but rather achieve an illusion of their reality, like a vivid memory, more real than the actual places themselves. For the first act, the director Tito Capobianco and I decided to make the action more intimate and to set it downstage through a grilled screen that separated the forestage and the altar from the nave arcade beyond. You could see over and through the altar beyond the nave arcade in perspective. The second and third acts were quite realistic sets. The entire production was a collaboration, if obliquely, with Roman, Renaissance, and Baroque architects, and for a brief view of Rome itself, a mirror of Piranesi. I tried to see the scenes through the eyes of these artists and with my feeling for the theatre to dramatize visually the mood of the turbulent score.

You did the original production of Good News in 1927, and you have also designed the new 1973–1974 production.

Yes. I was delighted I was asked to do it, and it was great fun. They wanted to set the musical in approximately the same time. I had only one sketch of the original production, which was the portal I designed. In the twenties, every musical had its own portal and the show played behind it. I found my original design in the Museum of the City of New York, actually, not in my collection. I had given the original sketch to them years ago. This is the only piece from 1927 in this new production.

In your career as a stage designer, you have been a consultant for many theatres. What were some you found interesting to work on?

I enjoyed working on Philharmonic Hall in Lincoln Center—or rather the Avery Fisher Hall, as it is called today—with Max Abramovitz, and the New York State Theatre with Philip Johnson. On the State Theatre, I was the theatre consultant on all the backstage planning, the space allocations, all the mechanical equipment, and the lighting layout. Then I was theatre consultant with Edward Stone for the John F. Kennedy Center for the Performing Arts in Washington. The Kennedy Center offered all kinds of interesting possibilities. The unfortunate, indeed the sad, thing about that, as well as the State Theatre in New York, is that the architect was not told who would use it and how and for what purposes. It is exceedingly difficult designing a theatre when you don't know whether it is going to be used primarily for theatre, opera, or dance. It becomes a compromise.

Something you have written sums up the role of the theatre designer. May I repeat it?

Yes, certainly.

"In our theatre, the stage designer is essentially an artist craftsman. He uses his head and his hands. He must have a knowledge of architecture and sculpture, painting and engineering, decorating and the graphic arts. He is at once a woodworker, a weaver, a dressmaker, a plumber, an upholsterer. He assumes many styles of production, working as a realist or surrealist, or as an expressionist or impressionist. Creating his sketches is the happiest and briefest part of the designer's work. Good scenic design is good thinking, with freedom of imagination supplemented by reasonable performance in execution.

"First let the designer pause and ask himself just how the scene should look, first to himself and then to the audience. A stage setting is rather like a 'still life' on the stage—'nature morte,' the French call it. The designer's own feeling for the play will determine the direction away from imitating reality which the production will follow. He will be guided by his own compass of intuition toward a determined feeling or mood for the production. By recalling in himself a feeling he has once experienced, he proceeds to dramatize that feeling for others who have experienced a similar feeling. The designer translates this feeling onto the stage in terms of color, form, line, and light so that an audience will realize clearly as the curtain rises that this scene before it is no ordinary scene, but something deeply felt, seen for the first time on any stage. The scene may be the heath of Lear's imagination, or the haunting rockery of the Madwoman of Chaillot, or the ominous dwelling of *The Crucible's* rockbound Puritans. The designer has wrought these scenes from the hearts of the characters who are to inhabit them. Yet while he has made these scenes inseparable with the actors, he has also identified them clearly with the audience's imagination. This is the designer's role in the theatre today."—Donald Oenslager 1902–June 21, 1975.

Stage design by Donald Oenslager
DON CARLOS by Giuseppe Verdi
Libretto by François Joseph Méry and Camille du Locle
Act I—Garden
Directed by Tito Capobianco

Hemis Fair '68
Produced by the San Antonio Symphony
San Antonio, Texas (1968)
(Photograph—Peter A. Juley and Son)

TEN
Creating sculptured scenery

A multitude of different materials are used for creating sculptured scenery for the theatre today. Wood, metal, plastics, plaster, fabrics, paints, dyes, and glues are combined with one another in numerous processes to achieve all kinds of shapes and effects. Although the methods and materials discussed in this chapter reflect those typically used for making scenery in the mid-1970s, new materials and techniques are constantly under experimentation.

Various plastic materials have become increasingly popular in scenic work. Although they have been used by industrial firms for some time, the use of plastics for scenery has come about in great part as a result of innovations and experiments by theatrical designers and craftsmen who have come up with fresh ideas, insisted on trying them, and found that they worked well. These successful experiments have become standard patterns for the execution of scenery.

The use of plastics as a material in the scenic studio is affected by the labor (time and money involved), the practicality (whether they will hold up well in the run of the show with handling and traveling), and the demand by the designer to use them specifically for effect. One designer will ask for a plastic material, like transparent vinyl hanging panels, to be used as it is; another may specify that a statue be carved of Styrofoam, although the audience viewing the sculpture onstage will not realize that it is a plastic (after the surface is covered with fabric and painted). While plastics may be lightweight and durable, they can also be fragile and often require framing and supporting. This is a situation that must be dealt with on each individual production.

While Styrofoam was used primarily to make simple stage props a few years ago, it has become an excellent material for creating large-scale units of sculptured scenery and sometimes even full stage settings themselves. Before carving Styrofoam in three-dimensional forms, large sheets and blocks are bonded together and then bonded to plywood that is supported by a wooden or aluminum framework. Styrofoam scenery is made in sections designed to dismantle like regular scenery for traveling and handling. Although sculptured Styrofoam scenery functions superbly for all types of theatrical production, including proscenium, thrust stage, and arena, it is extremely effective for presentations "in the round," where the audience can see the three-dimensional carving from various angles.

Setting by Robert O'Hearn
DIE FRAU OHNE SCHATTEN by Richard Strauss
Libretto by Hugo von Hofmannsthal
Directed by Nathaniel Merrill
The Metropolitan Opera, New York (1966)
(Photograph — Louis Mélançon)

Scene: Entrance to the underground temple.

Model by Herbert Senn and Helen Pond
LES TROYENS by Hector Berlioz
Libretto by the composer
Directed by Sarah Caldwell
Opera Company of Boston (1971)

Model by Peter Harvey
JEWELS
Music by Tchaikovsky
Choreographed by George Balanchine
New York City Ballet, New York State Theatre (1967)
(Photograph — Martha Swope)

Drapery wings — sculptured plastic and fiber
glass; jewels — clear vacuum-formed plastic.

Checklist for Creating Sculptured Scenery

Plastic Products

As the actual material or covered with another material or painted:
Styrofoam
Ethafoam
Celastic
Plexiglas and other acrylic sheets
Vacuum-formed plastics
Fiber glass and resin
Polyurethane foam (rigid or flexible)
Vinyl sheeting
Plastic rods, tubes, balls, blocks
Mylar
Polyethylene film

Metals

For frameworks, supports, armatures, or actual surfaces:
Steel pipes
Lengths of flat, round, or square iron
Sheet metal
Sheet metal ornaments
Pressed steel ceilings
Aluminum sheets, tubes, or channels
Expanded mesh wire
Wire forming cloth
Welded steel fabric
Chicken or turkey wire

Cast iron objects
Perforated metal sheets
Brass sheets, pipes
Tin, stainless steel, chrome

Woods

All kinds of wood for frameworks, bases, backings, sections, appliqués, turnings, and actual surfaces.

Board Products

Foam core board
Display foam board
Upson board

Plaster

Plaster of Paris for casting objects, making molds. Plaster bandages for casting and covering objects

Models and Molds

A combination of materials including:
Wood
Masonite
Plaster
Burlap
Plasteline
Metals
Styrofoam
Silicone mold compound
Latex (rubber mold compound)
Various plastics

Fabrics and Materials

For covering surfaces and for creating textures:
Burlap
Erosion cloth
Velour
Sharkstooth scrim
Linen scrim
Muslin
Canvas
Cheesecloth
Scenic netting
Sponges
Felt
Flannel
Rug padding
Carpet
Celetox panels
Scenic dope
Sawdust
Buckram
Shredded Styrofoam

Attachment of Pieces and Materials

Glues
Binders
Adhesives, cements
Resins
Nails
Screws
Staples
Wires, cables
Soldering
Welding
Brasing

Finishing Surfaces

Paint of all kinds including dyes, lacquers, and varnishes
Metallic finishes
Decorative effects such as sequins, mica, flitter, glass jewels

---

(Top left) Carousel horse for PETROUCHKA (1970), American Ballet Theatre. Styrofoam blocks were glued to three 3/4-in.-plywood sections, carved with sharp knives and narrow blades. Surfaces were sanded and details shaped by a soldering gun with a wire loop. Horse was covered with linen scrim and painted. (Left and above) Miniature Styrofoam figures for the Ferris wheel. (Photographs — John Keck)

STYROFOAM

Styrofoam is the trade name of a foamed plastic made from polystyrene (often called styrene). It is rigid, porous, and lightweight. Manufactured by the Dow Chemical Co., this foam is an expanded plastic that can be cut, carved, and sanded easily. For practicality in the theatre, the surface is usually covered with pieces of linen scrim or cheesecloth to strengthen it and to seal the surface before it is painted, although the surface is sometimes left uncovered when the show is opening in town and the Styrofoam scenery will not be moved around. If the Styrofoam surface is not to be covered but is to be painted, a coat of vinyl paint, a mixture of dope, or a mixture of plaster of Paris can be applied to seal the porous surface. A number of water-base paints like casein, vinyl, and latex can be used on the covered and primed surfaces. Paints that contain acetone or turpentine should never be put directly on the Styrofoam surface, as they will dissolve it.

Both blue and white Styrofoam are commonly used in scenic work. *Blue Styrofoam,* which is flame-retardant or self-extinguishing, comes in rigid sheets or in blocks with these maximum measurements: 16 inches by 6 inches by 9 feet long and 24 inches by 6 inches by 8 feet long. *White Styrofoam* or styrene is also rigid and flame-retardant and can be obtained in thicker sheets in sizes up to 48 inches by 96 inches by 20 inches thick.

Large Detailed Styrofoam Sculpture

From the very large to the very small, almost any kind of subject matter can be carved out of Styrofoam to create scenery for the stage. Designers have turned to designing not just scenic pieces but complete sculptural settings of Styrofoam. A few include Douglas W. Schmidt's enormous carved set for *Antigone* at the Repertory Company of Lincoln Center, a classical Greek wall of weathered and worn stone figures, and his less-massive setting for *Mary Stuart* (also for Lincoln Center), which was an elaborately shaped royal crest simulating carved wood. In 1968 Rouben Ter-Arutunian filled the Mark Hellinger stage with a gigantic façade that had all sorts of details (animals, trees, flowers, and small buildings) for the short-lived musical *I'm Solomon,* plus other large carved Styrofoam units in the show. All these stage settings were supported by a framework of wood constructed from full-scale drawings, and the thickness of the Styrofoam varied from 2 to 18 inches.

MAKING DRAWINGS FOR STYROFOAM SCULPTURE

To start work on large objects that are to be made of Styrofoam, full-scale drawings are made to show both the front elevation and the plan. If it is an intricate piece, the side view is also done, and sometimes a section view or views. These drawings, on brown Kraft paper, follow the set designer's drafting and show all necessary measurements and details for the building, including the contrasting thicknesses of Styrofoam to be used. Along with the drafting, research may be furnished by the designer or, on occasion, by the studio. When the scenic artist has finished the brown-paper drawings, all the lines of the elevation drawings are perforated with a pounce wheel so they can be easily transferred either onto wood for building or onto the face of the Styrofoam for carving. This is accomplished by placing the drawings on the surface of the Styrofoam and rubbing a charcoal pounce bag over the lines of small holes.

USING THE DRAWINGS FOR CONSTRUCTION

The perforated drawings are then given to the carpenter shop for building the supporting structure and for cutting out the basic shapes of Styrofoam. In the carpenter shop, the wooden framing is constructed first and is covered with $\frac{1}{4}$-inch plywood onto which the rigid Styrofoam is adhered. Several glues and adhesives are used to bond blocks or sheets of Styrofoam to wood. Mastic No. 11, a Dow product, is an excellent adhesive that takes hold immediately. White synthetic resin glues like Hewhold, Bergenbond, and Elmer's Glue-All can be used, but they require a much longer time for drying and holding than Mastic No. 11. Hot concentrated scenic glue, which must be applied in a hurry, works well and is fast, but is sometimes difficult and awkward to carve through, especially for sharp details. Small pieces of Styrofoam can be bonded together by spraying Krylon spray fixative on each of the two sides to be joined and then quickly holding them together for a few seconds.

DRAWING DIRECTLY ON THE STYROFOAM

Not all sculptured designs need perforated drawings, and often simple patterns and shapes can be drawn on the surface of the Styrofoam itself after it has been adhered to the built wings or set pieces. For any specifically designed profile edges that must be built first, a pounce drawing is needed. Such patterns as brick or fieldstone can be laid out easily with charcoal sticks according to the specific design; for these, the Styrofoam may be anywhere from $\frac{1}{2}$ inch to 2 inches thick. Whenever brick is being laid out directly on a Styrofoam surface, the vertical measurements are marked off on each side of the wing and guidelines are snapped through the points, both for horizontal mortar lines and for those in perspective. Drawing objects like fieldstone on the Styrofoam surface does not require the same mechanical layout; stone is frequently drawn almost completely freehand by using the sketch or drafting as a guide. This worked well for laying out the fieldstone fireplace unit (carved of Styrofoam, then covered with linen scrim) for Robert Randolph's Connecticut set in *Applause.*

A pounce for carving is sometimes drawn when there are several repeats to be made of an item, like letters and numbers, flowers and leaves, or pieces of period ornament. On other designs, pounce drawings may be done only for detailed subjects (large-scale faces, figures, animals) that are to go on a generally carved background (rough-pitted texturing, for example) that does not need a pounce. Usually, large details are easier to carve separately and glue into place.

CARVING LARGE DETAILED STYROFOAM SCULPTURE

When the finished built units have been covered with the flat layers or blocks of porous Styrofoam and are ready for carving, they are brought to the scenic department from the carpenter shop along with the original pounce drawings. These units are far more convenient to work on if they are laid on work horses rather than on the floor. Once they are positioned, the details to be followed for carving are transferred to the surface by using a perforated pounce and charcoal bag or by drawing directly on the surface of the Styrofoam. For freehand drawing, built units with Styrofoam are sometimes placed vertically if their size is not too great.

THE INITIAL CUTTING

After the drawing or pouncing is finished, cutting and carving may be started on the stretched-out unit or units. The outer edges (profile) of a large piece should always first be cut away if this has not already been done. This can be done in the carpenter shop with a bandsaw, or by the scenic artist with a long sharp knife (like a butcher knife), a regular handsaw, or an electric carving knife. Next, the charcoal lines on the surface that denote divisions of major areas are well defined by cutting and carving a V-shaped line over each of them. A long knife is good for this, and the V shape should be at least $\frac{1}{2}$ inch deep. This cutting helps emphasize the different planes to be carved and prevents the charcoal drawing from being lost while working on the sculpture.

ROUGH MODELING

Rough modeling in three-dimensional form is now ready to take place on the entire piece; this involves cutting away the excess Styrofoam and forming the overall basic shape of the sculpture so that sharp detailed carving can take place next. A handsaw is quite good for cutting away very large thick chunks of excess Styrofoam. Other tools used for cutting away smaller portions include 1-foot lengths of heavy metal bandsaw blades with improvised wooden handles, which provide flexible and easy cutting. Keyhole saws also work nicely for intricate cutting, as does a long sharp knife. If the surface is to be rough when finished rather than carved in fine detail, a rotary hand sander with a wire-brush attachment works beautifully for creating a rough texture. (Always wear a mask and goggles when using the sander.)

CARVING DETAILS

In carving pronounced details, many of the tools mentioned can be used—which ones depend on the scale and style of the sculpture. An electric soldering gun with a nicrome wire loop attached makes an excellent device for shaping and carving sharp details in Styrofoam. This wire heats up without getting soft and melts through the surface of the foam as the wire loop is hand-guided over the drawing. The degree of heat can be increased or decreased by shortening or lengthening the wire loop, and the hot wire should be tested on a piece of Styrofoam before carving is started. A kitchen

Douglas W. Schmidt's Styrofoam scenery for ANTIGONE (1971) at the Vivian Beaumont Theatre in Lincoln Center.

butcher knife with a newly sharpened blade makes a superior carving tool since it performs well when manipulated in a manner similar to sawing. When conditions permit, several long metal knives can be quite effective for carving the foam by placing them on a stove until the blades become very hot. Used in constant rotation so that a hot knife is always available, these tools slice through the Styrofoam very rapidly. Good organization and caution should always be exercised whenever this method of carving is done.

CREATING ROUGH TEXTURES

While the artist's technique of carving can be adjusted to execute a rough texture by the crudeness with which the Styrofoam is cut, tools are usually employed to point up the effect. An especially good tool is the "shaper" attachment used in an electric drill. This small metal cylinder is about $1\frac{1}{4}$ inches in diameter by 1 inch high, with a perforated surface similar to that of a cheese grater. It speedily grinds away the porous surface of the foam, leaving irregularly carved patterns. For large general areas (such as backgrounds for huge figures) where a random texturing is desired, the shaper can give enormous variety in the carving.

By first holding the shaper perpendicular to the line and then tilting it on an approximately 45-degree angle and keeping it that way, V-shaped cuts and curves can easily be made with the edge of the metal cylinder. Also, the metal cylinder (again tilted) can be dragged over the Styrofoam surface to produce a routed-

Steps of Execution:
1. Full-scale brown-paper pounces were made.
2. Large sheets and blocks of Styrofoam were glued on the large framed sections covered with plywood.
3. Pounce drawings, cut into workable sizes, were transferred with charcoal to Styrofoam surfaces.
4. Carving was done with saws, knives, wire brushes, a steel grinder in a high-speed drill, and pieces of coarse sandpaper. Larger areas of drapery were created by using long strips of velour dipped in scenic dope. Rolls of cotton were tucked under folds to keep them from falling down before they had dried and become firm.
5. Lacquer thinner was spattered sparsely on areas to produce an effect of aged ruins.
6. Scenic dope was brushed over the carved surfaces. (Model, left foreground, first photograph.)
7. The sculptures were painted with thin casein and vinyl colors and aniline dyes.
8. (Above) The carved and painted scenery onstage at the Vivian Beaumont Theatre. (Photographs—Arnold Abramson)

out half-round shape. Other interesting patterns can be created by arbitrarily raising the shaper slightly and letting it back down. In addition, the shaper can be employed similarly to grind away excess pieces of Styrofoam. Occasionally this is done initially on very large pieces where many variations are required on the overall surface. To dust off the excess Styrofoam that has collected on the sculpture during the grinding, a rubber hose attached to an air compressor is utilized periodically.

There are several other ways of achieving a textured surface on Styrofoam. A propane torch is an effective device for making rough and ir-

LARGE DETAILED STYROFOAM SCULPTURE WITH SMOOTH SURFACES
Rouben Ter-Arutunian's sets for the musical I'M SOLOMON (1968), showing enormous walls with elaborately carved details. Made of Styrofoam adhered to framed plywood, the carved surfaces were covered with patches of linen scrim, then painted.

(Above) Sculptured set pieces being executed.
(Below) View during set-up in the theatre.
(Photographs – Munro Gabler)

COVERING A CARVED ORNAMENT WITH PLASTER BANDAGES
Fast-setting Johnson & Johnson plaster bandage was cut from a 6-in. roll, dipped in water, and pressed onto a large carved Styrofoam ornament to serve as a smooth covering material. Imitation gold leaf was applied by:
1. Brushing on Haeuser's white Enamelac to seal plaster surface.
2. Brushing on a coat of orange shellac to give more body.
3. Applying Hastings Quick Drying Gold Size.
4. Applying the leaf.
5. Brushing on clear varnish.
(Photograph – Lynn Pecktal)

regular texturing by melting the surface of the Styrofoam with the lighted flame. A steel-wire brush with a bent handle is another implement that works well when it is brushed firmly and vigorously over the surface (often after the details have been carved) to give the appearance of aging and roughness. Lacquer thinner, which dissolves the Styrofoam wherever it is applied, can be spattered on sparingly with a brush to produce the appearance of decayed wood or crumbling stone. Krylon spray fixative also decomposes the rigid foam wherever it hits, and it is useful when designs are to be repeated in low-relief carving on the sculpture. With a regular stock stencil (ordinarily used for painting), the Krylon fixative can be sprayed through the openings, but they must be the proper size and style. The areas shielded by the stencil remain, while the cut openings allow the foam to be eaten away by the sprayed fixative. For some of the molding on Eoin Sprott's scenery for *The Masked Ball* (New York City Opera), an egg-and-dart stencil was used to make designs on a cornice that had first been carved of Styrofoam. This fast technique also works well with other types of stencil where low-relief carving is only $\frac{1}{4}$ to $\frac{1}{2}$ inch deep.

MAKING SMOOTHLY CARVED SURFACES

The process is more simple in creating smoothly finished Styrofoam surfaces. Here it is just a matter of how smooth and finely finished the details of a carving are designed to be. Among the tools needed to make the smooth surfaces are the metal rasp and the metal file, plus assorted weights of sandpaper, which are used with and without a wooden block. For small details, strips of sandpaper can be glued to short lengths of wooden molding and utilized as sanding tools; these molding shapes may consist of quarter-round, half-round, cove, and the like. They are usually around 1 foot long and from 1 to 2 inches wide. With these tools, you can consistently carve details that have sharp corners, flat members, or concave and convex curves.

COVERING THE SURFACE OF THE FINISHED SCULPTURE

Whether or not the carved Styrofoam unit is to be covered with a fabric depends mainly on how much it will be moved during the production's run, since the prime reasons for covering the sculpture are to protect it and help hold it together, as well as to give it a good painting surface. If a show is traveling to out-of-town

370

engagements, the Styrofoam scenery will be loaded and unloaded several times. Also, when a particular piece only plays onstage for part of a performance, more handling than normal is necessary to move it off and on. In both cases, the sculpture would definitely need to be covered. If the sculptured scenery remains onstage throughout the show and the play only has a limited run in town, such as one that might be presented by the New York Shakespeare Festival at Lincoln Center, covering would not necessarily be required.

Pieces of linen scrim or cheesecloth, cut into squares and rectangles with scissors, are ideal for covering the Styrofoam, particularly when you want to retain the sharp details of the carving. The sizes of these pieces are cut according to the scale of the details being covered, and it is really a matter of what works best for each individual area of the sculpture, since several different sizes of linen scrim can frequently be cut for one carved unit. For general covering, pieces cut approximately 6 by 8 inches work well, while smaller details may use 4-by-6-inch pieces or smaller. Large broad areas, especially if they are backgrounds carved in low relief, can require pieces as big as 12 inches square. The selvage edges should always be trimmed off, and if a heavier covering fabric is preferred, flannel is good.

These lightweight fabrics are adhered to the Styrofoam with scenic dope. (When you are making a batch, consult the section on mixing dope and its specific proportions.) The dope can be put on the scrim pieces with a brush, or sometimes the fabric can be dipped into the container of hot dope and then placed on the Styrofoam by hand. But a brush is necessary for pressing the pieces of fabric down into the contours of the carving, by stippling with the bristles, so that none of the details are lost. Allow at least a half-inch overlap on each new piece of material as it is put into place.

The dope mixture may be brushed over the surface of the applied fabric to produce additional texturing. Usually the dope is tinted with a color, so the sculpture receives a base coat at the same time the fabric is being put on. When it has dried, the covered Styrofoam is ready for the final painting.

ETHAFOAM

Ethafoam is an ideal material for creating sculptured scenery when flexibility is a factor. Another product of Dow Chemical, *Ethafoam* (low-density polyethylene) is the trade name of a plastic made in flexible round rods and flexible flat sheets. Both can be used advantageously on curved or round surfaces. This material is very easy to cut, bend, and glue into place. Ethafoam is made in flexible white sheets 2 inches by 24 inches by 108 inches long. It also comes in flexible white round lengths of 9 feet with diameters of $\frac{1}{4}$, $\frac{1}{2}$, and 1 to 6 inches. Diameters smaller than 1 inch are obtainable on spools of 1000-foot length. A few of the small sizes come in gray. Round lengths of Ethafoam work beautifully to simulate molding and ornamentation on scenery, especially on items like Gothic arches and the bases of columns. These round pieces can be cut into half-round or quarter-round and used with the flat flexible sheets to form many combinations on either round or flat surfaces.

Setting and lighting by James Tilton
THE GRASS HARP
Book and lyrics by Kenward Elmslie
Music by Claibe Richardson
Based on the novel and play
  by Truman Capote
Directed by Ellis Rabb
Costumes by Nancy Potts

Martin Beck Theatre
New York (1971)
(Photograph — James Tilton)

Bottom two-thirds of tree was bent steel pipes ($1\frac{1}{2} - \frac{1}{2}$-in. O.D.), top third lightweight Ethafoam rods $1\frac{1}{4} - \frac{1}{2}$-in. O.D.

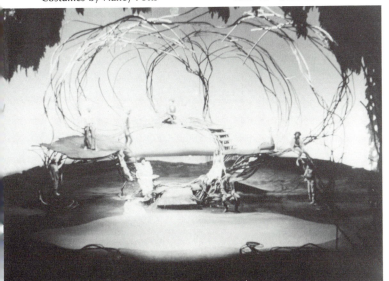

(Right) Ethafoam rods halved, glued, and nailed to Carl Toms' wooden fireplace for SLEUTH (1970); details rigid polyurethane foam. Flexible latex female mold rests on the boxed plaster mold. Scenic dope brushed on unit for texture, then water-base paints applied.
(Photograph — Lynn Pecktal)

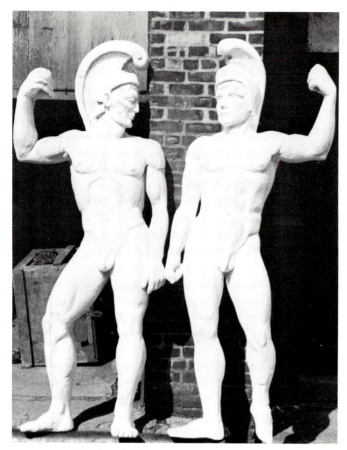

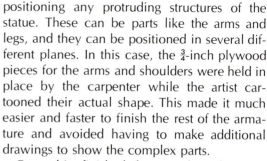

Life-size classical figures were carved from blocks of Styrofoam glued together on a wooden armature for THE YOUNG LORD (1973), designed by Helen Pond and Herbert Senn for the New York City Opera. The figures above, carved by John Keck and Bill Bellin, were covered with pieces of velour dipped in scenic dope. (Photograph—Lynn Pecktal)

SCULPTURED FIGURES IN FULL ROUND

Subjects for sculptured figures in full round may be the human figure, cherubs, mythical characters, and horses or other animals. These can be made life-size or oversize. Full-round sculpture, like half-round, requires that detailed drawings (front elevation, side elevation, and plan) be made by the scenic artist for his own use and for the carpenters, who need them for constructing the armature or basic framework.

The angel statue in the accompanying photographs is a typical example of full-round sculpture involving a combination of many types of materials and techniques. It was designed by Lloyd Evans for the New York City Opera's production of *Summer and Smoke*. Full-scale drawings were made on brown Kraft paper, then the outlines were perforated. On these pounces, vertical cores or sections of ¾-inch plywood were indicated for the basic armature, which the carpenters cut out and mounted on a wooden base with appropriate bracing. Frequently, while the initial framework is being assembled, it is best for a carpenter to work alongside the scenic artist as he is marking and

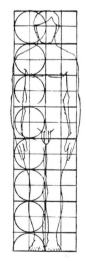

RELATIVE PROPORTIONS. Figures in heads and half heads.

positioning any protruding structures of the statue. These can be parts like the arms and legs, and they can be positioned in several different planes. In this case, the ¾-inch plywood pieces for the arms and shoulders were held in place by the carpenter while the artist cartooned their actual shape. This made it much easier and faster to finish the rest of the armature and avoided having to make additional drawings to show the complex parts.

Over this finished framework, galvanized forming cloth (wire in ½-inch squares) was used to model the general shape of the angel's body. It was attached to the wooden armature by staples and pieces of flexible wire. The statue's face, hands, and feet were carved entirely out of blue Styrofoam before they were positioned and fastened to the body, as was the large shell. All these details were sanded smoothly. Although much of this particular statue's body was clothed, other figures that are unclothed can be created in the same way. In many instances, a central core of ¾-inch plywood is profiled for the arms or legs with Styrofoam applied on both sides and then carved.

Before the wire modeling and Styrofoam details were completely covered, the angel's wings were made of two layers of ¼-inch plywood laminated together to produce a curved surface. The wings were fastened on the back with flat metal pieces on wood so they could detach for storage. Then, 2-inch round Ethafoam was cut in half and affixed onto the outer edge of the plywood wings with Mastic No. 11. The various feathers in the wings were made of heavy felt and glued into place.

All the final covering on the sculpture was applied by dipping the fabric into a mixture of hot dope (using the proportions for medium dope). For the heavy draping, suitable pieces of velour were torn, then dipped in the dope and draped over the modeled chicken wire while placing the nap of the fabric face down. To cover the Styrofoam details, small pieces of cheesecloth were placed in the dope and pressed onto the surfaces. Cheesecloth was used so the sharpness of the detail in the covering would not be lost. The hair and flowers on the statue's head were made by saturating small pieces of scrim and velour in the dope mixture, then modeling them in place. When dry, the whole surface of the covered statue became very firm, and it was sanded thoroughly before painting. On this particular piece of sculpture, flat white vinyl paint was applied as a base coat, then aniline dyes and casein paints were used for the finish.

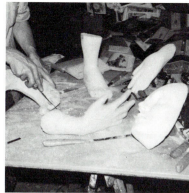

Lloyd Evans' full-round angel for SUMMER AND SMOKE (1972)

Steps of Execution:

1. Elevations. Chalk lines denote plywood armature sections.
2-3. Parts carved of blue Styrofoam (above).
4. The $\frac{3}{4}$-in. plywood armature was assembled; galvanized forming cloth, head, hands, and feet were attached.
5. Long velour strips saturated with scenic dope applied.
6. Curved wings were bolted on. Pieces of cheesecloth were placed on the head to see how the hair would fall and on the bosom to visualize the draped robe. (Left)
7. The painted statue mounted on a castered base.
8. Fine-combed textures were made in the wet scenic dope. (Sculpture by John Keck; photographs — Lynn Pecktal, Arnold Abramson)

CELASTIC

Celastic is an extremely versatile material to have on hand. It can be used for shaping objects in free-form sculpture, waterproofing the surfaces of finished props, making sculpture with negative and positive molds, and creating sculpture on an armature.

Celastic comes on rolls and is very simple to use. Pieces of the desired size are cut or torn from the roll of fabric (which is impregnated with a plastic coating) and are then dipped into a shallow container of the activator solution, Methyl-ethyl-ketone (MEK). The pieces of Celastic are placed in this solution just long enough to make them flexible and soft, and only need to remain for a few seconds before they are ready to be taken out and modeled into the desired shape. It takes about 30 minutes for the Celastic to dry firmly, and then the surface can be painted. Heavy-duty rubber gloves should *always* be worn to protect the hands when using Celastic in the activator solution.

Manufactured in three weights (light, medium, and heavy), Celastic comes in a gray color on 25-yard rolls. It is made in widths of 47, 32, and 16 inches.

The activating solution, Methyl-ethyl-ketone, can be obtained from local chemical supply houses or hardware stores.

Shaping Objects in Free-Form Sculpture

For shaping objects in free form, Celastic is well suited. It makes many diversified types and sizes of sculpture for the stage — such objects as draperies, swags, rosettes, flowers, leaves, and all kinds of ornament. Celastic is widely utilized for costume draping on figures and mannequins, especially in the display world. The medium-weight fabric works well for this and, like other fabrics, drapes better if the piece is placed so that it hangs diagonally.

When draping, always allow a little extra before cutting the fabric so the Celastic can hang with a good fullness. Once the piece is cut, dip it into the activator solution (MEK) for two or three seconds and hang it up to dry for a couple of minutes before you drape it. This lets it dry slightly and makes it much easier to work with. When it is ready, gather the piece of Celastic at one end, position it, and attach it on the surface by pressing down tightly. If the fabric is a large piece, it sometimes has to be stapled to the framework or armature. The fabric should fall gracefully and naturally while it is being arranged, so this should be done quickly. Then staple the remaining end. After the Celastic fabric has dried thoroughly, it holds each draped fold in place firmly.

Items in various shapes such as ribbons and bows, decorative tiebacks, pleated bands, and fringes can be cut out of the fabric and attached to other Celastic surfaces by putting them on while they are still wet with the activator solution. The pieces can also be modeled separately and attached after they have dried by simply pressing a rolled-up strip of wet Celastic between the finished appliqué and the already dried surface.

Waterproofing Surfaces on Props

If props that are made in the scenic studio are to come in contact with water or liquids during their use on stage, pieces of Celastic can be applied on them to produce a durable waterproof surface. These may be for kitchen and bathroom sinks constructed of wood, fountains of wood or similar materials, plaster statues, or mannequins made of papier-mâché. For these, light- or medium-weight Celastic is best to use, and the pieces should be torn according to the size of the details being covered. Celastic should not be put directly on a Styrofoam surface, as the activator solution will cause the Styrofoam to disintegrate.

Making Sculpture with Negative and Positive Molds

A negative mold is made when many duplicates of the sculptured object are needed. If a full-round object is being made, two negative molds (front and back) are necessary; a half-round piece of sculpture would require only one mold. The positive mold is somewhat easier, and takes less time, since the sculptured model is the mold itself and the Celastic is applied directly on it after it has first been coated with a releasing agent.

NEGATIVE MOLDS

Assume that a piece of sculpture like a full-round classical Greek bust is being cast. After the two negative molds of plaster have been made from the positive bust and are ready to be used, they must have a releasing agent applied so the Celastic sculpture will come out easily when it has dried. Aluminum foil carefully pressed into the contours of each mold can be used, or ordinary grease may be brushed on. Tear off the pieces of Celastic instead of cutting them; tearing gives the pieces an irregularly feathered edge and they show less on the finished sculpture. Now dip these pieces into the MEK activator and press them into the mold, overlapping each piece so that it holds sufficiently on the previous piece. Continue this until each mold is covered with Celastic.

By placing the front and back plaster mold together, the two halves of Celastic sculpture can be joined while still in the molds, provided they are constructed with an opening in the bottom large enough for you to work through. If so, strips of Celastic can be placed on the inside seam and left to dry before removing. If not, the two halves of Celastic may be removed when dry and the edges (seams) joined by placing strips on the outside surface of the hollow sculpture. Before painting the Celastic surface, you should sand it lightly.

THE POSITIVE MOLD

The same techniques are involved when a positive mold is being used. Depending on the shape, it can be made in one piece, cut in the back, and joined with strips, or made in two halves and joined at the seams. A positive mold is effective for sculpture that is half-round and needs only one or two repeats. For example, theatrical masks or parts of costume armor can be made by first shaping the molds in plasteline clay and then using them as the positive molds. Once the releasing agent is applied and the torn pieces of Celastic have been dipped in the activator solution and removed, they are carefully pressed onto the clay so the shape is not damaged.

Creating Sculpture on an Armature

When statues and figures are being made, they need an armature to support the basic shape of the sculpture. These are ordinarily made of metal, wood, or both. The shapes are modeled on these armatures or frameworks with chicken wire, forming wire, metal mesh, wood, or a combination, governed by the design and the

USING CELASTIC IN A PLASTER MOLD TO MAKE A PROP MASK

Steps of Execution:

1. Model was shaped in plasteline over a Styrofoam base, then centered in a 6-in.-deep wooden box (with removable bottom) to make plaster mother mold.
2. Inside of box and clay model were brushed with orange shellac.
3. Plaster of Paris, mixed with water, was poured into box over model to form mother mold. Model was separated from plaster mold and mold coated with shellac.

4. (Left) Aluminum foil, the releasing agent, was pressed into contours and taped on the mold. Torn strips of Celastic were dipped in a shallow pan of Methyl-ethyl-ketone, then pressed into contours of plaster mold.
5. (Center) The Celastic casting (right foreground) with aluminum foil not yet peeled off. White mask at left was created by using three layers of plaster bandage strips in same plaster mold (mold sprayed with Johnson's Pledge wax so plaster strips would not stick).
6. (Right) After foil was removed from Celastic casting, mask was sanded and trimmed. (Photographs—Lynn Pecktal)

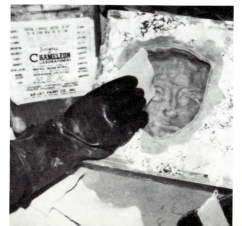
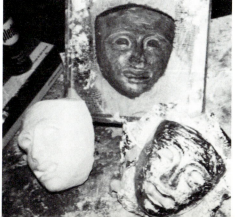

scale of the sculpture. After the initial modeling is completed, Celastic is applied over the shape, working with the previously mentioned techniques. For bulky props like rocks or tree stumps, the framework is constructed of wood and the same materials are used to form the basic shapes that hold the Celastic.

Other Uses of Celastic

In addition to theatrical work, Celastic is used extensively in display houses, where many similar objects of sculpture are created for both indoor and outdoor use. Displays made of Celastic can be found in amusement parks, fun houses, shopping centers, and in big department-store exhibits and windows, especially at Christmastime. Most notable each year are Lord and Taylor's, B. Altman's, and Macy's famous crowd-attracting Christmas window displays in New York City with their many small and elaborately dressed figures, moving mannequins, and props. A number of the little figures have costumes of Celastic constructed directly over the detailed mechanical parts that make the mannequins move.

Painting Celastic Surfaces

For painting Celastic surfaces, such paints as vinyl, acrylic, latex, and casein are easily applied. If a Celastic sculpture is to remain outdoors or if it has constant exposure to water, an oil-base paint should be used.

VACUUM-FORMING

Vacuum-forming involves the use of plastic to produce a three-dimensional hollow replica of an object. A mold is usually made according to the designer's specifications, but an ordinary firm object can also be used. This is a forming process whereby a plastic sheet (vinyl, styrene, or other) is softened by heat, drawn over or into a mold from which air is evacuated, creating a vacuum, and the pliable plastic sheet takes the shape of the desired mold. It needs only a minute or less for the molded plastic to cool.

For scenic use, molds are made of wood,

plaster, metal, clay, and the like without undercuts that would keep the shaped plastic from releasing from the mold when it has cooled. Tiny holes $\frac{1}{32}$ inch in diameter (similar to those on the top of the forming table) are drilled through a mold wherever there are any low depressions, so the plastic sheet can be drawn snugly into the contours of these areas. Commercially, the two basic vacuum-forming methods are straight vacuum-forming into a female mold with plug assists and drape vacuum-forming on a male mold. Toys, display packaging, and signs are a few of the products that are manufactured by vacuum-forming for industrial use by such large companies as Chanel Plastics.

Vacuum-forming is best suited for scenery or props in the theatre when a great many duplicates are needed. With the cost of labor and materials involved, the technique is not advantageous for the scenic studio doing commercial Broadway settings because they do not always require repetitious manufacture of the item. On an average, the demand is usually for three-dimensional objects of a very limited quantity. If so few copies of an object are to be made (like two, three, or four) it does not always pay for the time it takes to make a mold, go through the process of vacuum-forming, plus having to support and frame each of the hollow sculptures. But this depends on the nature of its design. It is another matter when a designer incorporates an enormous amount of vacuum-formed plastic into a stage setting, especially if it is to be used and realized as an actual plastic material and the effect cannot be created in any other way. When a scenic studio is doing a special job for a television commercial or a photography studio and the concerned companies do not mind the cost, a very large mold is sometimes created to be used for vacuum-forming a single copy of the object in plastic. This can be an item like a very oversized electric razor, which is made by vacuum-forming two halves and then joining them together.

Besides the number of objects to be duplicated, another consideration in the theatre is the practical aspect of whether the vacuum-formed objects will hold up with handling and traveling during the run of the production, including out-of-town, New York, and repertory. Although it varies with the item, most pieces of vacuum-formed plastic used as scenery need to have some kind of support or framing unless they are free-hanging. For instance, to support hollow replicas of half-round balusters may re-

Typical vacuum-formed objects are plastic bricks and sections of radiators. The bricks are $7\frac{1}{4}$ by $2\frac{1}{4}$ by $\frac{3}{8}$ in. in relief and the radiator parts are 35 by $7\frac{1}{4}$ by $1\frac{1}{2}$ in. in relief.
(Photograph – Lynn Pecktal)

For a basic set at the American Shakespeare Festival in Stratford, Conn. (1960), Rouben Ter-Arutunian devised a hanging arrangement of vacuum-formed plastic shapes. (Left) One of the dimensionally textured plastic patterns as it appeared before excess was trimmed off and desired shape cut. After shapes were cut, they were laid in place on the floor and wired together. A portion of the shapes was hung in the studio to see how it looked as a unit.
(Photographs – Munro Gabler)

quire profiles of plywood in back to hold them firmly. Also, any portions left hollow can easily get mashed when they are in use. If the vacuum-formed object must also be filled with some material like polyurethane foam or plaster to make it solid, it is often much simpler in the beginning to turn the baluster on a lathe, either using all wood or possibly using layers of Styrofoam affixed to a wooden core. On other items, like ornament that have been vacuum-formed in low relief, there may not be a big problem because the object can be fastened onto a solid surface of woodwork or on a hard-covered flat. It must nevertheless be packed, moved, and stored with care. Unlike Broadway, a good number of university and resident theatre companies are experimenting with vacuum-forming and some are purchasing or making their own equipment. This may work well for them, since they do not always have to contend with planning for a long-running pro-

duction and the high cost of time and labor in producing it. Another plus factor is that these theatres may count on reusing the vacuum-formed objects in other shows.

The average scenic studio does not have vacuum-forming facilities. When vacuum-formed plastic objects are needed, the scenic shop has them done by a firm that can either custom-make them from a mold created by the studio's artists (for example, a capital for a column per the designer's drawing) or from the firm's own stock molds (like sheets of brick and mortar). Firms that may do this include the NBC-TV Shop in Brooklyn, which has one of the largest machines for vacuum-forming (8 feet wide by 16 feet long).

Although the idea of vacuum-formed plastics is becoming ever more popular, some designers began using them several years ago. As early as 1960, Rouben Ter-Arutunian made effective use of vacuum-formed plastic shapes when he designed a background for the American Shakespeare Festival at Stratford, Connecticut. He utilized various potato-chip or petal shapes cut from a single vacuum-formed pattern in a milky translucent plastic, attached with wire for hanging. In 1961 David Hays created an interesting stage setting for the New York City Ballet *Electronics* in which he devised a hanging arrangement of long transparent vinyl forms similar in shape to logs with a rough texture. These were also connected together and held in place with wire.

MAKING A LATEX MOLD

A latex mold is used when several repeats of an object are needed, and may be for practically any item from a bracket support to a capital to a balustrade turning. Items being cast usually have carved surfaces or ornamentation, and latex is excellent for forming a flexible mold, because this rubberlike material can be easily peeled back to release the newly fin-

Setting and lighting by James Tilton
THE MERCHANT OF VENICE by
   William Shakespeare
Directed by Ellis Rabb
American Conservatory Theatre
Geary Theatre, San Francisco (1970)
(Photograph – James Tilton)

Rigid white plastic (polyvinyl chloride) tubes, $2\frac{3}{8}$ in. O.D., were used to form the arches in Tilton's modern-day setting for Portia's yacht. The arches were shaped by pouring hot sand into straight plastic tubes and bending them around forms attached to the floor. In the background, black-and-white photographs of Venice were projected from the rear onto three screens of Polacoat.

Lengths of bamboo are simulated with iron tubing when strength is needed. Rubber molding compound (liquid latex), for making flexible molds, is shown creating the bamboo joints.

Steps of Execution:

1. (Left) A model of long clay ridges (plasteline) shaped on Masonite.
2. From this, a plaster female mold, framed in wood (top left) was made (no releasing agent like vaseline since plasteline is grease-based).
3. After mold dried, a layer of liquid latex was brushed on the plaster surface and left to dry. More latex, mixed with filler compound to thicken it and speed application, was brushed on top of first layer.
4. (Center) Strips of the flexible latex were adhered to the metal with Scotch Spray Adhesive 77.
5. (Right) Lengths of the latex were cut to fit the iron tubing's diameter and applied, then painted. (Photographs — Arnold Abramson)

ished casting. Latex also works well when there are some undercuts, since a mold of firm material would hold these and not readily allow separation from the mold. The latex mold is referred to as the female, while the model (from which the mold is made) is called the male. Allow two or three days for making the model and the mold.

Preparation before Making the Model

Although a designer may occasionally select a piece of work and have it sent to the studio to serve as a model, most of the time he designs and drafts exact specifications for making a model. From these, full-scale drawings are made by the scenic artist, who refers to them often when checking on proportions, shapes, and measurements.

Before the actual model is started, further preparations must be made. A panel of $\frac{1}{4}$-inch Masonite should be cut for the model to rest on. To determine the size of the panel, measure the overall model (length and width) and add at least a couple of inches around all four sides of the model. This allowance is for the sides and mold that are added later. (If your model is a support bracket that measures 6 inches wide by 8 inches long, you would need a Masonite board approximately 10 inches wide by 12 inches long.) Using the smooth side of the Masonite face up, the model is centered on the panel as it will be when cast. While the model is shaped on this panel and remains on it during application of the latex mold, the Masonite also serves as the bottom of the box form needed for making the second mold. The purpose of this additional mold is to provide a more rigid material that will hold the flexible latex mold in shape when casting a new model. This is formed with plaster of Paris and is known as the "mother" mold.

In order not to disturb the finished model on the Masonite panel, the box form for the plaster mold should be planned so the sides, still together in a rectangle or square, are disassembled from the bottom when shaping the model and easily reassembled after it is finished. To make the sides, use $\frac{3}{4}$-inch boards with their lengths cut to fit on the panel. The height of the boards should be an inch above the highest point on the model. When attaching the bottom, use wood screws to produce a tight fit, as this is necessary when the plaster is poured into the box form.

Shaping the Model

The model on which the latex is applied to make the mold can include wood, metal, plaster, marble, glass, and clay. Plasteline clay is one of the most frequently used materials when a detailed model has to be made. Roma Plastilina and Plasticum are two brands of good-quality plasteline clays that will not harden. Roma Plastilina, made in a gray-green color, comes in different consistencies: No. 1. Extremely Soft; No. 2. Medium (slightly firmer, for average use); No. 3. Medium (firm, for smaller models); and No. 4. Extra Hard (for very small models). Plasticum is made in gray, white, gray-green, and terra cotta. Both clays are packed in 2-pound bricks.

Work on the plasteline is done with the hands and with standard modeling tools. Wooden sculpture tools are good for pressing and smoothing the clay, and tools that have wire loops are most helpful for cutting out portions. For slicing through large areas of plasteline, a heavy flexible wire fastened on two sticks works well. If the plasteline is too firm for working easily or has become so with age, it can be softened by kneading it with Neat's foot oil. A small dish of alcohol is very useful for dipping your fingers and tools into while working. It softens the surface momentarily and lets the tools slide easily, achieving a smoother surface. The alcohol evaporates quickly, and the plasteline goes back to its firm consistency. Neat's foot oil (the true solvent) is not used for this, as it would tend to remain and gradually make the surface mushy.

The size of models varies a great deal. If you are doing a model like a rosette, the entire piece is made of clay. When a sizable model such as an Ionic capital is being done, the basic form is often shaped with a firm material like Styrofoam and details are added afterward in plasteline clay. Any exposed surface of the porous Styrofoam should have a smooth finish like the clay. Once the Styrofoam is carved and sanded, a smooth finish can be achieved by brushing white spackle paste on it. After it has dried, the Styrofoam can be sanded and then painted with white vinyl paint to seal the surface.

For making a long or low model, cut the base out of a piece of $\frac{1}{2}$-inch or $\frac{3}{4}$-inch plywood; the clay details are added directly on the wood. Clear shellac can be brushed on both the wood and finished clay. Sometimes the completed model is a combination of wood and Styrofoam and plasteline clay.

Applying Latex on the Model

After the model has been finished with a smooth surface, it is ready to have latex applied, and a releasing agent is not ordinarily needed on a smooth model. The latex, which comes in liquid form, is called rubber molding compound and is put on with a brush. Pliatex and Flex-Mold are two trade names for this.

The important factor in making a latex mold is the length of the drying time, because the mold is built up by brushing on successive coats of the liquid latex. You must take care not to make each coat too thick, and always allow it to dry thoroughly between coats. Depending on room temperature, allow at least two days for drying, since the mold is normally built up to a total thickness of $\frac{1}{4}$ inch, which usually means applying four coats of latex when you figure that each layer adds about $\frac{1}{16}$ inch.

For filling any undercuts after $\frac{1}{4}$-inch latex thickness has been applied, a filler is mixed with the rubber-molding compound to thicken it. A good filler is Paste Maker, a product of Pliatex that is available at sculpture-supply houses. There must not be any undercuts on the outer surface of the latex mold or it will not separate from the plaster mold.

After the latex is applied, the wooden sides are attached to the Masonite panel on which the model and latex mold are positioned. It is helpful to drive a couple of nails horizontally through each side of the box frame to hold the plaster of Paris after it has hardened. The nails keep the mother mold in the framing when it is turned upside down for a new casting. It is now ready for the plaster of Paris to be mixed and poured over the latex mold in the box frame.

Mixing Plaster of Paris with Water

Before starting to mix plaster of Paris, estimate the approximate amount of plaster needed for the finished batch, and this comes with experience. When the amount is decided, definite proportions are used. To make a full container (in a selected size) of mixed plaster, fill $\frac{1}{3}$ of the container with water. Then add the plaster until the volume has been increased by $\frac{2}{3}$. (In other words, to make 3 gallons of mixed plaster, select a 3-gallon container and use 1 gallon of water.) Use warm water. Hot water makes the plaster set too fast and cold water slows the setting.

Once the mixing of the plaster is started, it *must* be followed through to completion without stopping. To start mixing, pour the water into a clean porcelain or plastic container. Sift the plaster in evenly by hand, working it all over the entire area of water. Continue with this sifting until the powdered plaster reaches the surface level of the water and all the water is absorbed. A large handful of powder should not be emptied into the water, because dry lumps will form down inside. Do not stir until all the plaster is in. It will not set before it is stirred. When ready, stir carefully by hand or with a brush, trying not to let bubbles form. The mixture of plaster of Paris and water should be stirred a minute or so, then be poured immediately into the box framing over the latex mold. Remember that once stirring begins, and the longer it continues, the faster the setting when the stirring is stopped.

Pouring Plaster to Form the Mother Mold

During the pouring of the plaster, strips of burlap can be put in the center of the wet plaster to add strength to the mold. These should be precut according to the size and shape of the mold and be ready to use. Working rapidly, fill the box frame completely with the mixed plaster until it is even with the top.

While doing this, quickly place the burlap strips down into the center of the wet plaster. When the framed box is full, shake it slightly to help the bubbles rise to the top. A piece of cardboard with a straight edge or a wooden lath works well to level off the plaster with the top of the framing.

After the plaster mother mold has set (45 minutes to an hour), the model should be removed at once. Carefully turn it over and take off the Masonite panel. If the model and latex mold did not lift out with the panel, remove them now. Continue by next separating the latex mold from the model, and clean out any excess plasteline clay in the mold. Ordinarily, it takes 24 hours for all the water in the plaster mold to dry out completely.

As a preservative for the plaster mother mold, apply two coats of clear white shellac (using 1 part clear white shellac to 1 part denatured alcohol), but if time is pressing, this can be omitted. If you have shellacked the mother mold and it has dried, the latex mold can be placed in the mother mold and the new objects are now ready to be cast. Among the materials that can be used to make a casting in the latex mold are plaster of Paris, pressed paper, and polyurethane foam. (If casting numerous objects with polyurethane foam, molds of silicone, aluminum, or fiber glass are better than latex because they are much more durable.) Johnson's Glo-Coat wax in a spray can is an ideal releasing agent for coating the mold before using these materials, although plaster does not necessarily need it. The plaster for the objects to be cast is mixed and poured into the latex mold the same way as for the mother mold, and strips of burlap are also put into it to strengthen the cast object. Sculpture House and Sculpture Services, Inc., are two New York suppliers of sculpture materials and equipment. In addition the National Sculpture Society's booklet *Classified Index of Services, Materials and Equipment* is a fine source for information on sculpture. This comprehensive listing includes the names and addresses across the country where service, equipment, and materials can be obtained. Among these are metals, plastic, stone, wood, clay, plaster, burlap, as well as plaster casters, bronze casters, and mold makers, plus many others. For miscellaneous information, contact: Art & Sculpture Inquiry Office, U. S. Steel Corp., Rm. 1100, 208 South LaSalle Street, Chicago, Ill. 60604.

CASTING A DRAPERY SWAG WITH PLASTER BANDAGE IN A PLASTER MOLD

Steps of Execution:

1. A plaster mold in a wooden box ($35\frac{1}{2}$ in. by $58\frac{1}{2}$ by $2\frac{1}{2}$ deep) was made after swag model was shaped in Styrofoam and sanded.
2. Two coats of white vinyl paint applied to fill the porous Styrofoam, then two coats of orange shellac. Model next placed in a wooden box, also shellacked.
3. Johnson's Pledge wax sprayed on shellacked model before the mixed plaster was poured to form the mother mold.
4. After model was separated from mother mold, the mold was given two coats of orange shellac.
5. (Left) Johnson's Pledge wax sprayed on mold before applying plaster strips (5 in. wide). Strips dipped in warm water, one at a time, and pressed into mold with a brush.
6. (Center) Strips (three to four layers) pressed in the mold and continued past edge of the swag so casting could be lifted out. Two double-folded strips pressed around edge of drapery for strength. More strength added with heavy burlap pieces dipped in plaster.
7. (Right) Finished castings of joined swags. Each swag backed with $\frac{1}{2}$-in. plywood attached with $2\frac{1}{2}$-in.-wide plaster strips wrapped around extreme edge of swag and edge of plywood. Patterns in castings were from dye in the burlap bleeding through the plaster. (Photographs — Lynn Pecktal)

Steps of Execution:

1. Plaster of Paris, mixed in a plastic container.
2. Plaster quickly poured into flexible latex mold, shown resting in plaster mother mold framed with wood. (Releasing agent not used.)
3. When hardened, cast and mold lifted from mother mold and latex mold peeled from object. Plaster relics adhered to well with Mastic No. 11. Strips of bandage were dipped into water and pressed around edges to help hold relic on facing and seal cracks. For a rough-textured surface, scenic dope was brushed over well.
4. Well painted with aniline dyes and casein paints. (Photographs — Lynn Pecktal)

SILICONE FLEXIBLE MOLD

A silicone mold is much more durable than a latex mold, but it is also far more costly. It can be used for casting a large quantity of objects with such materials as plaster of Paris and polyurethane foam. If you plan to make a silicone mold, the same basic procedure is followed as for a latex mold, except that (1) the silicone compound is poured over the model in one continuous process, whereas the latex compound is built up over the model in several successive coatings and (2) a latex mold requires that a plaster mother mold be made, whereas the silicone mold does not necessarily need a plaster mother mold. It takes at least two or three days for the silicone mold to cure completely.

Other material like fast-setting plaster bandages can be used to cast objects. The plaster bandages — which come on a roll — are cut into pieces, dipped into water, and pressed into the contours of the mold to produce a hollow-cast object. The use of polyurethane foam in the mold is considerably more complex. The silicone mold must fit tightly into the wooden box (used to make the mold) and have a hinged wooden lid with holes drilled in to allow the excess foam to escape. Heavy-duty iron clamps are needed to hold the lid down tightly once the foam has been poured in the mold.

POLYURETHANE FOAM

Polyurethane foam is included in this section only as a basis for experimentation. It is not recommended unless you have a very good budget and a lot of time. Because there are so many variables involved in the process, it does not always function as well in a theatrical scenic studio as in a commercial or industrial situation, where conditions are set up especially for the process. If you are planning to use it, you should follow the instructions available where you purchase your materials. Complete information can be obtained from Reichhold Chemicals, Inc., White Plains, New York 10602. The main advantage in using polyurethane foam for scenery work exists when many rigid and solid

duplicates of an object are needed — such items as carved ornament, balusters, statues or gargoyles. For only one, two, or three objects, it would be practical to hand-carve them out of Styrofoam, unless a more rigid material is required. Since this process is time-consuming, especially in getting everything ready before you actually use the foam, you will find that the experience of doing it yourself is the best teacher. (See following page.)

Almost any kind of paint can be applied on the polyurethane castings. The resin and the activator come in 1-gallon and 5-gallon sizes and 55-gallon drums. Two 5-gallon containers weigh 90 pounds.

FIBER GLASS

Fiber glass is another good material for sculptured scenery, but it is seldom used in the commercial scenic studio because of the expense and the lack of demand. The Metropolitan Opera shop, where the repertory situation and special needs have given rise to extensive facilities, does create scenery with fiber glass. In the average scenic studio, however, fiber glass is used mainly for making rigid sculptured objects on a one-shot basis and for a durable covering material on firm objects. It can also be used in or over a mold to make duplicates of objects, but more often this is done by vacuum-forming if the items are to be translucent and hollow or with materials like polyurethane foam or plaster if they are to be opaque and solid. If you need a very strong material, fiber glass is excellent.

Fiber glass comes in several types and weights: fiber glass cloth (light, medium, heavy, extra-heavy), mat, chopped, or woven roving. Application involves using a solution consisting of a fabricating resin and catalyst hardener (polyester resin and hardener or epoxy resin and hardener). Once the solution has been mixed, it is applied on the flexible fiber glass to saturate and bond it together permanently, and it produces an extremely hard surface when it cures. It is necessary to catalyze the resin so that it hardens to the proper consistency, and specific proportions are required for mixing. Since the proportions can vary according to the temperature, the manufacturer, and the setting time you desire, follow the instructions that come with the materials. A good source for fiber glass products, resin, and catalyst hardener is the Industrial Plastics Supply Co.

CREATING A FLEXIBLE SILICONE MOLD TO CAST PLASTER ROSETTES. Left above: Silicone Flexible Mold Compound (RTV-630A and curing agent RTV-630B) from a kit were mixed and poured over the rosette model (18-in. diameter by 1½ in.) in a wooden box. Several cans of compound were required for a continuous pouring to get a silicone mold 2 in. thick. Below: (Top left) Rosette model of Styrofoam; ring and base of wood. (Bottom) Cured flexible silicone mold, made from the model. (Top right) Plaster rosette, made from the mold. Hollow castings were made with plaster bandage (two layers) in small pieces, dipped in water, and pressed into the mold's contours. (Photographs — Lynn Pecktal)

After this Styrofoam figurehead (right) was carved and covered with scraps of linen scrim, polyester resin (ordinarily used for fiber glass) was brushed on the surface to give added strength, then it was painted. Designed by Eoin Sprott for the New York City Opera's UN BALLO IN MASCHERA (1971). (Photograph — Arnold Abramson)

Polyurethane foam was selected for the many dimensional and durable balusters in Carl Toms' setting for SLEUTH (1970), New York production. Shown: latex mold resting in the plaster mother mold, a casting, and the finished unit.

Steps of Execution:

1. Baluster model made of Styrofoam on profiled plywood base with plasteline details, then latex mold and a plaster mother mold made for it to rest in. Plaster was poured over the latex mold (with model) and allowed to set in a wooden box (sides 1-in.- and top ½-in.-plywood, top hinged). So the rising foam would be confined to the mold, large clamps held the box lid tightly. Small holes were drilled in the top to let excess foam escape.

2. The foam expands faster with increased heat and room temperature should be 70 to 90 degrees. For heat, infrared lamps were placed 18 in. above latex mold before pouring.

3. Two liquid ingredients were mixed to make the polyurethane foam. Proportions: 1 part resin (Polyite 43-718) to 1 part activator (Polyite 34-842). To find amount of solution needed: fill mold with water, pour into container and measure, add 10 percent for residue in mixing can. (Two pounds solution for 1 cubic ft.)

4. Releasing agent: Johnson's Glo-Coat sprayed on mold just before pouring.

5. Mixing and pouring requires fast work and precise measuring of resin and activator. While weighing is the most accurate, two 20-oz. cans were used here to measure resin and activator separately. The measured resin was poured first into a 46-oz. can, then the activator. The two were combined speedily with a mixer bit in a heavy-duty hand drill a few moments, then the solution was poured quickly into the latex mold and the lid tightly clamped. Time for mixing, pouring, rising, and curing for each casting: about 15 minutes.

6. Lid unclamped, latex mold with casting lifted out and peeled back. Each casting was nailed to a wooden profiled baluster. After spackling and sanding any holes, balusters were painted with an opaque shellac color, an undertone for an oil and turpentine stain applied next to simulate grained wood.

(Photographs — Lynn Pecktal, Arnold Abramson)

382

Details on this prop chariot were covered with fiber glass for durability.

Steps of Execution:

1. A perforated pounce was made for details.
2. Top (left) Details carved out of $\frac{1}{2}$-in. display foam after heavy paper on both sides was peeled away, making the foam semiflexible. Ornaments shaped with long knives and sandpaper, then adhered with Mastic No. 11 to the curved front (built by laminating three layers of $\frac{1}{8}$-in. plywood) and sides.
3. (Right) Chopped fiber glass was scattered over the surface, then polyester resin was brushed on to saturate and cement it, while a stippling techinque with the brush was used to get the fiber glass into the contours of the carving. Proportions for mixing: 1 qt. polyester resin to $1\frac{1}{2}$ tsp. catalyst hardener. The resin was poured from its container and measured in a 1-qt. tin can, poured into a disposable 1-gal. can; $1\frac{1}{2}$ tsp. hardener added, and mixture stirred thoroughly with a wooden stick. Small amounts were mixed for a working time of about 15 minutes. Finish quickly and mix a new batch if needed because the resin starts to set in the container before it begins to harden on the fiber glass. After the resin-covered surface had set and cured, it was sanded lightly with an electric sander.
4. Bottom (left) Chariot coated with oil paint.
5. (Right) Overpainting applied with same paint.
(Photographs — Lynn Pecktal)

 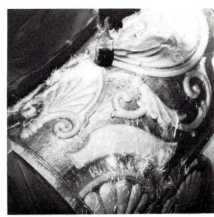

For other scenery, objects like rocks, stone walls, and treetrunks can also be made by placing pieces of fiber glass over a framework of chicken wire or wire forming cloth, whereby the frame becomes part of the object when the fiber glass is fabricated with the resin. While fiber glass can be used effectively for these, unless they must be extra-strong or translucent, they can be created from ragging and scenic dope, which is much less expensive and less time-consuming. If a mold is being made with fiber glass over an object that has a smooth surface, polyethylene film or Saran wrap can be used as a releasing agent. Fiber glass can easily irritate the skin, so gloves should be worn when using it. If finished surfaces are to be sanded with an electric sander, a face mask should always be worn to keep the mouth and nose free of the tiny particles of fiber glass and cured resin. Brushes that have been in resin can be cleaned immediately after use with acetone.

USING ACRYLIC PLASTICS

Plexiglas (Rohm & Haas), Lucite (duPont), and Acrylite (American Cyanamid) are trade names of the acrylic plastics most commonly used for the stage. They are available in sheets of various sizes and weights. Plexiglas is probably the best-known acrylic plastic. It is made in sheets of clear, frost, white, and a wide variety of colors that may be either translucent, opaque, semiopaque, or transparent. Besides the smooth sheets, Plexiglas with a rippled surface on both sides is made in many colors. Other patterns are available with surface textures on one or both sides. Plexiglas can be cut with a bandsaw or table saw, drilled into, or sanded wet or dry. A frosted effect can be created on a clear plastic sheet by sanding one or both sides. The plastic sheets can also be heated and shaped.

For scenery, acrylic plastics are utilized in numerous capacities. Clear and frosted sheets are used to simulate all types of glass in windows, doors, and transoms that have stained-glass designs and decorative ornaments painted on them. Many exciting effects can be created when these plastics are illuminated on stage by special animated lighting, while other typical uses include making signs of all descriptions and devising decor for settings in barrooms, cafés, discothèques, and for theatre marquées. Profiled lampshades for chandeliers and sconces are regularly cut out of acrylic sheets, as are profiles of items such as icicles and fallen snow on window mullions. Often Plexiglas sheets are supported by an aluminum framework and used for walls or for hanging pieces in musicals. Robert Randolph designed hanging pieces and colorful walls of Plexiglas panels attached to platforms for *70 Girls 70,* while Robin Wagner used a multitude of small pieces of $\frac{1}{8}$-inch-thick translucent Lucite to create a curved back wall of tiny city skyscraper windows for the musical *Seesaw*. The many Lucite windows in *Seesaw* were suspended by attaching each at the top with Sta-kon fasteners to $\frac{1}{16}$-inch steel cables stretched vertically. Acrylic sheets are even utilized for making furniture. In John Bury's set for *Old Times*, a cocktail table and two night tables were made in forced perspective using $\frac{1}{4}$-inch Plexiglas. Pieces for the tables were marked out with the masking paper that comes on the Plexiglas and then cut out with a bandsaw. The edges were smoothed with a plane and the pieces were put together and clamped in place. For bonding the edges together, an ethylene dichloride cement was applied with an eyedropper.

Mirrored Plexiglas also works beautifully for some productions. Rouben Ter-Arutunian designed an interesting arrangement of mirrored Plexiglas shapes with a raked platform for the Robert Joffrey ballet's *The Relativity of Icarus*. Shapes of mirrored Plexiglas (framed and supported by wood and metal) were positioned in various planes above and below a tilted oval platform covered with canvas and painted aluminum (bronze powder and lacquer).

Many of these plastic sheets are manufactured with masking paper on one or both sides, although some have it on neither. The masking paper is most useful for drawing or pouncing designs on before it is removed from the plastic. These drawn patterns may be cut out of the masking paper with an X-Acto knife and easily peeled off, leaving the background to mask unpainted areas. This technique is especially good when painting lettering; either the lettering or the background can be masked out by the remaining paper.

A corrugated plastic sheet is also available in different sizes, providing a good linear pattern for walls or roofs. In a section view this pattern looks like a serpentine wall. Other plastic products sometimes employed for special props are half-round rods, square rods, tubing, and acrylic balls.

PAINTING ON PLASTICS

Several kinds of paint can be selected for painting on plastics. These are determined by the desired effect and sometimes by what is on hand in the studio. Vinyl, latex, acrylic, shellac, and lacquer can be used. Vinyl, latex, and acrylic are usually applied by brush (or by sponge or paint roller if texturing is desired). Lacquer and shellac are best applied by a hand spray gun or spray can when a smooth finish is required, because they dry fast and application by brush is difficult. For putting on small areas of lacquer or shellac, a Jet-Pak Sprayon kit is effective. The kit contains a head assembly, glass jar with lid, and a can of propellent. Each can sprays up to one pint of liquid, thinned to a proper consistency.

Although they are expensive for doing large areas of scenic work, acrylic polymer plastic colors in tubes or jars are ideal for painting on plastics, especially Plexiglas, Lucite, and the like. Hyplar and Liquitex are two name brands available in a wide selection of colors. They can be thinned with water to make glazes, or they can be put on thickly.

Spray Mark is a brand of acrolite transparent dye in spray cans that comes in many colors, and very unusual effects may be obtained by spraying one color over another. Besides plastics, these dyes can be put on metal and tin. For doing transparent drawing on plastic like Mylar, felt-tip pens such as Flo-master perform splendidly. Aniline dyes are frequently used for transparent painting on plastics, but they need a binder to make them hold to the surface. Water-soluble dyes can be mixed with clear gloss vinyl and lacquer-soluble dyes can be mixed with clear lacquer.

MYLAR

Mylar is a plastic with a highly reflective surface that gives a mirrorlike appearance. For this reason it is usually used on the stage in a very stylized production or where only small amounts are used for props or decoration.

The most popular kind of Mylar for theatrical use is manufactured in a roll that comes 54 inches wide. It may be purchased by yard or roll, which holds 75 yards. This plastic is easy to cut, fold, and apply as the weight and flexibility is similar to that of a very heavy kitchen oilcloth.

Mylar is a favorite material for use in the field of display, where it covers walls, floors, or display cases to simulate a brightly mirrored surface. Unlike those for the stage, where the scenery must be constructed to hold up well during handling and moving, display materials do not always have to meet durability requirements.

Applying the Mylar to a Surface

Whenever Mylar is to be attached to walls, facings, and other flat scenery, the best way is to glue or cement it to the surface. In preparing them for application, all Mylar pieces should first be laid out and cut according to the needs of the design. Weldwood contact cement (which is used for formica) is ideal for adhering the Mylar to a wooden surface. It should be applied on the wood with a brush and left a few moments to dry before putting the Mylar pieces in place, which are then smoothed out by hand in all directions. Although a white synthetic glue that dries clear can also be used, it takes longer to dry. If the pieces of Mylar are large, they should also be stapled on the extreme edges to help keep them in place when using this glue. For attaching very small pieces of Mylar, a spray adhesive such as Scotch spray mounting adhesive is effective. Spray on the back of the Mylar, then onto the wooden surface where it is to go. Allow both surfaces to become slightly "tacky" before pressing on the Mylar.

Painting Mylar

Since thin transparent colors are usually the ones most preferred for Mylar, lacquer is excellent for painting it. Aniline dyes (those soluble in lacquer) are mixed with clear gloss lacquer to make the transparent colors. This is done by first pouring a bit of the lacquer into a

container, adding a pinch of aniline dye, stirring, then thinning it with lacquer thinner (as desired) to lighten the color. Clear white shellac can also be thinned with alcohol and mixed with aniline dyes (those soluble in alcohol) to create transparent colors. Often pieces of Mylar in contrasting colors are cut and applied with Scotch spray adhesive to the painted surface. A thin transparent bath of lacquer or shellac colors may be spattered over the surface.

METAL SCENERY

While metal has been used to support scenery for many years, it is now being increasingly used as a material for the stage scenery itself. Highly stylized and abstract settings of metal are frequently designed for both dramatic presentations and the musical comedy stage. It is not unusual to see stage settings like Ming Cho Lee's for *Two Gentlemen of Verona* or *Julius Caesar* (at the New York City Opera) constructed almost entirely of metal, with elaborate steel scaffolding spanning a distance of 25 to 30 feet above the deck. Emanating from many of these structures are cantilevered platforms and twisted circular stairways. Such geometric shapes as ovals, circles, diamonds, and diagonals are often worked as braces into classical or contemporary designs so their placement gives support and strength to the structure as well as being esthetically pleasing.

Steel pipes and aluminum tubing in various diameters ordinarily go into the construction of a skeletonized metal setting. They offer excellent support for wooden platforms, stairways, and ramps. Whether a scenic creation is realistic or abstract, any number of metals can work beautifully for surface materials. Among them are sheet metal, expanded mesh wire, aluminum sheeting, tin, and galvanized turkey wire. For more detailed work, lengths of flat, round, or square steel are used to shape such set props as chandeliers, sconces, and ornate grillwork; all have thin graceful lines yet require strength.

Painting Metal Scenery

Metal scenery must always be thoroughly cleaned of dirt, grease, and rust before painting. Carbon tetrachloride, a nonflammable drycleaning agent, works well for this and is applied simply by pouring it on a cloth and rubbing it over the surface of the metal.

In scenic work, it is standard procedure to give metalwork a base coat of shellac, mixed so that it is close to what the final coat is going to be. Dry colors, first dissolved in alcohol, can be

Setting by John Scheffler
THE BALCONY by Jean Genêt
Directed by D. Brook Jones
Lighting by Joe Pacitti
Cincinnati Playhouse in the Park (1969)
(Photograph — Walter Burton)

Scene: A brothel in Paris during a revolution. Materials included rusty metal grillwork, cracked mirror panels, and stained wooden units.

mixed with shellac (clear white, orange, or opaque white Haeuser's Enamelac), according to the chosen color. Vinyl paint can also be used for laying in the metal but does not hold as well as shellac. After the base coat has been laid in, overpainting is usually done with vinyl, latex, or casein. Always try a sample of the paint on the metal surface to see how it holds before starting to do extensive painting. If it does not seem to adhere well, the metal may have to be treated.

Treating Metals to Make the Paint Hold

Metal Treat is the trade name of a solution that can be applied on metal surfaces, especially galvanized metal and aluminum, so paint will adhere to them. When you are treating metal surfaces before painting, be sure they are clean. A 1-pint container of concentrated Metal Treat thinned with water makes 1 gallon of the solution to be used, mixed in these proportions:

1 part *METAL TREAT*	
to	FOR MIXING A SOLUTION OF METAL TREAT
7 parts *WATER*	

The solution can be applied by brush, spray, or dipping. Allow the surface to dry thoroughly before starting to paint, and wear rubber gloves when there is prolonged use with the hands.

Treating Metals to Prevent Rust

Metal Treat also prevents rust from forming under the base coat on iron and steel. To remove rust with this solution, wipe it on full strength, then wait for the rust to dissolve. Wash with clear water to neutralize the acid.

Sheet Metal Ornaments

To supplement realistic details on scenery, architectural sheet metal ornaments can be added to the built work to give an even more authentic look. Made by commercial firms, these three-dimensional classical ornaments are selected by the designer to fit the period and scale of the setting, and there is a wide range from which to choose. Although the ornaments may be expensive for use in only one show, it is advantageous to have them on hand in a repertory or stock company, since they can be changed around and painted for several different productions.

On wooden-covered wings or set pieces, ornaments may be garlands and festoons applied to embellish built panels, carved moldings for the wainscoting, or elaborate capitals for columns. For metal scenery, small pieces of decorative ornament such as rosettes, leaves, and half balls are added to steel grillwork designs. The scenic studio usually keeps a stock assortment of the smaller ornaments on hand to use when making up prop chandeliers and wall sconces (either metal or wood), and for applying on furniture that is constructed there. One of the best-known sources for purchasing sheet metal ornament is Kenneth Lynch and Sons, Wilton, Conn.

Another company that makes architectural steel products is J. G. Braun Co., West Caldwell, N.J. or Skokie, Ill. The J. G. Braun stock products include steel cornice moldings, cove-and-panel moldings, steel treillage, and baluster spindles. Among the smaller items of ornamental steel stamping are leaves, rosettes, and balls. Other products can be obtained in aluminum, bronze, and malleable iron, and Braun also manufactures a wide range of small brass ornaments.

Pressed-Steel Ceilings

Pressed-metal ceilings are used in much the same way as are sheet-metal ornaments, and are applied on both the ceiling pieces and the

A few of the many sheet-metal objects that can be used to supplement dimensional details on scenery. The support at the lower left comes in three pieces, as does the one above right, which is shown assembled. (Photograph—Lynn Pecktal)

walls to add an extra touch of realism or period flavor to such stage sets as bars and restaurants, brownstone interiors, and old-fashioned ice cream parlors. Pressed ceilings and walls are highly favored by architects and designers for restorations, boutiques, cafés, and amusement centers. Some patterns of the pressed steel can even be used in homes to simulate wall tiles.

While flat ceilings and walls can be painted effectively with a stencil to achieve these patterns, stage designers occasionally prefer to use the actual pressed steel. The real patterns work well except when a setting is designed to have the walls and ceiling in sharp perspective. Since the typical pressed-steel designs are usually laid out in squares, they can easily call attention to the fact that they are not in perspective. If these patterns are painted on the flat scenery, the lines can be drawn to the desired vanishing point in particular set pieces.

Although the amount of pressed-steel material needed for a setting can only be figured from the designer's drafting, it is estimated commercially by the unit of measure for steel ceilings, which is 100 square feet and is referred to as a "square." Furring strips and nails are necessary for commercial attachment, whereas for scenery, construction is to the exact size of the designs. The Wheeling Corrugating Company manufactures a wide assortment of steel ceilings and accessories—pressed-steel plates, panels, cornices, and moldings that come in assorted sizes. Average measurements of the steel panels and plates are 24 by 24 inches, 24 by 48 inches, and 24 by 96 inches; average depth is $\frac{1}{2}$ inch. Multiples can be 3, 6, 12, and 24 inches, depending on the particular pattern. Cornices vary from $1\frac{1}{4}$ to $11\frac{1}{8}$ inches in depth, and inner and outer miters (for inside and outside corners) are made to accompany the cornices. Molding and nosing are included among the selections. A firm that deals in the Wheeling steel products is Barney Brainum-Shanker Steel Co., Inc., Glendale, N.Y.

An undercoat is needed on these steel products so that water paints can be put on. Shellac (usually opaque) is applied as a base. Since dimensional steel patterns tend to become flat under normal stage light, the finished painting ordinarily involves modeling them over the base coat to emphasize the design and depth by using highlights, shadows, and cutting lines. After the detailed painting is finished, it is toned and antiqued.

Setting by Boris Aronson
J.B. by Archibald MacLeish
Directed by Elia Kazan
Lighting by Tharon Musser
ANTA Theatre, New York (1959)
(Photograph—Robert Galbraith)

"My main approach in designing J.B. was simplification. J.B. is a dramatization of issues, not a circus story. I avoided the glamorous elements of the circus. I skeletonized the props and used the three rings as representative of the performance areas in J.B.'s life. Each piece was both a part of the circus and a part of the theme."

— Boris Aronson

A Conversation with ROBIN WAGNER

Robin Wagner chatted with the author in the designer's apartment in Manhattan's Greenwich Village. Born in California, Wagner studied at the School of Fine Arts in San Francisco. He has designed the settings for many shows both on and off Broadway. His first Broadway assignment was for the drama *The Trial of Lee Harvey Oswald* at the ANTA Theatre in 1967. He has also designed scenery for the Repertory Company of Lincoln Center, the American Shakespeare Festival at Stratford, Connecticut, and for many regional theatres, including Washington's Arena Stage and the Fred Miller Theatre in Milwaukee. Robin Wagner has collaborated with director Tom O'Horgan on several shows, and since creating the scenery for the original Broadway production of *Hair* he has designed and supervised fourteen separate productions of that particular show. He won the Joseph Maharam Award for the settings he designed for *Seesaw* in 1973 and the Drama Desk Award for *Lenny* in 1972. Among his design credits are:

Broadway:
Mack and Mabel (1974)
Full Circle (1973)
Seesaw (1973)
Rachael Lily Rosenbloom and Don't You Ever Forget It! (1973)
Sugar (1972)
Lysistrata (1972)
Jesus Christ Superstar (1971)
Lenny (1971)

Inner City (1971)
Promises, Promises (1968)
The Great White Hope (1968)
Lovers and Other Strangers (1968)
Hair (1967)
The Trial of Lee Harvey Oswald (1967)
The Repertory Theatre of Lincoln Center:
Galileo (1967)
The Condemned of Altona (1966)

Off-Broadway:
A Chorus Line (1975)
The Rise and Fall of the City of Mahagonny (1970)
A View from the Bridge (1965)
Between Two Thieves (1965)
In White America (1963)
Cages (1963)
The Prodigal (1960)
Waiting for Godot (1958)

Setting by Robin Wagner
JESUS CHRIST SUPERSTAR
Lyrics by Tim Rice
Music by Andrew Lloyd Webber
Directed by Tom O'Horgan

Costumes by Randy Barcelo
Lighting by Jules Fisher
Universal Amphitheatre
Los Angeles, California (1972)
(Photograph — Marc Cohen)

When you first got involved with the theatre, were you in high school or in college?

I was out of high school waiting for my draft notice, and one of the things we used to do in San Francisco was to go to anything that was happening around town. I had always been an art student of sorts, but I never had any particular interest in the theatre. And one evening, a group of us sneaked into the opera house and sat in little rooms behind the boxes. We just went in the place to drink and raise hell. And I looked out and saw this ballet going on and I got kind of interested because there were all these girls in it. The next night I went back with two of the guys and this time, we watched it. There was a backdrop behind the ballet, and I thought, "Geez! I could do that. That's really awful!" To show how unsophisticated my tastes in art were, it turned out later that this was the ballet called *Aleko* that had been designed by Chagall. I just had no idea who Chagall was.

What happened then?

I saw this ad in a local paper in San Francisco saying they wanted a designer at the Golden Gate Opera Workshop at the YMCA. So I said to this one other guy who kind of acted interested, "Let's go down and tell them we're designers. They'll never know the difference." We didn't know until later that they could never get a designer or technician or anybody to go backstage to help. We thought we were taking over and conning this guy, but we were the patsies. And we literally worked our asses off for six weeks to make some scenery for him. We painted it and did everything. It was corrugated cardboard, and as it turned out, it looked pretty good. It was for a one-act opera. But I didn't know opera and I had never been to the theatre, I was nineteen at the time.

Where did you go from there?

Because of this opera workshop, I heard about another group that needed someone to run lights. This was at the Theatre Arts Colony. So I went over there and started running lights. Then I got with this group called the Contemporary Dancers where I met J. Marks, a fellow who was just beginning to form a company that was doing full-length evenings of dance dramas. It was the first thing of that kind in San Francisco. I got into that and started doing scenery. He was light years ahead of anything that I had conceived of in scenery. So I started picking up the whole visual

Setting by Robin Wagner
JESUS CHRIST SUPERSTAR
Lyrics by Tim Rice
Music by Andrew Lloyd Webber
Directed by Tom O'Horgan

Costumes by Randy Barcelo
Lighting by Jules Fisher
Mark Hellinger Theatre, New York (1971)
(Photograph—Marc Cohen)

thing and I became aware of what was going on. Then the actor's workshop gave me a call to do a set for *Waiting for Godot* in San Francisco. I went to see Herbert Blau and he brainwashed me for about eight weeks and fed me Becket and all the 1930s crazies. And out of it came a kind of set. By this time I was really interested. I started seeing everything and began working in all the other groups in the area. I just worked very hard for about five years for no money. Then one day, I decided I would come back to New York. This came out of this production of *Waiting for Godot*. It went to the Brussels World's Fair and I came East with it. I saw everything that was in New York and I stayed and started working Off Broadway.

What was your first Off-Broadway production?

Well, the *Godot* played here, that was the first thing. Then I did a show called *And the Wind Blows* at the St. Marks Playhouse in 1959 and I just kept doing Off-Broadway things—*The Prodigal, Between Two Thieves*. I did 18 to 20 Off-Broadway shows, then I got into the union.

Did you start assisting designers then?

About two years later. When I first got in the union I was working as a painter in television doing commercials. I had written a lot of letters to designers. I

really wanted to work with a Broadway designer. And one of the people who called back (you know, after millions didn't) was Ben Edwards, and I was with him for three years while I continued my Off-Broadway shows. After a while, I started doing regional theatre and I was flying all around, so I couldn't work for Ben any more. That period of time went by and I started working for Oliver Smith, and I was also with him for three years.

What would you call your first big show in New York?

The first one I did was *The Condemned of Altona* at Lincoln Center in 1966. That's because Blau and Irving took over Lincoln Center and I was one of the few people they knew in New York. They just called me and said, "Come over and do this." I also did *Galileo* there. Now all the time I was doing this, I was at Arena Stage in Washington, where I was their staff designer for three years.

Did you get the Washington job as a result of your Off-Broadway work in New York?

That came through Ed Sherin. I worked with him in stock when he was about to do *Major Barbara* in Milwaukee at the Fred Miller. I said, "Gee, I can't go," and he said, "But let's work it out together." So I sort of designed it by mail

Setting by Robin Wagner
LENNY by Julian Barry
Music by Tom O'Horgan
Based on the life and words of Lenny Bruce
Directed by Tom O'Horgan

Lighting by Jules Fisher
Costumes by Randy Barcelo
Brooks Atkinson Theatre, New York (1971)
(Photograph — Martha Swope)

and he went out and carried it through and it worked very well. We also did an Off-Broadway show together called *The White Rose and the Red,* which was a War of the Roses thing. Then Ed asked me to come down to Washington and do *Dark of the Moon,* and I did. We tore the stage up and redid the whole place and it was very successful.

You got most of your practical experience Off Broadway.

Yeah, and a little in San Francisco, but mostly Off-Broadway here. I also met a lot of people I still work with. The people who produced *Charlie Brown* were doing a show called *The Trial of Lee Harvey Oswald* and they couldn't get a designer for it. So by way of the grapevine, I think it was through Jules Fisher, I was available. And that was my first Broadway show. I was still living and working in Washington and doing Lincoln Center things, so I was commuting and was in the airport like every day. I moved back to New York after that.

When did you begin working with Tom O'Horgan?

Well, Dick Osorio, the same manager for the *Lee Harvey Oswald,* was working for Michael Butler and they were trying to put *Hair* on Broadway. And here again, they couldn't find a designer. Another designer turned the show down because it wouldn't be reviewed. It had already played the Public Theatre and had also played the Cheetah, and so

nobody wanted to touch it, evidently. At least that's the word I got. So I went over and Osorio said, "Look, we don't have any money, but if you're not busy, do it." It was all verbal, you know, word of mouth. I met Tom and just had a great time. We both got very excited. So we did it and it sort of evolved in the theatre. It was a very fine experience. Out of that I have just continued working with him. Every time he's worked, he's asked me to do the show.

How did you start out with O'Horgan on your approach to Superstar?

That part's really hard when you describe an O'Horgan show. What happens with Tom and me is that we just sit and talk, and we just throw out any wild ideas that come up. For instance, when we were working on *Superstar* for Los Angeles, one of the things we had was a tower of people for the Crucifix. This came about out of our going to see *King Kong* together, and we were talking about Christ climbing up the cross and being shot down by biplanes, and we just got to throwing everything into it. *Lenny* came out the same way. He had seen *North by Northwest,* and when we met he said, "I saw this strange movie last night." In this movie a man crawls across the face of Mount Rushmore, and so we started talking about that and he said, "By the way, I'm going to do this show called *Lenny.*" We talked and I said, "Well, how do you feel about it?"

And he said, "Well, it should have a monumental feeling." I said, "What about Mount Rushmore?" And he said, "What about Mount Rushmore?" And we used it.

Your ideas flow out of things that are happening?

Yes, and they change. We'll leave with a seed of an idea, then I'll get a call in the middle of the night, or he'll get a call from me in the middle of the night, and it's developed into something, obviously. So I can never say I know where this comes from, because you never know. And I feel Tom is the same way. He's very open and very free about using anything that he feels is good. So if you come up with a seemingly crazy idea and it works for him, he wants it and you use it. He has absolutely no ego that way. A lot of directors are impacted with a kind of protective ego thing that they must use only ideas which are their own, and they can say, "I thought of this," and then they have a problem. Tom has none of that problem. It flows so openly. For instance, one thing he did say is someone had made a comment in an interview that I had a tendency to overdesign and Tom's comment was, "No one can overdesign for me." And he's like that. I think his openness is purely creative. He wants to make something exciting. And the derivation of the genesis of ideas is second to the excitement of the events in the show.

There is another thing that happens in O'Horgan productions which is confusing sometimes, and I'll give you a great example of it. The chrysalis thing in *Superstar* when Christ rises out of the ground is a combination of scenery, costumes, properties, and electrics. And there is no line. I know the source of the ideas is from the *Hellstrom Chronicles* when the cocoon turns into a butterfly. The source of a lot of stuff in that show was from insect life or fossil life, and from early life. It was almost as though someone twenty thousand years in the future viewed a myth from the past called "Jesus Christ" and they had it mixed up with the Stone Age and the prehistoric Pliocene Period, and also with two thousand years after Christ. In other words, this is so distant a point that it is all one period. And it is sort of the genesis of the whole design for *Superstar.*

That was your overall concept for

Jesus Christ Superstar?

It's all life from all time and it's a myth from all time.

That was the fetus of it, and from there we could go in any direction, wherever it was—what was exciting and still related to this concept of the Christ myth. But back to the chrysalis, it's a thing which grows out of the ground on an electric piston arm or an elevator which is run electrically. It's a piece of machinery which is built by carpenters and it comes up through a hole in the floor. And on it sits a prop, an encasement which is put together with hinges and which has different devices in it. It is raised up electrically out of the floor; it's opened by the actors manually. Inside of it is a costume which is gradually peeled away until it reaches a certain point in space when it becomes a cape, which in essence is a scenic piece. So it's going through the transition from a piece of mechanical apparatus into a property, into a costume, into an electrical apparatus, into a piece of scenery again. Then all the time containing a human being which is an actor. So there is no real line.

This is a separate piece that lifts off?

Yes, each piece in that. And the genesis of that piece, again, went through everybody, and it just was passed from hand to hand, everyone lending some ideas, another way to do it to the point where you don't know, again, who did the work, but the guiding hand was Tom's.

And you don't get uptight if someone makes suggestions to you?

Oh, no, I think it's wonderful. I think Randy Barcelo had some great ideas in *Lenny* and he had some great ideas in *Superstar*. I, in turn, had costume ideas which are in the show. The same was true in *Lenny*. Tom is always filtering and passing and weaving all these things together. And we do the same, I think. We get directoral ideas which even get woven into the direction. Randy also had some ideas. And Jules Fisher, who did the lighting for both shows, is always in there moving in and out, you know: "Do a scene like this and this can happen with the light." And I like to get my hand into lighting—"Can we make a lamp that will do this?" And Jules does that same kind of open-field work. So it's like a lot of people climbing a mountain together, and hopefully arriving at the top because we are helping each

Setting by Robin Wagner
LENNY by Julian Barry
Music by Tom O'Horgan
Based on the life and words of Lenny Bruce
Directed by Tom O'Horgan

Lighting by Jules Fisher
Costumes by Randy Barcelo
Pictured: Cliff Gorman and company
Brooks Atkinson Theatre, New York (1971)
(Photograph—Martha Swope)

other up and moving each other around. For me, it's the only really exciting way to work. On the basis of other shows that I've done I function better; my product is better and I'm much more enthusiastic about working on it. Because I know that the realization is going to be greater than I'm giving, because everyone else is doing the same thing. It's like the old Gestalt idea that the whole is always greater than the parts. I think if it's woven together beautifully, you can't distinguish which hands wove where. You just end up with this kind of marvelous garment sometimes.

You also had a great deal of mechanical apparatus in other parts of Superstar. *How did the idea of the front walls come about?*

That happened in an audition. We were sitting in the theatre in a very early audition. Tom and I were sitting down in the second row. We had been up in the balcony, and we saw this little man walk across the stage with a broom. The theatre was entirely empty. And then we were sitting down in the first row, and we started talking about the scale of people in the space. Now, we were sitting in the second row. What if we could view what we had seen from the balcony in the first row? What if the stage were kind of straight up and down, and what if there were a man walking across it with a broom? What if he were crawling across on his hands and knees, what

if all the actors came on like insects crawling down the stage, and the stage was presented to you in a fashion that you hadn't seen it in before? It would be as though you were viewing it from the air. And the correction for the audience would be, instead of lifting the audience up to view it from the air, you just lift up the stage so the audience could view it and then tip it back. And in the balance of the conversation, Tom said, "Well, is that possible?" which is Tom's classic question. And I sort of said, "Well, I don't know why not." So the next thing, we got Pete Feller on the phone trying to find out about pistons.

How is that operated?

It's operated on cherrypicker pistons. They are pistons which come out of each other and go up twenty-eight feet, and it drops from twenty-eight feet down to nothing. And each of these panels weighs about two tons. There are three panels. We had to divide them into three. There was no other way to do it.

Do you have a rough texture on the front of them?

Yeah. Actually, we needed something that the actors' feet would grab on on extreme angles. And we experimented with rubber straight on the wood, but we found it would tear up, so Matty [Slachmuylder], the supervising scenic artist at Feller's, permeated indoor-outdoor carpet with rubber, and then we painted on it. We found a kind of technique or style. I didn't know what it was from and Tom didn't know what it was from. But after we both saw it, Tom said, "It's Blake!" And I looked at Blake drawings after we saw that, and we started using more Blake and we got Blake all over the place, because we realized there was some link in there. Then out of that came ideas and certain wonderful things that happened in Blake that came into the staging.

You also have a great many people coming down from the grid. Did you have special rigging?

Oh, yeah. The rigging is very complicated in *Superstar*. We have three catwalks—one for Judas when he hangs, one for the priests when they come down upstage in their bone bridge, and one downstage which is a hanging unit made of bones. I mean it's made out of Styrofoam. They're all dinosaur bones and the dinosaur's femurs. And the one upstage is a sort of brontosaurus mask and also made with a dog bone.

And you had certain relationships in mind?

We knew where the relationships were. It's not always certain that the audience knows, but I don't know how much they question it in that the elements are related to each other. It's not easy to link the relationships, but they're there. And in that there's a little bit of esoterica perhaps that has caused whatever criticisms of that aspect of it, that has come out of people's not knowing what it is. And there is a possibility that they don't. But must you always know what something is in order to experience it? Tom does work on an emotional level. He's trying to reach feelings. He's really anti-intellectual from that point of view. And I don't think he was particularly concerned about making things easily understood as much as he was to create an event which could be felt. And I think there are moments in *Superstar* which are full of feeling.

It does promote feeling from a purely visual point of view. But sculpturally, it is not particularly interesting and from the point of view of static painting it is not particularly interesting. I think that things do happen in space in a way which is interesting and are related only to the stage—not related to painting, sculpture, or to any other form, except to the form of the theatre. And I think that's a completely unexplored and undefined direction that designers

could go after and discover: What is the visual esthetic of the theatre? Where is it? What does it mean? How is it related to space, the dynamics, to the actor? How is it related to music or whatever is happening?

What about the upstage shaft that comes through the center opening of the cyc?

Well, that's another piston. That's also a piston which comes out of itself. It's stored in about eight feet upstage and it comes about forty feet downstage with Christ on it. It's a telescoping piston and it will carry exactly 140 pounds, which is the weight of Christ. It couldn't have had another two pounds on it. In fact, we had to cut some lasers off. We had some lasers mounted on the back.

What do you mean by lasers?

Laser beams. And if it had another two, it wouldn't move. Because with this extension, the weight on it was just enough so that it would telescope back into itself. It was originally designed to pick him up from the other telescope downstage, which would go twenty-four feet in the air from the basement. He would be picked up by it and go off into the distance upstage. Now we couldn't make the change. The music didn't hold long enough. But as it turned out dramatically, it wasn't as good to go upstage as it was to come downstage.

And that's the other element of design which I think is terribly important. And that's when you freeze a design. When you are working with very rigid ideas that are interstructured and are interwoven so they can only work one way, then you stop a creative process which is only really coming into being when it gets onto the stage with its scenery and its elements. And that is the point when it should be explorable, and at a time when it should be able to explode into completely undiscovered lands. And by using single outlets which have their own life and their own function and yet can come together, I think opens up a whole range of design which is also unexplored.

Musicals have been stuck for years, because this set can't play until set A has played. And set B is locked in behind set A, instead of letting set A, set B, and set C play anywhere, anytime, and let the events decide what is going to happen on the stage. I think those things are only really discovered and formed when you're on stage.

Did you also throw out a lot of ideas?

Well, the only thing we had left in the alley after *Superstar* was a cape which couldn't be manipulated by the actors. It was going to walk around behind Pilate. But the elements were designed in such a manner that they could work at any time, and there was that possibility. And Tom and his actors work that way. Why should he be held down by a set which has to come down and go back mechanically? It should be able to happen like life happens. At least it's spontaneous when you're creating the work, and then hopefully, there will be some organization to it so that it continues that kind of pattern.

So it's difficult for me to say what the process of work is in *Superstar*. Because I know it came out of dozens of sessions where we were throwing out things and going to museums and digging up fossil books, and what does it mean, how does it relate to this? Tom always likes to find the relationships and put them together and make them into something beautiful. And as a consequence, the work that I have been doing I feel has less to do with stage design than it does to do with helping create theatrical events, and really trying to materialize ideas on the stage. I don't ever feel that I'm restricted to using any particular design or style or not to use any particular design style. It should, and hopefully does, grow out of the director and the work. And if it can be that, I think it's ideal.

Then you're not primarily concerned with style.

I used to have a great deal of concern about not having a style when I was first starting out. I hadn't been trained as a designer and I always felt that good designers have a portfolio, and a portfolio showed a very definite style and very strong point of view and an attitude towards the stage. Since that time, I've come all the way around to the point where I feel that the designer should have no portfolio. I feel the set, if it really lives, if it really has a moment of life on the stage, should be the same kind of moment that the actor has or the director has. But it shouldn't be something you can put in a picture frame or something that you can put in a box and say, "This is a set." I think its moment of life is when it is in movement or when it's helping create a certain excitement. If you can epitomize those moments, then you'd say, "That's the design." But those moments are in space and they are in movement and they are organic to the lighting, organic to the action, and to the staging. And when all of those elements come together, then you have exciting design.

The designer shouldn't impose a style. I think that that should grow from the show or the director, depending which is stronger. But I don't think that style should be left out of the theatre. What I feel that I want to do is to allow the design to help in whatever way I can to make the events take place. And whatever it looks like, it looks like. If it looks tacky, it looks tacky. If it brings life to the stage, then I think it's providing the one thing that you can't give it in any other medium, and that is, creating life on the stage in a very exciting ambiance with a live audience, live action, and anything that can happen at any moment. And hopefully, you design to help that, support that, and add an element of its own. But I don't think it should be fixed. If you're looking at a photograph of a production, it would be like looking at a picture of actors, not acting. It should have no more interest than that and no less. But if it's all finished and it doesn't need movement and light in it, then somehow, it's failed me.

You're not so concerned with a design being exactly like what you have on that piece of paper?

I've not been able to explore this fully, but God knows, in the last six or seven shows that I've done, it's been explored. If the scenic artist has some technique, some idea, some way of doing something which I don't have, I want him to bring all of his creative forces to that. And a lot of people think it's a cop-out, you know, when I've said this to the scenic artist, "Do it the way you would as long as it relates to this." I want his gift also. And I think this is true of stagehands and machinery and everything else. Every time you can bring another human being's touch into the production, the more lifelike it becomes. I think uniformity of style is a bore. And the same thing is true with machinery. If you can do it by hand, don't do it with machinery. There's a sensitivity and a rhythm and an understanding that a stagehand has that can bring another element into the production that a machine can't do.

I'm relating this back to what happened in the different productions of *Hair*. I would never go out to the scenic studio until it was almost finished, and I would see all kinds of marvelous things that people were bringing to it which were not in my head but which related. A lot of scenic artists in New York are capable of doing that and they bring a fantastic talent to the work.

My assistants are the same way. I don't think of them as assistants. I think of them as associates, because they are always bringing in elements and ideas. Marge Kellogg, Ralph Funicello, John Kasarda, and Dave Chapman are marvelous people, and they bring all kinds of things to work. They are all designers on their own. I know as a draftsman that you can work either way. I know that Oliver Smith used to let me open up and do things within the framework, and if he didn't like it, he would say, "Robin, that's clunky." And he'd scratch it out and have me do it over six times.

Do you build models for most of your shows?

Yes, for every show. I don't do drawings any more. I haven't drawn anything for years. I do sketches and work in models, and we draft from the model.

You have done musicals such as Promises, Promises *and* Sugar. *How do you feel about these as opposed to the type of theatre you have been discussing?*

They are totally disassociated shows.

They have nothing to do with each other. And I don't think they have a lot to do with the kind of theatre I'm talking about. *Promises* had more. There's not much I can say about *Sugar*, because I went in after another designer. I used basically his ground plan, because it was built and the machinery was built. As a consequence, I was just exploring director's problems and trying to make it flow. I really understand the other designer's problem now, and why he was where he was at on that show at that point. Had I known it, I probably wouldn't have gone in on it. But at that particular time, I was doing nothing and I thought, well, what the hell? But I wasn't at all satisfied with it because it was done in three weeks under the worst possible circumstances and it was just chaos. And I don't like to work that way. I wasn't working with any love or any feeling. In a way, I've gotten a reprieve. I am doing a show with the same director, Gower Champion, called *Mack and Mabel,* and it's one of the most creative experiences I've ever had.

Is it necessary to go to college to get a background for the theatre?

Well, I don't know. You see, that's a bad question for me, because I didn't, and as a consequence, I feel that I have missed learning some things that would have been helpful to me. But at the same time, I feel that I was not put into a bag, which I think is a great danger— of being trained very carefully, very

Setting by Robin Wagner
MARY C. BROWN AND THE HOLLYWOOD SIGN
Directed by Tom O'Horgan
Costumes by Randy Barcelo

Lighting by Jules Fisher
Shubert Theatre, Century City
Los Angeles, California (1972)
(Photograph—Marc Cohen)

well. I've had people work for me who are really concerned about having trained with certain designers at schools, because their style is imposed on them. And it takes quite a while to dispose of that style and find their own. But then, maybe the discipline is good and only the real talents will emerge. I think very simply it's a question of where you're headed. If you're headed into a school, you go to school, and if it's into work, you go to work. As far as regional theatre goes, I think it's great if it's good and exciting theatre. The only thing that really counts is that you really love what you're doing. If you're bored, you're in the wrong place.

I think young people should see everything they can see, and I think the designer should really get into directors' heads, because ultimately, there's a source there that you can just keep tapping forever. This has been true with every director I have worked with. The more you can begin to understand how his mind functions from the staging point of view, then you begin exploring that world. Stage directing has its own world, its own way of looking at things. I think it's just valuable to work with as many people, as many theatres, and as many forms as you can. No form should be cut out. You shouldn't specialize, because you're forced into that soon enough. Somebody pockets you into a category and that's what you do, which is really hell.

Do you have any preference about designing for a specific type of theatre, like plays or musicals?

No. I think theatre is theatre. I have no preferences at all. If it's exciting and makes an audience feel more alive and reveals something to them in some magical way, then its place is justified. I have a feeling that we are going to see more of opera in a different way, because the musical seems to have reached the extent of its particular form.

All I know is, if I project myself fifty years into the future and look at this period of theatre, I really wonder if we are going to discuss Broadway as being theatre or if we're going to discuss Bob Dylan, Bangladesh, the Beatles, that whole world. Then conceivably *Superstar*, as far as it comes out of a concert. That's where the audience is and that has the voice that the theatre has had in the past, historically. It is a far-reaching voice and one that has dramatic as well as political overtones. It has power—a theatre power. And until the theatre reaches that importance again and stops being a dilettante entertainment, which I think it has become on Broadway, then it has lost its balls. It doesn't have what it should have, what has made it last through the centuries. And it has to go to that point.

The first time I saw *Superstar* in concert was in Chicago. There were twenty-two thousand people walking there with knapsacks and their grass and their wine in an outdoor amphitheatre. And there was an excitement in the air. There was nothing on stage but an orchestra and twenty singers. Kids of ten to old people in wheelchairs were everywhere. I sat down and I looked at it and felt what was happening. I looked up on the stage and saw the orchestra and I saw these people with microphones standing on a platform and it occurred to me that in history there was another kind of theatre like that, only they had a mask with a megaphone built into it. And they stood in heroic postures and they spoke about legends and myths. They spoke about things of overwhelming importance. It was the Greek theatre. Somehow the concert had a leaning to that form which could be explored, perhaps, which could become another kind of theatre. And every great theatre has had an importance. We have to help create that in ours.

Setting by Robin Wagner
JESUS CHRIST SUPERSTAR
Lyrics by Tim Rice
Music by Andrew Lloyd Webber
Directed by Tom O'Horgan

Costumes by Randy Barcelo
Lighting by Jules Fisher
Universal Amphitheatre
Los Angeles, California (1972)
(Photograph—Marc Cohen)

Stage Designers

Broadway Stage Designers

Biographical information about the ten designers whose conversations with the author appear in the body of the book precedes each conversation. Production credits may include settings, lighting, and costumes (one or more categories) Abbreviations used here: setting (s), costumes (c), lighting (l), or supervision (sup.).

ALSWANG, Ralph B. 1916 in Chicago, Ill. Ed. Goodman Theatre, Chicago Art Institute. Productions include: *Home of the Brave, Strange Bedfellows, Peter Pan, Tickets Please, King Lear, The Mikado. Two's Company, The Rainmaker, Catch a Star, The Tunnel of Love, The First Gentleman* (also co-presented), *Sunrise at Campobello, A Raisin in the Sun, The Girls Against the Boys, Come Blow Your Horn, Beyond the Fringe* (l), *The School for Scandal* (l), *The Committee, The World of Charles Asnavour, Hostile Witness, Fun City.* Designed for Mark Taper Forum, Center Theatre Group, Los Angeles. Designed the Uris Theatre in New York.

ARMISTEAD, Horace B. 1898 in Yorkshire, England. At 15 apprenticed to Helmsley's Scenic Studio in London where productions for Convent Garden, the Old Vic, St. James, and other notable playhouses were designed. Ed. London Polytechnic. Designed productions of Gilbert and Sullivan and famous pantomimes in England. In 1925 he came to Boston to be technical advisor at the Fine Arts Theatre. Later joined Civic Repertory Theatre (N.Y.) under Eva Le Gallienne. New York productions include: *What Big Ears, Regina, The Telephone* and *The Medium, Punch and the Child, Arms and the Girl, The Nutcracker, Gounod Symphony.* Metropolitan Opera productions: *Cavalleria Rusticana, Pagliacci, The Rake's Progress, Pelléas et Mélisande.* Taught at Boston University.

ARONSON, Boris B. 1900 in Kiev, Russia. Ed. State Art School, School of the Theatre, Kiev, and School of Modern Painting, Moscow. First New York show: *Day and Night,* Unser Theatre, Bronx, N.Y., 1924. Among numerous productions are: *Three Men on a Horse, Awake and Sing, Cabin in the Sky, R.U.R., Sadie Thompson, Detective Story, Season in the Sun, The Country Girl, Barefoot in Athens, I Am a Camera, The Rose Tattoo, The Crucible, My Three Angels, Bus Stop, A View from the Bridge, The Diary of Anne Frank, Orpheus Descending, The Rope Dancers, J.B., A Loss of Roses, Flowering Cherry, A Gift of Time, Do-Re-Mi, Fiddler on the Roof, Incident at Vichy, The Price, Cabaret, Zorba, Company, Follies, A Little Night Music.* Metropolitan Opera: sets and costumes for *Fidelio* and *Mourning Becomes Electra.* Ballet: *Tzaddik,* Eliot Feld Ballet. Awards: five Tonys— *Rose Tattoo, Cabaret, Zorba, Company,* and *Follies;* a Guggenheim Fellowship, Ford Grant, American Theatre Wing Award, Brandeis University Award, New York Critic's Poll as Best Designer for *Follies.* Maharam Awards for *Cabaret* and *Follies.*

BEATON, Cecil B. 1904 in London. Ed. Harrow, St. John's College, Cambridge. First Broadway show: *Lady Windermere's Fan* (s, c), 1946. New York productions include: *The Cry of the Peacock* (s, c), *The Grass Harp* (s, c), *Quadrille* (s, c), *Portrait of a Lady* (c), *The Chalk Garden* (s, c), *My Fair Lady* (c), *Saratoga* (s, c), *Look After Lulu* (s, c), *Dear Liar* (c), *Tenderloin* (c), *Coco* (s, c). Metropolitan Opera productions: *Vanessa, Turandot.* Has designed for films: *Gigi, My Fair Lady, The Doctor's Dilemma.* Has designed sets and costumes for many productions in London including his first production *Follow the Sun,* 1935, *The Return of the Prodigal, Charley's Aunt, Love's Labor's Lost.* Has designed sets and costumes for the ballet *Marguerite and Armand* at Convent Garden. He received the N.Y. Drama Critic's Award for best costume designer, *My Fair Lady,* 1956, and best scenic and costume designer, *Saratoga,* 1959; an Academy Award for *My Fair Lady,* 1965, and *Gigi* (costumes), 1958. He is also a photographer, illustrator, author.

BURLINGAME, Lloyd B. 1934 in Washington, D.C. Ed. Carnegie Tech. First Broadway show: *Lock up Your Daughters* (s, l), 1960. Productions include: *Love Is a Time of Day* (s, c, l), *Hadrian VII* (l), *Rockefeller and the Red Indians* (l), *Joe Egg* (l), *There's a Girl in My Soup* (l), *Keep It in the Family* (s, l), *The Astrakhan Coat* (s, c), *The Loves of Cass McGuire* (s, l), *Help Stamp Out Marriage* (l), *Philadelphia, Here I Come!* (s, c, l), *First One Asleep, Whistle* (s, l), *Marat/Sade* (l), *Inadmissible Evidence* (l), *The Right Honorable Gentleman* (l), *Boeing-Boeing* (l), *Alfie* (s, c), *Lady of the Camellias* (l). Off Broadway includes: *Arms and the Man* (s, c), *The Great Western Union* (s, c), *The Secret Life of Walter Mitty* (s, l), *The Alchemist* (s, l), *Pimpernel* (s, l). Has designed for the Repertory Theatre/New Orleans, San Francisco Opera, Chautauqua Opera, Boston Opera, Peabody Art Theatre. Chairman of design dept., School of the Arts, New York Univ.

BURY, John B. 1925 in Wales. Ed. Hereford Cathedral School and Univ. College, London. First Broadway show: *Oh, What a Lovely War,* 1964. New York productions include: *The Homecoming, The Rothchilds* (s, c), *The Physicists, A Doll's House* (s, l, c), *Hedda Gabler, Old Times* (s, l). O-B: *The Blood Knot.* Other productions include: Royal Shakespeare Company (Head of design 1964– 1968); *Measure for Measure, Macbeth, The Physicists, The Collection, Julius Caesar, The War of the Roses, Indians, A Delicate Balance, Landscape, Silence;* Theatre Workshop Company at the Theatre Royal, Stratford, *Richard II, Volpone, Edward II, A Taste of Honey, A Christmas Carol, Oh, What A Lovely War;* Convent Garden, *Moses and Aaron, The Magic Flute, The Knot Garden, A Midsummer Night's Dream, Tristan und Isolde.* Has also designed the film *A Midsummer Night's Dream.* Received the Plays and Players Best Designer Award for *Silence,* 1969.

CONKLIN, John B. 1937 in Farmington, Conn. Ed. Yale Drama School, Yale College. First Broadway show: *Tambourines to Glory,* 1963, followed by *Lorelei, Scratch, Au Pair Man* (Lincoln Center). O-B: *The Firebugs, The Play of Herod, The Way of the World.* Has designed for the American Opera Society, Santa Fe Opera, Baltimore Civic Theatre, Washington Opera Society, Houston Opera, Minnesota Opera Company, Princeton's McCarter Theatre, Seattle Repertory Company, Williamstown Theatre, New York City Opera, Theatre of the Living Arts, Arena Stage, Studio Arena, San Diego Shakespeare Festival, Long Wharf Theatre, Hartford Stage Company, Joffrey Ballet: *Double Exposure;* Pennsylvania Ballet: *Swan Lake, Nutcracker Suite;* London's Royal Ballet: *Grand Tour.* Visiting professor of design at Temple University.

ECKART, William and Jean Jean Eckart B. 1921 in Chicago, Ill. Ed. Newcomb College and Yale Drama School. William Eckart B. 1920 in New Iberia, La. Ed. Tulane and Yale Drama School. As a team, productions include: *Glad Tidings, Oh, Men! Oh, Women!, The Golden Apple, Damn Yankees* (s & c), *Once upon a Mattress, Oh Dad, Poor Dad, Mama's Hung You in the Closet and I'm Feelin' so Sad, Fiorello, Flora, the Red Menace, Mame, Hallelujah Baby, She Loves Me, Fade Out—Fade In, L'il Abner, Of Mice and Men* (revival). Motion pictures: *Pajama Game, Damn Yankees.* Donaldson Award for *The Golden Apple,* 1954.

EIGSTI, Karl B. 1938 in Goshen, Ind. Ed. Indiana and American Univs. First Broadway show: *Inquest,*

1970, followed by *Grease* (l), *Othello, Henry V.* O-B productions include: *Nourish the Beast, The Karl Marx Play, The House of Blue Leaves, Boesman and Lena.* Has designed for Arena Stage, Tyrone Guthrie Theatre, American Place Theatre, Long Wharf Theatre, Studio Arena, Actors Theatre of Louisville, Theatre of the Living Arts. Awards: Fulbright for study in England. Instructor at New York University School of the Arts.

ELDER, Eldon B. 1924 in Atchison, Kan. Ed. Denver Univ. and Yale Drama School. First Broadway show: *The Legend of Lovers,* 1951. Productions include: *Dream Girl, Idiot's Delight* (revivals), *Venus Observed, Time Out for Ginger, Take a Giant Step, The Girl in Pink Tights, Phoenix '55, The Young and the Beautiful, Shinbone Alley, The Affair, Blasts and Bravos: An Unpleasant Evening with H.L. Mencken, A Family and a Fortune, A Whitman Portrait, Will Rogers' U.S.A.* Has designed for the New York Shakespeare Festival, American Shakespeare Festival, Baltimore's Center Stage, Seattle Repertory Company, St. Louis Municipal Opera, San Francisco Opera, Santa Fe Opera and for television. Awarded Ford Foundation Grant for Theatre Design, 1960. He is currently professor of stage design at Brooklyn College.

ELSON, Charles B. 1909 in Chicago, Ill. Ed. Univs. of Ill. and Chicago, Yale Drama School. Productions include settings for *As You Like It* (1945), *Hidden Horizon, Duet for Two Hands* (& l), *The First Mrs. Frazier, Power without Glory, Private Lives, Nina, His and Hers, Champagne Complex, The Lovers, La Plume de Ma Tante, Lysistrata, The Deep Blue Sea* (& l). Lighting includes: *Regina, An Enemy of the People, The Rose Tattoo, Compulsion, Blue Denim, Maria Golovin, First Impressions, Wildcat, Troilus and Cressida, Henry IV—Part I, Richard II, Photo Finish.* Metropolitan Opera productions: *Lohengrin, Don Giovanni, Norma, The Flying Dutchman.* Has taught at the Univs. of Iowa and Okla., Yale, and Hunter College.

EVANS, Lloyd B. 1932 in Mt. Morris, Mich. Ed. Univ. of Michigan School of Music and Yale Drama School. First New York show: *Color of Darkness,* 1963. Has designed settings and costumes for many New York City Opera productions: *Don Giovanni, Summer and Smoke, Albert Herring, Pelléas et Mélisande, Il Barbiere di Siviglia, La Bohème, Pagliacci, Cavalleria Rusticana, Madama Butterfly, Medea;* s only for *Rigoletto, Pirates of Penzance, Die Fledermaus, L'Incoronazione di Poppea;* c only for *Ariadne auf Naxos.* Also designed for St. Paul Opera Association, Caramoor Musical Festival, Jacksonville Symphony Orchestra, Corporacion de Arte Lirico (Santiago, Chile). Production designer for *Love of Life,* CBS television drama.

FOX, Frederick B. 1910 in New York City. Ed. Phillips Exeter Academy, Yale University, National Academy of Design. First Broadway show: *Farewell Summer,* 1937. Productions include: *Johnny Belinda, The Two Mrs. Carrolls, Anna Lucasta, Darkness at Noon, The Climate of Eden, The Seven Year Itch, King of Hearts, Anniversary Waltz, Lunatics and Lovers, The Hostage, Send Me No Flowers, From the Second City.* Metropolitan Opera (s & c): *Andrea Chenier, Tosca, Simon Boccanegra.* Donaldson Award for *Darkness at Noon,* 1951. Has also designed for television.

GORELIK, Mordecai B. 1899 in Minsk, Russia. Ed. Pratt Institute. Studied with Robert Edmond Jones, Norman Bel Geddes, and Sergei Soudeikine.

First Broadway show: *Processional*, 1925. Productions include: *Casey Jones, Loudspeaker, Success Story, Men in White, All Good Americans, Sailors of Cattaro, Golden Boy, Tortilla Flat, Thunder Rock, All My Sons, The Flowering Peach, A Hatful of Rain.* Motion Pictures: *Days of Glory, None but the Lonely Heart.* Awards: Guggenheim Foundation Fellowship, 1936; Rockefeller Foundation Grant, 1949. Has taught at many schools including: School of the Theatre, New York; American Academy of Dramatic Arts; Miami, Toledo, Brigham Young, and New York Univs., Southern Illinois Univ. Author of *New Theatres for Old,* 1940.

HARVEY, Peter B. 1933 in Quirigua, Guatemala. Ed. Univ. of Miami. First Broadway show: *Baby Want a Kiss,* 1964. Productions include designing the scenery and costumes for *The Children's Mass, The Survival of St. Joan, Crisscrossing* and *Watercolor, Transfers, Park, Dames at Sea* (also London and San Francisco), *Sweet Eros/Witness, Red Cross/Muzeeka, The Boys in the Band* (& l) in New York, also Boston, Hollywood, London (& l), and Copenhagen (s & l); *The Butter and Egg Man, The Mad Show, The Sweet Enemy, The Immoralist.* Costumes for *All in Good Time.* Also has designed the scenery for *Sextet, Black Picture Show, La Bohème* and *Don Pasquale* (Brooklyn Lyric Opera), *Johnny Johnson, The Nuns, One Night Stands of a Noisy Passenger.* Has designed *Jewels* (s), *Pas de Deux & Divertissement* (s), *La Guirlande de Campra* (s & c), *Brahms-Schoenberg Quartet* (s) for New York City Ballet; *Concerning Oracles* for Metropolitan Opera Ballet. Has designed for Lincoln Center Repertory Company, Cincinnati Playhouse in the Park, Tulsa Opera, Robert Joffrey Ballet Company, Studio Arena, Annenberg Center, and for television. Instructor of stage and costume design at Pratt Institute.

HAYS, David B. 1930 in New York City. Ed. Harvard, Yale, and Boston Univ. Fulbright scholarship to study in London at the Old Vic, 1952–1953. First New York design: *The Cradle Song* (s & l), 1955. Productions include: *The Iceman Cometh, Long Day's Journey into Night, Hamlet, A Midsummer Night's Dream, The Quare Fellow, The Tenth Man, The Cradle Will Rock, All the Way Home, Gideon, No Strings, Desire Under the Elms, Marco Millions, The Changeling, Tartuffe, Dinner at Eight, Saint Joan, A Cry of Players, The Miser, The Gingerbread Lady, Two by Two,* the musical *Gone with the Wind.* Has designed for the New York City Ballet, American Shakespeare Festival, Repertory Theatre of Lincoln Center, the Metropolitan Opera, among others. Two Obie Awards for *The Quare Fellow* and *The Balcony. Variety* New York Drama Critics Poll for *No Strings.* Has been an instructor in stage design at New York Univ., Circle in the Square, and Boston Univ. He is currently director of the National Theatre of the Deaf.

HEELEY, Desmond B. in Staffordshire, England. Ed. Ryland Art School near Birmingham. First Broadway show: *Rosencrantz and Guildenstern Are Dead,* 1967. Also designed costumes for the musical *Cyrano.* Settings and costumes at the Metropolitan Opera for *Pelléas et Mélisande* and *Norma.* Has designed many shows for the London stage including The Old Vic, H. M. Tennent, Ltd., Sadler's Wells. Also designed for Glyndebourne, England, Shakespeare Festival Theatre, Stratford Ont., Canada. Awarded two Tonys for sets and costumes for *Rosencrantz and Guildenstern Are Dead,* 1968.

HORNER, Harry B. 1912 in Holič, Czechoslovakia. Ed. Univ. Vienna. Studied at Reinhardt's Theatre Academy. Brought to America by Reinhardt to be assistant director and designer of *The Eternal Road.* Productions include settings for: *All the Living, Jeremiah* (& c), *Family Portrait* (& c), *Reunion in New York, Lady in the Dark, Let's Face It, Banjo Eyes, Heart of a City, Star and Garter, Winged Victory, Joy to the World, Tovarich, Hazel Flagg* (& l), *How to Make a Man, Idiot's Delight.* Film designs include: *Our Town, The Little Foxes,*

The Heiress, Born Yesterday. Has also directed and produced films; directed productions for stage and television. Two Academy Awards for *The Hustler* and *The Heiress.*

JAMPOLIS, Neil Peter B. 1943 in Brooklyn, N.Y. Ed. Art Institute of Chicago. First Broadway show: *Borstal Boy* (s & l) 1969, followed by *Crown Matrimonial* (s, c sup., & l), *Brief Lives* (l), *Let Me Hear You Smile* (l), *Butley* (l & c), *Emperor Henry IV* (l, sup.), *Warp* (sup.), *To Live Another Summer, To Pass Another Winter* (s, l), *Wild and Wonderful, Wise Child* (l), *Les Blancs* (l), *Earl of Ruston* (s, l, c), *Canterbury Tales* (l). O-B includes: *The Wager* (l), *One Flew Over the Cuckoo's Nest* (s, c, l), *Show Me Where the Good Times Are* (l), *Tea Party* and *The Basement* (l), *The People vs. Ranchman* (l), *Little Murders* (l), *War Games* (s), *In the Bar of a Tokyo Hotel* (s, l), *Rondelay* (l). Has designed for the Hartford Stage Company, Netherlands Opera, Santa Fe Opera, Metropolitan Opera (projections, scenic & costume designs for *Macbeth,* 1973). Tony and Drama Desk Awards for lighting for *Sherlock Holmes,* 1975.

JENKINS, David B. 1937 in Hampton, Va. Ed. Earlham College, Indiana Univ., and Yale Drama School. First Broadway show: *The Changing Room,* 1973, followed by *The Freedom of the City, Rodgers and Hart.* Has designed for Long Wharf Theatre. Arena Stage, Theatre of the Living Arts, McCarter Theatre, Trinity Square Repertory Company, Cincinnati Playhouse in the Park, Goodman Theatre, Les Ballets Canadiens, American Shakespeare Festival. Television: WNET-TV Theatre in America Series — *The Widowing of Mrs. Holroyd.*

JENKINS, George B. 1910 in Baltimore, Md. Ed. Univ. of Pennsylvania. First Broadway show: *Early to Bed,* 1943. Productions include: *Mexican Hayride, I Remember Mama, Dark of the Moon, Allah Be Praised, Memphis Sound, The French Touch, Strange Fruit, Lost in the Stars, The Bad Seed, The Happiest Millionaire, The Curious Savage, The Immoralist, Too Late the Phalarope, The Desk Set, Bell, Book, and Candle, Cue for Passion, Generation, Wait Until Dark, Two for the Seesaw, Once More with Feeling. Song of Norway* for the Jones Beach Theatre. Has designed many films, among them *The Best Years of Our Lives, The Secret Life of Walter Mitty, 1776, Funny Lady.*

KECK, John William B. 1929 in New York City. Ed. at the High School of Music and Art and Pratt Institute. Son of sculptor Charles Keck. Master scenic artist for McDonald-Stevens (1954–1956) and Nolan Scenery Studios (1956–1973). Became Art Director for Radio City Music Hall, August 1973. Has also designed the settings for rock concerts at the Music Hall: Aretha Franklin, The Jackson Five, Sly and the Family Stone, and Marvin Gaye; settings for *Oklahoma* and *Fiddler on the Roof* for Guy Lombardo's productions at Jones Beach Theatre.

KERZ, Leo B. 1912 in Berlin, Germany. Ed. Friedrich Ebert Oberreal Schule and Academy of Arts and Science, Berlin; studied with Brecht. First Broadway show: *Antony and Cleopatra,* 1947. Productions include: *A Long Way Home, Clerambard, Moonbirds, Rhinoceros, Victim, The Sacred Flame;* Metropolitan Opera: *Parsifal, The Magic Flute;* New York City Opera: *Orpheus in the Underworld, Susannah, The Tempest;* San Francisco Opera Association: *Troilus and Cressida, Macbeth, Aïda, Lohengrin, Der Rosenkavalier.* Music Critic's Award for direction of *Susannah,* 1956; The Outer Circle Award for *Rhinoceros,* 1961. Among his film designs are *The Goddess, Middle of the Night, This Is Cinerama.* Has been staff designer for CBS-TV. Taught at the Dramatic Workshop of the New School for Social Research, Montana State Univ., Univ. of Warsaw, Univ. of Krakow.

LARKIN, Peter B. 1926 in Boston, Mass. Ed. Deerfield Academy and Yale Drama School. Productions include: *The Wild Duck, Dial M for*

Murder, The Teahouse of the August Moon, Ondine, Mary Martin's *Peter Pan* (stage and television), *Inherit the Wind, No Time for Sergeants, Shangri-La, New Faces of 1956, Compulsion, Blue Denim, Goldilocks, First Impressions, Greenwillow, Wildcat, Marathon '33, The Seagull, The Crucible, Ring Round the Moon, She Stoops to Conquer, Scuba Duba, Sheep on the Runway, Les Blancs, W. C., Twigs, Thieves.* Four Tony Awards for *No Time for Sergeants, Inherit the Wind, Ondine,* and *The Teahouse of the August Moon.* Two Donaldson Awards for *The Teahouse of the August Moon* and *Ondine.* Maharam Award for *Les Blancs.*

LOQUASTO, Santo B. 1944 in Wilkes-Barre, Pa. Ed. at the Yale Drama School and King's College. First Broadway show: *Sticks and Bones,* 1972 (from the Public Theatre), followed by *That Championship Season* (also from the Public Theatre), and *The Secret Affairs of Mildred Wild.* For the N.Y. Shakespeare Festival at Lincoln Center: *A Doll's House, The Dance of Death, The Tempest, Boom Boom Room, Macbeth, Pericles, What the Wine-Sellers Buy.* N.Y. Shakespeare Festival in Central Park: *King Lear, As You Like It.* Designed *La Dafne* for N.Y. Pro Musica at the Spoleto Festival of Two Worlds. Also designed for the Arena Stage, Yale Repertory Theatre, Hartford Stage Company, Williamstown Theatre, Long Wharf Theatre, Charles Playhouse, Mark Taper Forum, San Francisco Spring Opera, Opera Society of Washington, Chelsea Theatre Center. Drama Desk Awards for *Sticks and Bones* and *That Championship Season.*

LUNDELL, Kert B. 1936 in Malmö, Sweden. Ed. Goodman School of Drama, Art Institute of Chicago; Yale Drama School. First Broadway show: *The Investigation,* 1966. Productions include: *The Sunshine Boys, Hughie/Duet, The Night that Made America Famous, Ain't Supposed to Die a Natural Death, Don't Play Us Cheap, The Lincoln Mask, Under the Weather, Solitaire/Double Solitaire, Carry Me Back to Morningside Heights.* O-B: *Fragments, House of Flowers.* Many productions at the American Place Theatre include: *The Kid, Fingernails Blue as Flowers, Sleep, Ceremony of Innocence, Posterity for Sale, La Turista, The Displaced Person, Journey of the Fifth Horse, Hogan's Goat.* Also designed for The Scandinavian Theatre Co. (Stockholm), The Groot Limburg Toneel (The Netherlands), St. Louis Municipal Opera, Arena Stage, Long Wharf Theatre, Milwaukee Repertory Co., Baltimore's Center Stage, Trinity Square Repertory Co. Maharam Award for best set for *Ain't Supposed to Die a Natural Death,* 1972.

MESSEL, Oliver B. 1905 in London, England. Ed. Eton. Productions include *Cochran's Revue 1926* (and *1930, 1931), Helen, The Miracle, The Country Wife,* the ballet *Paolo and Francesca, A Midsummer Night's Dream, The Tempest, The Rivals, The Sleeping Beauty, The Lady's Not for Burning, Ring Round the Moon, Le Bourgeois Gentilhomme,* the operas *The Magic Flute, The Queen of Spades, Idomeneo, The Marriage of Figaro, Der Rosenkavalier.* Among N.Y. productions: *The Play's the Thing, Romeo and Juliet, The Little Hut, The Dark Is Light Enough, House of Flowers, Rashomon, Traveller Without Luggage, Metropolitan Opera, The Marriage of Figaro.* Films include: *Romeo and Juliet, Caesar and Cleopatra, Suddenly Last Summer.* Designed interiors for the Billy Rose National Theatre. Author of *Stage Designs and Costumes,* 1934.

MITCHELL, David B. 1932 in Honesdale, Pa. Ed. Boston Univ. First Broadway show: *How the Other Half Loves,* 1971, followed by *The Incomparable Max.* Productions include: designs for the New York Shakespeare Festival — *Little Black Sheep, Short Eyes, Hamlet, Trelawny of the Wells, The Basic Training of Pavlo Hummel,* mobile theatre productions of *Macbeth* and *Volpone.* O-B: *Steambath, Colette.* Opera: *Mefistofeles* (New York City Opera), *Aïda* (Deutche Oper, Berlin), *Il Trovatore* (Paris Opera), *Macbeth* (Washington Opera, Houston Grand Opera, Philadelphia Opera), *Manon* (San Francisco Opera), *Boris Godunov* (Cincinnati Opera and Canadian Opera). Has also designed for Pennsylvania Ballet and Charles Playhouse.

MITCHELL, Robert D. B. 1929 in Rutherford, N.J. Ed. Yale and Columbia, Lester Polakov's Studio of Stage Design. First Broadway show: *The Sudden and Accidental Re-education of Horse Johnson,* 1968. Productions include: *Medea* (Joseph E. Levine's Circle in the Square), *The Bacchae* (Lincoln Center), *The Lottery* and *L'Absence* (Harkness Ballet), *Cantique des Cantiques* and *Ceremonie* (Les Grands Ballets Canadiens), *La Peri* (Paris Opera Ballet, National Ballet of Washington, D.C.), *In Retrospect* (Pennsylvania Ballet), *Pie X* (Ballet, Walnut St. Theatre, Philadelphia). Also designed for Zellerbach Theatre and Harold Prince Theatre (Annenberg Center, Philadelphia), American Place Theatre, Chelsea Theatre Center (BAM), Minneapolis Theatre Company, Hedgerow Theatre, and O-B. Has been a theatre design consultant.

MORCOM, James Stewart B. 1906 in Covington, Ky. Ed. Grand Central Art School, and John Murray Anderson-Robert Milton School of the Theatre. First New York show: *Five Kings* for Orson Welles' Mercury Theatre Group, 1939. First Broadway show: *Native Son,* 1941. Ballet: *Time Table* for Ballet Caravan, *Symphonie Concertante* for the New York Ballet. Assistant Art Director Roxy Theatre, 1927–1932. Costume Designer for Radio City Music Hall, 1947–1950. Art Director Radio City Music Hall, 1950–1973. Designed settings for *The King and I* and *Carousel* at Jones Beach Theatre.

MORRISON, Paul B. 1906 in Altoona, Pa. Ed. Lafayette College. First Broadway show: Costumes for *Thunder Rock.* Productions include: (s, l, & c): *Walk into My Parlor, I'll Take the High Road, Four Saints in Three Acts, On Borrowed Time, The Confidential Clerk, Abie's Irish Rose, The Loud Red Patrick;* (s & l): *Hedda Gabler, Billy Budd, Affairs of State, The Tender Trap, Rape of the Belt, The Jockey Club Stakes;* (l & c): *Bus Stop, Golden Boy;* (l): *Candide, The Flowering Cherry, A Man for All Seasons;* (l & s, sup.): *Tamburlaine, Separate Tables, Cranks, The Visit, Much Ado about Nothing, The Caretaker.* Head of Theatre Dept., Barnard College, 1936–1941. Became executive director of the Neighborhood Playhouse School of the Theatre, 1962.

O'HEARN, Robert B. 1921 in Elkhart, Ind. Ed. Indiana Univ. and the Art Students League, N.Y. First Broadway show: *The Relapse,* 1950, followed by *Love's Labor's Lost* (s), *A Date With April* (s), *Festival* (s & l), *Othello* (s), *Henry IV, Part 1* (s), *Child of Fortune* (s & l), *The Apple Cart* (s & l). Sets and costumes for the Metropolitan Opera: *L'Elisir d'Amore, Parsifal, Der Rosenkavalier, Hansel and Gretel, Die Frau ohne Schatten, Samson et Dalila, Aïda, Die Meistersinger von Nürnberg, Queen of Spades, The Marriage of Figaro, Boris Godunov* (unproduced). Among others, has designed for American Ballet Theatre, Washington Opera Society, San Francisco Opera, Central City Opera, Boston Opera, Vienna Volksoper, Bregenz Festival (Austria), Saratoga Theatre, Olney Theatre, Green Mansions Playhouse.

PITKIN, William B. 1925 in Omaha, Neb. Ed. Universidad Nacional de Mexico, Univs. of Texas and New Mexico, Bard College. First New York show: *The Three Penny Opera,* Theatre de Lys, 1954. Productions include: *La Ronde, Child of Fortune* (c), *The Potting Shed, A Moon for the Misbegotten, The Cave Dwellers, Invitation to a March, The Conquering Hero* (with Jean Rosenthal), *The Beauty Part, The Impossible Years, Adaptation Next,* and *Comedy.* Has also designed for the American Ballet Theatre: *Coppelia;* Eliot Feld Ballet: *The Maids;* City Center Joffrey Ballet: *La Fille Mal Gardée* and *Cakewalk;* San Francisco Ballet; London's Royal Ballet; New York City Opera: *Die Fledermaus;* Washington Opera Society: *Madama Butterfly;*

American Shakespeare Festival, National Repertory Theatre, National Shakespeare Company, Berkshire Theatre Festival, Children's Theatre, and Nicolo Marionettes.

POLAKOV, Lester B. 1916 in Chicago, Ill. Studied painting and drawing with George Grosz in N.Y., stage design with Milton Smith at Columbia. Designed productions for the Morningside Players at Columbia Univ. 1934–1945, at the same time working on Broadway productions. First New York shows: Costumes for *Reunion in New York,* 1940, and *Crazy with the Heat,* 1941. Productions include: *Call Me Mister* (s), *Crime and Punishment* (c, l), *Member of the Wedding* (s, c, l), *Mrs. McThing* (s, l), *The Emperor's Clothes* (s, l), *The Empire Builders* (s, c, l), *Great Day in the Morning* (s, l). Has designed scenery for *The Beggar's Opera* and *The Bartered Bride* at Sarah Caldwell's Opera Company of Boston. Paintings and scene designs exhibited widely in galleries since 1950. Director of the Studio and Forum of Stage Design in N.Y.C., established 1958.

RITMAN, William B. 1928 in Chicago, Ill. Ed. Goodman School of Drama. Productions include: *Same Time, Next Year; Find Your Way Home, Noel Coward in Two Keys, My Fat Friend, 6 Rms Riv Vu, Play It Again, Sam; Moonchildren, The Sign in Sidney Brustein's Window, Bob and Ray—the Two and Only, What the Butler Saw, We Bombed in New Haven, Lovers, Loot, The Birthday Party, Johnny No-Trump, Who's Afraid of Virginia Woolf?, Tiny Alice, A Delicate Balance, Everything in the Garden, The Killing of Sister George, The Zoo Story, Krapp's Last Tape, Happy Days, The Collection,* and *The Dumbwaiter.* Designed the lighting for *Sleuth.* Has also designed for Arena Stage, Studio Arena, and the American Shakespeare Festival: *Mourning Becomes Electra* and *Major Barbara.*

ROTH, Wolfgang B. 1910 in Berlin, Germany. Ed. Academy of Arts, Berlin. N.Y. productions include: *The Deadly Game,* 1940 (s, l), *Yellow Jack, Androcles and the Lion, Porgy and Bess* (national and international touring company), *Oh, Mr. Meadowbrook!, Cock-a-Doodle-Doo, Twentieth Century, Medea, Brecht on Brecht, Johnny Johnson, Good Woman of Setzuan, The Tower Beyond Tragedy, Now I Lay Me Down to Sleep, School for Wives, The Littlest Circus* (created and designed), *Bernadine, The Typists, The Tiger* (double bill), *The Cannibals.* Has designed in Germany, Austria, Switzerland and for cabaret, film, opera, operetta, circus, vaudeville. Has designed for the Metropolitan Opera: *Don Pasquale, Tristan und Isolde;* American Repertory Theatre, ANTA Play Series, ANTA Experimental Theatre, Boston Repertory, for ballet, television and films. Is also known for paintings, drawings and architectural designs.

SCHMIDT, Douglas W. B. 1942 in Cincinnati, Ohio. Ed. New Hampshire and Boston Univ. First Broadway show: *Paris Is Out,* 1970. Productions include: *Grease, The Country Girl, A Streetcar Named Desire* (revival), *Love's Suicide at Schofield Barracks, Veronica's Room, Over Here!* Resident designer for Lincoln Center Repertory Company; many productions include: *The Time of Your Life, The Good Woman of Setzuan, Antigone, Playboy of the Western World, Enemy of the People, A Midsummer Night's Dream, Operation Sidewinder, Narrow Road to the Deep North.* Also designed for Juilliard Dance Co., Juilliard Opera Theatre, New York Shakespeare Festival, The Public Theatre, Tyrone Guthrie Theatre, Baltimore Center Stage, Theatre of the Living Arts, Cincinnati Playhouse in the Park, the Music Theatre of Tanglewood, Arena Stage. Has been instructor at Columbia, Circle in the Square, and Studio and Forum of Stage Design.

SENN, Herbert (as team with Helen Pond) B. 1924 in Ilion, N.Y. Ed. Columbia University. *POND, Helen* B. 1924 in Shaker Heights, Ohio. Ed. Ohio State and Columbia. First Broadway show: *What Makes Sammy Run?,* 1964, followed by *No Sex*

Please, We're British; Roar Like a Dove, Noel Coward's Sweet Potato. Over 25 O-B productions include: *Berlin to Broadway, Oh, Coward, The Idiot, The Brothers Karamazov, Gay Divorcé, By Jupiter, The Boys from Syracuse* (also for London's Theatre Royal, Drury Lane and for production in Australia). Designed *Jacques Brel Is Alive and Living in Paris,* The Duchess Theatre, London. New York City Opera: *Ariadne auf Naxos, The Young Lord.* Opera Company of Boston: *Les Troyens, War and Peace.* American National Opera Company: *The Rake's Progress.* Boston Ballet: *Giselle* and *Les Sylphides.* Designed Offenbach's musical *Voyage to the Moon* for two command performances at the White House. Team has designed scenery for ten productions each summer at the Cape Playhouse, Dennis, Mass., for the past 19 years.

TAYLOR, Robert U. B. 1941 in Lexington, Va. Ed. Univ. of Pennsylvania, Pennsylvania Academy of Fine Arts, Yale Drama School. First Broadway show: *Unlikely Heroes,* 1971, followed by *Raisin.* Productions include: *Fashion, The Beggar's Opera, Saved, Coocooshay, Touch, Istanbul, The Vest, The Bench, The Judas Applause, Lady Day.* Also designed for Arena Stage, Playhouse in the Park, Goodman Theatre, McCarter Theatre, Shaw Festival (Canada), New Haven Opera Society, Tyrone Guthrie Theatre, Loeb Repertory Theatre (Harvard), Hunter College, Wheaton College, Connecticut College, St. Cloud College, N.Y. State College, Univ. of Pennsylvania, City Island Theatre, Peterborough Players. Drama Desk Award and Maharam Award for Best Scenery 1971–1972, *Beggars Opera.*

TILTON, James F. B. 1937 in Rochelle, Ill. Ed. Univ. of Iowa. First Broadway show: *You Can't Take It with You,* 1965. Productions include: *Seascape, The Merchant of Venice, Oh! Calcutta!* (also Off-Broadway, Los Angeles and San Francisco), *The Grass Harp, The School for Wives, Harvey, Private Lives, Hamlet, Cock-a-Doodle Dandy, The Cocktail Party, The Misanthrope, The Cherry Orchard, Exit the King* (1), *The Show-Off, Pantagleize, The Wild Duck, War and Peace, We Comrades Three, School for Scandal, Right You Are.* O-B includes: *The Inspector General, The Seagull, Rainbow, The Criminals, Ballad for a Firing Squad, The Lower Depths, Scapin* and *Impromptu de Versailles.* Has also designed for the Professional Theatre Program-Univ. of Michigan, American Conservatory Theatre, Asolo Theatre, Front Street Theatre, Shaw Festival (Canada), Huntington Hartford Theatre, Kansas City Opera, the film *Dear, Dead Delilah.*

TOMS, Carl B. 1927 in Kirkby-in-Ashfield. Ed. Mansfield College of Art, the Royal College of Art, and the Old Vic School. First New York production: *Sleuth,* 1970. Productions include *Vivat! Vivat Regina!, Sherlock Holmes* (Tony Award for best scenery, 1975), *I Puritani* and *Der Meistersinger* for New York City Opera. Has designed many productions for the West End, the Edinburgh Festival, the National Theatre (*Cyrano de Bergerac, Love's Labor's Lost*), the Chichester Festival Theatre (*Antony and Cleopatra, The Magistrate, Vivat! Vivat Regina!, The Alchemist*), the Welsh National Opera (*Falstaff*), opera and ballet for the Royal Opera House, Glyndebourne and Sadler's Wells, among others. Has designed for films and for television. Design consultant for the Investiture of the Prince of Wales at Caernarvon Castle. Has been Head of Design for the Young Vic Theatre.

WALTON, Tony B. 1934 in Walton-on-Thames, England. Ed. Radley College, City of Oxford School of Technology, Art and Commerce; the Slade School of Fine Arts. First New York show: *Conversation Piece,* 1957. Productions include: *Chicago, Pippin,* Bette Midler's *Clams on the Half-Shell Revue, The Apple Tree, The Rehearsal* (c), *Golden Boy, A Funny Thing Happened to Me on the Way to the Forum, Once There Was a Russian, Valmouth.* He has also designed many London productions including *The Ginger Man, Pieces of Eight, Caligula, Fool's Paradise, The Pleasure of His Company, The*

Most Happy Fella, and opera and ballet at Convent Garden and Sadler's Wells. Has also designed for films: Mary Poppins, The Seagull, Fahrenheit 451, A Funny Thing Happened to Me on the Way to the Forum, Petulia, The Boy Friend, as well as designing for television. Has also directed and produced.

WEXLER, Peter B. 1936 in New York City. Ed. Univ. of Michigan's School of Architecture and Design, Yale Drama School. Productions include: The Happy Time (s), A Joyful Noise (s, l), Minnie's Boys (s), War and Peace (s), Brecht on Brecht (s, l), The White Devil (s), The Trial of the Catonsville Nine in N.Y., Los Angeles (and the film); Camino Real (s, c) and In the Matter of J. Robert Oppenheimer for Lincoln Center Repertory Company.

Among productions for the Mark Taper Forum (Los Angeles): Mass (s), The Devils (s, l, c), The Marriage of Mr. Mississippi (s, l, c), Chemin de Fer (s), Uncle Vanya (s, l), Murderous Angels (s), Rosebloom (c). Opera credits include: Metropolitan Opera — Les Troyens (s, c, visual effects); Central City Opera — Curlew River (s, c); Washington Opera Society — The Magic Flute (s, l); New York City Opera — Lizzie Borden (s, l). Has also designed for the Goodman Theatre, for the Corpus Christi Symphony Orchestra, for television, and for the New York Philharmonic Promenades (s, l, interior & exterior graphics). Drama Desk Award and Maharam Award for The Happy Time (best designer of musical, 1968).

WITTSTEIN, Ed B. 1929 in Mt. Vernon, N.Y. Ed.

Parsons School of Design, New York Univ. Cooper Union. First Broadway show: Kean (s & c), 1961. Productions include: Ulysses in Nighttown, Happy Birthday, Wanda June; Blood Red Roses, Celebration, You Know I Can't Hear You When the Water's Running, The Man in the Glass Booth, Bravo Giovanni (c). Off-Broadway: The Last Sweet Days of Isaac, Little Murders, The Fantasticks. Motion pictures include: The Seven-ups, Bananas, Don't Drink the Water. NBC-TV opera productions: La Bohème, La Traviata, Cosi Fan Tutti, Cavalleria Rusticana, The Love of Three Kings, and other television productions. Has also designed for the American Shakespeare Festival, New York City Opera, Cincinnati Playhouse in the Park, restaurant interiors, cabaret revues, productions abroad.

Important Earlier Twentieth-Century Stage Designers

ARMSTRONG, Will Steven (1930–1969) B. New Orleans, La. Ed. Louisiana State and Yale. Productions include: The Andersonville Trial, 1959, Caligula, Carnival, A Cook for Mr. General, Subways Are for Sleeping, I Can Get It for You Wholesale, Tchin-Tchin, Dear Me, the Sky Is Falling; One Flew Over the Cuckoo's Nest, Nobody Loves an Albatross, Semi-Detached, The Passion of Josef D., The Three Sisters, I Had a Ball, Ready When You Are, C.B.; The Front Page, Forty Carats, The Lion in Winter. Designed for: American Shakespeare Festival, Stratford, Conn., Williamstown Theatre, National Repertory Theatre, New York City Opera, Phoenix Theatre as well as London productions. Awards: Obie Off-Broadway Award for Ivanov, 1959, Tony Award for Carnival, 1962.

AYERS, Lemuel (1915–1955) B. New York City. Ed. Princeton and Iowa Univ. First Broadway shows: Revivals of Journey's End and They Knew What They Wanted, 1939. Productions include: Angel Street, The Pirate, Lifeline, The Willow and I, Harriet, Oklahoma, Song of Norway, Bloomer Girl, St. Louis Woman, Cyrano de Bergerac, Inside U.S.A., Kiss Me, Kate, My Darlin' Aida, As You Like It, Kismet, The Pajama Game, Camino Real and The Merchant of Venice for the NYC Drama Co. Co-producer with Saint Subber for Kiss Me, Kate and Out of This World.

BARRATT, Watson (1884–1962) B. Salt Lake City, Utah. Ed. Chase School of Art and Howard Pyle Illustration School. First Broadway show: Sinbad, 1918. Productions include: The Student Prince, Blossom Time, Scarlet Sister Mary, Artists and Models, Three Waltzes, Bachelor Born, The White Seed, The Time of Your Life, The Importance of Being Earnest, Love's Old Sweet Song, Magic, Hello, Out There; Ziegfeld Follies, Rebecca, Flamingo Road, January Thaw, Little A, Hedda Gabler, Ghosts. Designed Winter Garden shows from 1918 to 1928; art director and assistant manager of St. Louis Municipal Outdoor Opera for many years.

BEL GEDDES, Norman (1893–1958) B. Adrian, Mich. Ed. Cleveland School of Art, Chicago Art Institute. First New York production: Shanewis, Metropolitan Opera, 1918. Designed more than 200 productions, which include: The Miracle and The Eternal Road for Max Reinhardt; Divine Comedy, The Rivals, The School for Scandal, Jeanne d'Arc, Arabesque, Ziegfeld Follies, Lysistrata, Flying Colors, Hamlet (also directed and produced), Dead End, Iron Men, Siege, The Truth about Blayds, Lady Be Good, Strike up the Band, Fifty Million Frenchmen, Sons and Soldiers. Settings for films: Feet of Clay, 1924, The Sorrows of Satan, 1926. Published a book on Dante's Divine Comedy, 1924. Created futurama "Highways and Horizons" for the 1939 World's Fair. Also designed commercial items like autos, scales, beds, and radios. He supervised draftsmen who made the drawings for his theatres, hotels, television stations, and trains.

BERMAN, Eugene (1899–1972) B. St. Petersburg, Russia. Ed. Academie Rancon, Paris. First stage designs: Hartford Musical Festival, Hartford, Conn., 1939. As an artist, exhibited at the neo-romantic show at the Duret Gallery in 1926 with Christian Bérard, Tchelichew, and his brother Leonid; had numerous exhibits in Paris, London, Chicago, Boston, San Francisco, Los Angeles, Rome, Turin, Palmero, and Madrid; author of The Graphic World of Eugene Berman. Designed settings and costumes for Metropolitan Opera's Rigoletto, La Forza del Destino, Il Barbiere di Siviglia, Don Giovanni, Otello. American Ballet Theatre: Romeo and Juliet, Giselle, Concerto Barocco. Ballet Russe de Monte Carlo: Danses Concertantes, Le Bourgeois Gentilhomme, Devils' Holiday. Società Filarmonica di Roma: Renard. Sadler's Wells Ballet and La Scala: Ballet Imperial. New York City Ballet: Pulcinella.

BERNSTEIN, Aline (1882–1955) B. New York City. Ed. New York School of Applied Design. Began designing costumes at the Neighborhood Playhouse, Grand St., N.Y., for The Little Clay Cart, 1924, followed by costumes for Reinhardt's The Miracle, 1924. Designed settings for Theatre Guild: Caprice, Reunion in Vienna; Gilbert Miller: Tomorrow and Tomorrow, The Animal Kingdom; Civic Repertory Theatre: The Cherry Orchard, The Sea Gull, Camille, Peter Pan, Romeo and Juliet, Liliom; Herman Shumlin: Grand Hotel, Clear All Wires, The Late Christopher Bean, Firebird, A Good Woman, For the People, Thunder on the Left, Mackerel Skies, Judgment Day, The Children's Hour, Night in the House. Costumes for: The Little Foxes, Harriet, Regina, The Eagle Has Two Heads.

CHANEY, Stewart (1910–1969) B. Kansas City, Mo. Ed. Yale and with Andre L'Hote. First Broadway show: The Old Maid, 1935. Productions include: Life With Father (s, c), Blithe Spirit, Appollon Museagate (ballet, Met. Opera House), Faust (opera, Covent Garden), The Rivals (Old Vic), Twelfth Night, Voice of the Turtle, Jacobowsky and the Colonel, The Late George Apley (s, c), The Winter's Tale, I Know My Love, The House of Bernarda Alba (s, c, also co-produced), The Moon Is Blue, Arsenic and Old Lace, Shumann Concerto (s, c, ballet, Met. Opera House), Late Love (s, l), Sherlock Holmes (s, l, c), The Bad Seed (London), The Hidden River (s, l), The Summer of Daisy Miller (co-produced). Also designed for films and television. Guggenheim Fellowship for European theatre study, 1937.

DREYFUSS, Henry (1904–1972) B. New York City. Ed. Occidental College, Pratt Institute. Productions include: Beau Gallant, 1926, Hold Everything, Remote Control, Boundry Line, The Last Mile, Fine and Dandy, Blind Mice, Pagan Lady, Sweet Stranger, An Affair of State, This is New York, Kiss of Importance, Philip Goes Forth, The Gang's All Here, The Man on Stilts, The Cat and the Fiddle, Strike Me Pink, Continental Varieties (also dir.), Paths of Glory. Designed stage equipment and

lights for RKO theatres, the Perisphere for the 1939–1940 N.Y. World's Fair, designed for the Chicago Century of Progress. Entered industrial design.

JOHNSON, Albert (1910–1967) B. La Cross, Wis. Studied stage design with Norman Bel Geddes. First Broadway show: The Criminal Code, 1929. Productions include: Three's a Crowd, The Band Wagon, Waltzes from Vienna (London), The Mad Hopes, Face the Music, Foreign Affairs, Exit the Queen, Americana, As Thousands Cheer, Let 'Em Eat Cake, The Ziegfeld Follies, Union Pacific (Ballet Russe de Monte Carlo), Life Begins at 8:40, The Great Waltz, Revenge with Music, Jumbo, Between the Devil, The Skin of Our Teeth, You Never Know, Leave It to Me, Great Lady, Sing out, Sweet Land; Of Thee I Sing, Two Blind Mice, What Did We Do Wrong?, George White's Scandals. Designed for Ringling Brothers, Barnum and Bailey Circus, many productions for Radio City Music Hall, numerous outdoor amphitheatre productions, including Show Boat at Jones Beach.

JONES, Robert Edmond (1887–1954) B. Milton, N.H. Ed. Harvard. First Broadway show: The Man Who Married a Dumb Wife (s, c), 1915. Productions include: Hamlet, The Jest, Desire Under the Elms, The Green Pastures (revival), Mourning Becomes Electra, Camille, Ah, Wilderness!, A Night over Taos, Mary of Scotland, Othello, The Sea Gull, The Philadelphia Story, Without Love, Helen Goes to Troy, Lute Song. Beginning in 1925 he was associated with Kenneth MacGowan and Eugene O'Neill on several plays at the Greenwich Village Playhouse. He staged many of O'Neill's plays. Designed in Hollywood where he helped develop technicolor. With Kenneth MacGowan, author of Continental Stagecraft, 1922. Author of The Dramatic Imagination, 1941, Drawings for the Theatre, 1925.

KARSON, Nat (1910–1954) B. Zürich, Switzerland. Ed. Chicago Art Institute. First Broadway show: Waltzes in Fire, 1934. Designed the sets for the Federal Theatre Negro Company production of Macbeth. Art director for Radio City Music Hall for seven years. Painted murals for Chicago World's Fair, 1933. Hamlet at the Kronborg Festival, Elsinore, 1947, was a great success.

KENNY, Sean (1932–1973) B. Tipperary, Ireland. Ed. St. Flannan's College and School of Architecture, Univ. of Dublin. Pretheatre work as an architect, with Frank Lloyd Wright. First Broadway show: Stop the World—I Want to Get Off, 1962, followed by Oliver!, 1963. Tony Award for best sets for Oliver! in 1963. Designed sets for more than 30 West End productions, London. Redesigned Old Vic Theatre (now National Theatre), London. Designed mechanized multilayer stage for the Casino de Paris in Las Vegas; the Gyroton, the spectacular ride at Expo 67 in Montreal; an all-glass underwater restaurant in Nassau, the Bahamas. Designed for television and a film.

ROSENTHAL, Jean (1912–1969) B. New York City. Ed. Yale, the Neighborhood Playhouse School of the Theatre. First New York show: production supervisor for the Federal Theatre Negro Company production of Macbeth, 1936. Designed lighting for more than 200 shows including Hello, Dolly!, Cabaret, Plaza Suite, Fiddler on the Roof, The Sound of Music, Ballets: USA; West Side Story, A Hole in the Head, The Great Sebastians, The Saint of Bleeker Street, House of Flowers, Quadrille, Redhead, Take Me Along, The Apple Tree, Dear World, The Dark at the Top of the Stairs, Destry Rides Again, Caligula, The Disenchanted. Lighting director for the New York City Ballet, American Shakespeare Theatre, Dallas Opera Company, Martha Graham Company. Lighting consultant to many schools, theatres, theatre architects, and firms.

ROSSE, Herman (1887–1965) B. The Hague. Ed. South Kensington College of Art in England, Stanford Univ. An architect, he designed more than 200 sets for the stage and screen. Productions include: Casanova, The Swan, several Ziegfeld Follies, The Great Magoo, Ulysses in Nighttown (O-B). Awarded an Oscar for first film, King of Jazz, 1930. Taught at the Univ. of Calif., headed the design dept. at the Art Institute in Chicago. Scenic designer for 10 years at the Paper Mill Playhouse, Millburn, N.J. Author of Masks and Dreams with Kenneth MacGowan. Designed medallions for the American Theatre Wing's annual Antoinette Perry (Tony) Awards.

SIMONSON, Lee (1888–1967) B. New York City. Ed. Harvard. Started with the Washington Square Players and became one of the founders and directors of the Theatre Guild, 1919. Did settings for Guild productions from 1919 to 1940 (and other Broadway plays). Productions include: The Faithful, The Power of Darkness, The Dance of Death, Heartbreak House, Mr. Pim Passes By, Liliom, He Who Gets Slapped, Back to Methuselah, R.U.R., The Tidings Brought to Mary, Peer Gynt, The Adding Machine, The Goat Song, Marco Millions, Volpone, Faust, Dynamo, Roar China, The Apple Cart, Hotel

Universe, Elizabeth the Queen, Idiot's Delight, Amphytrion 38, Madame Bovary, The Road to Rome, The Good Earth, As You Like It, The School for Husbands, Days without End. Designed the Ring cycle for the Metropolitan Opera, 1947. Editor of Creative Art magazine. Author of The Stage Is Set, 1932, Part of a Lifetime, 1943, and The Art of Scenic Design, 1950.

SOUDEIKINE, Sergei (1882–1946) B. Tiflis, Russia. Ed. Moscow and Paris. First designed sets for Maeterlinck's plays. Designed sets for the Metropolitan Opera, sets and costumes for the Mordkin Ballet: Dionysus, La Fille Mal Gardée, Giselle, Trepak; the American Ballet: Reminiscence; Ballet Theatre: La Fille Mal Gardée (revival), and for the original Ballet Russe: Paganini. Also designed Porgy and Bess.

SOVEY, Raymond (1897–1966) B. Torrington, Conn. Ed. Columbia. First Broadway show: Costumes for George Washington, 1920. Productions include: Strictly Dishonorable, The Vinegar Tree, Strike up the Band, The Inspector General, Green Grow the Lilacs, The Petrified Forest, Ladies in Retirement, The Hasty Heart, State of the Union, The Heiress, For Love or Money, Edward My Son, The Cocktail Party, Ring Round the Moon, The Green Bay Tree, Gramercy Ghost, Gigi, Witness for the Prosecution, The Chalk Garden, The Great Sebastians.

THOMPSON, Woodman (1889–1955) B. Pittsburgh, Pa. Ed. Carnegie Inst. of Technology. Designed sets and costumes for many productions including Beggar on Horseback (1924), Firebrand, Iolanthe, The Warrior's Husband, Candida, The Magnificent Yankee. Also sets for The Desert Song, Habitual Husband, What Price Glory?, The Merchant of Venice, Lady Jane, The Bishop Misbehaves, Tomorrow's Holiday, The Ghost of Yankee Doodle, Hear the Trumpet. Designed for Ballet Theatre, Metropolitan Opera. Taught at the School of Dramatic Arts, Columbia Univ.

THROCKMORTON, Cleon (1897–1965) B. Atlantic City, N.J. Started as a landscape and figure painter. First New York production: The Emperor Jones, Provincetown Playhouse, 1920. Productions include: Porgy, All God's Chillun Got Wings, The Old Soak, In Abraham's Bosom, The House of Connelly, Springtime for Henry, The Silver Cord, Alien Corn, Noah, Bitter Oleander, Bride of the Lamb, Criminal at Large, Another Language, The Russian People, Mr. Sycamore, Across the Boards, Nathan the Wise. Also executed the settings for many other productions in his studios, and supplied theatrical equipment.

URBAN, Joseph (1872–1933) B. Vienna. Ed. Vienna Academy of Fine Arts, Polytechnic. An architect and book illustrator before working in theatre. Began theatre designing in the Hofburgtheatre, Vienna, 1904. Came to America in 1911 as artistic director of the Boston Opera House, also supervising the execution and painting of scenery. Productions include: Pelléas et Mélisande, Hansel and Gretel, Tristan und Isolde. Later came to New York as a designer for Ziegfeld and to the Metropolitan Opera. Broadway productions include: The Garden of Paradise, Macbeth, The Merry Wives, Twelfth Night, Caliban; Don Giovanni at the Metropolitan Opera. Had his own American scenic studio. Did 40 to 50 productions in Austria and Germany beginning in 1917. Interested in the problems of modern architecture. Designed the Ziegfeld Theatre (1927) in New York for presenting spectacular revues.

VERTÉS, Marcel (1895–1961) B. Hungary (French citizen). Began career under sponsorship of Ferenc Molnár in Paris showing, 1920. Productions include sets and costumes for: Broadway musical Seventh Heaven (1955), ballets Bluebeard and Helen of Troy, La Belle Helene—Paris Opera, film Moulin Rouge (awarded two Oscars: s, c). Designed 800 costumes for Ringling Brothers and Barnum and Bailey Circus, 1956. Also a book illustrator and artist.

Noted International Scenic Designers, Artists, and Architects

The works of the following are suggested for study:

Adolphe Appia (1862–1928) Swiss scenic designer.
Léon Bakst (1866–1924) Russian artist, scenic and costume designer.
Alexandre Nikolayevich Benois (1870–1960) Russian scenic designer and painter.
Jean Berain (1640–1711) French designer.
Christian Bérard (1902–1949) French artist, scenic and costume designer.
Bibiena family (17th and 18th centuries) Italian family of stage designers and architects who worked in Italy, Austria, Germany.

Jacques Callot (1592–1635) French engraver and designer.
Edward Gordon Craig (1872–1966) English scenic designer.
Bernardino Galliari (1707–1794) Italian scenic designer.
Inigo Jones (1573–1652) English architect, scenic designer.
Theodore Komisarjevsky (1882–1954) Russian director, scenic and costume designer, and artist.
Andrea Palladio (1518–1580) Italian architect.
Baldassare Peruzzi (1481–1536) Italian architect and designer.
Giovanni Battista Piranesi (1720–1778) Italian designer, architect and engraver.

Andrea Pozzo (1642–1708) Italian designer, architect.
Vincenzo Scamozzi (1552–1616) Italian architect.
Sebastiano Serlio (1475–1554) Italian architect, painter, critic.
Pavel Tchelitchew (1898–1957) Russian born American painter, draftsman, and stage designer.
Giacomo Torelli (1608–1678) Italian scenic designer.
Gaspare Vigarani (1586–1663) Italian architect.
Giacomo Barocchio Vignola (1507–1573) Italian architect.
Rex Whistler (1905–1944) English stage designer.

International Contemporary Stage Designers and Artists

James Bailey B. London, 1922. Artist, stage designer.
Nicola Benois B. St. Petersburg, Russia, 1901. Stage designer.
Yves Bonnat B. Voiron, France, 1912. Stage designer, writer.
Peter Brook B. London, 1925. Stage designer and director.
Edward Burra B. 1905, London. Artist, stage designer.
Marc Chagall B. Vitebsk, Russia, 1887. Painter, scenic and costume designer.
William Chappell B. Wolverhampton, England, 1908. Stage designer, dancer, director.
Antoni Clavé B. Barcelona, Spain, 1913. Stage designer.
Attilio Colonnello B. Milan, 1931, Stage designer.
Giorgio de Chirico B. Bolo, Greece, 1888. Painter, graphic artist, stage designer.
Lila de Nobili B, Lugano, Italy, 1916. Stage des.

Sven Leonard Erixson B. Tumba, Sweden, 1899. Stage designer.
Erté (Romain de Tirtoff) B. St. Petersburg, Russia, 1892. Fashion designer, illustrator. Scenic and costume designer.
Roger Furse B. Ightham, England, 1903. Painter, scenic and costume designer.
Rudolf Heinrich B. Halle, Germany, 1926. Stage designer.
Anthony Holland B. Macclesfield, England, 1912. Stage designer.
Leslie Hurry B. London, 1909. Stage designer.
Ralph Koltai B. Berlin, 1924. Stage designer.
Osbert Lancaster B. London, 1908, Stage designer.
Emanuele Luzzati B. Genoa, Italy, 1921. Stage designer.
Tanya Moiseiwitsch B. London, 1914, Scenic and costume designer.
Beni Montresor B. Bussolengo, Italy, 1926. Scenic and costume designer, and book illustrator.

Teo Otto B. Remscheid, Germany, 1904. Stage designer.
Reece Pemberton B. Tamworth, England, 1914. Stage designer.
John Piper B. London, 1903. Painter, illustrator, stage designer, writer.
Jean-Pierre Ponnelle B. Paris, 1932. Stage designer.
Malcolm Pride B. London, 1930. Stage designer.
Loudon Sainthill B. Hobart, Tasmania, 1919. Stage designer.
Per Schwab B. Stockholm, 1911. Stage designer.
Josef Svoboda B. Cáslav, Czechoslovakia, 1920. Stage designer.
George Wakhevitch B. Odessa, Russia, 1907. Stage designer.
Michael Warre B. London, 1922. Stage designer, director.
Franco Zeffirelli B. Florence, Italy, 1923. Stage designer, director.

Sources, Manufacturers, Studios, Costume Houses

Popular sources for finding special materials that may not be available locally are listed. For other sources of scenic materials, supplies, scenic studios, and costume houses in the United States and Canada, consult *Simon's Directory of Theatrical Materials, Services and Information*, published by Package Publicity Service, Inc., 1564 Broadway, New York, N.Y. 10036.

Sources and Manufacturers of Scenic Supplies

Aniline dyes
(also see Paints)
Bachmeier and Co.
154 Chambers St.
New York, N.Y. 10007
(212) RE 2-3621
Fezandie and Sperrle
103 Lafayette St.
New York, N.Y. 10013
(212) 226-7653

Architectural steel
J. G. Braun Co.
4 Fairfield Crescent
West Caldwell, N.J. 07006
(201) 575-0800
(212) 285-9757

Artificial flowers, plants
Decorative Plant Corp.
136 West 24 St.
New York, N.Y. 10011
(212) WA 4-4405
Modern Artificial Flowers and Displays
457 West 46 St.
New York, N.Y. 10036
(212) CO 5-0414

Celastic
Messmore and Damon Co.
530 West 28 St.
New York, N.Y. 10001
(212) 594-8070
Mutual Hardware
5-49 Ave.
Long Island City, N.Y. 11101
(212) EM 1-2480

Concentrated rubber latex, Sobo Quik (flexible white resin glues)
Sloman's Labs
32-45 Hunters Point
Long Island, City, N.Y. 11101
(212) 784-0205

Fabrics, stage curtains, draperies, backdrops
Astrup Co.
12 Parkway Pl.
Edison, N.J. 08817
(201) 225-1776
(muslin and canvas)
Dazian's Inc.
40 East 29 St.
New York, N.Y. 10016
(212) 686-5300
Also: Boston, Chicago, Miami, Los Angeles, Washington, D.C., San Francisco
(fabrics, trims of all sorts)
J. C. Hansen
423 West 43 St.
New York, N.Y. 10036
(212) CI 6-8055
(cycs, scrims, ground cloths, draperies, backdrops)
M. H. Lazarus and Co.
516 West 34 St.
New York, N.Y. 10001
(212) 736-6200
(theatrical fabrics)
Mutual Hardware
See address under Celastic
(draperies, curtains, scrims, backdrops, cycs)

Paramount Theatrical Supplies
32 West 20 St.
New York, N.Y. 10011
(212) CH 3-0765
(backdrops, cycs, scrims, fabrics)
Rose Brand Textile Fabrics
138 Grand St.
New York, N.Y. 10013
(212) CA 6-3710
(muslin, canvas, others)
Frank W. Stevens
544 West 30 St.
New York, N.Y. 10001
(212) LO 3-0066
(draperies, curtains, painted backdrop rentals)
Theatre Production Service
26 South Highland Ave.
Ossining, N.Y. 10562
(914) 941-0357
(draperies, curtains, backdrops, cycs, muslin, canvas)
I. Weiss and Sons
445 West 45 St.
New York, N.Y. 10036
(212) CI 6-8444
(cycs, scrims, muslin, canvas, ground cloths, backdrops, draperies)

Fluorescent and luminous paints
Stroblite Co.
10 East 23 St.
New York, N.Y. 10010
(212) 677-9220

Furniture and props (antiques, period pieces, objets d'art)
Encore Studio
410 West 47 St.
New York, N.Y. 10036
(212) 246-5237
Newel Art Galleries
877 Second Ave.
New York, N.Y. 10017
(212) 758-1970

Gray bogus paper
Gilshire Corp.
220 Fifth Ave.
New York, N.Y. 10001
(212) MU 6-4864

Iron-on Fabric
Peters Brothers Coating and Laminating Co.
95 Dobbin St.
Brooklyn, N.Y. 11222
(212) 389-5445

Japan colors
Ronan Superfine Japan Colors
T. J. Ronan Paint Corp.
749 East 135 St.
Bronx, N.Y. 10454
(212) 292-1100

Materials for models (miniature furniture, decorative papers)
The Peddler's Shop
12408 East 46 Terrace
Independence, Mo. 64050
(816) FL 3-0683

Metal ornaments
Kenneth Lynch and Sons
78 Danbury Road
Wilton, Conn. 06897
(203) 762-8363 (212) 585-3095

Mylar
Dazian's Inc. (See Fabrics)

Paints, aniline dyes, glues, brushes, bronze powders, gold leaf, other scenic supplies
M. Epstein's Son
809 Ninth Ave.
New York, N.Y. 10019
(212) CO 5-3960
Gothic Color Co.
727 Washington St.
New York, N.Y. 10014
(212) 929-7493
Paramount Theatrical Supplies
32 West 20 St.
New York, N.Y. 10011
(212) CH 3-0765
Theatre Production Service
26 South Highland Ave.
Ossining, N.Y. 10562
(914) 941-0357
S. Wolf's Sons or Playhouse Colors
771 Ninth Ave.
New York, N.Y. 10019
(212) 265-2066

Paper board specialists (foam core and display foam)
Henry Fuchs and Son
94 Ninth St.
Brooklyn, N.Y. 11215
(212) 499-8600

Paper Tubes
Hudson Paper Tube Co.
372 Broome St.
New York, N.Y. 10013
(212) CA 6-3858

Perforated metals
Harrington and King Perforating Co.
East Crescent Ave. at Arrow Rd.
Ramsey, N.J. 07446
(212) 682-1255

Plastic adhesives
Schwartz Chemical Co.
50-01 Second St.
Long Island City, N.Y. 11101
(212) 784-7592

Plastic products, materials
Acme Foam Corp.
57-02 48 St.
Maspeth, N.Y. 11378
(212) 361-0707
Alfred Haussmann
2 Hamburg 70
Tonndorfer Hauptstrasse 79
West Germany
Industrial Plastic Supply Co.
324 Canal St.
New York, N.Y. 10013
(212) 226-2010
National Distributing Co.
50 Maple St.
Norwood, N.J. 07648
(212) PE 6-5555
(201) 768-2500
Styro Sales
25-34 50 Ave.
Long Island City, N.Y. 11104
(212) ST 6-1791

Pressed metal
Barney Brainum-Shanker Steel Co.
70-32 83 St.
Glendale, N.Y. 11227
(212) 894-5581

Resin Glues
Bergen Glue Corp.
Ridgefield, N.J. 07657
(Bergenbond)
(201) 943-1130
Dunn's Woodhesive
Ridgefield, N.J. 07657
Gill Chemical Products
366 McGuinnes Blvd.
Brooklyn, N.Y. 11222
(212) EV 3-4399
(Mend-All)
C. B. Hewitt and Brothers
Ridgefield, N.J. 07657
(Hewhold)

Sculpture supplies, information
Sculpture House
38 East 30 St.
New York, N.Y. 10016
(212) OR 9-7474
Sculpture Services
9 East 19 St.
New York, N.Y. 10003
(212) 254-8585

Sequins, beads, spangles, decorative items
LeeWards
1200 St. Charles
Elgin, Ill. 60120
(312) 697-1800

Shellac (also paint stores)
Mantrose-Haeuser
99 Park Ave.
New York, N.Y. 10016
(212) 687-2762

Spray guns
Binks Manufacturing Co.
9201 Belmont St.
Franklin Park, Ill. 60131
(312) 671-3000
(312) 992-3900 Chicago
DeVilbiss Co.
300 Phillips Ave.
Toledo, Ohio 43612
(419) 474-5411

Staplers, hammer tackers
Arrow Fastener Co.
271 Mayhill
Saddle Brook, N.J. 07662
Duo-Fast Fasteners Corp.
3702 River Rd.
Franklin Park, Ill. 60131
(312) 678-0100

Trimmings, fringes, braids, lace, and so on
M & J Fifth Ave.
395 Fifth Ave.
New York, N.Y. 10016
(212) 683-9320
M & J Trimming
1008 Sixth Ave.
New York, N.Y. 10018
(212) 244-7072

Vinyl paints (see also Paints)
Flo-Paint
5-49 Ave.
Long Island City, N.Y. 11101
(212) EM 1-2480

Wallpaper paste (Glutoline)
The Henneux Co.
330 West 72 St.
New York, N.Y. 10023
(212) 799-3333

Theatrical Scenic Studios in the New York City Area

Atlas Scenic Studios, Ltd.
10 Wall St.
Norwalk, Conn. 06854
(203) 874-2130

Design Associates Scenic Studios
76 South Union St.
Lambertville, N.J. 08530
(609) 397-1588

Hart Scenic Studio
35-41 Dempsey Ave.
Edgewater, N.J. 07020
NYC: (212) 947-7264

Lincoln Scenic Studios
440 West 15 St.
New York, N.Y. 10011
(212) 255-2000

Messmore and Damon Co.
530 West 28 St.
New York, N.Y. 10001
(212) 594-8070

Metropolitan Opera Scenic Studio
1865 Broadway (Lincoln Center)
New York, N.Y. 10023
(212) 799-3100

Nolan Scenery Studios
1163 Atlantic Ave.
Brooklyn, N.Y. 11216
(212) ST 3-6910

Theatre Techniques (formerly Feller's)
Hanger E, Stewart Airport
Newburgh, N.Y. 12550 Box 6087
(914) 564-6450

Theatrical Equipment Corp.
209 South Fehr Way
Bay Shore, N.Y. 11706
(516) 242-5400

Variety Scenic Studio
25-10 Borden Ave.
Long Island City, N.Y. 11101
(212) 392-4747

Also:
National Scenery Shop
8409-B Terminal Rd.
Newington, Va. 22150
(703) 550-9757

Theatrical Costume Houses in New York City that execute clothes for the stage

Brooks-Van Horn Costumes
117 West 17 St.
New York, N.Y. 10011
(212) 989-8000

Ray Diffen
121 West 17 St.
New York, N.Y. 10011
(212) 675-2634

Eaves Costume Co., Inc.
423 West 55 St.
New York, N.Y. 10019
(212) PL 7-3730

Grace Costumes Inc.
254 West 54 St.
New York, N.Y. 10019
(212) JU 6-0260

Barbara Matera Ltd.
311 West 43 St.
New York, N.Y. 10036
(212) 765-4865

Stage Lighting Equipment Sources

Altman Stage Lighting Co., Inc.
57 Alexander St.
Yonkers, N.Y. 10701
(914) LO 9-7777

American Stage Lighting Co., Inc.
1331C North Ave.
New Rochelle, N.Y. 10804
(914) 636-5538

Bash Stage Lighting Co.
715 Grand St.
Hoboken, N.J. 07423
(201) 659-2199

Berkey Colortran, Inc.
25-15 Woodside
Queens, N.Y. 11377
(212) 721-3434

Capital Stage Lighting Co., Inc.
509 West 56 St.
New York, N.Y. 10019
(212) 246-7770

Four Star Stage Lighting, Inc.
585 Gerard Ave.
Bronx, N.Y. 10451
(212) 993-0471

Kliegl Bros. Universal Elec.
Stage Lighting Co., Inc.
32-32 48 St.
Long Island City, N.Y. 11103
(212) 786-7474

Skirpan Lighting Control Corp.
41-43 24 St.
Long Island City, N.Y. 11101
(212) 937-1444

Strand Century, Inc.
20 Bushes Lane
Elmwood Park, N.J. 07407
(201) 791-7000 (212) 947-2475

Times Square Stage Lighting Co., Inc.
318 West 47 St.
New York, N.Y. 10036
(212) 541-5045

Also:
Mutual Hardware Corp.
Paramount Theatrical Supplies
Theatre Production Service
(See addresses opposite page)

Stage Hardware and Equipment Sources

American Stage Equipment & Iron
Works
805 E. 134 St.
Bronx, N.Y. 10454
(212) CY 2-8670

Also:
Mutual Hardware Corp.
Paramount Theatrical Supplies
Theatre Production Service

Sound Equipment Sources

Masque Sound & Recording Corp.
331 West 51 St.
New York, N.Y. 10019
(212) CI 5-4623

Sound Associates, Inc.
432 West 45 St.
New York, N.Y. 10036
(212) 757-5679

Costume Fabric Sources

S. Beckenstein, Inc.
130 Orchard St.
New York, N.Y. 10002
(212) 475-4525

Dazian's Inc.
40 E. 29 St.
New York, N.Y. 10016
(212) 686-5300

Far Eastern Fabrics, Inc.
171 Madison Ave.
New York, N.Y. 10016
(212) MU 3-2623

Gladstone Fabrics
16 West 56 St.
New York, N.Y. 10019
(212) 765-0760

Rose Brand Textile Fabrics
138 Grand St.
New York, N.Y. 10013
(212) CA 6-3710

Stroheim and Romann
10 W. 20 St.
New York, N.Y. 10011
(212) 691-0700

Stage Makeup Sources

Ben Nye Makeup
11571 Santa Monica Blvd.
Los Angeles, Calif. 90025
(213) 478-1558

Bob Kelly Cosmetics
151 West 46 St.
New York, N.Y. 10036
(212) 245-2237

Makeup Center Ltd.
150 West 55 St.
New York, N.Y. 10019
(212) 977-9494

Mehron, Inc.
325 West 37 St.
New York, N.Y. 10018
(212) 524-1133

Stein Cosmetic Co.
430 Broom St.
New York, N.Y. 10013
(212) 226-2430

Zauder Bros. Inc.
902 Broadway
New York, N.Y. 10011
(212) 228-2600

Professional Resident and Repertory Theatres

Listed alphabetically by state and town.

Arizona Civic Theatre
2719 East Broadway
Tucson, Ariz. 85716

South Coast Repertory
1827 Newport Boulevard
Costa Mesa, Calif. 92627

L.A. Free Shakespeare Festival
P.O. Box 1951
Los Angeles, Calif. 90028

Mark Taper Forum
(Center Theatre Group)
135 N. Grand Ave.
Los Angeles, Calif. 90012

Old Globe Theatre
P.O. Box 2171
San Diego, Calif. 92112

American Conservatory Theatre
450 Geary Street
San Francisco, Calif. 94102

Hartford Stage Company
65 Kinsley Street
Hartford, Conn. 06103

Long Wharf Theatre
222 Sargent Drive
New Haven, Conn. 06511

Yale Repertory Theatre School of
Drama
Yale University
New Haven, Conn. 06520

American Shakespeare Festival
1850 Elm Street
Stratford, Conn. 06497

Eugene O'Neill Memorial Theatre
P.O. Box 206
Waterford, Conn. 06385
N.Y.C. address:
1860 Broadway
New York, N.Y. 10023 (summer)

Arena Stage
Sixth and M Streets, S.W.
Washington, D.C. 20024

D. C. Black Repertory Company
4935 Georgia Ave., N.W.
Washington, D.C. 20011

Players Theatre of Greater Miami
c/o Museum of Science
3280 S. Miami Ave.
Miami, Fla. 33129

Asolo Theatre Festival
P.O. Box Drawer E
Sarasota, Fla. 33578

Goodman Theatre Company
200 S. Columbus Dr.
Chicago, Ill. 60603
Professional Performing Co. of the
Drama Guild of Kennedy-King College
6800 S. Wentworth Ave.
Chicago, Ill. 60621
Indiana Repertory Theatre
411 E. Michigan St.
Indianapolis, Ind. 46204
Actors Theatre of Louisville
316–320 W. Main St.
Louisville, Ky. 40202
Theatre at Monmouth, Inc.
Cumston Hall
Monmouth, Me. 04295
Center Stage
31 E. North Ave.
Baltimore, Md. 21202
Theatre Company of Boston
Boston Center for the Arts
551 Tremont St.
Boston, Mass. 02116
Stage West
1511 Memorial Ave.
West Springfield, Mass. 01089
Meadow Brook Theatre
Oakland University
Rochester, Mich. 48063
Guthrie Theatre
725 Vineland Place
Minneapolis, Minn. 55403

Missouri Repertory Theatre
University of Missouri
5100 Rockhill Rd.
Kansas City, Mo. 64110
Repertory Theatre of Loretto-Hilton
130 Edgar Rd.
St. Louis, Mo. 63119
McCarter Theatre Company
Princeton University, Box 526
Princeton, N.J. 08540
New Jersey Shakespeare Festival
Drew University
Madison, N.J. 07940 (summer)
Cohoes Music Hall
Cohoes, N.Y. 12407
Bil Baird Marionette Theatre
59 Barrow St.
New York, N.Y. 10014
City Center Acting Company
130 W. 56 St., Fifth Floor
New York, N.Y. 10019
Negro Ensemble Company
St. Mark's Playhouse
133 Second Ave.
New York, N.Y. 10003
New York Shakespeare Festival
(Delacorte and Mobile Theatres)
The Public Theatre
425 Lafayette St.
New York, N.Y. 10003 (summer)
Performing Arts Foundation (PAF)
185 Second St.
Huntington Sta., N.Y. 11746

Puerto Rican Traveling Theatre Co.
124 W. 18 St.
New York, N.Y. 10011 (summer)
Roundabout Theatre
307 W. 26 St.
New York, N.Y. 10001
GeVa
168 Clinton South
Rochester, N.Y. 14604
Rochester Shakespeare Theatre
50 Plymouth Ave. North
Rochester, N.Y. 14614
Syracuse Stage
University Regent Theatre
820 E. Genesee St.
Syracuse, N.Y. 13210
Playhouse in the Park
962 Mount Adams Circle
Cincinnati, Ohio 45202
Cleveland Play House
2040 E. 86 St.
Cleveland, Ohio 44106
Great Lakes Shakespeare Association
Lakewood Civic Auditorium
Franklin Blvd. and Bunts Rd.
Lakewood, Ohio 44107 (summer)
Fulton Opera House
12 N. Prince St.
Lancaster, Pa. 17607 (summer)
Philadelphia Drama Guild
Room 609, 1601 Walnut St.
Philadelphia, Pa. 19103

Pennsylvania State Festival Theatre
103 Arts Building
University Park, Pa. 16802
(summer)
Trinity Square Repertory Theatre
201 Washington St.
Providence, R.I. 02903
Department of Speech and Theatre
University of Tennessee
Knoxville, Tenn. 37916
Theatre 3
2800 Routh St.
Dallas, Tex. 75201
Alley Theatre
615 Texas Ave.
Houston, Tex. 77002
Champlain Shakespeare Festival
Royall Tyler Theatre
University of Vermont
Burlington, Vt. 05401 (summer)
Barter Theatre
Abingdon, Va. 24210
Virginia Museum Theatre
Boulevard and Grove Aves.
Richmond, Va. 23221
Seattle Repertory Theatre
Queen Anne Station, P.O. Box B
Seattle Center
Seattle, Wash. 98109
Milwaukee Repertory Theatre
Performing Arts Center
929 N. Water St.
Milwaukee, Wisc. 53202

Selected Bibliography

SCENERY

Ashworth, Bradford. *Notes on Scene Painting.* New Haven, Conn.: Whitlock's, 1952.

Bablet, Denis. *Edward Gordon Craig.* New York: Theatre Arts Books, 1967.

Bay, Howard. *Stage Design.* New York: Drama Book Specialists, 1974.

Bruder, Karl C. *Properties and Dressing the Stage.* New York: Richards Rosen Press, 1969.

Burdick, Elizabeth B., Peggy C. Hansen, and Brenda Zanger (eds.). *Contemporary Stage Design U.S.A.* Middletown, Conn.: Wesleyan University Press, 1974.

Burian, Jarka. *The Scenography of Josef Svoboda.* Middletown, Conn.: Wesleyan University Press, 1971.

Burris-Meyer, Harold, and Edward C. Cole. *Scenery for the Theatre,* 3d ed. Boston: Little, Brown, 1972.

————. *Theatres and Auditoriums,* 2d ed. New York: Reinhold, 1964.

Craig, Edward Anthony. *Gordon Craig; The Story of His Life.* New York: Knopf, 1968.

Craig, Edward Gordon. *On the Art of the Theatre.* New York: Theatre Arts Books, 1957.

Gillette, A. S. *An Introduction to Scene Design.* New York: Harper, 1967.

————. *Stage Scenery: Its Construction and Rigging,* 2d ed. New York: Harper, 1972.

Graves, Maitland. *The Art of Color and Design.* 2d ed. New York: McGraw-Hill, 1951.

Hainaux, Rene (ed.). *Stage Design throughout the World since 1935.* New York: Theatre Arts Books, 1964.

————. *Stage Design throughout the World since 1950.* New York: Theatre Arts Books, 1964.

————. *Stage Design throughout the World since 1960.* New York: Theatre Arts Books, 1972.

Heffner, Hubert, Samuel Selden, and Hunton Sellman. *Modern Theatre Practice.* New York: Appleton-Century-Crofts, 1959.

Jones, Robert Edmond. *The Dramatic Imagination.* New York: Theatre Arts Books, 1941.

————. *Drawings for the Theatre.* New York: Theatre Arts Books, 1970.

Joseph, Stephen. *New Theatre Forms.* New York: Theatre Arts Books, 1968.

Kenton, Warren. *Stage Properties and How to Make Them.* London: Pitman, 1964.

Komisarjevsky, Theodore, and Lee Simonson. *Settings and Costumes of the Modern Stage.* New York: Benjamin Blom, 1966.

Mielziner, Jo. *Designing for the Theatre.* New York: Atheneum, 1965.

————. *The Shapes of Our Theatre.* New York: Crown, 1970.

Oenslager, Donald. *Scenery Then and Now.* New York: Russell & Russell, 1966.

————. *Stage Design: Four Centuries of Scenic Invention.* New York: Viking, 1975.

Parker, W. Oren, and Harvey K. Smith. *Scene Design and Stage Lighting,* 3d ed. New York: Holt, Rinehart and Winston, 1974.

Phillippi, Herbert. *Stagecraft and Scene Design.* Boston: Houghton Mifflin, 1953.

Rosenfeld, Sybil. *A Short History of Scene Design in Great Britain.* Totowa, N.J.: Rowman and Littlefield, 1973.

Rowell, Kenneth. *Stage Design.* London: Studio Vista, 1968.

Schubert, Hannelore. *The Modern Theatre: Architecture, Stage Design, Lighting.* New York: Praeger, 1971.

Seldon, Samuel, and Tom Rezzuto. *Essentials of Stage Scenery.* New York: Appleton-Century-Crofts, 1972.

————, and H. D. Sellman. *Stage Scenery and Lighting.* New York: Appleton-Century-Crofts, 1958.

Simonson, Lee. *The Art of Scenic Design.* New York: Reinhold, 1968.

————. *Part of a Lifetime.* New York: Duell, Sloan and Pearce, 1943.

————. *The Stage Is Set.* New York: Theatre Arts Books, 1964.

Volbach, Walter R. *Adolphe Appia, Prophet of the Modern Theatre: A Profile.* Middletown, Conn.: Wesleyan University Press, 1968.

Warre, Michael. *Designing and Making Stage Scenery.* London: Studio Vista, 1966.

Welker, David. *Theatrical Set Design: The Basic Techniques.* Boston: Allyn & Bacon, 1969.

LIGHTING

Burian, Jarka. *The Scenography of Josef Svoboda.* Middletown, Conn.: Wesleyan University Press, 1971.

Fuchs, Theodore. *Stage Lighting.* New York: Benjamin Blom, 1963.

McCandless, Stanley. *A Method of Lighting the Stage,* 4th ed. New York: Theatre Arts Books, 1958.

————. *A Syllabus of Stage Lighting.* New Haven, Conn.: Published by the author, 1949.

Parker, W. Oren, and Harvey K. Smith. *Scene Design and Stage Lighting,* 3d ed. New York: Holt, Rinehart and Winston, 1974.

Pilbrow, Richard. *Stage Lighting.* New York: Van Nostrand, 1970.

Rosenthal, Jean, and Lael Wertenbaker. *The Magic of Light.* Boston: Little, Brown, 1972.

Rubin, Joel E., and Leland H. Watson. *Theatrical Lighting Practice.* New York: Theatre Arts Books, 1954.

Sellman, Hunton D. *Essentials of Stage Lighting.* New York: Appleton-Century-Crofts, 1972.

Wilfred, Thomas. *Projected Scenery.* New York: Drama Book Specialists, 1965.

Williams, Rollo G. *The Technique of Stage Lighting,* 2d ed. New York: Pitman, 1958.

COSTUME

Boucher, François. *20,000 Years of Fashion*. New York: Abrams, 1966.

Brooke, Iris. *Footwear: A Short History of European and American Shoes*. New York: Theatre Arts Books, 1972.

———. *A History of English Costume*. New York: Theatre Arts Books, 1972.

———. *Medieval Theatre Costume*. New York: Theatre Arts Books, 1968.

———. *Western European Costume I: Its Relation to the Theatre; 13th–17th Centuries*. New York: Theatre Arts Books, 1964.

———. *Western European Costume II: Its Relation to the Theatre; 17th–19th Centuries*. New York: Theatre Arts Books, 1966.

Buchman, Herman. *Film and Television Makeup*. New York: Watson-Guptill, 1973.

———. *Stage Makeup*. London: Pitman, 1972.

Davenport, Millia. *The Book of Costume*. New York: Crown, 1948. 2 vols.

Ewing, Elizabeth. *Underwear: A History*. New York: Theatre Arts Books, 1972.

Fernald, Mary, and Eileen Shenton. *Costume Design and Making*. New York: Theatre Arts Books, 1967.

Gorsline, Douglas. *What People Wore*. New York: Viking, 1952.

Holding, T. H. *Uniforms of the British Army, Navy and Court*. New York: Theatre Arts Books, 1972.

Kelly, F. M. *Shakespearean Costume*. New York: Theatre Arts Books, 1970.

Komisarjevsky, Theodore. *The Costume of the Theatre*. New York: Holt, Rinehart and Winston, 1932.

Miller, Edward. *Textiles*. New York: Theatre Arts Books, 1969.

Moulton, Bertha. *Garment Cutting and Tailoring for Students*. New York: Theatre Arts Books, 1968.

———. *Simplified Tailoring*. New York: Theatre Arts Books, 1969.

Motley. *Designing and Making Stage Costumes*. New York: Watson-Guptill, 1974.

Payne, Blanche. *History of Costume from the Ancient Egyptians to the Twentieth Century*. New York: Harper, 1965.

Perrottet, Philippe. *Practical Stage Make-up*. New York: Reinhold, 1967.

Russell, Douglas A. *Stage Costume Design: Theory, Technique and Style*. New York: Appleton-Century-Crofts, 1973.

Scott, A. C. *Chinese Costume in Transition*. New York: Theatre Arts Books, 1960.

Spencer, Charles. *Erté*. New York: Clarkson N. Potter, 1970.

Waugh, Norah. *Corsets and Crinolines*. New York: Theatre Arts Books, 1970.

———. *The Cut of Men's Clothes, 1600–1900*. New York: Theatre Arts Books, 1964.

———. *The Cut of Women's Clothes, 1600–1930*. New York: Theatre Arts Books, 1968.

Wilson, Eunice. *A History of Shoe Fashions*. New York: Theatre Arts Books, 1972.

GENERAL

Aronson, Joseph. *The New Encyclopedia of Furniture*. New York: Crown, 1967.

Berman, Eugene. *The Graphic Work of Eugene Berman*. New York: Crown, 1971.

Brockett, Oscar G. *The Theatre: An Introduction*. 3d ed. New York: Holt, Rinehart and Winston, 1974.

Croy, Peter. *Graphic Design and Reproduction Techniques*. London: Focal Press, 1968.

Davey, Norman. *A History of Building Materials*. New York: Drake, 1971.

Farber, Donald C. *Producing on Broadway*. New York: DBS Publications, 1969.

Fryklund, Verne C., and Frank R. Kepler. *General Drafting*, 4th ed. Bloomington, Ill.: McKnight and McKnight, 1969.

Goldscheider, Ludwig. *Michelangelo*. Greenwich, Conn.: New York Graphic Society, 1963.

Goodrich, Anne. *Enjoying the Summer Theatre of New England*. Chester, Conn.: Pequot Press, 1974.

Gorelik, Mordecai. *New Theatres for Old*. New York: Samuel French, 1940.

Guptill, Arthur L. *Watercolor Painting Step-by-Step*, 2d ed. New York: Watson-Guptill, 1967.

Hall, Ben M. *The Best Remaining Seats*. New York: Bramhall House, 1961.

Hollander, Harry B. *Plastics for Artists and Craftsmen*. New York: Watson-Guptill, 1972.

Kay, Reed. *The Painter's Guide to Studio Methods and Materials*. Garden City, N.Y.: Doubleday, 1972.

Luzadder, Warren J. *Fundamentals of Engineering Drawing*, 6th ed. Englewood Cliffs, N.J.: Prentice-Hall, 1971.

Mayer, Ralph. *The Artist's Handbook of Materials and Techniques*, 3d ed. New York: Viking, 1970.

Meilach, Dona Z. *Creating with Plaster*. Chicago: Reilly and Lee, 1966.

Mendelowitz, Daniel M. *Drawing*, 2d ed. New York: Holt, Rinehart and Winston, 1975.

Newman, Thelma R. *Plastics as an Art Form*. Philadelphia: Chilton, 1969.

Novick, Julius. *Beyond Broadway*. New York: Hill & Wang, 1968.

Pluckrose, Henry. *Introducing Acrylic Painting*. New York: Watson-Guptill, 1968.

Rich, Jack C. *The Materials and Methods of Sculpture*. New York: Oxford University Press, 1959.

Svensen, Carl Lars, and Edgar G. Shelton. *Architectural Drafting*. New York: Van Nostrand, 1948.

Time-Life Encyclopedia of Gardening. New York: Time, Inc., 1971.

Whiton, Sherrill. *Elements of Interior Design and Decoration*. Philadelphia: Lippincott, 1963.

HELPFUL RESEARCH BOOKS

These inexpensive paperback books, published by Dover in New York, are especially good for both the stage designer and scenic artist.

American Architecture
  Edmund V. Gillon, Jr.
America's Old Masters
  James Thomas Flexner
Architectural and Perspective Designs
  Giuseppe Galli-Bibiena
The Architecture of Country Houses
  A. J. Downing
Art Nouveau: An Anthology of Design and Illustration from the Studio
  Selected by Edmund V. Gillon, Jr.
The Artistic Anatomy of Trees
  Rex Vicat Cole
Baroque Cartouches for Designers and Artists
  Designed and engraved by Johann Ulrich Krauss

Will Bradley—His Graphic Art
  Edited by Clarence P. Hornung
The Cabinet Maker and Upholsterer's Drawing Book
  Thomas Sheraton
Cast-Iron Architecture in New York
  Margot Gayle and Edmund V. Gillon, Jr.
Decorative Antique Ironwork
  Henry René d'Allemagne
Early American Rooms—1650–1858
  Russell Hawes Kettell
The Fantastic Engravings of Wendel Dietterlin, a reprint 1598 edition of his architectura.
The First World War in Posters
  Selected and edited by Joseph Darracott

Handbook of Ornament
  Franz Sales Meyer
Handbook of Plant and Floral Ornament
  Richard G. Hatton
How to Know the Ferns
  Frances Theodora Parsons
Lost Examples of Colonial Architecture
  John Mead Howells
Maximilian's Triumphal Arch
  Woodcuts by Albrecht Dürer and Others
The Modern Builder's Guide
  Minard Lafever
Montgomery-Ward & Co.
  Catalogue and Buyer's Guide Spring and Summer—1895 introduction by Boris Emmet

New York in the Thirties
  Berenice Abbott
Old New York in Early Photographs
  Mary Black
Pattern Design
  Archibald H. Christie
Pictorial Calligraphy and Ornamentation
  Selected by Edmund V. Gillon, Jr.
The Triumph of Maximilian I
  Hans Burgkmair and Others
Victorian Cemetery Art
  Edmund V. Gillon, Jr.
Victorian Stencils for Designs and Decoration
  Selected by Edmund V. Gillon, Jr.

USEFUL CATALOGS

Almac Plastics. Almac Plastics, Inc., 47–42 37 St., Long Island City, N.Y. 11101.

American Scenic. American Scenic Co., 11 Andrews St., P.O. Box 283, Greenville, S.C. 29602.

Architectural & Decorative Sheet Metal Ornaments. Kenneth Lynch & Sons, Wilton, Conn. 06897.

Architectural Steel. J.G. Braun Co., 7540 McCormick Blvd., Skokie, Ill., 60076 or 4 Fairfield Crescent, West Caldwell, N.J. 07006

Art Supplies. Art Brown & Bros., 2 West 46 St., New York, N.Y. 10036.

Binks Spray Systems Catalog. Binks Manufacturing Co., 9201 Belmont St., Franklin Park, Ill. 60131.

Flax Artist's Materials. Sam Flax Inc., 25 East 28 St., New York, N.Y. 10016.

Letraset USA Graphic Art Products. Letraset USA, Inc., 33 New Bridge Road, Bergenfield, N.J. 07621.

Maxwell Illustrated Catalog of Moldings. Maxwell Lumber Co., 211 West 18 St., New York, N.Y. 10011.

Paramount Theatrical Supplies. Alcone Co., Inc., 32 West 20 St., New York, N.Y. 10011.

Playhouse Colors. Playhouse Colors, 771 Ninth Ave., New York, N.Y. 10019.

Scenic Artist's Handbook. Gothic Color Co., Inc., 727–729 Washington St., New York, N.Y. 10014.

Theatre Production Service. Theatre Production Service, 26 South Highland Ave. Ossining, N.Y. 10562.

Theatrical Equipment & Supplies. Mutual Hardware Corp., 5–45 49 Ave., Long Island City, N.Y. 11101.

Tools, Materials, & Accessories for Sculptors. Sculpture House, 38 East 30 St., New York, N.Y. 10016.

TOPICAL PUBLICATIONS

Theatre Crafts
Theatre World
Opera News
Dance Magazine
Dance World
A Pictorial History of the American Theatre

POPULAR SOURCE FOR ALL KINDS OF THEATRE BOOKS

Drama Book Shop, Inc.
150 West 52 St.
New York, N.Y. 10019
(212) JU 2-1037

Index

Page numbers in italic indicate black-and-white illustrations or caption references; those in boldface, one or more color illustrations on following pages.

The author

Lynn Pecktal, a native of Kingsport, Tennessee, began designing scenery professionally at Robert Porterfield's Barter Theatre, the State Theatre of Virginia, while still an undergraduate at Emory and Henry College, from which he received a bachelor of arts degree, then did graduate work in stage design with Donald Oenslager at the Yale Drama School. He has designed settings for more than 100 legitimate stage productions, including the stage scenery for the sound and light show in the restored Ford's Theatre in Washington and sets for *Lucia di Lammermoor* in Santiago, Chile. He was an assistant to Jo Mielziner and Eugene Berman and has lectured at a number of universities. For several years he has also been associated with Nolan Scenery Studios in New York. In 1977 he was scenery supervisor for the Broadway production of *Dracula.* Mr. Pecktal lives in Manhattan with his wife and sons.